FASCISM

Critical Concepts in Political Science

Other titles in this series

Revolution
Edited by Rosemary H. T. O'Kane
4 volume set

International Relations
Edited by Andrew Linklater
5 volume set

Nationalism
Edited by John Hutchinson and Anthony D. Smith
5 volume set

Liberalism
Edited by G. W. Smith
4 volume set

Global Governance
Edited by Timothy Sinclair
4 volume set

Socialism
Edited by Jeremy Jennings
4 volume set

Welfare and the State
Edited by Nicholas Deakin, Catherine Jones-Finer and Bob Matthews
5 volume set

FASCISM

Critical Concepts in Political Science

*Edited by Roger Griffin with
Matthew Feldman*

Volume IV

The 'Fascist Epoch'

LONDON AND NEW YORK

First published 2004
by Routledge
11 New Fetter Lane, London EC4P 4EE

Simultaneously published in the USA and Canada
by Routledge
29 West 35th Street, New York, NY 10001

Routledge is an imprint of the Taylor & Francis Group

Selection and Editorial Matter © 2004 Roger Griffin; individual
contributors retain copyright in their own material.

Typeset in Times by RefineCatch Limited, Bungay, Suffolk
Printed and bound in Great Britain by MPG Books, Bodmin, Cornwall

All rights reserved. No part of this book may be reprinted or
reproduced or utilised in any form or by any electronic, mechanical, or
other means, now known or hereafter invented, including photocopying
and recording, or in any information storage or retrieval system,
without permission in writing from the publishers.

British Library Cataloguing in Publication Data
A catalogue record for this book is available from the British Library

Library of Congress Cataloging in Publication Data
A catalog record for this book has been requested.

ISBN 0–415–29015–5 (Set)
ISBN 0–415–29019–8 (Volume IV)

Publisher's Note
References within each chapter are as they appear in the original
complete work.

CONTENTS

VOLUME IV THE 'FASCIST EPOCH'

Acknowledgements	viii
Introduction ROGER GRIFFIN	1

PART 9
European fascisms — 13

9.1	*Fascist regimes*	15
55	*Italy:* **Fascism in power: the totalitarian experiment** EMILIO GENTILE	17
56	*Germany:* **The essence of Nazism: form of fascism, brand of totalitarianism, or unique phenomenon?** IAN KERSHAW	47
9.2	*Fascisms under authoritarian conservatism*	75
57	*Portugal:* **National Syndicalism and international fascism** ANTONIO COSTA PINTO	77
58	*Spain:* Conclusion to *Fascism in Spain 1923–1977* STANLEY G. PAYNE	91
59	*Hungary:* **Extract from 'Hungary'** IGOR DÉAK	102
60	*Romania:* **Extract from 'Characteristics of Rumanian fascism'** RADU IOANID	119

CONTENTS

9.3	*Fascisms under liberalism*	143
61	*Great Britain:* **The black-shirted utopians** PHILIP M. COUPLAND	145
62	*Finland:* **Extract from 'From white to blue-and-black: Finnish fascism in the inter-war era'** LAURI KARVONEN	164
63	*Sweden:* **Swedish fascism – why bother?** LENA BERGGREN	177
64	*France:* **The Croix de Feu: Bonapartism, national populism or fascism?** KEVIN PASSMORE	202
9.4	*'Parafascism'*	229
65	*Nazi-occupied France:* **Vichy and fascism** JULIAN JACKSON	231
66	*Ireland:* **Extract from 'Connections with fascism'** MIKE CRONIN	247

PART 10
Fascism in Latin America 267

67	*Brazil:* **Extract from 'Fascism and authoritarianism in Brazil under Vargas (1930–1945)'** HELIGO TRINDADE	269
68	*Chile:* **A case of non-European fascism: Chilean National Socialism in the 1930s** MARIO SZNAJDER	304
69	*Argentina:* **The fascist and populist syndromes in the Argentine revolution of the right** ALBERTO SPEKTOROWSKI	328

PART 11
Fascism in Africa, Asia and the USA 357

70	*South Africa:* **The Berlin connection** PATRICK J. FURLONG	359

CONTENTS

71 *China:* **Blue Shirts, Nationalists and nationalism: fascism in 1930s China** — **384**
FAN HONG

72 *Japan:* **Japanese fascism and the Tennō imperial state** — **403**
TETSUNARI MATSUZAWA

73 *Japan:* **Fascism from below? A contemporary perspective on the Japanese right 1931–1936** — **419**
GREGORY J. KASZA

74 *USA:* **Extracts from 'The Coming American Fascism'** — **438**
LAWRENCE DENNIS

ACKNOWLEDGEMENTS

The publishers would like to thank the following for permission to reprint their material:

Emilio Gentile, 'Fascism in power: the totalitarian experiment', in Adrian, Lyttelton (ed.), *Liberal and Fascist Italy 1900–1945*, Oxford: Oxford University Press, 2002, pp. 139–174. Reprinted by permission of Oxford University Press.

Ian Kershaw, 'The essence of Nazism: form of fascism, brand of totalitarianism, or unique phenomenon?', *The Nazi Dictatorship: Problems and Perspectives of Interpretation*, 4th edn, London: Arnold, 2000, pp. 20–46. Copyright © Ian Kershaw. Reproduced by permission.

Social Science Monographs for permission to reprint António Costa Pinto, 'National Syndicalism and international fascism', *The Blue Shirts: Portuguese Fascists and the New State*, Boulder, Social Science Monographs, 2000, pp. 225–43.

Stanley G. Payne, 'Conclusion', *Fascism in Spain 1923–1977*, pp. 469–79, © 1999. Reprinted by permission of The University of Wisconsin Press.

University of California Press for permission to reprint Igor Déak, extract from 'Hungary', *The European Right*, Berkeley and Los Angeles: University of California Press, 1965, pp. 383–405.

East European Monographs for permission to reprint Radu Ioanid, extract from 'Characteristics of Rumanian fascism', *The Sword of the Archangel: Fascist Ideology in Romania*, Boulder East European Monographs, 1990, pp. 126–48.

Reproduced with permission from Philip M. Coupland, article 'The blackshirted utopians', *Journal of Contemporary History* 33 (2) (1998): 255–72. Copyright © Sage Publications Ltd, 1998, by permission of Sage Publications Ltd.

ACKNOWLEDGEMENTS

The Finnish Society of Sciences and Letters for permission to reprint Lauri Karvonen, extract from 'From white to blue-and-black: Finnish fascism in the inter-war era', *Commentationes Scientiarum Socialium* 36 (1988): 18–29.

Reproduced with permission from Lena Berggren, 'Swedish fascism – why bother?', *Journal of Contemporary History* 37 (3) (2002): 395–418. Copyright © Sage Publications Ltd, 2002, by permission of Sage Publications Ltd.

Kevin Passmore, 'The Croix de Feu: Bonapartism, national populism or fascism?', *French History* 9 (1) (1995): 67–92. Reprinted by permission of Oxford University Press.

Taylor & Francis for permission to reprint Julian Jackson, 'Vichy and fascism', in Edward Arnold (ed.) *The Development of the Radical Right in France 1890–1995*, London: Routledge, 2000, pp. 153–71.

'Connections with fascism', from *The Blueshirts and Irish Politics* by Mike Cronin (Four Courts Press, Dublin, 1997) is reproduced by kind permission of the publisher, Four Courts Press.

Social Science Monographs for permission to reprint Helgio Trindade, extract from 'Fascism and authoritarianism in Brazil under Vargas (1930–1945)', in Stein Ugelvik Larsen (ed.) *Fascism outside Europe: The European Impulse against Domestic Conditions in the Diffusion of Global Fascism*, Boulder Social Science Monographs, 2001, pp. 491–528.

Reproduced with permission from Mario Sznajder, article 'A case of non-European fascism: Chilean National Socialism in the 1930s', *Journal of Contemporary History* 28 (1) (1993): 269–96. Copyright © Sage Publications Ltd, 1993, by permission of Sage Publications Ltd.

Social Science Monographs for permission to reprint Alberto Spektorowski, 'The fascist and populist syndromes in the Argentine revolution of the right', in Stein Ugelvik Larsen (ed.) *Fascism outside Europe: The European Impulse against Domestic Conditions in the Diffusion of Global Fascism*, Boulder Social Science Monographs 2001, pp. 529–60.

Patrick J. Furlong for permission to reprint Patrick J. Furlong, 'The Berlin connection', *Between Crown and Swastika: The Impact of the Radical Right on the Afrikaner Nationalist Movement in the Fascist Era*, Johannesburg: Witwatersrand University Press, 1991, pp. 70–96.

Frank Cass Publishers for permission to reprint Fan Hong, 'Blue shirts, Nationalists and nationalism: fascism in 1930s China', in J. A. Mangan (ed.) *Superman Supreme: Fascist Body as Global Icon – Global Fascism*, London: Frank Cass, 2000, pp. 205–26.

ACKNOWLEDGEMENTS

The Japanese Studies Centre for permission to reprint Tetsunari Matsuzawa, 'Japanese fascism and the Tennō imperial state', trans. Valerie McGown, Papers of the Japanese Studies Centre 10, Melbourne: Japanese Studies Centre, 1984, pp. 1–15.

Reproduced with permission from Gregory J. Kasza, 'Fascism from below? A comparative perspective on the Japanese right 1931–1936', *Journal of Contemporary History* 19 (3) (1984): 607–29. Copyright © Sage Publications Ltd, 1984, by permission of Sage Publications Ltd.

Disclaimer

The publishers have made every effort to contact authors/copyright holders of works reprinted in *Fascism: Critical Concepts in Political Science*. This has not been possible in every case, however, and we would welcome correspondence from those individuals/companies who we have been unable to trace.

INTRODUCTION

Roger Griffin

This volume is in marked contrast to the other four. The others are concerned with the complex process of 'idealizing abstraction' involved in generalizing about fascism. This selection, on the other hand, focuses on fascism as an umbrella term covering a large number of highly distinctive political movements that appeared in the period 1918–45, or what has been called the 'fascist epoch' (e.g. in Nolte, 1965). Over and above the intrinsic fascination that its particular manifestations may hold to some readers, this series of rapid sorties into eighteen quite different socio-political environments that hosted (putative) fascist movements serves an important methodological function. It aims to impress on those who are tempted to generalize about fascism as if it were a homogeneous, clearly defined 'it' that the term embraces a host of heterogeneous, highly textured singularities.

The process of identifying singular movements or regimes as 'fascist' is not only contentious (the main theme of Volume I), but each has to be understood in its uniqueness as well as in its 'generic aspect' if significant features of its exceptionalness and concrete historicity are not to be lost sight of and sacrificed to the 'will to abstraction' so rife in some areas of the human sciences. As James Barnes, one of the most articulate English proponents of a 'universal fascism', put it in 1928, 'Fascists in each country must make Fascism their own national movement, adopting symbols and tactics which conform to the traditions, psychology and tastes of their own land' (Barnes, 1928: 240). Therefore, one of the main skills needed for comparative fascist studies is to be able to distinguish the core from the contingent elements of a national milieu or historical era.

There is a second item on the 'hidden agenda' of this volume. One of the basic premises of this anthology has been that fascist studies has only recently started to 'come of age' as a mature field of academic enquiry. A sign of its immaturity in the past was the way it succeeded in generating a steady flow of definitions and theories of fascism which suffered the indignity of being 'snubbed', or ignored altogether, by most historians investigating particular phenomena that within fascist studies would widely be considered examples of it ('putative fascism') and hence falling within their remit. This was the fate even of definitions proposed by Ernst Nolte, Zeev Sternhell and James Gregor which became famous within the specialism, not to mention those offered by a number of less famous contributors (e.g. Paul Hayes, 1973; Alan Cassels, 1975; Neil O'Sullivan, 1983). Indeed, it is only with the emergence of the new consensus that this situation is starting to change, so that the prospect is now opening up of a generally harmonious relationship between the 'nomothetic' search for general historical patterns when fascism is studied as a generic phenomenon (the province of the political and social scientists and historians drawn to comparative studies) and the 'idiographic' concern of historians to capture the past 'as it actually was'. Though few of the following texts have been written in the light of the 'new consensus', read in conjunction with selections from other volumes their very presence in the collection is a tacit appeal for a healthy synergy between theorizing and empiricism, the suggestion being that the analytical focus would have been even sharper had the lens (or lenses) of the new consensus been applied.

One historian demonstrating this synergy throughout his work is Emilio Gentile. As an integral part of his lifelong academic quest to understand Fascism he has made sustained excursions into the theory of the state, modernity, nationalism, political religion, totalitarianism and fascism itself in order to refine the generic concepts so central to his investigation, which are then applied fruitfully to the singularities of Mussolini's regime. It is thus appropriate to open Volume IV with his synoptic chapter on the Fascist regime (55) which applies his theory of totalitarianism (39) to revealing the deep structure of the Fascist state, in particular its bid to bring about an 'anthropological revolution' in the social and political culture of modern Italians. In doing so it displays good practice in synthesizing the nomothetic and the idiographic to probe into the phenomenon that, for good or ill, originally bequeathed the generic term 'fascist' in the first place, one we cannot simply dispense with or censure from the political lexicon, no matter what some academics such as Gilbert Allerdyce (I, 8) have hoped in the past. The unique texture of Mussolini's regime is thus illuminated by the sensitive handling of generic concepts in a spirit profoundly compatible with the 'new consensus' established in Volume I.

This is followed by a chapter (56) demonstrating just how complex a taxonomic process is involved (whether consciously or not) once the term is used 'generically' for any singularity outside Italy. Under the magnifying glass here is Nazism, although the same theoretical issues are raised in principle by all of the movements and regimes considered in the rest of this volume. In this chapter on various aspects of the convoluted academic debate surrounding the nature of Nazism, Ian Kershaw provides a guide to the issue of whether the Third Reich is to be seen as 'a unique phenomenon', 'a form of totalitarianism' or 'a form of fascism'. It is an important piece, not only because of the magisterial way he summarizes a vast secondary literature offering many contrasting positions before arriving at his own carefully formulated judgements, but because of the lucidity with which he makes three crucial points, namely a) there is no contradiction between the uniqueness of a historical singularity and its location within a generic phenomenon, so the undoubted uniqueness of Nazism's racial state and the exceptional scale of its mass production of atrocities are no reasons in themselves for its exclusion from the generic category of 'fascism'; b) what determines whether Nazism should be seen as 'fascist' or 'totalitarian' depends on the way these terms are defined as well as on the heuristic value of applying them to Nazism in terms of increased understanding of concrete realities; and c) if the definition of fascism proposed by the 'new consensus' (it is not called that by Kershaw) is applied, then Nazism is 'self-evidently' fascist (see Kershaw's note 60). I would add as my own footnote that if Emilio Gentile's definition of 'totalitarianism' is applied (III, 39), then Nazism is equally 'self-evidently' both totalitarian and fascist (while of course still being unique).

Bearing these methodological strictures in mind, the 'grand tour' of the extraordinarily varied species of fascism can begin. The terrain is vast, and a number of European countries which hosted fascist movements will be simply ignored (for a more comprehensive panorama of European fascisms in this period see Carsten, 1967; Blinkhorn, 2000; Morgan, 2002). The first stop is Portugal (57), which in 1932 witnessed the attempts by Rolão Preto's blue-shirted National Syndicalist movement to wrest power from Salazar's conservative regime which was increasingly modelling itself on Fascism in Italy, but which lacked any real commitment to a socio-cultural revolution. The conditions in which the NS might have achieved a mass base never materialized and it was easily neutralized by the 'New State', which never felt under any pressure to make concessions. In this extract António Costa Pinto establishes the parallels and contrasts between National Syndicalists and other European fascisms.

The situation of fascism in Spain (58) is different if only because in the exceptional circumstances of the Civil War (1936–9) the Falange acquired a sufficiently impressive mass following for Franco to absorb it into the right-wing regime that he established rather than neutralize it. This text forms the conclusion to a history of Spanish fascism by Stanley Payne, who has arguably done more than any other practising 'idiographic' historian to encourage the academic debate over the term fascist to progress towards methodological maturity and definitional clarity (see I, 4, 11). It illustrates the importance of demarcating the revolutionary palingenetic politics of fascists from the policies of radical right-wing conservatives, even when, like Franco, they go to great lengths to modernize authoritarianism and co-opt some of 'genuine' fascism's dynamism in order to make it more palatable to the age of the masses and 'youth' (to produce what has been called a 'parafascist' regime: Griffin, 1991, ch. 5).

INTRODUCTION

The extract from Igor Déak's chapter on radical right politics in Hungary (59) exhibits yet another permutation typical of the fate of fascism under authoritarianism. As in Portugal, an authoritarian right-wing regime (in this case that of Admiral Horthy and his anti-Semitic prime minister Gömbös) created an environment whose essential conservatism was deeply inhospitable to the revolutionary project of fascist movements. The various rural and urban attempts to emulate Nazism were thus pathetic failures, even the most 'successful' one, the Arrow Cross movement, whose leader, Szálasi – like De Ledesma and Antonio Primo de Rivera in Spain – had been at pains to create a national rebirth adapted to his own political culture and historical situation. It was only when the Third Reich ousted Horthy, who had resisted total capitulation to Nazi demands to the last, that Szálasi was given the chance to become head of state, or rather the nominal head of a Nazi puppet state, something he would never have achieved but for the determination of the Third Reich to see the Final Solution through even when defeat was inevitable.

The Romanian variant of fascism came much closer than National Syndicalism, Falangism or Hungarism to securing a share of state power through its own momentum as a populist movement. By 1937 the Iron Guard had gained enough popular support for attempts to be made by both King Carol and General Antonescu to absorb it into conservative authoritarian regimes (a tactic which, if successful, would have emulated Franquist Spain's emasculation of the Falange). This extract (60) from Radu Ioanid's book on the history of the Iron Guard (the Legion of the Archangel St Michael) identifies its main ideological components, some of which are familiar in other variants of fascism (e.g. its anti-Semitism). Others, however, are peculiar to it, notably the assimilation of Romanian orthodox Christianity in order to transform its theology 'into a political instrument' – though even here there are parallels elsewhere, such as in the Falange's appropriation of Catholicism (58), the Croatian Ustaše's close collaboration with Catholic clergy (Glenny, 2000) and the 'radical religion' of the USA's contemporary racist right (Kaplan, 1997, 2000).

It was within a liberal democracy undergoing a structural crisis that fascism had its best chance of challenging the state successfully, and even in such a situation it only managed to conquer power in two countries, Italy and Germany. Where the structural factors of systemic crisis were weak, as in England, it could pose no real threat to the status quo. Oswald Mosely made a sustained attempt before the Second World War to use his British Union of Fascists to tailor Fascism, with an increasing admixture of Nazism as the 1930s wore on, to the national context in order to realize his dream of a 'Greater Britain', but remained successfully marginalized. Philip Coupland's article (61) on the utopianism of the BUF reveals the blend of 'generic' traits of its programme (e.g. the cult of leadership, masculinity, the paramilitarism, the dream of emulating a former golden age) with highly idiosyncratic, culture-specific mythic components to be found in all specimens of the genus. (His article is to be read in conjunction with III, 52, the BUF's vision of rebirth being the corollary of its obsession with reversing Britain's decadence that is the theme of Linehan's chapter.)

Lauri Karvonen's article on fascism in Finland (62) deals with a more 'successful' movement, but still underlines just how difficult it was for an ultra-nationalist movement to achieve power even in the wake of a civil war and against a background of intense ideological polarization, 'unsated' nationalist ambitions and socio-economic crisis. To corroborate the importance of the dependency of the strength of a fascist movement on a perceived state crisis, Lena Berggren's article (63) shows that Sweden's internal stability meant that the government was never even remotely threatened by a fascist revolution. Nevertheless, given the comparative lack of factors causing structural dysfunction or widespread sentiments of unsated nationalism in inter-war Sweden, she also reveals a more sizable and variegated fascist constituency than conforming stereotypes about Swedish democracy or national character may suggest. Her article is also important because it underlines the need for a sound comparative and conceptual framework in order for Swedish fascism to be properly investigated, and makes the plea for insights drawn from the 'new consensus' to be imported into the Swedish academic community. It also stresses how we do need to 'bother' about apparently peripheral manifestations of fascism in order to refine collective understanding of the generic phenomenon.

With Kevin Passmore's article on the paramilitary league (64), the Croix de Feu, we move to another example of fascist and putative fascist movements arising in a liberal democracy, this time one which underwent a structural crisis sufficiently strong by the mid-1930s to enable heterogeneous anti-systemic movements of the far right to gain a considerable following as ideological, paramilitary and party-political movements, generating a far greater sense of threat to liberal democracy than their Swedish counterparts. However, even at the peak of the democratic crisis in 1934, these forces never coalesced into a single mass movement comparable to Fascism or Nazism. Moreover, such is the richness and complexity of the French revolutionary, authoritarian, ultra-nationalist and racist tradition that the taxonomic problems posed by each manifestation of putative fascism are considerable. Nor are they made easier to solve by the deep polarization between experts on the French inter-war radical right in the way they conceptualize key terms. Passmore's article is exemplary in his attempt to balance the nomothetic and the idiographic, both to illuminate the nature of the Croix de Feu and to establish its relationship both to French history and to international fascism.

The essay by Julian Jackson on the Vichy regime (65) provides yet another case study in applying the concept of generic fascism to France. Pétain's regime collaborated extensively with the Third Reich, but a general consensus has grown up that it lacked the revolutionary zeal or radicalism to count as fascism, more resembling in its core values Salazar's New State. Yet

INTRODUCTION

in Jackson's analysis a more complex picture emerges of a regime whose rhetoric contained strong elements of palingenetic myth, launched some fascist policies and confirmed the convictions of those who wanted to bring France into the mainstream of what seemed at the time an increasingly fascist Europe. Even if, as he concludes, fascism always played a 'subordinate role' in Vichy, its zeal in collaborating with the Final Solution should not be overlooked, underlining the fact that crimes against humanity were not a monopoly of the fascist right and communist left.

If Vichy turns out to be a particularly intricate example of a parafascist regime, then Mike Cronin's article adds a new twist to the taxonomic complexities of this area of comparative history. It postulates that the Irish Blueshirts, even if some key elements in the leadership – notably its leader Eoin O'Duffy – were undoubtedly fascists, are best seen as a parafascist movement (66). In particular, their commitment to the creation of a corporate state is to be associated more with the official economic theory of the Vatican and with the statist planned economy adopted in Salazar's Portugal than with the Italian Fascist state. Significantly, the radicalness of O'Duffy's views led him eventually to resign in 1934 as President of Fine Gael, the political party associated with the Blue Shirts, at which point he created the National Corporate Party (the Greenshirts) which had an overtly fascist political agenda. Equally significantly the NCP had a derisory impact on Irish politics.

After our whistle-stop tour of Europe, taking in a handful of the many fascist movements that sprang up in the 'era of fascism', we move to the Americas. If the popular mind tends to equate Latin American dictatorships with fascism, many well-established historians have betrayed their ethnocentrism by considering fascism an exclusively European phenomenon. It is thus instructive to read in an extract of Helgio Trindade's extensive chapter (67) on the Brazilian Integralist Action movement (AIB) a detailed evocation of the ideology, theory of state, organizational structure and political religion of a movement that undoubtedly conforms to the 'new consensus' definition (even if Trindade himself is oblivious of it and uses instead a loose checklist of definitional traits broadly corresponding to it). Not only does the AIB emerge as a movement of populist rebirth nationalism fully adapted to the unique historical conditions of Brazil, it also demonstrates an explicit linkage between modernism and fascism in the ideological career of its leader, Plínio Salgado, a member of the intelligentsia who believed the world was witnessing the birth pangs of the 'fourth era of humanity'. Despite becoming Brazil's largest mass movement of the inter-war years, its assault on state power in 1937 was easily quelled by Vargas' authoritarian regime, once more confirming the fundamental antagonism in the relationship between fascism and conservatism encountered in Europe.

Mario Sznajder's article on Chile's Movimiento Nacional Socialista (MNS) (68) traces the history of a movement that, despite its name, modelled itself not on Nazism as such, but on a vision of itself as a Latin American counterpart of the regenerative nationalisms of European fascism, helping modern humanity to resolve the perceived crisis of civilization. (The fact that the movement nevertheless called itself National Socialist shows that by the 1930s it was a commonplace for the radical right to consider Nazism a permutation of the same force that had given rise to Italian Fascism, otherwise the British Union of Fascists would not have changed its name to the British Union of Fascists and National Socialists.) As a result MNS ideologues adapted the notion of national revolution to the concrete circumstances prevailing in 1930s Chile. Its retention of Catholic values (if not faith) and rejection both of imperialism and of the notion that there was any sort of racially or culturally ideal-typical or racially pure Chilean to serve as the embodiment of the revolutionary project are significant departures from both Fascism and Nazism. Another peculiarity is that the leader of the MNS was still able to continue his parliamentary career after giving the orders triggering an abortive and ruthlessly suppressed military coup in September 1938, and eventually transformed the MNS into the Vanguardia Popular Socialista. By this time it had shed all traces of revolutionary nationalism, bearing out Sznajder's thesis that Chilean Nacism stood 'somewhere between fascism and the radical right'.

A Latin American country that has generated putative fascist political phenomena even more resistant to watertight categorization is Argentina. There has been much speculation about whether Peronism is to be seen as a form of fascism, with experts producing contrasting analyses (e.g. Lipset, 1960; Hennessy, 1979). Alberto Spektorowski's article (69) makes a convincing case for seeing the Grupo de Oficiales Unidos, the military faction that seized power in June 1943, as consciously pursuing a policy of tailoring European fascist principles to the peculiar situation of Argentina and creating a national revolution having as much to do with a regenerative communal ethos as with institutional and economic reform. In doing so it was building on a vision of national modernization pioneered in the 1930s, synthesizing the populist left and integralist right wings of Argentinian nationalism and in a manner profoundly influenced by the example of Fascist Italy. It further implies that the Peronist regime that succeeded it after February 1946, with its unique blend of syndicalism, corporatism, nationalism, militarism, constitutionalism, authoritarianism and populism, started out as a fascist 'revolutionary' order imposed from above, adapting its original fascist radicalism to the ending of the 'fascist epoch' in Europe and the victory of liberal capitalism in the West (a similar accommodation was made by the authoritarian regimes of Franco and Salazar, which progressively shed their parafascist trappings after 1943).

The one state in Africa in the fascist epoch which provided an ideal habitat for the growth of ultra-nationalist ideologies on the European model on a par with Brazil or Argentina was South Africa. The Ossewabrandwag

(Oxwagon Sentinel, or OB) was the most famous movement of Afrikaaner nationalism, and crystallized longings widespread among the Boers for a homeland based on a religious, cultural, linguistic and racial homogeneity unthinkable under British colonial rule (Bunting, 1969; Bloomberg, 1981). Its ideology attached profound importance to a fundamentalist version of Dutch Reformist Christianity as an indicator of national identity and a basis of spiritual values, giving it a distant affinity with the Finnish Lapua movement, the Spanish Falange and the Romanian Iron Guard, all of which also incorporated politicized versions of Christianity into the mythic articulation of their national cause. Patrick Furlong's chapter (70) illuminates one episode in the genesis of the OB, namely the growing impact of Nazism on the Afrikaaner community, which helped crystallize its sense of humiliation and marginalization at the hands of the British during the 1899–1902 Boer War into a highly idiosyncratic fascist programme of ethnic exclusiveness and national rebirth. Its emphasis on the sanctity of peasant life is reminiscent of the extreme anti-urban *völkisch* and Blood and Soil strands of Nazi ideology embodied in Walter Darré's version of Nazism.

So far all the putative fascisms considered have emerged either in European societies or in former colonies deeply influenced by the legacy of European rule. It thus challenges some deeply held preconceptions about the geographical diffusion of fascism (which even an expert as distinguished as Renzo de Felice claimed was confined to inter-war Europe) to read Fan Hong's article (71). China is conspicuous by its absence from the 'classic' major collections of essays about international fascism (e.g. Turner, 1975; Mosse, 1979; Larsen *et al.*, 1980). Yet here a scholar consciously applying the new consensus on fascism shows just how indebted not one, but two movements sponsored by Chiang Kai-shek's Nationalist Party government were to European fascist models, namely the Blue Shirts and the New Life movement. Nationalist Party leaders had received material help from Nazi military advisors and were deeply impressed by the continuous displays of youthful, disciplined nationalism being staged at the time in both the Fascist and the Nazi regimes. Indeed, the Blue Shirt leaders were so struck by their palingenetic ethos that they could declare that 'fascism is the only tool of self-salvation of nations on the brink of destruction', a belief that provides further empirical corroboration to the new consensus. Though both movements were eclipsed by the United Front formed to fight the Japanese in 1937, they represent yet more cases of deliberate attempts to adapt the mythic core of fascism *as fascists themselves perceive it*, namely palingenetic ultranationalism, to the conditions prevailing in a particular country. Another important feature of the Chinese example is that the two movements are promoted by a nationalist regime from above, but not in the parafascist spirit of Spain, Romania or Vichy in order to create a revolutionary populist façade. Rather, as in Argentina, fascism seems to have been encouraged as part of a genuine attempt by the state to mobilize revolutionary enthusiasm among the masses for the nationalist cause and accelerate the process of transition from a traditional to a modern society (there are parallels here with the Leninist theory of socializing the masses from above after the conquest of power).

If some readers have been disoriented by evidence of fascism arising in a country where few would expect to find it, their sense of being on familiar ground will probably return with Tetsunari's article (72). Once the attack on Pearl Harbor had brought Japan into the Second World War on the side of the Axis Powers it was naturally closely identified with fascism, especially since the pervasive militarism of the regime and the ruthless brutality of its imperialism was so reminiscent of the behaviour of the Nazis in Eastern Europe. It will thus raise few eyebrows, then, if the article simply assumes the existence of a Japanese fascism without 'problematizing' the term, locating its distant roots in the hostility to 'outsiders' that was intrinsic to the feudal system. This xenopbobia then became perpetuated and formalized within the state system which had emerged by the early twentieth century to underpin Japan's transformation into a modern nation-state, a unique blend of social integration, ultra-conservatism and industrialization given cultural cohesion by the institution of the divine Emperor, referred to here as the '*Tennō* imperial state'. According to Tetsunari two fascist movements then arose at the end of the 1920s as a response to the perceived threat of the imminent collapse of the *Tennō* system, one advocating a 'return to the origins' (reminiscent of the Nazi Blood and Soil faction), and the other calling for a vision of 'controlled development' (*tōsei*) embracing a vast scheme of imperial conquest based on a sense of Japan's racial superiority and destiny of historical greatness (something much closer to mainstream Nazism). It was the growing domination of government policy by the 'tōsei' faction after the Manchurian Incident of 1931 that accounts for the metamorphosis of the *Tennō* state into an aggressively expansionist, militarist, racist and fully fascist regime after 1931.

Yet any feeling of being on terra firma in this account of Japanese fascism is immediately undermined by Gregory Kasza's article (73). Tetsunari's analysis has clearly been influenced by the Western Marxist tradition that equates fascism with aggressive nationalism, imperialism and racism. Thus the rise of fascism in Japan is associated with the state crisis and rising class tensions of the 1920s. Kasza, a US scholar, approaches the topic from a quite different perspective. Fully aware of the need of a solid 'nomothetic' base if a European term is to be meaningfully applied idiographically to such a deeply un-European context, he avails himself of the most sophisticated tripartite 'typological definition' of fascism then available, namely the one offered by Payne (Payne, 1980), to tackle what is for him a question defying simple answers. He then conscientiously sets about the delicate task of identifying the existence of unmistakably fascist elements in 1930s Japan, which by then had become an aggressively imperialist, authoritarian state and hosted a thriving radical right culture made up of countless factions pursuing different ideals of Japan's path to greatness, each using different tactics to realize them.

So great is the taxonomic problem posed that Kasza has to supplement Payne's three-part model of the modern radical right with a new category in order to do justice to the complexity of the reality he encounters. The bottom line after this painstaking analysis is that fascism as a mass-mobilizing myth of national rebirth, conceived in a way that would make a clean break with traditional conservatism (in Japan's case embodied in a divine Emperor), is practically non-existent: the radical right's identification of the constitution with the Emperor made 'any proposal for a radically new political regime' unthinkable. As for the imperial state itself, it did not need fascism to pursue its delusions of imperial grandeur. The powerful currents of fascism that featured in Tetsunari's article suddenly evaporate in Kasza's, a sober reminder of just what a methodologically treacherous terrain fascist studies are for all those who would wish to explore them.

Our grand tour of the fascist epoch ends with a glimpse of what might have been. By mid-1935 Italy and Germany had become seemingly impregnable fascist regimes, much of the rest of Europe was in political turmoil and the effects of the Depression were still being felt throughout the capitalist world. At a time when Roosevelt's New Deal was being widely seen as a form of state intervention inspired by Fascism and Nazism, it was possible for cultural pundits to believe that they were experiencing the collapse of liberal capitalism, thus confronting all liberal elites with the stark choice between communism and a form of fascism so well adapted to the circumstances of the nation that it did not even use the name. The extract chosen from Lawrence Dennis' book, *The Coming American Fascism* (74), is part of a sustained plea for the USA's ruling elites to turn from liberalism while there is still time and impose a fascist regime from above, a scenario that is reminiscent of what was partially realized by the GOU coup in Argentina in 1943 (see 69). Dennis argues that only by doing so would they avoid another disastrous 'holy war' (the allusion is to the First World War into which the USA had been lured twenty years earlier) to make the world safe for liberalism, a catastrophic turn of events which would in practice only mean handing civilization over to Russia's Red Army.

No matter how absurd such a scenario seems in hindsight (though elements and ingredients of fascism certainly surfaced in Depression-struck North America (Warren, 2001), it serves as a powerful symptom of how widespread the sense of the decay of the liberal West had become on the eve of the Second World War, generating a diffuse 'sense-making crisis' (see II, 28) that made fascism seem to be the only alternative to the triumph of communism and the source of salvation from the total collapse of civilization. (For another testimony to the prevalence of this mood it is worth reading H. G. Wells, *The Shape of Things to Come* (1933).) Dennis suggests in the introduction to his book that an American fascism might be so well adapted to the particular situation of the USA that it would probably deny it was in fact fascism at all (the Falange also denied its fascist credentials so as not to be perceived as 'foreign' and hence un-Spanish). This, of course brings us back to a central theme of these volumes in the Critical Concept series, namely the need to have a clear heuristic definition of fascism so that its permutations can be recognized even when they are heavily disguised or assume unfamiliar external forms. It is an issue that assumes particular importance in Volume V of this collection, which deals with fascism's evolution after the defeat of the Axis Powers in 1945.

Part 9

EUROPEAN FASCISMS

9.1 Fascist regimes
9.2 Fascisms under authoritarian conservatism
9.3 Fascisms under liberalism
9.4 'Parafascism'

9.1

Fascist regimes

55

FASCISM IN POWER

The totalitarian experiment

Emilio Gentile

Source: Adrian Lyttleton (ed.) *Liberal and Fascist Italy 1900–1945*, Oxford: Oxford University Press, 2002, pp. 139–74.

WHY TOTALITARIAN?

Historians have variously described Italy's Fascist regime as an authoritarian nationalist regime, as a personal 'monocracy', a 'tendentially totalitarian State', 'an imperfect totalitarian state', and as an 'incomplete totalitarian state'. Others have simply described Fascism as *Mussolinismo*, arguing that Mussolini created a personal dictatorship based on an alliance with the traditional institutions of the Italian monarchist state that left the fundamental structures of the old regime virtually unchanged. To support this, they claim that Mussolini carried out the 'political liquidation' of the Fascist Party, which he then turned into a vast bureaucracy whose function was simply to orchestrate parades, organize consensus, create jobs and positions.

Until quite recently these interpretations of the nature of the Fascist regime were endorsed by a majority of historians, but studies published since the 1970s have forced us to reassess many of the most fundamental features of the regime and the role of the Fascist Party. These recent studies have made available important new information and new understanding on aspects of the regime that range from the role of ideology to institutional organization, and from mass politics to foreign policy, which indicate that Italian Fascism is best understood and interpreted as 'Italy's road to totalitarianism'.[1]

Since the term 'totalitarianism' has given rise to endless controversy, we must start by defining the meaning that will be attached to it in this chapter. The terms 'totalitarian', 'totalitarianism', 'total dictatorship', and 'party-state' were first invented in the years between 1923 and 1925 by the intellectual and political opponents of Fascism. They used these terms to pinpoint what made the Fascist dictatorship different from traditional dictatorial governments. The most novel feature of what many anti-Fascists were already calling a new 'experiment in government' was seen to be the determination to concentrate a total monopoly of political power in the hands of a single political party which was committed to imposing its ideology as a form of secular religion. In April 1923 the anti-Fascist historian Luigi Salvatorelli wrote that Fascism aimed at achieving 'a total party dictatorship': 'it aims at the dictatorship of the party and the establishment of a "single party", which means the suppression of all other political parties, or in other words the end of political life as it has been understood in Europe over the last century'.[2]

In October of the same year the liberal anti-Fascist Giovanni Amendola, who was probably the inventor of the term 'totalitarian', insisted that the fundamental feature of the Fascist movement was a ' "totalitarian spirit" which means that in future no day would dawn without being greeted with the Roman-style Fascist salute' and which had unleashed in Italy 'a particular form of "war of religion" in the attempt to impose its ideology as a form of faith to be obligatory for all Italians'.[3]

A few months earlier a Catholic anti-Fascist had written of Mussolini's claims to be 'the only interpreter and repository of the new religion of the fatherland':

'we are faced by a new dogmatic religion equipped with its own sacraments and its own infallible leader. Anyone who fails to love the fatherland in the ways desired by Benito Mussolini and in conformity with the rites that he has established is a heretic to be consigened to the purifying fire of the muskets of the national militia.'[4]

Early in 1925 and before Mussolini's speech of 3 January that set out the totalitarian programme that opened the way to the one-party state, the Marxist Lelio Basso had written:

> The Fascist state no longer limits itself to defending the established order by means of a legal system devised for that purpose.... It now claims to represent the entire people and therefore excludes the possibility that there could be any political movement opposed to it or different from it, and should such a movement meekly show itself, it will immediately attempt to destory it totally. When we have reached the point when the institutions that in theory embody the three powers of the state (the monarchy, the parliament and the magistracy, as well as the armed forces which translate their will into action) become the instruments of a single party that claims to be the interpreter of a unanimous will and of an undivided totalitarianism that shuts out the possibility of any further progress, we can confidently claim that the crisis of the state will have reached its climax and that the only alternatives

remaining will be that either the crisis is resolved or that the state collapses.⁵

The term 'totalitarian' and its derivatives began to be used by the Fascists themselves after 1925, who adopted it as a badge of identity that defined their own conception of politics and of the state. This was based on the idea that all power should be concentrated in the hands of the party and its leader, and that the *fascistizzazione* of Italian society would be achieved through the expansion of the power exercised by the Fascist Party. This would extend to every aspect of social life to bring about what Mussolini referred to as 'the reformation of the character of the Italians' that was needed to make the Italians a race of conquerors and rulers.

In the following years, the anti-Fascists took up the concept of the totalitarian state and regime to describe all new one-party regimes. Luigi Sturzo, the founder of the Catholic Popular Party (PPI) who had been forced into exile in 1924, wrote in 1926, for example, that Fascism was advancing along the path 'towards "totalitarianism and absolutism" '.

During his imprisonment in the early 1930s Antonio Gramsci would also formulate a concise definition of the concept of 'totalitarian politics':

> It is always the case that an individual belongs to more than one particular association and is often a member of associations that are in conflict with one another. The tendency of a totalitarian political system is to ensure (i) that the members of a given political party find within this single party the satisfactions that they had previously derived from a range of different organizations, thereby breaking the ties that previously connected these individuals to external cultural organizations; (ii) to destroy all other forms of organization or to incorporate them into a system which is controlled exclusively by a single party.⁶

After the Second World War, however, the term 'totalitarianism' and its derivatives lost their original meanings and became part of the armoury of Cold War propaganda and invective, and as a result were discredited as models for political or hisotrical analysis. But the abuse and misuse of the terms in that period is no reason for banning them forever, and so long as they are understood in the terms in which they were originally defined by the opponents of the Italian Fascists they remain essential for understanding the nature of Fascism in Italy.

Totalitarianism and the nature of Fascist politics

The development of the Fascist regime in Italy is best studied, therefore, in terms of the concept of 'totalitarianism' as it was defined by those who first devised the term and with the meanings illustrated in the quotations cited above. This offers a valid explanation not only of the nature, but also of the dynamics of Fascism in power. Here 'totalitarianism' has the meaning of an experiment in political power undertaken by a revolutionary party with an integralist understanding of politics. The objective was to establish monopolist control over all forms of political power. Once that had been achieved by legal and illegal means, the aim was to destroy or radically transform the existing political system in order to create a new state organized around a single political party, flanked by the apparatus of a police state, and by the systematic use of terror to prevent or repress all forms of opposition and dissent.

The origins, nature, and dynamic of the Italian experiment in totalitarianism cannot be understood, however, without taking account of the specific nature of the political party from which it originated. The central objective of the totalitarian party, beyond the acquisition of a monopoly of political power, is to conquer and change society, in other words to subordinate, integrate, and regiment those governed on the basis of an ideology that asserts the *primacy of politics* in every aspect of human life. Totalitarian politics are based on the idea that the meanings and purpose of human life are expressed in myths and values that constitute a secular religion whose aim is to make the individual and the masses one. It therefore aims to bring about an *anthropological revolution* that will create a new type of human being, totally dedicated to achieving the political aims of the totalitarian party.

The concept of totalitarianism that we shall use in this chapter is not intended to imply, however, any underlying similarity between different totalitarian regimes. Defining totalitarianism as an experiment in political domination serves above all to emphasize that this was a *continuing process*, and hence it cannot meaningfully be judged to have been 'complete' or 'perfect'. No historical example of a totalitarian regime can be considered to have been 'complete' or 'perfect', because these are categories that exist only as abstract ideal-type models of the totalitarian state. History, by contrast, provides us with no examples of totalitarian experiments that were not subject to limitations, obstacles and resistance.

Nor was the Fascist totalitarian experiment limited simply to internal politics. Indeed, Fascist foreign policy was driven by the same objectives and its aim was to create an empire. The ultimate failure of Fascism was inseparable, therefore, from the ambitions for totalitarian power which drove the regime continuously to seek to acquire ever greater internal power and at the same time committed it to the pursuit of aggrandisement and territorial conquests overseas.

Mussolini and Fascism

The Fascist totalitarian experiment was closely associated with Mussolini, but was never simply Mussolini's personal creation. It has to be remembered that while Mussolini had been the original founder of the Fascist movement in 1919, he was not the main cause of its expansion or success after 1920. Fascism became a mass movement after 1920 as a result of what was termed *squadrismo*, the creation of para-military squads, each with their own charismatic local leader, organized at a provincial and local level. As a result, Mussolini had found himself faced by a major rebellion in the summer of 1921 when the provincial leaders of Fascism opposed his decision to enter into a 'pact of pacification' with the Socialists. Even after he came to power, Mussolini had to bow to the integralist Fascists who were demanding a much faster seizure of power by the Fascist Party and the immediate transformation of the liberal regime into a new state that would be controlled by the Fascist Party. Until as late as 1926 Mussolini was still not recognized as the unchallenged leader by many of the leaders of 'provincial Fascism'.[7]

In 1919 the Fascist movement had been born as an 'anti-party' that looked to recruit those who had no place in traditional political parties. Fascism was presented as a pragmatic, anti-dogmatic, anticlerical, and republican political movement that advocated radical institutional, economic, and social reform. The Fascists were contemptuous of parliamentary government and liberalism; they supported the activist politics of minority groups and were prepared to use violence and the politics of the street both in support of Italy's territorial demands at the Peace Conference and to combat the socialists.

Between 1919 and 1920 Fascism was of little significance, however. Its expansion began only after the collapse of the workers' occupation of the factories in the autumn of 1920, at which point the Fascists placed themselves at the head of the bourgeois reaction. It was at this point that Fascist squads, now armed and organized on a para-military basis, began a series of violent offensives that in the space of only a few months shattered the workers' organizations in the Po Valley and in central Italy, where they had previously been strongest and most numerous. This *squadrismo* was the real beginning of Fascism as a mass movement.

After 1920 the expansion of the Fascist movement was extremely rapid. Membership rose from 20, 165 in December 1920 to 187,588 in May 1921 when the Fascists took part in the parliamentary elections and returned thirty-five deputies. But this mass party was already something quite different from the original Milanese fascism, and was essentially a composite of many different 'provincial fascisms' whose principal strength came from the Po Valley and Tuscany. By contrast, the Fascists had made little impact in the industrial regions and were virtually non-existent in the south, except for Apulia.

Strengthened by this rapid expansion, the Fascists fought the election campaign of 1921 on the slate of the 'National Coalition' headed by the Prime Minister Giovanni Giolitti. The aged statesman believed he could put an end to *squadrismo* by bringing the Fascists into the parliamentary system, but the plan failed. The Fascists obtained thirty-five seats, but Mussolini used this electoral success to force the collapse of Giolitti's government while the squads kept up their violent attacks on the socialists, communists, republicans, and the anti-Fascists in the Catholic PPI. A new government headed by Ivanoe Bonomi (June 1921–February 1922) tried to end the political violence by sponsoring an agreement between the Fascists, the Socialists, and the leaders of the principal trade union, the General Confederation of Workers (CGL) to abjure violence which was signed on 3 August 1921. This was the 'pacification pact' that the majority of the leaders of provincial *squadrismo*, including Pietro Marsich, Dino Grandi, Italo Balbo, and Roberto Farinacci, rejected outright, openly challenging Mussolini's right to act as leader of the Fascist movement. The crisis was one of the most critical points in the history of Fascism, and ended in a compromise reached at the congress held in Rome in November 1921. Mussolini's role as leader or 'duce' was recognized, but in return the movement was transformed into a political party, the Partito Nazionale Fascista (PNF), and the leaders of the squads forced Mussolini to abandon the pacification pact and acknowledge that *squadrismo* was the essence of the new party.

As a social movement, the main support for Fascism came from both the traditional and newer urban and provincial middle classes. The middling groups in Italian society had expanded notably in the early decades of the twentieth century. Between 1901 and 1921 they had risen from 51.2 to 53.3 per cent of the active population, in contrast to the wealthier bourgeoisie that had remained at 1.7 per cent while the working class had dropped from 47.1 to 45.0 per cent. The expansion of the lower middle-classes had been most marked in the North (10%), in comparison with 7.1 per cent in Central Italy and only 2.0 per cent in the South. The largest contribution to this expansion had come from new landowners, who had risen from 18.3 per cent in 1911 to 32.4 per cent in 1921. The expansion in the peasant middle classes was concentrated primarily in Lombardy (increasing from 18.29% to 26.54%), in Emilia (from 13.33% to 20.26%), and in the Veneto (from 22.59% to 29.53%), that is to say precisely in the regions where Fascism had first developed as a mass movement. The vast majority of the organizers of the *Fasci* and leaders of *squadrismo* were from the lower middle classes. In 1922 of 127 national and provincial political officers, 77 per cent had lower middle class backgrounds as opposed to only 4 per cent from bourgeois families, while only one federal secretary was a worker. In terms of occupations, there were lawyers (35%), journalists (22%), teachers (6%), employees (5%), engineers (4.7%), army officers (4.7%), insurance agents (3%), and farmers (3%). Of some thousand Fascist leaders who ran local organizations, 80 per cent came from lower middle class backgrounds, 10.5 per cent from the bourgeoisie, and only 5 per cent were proletarians: the occupational groups most strongly represented were public employees (12%), students (9.5%), lawyers (9%), landowners (7.62%), artisans (7%), teachers (7%), farmers (6.7%), accountants (6%), manual workers (5%), and engineers (3.65%).

Youth was also a distinctive feature of the new movement. Of the thirty-five deputies elected in 1921, four were younger than 29 (which meant that they were below the legal age to be elected), and fourteen were aged between 30 and 40. Of the 101 federal secretaries in office before the 'March on Rome', half were under 32 years of age. Overall, the average age of the leaders of the Fascist federations was 31.8. The average age of the members of the National Directorate of the PNF, when it was founded, was 32.9, in contrast to an average of 45.2 for the Socialist Party, 37.7 for the Popular Party, and 36.7 for the Communist Party.

The 'militia-party' and the seizure of power

The youth of the new party gave the violence of the Fascist squads and the hostility towards liberal democracy the appearance of a generational revolt and almost of a struggle between two different and incompatible 'anthropological types'. The Fascists hated their adversaries on the left, the socialists and the communists, whom they considered as human beings with quasi-animal features that made them uniquely bloodthirsty and destructive. But they also despised the liberal bourgeoisie, whom they portrayed as timid and superannuated politicians with no sense of idealism or grandeur, because they had degenerated and been corrupted by the politics of compromise and clientelism.

The majority of the militants of the PNF had served in the Great War, which for many of them had been a genuine initiation into politics. As a result Fascism had come into being as a militia-party, not because the Fascist Party had an armed paramilitary force from the start but because Fascism made the *militarization of politics* its key identifying feature. Fascism institutionalized the militarization of politics through its organizational structures, through its ideology, values, and patterns of behaviour, and through the methods of political combat it used. Fascist culture rejected rationalism, exalted mythical thought, and set up as the highest form of political consciousness a secular religion rooted in a cult that combined worship of the fatherland with the community sense of camaraderie, the ethic of combat and the principles of hierarchy. The nationalist and anti-democratic ideology of the militia-party was expressed through myths, rituals, symbols, and a 'lifestyle' in which the militarization and the *sacralization of politics* were combined in ways that were both original and effective.

This continued to be the essential distinguishing feature of Fascism after the establishment of the regime. The Fascists claimed a 'privileged difference' that set them apart from all other political parties, and they saw themselves as a *new aristocracy* that had been forged in the wartime experience of the trenches and during the civil war against the 'internal enemy' that had followed. The Fascist mission was to regenerate politics and create a new state founded on the dogma of the nation and on the privileged role of the Fascist Party, which was the only party capable of expressing the will of the nation. For that reason, the Fascist Party alone had the right to govern Italy and lead it to the conquest of new greatness. While they condemned bourgeois society as materialist and individualist, the Fascists none-theless defended private property and praised the leadership qualities of the productive bourgeoisie. While they advocated the need for inter-class co-operation (*corporativism*), they accepted that the sub-ordination of the working class to the bourgeoisie was the best way to maximize production (*productivism*) and hence to provide the material resources needed to make Italy a great power and to support imperial expansion. With regard to the liberal state, the Fascists also asserted their privileged diversity which, they claimed, placed them above the law because they were the sole interpreters of the will of the nation. All this, in short, served to legitimate violence and the domination which the Fascist Party had imposed over many regions of northern and central Italy, to the resounding cheers of the bourgeois nationalists and the consent, from motives either of sympathy or weakness, of the political and military authorities, who looked on the Fascists as defenders of the fatherland and of order.

By 1922 the PNF already had over 200,000 members, a private army, women's and youth associations, and trade unions with over half a million members. It was the most powerful and dynamic political party at a moment when all the other Italian political parties, and especially those of the left, were in crisis caused by internal divisions that made them more interested in fighting amongst themselves than in uniting against the Fascists. But they were also subject to unrelenting violence from the Fascist squads. Throughout most of northern and central Italy the PNF had by now established unchallenged control and was beginning to operate like a state within a state. To flout their strength and to challenge the liberal state, the *squadristi* staged carefully orchestrated occupations of whole towns, cities, and provinces to force the resignation of administrations run by their political opponents, or to obtain concessions from the government and even, as occurred in Bologna in 1922, to demand and obtain the removal of a government prefect deemed to be hostile to Fascism. The Fascist Party openly avowed its aversion to democracy and the liberal state: Democracy, Mussolini stated in August 1922 'has done its work. The century of democracy is over. Democratic ideologies have been liquidated.'[8]

In preparation for the seizure of power, the militia-party took responsibility both for defending the existing institutional, economic and social structures and for implementing a political revolution through which a new state would be constructed that neither in theory nor in practice would tolerate the coexistence of any other political parties. As far as outlook, organization, methods of political conflict, and ideology were concerned, the blueprint for the future Fascist totalitarian experiment had already been drawn up within the party. In July 1922 the anti-Fascist paper *La Stampa* noted that:

> Fascism is a movement that strives with all its means to gain control over the state and the entire life of the nation in order to establish an absolute and unique dictatorship. The fundamental means for achieving this, in the programme and in the intentions of the leaders and their followers, is the complete suppression of all public and private constitutional liberties, which is to say the destruction of the Constitution and the entire liberal state that was the creation of the Italian Risorgimento. Once that dictatorship is established, for any institution to exist it must take no action nor utter any word except that of total dedication and obedience to Fascism. Only at that point will it be prepared to suspend the use of violence, for lack of targets, while always reserving the right to revive it at the first sign of any new resistance.[9]

The project for the March on Rome came about after the failure of an attempt by the Alliance of Labour to organize a 'legalitarian strike' in protest at Fascist violence early in August 1922. The PNF reacted by taking violent reprisals and destroying what remained of the workers' organizations. Once again the weakness of the liberal state was evident, as was the inability of the anti-Fascist parties to reach any agreement that might have given rise to a government capable of restoring the authority of the state. During the summer and autumn of 1922 and right up to the March on Rome, the Fascists continued to wage a violent offensive against their political opponents and against those representatives of the state who failed to support them, while the Liberal government proved completely unable to check the escalating violence of the *squadristi*. The PNF now developed new tactics for the revolutionary seizure of power that combined terrorist actions with political manoeuvres. Fascist insurrections in many cities in northern and central Italy led to the occupation of many government buildings, post offices, and railway stations and would certainly have collapsed had there been a direct confrontation with the army. But the Fascists succeeded because they were able to sow confusion within the highest political levels of the state, while Mussolini was at the same time negotiating his rise to power with the leaders of the Liberal regime and the world of business and finance.

For that reason, the March on Rome brought the highest returns at minimal risk. It wrecked attempts to form a new government led by Salandra or Giolitti, which the monarchy together with many industrialists and moderate Fascists would have supported, and resulted instead in a government headed by Mussolini, when the king refused to end the Fascist insurrection by proclaiming a state of emergency. On 31 October Mussolini formed his government, which included Liberals, the Popolari, Democrats, and Nationalists.

With overwhelming majorities it obtained votes of confidence in both the Chamber of Deputies and in the Senate that conceded full powers to enable the new prime minister to implement fiscal and administrative reforms. But parliamentary approval could not hide the gravity of what had happened. For the first time in the history of European liberal democracy, government had been entrusted to the leader of a militia-party whose parliamentary representation was small, which openly repudiated liberal democracy, exalted the militarization of politics, and proclaimed its revolutionary determination to bring authoritarian changes to the state.

The timing of the consolidation of the Fascist seizure of power was determined by the expansion of Fascist power and the introduction of laws that effectively destroyed the parliamentary system. In the first phase, Mussolini established a political coalition with the parties willing to collaborate with him while at the same time working to disunite them, and he also brought the Nationalist Association into the PNF (February 1923). Legal means of repression were used against the anti-Fascist parties, but they continued to be the targets of the violence of the *squadristi*. The same combination of terrorism and government intervention was used by the Fascists to rapidly complete the seizure of control of local government. Immediately after the March on Rome Mussolini launched the Fascist takeover of the southern provinces. This was again achieved by using the powers of the state exercised in each province by the prefect, together with the creation of new *Fasci* in the South which recruited the local notables and the mass of new lower middle class and bourgeois militants eager for positions and power.

This caused a major crisis for the Fascist Party, however, as thousands of new adherents rushed to jump on the bandwagon, and the rapid expansion in membership split the party into rival camps of moderates and intransigents. In many provinces dissident and independent *Fasci* were formed that opposed the line of the party and the government, and appealed instead to the ideals of what was vaguely defined as 'original fascism'.

The central conflict was between the 'revisionism' of those who advocated the normalization and demilitarization of the PNF and the 'integralism' of the intransigent Fascists who insisted on the supremacy of the 'militia-party' and were determined to continue to use violence until the Fascist revolution had brought about the total conquest of power and had created a new state. After the March on Rome Mussolini had tried to deprive the PNF of its independence and subordinate it to his command. In December 1922 he established a new institution, the Fascist Grand Council, of which he was president, and which included the leaders of the party and the party representatives who held office in the government. The new body took over control of the party and also acted as a form of 'shadow government' in which the laws that would transform Italy's parliamentary democracy were first drafted, before being submitted to the cabinet and being approved by the parliament. The first of these laws established the MVSN (Voluntary Militia for National Security, 14 January 1923) which legalized the squads but placed them under the control of the head of the government.

Mussolini tried to keep an ambiguous stance between the politics of terrorism and normalization, therefore, alternatively backing then restraining the violence of the squads as circumstances required. But his principal objective was always to strengthen his own power through a compromise with the traditional élites. In order to acquire a larger and stronger parliamentary majority he introduced an electoral reform, known as the Acerbo Law, which had been drafted by the Fascist Grand Council and which assigned additional seats to the coalition that gained the highest number of electoral votes. The law was approved by the Chamber of Deputies in July 1923 and first came into effect in the elections of April 1924. These were held in a climate of extreme violence and intimidation, and returned an increased government majority that was now composed mainly of Fascists, who received many more votes than the representatives of the old Liberals who were still supporting the government.

The assassination on 10 June 1924, immediately after the elections, of the socialist deputy Giacomo Matteotti by a group of *squadristi* acting on orders from Mussolini's closest advisers provoked a huge outcry that seriously shook Mussolini's government. A majority of the anti-Fascist deputies decided to leave their seats in parliament until a new government capable of restoring order and ending Fascist violence could be formed. The government was now also losing support amongst those political parties that had originally supported the Fascists, and was also being opposed by the bourgeois press and by many industrialists. Demands were growing for the restoration of constitutional government and the rule of law, as well as an end to Fascist violence.

Mussolini was only able to avoid disaster because the anti-Fascist opposition proved incapable of taking political advantage of the situation, and above all because the monarchy and those who looked to it for political leadership were willing to continue supporting the government on the condition that it would implement a policy of normalization and bring Fascist illegality to an end. The Matteotti crisis had, however, given the integralist Fascists, and especially the leaders of the provincial squads (or *ras* as they were called by the anti-Fascists), the opportunity to regain the initiative. At the end of 1924 it was they who demanded that the Duce take the decisive steps toward setting up the forms of authoritarian government that would provide the basis for the dictatorship of the party.

Mussolini's speech to the Chamber of Deputies on 3 January 1925 was the authoritarian step that made possible the consolidation and strengthening of Fascist power. The Interior Ministry was placed under the former nationalist, Luigi Federzoni, who took charge of the repression of the anti-Fascist political parties, but was also useful to Mussolini for keeping the Fascist extremists in check. But in this new phase of consolidation and expansion of

Fascist power Mussolini also needed the support of the *squadristi* and their bosses. In February 1925 Roberto Farinacci, the principal spokesman of integralist Fascism, was appointed secretary of the PNF. Within only a few months, he had restored the internal unity and discipline of the party and became the principal supporter of radical measures aimed at destroying the remains of political opposition and establishing a one-party regime. Farinacci had his own view of the totalitarian party which, he believed, should retain its autonomy from the government, so that he as secretary of the PNF, or 'head of the party', would be on the same political level as Mussolini, the 'head of the government'.

This was a division of power that the Duce found totally unacceptable and, once the authoritarian reorganization of the state had concentrated all executive power in Mussolini's hands and consolidated his personal power, Mussolini sacked Farinacci and replaced him with Augusto Turati. Turati was another leading integralist, but was more prepared to work with the Duce in transforming the state into a one-party regime. He held the position until October 1930 and played a decisive role in the reorganization of the party, leading a massive operation to purge the party of corruption and indiscipline, which made it easier to install the PNF as the fundamental and essential pillar of the new regime.

The foundations of the Fascist regime

The transformation of the Italian political system into a single party state was achieved through a 'legal revolution', in which the Italian parliament gave its full approval to a complex of authoritarian laws, most of which were drafted by Alfredo Rocco, the architect of the Fascist state. These effectively destroyed the liberal constitutional regime that had taken shape in the sixty years after Italy's unification in the mid-nineteenth century, yet left the façade of a constitutional monarchy intact. The laws of 24 December 1925 and 31 January 1926 established the supremacy of the executive power and the subordination of all ministers of state, as well as the parliament, to the authority of the head of the government who was responsible only to the king.

Local administration was also reorganized along authoritarian lines, and the law of 4 February 1926 replaced formerly elected mayors with the new office of *podestà*, a position filled by royal nomination, which became effectively a dependency of the provincial prefects whose powers had also been greatly increased by the law of 3 April 1926. The law of 25 November 1926 brought the freedom of association to an end, but even before the authoritarian coup of 3 January 1925, the anti-Fascist political parties had in practice been hardly able to engage in any activity. Immediately after the March on Rome over 70 per cent of the leading figures in the PCd'I had been arrested, and Luigi Sturzo, the founder of the PPI, had been forced into exile. Leading anti-Fascists like Giovanni Amendola and Piero Gobetti suffered repeated and brutal beatings and both were to die in exile in 1926 from the injuries they had received.

At the end of 1926 the secretary of the PNF announced that since the deputies of the anti-Fascist opposition parties had all been removed from parliament, all parties other than the PNF were now illegal. The press was brought under tight Fascist control and the opposition papers were either suppressed or else changed ownership and came into line with Fascist directives. No form of criticism of the government or of the state or its representatives was permitted after the law of 25 November 1926 which also reintroduced the death penalty for crimes against the state and established a special Tribunal composed of officers of the Fascist Militia and the armed forces, with jurisdiction over all crimes against the state or the regime.

The trade unions were also brought under the authoritarian control of the state. The law of April 3 1926 on labour relations made strikes illegal and created a 'magistracy of labour' to resolve all disputes between labour and employers. Eleven trade unions received legal recognition, and these were all Fascist organizations. The Confederation of Fascist Trade Unions that had been set up in 1922 had become a powerful organization and was led by Edmondo Rossoni. Rossoni was committed to the ambitious plan of implementing an integralist form of syndicalism that would have brought all workers and employers under the control of his federation. But in 1928 Mussolini destroyed this project when he insisted that the federation should be broken up into smaller organizations. The abandonment of the programme of Fascist syndicalism was to the advantage of the employers, and for the workers was only partially compensated by the social and welfare policies of the regime, consisting in the establishment of collective contracts, of measures to reduce unemployment, and the organization of workers' free time through the activities of the Opera Nazionale Dopolavoro.

The regime hailed its law on the trade unions as the first step towards the realization of a new corporate order that would lead to what the Charter of Labour (21 April 1927) called the 'united organization of all forces of production'. A Ministry of Corporations was established in 1926 and the National Council of Corporations created in 1930 was designed to be the central constitutional body of the new state, although the corporations themselves did not come into being until 1934.

The law of 17 May 1928 completed the reorganization of political representation by creating a single national electoral College and assigning to the Fascist Grand Council the right to select candidates for the Chamber from the names put forward by the Fascist trade unions and other bodies. This meant that the 'electors' were presented with a single list of deputies which they had to either approve or reject en bloc. The law of 9 December 1928 made the Grand Council the supreme body of the regime, with powers to amend the constitution, to draw up and revise a list of persons to succeed

Mussolini as head of the government (the list was never drawn up), and to intervene in the succession to the throne. Since this law infringed the prerogatives of the monarchy it provoked strong, but ineffective, protests from the king.

The regime met no serious opposition from established institutions or from traditional economic and social interests as it set about demolishing the liberal state. The monarchy, the armed forces, and the industrial and agrarian bourgeoisie accepted the demise of parliamentary government with little evident sign of regret, and seemed more impressed by the advantages that the new regime had brought them by restoring order and discipline in Italian society, and in particular over the workers. These groups complacently assumed that once the Fascists had acquired a monopoly over the exercise of power, their political ambitions would be fully satisfied.

The crowning moment of the consolidation of the Fascist regime came with the plebiscitary elections held on 24 March 1929, when the Italians were called to express their opinion of the list of new deputies selected by the Grand Council with a single vote of 'Yes' or 'No'. 8,661,820 votes were cast, 98.34 per cent of which were 'Yes', with some 8,209 spoiled votes, and a mere 135,773 'No'—less than 1.57 per cent, and mainly from the North which accounted for 84.7 per cent of the contrary voters. The victory was a foregone conclusion, given the new circumstances of the dictatorial regime, that had by now fully consolidated the structures by which it controlled society, and which had in addition the support of a large part of the bourgeoisie and middle classes. Furthermore, the elections were held little more than a month after the signing of the Lateran Pacts (on 11 February 1929), which had gained the Fascist regime recognition by the Church and hence the support of the majority of the clergy and the faithful. The next plebiscite for elections to the Chamber of Deputies was held in 1934, and produced results that brought the 'Yes' vote even closer to 100 per cent.

Approval by plebiscite in no way attenuated the nature of the police state that Fascism had assumed from the start and which it would never abandon. Police repression took the place of the violence of the squads and was used to destroy any form of dissent, anti-Fascist organization, or activity. When the opposition political parties were suppressed, many of the leading anti-Fascists were sentenced to long terms in jail. This was the fate of Antonio Gramsci, the former secretary of the PCd'I. Other anti-Fascist political leaders and intellectuals like the socialist Filippo Turati, the former Prime Minister Francesco Saverio Nitti, and the historian Gaetano Salvemini managed to flee abroad where together with thousands of other anti-Fascist exiles they took up their struggle against the regime. Their arms were mainly books, lectures, and newspaper articles in which they tried to alert Western public opinion, which was often indifferent if not outright sympathetic to Fascism, to the danger that Fascist totalitarianism posed not just for Italy but for democracy and peace in Europe as a whole. In Italy, however, militant anti-Fascism existed only in tiny clandestine groups. But although intellectual anti-Fascism was very rare and was almost inevitably silenced by the punishment of house arrest or prison, it found an eloquent voice in the philosopher Benedetto Croce. The regime did not try to silence Croce partly because of his international reputation, but also because he was probably not considered to be politically dangerous.

In 1927 an Anti-Fascist Concentration was founded in Paris by the Italian socialist and republican exiles, but down to 1934 the communists continued to follow Stalin's orders and remained both isolated from, and hostile to, the other Italian anti-Fascist parties. In the clandestine struggle against Fascism, however, the communists and the militants of the liberal socialist movement known as Justice and Liberty (Giustizia e Libertà), which operated in Italy through small groups of activists that disseminated anti-Fascist propaganda, were the most active and best organized. But the police always caught up with them and their clandestine operations had become impossible by the beginning of the 1930s because of the efficiency of the regime's apparatus of repression, which relied on both the traditional police and on new secret police units known as OVRA that operated both in Italy and abroad amongst Italian anti-Fascist exiles. Between 1922 and 1943 the police opened 114,000 new files on 'subversives' (there had been only 40,000 in the previous period) and these included militant anti-Fascists, their families, and other potential opponents. Even though the Italian totalitarian experiment did not resort to the mass terror and killings used by other totalitarian regimes, the repression of any form of opposition or dissent and the constant threat of violence were permanent features of Fascism. Between 1928 and 1932 the Special Tribunal issued only nine death sentences for political crimes, five of which were for Slavs accused of terrorist actions, and none before 1941. But between 1928 and 1943, 5,319 individuals appeared before the Special Tribunal of whom 5,155 received a total of 27,735 years of prison sentences, including seven condemnations to life imprisonment. Between 1926 and 1943 some 15,000 Italians were in addition subject to *confino*, which meant that they lost their jobs and were obliged to live under house arrest somewhere far distant from their normal place of residence.

The party in the Fascist regime

Under the leadership first of Turati and then of Giovanni Giuriati, who served as national secretary from 1930 to 1931 and continued the purges and the work of reorganizing the party, the PNF was placed at the centre of the new political system where it was rigidly subject to control by the Duce who became its sole and unchallenged leader. Mussolini proclaimed that in the Fascist regime the party was subordinate to the state just as the PNF's representative in each province, the federal secretary, was subordinate to the senior representative of the state, the prefect. But this claim was continuously overturned in practice. The prefect was not the representative of an abstract state that existed over and above political parties. The subordination of the party to the state was a rhetorical fiction as the dual nature of Mussolini's power as head of the government and head of the Fascist Party made evident, and it was this double set of powers that makes it unrealistic and historically inaccurate to draw any firm distinction between the Duce and the party as if they were in reality different entities.

Behind the façade of the regime's monolithic unity there were constant conflicts between the party and traditional institutions, which Mussolini neither wanted nor was able to stop. The conflicts between the provincial *federali* and the prefects, for example, continued until the last days of the regime. An attempt was made to solve the problem by choosing political prefects, in other words, men from the party: but this often simply created new causes of conflict with the *federali*. By 1935 over half the prefects were no longer career administrators, and already in 1934 out of a total of 65 prefects, 31 had backgrounds in public administration against 34 who were political nominees, 10 of whom had been *squadristi* and 13 provincial secretaries of the PNF. Of the total number of 79 Fascist prefects appointed between 1922 and 25 July 1943, 37 were still in office in July 1943. The political prefects were especially prominent in the major regional administrative centres like Milan, Genoa, Turin, Naples, and Palermo. The subordination of the *federali* to the prefect was not laid down in any law, nor was it part of the constitution of the PNF, which placed the federal secretaries directly under the orders of the National Secretary.

The party acknowledged its subordination to the state, but with reference to the myth of the Fascist state and not to the monarchic state. Particularly under the leadership of Achille Starace (National Secretary, 1932–9), the party conducted a tenacious, gradual and unremitting campaing of internal subversion against the old monarchist state, and as a result acquired ever-wider powers within the new totalitarian state. In 1937 the secretary of the PNF acquired the powers and responsibilities of a minister of state, while in the new constitution of 1938 the PNF was officially declared to be the 'only party', and its functions were defined specifically as 'the defence and strengthening of the Fascist revolution and the political education of Italians'. In 1941 the new PNF secretary, Adelchi Serena (1940–1), took a further important new step towards the totalitarian transformation of the state by creating a special party office with responsibility for preparing legislative reforms that would 'strengthen the position of the party in the state'. These included the law of 29 November 1941 requiring that the party be consulted before nominations were made for any public or political office. In the same year, and in anticipation of the victorious conclusion of the war, the party prepared a radical plan that would transform the PNF into an élite organization, together with a project for the reform of the state whose constitution would acknowledge the primacy of the PNF as 'the motor of the state'. The proposal envisaged that the Ministries of the Interior and Popular Culture would be controlled by the PNF, that the dual powers of the provincial *federali* and prefects would be resolved by instead creating a single representative of the PNF in each province, and that the secretary of the PNF would be recognized in the constitution as the most senior Fascist *gerarca* after the Duce.

The PNF's strategy for expansion

The symbiosis of state and party was the central characteristic of the Fascist regime. The intervention of the PNF reflected the presence of a new ruling caste whose power derived from control over the party bureaucracy, which was constantly trying to take over the state bureaucracy, or, if this proved impossible, to undermine its authority. From Farinacci to Serena, every leader of the PNF sought to expand the power of the party not only at the expense of traditional state institutions, but of all other institutions of the regime and Italian society. This strategy of expansion was gradual and advanced at speeds that were determined by changing national and international circumstances, but it was constant, unremitting, and resulted in mounting successes that brought the party ever-wider control over both the state and Italian society.

In the case of traditional institutions that the party was unable to get rid of quickly, its tactic was either to bring them under Fascist control or suppress them. The strategies of expansion were constantly being adapted according to time and circumstance to avoid provoking unnecessary reactions or resistance. In the case of the Chamber of Deputies and Senate, for example, the PNF's strategy of expansion followed two quite different tactics that were determined by the different political character of the two institutions, the former being elective, whereas the second was filled by life-time nomination.

Following the reform of political representation and the elections of 1929, the *fascistizzazione* of the Chamber of Deputies was virtually complete. The PNF then proposed a new reform that would abolish the Chamber of Deputies and replace it in 1939 with a Chamber of Fasci and Corporations in which all vestiges of the principles of parliamentary representation would totally disappear. The new Chamber was a direct offshoot of the PNF and of the corporations controlled by the PNF. The party secretary was also given the power to impose punishments on the deputies and senators, and the statutes of the new Chamber laid down that any deputy who was suspended or expelled from the party was prohibited from continuing his parliamentary duties.

In the case of the Senate, the PNF instead adopted a tactic of infiltration resulting in a gradual process of *fascistizzazione* through the nomination of new senators. Between the March on Rome and February 1943, 596 new senators were nominated (in comparison with 398 between 1901 and 1914).

This influx of Fascist senators was reinforced by the activity within the Senate itself of the Association of Senators, all of whom were members of the PNF. As a result, by the end of the 1930s the *fascistizzazione* of the Senate had been virtually completed.

New and greater possibilities for expanding the power of the PNF were offered by the various state agencies that operated in sectors ranging from agriculture to social welfare, from culture to tourism, from industry to public works, and from trade to transport. Under the Fascist regime these bodies multiplied much faster than in the past. Between 1901 and 1921, 102 new government agencies had been created, in contrast to 353 between 1922 and 1943. The creation of what came to be called the 'parallel bureaucracy' by the Fascists began immediately after the March on Rome and continued at varying speeds well after the establishment of the regime. In some cases the Fascists retained the managers appointed by previous Liberal governments because of their technical skills, providing that they were prepared to accommodate to the new regime and show loyalty to the PNF by becoming members of the party. But the majority of state agencies were managed and controlled by men chosen by the Fascist Party. Even in the case of the state bureaucracy, which for reasons of practicality and convenience Mussolini wished to keep out of the control of the party, the PNF gained increasing influence through the Association of State Employees which the party controlled. PNF representatives were to be found everywhere: in the central administration of the state, in the provincial administration, from the Higher Council for Schools to the Higher Council for Public Health, from the National Research Council to the Commission of Theatre and Cinema Censors, from the commissions that awarded literary prizes to those responsible for overseeing wholesale fish and grain markets, from committees responsible for tourism to those for fairs and exhibitions.

The influence, control, and interference of the Party gradually also extended to sectors that had previously been outside the party's control, notably the magistracy. Membership of the PNF became an essential prerequisite for career advancement for judges, while measures were adopted to subject magistrates to close Fascist surveillance, and after 1939 all judges were required to undergo political and ideological retraining programmes and to attend special courses designed by Fascists.

The PNF's strategy of expansion was not as immediately successful in every branch of the traditional State as many integralist Fascists desired. The armed forces, for example, retained their independence, even though they were increasingly subject to Mussolini who as head of the government was also Minister for the Army and Navy. But the military was not an obstacle to the expansion of the totalitarian state. In 1933 army officers were permitted to join the PNF and in 1936 the requirement of PNF membership for civil servants was extended to officers and non-commissioned officers in the Finance Guards and to army officers.

Between regimentation and consensus: the *fascistizzazione* of the Italians

To celebrate its first decade in power and to demonstrate its solidity and security, the regime in 1932 offered a general amnesty to political prisoners. Under Starace's leadership, new efforts were also being made to intensify the *fascistizzazione* of the Italians through the various forms of regimentation controlled by the party and by the organization of consensus that focused increasingly on the myth and the cult of the Duce. In addition to his institutional role as permanent head of state, Mussolini's charismatic role was accentuated through the development of the cult of the *littorio*. This was a secular Fascist political religion, with its own creeds, myths, rites and symbols that came to play the fundamental role in integrating the Fascist state and the single mass political party. The Duce's frequent public rallies were the culminating point in the organization of consensus, and in these carefully prepared and choreographed settings the emotional meeting of the leader and the masses offered a dramatic and mystical symbol of the unity of the nation expressed by its highest interpreter.

The cult of the *littorio* took a central place in the organization of consensus and derived from the notion that the masses were an aggregate governed by mythical and irrational forces. This made them incapable of developing an independent political awareness derived from a sense of individual responsibility that would enable them to engage directly in the choice of their own rulers. Instead, a conformist mentality could be inculcated in the individual and the masses, as throughout their entire existence they would be subject to parallel processes of regimentation, indoctrination, and integration in accordance with the values and principles of the totalitarian party. This project was premissed on the notion of the primacy of the political, or in other words the total assimilation of the private to the public and with it the total subordination of all those values belonging to the private sphere (religion, culture, morality, love, and so forth) to the supreme political value which was embodied in the state alone, the supreme entity before which individuals and society were no more than the instruments through which the state achieved its objectives of greatness. Within this perspective of totalitarian Fascism, politics was an all-embracing experience that alone gave meaning and purpose to human existence. This could only be achieved within the specific context of the Fascist state and through the constant activity of the single state party, whose task it was to organize and educate the masses in order to transform Italians into a totalitarian community united by a single faith, disciplined in every aspect of their lives and totally subordinated to the will of the Fascist Party, which was committed to the achievement of power and expansion.

Seen in these terms, mass politics in Fascist Italy took the form of permanent totalitarian education. Different means with different objectives were used depending on the sections of the population that were addressed, but this operation of totalitarian education was conducted by every institution of the Fascist state, from elementary schools to the Opera Nazionale Dopolavoro that had been created to organize the leisure time of Italian workers. But the key role of 'The Great Pedagogue' of the masses belonged to the PNF. 'Political education' in Fascist Italy revolved around the Fascist understanding of the relationship between politics and the masses. To educate Italians politically meant nurturing in each individual the mentality of the 'citizen-soldier' whose entire existence must conform to the simple dogma: 'believe, obey, and fight'.

In line with these principles, Fascism set out to indoctrinate the masses and especially the younger generations. The *'fascistizzazione'* of young Italians of both sexes between the ages of 6 and 18 was entrusted to the Opera Nazionale Balilla and then after 1937 to the Gioventù Italiana del Littorio (GIL) which brought all the Fascist youth movements together under the leadership of the PNF. Within the broader project of regimentation and the organization of consensus, the *fasci femminili* had a more specific role. Fascism ostentatiously worshipped male virility and was explicitly anti-feminist. All forms of political activity were reserved exclusively for males, while the role of woman was that of spouse, mother, and teacher, and hence always subordinate to that of the male. At the same time, Fascist politics also gave women new, albeit highly contradictory, functions both in the home and in the totalitarian state. As wife and mother, women were entrusted with the task of producing children for the fatherland and providing them with their first training and education, while as members of the party they were also militants committed to creating the Fascist 'new man' and hence with responsibilities that went far beyond the family. This meant that as well as the traditional model of the woman as mistress of the household and guardian angel of the home, the party's mission also created the alternative model of the Fascist 'new woman', who, although confined exclusively to the spheres of welfare and education, was nonetheless actively engaged in party work. This resulted in the mobilization of women outside the traditional private sphere of the family, and gave militant Fascist women, and especially younger women, opportunities Fascist women, and especially younger women, opportunities to take part in the great enterprise of the *fascistizzazione* of the masses.

The totalitarian party was the first attempt to impose a single form of organization on all Italians based on rigidly centralized principles that aimed at creating a single mass ideological identity. It is still difficult to measure the effectiveness of these attempts to organize consensus on those who for nearly twenty years were subject daily to the incessant hammering of pervasive and omnipresent propaganda. The party was a capillary organization that operated uniformly throughout Italy and involved all Italians in an experiment in political socialization that had no precedent in Italian history. But the impact and effectiveness of these policies on a population that had no opportunity to escape the tentacles of the party or to stand aloof from the regime—except at the risk of being ostracized from all forms of public life, and probably also the loss of a job—varied from city to city, province to province, region to region, and from one period to another. Reactions also differed according to generations, and the reactions of those who had known parliamentary government and competition between rival political parties and who had possibly been themselves victims of Fascist violence were different from those of the younger generations, who had grown up knowing only the totalitarian regime, and who had been educated in the noise and clamour of Fascist triumphalism. Resistance to the organizations of consensus was greatest in those regions where there had previously been strong Catholic associations, or where there was still some memory of the now prohibited former political parties. In the more backward regions, and especially in the South, the party also found it very difficult to organize and mobilize the population except in the larger cities. But even anti-Fascist observers were agreed in the 1930s that the regime's initiatives in welfare and in the organization of leisure activities had enabled it, as one Communist observer noted in 1932, 'to succeed in influencing the greater part of the masses with its ideology'.[10] It was because of the regime's success in regimenting and organizing the masses that the leaders of the Communist Party decided in the second half of the 1930s to adopt the tactic of infiltrating Fascist organizations to try to reach 'our brothers in black shirts'.

More than in any other field, the party was especially intransigent and integralist when it came to education. This led to direct confrontation with Catholic Action, its most powerful rival, which in 1931 caused a major conflict with the Catholic Church when the regime asserted the party's exclusive role in the education of the young. During the 1930s the Party's role in education had been systematically strengthened with the expansion of the Fascist youth organizations. This too was ground on which the party did not hesitate to openly challenge the Catholic Church, and in 1938 it again asserted its right to monopolize the education of Italian youth in the values of its own ideology. While the regime looked on Catholicism as a useful tool in the bid to organize consensus, it also held Fascism to be the secular religion of the nation and of the state, that demanded the undivided devotion of all citizens.

The new oligarchy

By the end of the 1930s the tentacles of the party had come to reach every part of Italian society. As one Communist militant wrote in November 1938:

> Fascism keeps the entire life of the Italian people under strict control, and the great mass of the petty bourgeoisie, workers, peasants

and intellectuals can only live by submitting themselves to the controls imposed by Fascism. The organization of the state makes it impossible, except in the most exceptional circumstances, for anyone to live outside its parameters or outside the control exercised by the Fascist Party and its various organs. There is no alternative: whoever has to live in Italy has to adopt the Fascist label.[11]

One of the leaders of the liberal-socialist organization, Giustizia e Libertà, reached similar conclusions in the same year:

> Fascism does not oppress and control simply by means of its police apparatus: it oppresses and controls by means of its trade unions, through its schools, through its footholds in industry and the banks, through the vast bureaucracy that it has created, directs and maintains, through the press and the radio. The whole country is swallowed up by this apparatus: any manifestations of protest or lack of loyalty are reported immediately to the centre and are then suppressed through the use of those forms of aggression against which the discontent was originally directed.[12]

Membership of the Fascist Party had become an indispensable pre-requisite for anyone seeking to enter any form of public or local government service, in local or para-state agencies. A circular issued by the Interior Ministry in 1937 declared that the PNF membership card had the same status as an identity card, while the Party's constitution of 1938 declared that anyone 'who ceases to be a member of the Partito Nazionale Fascista is to be relieved of all positions and responsibilities he may perform'.

The leaders of the party and its principal organizations now formed a new oligarchy of privileged citizens. In the GIL alone there were 33,958 officers and 250,000 male and female youth leaders. The totalitarian party also gradually transformed the traditional local élites, who were replaced with new men who saw themselves as part of the new Fascist aristocracy, and enjoyed the prestige and authority, and to a lesser extent the power, which derived from the totalitarian party.

Control of the party, and hence of the regime, remained almost entirely in the hands of the political class from which Fascism had originated. Of the members of the Fascist Grand Council in office between 1923 and 1943, nearly 70 per cent had been members of the original *fasci di combattimento* between 1919 and 1922, hence from before the March on Rome, and of these about 40 per cent had been *squadristi*. They came predominantly from Emilia-Romagna (18.0%), Tuscany (11.3%), Lombardy (9.8%), and the Veneto (9.0%). 81.4 per cent of the National Directorate had been party members before the March on Rome and 59.2 per cent had been *squadristi*, while 65 per cent were army veterans. Of the federal secretaries, those who had joined the party before the March on Rome amounted to 74.5 per cent, and 44 per cent had been *squadristi*, while the regional breakdown showed the same pattern as for the Fascist Grand Council and the National Directorate.

Within this oligarchy of 'Fascists of the first hour' the only form of renewal was by the recruitment of new senior figures from the youth organizations, although in practice very few younger people joined the Fascist aristocracy. The number of Fascist federal secretaries coming from the new generation that had entered the party after 1926 in what was called the ritual of the 'Fascist call-up' were only thirty two. The Fascist University Groups (GUF) were the principal hothouse for rearing new party officials, and provided fifty-four federal secretaries, ten members of the National Directorate, six inspectors of the PNF, two deputy-secretaries, and one National Secretary.

This was the cause for growing criticism of the 'bureaucratization' of the party and the regime from within the Fascist youth movements in the late 1930s and of demands for renewal of the executive class. These signs of unrest and impatience on the part of some of the younger Fascists were mainly limited to university students. They never constituted a challenge either to the regime or to the fundamental principles of the totalitarian experiment which these younger Fascists simply wished to speed up and make more radical through new reforms and social policies designed to reshape the Italian character and hence bring into being the Fascist 'new man'.

The anthropological revolution

At the final Congress of the PNF held in Rome in June 1925 Mussolini had stated

> what we describe as our ferocious totalitarian determination will now be pursued with even greater ferocity; it will be the compass and the predominating concern of all our actions. There must be Fascist Italians, just as the Italians of the Renaissance and of Ancient Rome shared unmistakable characteristics ... by means of a process of unrelenting and tenacious selection we will create the new generations in which each person will have a clearly defined role. I take pleasure at times in the idea of generations created in a laboratory. To create, that is to say, a class of warriors constantly prepared to die; a class of inventors able to reveal the secrets of every mystery; a class of judges, a class of great leaders of industry, of great explorers, and great governors. It is through such forms of methodical selection that outstanding professional cadres are created, and it is they in turn who create empires.[13]

From as early as 1925, therefore, the project for the totalitarian anthropological revolution that Fascism planned to implement through the new political system that was to be established was already fully developed, and the implementation of this project had already been assigned to the party. The new Fascist totalitarian state was to be the laboratory in which the 'new Italian', totally dedicated to the achievement of the imperial ambitions of the Duce and the Fascist Party, was to be created. The regime's whole system of mass organization, from primary schooling to the organization of leisure time, was developed around this single goal.

The experiment in anthropological revolution was intensified when the regime opened up a new campaign for the 'reform of social behaviour' directed against the bourgeoisie and introduced the racial and anti-Semitic laws at the end of the 1930s. The regime's racial programme had taken coherent and systematic shape after the war in Ethiopia, and the measures against the Jews were a later extension of this. Until, the late 1930s the regime had not given particular priority to racism in its policies, although it had frequently emphasized the need to improve the Italian race and in its colonial undertakings had always followed typically colonial and racist criteria and had perpetrated acts of deliberate savagery during the war and against the indigenous peoples in Libya and Ethiopia. Fascism had not originally been an anti-Semitic movement and although it did contain some anti-Semitic groups they had little influence. There were a number of Jews amongst the founders of the *fasci di combattimento*, as well as in the Fascist Party and the government. In 1932 Mussolini had publicly poured scorn on German racism, claiming that pride in the nation gained nothing from 'the delusions of race' and he had denied that anti-Semitism existed in Italy. Many foreign Jews fleeing from Nazi persecution had found refuge in Italy, until anti-Semitic legislation (which originally found support amongst only a handful of fanatics) was officially introduced in 1938. But on 14 July 1938 the government published the *Manifesto on Race* and on 19 July the Demographic Service of the Interior Ministry was renamed the Central Directorate for Demography and Race. On 6 October, with opposition only from Balbo, De Bono, and Federzoni, the Fascist Grand Council approved the *Manifesto on Race* which prohibited Italians entering into marriage with 'elements belonging to the Hamitic, Semitic, or other non-Aryan races', banned foreign Jews from entering Italy and ordered the expulsion of those who had done so, and set out the restrictions to be imposed henceforth on Italian Jews. On 17 November the decision of the Grand Council became the law of the Italian state.

Although the anti-Semitic laws of 1938 were certainly a consequence of Mussolini's alliance with Germany, they were neither requested nor imposed by Italy's Nazi ally. The laws were freely and knowingly imposed by Mussolini for political and ideological reasons that had more to do with his desire to compete with, rather than imitate, German National Socialism,

Mussolini's main concern was to emphasize how the 'spiritual' racism of Fascism differed from the 'biological' racism of the Nazis, and to underline that difference he used the slogan that the aim of Fascist anti-Semitism was to 'discriminate not persecute', as if discrimination was not both premiss and part of the persecution inherent in Fascism's totalitarian logic.

Totalitarian 'Caesarism' and the monarchy

As the experiment in totalitarianism took shape, the Fascist state took on a political form that is best described as 'totalitarian Caesarism', in other words a charismatic dictatorship rooted in a complex institutional structure whose foundations lay in the single party and in the subordination and total assimilation of Italian society into the state through the organization and mobilization of the masses. The concentration of power in the person of the Duce had never been the result simply of Mussolini's personal qualities. The Fascist definition of the role and nature of the party and the state meant that the leader must be the central and fundamental feature of the new state to personify the principle of undivided authority on which the totalitarian state was premissed. After 1938 leading lawyers began to argue the need for a new constitution in line with the realities of the new Fascist political system, which they too now defined as a totalitarian state. This need became even more pressing in 1939 when the Chamber of Deputies was finally abolished and replaced by the Chamber of Fasci and Corporations. This reform finally consolidated the Duce's institutional position. A review of legislation since 1939, published in 1941 by the Senate and the Chamber of Fasci and Corporations, devoted a whole chapter to the institutional position of the 'Duce of Fascism, the Head of the Government' who was described as 'The Supreme Leader of the Regime, which now inseparably represents the State'.[14] In a text published by the PNF, the Duce was described as 'the Head of State'.

In this programme for the totalitarian revolution, the monarchy had clearly become redundant. The majority of Fascists would have been happy to see it abolished, and although Mussolini confided with only his closest advisers, he too was working in this direction and there is ample and reliable evidence that he was simply waiting for the right moment to get rid of the monarchy, which he considered to be an insufficiently trustworthy institution to include in the Fascist state of the future.

In the so-called 'dyarchy' between the Duce and the king, which after the fall of the regime Mussolini would invoke in an attempt to mitigate his own responsibilities as dictator, effective power was in the hands of the Duce. The king in formal terms remained the head of state, but was either not concerned or not able to prevent or slow down the systematic destruction of the constitutional order. Victor Emanuel III made no effort to oppose the Fascist anthropological revolution, however, even when it assumed its most extreme form with the introduction of the racial and anti-Semitic laws. The prestige of the monarchy also suffered an immense blow when on 30 March 1938 the Senate and the Chamber of Deputies approved by acclamation a law creating the title of First Marshal of the Empire, the highest rank in the military hierarchy, which was bestowed contemporaneously on the king and on Mussolini. As soon as Italy entered the Second World War in June 1940, Mussolini deprived the king of his role as supreme military commander. The army remained loyal to the monarchy, but with some minor exceptions there is no evidence that the military hierarchy ever tried to resist the growing power or the policies of the Duce, who for most of the twenty years of Fascist rule held the Ministries for the Army and Navy. At no time did any senior army or naval officer appeal to the king against Mussolini's decisions, even when these affected the armed forces and the future of the nation most seriously. Nor were the armed forces impermeable to the process of *fascistizzazione* and the influence of the Fascist Party.

However reluctant, the acquiescence of the monarchy and the institutions that supported it when faced by Mussolini and the implementation of the totalitarian experiment was the principal feature of the relationship between 'totalitarian Caesarism' and the monarchy. When after the end of the Second World War the king was called on to give an account of the ways in which the monarchy had tried to oppose the advance of Fascist totalitarianism, the only example he was able to give was that he had succeeded in delaying the introduction of a decree limiting the freedom of the press by a year, from 1923 to 1924. The king himself confessed his impotence in the face of Fascism: 'At that time—he said—it was not possible to oppose the Head of the Government.'[15]

Crisis, defeat, and the end of Fascism

It was military defeat, not the Resistance nor opposition by the monarchy, by the armed forces, by the Church, or economic interest groups, that brought down the Fascist regime. The rest only became factors once military defeat seemed inevitable and once the myth of the Duce had disintegrated.

The Allied invasion of Sicily (10 July 1943) precipitated the collapse of the regime, which by that time had almost completely lost the consensus that it had succeeded in imposing in the course of twenty years of regimentation and repeated triumphs, real or imagined. However, there had been signs that the regime was in crisis even before Italy entered the war. These were evident in growing popular concern about the regime's continuous war-making, that was heightened by the threat of a new world war. But there was also growing resistance to the totalitarian experiment and to the invasive and domineering presence of the Fascist Party in every aspect of public and private life. Rather than protest or opposition, this discontent gave rise to a sense of apathy and resignation, a situation that was vividly described in the report of a police informer in January 1939:

> Many are criticizing the Fascist Regime for forcing all citizens to join different organizations which draw them into ever narrower circles that limit and control every form of activity. It is said that this desire to organize every form of individual activity is crushing freedom and suffocates every type of initiative, and people are no longer willing to put up with the restrictions imposed on them and the interference of the Regime in every form of activity, and especially those where outside interference seems least easy to justify. Some now say that this is a system of repression that is becoming increasingly unbearable. For the present, people are putting up with it out of fear and are careful not to show their opposition openly, but it seems likely that were some setback to seriously shake the Regime there might well be a violent reaction against this repression.[16]

Concern and hostility towards the intensification of the totalitarian policies of the regime was also increasing in Church circles in the late 1930s. Another Fascist police report of January 1939 stated that in the Vatican 'Mussolini no longer has the prestige he once enjoyed. The Jewish question and the persecution of the Jews lies at the root of this discontent, and they say that, like the decrees of a Roman emperor, these measures could in the future be applied to anyone since there are no longer any constitutional guarantees.'[17]

In a speech to the Lombard Episcopal Conference held in the same month, the Cardinal of Milan declared that the policy of conciliation between the Church and the regime had failed, and he warned of the danger that the 'Fascist religion' was seeking to turn the state into a divinity:

> The Catholic Church is confronted today not so much by a new Fascist state—since that was already in existence in the year when the Concordat was agreed—but by an imperialist philosophical and religious system which, although it does not say so in words, implicitly rejects the Apostolic Creed, the spiritual transcendence of religion, the rights of the Christian family and of the individual. The Apostolic Creed and a Catholic Church of divine origin are now confronted by a Fascist creed and a totalitarian state which, just as Hegel had predicted, now claims for itself the attributes of divinity. In religious terms, the Concordat has been stripped of its substance.[18]

As Italian intervention in the European war drew closer, feelings of hostility towards the regime increased in industrial and business circles as well, but again never to the point of clearly formulated political opposition. One of Italy's leading industrialists, Ettore Conti, noted in his diary on 2 January 1940, for example:

We may well be on the verge of war: but never has the country wallowed in such a state of apathy and inertia: never has Fascism been held in lower esteem by the Italians. The failings of the dictatorship are now finally evident to all, even to those who had supported it in good faith. . . . The gradual but constant worsening of the quality of the leadership, the insolence of the senior officals in every branch, the spread of profiteering combined with the most idiotic constraints imposed on every aspect of private life have turned the Italians into an amorphous herd that has no sense of will, of faith or aspiration.

And with the country in this state, they want to take us to war![19]

The military defeats that piled up as soon as Italy entered the war plunged the regime into a crisis that proved catastrophic. Military defeat caused consensus to disintegrate rapidly, except during a few brief moments of revived enthusiasm aroused by the news of some minor military success. But the crisis of the regime during the war was made more serious by the simultaneous crisis of the Fascist Party. The PNF lost its most militant and convinced members, who immediately enrolled for active service, and at the same time was burdened with new and ever growing assignments on the 'home front'. With the onset of the war Mussolini repeatedly changed the leadership of the party, with no less than four new National Secretaries in the space of three years, which disorientated the entire organization and lowered its standing in public opinion. Another clear sign of the crisis of the regime was the revival of anti-Fascist activities and the clandestine reorganization of the opposition parties in 1942. The strikes in the factories in northern Italy in March 1943 were the result of economic rather than political grievances, but they too played an important role in precipitating the final crisis of the regime.

The regime finally fell on 25 July 1943 when the Duce, who had been abandoned by the majority of the Grand Council, was deposed by the king and arrested. A new government was set up headed by General Pietro Badoglio, who ordered the dissolution of the Fascist Party and began the negotiations with the Allies for Italy's surrender which resulted in the armistice of 8 September.

Shortly after a new Fascist state that called itself the Italian Social Republic (RSI, but it was also known as 'the Republic of Salò') was set up at the instigation of Hitler after German troops had liberated Mussolini. It lasted from 13 September 1943 to 25 April 1945 and was the final attempt to revive Fascism by taking it back to its republican origins. This left Italy divided into two separate states, the RSI in the North and the Kingdom of the South, and marked the start of a civil war between Fascists and anti-Fascists. The former, had a variety of military and paramilitary organizations (the army, the Republican National Guard, the *Brigate Nere, Decima Mas*), while anti-Fascists joined the different armed partisan groups of the Resistance or the reconstituted royal army in the South. The RSI was run by a Duce who by now believed himself to be politically finished and with no real independence or authority. It was based on a cluster of rival forces and institutions that were constantly competing with one another for political and military reasons, even though they were able to provide some degree of administrative organization and to assert their independence from their German ally, who directly controlled large areas of north-eastern Italy. The volunteers who rallied to the RSI included both old and young Fascists, among them the philosopher Giovanni Gentile, who was killed in 1944, together with men and officers from the regular army. There were also many young people and teenagers of both sexes who had grown up in the climate of totalitarian indoctrination and who were moved by a genuinely romantic form of patriotism. But above all, the Republic of Salò provided the opportunity for the re-emergence and domination of the most intransigent and violent tendencies in totalitarian Fascism. The anti-bourgeois and socialistic tendencies that had gained increased prominence in the final years of the regime now sought to give republican Fascism a new revolutionary and anti-capitalist character. They gave new impetus to the irrational and mystical elements of Fascist militancy that worshipped patriotism, the defiance of death, the ethic of sacrifice, the warrior spirit, and the cult of violence, which became the watchwords of the militia-party reestablished by the new Republican Fascist Party. The RSI also revived and intensified the campaign against the Jews by bringing in even more severe anti-Semitic legislation and stepping up the persecution of the Italian Jews. Between 1943 and 1945 more than 7,000 Jews were deported, of whom only 610 ever returned to Italy from the death camps where 6,885 would die.

Completely controlled by the Germans for whom its sole purpose was to provide assistance in the operations against the partisans, the RSI finally collapsed following the victory of the Allies and the Resistance forces which ended with Italy's liberation on 25 April 1945. On 28 April Mussolini was captured and shot: his body, hanging by the feet, together with those of other Fascist leaders, was later put on public display in the centre of Milan.

Notes

1 For bibliographical references, please refer to the Further reading section.
2 'Secondo tempo', in *La Stampa*, 25 Apr. 1923.
3 [G. Amendola], 'Un anno dopo', in *Il Mondo*, 2 Nov. 1923, in id., *La democrazia italiana contro il fascismo, 1922–1924* (Milan–Naples, 1960), p. 193.
4 N. Papafava, 'Il fascismo e la costituzione', in *Rivoluzione Liberale*, 23 Aug. 1923.
5 Prometeo Filodemo [L. Basso], 'L'antistato', in *Rivoluzione Liberale*, 2 Jan. 1925.
6 A. Gramsci, *Quaderni del carcere*, Vol. II, ed. V. Gerratana (Turin, 1975), p. 800.
7 See E. Gentile, 'Mussolini's Charisma', *Modern Italy*, Nov. 1998, 219–35.
8 B. Mussolini, 'Fiera di "Demos"' in *Il Popolo d'Italia*, 19 Aug. 1922.

9 'Il Governo e la Destra', in *La Stampa*, 18 July 1922.
10 Istituto A. Gramsci, Archivio del partito comunista, 1138/1.
11 'Qual è la vera situazione presente', 16 Nov. 1938, cited in S. Colarizi, *L'Italia antifascista dal 1922 al 1940*, Vol. II (Rome–Bari, 1976).
12 Report of Alberto Cianca, 13 June 1938, in Colarizi, *L'Italia antifascista*, p. 386.
13 B. Mussolini, *Opera Omnia*, 35 vols., eds. D. and E. Susmel (Florence, 1951–63), vol. XXI, 362.
14 *La legislazione fascista nella XXIX Legislatura 1934–1939 (XXII–XVII)*, Vol. 1 (Rome, s.d.), p. 13.
15 P. Puntoni, *Parla Vittorio Emanuele III* (Bologna, 1993), pp. 291–8, 321.
16 Report from Florence, 5 Jan. 1939, in Archivio Centrale dello Stato, Divisione Polizia Politica 1927–1944, b.220.
17 Ibid.
18 Cited in P. Beltrame-Quattrocchi, *Al di sopra dei gagliardetti* (Casale Monferrato, 1985), pp. 260–2.
19 E. Conti, *Dal taccuino di un borghese* (Milan, 1946), pp. 673–4.

56

THE ESSENCE OF NAZISM

Form of fascism, brand of totalitarianism, or unique phenomenon?

Ian Kershaw

Source: Ian Kershaw, *The Nazi Dictatorship: Problems and Pespectives of Interpretation*, 4th edn, London: Arnold, 2000, pp. 20–46.

There has been debate since the 1920s about the nature and character of the Nazi phenomenon – how it ought to be located in the context of the strikingly new political movements which, since the Bolshevik Revolution of 1917 and five years later Mussolini's 'March on Rome', had been recasting the shape of Europe. While Comintern theorists in the 1920s were already categorizing Nazism as a form of fascism engendered by capitalism in crisis, bourgeois writers a little later were only beginning to associate Right and Left as the combined totalitarian enemies of democracy. The debates were, of course, considerably broadened during the years of Nazi rule: on the one hand through the finalizing of the Comintern definition of fascism in 1935 and through analyses of fascism by left-wing theorists exiled in the West; and on the other hand through a growing readiness in the western democracies and in the USA to view Nazism and Soviet Communism as two sides of the same totalitarian coin – a view seemingly confirmed by the Nazi-Soviet Non-Aggression Pact of 1939. Though this line was naturally played down from 1941 onwards, it re-emerged all the more strongly with the onset of the Cold War in the later 1940s. During the Cold War era, left-wing interpretations of Nazism as a form of fascism lost their influence, while totalitarianism theories enjoyed their hey-day and came gradually under fire – crumbling beneath the weight of accumulating detailed research – only in the period of growing detente, increasing introspection and criticism of western society and governments, and then the upheavals in universities and intellectual currents in the later 1960s. Revival of interest in fascism as a generic problem was reflected in a burgeoning output of studies not only from the Left but also from liberal writers, setting the 'totalitarianism' theorists on the defensive, though there was some retrenchment in the 1970s as weaknesses of the comparative fascism approach became increasingly visible.

The debate about fascism and totalitarianism was kept alive, too, by its relationship to a third strand of interpretation which proved highly influential: that Nazism can only be explained as a product of the peculiarities of Prussian-German development over the previous century or so. Such an interpretation was, however, itself advanced in two quite distinct and opposed forms.

Social historians, concentrating on the *causes* of Nazism, emphasized a specific path of modernization in Germany in which, far more so than was the case in western societies, pre-industrial, pre-capitalist, and pre-bourgeois authoritarian and feudal traditions survived in a society which was never truly bourgeois, existing in a relationship of tension with a modern, dynamic capitalist economy and finally exploding into violent protest when that economy collapsed in crisis. Less the nature of German capitalism than the strength of pre-modern forces in German society determined the road to Nazi victory in 1933. Though stressing the peculiarities of the German development, exponents of such an interpretation pointed to obvious parallels in other societies, for instance in Italy, and regarded Nazism, for all its singular characteristics, as a form of fascism in terms of its socio-economic origins and formation, seeing also no necessary incompatibility with elements of the totalitarianism theory in terms of certain components of rule.[1]

This emphasis upon a 'failed bourgeois revolution' and the dominance of pre-industrial, neo-feudal structures in explaining a German 'special path' of development was, however, subjected to a frontal attack.[2] The alternative position stressed in contrast the *bourgeois* character of late-nineteenth-century German society and politics and – implicitly rather than explicitly – the need to explain Nazism not through 'German peculiarities' but through the particular instabilities of the form of capitalism and capitalist state which existed in Germany. It might be thought that this line of argument – whatever its merits – only brought one back to a slightly different set of questions about 'peculiarities' in order to answer the obvious problem about why Germany alone of all the highly advanced industrial capitalist economies – Italy, though making great advances in industrialization before the War, could not rank with the major industrial economies – produced a fully-blown 'fascist' dictatorship. The heated (if somewhat artificial) debate on the 'special path' of Germany's development was concerned more with interpreting the Imperial period than the Third Reich. Despite its obvious connotations for understanding the origins of Nazism, it need occupy us no longer here – not least because historians on both sides of the debate fully accept that, for all its singular characteristics, Nazism belongs to a wider category of political movements which we call 'fascist'. The German 'peculiarities' under question in this controversy are those which set Germany apart from western parliamentary democracies, not from Italian or other manifestations of fascism.

A different and more exclusive emphasis upon the singularity of Nazism as the product of recent Prussian–German history has been an important focus of the interpretation of some of the leading West German political historians in their analyses of the character and nature of Nazi rule. According to such an interpretation, Nazism was *sui generis* – altogether a unique phenomenon, emerging from the peculiar legacy of the Prusso–German authoritarian state and German ideological development, but owing its uniqueness above all to the person of Hitler, a factor of overriding importance in the history of Nazism and one which is incapable of being ignored, played-down, or substituted. So singular was Hitler's ideological and political contribution to the shaping and direction of the Nazi movement and then the Nazi State that any attempt to label National Socialism as 'fascism', thus placing it in comparison with other 'similar' movements, is meaningless and implies, moreover, the 'trivialization' of Hitler and Nazism. Rather, so completely interwoven was National Socialism with the rise, fall, political aims, and destructive ideology of this unique personality, that it is legitimate to speak of Nazism as 'Hitlerism'. Though excluding vehemently any possibility of regarding 'Hitlerism' as a type of fascism, exponents of this interpretation nevertheless attached one important strand of comparison, arguing that the form and nature of Nazi rule made it essential to regard Nazism as a brand of totalitarianism alongside Soviet Communism (in particular Stalinism).[3]

In this chapter I shall first summarize briefly the stages of development and the main variants of interpretation within the 'totalitarianism' and 'fascism' approaches. There is by now a wide literature examining and describing these approaches in detail, so that I shall offer as brief an outline as possible for purposes of orientation. Secondly, I shall attempt to evaluate the strengths and weaknesses of the concepts in their application to Nazism. Finally, in the light of discussion of totalitarianism and fascism I shall return to consider the argument for the singularity of Nazism in the context of the 'peculiarity' of German development.

Totalitarianism

It is mistaken to regard the totalitarianism concept as simply a product of the Cold War, though that was indeed the period of its full flourishing. Its usage is in fact almost as old as that of fascism, dating back to the 1920s. And though slightly later on the scene than fascist theorems, the totalitarianism approach came earlier to gain general acceptance as an 'established' and 'establishment' theory before being subjected to a damaging challenge in the 1960s. I shall deal, therefore, with totalitarianism first.

The term was coined in Italy as early as May 1923 and used initially as an anti-fascist term of abuse. In order to turn the tables on his opponents Mussolini usurped the term in June 1925, speaking of the 'fierce totalitarian will' of his Movement. Thereafter, it was used in positive self-depiction by Mussolini and other Italian fascists, then later by German legalists and by the Nazis. Gentile, the chief ideologue of Italian fascism, also employed the term on numerous occasions, though in a more étatist sense, implying an all-embracing state which would overcome the state-society divide of weak pluralist democracies. The two notions, this étatist one and Mussolini's implication of the dynamic revolutionary will of the Movement, existed side by side. The German usage was somewhat different, but related and with the same dual approach. Ernst Jünger was one of a number of writers already coining the notion of 'total war' and 'total mobilization' in the 1920s – a term with dynamic, revolutionary implications. Around the same time Carl Schmitt, Germany's foremost legal theorist, was developing the concept of power politics based on a friend-foe relationship, into which he fitted, as the historical antithesis to the liberal pluralization of the state, the 'total state of identity of state and society'. Both forms, therefore, the 'actionist' and the 'étatist', existed before the Nazis came to power and were incorporated into Nazi usage (though the word 'totalitarian' was, in fact, seldom used by the Nazi leadership).[4]

First usage of the word 'totalitarianism' to bracket together fascist and communist states seems to have been in England in 1929, although several years earlier Nitti, the former prime minister of Italy was among those making structural comparisons between Italian fascism and bolshevism. In the 1930s and 1940s the concept was also applied by notably left-wing analysts of fascism such as Borkenau, Löwenthal, Hilferding, and Franz Neumann as a tool for characterizing what they saw as the new and specific in fascism (or Nazism) alone, without the comparative element of extension to Soviet Communism. Franz Neumann, for example, built his application of the term in his masterly *Behemoth* on the contemporary fascist self-stylization and the notion of the collapse into chaos of the Schmitt 'total state' under the 'totalitarian' drive of the Nazi movement.[5] At the same time the dominant usage of the adjective 'totalitarian' to link fascism and Nazism with communism was already gaining ground in Anglo-Saxon countries in the 1930s, boosted by German exile writing, the Stalinist terror, and the Nazi-Soviet Pact. The way was being paved for the emergence of the fully-fledged totalitarian model of the early post-war era, popularized in different ways above all by Hannah Arendt and Carl Friedrich.

Hannah Arendt's *Origins of Totalitarianism* is a passionate and moving denunciation of inhumanity and terror – depersonalized and rationalized as the execution of objective laws of history. Her emphasis on the radicalizing, dynamic, and structure-destroying inbuilt characteristics of Nazism has been amply borne out by later research. However, the book is less satisfactory on Stalinism than on Nazi Germany. Moreover, it offers no clear theory or satisfactory concept of totalitarian systems. And its basic argument explaining the growth of totalitarianism – the replacement of classes by masses and the emergence of a 'mass society' – is clearly flawed.[6]

Carl Friedrich's publications, written from a standpoint of constitutional theory, were even more influential than Hannah Arendt's. Every subsequent writer on totalitarianism has had to confront Friedrich's work, and especially his famous 'six-point syndrome' highlighting what he saw as the central characteristics of totalitarian systems (an official ideology, a single mass party, terroristic police control, monopoly control over the media, a monopoly of arms, and central control of the economy). The main weaknesses of the Friedrich model have frequently been pointed out. It is above all a static model, allowing little room for change and development in the inner dynamics of a system, and it rests on the exaggerated assumption of the essentially monolithic nature of 'totalitarian regimes'. His model has, therefore, come largely to be rejected even by those scholars still operating with a totalitarianism approach.[7]

Following the stabilization of the USSR in the post-Stalin era, totalitarianism theorists tended to concentrate attention far more on current eastern-bloc regimes rather than on the dead Nazi system, and divided into those who broadened the totalitarianism concept to include all manifestations of communist rule and those who limited it in the main to Stalinism. In both cases, however, the comparison with fascist systems was at least implicitly preserved.[8]

In the meantime, totalitarianism had been adopted in the 1950s as the fundamental prop of leading scholarly interpretations of Nazism, as in the classic pioneering works of Karl Dietrich Bracher. A political scientist himself, Bracher has pointed out the caution needed in developing a general theory of totalitarianism through constitutional or sociological categories resting on all too meagre empirical historical research. Such research was vital, in his view, to reveal the many varied forms of totalitarian rule, but would confirm the essential similarity in the techniques of rule of the Bolshevik/communist and Nazi/fascist systems. Bracher was unwilling to tie himself to the static, constitutive, and insufficiently differentiated features of the Friedrich model which could do scant justice to the 'revolutionary dynamic' which he saw as the 'core principle' distinguishing totalitarian from other forms of authoritarian rule. The decisive character of totalitarianism lay for him in the total claim to rule, the leadership principle, the exclusive ideology, and the fiction of identity of rulers and ruled. It represents a basic distinction between an 'open' and a 'closed' understanding of politics.[9] The fundamental value of the totalitarianism concept resides therefore in its ability to recognize the primary distinction between democracy and dictatorship. Though Bracher sees that, as in all political and social theories which go beyond simple description, totalitarianism theories have their weaknesses, he claims that now as before, even after Hitler and Stalin, there is 'the phenomenon of totalitarian claims to rule and the tendency to the totalitarian ... temptation' (which in this context he goes on to associate with the New Left among German intellectuals and also with the growth of terrorism of Left and Right in the Federal Republic in the 1970s).[10] In his view, the primary question of the totalitarian character of political systems cannot be shirked either in the interest of scholarly clarity and objectively, or in view of the political and human consequences of such dictatorships and the tendencies towards totalitarianism in present-day society.

Though other eminent scholars have applied and continued to apply the concept of totalitarianism to characterize what they see as the essence of the Nazi system, it suffices here to summarize Bracher's use of the concept. Not only was he at the pinnacle of scholarship on Nazism from the 1950s to the 1970s, but he also consistently argued the case for totalitarianism within the framework of understanding different models of political domination and was more than any other historian instrumental in the retention and even revival of the totalitarianism concept in its application to Nazism. However, doubts must remain about Bracher's employment of a rather undifferentiated divide between 'open' and 'closed' understandings of politics as a key ordering principle for defining totalitarianism, about his lack of clear distinction between totalitarianism as a tendency and as a system of rule, about the arguable value of the concept of 'revolutionary dynamic' when applied to various societies which Bracher would regard as 'totalitarian', and, fundamentally, about the attribution of relatively superficial common characteristics to regimes revealing many significant differences of organization and aim.

We can turn now to a brief outline of opposed interpretations locating Nazism in the family of inter-war European fascisms, rejecting at the same time the comparison with Soviet Communism inherent in the totalitarianism approach.

Fascism

A new wave of interest in fascism as a phenomenon experienced in most countries of inter-war Europe was prompted in no small measure in the 1960s by the appearance of Ernst Nolte's highly influential book *Der Faschismus in seiner Epoche* in 1963.[11] Within five years several major international conferences had been held, numerous anthologies were in print containing studies of the nature and manifestation of fascist movements throughout Europe, and a considerable scholarly literature had built up.[12] Scholarly interest in comparative fascism merged with, and was then in part overtaken by, political interest on the Left in the later 1960s during the period of the 'New Left' challenge to the values of contemporary liberal-bourgeois society. The political conditions of the 1960s spurred and steered, therefore, a revival of marxist theories of fascism derived from the writings of contemporary marxist analysts of the fascist phenomenon alongside the proliferation of non-marxist interpretations of fascism.[13] In the case of both marxist and non-marxist interpretations, it can generally be said that, as with totalitarianism, most of the strands of the debate reach back practically as far as the phenomenon of fascism itself.

Marxist theories

The first serious attempt to explain fascism in theoretical terms was undertaken by the Comintern in the 1920s. The Comintern understanding, initially of Italian fascism, was founded on the notion of a close instrumental relationship between capitalism and fascism. Derived from the Leninist theory of imperialism, the theory held that the coming inevitable collapse of capitalism fostered an increased need on the part of the most reactionary and powerful groups within the now highly-concentrated finance capital to secure their imperialist aims by manipulating a mass movement capable of destroying the revolutionary working class and therefore of safeguarding in the short-term capitalist interests and profits to be achieved through expansion and war. Fascism was thus the necessary form and final stage of bourgeois-capitalist rule. According to this interpretation, therefore, politics was a direct function of economics and wholly subordinated to it; the fascist mass movements were a product of capitalist manipulation; fascist rule served the function of bolstering profit; fascist leaders were thereby the 'agents' of the capitalist ruling class. The key question to be asked was: to whose advantage did the system work? And the answer left no doubt as to the intrinsic link between the fascist lackeys and the capitalist rulers. Though a short summary can do scant justice to the debates within the Comintern and to the varied glosses and interpretations which were advanced (the most far-sighted and nuanced by Clara Zetkin), it can be said that the view just described prevailed in essence to be encapsulated at the thirteenth plenary meeting of the Executive Committee of the Communist International in December 1933, and in its final form in the Dimitroff definition of 1935, mentioned in chapter 1. It remained the basis of Soviet and East German writing on Nazism down to the recent upheavals in eastern Europe.[14]

The contemporary dominance of the 'orthodox' Comintern thinking meant that 'nonconformist' marxist interpretations often received less attention than they merited at the time. The subtle interpretations, for example, of the KPD 'renegade' August Thalheimer, excluded from the Communist Party in 1928, and the Austrian theorist Otto Bauer received due recognition only during the revival of fascist studies in the 1960s and 1970s, though their influence on recent western marxist interpretations of fascism has generally been greater than the Comintern formulation.

Thalheimer, in a series of essays published in 1930 but gaining full recognition only in the late 1960s, and Bauer, in an essay printed in 1924 and elaborated upon in a chapter of a book written in 1936, both based their understanding of fascism on Marx's writing on Bonapartism, in particular his *Eighteenth Brumaire of Louis Bonaparte*, written immediately after the *coup d'état* of 2 December 1851. Though neither equated Bonapartism with fascism (which at the time of their original publications remained chiefly in its Italian manifestation), both saw in Marx's interpretation of the French *coup d'état* a significant pointer to understanding the mechanics of the fascist relation to the capitalist ruling class. Marx's work had rested on his assertion that the mutual neturalization of the social classes in the struggle for power in France had enabled Louis Bonaparte, supported by the lumpenproletariat and the mass of apolitical peasant small-holders, to build the executive authority of the State into a relatively independent power. Applying Marx's analysis to fascism allowed Thalheimer and Bauer to distinguish between the social and political domination of the capitalist ruling class, to give weight to the autonomous importance of the fascist mass backing, to see fascism as only one of a number of possible ways out of the crisis of capitalism and by no means the equivalent of the final stage of capitalism *en route* to socialism, and, finally, to give weight to the relative autonomy of the fascist executive once in power. In each case, this interpretation brought them in direct conflict with the 'orthodox' Leninist line (though in his last writings in 1938 Bauer played down Bonapartism and came much closer to a Leninist analysis of imperialism). The crucial point was the dialectical relationship between the economic rule of the 'big bourgeois' and the political supremacy of the fascist 'ruling caste', financially supported by capitalists but not created by them. Though petty bourgeois in composition, the fascist party in power was bound, however, to become the instrument of the economic ruling class, especially its more warlike elements, but the inner contradictions within the system which would result in clashes of interest between the fascist caste and the capitalist ruling class could only be soluble through war.[15]

While the Comintern theory remained, until the upheavals of 1989, operational in the GDR as the key to an understanding of fascism, variants of the Bonapartist approach (such as can also be seen in Trotsky's perceptive writings on fascism[16]) have greatly influenced the theoretical writings of western marxists since the 1960s. In addition, however, writing on fascism on the Left was significantly affected by a third major strain of marxist fascism interpretation, derived from Gramsci's work (in particular his concept of 'bourgeois hegemony') and articulated by Nicos Poulantzas, whose interpretation we will consider more closely in Chapter 3.[17] The neo-Gramscian approach lays far more emphasis than other marxist interpretations on the conditions of *political* crisis, arising when the state can no longer organize the political unity of the dominant class and has lost popular legitimacy, and which make fascism attractive as a radical populist solution to the problem of restoring the dominant class's 'hegemony'. Marxist interpretations of fascism, briefly described here, will concern us in the following chapter when we deal with the relationship of politics to economics in the Nazi system of rule.

Non-marxist interpretations

While, as I have indicated, most recent marxist interpretations of fascism have adopted or built upon theories which were current in the 1920s and 1930s, early 'bourgeois' or non-marxist interpretations – few if any of them actually amounting to a *theory* of fascism – have generally been found seriously wanting by later scholarship. The 'moral crisis of European society' view, for instance, favoured by Croce, Meinecke, Ritter, and later Golo Mann, has had only the most indirect impact upon later non-marxist fascism interpretation. Wilhelm Reich's attempt to combine marxism and freudianism in interpreting fascism as a consequence of sexual repression, and Erich Fromm's collective psychology approach arguing for an 'escape from freedom' to take refuge in submission, have also provided little methodological impetus for current analysis of fascism. Only Talcott Parsons' approach through the 'anomie' of modern social structures and the conflict-laden coexistence of traditional, archaic value-systems and modern social processes can be said to have 'left an indelible imprint' on later non-marxist analyses of fascism linked to theories of modernization.[18] Non-marxist scholarship on comparative fascism, since its revival in the 1960s, found its drive chiefly from three different directions: from the 'phenomenological' history of ideas approach emanating from Ernst Nolte's work; from a number of varied 'structural-modernization' approaches; and from 'sociological' interpretations of the social composition and class base of fascist movements and voters.

Nolte's self-proclaimed 'phenomenological method' seems to amount in practice to little more than taking the self-depiction of a phenomenon seriously – in this case the writings of fascist leaders. Biting critics have suggested that it turns out 'to be essentially Dilthey's good old method of empathy', or 'little more than historicism in fancy dress'.[19] Nolte gives little serious consideration to the social foundations of fascism, since he finds socio-economic explanations of fascism inadequate. Rather, his analysis of the development of fascist ideas brings him to what he rather grandiosely calls a 'metapolitical' conception of fascism as a generic and autonomous force. In a somewhat mystical and mystifying conclusion, he sees fascism as 'practical and violent resistance to transcendence'. By 'transcendence' he understands a twofold process of mankind's quest for emancipation and progress (which he terms 'practical transcendence'), and of man's search beyond this world for salvation, 'reaching out of the mind beyond what exists and what can exist toward an absolute whole' – i.e. belief in God and after-life (which he calls 'theoretical transcendence'). Fascism is in essence, therefore, anti-modernist; but in the emphasis on the notion of 'violent resistance to transcendence', Nolte distinguishes fascism from mere 'reaction' and sees it as a European movement which was both anti-traditional and anti-modern, which, in rejecting first and foremost its mirror image of communism, at the same time threatened also the existence of bourgeois society. Finally, in his stress on 'fascism in its epoch' (the original German title of his major work), Nolte is claiming that fascism was historically time-bound, that 'it would not be possible for the "same" sociological configuration in a different period and under other world conditions to produce an historically relevant phenomenon that can qualify as fascism, at least not . . . in the form of European national fascism.'[20]

Nolte's was an important book and, as mentioned earlier, stirred up interest in the problem of generic fascism more than any other single work of the 1960s. But it is difficult to see that either methodologically or in terms of its conclusions it has gained a wide following. Other writers on comparative fascism, also working from the self-image of the fascists, have argued that fascism was revolutionary rather than backward-looking, that it 'looks much like the Jacobinism of our time'.[21] Secondly, the omission of detailed analysis of the nature and dynamics of the socio-economic foundation of fascist movements is a significant limitation of Nolte's work. Finally, from a different perspective it has been questioned whether Nolte has done more than describe similar manifestations of a type of political system which he calls 'fascism', but which showed vitally different degrees of intensity throughout Europe, in other words missing the point that the differences outweigh the similarities, which would call into question the very existence of the phenomenon itself.[22]

The second major non-marxist *group* of approaches (for they contain many varied nuances and differences of emphasis) is that linked to modernization theories, in which fascism is seen as one of a number of different paths along the route to modern society. In one variant of the modernization approach, which Klaus Hildebrand has dubbed the 'structural-functional theory', fascism is regarded as 'a special form of rule in societies which find themselves in a critical phase of the process of social transformation to industrial society and at the same time objectively or in the eyes of the ruling strata are threatened by the possibility of a communist upheaval'.[23] Fascism gains its chief impetus, in this view, from the resistance of residual 'élites to the egalitarian tendencies of industrial society. Other approaches see fascism as a form of developmental dictatorship (Gregor), as primarily a phenomenon encountered in agrarian societies in a particular phase of their transition to modernization (Organski), or as a product of the road to modernism of an agrarian society which has encountered only 'revolution from above', resulting in revolutionary unrest – with temporary modernizing force – of a thoroughly reactionary class (the peasantry) which is doomed to extinction (Barrington Moore).[24]

The main problem of the 'structural-functionalist' approach seems to lie in its over-emphasis on the resistance of the ruling élites to change at the expense of the weight to be attached to the autonomous dynamism of the fascist mass movements themselves. Coupled with this is the difficulty of establishing which states afflicted by fascism were precisely in this process of transition to a pluralistic industrial society. At best this seems to apply to Italy and Germany, though the degree of the transition was so different in the two countries that doubts remain about the value of the 'model'.[25] The chief difficulty with those modernizing theories which place fascism chiefly in an agrarian context is that they seem scarcely to apply to the German case, where Nazism developed in a highly-industrialized society. Significantly, Organski – one of the most prominent exponents of this approach – leaves Germany out of his model, while Barrington Moore's stimulating and wide-ranging analysis of different patterns of modernizing development rooted in the varied nature of the power base of the landed élites greatly over-emphasizes the importance of feudal traditions to the success of fascism, correspondingly underrating significantly the relationship to the dynamics of a fully-fledged capitalist economy and bourgeois society. Such modernization approaches as concentrate specifically upon Germany (e.g. the works of Dahrendorf and Schoenbaum[26]) are not concerned with a theory of fascism, but rather with the modernizing impact (if largely unintended) of Nazism itself. These interpretations are evaluated in chapter 7.

A third influential non-marxist approach to fascism has been Seymour Lipset's 'sociological' interpretation of fascism as lower-middle-class radicalism – the 'extremism of the centre', as he dubbed it.[27] According to this view, fascism arose when mounting economic distress and a perceived threat both from big capital and organized labour forced middle-class strata which had previously supported centrist liberal parties to turn to the extreme Right. Such an interpretation has in recent years come under fire from various directions. First, it has been shown that the lower-middle-class vote in Germany before the rise of Nazism – and Lipset's argument was heavily based upon the German case – went to parties which in no sense could be regarded as 'liberal' or moderate centrist parties, but were distinctly rightist (authoritarian, nationalist, and often racist) in complexion. A vote for a fascist party was in fact the end of a long process of gradual rightwards shift in voting patterns.[28] Secondly, the Nazi Party received its main voter support in large cities – as has recently been demonstrated – from well-to-do districts representing the established upper bourgeoisie not the precariously placed or declining lower-middle-class social groups of the classic Lipset theory, while at the other end of the social scale the Nazis gained a higher level of backing from the working class (if not making serious inroads into 'organized' labour) than had been presumed.[29] Finally, it has been objected, exclusive concentration on the political behaviour of the lower-middle-class ignores completely both the role of the élites in bringing fascism to power and also the obvious subordination of lower-middle-class interests to those of big capitalism during the regime phase of fascism.[30]

It has not been my intention to attempt a full critique of the widely differing interpretations of fascism, but rather to illustrate the fact that, despite considerable advances in developing sophisticated typologies of fascist movements, there is no prospect in view of any theory of fascism which might win universal approval. No single marxist theory can command general acceptance even among marxist scholars, while some of the weaknesses and criticisms of 'bourgeois' interpretations have been indicated. Finally, as mentioned earlier, some leading scholars – whether favouring a 'totalitarianism' approach or not – question the whole basis of studies of comparative fascism, arguing that profound differences between the 'fascist' movements render any concept of generic fascism meaningless.

Following this brief description of the stages of development of the concepts of totalitarianism and fascism, we can now turn to consider critically whether either model type satisfactorily embraces the phenomenon of Nazism.

General reflections on the concepts of 'totalitarianism' and 'fascism'

Neither 'totalitarianism' nor 'fascism' is a 'clean' scholarly concept. Both terms have, from the beginning of their usage, served a double function: as an ideological instrument of negative political categorization, often serving in common parlance as little more than 'boo-words'; and as a heuristic scholarly device used in an attempt to order and classify political systems. It is as good as impossible to treat them as 'neutral' scholarly analytical tools, detached from political connotations. Scholarly debate about the use of the terms illustrates above all the closeness of the mesh of history, politics, and language.[31] This is reflected, too, in the lack of agreement about precise definitions as well as usages of the terms.

Furthermore, there is often less than clarity about the link between concept and theory. If 'theory' is taken to be a system of interrelated statements, deriving from and based upon each other, with general explanatory power, and 'concept' as an abstract linguistic short-cut, without independent standing and offering no systematic explanation, then it could be argued that in the case of totalitarianism Friedrich produced a conceptual definition, but one which does not provide a genuine theory of totalitarianism. In the case of fascism, most non-marxist approaches, as mentioned earlier, are essentially descriptive and rest on no clearly-defined theoretical premises, while marxist approaches derive from theoretical positions but the applied theory is not always based upon a clear conceptual definition and sometimes even upon what comes close to a tautological one.[32]

Though both 'fascism' and 'totalitarianism' approaches seek to provide typologies of political systems, these are of quite a different kind. The emphasis in fascism 'theories' is upon fascist *movements* – upon the conditions of growth, aims, and function of these movements as distinct from all other forms of political organization. (Though this is also true of the Comintern theory and its later application, much more emphasis has generally here been attached to the nature of fascist dictatorship rather than to the 'movement' phase.) Totalitarianism models, on the other hand, are practically by definition largely uninterested in the pre-power phase, except in so far as it betrays 'totalitarian' ambitions. The focus is rather on *systems* and *techniques of rule*. Many questions, therefore, of vital importance to the analyst of fascist movements – regarding, for instance, the socio-economic 'causes' of fascism, the social composition of fascist parties, and the relationship of fascist movements to the existing 'ruling class' – are of little importance to the totalitarianism theorist. Significant concerns in the totalitarianism approach, on the other hand, such as the existence of a single monopoly party, plebiscitary legitimation of rule, or the dominance of an official ideology, are usually regarded as secondary by analysts of fascism, who stress rather the major differences in the aims, social base, and economic structures of fascist and communist regimes.

Both 'fascism' and 'totalitarianism' are concepts extending beyond single systems of rule to 'generic types'. As such, they both demand rigorous comparative method. Yet in practice, thorough comparative analysis has often been lacking, particularly so in the totalitarianism model, and both approaches have traditionally been top-heavy in their reliance on the case of Nazi Germany.[33] Valuable systematic comparative research has been undertaken in recent years into the structure of fascist movements,[34] but much comparative work remains to be done on the character of fascist institutions in power. From the totalitarianism perspective, research into Stalinist government and society has reached nowhere near the level of penetration of that into the Nazi Regime, and comparisons are in practice often highly superficial.[35]

Despite the fact that the concepts are politically irreconcilable – protagonists of a general fascism concept rest their position upon the view that right-wing dictatorships are *fundamentally different* from left-wing dictatorships, while protagonists of a totalitarian approach begin with the premise that fascist and communist dictatorships are *basically similar* – prominent German scholars have claimed the indispensability of both concepts in analysing modern political structures and have argued that it is possible to apply both approaches in different ways in examining Nazism.[36] This seems to attract the difficulty of applying *comparative* concepts to a single phenomenon while leaving unresolved the problem of whether the comparative concept itself is a valid one. Nevertheless, that each of the concepts undeniably contains political overtones does not in itself disqualify them from having scholarly value and intellectual validity. Hence, there remains the need to test the explanatory value of each of the terms as vehicles for assessing the essential character of Nazism.

Nazism as totalitarianism?

Critics of the totalitarianism concept fall into two main categories: (a) those who reject categorically any deployment of a concept or theory of totalitarianism; and (b) those who are prepared to concede it some theoretical validity, but who regard its practical deployment as a tool of analysis as limited in potential. The arguments in favour of the second position are, in my view, more convincing.

(a) Categorical rejection of totalitarianism as a wholly worthless concept is usually pressed on the following grounds:[37]
  (i) Totalitarianism is no more than a Cold War ideology, devised and deployed by western capitalist states in the 1940s and 1950s as an anti-communist instrument of political integration, and continuing to be used as such to the present day. Apart from the fact that, as we have seen, the concept and its application existed long before the Cold War, the undoubted and usually crude political use to which it was put in the Cold War of itself no more deprives totalitarianism of potential value as a scholarly analytical tool than the often equally crude political exploitation of the term 'fascism' robs theories of fascism of any validity.
  (ii) The totalitarianism concept treats the form – the outward shape of the systems of rule – as content, as their essence. As a result, it fully ignores the completely different aims and intentions of Nazism and Bolshevism – aims which were wholly inhumane and negative in the former case and ultimately humane and positive in the latter case. The objection is not altogether convincing. As Adam has pointed out,[38] the argument is based upon a deduction from the future (neither verifiable nor falsifiable) to the present, a procedure which in strict logic is not permissible. There is also a presumption that form and content can be so dissociated from each other that a comment on the form says nothing about the content – a point rejected even by materialist dialectics. Furthermore, the emphasis upon the ultimate humanity of Bolshevism contrasted with the inhumanity of Nazism correlates a presumed idealistic intention of the one system with the known reality of the other, and shirks the question of possible actual similarities in techniques of domination between the Stalinist and Hitler regimes. The purely functional point that communist terror was 'positive' because it was 'directed towards a complete and radical change in society' whereas 'fascist (i.e. Nazi) terror

reached its highest point with the destruction of the Jews' and 'made no attempt to alter human behaviour or build a genuinely new society'[39] is, apart from the debatable assertion in the last phrase, a cynical value judgement on the horrors of the Stalinist terror.

(b) Four substantial criticisms are raised by those who do not reject the totalitarianism model out of hand, but see its application as very limited:

   (i) The concept of totalitarianism, however defined, can only unsatisfactorily grasp the peculiarities of the systems it attempts to classify. Broszat pointed out, for instance, in the introductory remarks to his masterly analysis of the 'Hitler State', the difficulty of locating the amorphous structurelessness of the Nazi system in any typology of the rule.[40] The totalitarianism concept can, in fact, only speak in a generalized and limited fashion about the similarities of systems, which on closer inspection are so differently structured that comparisons are forced to remain highly superficial. Hans Mommsen has indicated, for example, how different the Nazi Party and the Soviet Communist Party were from each other in structure and function, and how little it says, therefore, simply to refer to both Nazi Germany and Soviet Russia (even confining the treatment to the Stalinist period) as 'one-party states'.[41] Equally significant were the major differences in the essential character of leadership in the two states, so that the roles of Hitler and Stalin can only with difficulty be typified as those of 'totalitarian dictators'. And the fundamental contrasts in the control of the Nazi and Soviet economies are an even more striking example of highly misleading generalizations emanating from the totalitarianism approach – in this instance about centralized 'totalitarian' economies.

   (ii) The totalitarianism concept cannot cope adequately with change within the communist system. The extension of the concept to post-Stalinist USSR and other eastern-bloc states is forced to see the essence of totalitarianism as lying elsewhere than in the specific features of Stalinism usually taken to be comparable with Nazism (e.g. terror, leadership cult etc.). Still retaining the implicit (if not explicit) linkage with Nazism and other 'right-wing dictatorships', such attempts often rapidly widen into outright absurdity.

   (iii) The decisive disadvantage of totalitarianism as a concept is that it says nothing about socio-economic conditions, functions, and political aims of a system, but is content to rely solely upon emphasis of techniques and overt forms of rule (exclusivity of ideology, tendency to comprehensive mobilization etc.).[42] Since one of the most obvious and striking differences between the Nazi and the Soviet systems lies in the socio-economic sphere, it has been pointed out that 'the value of an analysis which ignores the relations of production and the resulting social structure of the two systems is strictly limited'.[43]

(iv) The legitimacy of the totalitarianism concept rests upon the upholding of the values of western 'liberal democracy' and the distinction between 'open' and 'closed' government, between 'shared' and 'unified' power. There is, however, built into the totalitarianism concept an ambivalence between describing historically real systems of rule (Nazism, 'Stalinism') and being widened out into a 'tendency' which extends to so many modern dictatorships and even to sections of society within western democracies that the concept loses much of its analytical value.[44]

These criticisms are generally advanced by those who nevertheless would not wish altogether to discard the concept of totalitarianism. They claim – and I would agree with their argument – that it is in itself a wholly legitimate exercise, whatever essential differences existed in ideology and socio-economic structures, to compare the forms and techniques of rule in Germany under Hitler and the Soviet Union under Stalin; and that a new scale and concept of the development of force in governmental systems, in attempted comprehensiveness of control and manipulation, in methods (based on modern technology) of dynamic plebiscitary mobilization of the population behind its rulers, and a radical intolerance of any focus of coexisting alternative loyalties or any form of institutional 'living space' except under the regime's own terms, corresponding therefore to the *attempted* politicization of all facets of social experience, can justifiably be seen in both systems. The spectrum of dissent ranging to 'resistance' in Nazi Germany (and *pari passu*, though so far little analysed, in Stalin's Russia) can in fact only be understood in the light of the relationship to the demands of a regime which made a 'total claim' on behaviour and manifestations of outward conformity, hence creating nonconformist and oppositional behaviour which even in other authoritarian systems would not have been politicized and turned, thereby, into political dissent.[45] If the redundant echoes of 'atomized mass society' theories can be dispensed with, then it may indeed be at the social rather than the institutional level that, if not the full-blown, politically loaded, concept of totalitarianism, then the more modest notion of the 'total claim' of a regime on its subjects could prove heuristically useful in a comparative analysis of behavioural patterns – acclamatory and oppositional – in quite differently structured societies and political systems.[46] Even the posing of an extreme 'total claim' might then be seen as symptomatic of the 'crisis management' of regimes in transitory, unstable periods rather than as lasting characteristics of rule.

Beyond this, it seems to me that depictions of Nazism as a 'totalitarian system' are best avoided, not simply because of the inescapable political colouring attached to the label 'totalitarianism', but because of the weighty conceptual problems which the term poses and which have been outlined above. There remains a final possibility of deploying the concept in a non-comparative sense, restricting its usage to Nazi/fascist systems alone and reverting to something like its earlier usage by Franz Neumann and others in distinguishing phases of development in the impact of a dynamic mass movement with 'total' claims upon the legislative and executive structures of the state. Broszat's analysis of the Nazi state, for instance, uses the adjective 'totalitarian' divorced from comparison with the USSR to distinguish the more radical phase of Nazi government after 1937–8 from the earlier merely 'authoritarian' phase.[47] Quite apart from the question of attaching distinctive labels to the periods of the Third Reich before and after 1937–8, and of ridding 'totalitarianism' of its usual comparative connotations with the USSR, it might be seriously doubted whether, in dealing with the Nazi state alone, the adjective 'totalitarian' is needed at all simply as a synonym for progressively radicalizing dynamism. Others, developing the same line of interpretation, find the term wholly redundant.[48]

All in all, the value of the totalitarianism concept seems extremely limited, and the disadvantages of its deployment greatly outweigh its possible advantages in attempting to characterize the essential nature of the Nazi Regime.[49]

Nazism as fascism or unique phenomenon?

Opponents of the use of a generic concept of fascism advance two principal and serious objections to the ranking of Nazism as fascism: firstly – an objection I find justified – that the concept is often extended in inflationary fashion to a wide variety of movements and regimes of wholly disparate character and significance; and secondly, but in my view less persuasive, that the concept is unable to satisfactorily embrace the singular characteristics of Nazism, and that the differences between Italian fascism and German National Socialism significantly outweigh whatever superficial similarities they might appear to possess.

(a) The first criticism pertains particularly, though not solely, to marxist interpretations of fascism. The intrinsic relationship between fascism and capitalism in the marxist-leninist version of fascism theory, for instance, extends the notion of 'fascist dictatorship' to cover numerous kinds of repressive regime, and no fundamental distinction is drawn between military dictatorships and mass-party dictatorships in terms of the essence of rule. Since, according to this view, the mass base of a fascist party is a manipulated product of the ruling capitalist class without any autonomous force, the importance of the mass movement (which most non-marxist analysts would regard as a significant difference between military authoritarian regimes and fascist regimes) recedes.

Hence, GDR scholars classed such disparate regimes as existed in Poland, Bulgaria, and Hungary in the inter-war period, in Portugal under Salazar and Caetano and Spain under Franco, in Greece under the Colonels, Argentina under the Generals, Chile under Pinochet, and other South American dictatorships, as 'fascist' alongside 'Hitler Fascism'.[50] Decisive for GDR historians was not the outward form of the dictatorship, but its essence as the weapon of the most aggressive elements of finance capital. Nevertheless, GDR scholarship did come to distinguish very clearly between two basic types of fascist dictatorship; the *normal* form – usually a military dictatorship – in countries with relatively unadvanced capitalist economies; and the *exceptional* form – mass-party fascism – of which only the two examples of Italy and Germany have so far been experienced, both arising in highly unusual conditions within the framework of a complete national crisis.[51] Consideration of the relationship between capitalism and Nazism, on which this theory rests, will have to wait until the following chapter. It suffices here to say that, however unconvincing the underlying principles are, GDR interpretations compared very favourably with the writings of parts of the 'New Left' in the Federal Republic, where the concept of fascism was extended to any form of 'repressive' government which serves to uphold the domination of economic power-groups, thus allowing western capitalist systems – and the Federal Republic in particular – to be dubbed 'fascist' or at least 'fascistoid' or 'proto-fascist'.[52] In such cases, where the fascism concept is widened in hopelessly nebulous fashion, it seems perfectly correct to speak of a trivialization of the horror of Nazism.

(b) The second, related, criticism claims that no theory or concept of generic fascism can possibly do justice to the peculiarities and unique characteristics of Nazism. While movements calling themselves fascist or national socialist existed in most European countries outside the Soviet Union in the inter-war period, it is widely accepted that fully-fledged, self-sustaining fascist dictatorships deriving their impetus from mass parties consolidated power only in Italy and Germany (leaving aside puppet or quisling governments of the war years). A comparison of fascism in all its stages can accordingly be made only for the systems in these two countries.[53] Yet in the eyes of some leading authorities, the differences between the two regimes were so profound that the term 'fascism' should be reserved for the Italian system under Mussolini, while Nazism should be called 'National Socialism' and regarded as a unique phenomenon (though, interestingly enough, falling in terms of techniques of rule within the category of 'totalitarian systems'). Since, in this view, the generic concept of fascism does not even apply to the two leading species within the genus, it had better be discarded altogether. The central differences emphasized in this argument focus on the dynamic nature of the Nazi race ideology, which had no exact parallel in Italian fascism; on the discrepancy between Nazi elevation of the *Volk* over the state, contrasted with Italian fascist étatism; on the anti-modern, archaic aims and ideology of Nazism compared with the modernizing tendencies of Italian fascism; on the totality of the Nazi conquest of state and society as against the far more limited penetration of the established order by the Italian fascists; and, not least, on the contrast between a relatively 'traditional' imperialistic policy on the part of Italy, and a qualitatively different drive for racial domination, eventually of the whole world, by the Nazi regime. And since this last and most crucial distinction is, according to such interpretations, attributable directly to Hitler himself, it is claimed that 'the case of Hitler' was unique, and cannot be subjected to the generalizations of comparative fascism, not even to a comparison limited to Italy and Germany.[54]

These criticisms cannot be lightly passed over. Indeed, examination of two central issues – the relationship between capitalism and Nazism, and the personal role of Hitler in the Nazi system – form the direct subject of later chapters. There is space here only for a number of general observations about the criticisms of the generic fascism approach, related to the alternative possibility of emphasizing the uniqueness of Nazism.

A number of the supposed major difference between Nazism and Italian fascism are open to debate. This would apply, for instance, to the stress on the 'backward-looking' nature of Nazism in distinction to the 'modernizing' pressures of fascism in Italy. Research has called such a distinction increasingly into question, as chapter 7 indicates.[55] Quite apart from such qualification, the uniqueness of specific features of Nazism would not of itself prevent the location of Nazism in a wider genus of political systems. It might well be claimed that Nazism and Italian fascism were separate species within the same genus, without any implicit assumption that the two species ought to be well-nigh identical. Ernst Nolte has stated that the differences could easily be reconciled by employing a term such as 'radical fascism' for Nazism.[56] Winkler has indicated that for him Nazism was 'also but not only "German fascism" ',[57] while Juan Linz regarded it as a 'distinctive branch grafted on the fascist tree'.[58] Jürgen Kocka, in a subtle essay on the causes of Nazism, again sees no incompatibility between the unique features of National Socialism in Germany and its attribution to a broader class of generic fascism, indispensable for putting the Nazi phenomenon in a wider than purely national perspective and understanding the social and political contexts in which such a movement could arise and take power.[59] Such approaches rightly stress the significant similarities between Nazism and the many movements (above all the Italian one) which called themselves fascist. Such similarities included: extreme chauvinistic nationalism with pronounced imperialistic, expansionist tendencies; an anti-socialist, anti-marxist thrust aimed at the destruction of working-class organizations and their marxist political philosophy; the basis in a mass party drawing from all sectors of society, though with pronounced support in the middle class and proving attractive to the peasantry and to various uprooted or highly unstable sectors of the population; fixation on a charismatic, plebiscitarily legitimized leader; extreme intolerance towards all oppositional and presumed oppositional groups, expressed through vicious terror, open violence, and ruthless repression; glorification of militarism and war, heightened by the backlash to the comprehensive socio-political crisis in Europe arising from the First World War; dependence upon an 'alliance' with existing élites – industrial, agrarian, military, and bureaucratic – for their political breakthrough; and at least an initial function – despite a populist-revolutionary, anti-establishment rhetoric – in the stabilization or restoration of social order and capitalist structures.[60]

The establishment of fundamental generic characteristics linking Nazism to movements in other parts of Europe allows further consideration on a comparative basis of the reasons why such movements were able to become a real political danger and gain power in Italy and Germany, whereas in other European countries they mainly remained an unpleasant, but transitory irritant. Among other things, one would undoubtedly have to lay stress on features prominent, though in different strengths, in both Italy and Germany before the First World War and massively accentuated through the traumatic consequences of the War itself. Common to both countries were the powerful imperialist–expansionist strains pronounced among the ruling élites and bolstered by the widespread extreme chauvinism in the bourgeois classes of these new states – self-perceived 'have-not nations'; the co-existence and conflict of highly modern strands of development and powerful remnants of archaic social structures and value-systems in societies simultaneously undergoing the process of national integration, transition to a bourgeois constitutional state, and rapid industrialization;[61] and finally, but not least, deeply fractured political systems, whose splintered parliamentary structures reflected deep social and political cleavages, fostering the feeling that a strong, but 'populist', leadership was necessary to impose unity 'from above' – in the first instance by crushing those standing in the way of unity, primarily 'the marxist Left'. The different scale of the social and political conflict spheres in Italy and Germany helps explain the different level of radicalization in the two countries when beset by different, though related, comprehensive crises of the political system – directly unleashed by the War in the Italian case, unfolding, after a long period of political instability, during the world economic crisis in Germany.

It is within this perspective, rather than divorced from it in an emphasis upon Nazism as an altogether unique phenomenon, that the peculiarities of the German radical variant of fascism can be brought out by analysis of the specific features of the German political culture and its relationship to socio-economic structures. There need be no contradiction, therefore, between acceptance of Nazism as (the most extreme manifestation of) fascism and recognition of its own unique characteristics within this category, which can only properly be comprehended within the framework of German national development.

Such an argument would not, however, satisfy Bracher, Hildebrand, Hillgruber, and others, who would argue that Nazism was not only in form, but in essence a uniquely German phenomenon, and that this essence or uniqueness was located in the person and ideology of Adolf Hitler. This personalization of the essence of Nazism is, in fact, at the crux of the debate over the historical place and characterization of Nazism. The major differences do not lie in explaining Nazism's origins and the circumstances of its rise to power. Bracher has tended to emphasize the specific features of German-Austrian ideological development in order to lay full weight on the racial-*völkisch* dimension of Nazi ideology; Hillgruber and Hildebrand have stressed the particular constellation of German power-politics and the overwhelming continuities between 1871 and 1933 (only to be broken thereafter) intrinsic to the Prussian–German State.[62] These are important strands of an overall explanation of Nazism and, despite differences of emphasis, are generally compatible with those works – for example, by Wehler, Kocka, Puhle, and Winkler[63] – which look rather to Germany's specific socio-economic structures as the focal point of their explanations. Yet this later group have no hesitation in accepting Nazism, for all its singularities, as a form of fascism; while the former group deny this categorization and insist that it was *sui generis*. The breaking-point is clearly 'the case of Hitler': whether Nazism can be set aside from fascism in Italy and elsewhere because it was *in its essence* 'Hitlerism'. According to the latter approach, not the causes of Nazism's rise but the character of the dictatorship itself is decisive. And here, the difference between Italian fascism and Nazism, whose rule rested on the implementation of the ideas and policies of the monocratic dictator, Hitler, were fundamental.[64]

This 'Hitler-centrism' is itself an understandable over-reaction against some crude left-wing interpretations which reduced Hitler to a mere cipher. However, irreplaceable though Hitler undoubtedly was in the Nazi movement, the equation Nazism = Hitlerism unnecessarily restricts the vision and distorts the focus in explaining the origins of Nazism; deflects away from rather than orientates towards consideration of the political manifestations in other European countries which shared (and continue to share today) important affinities and common characteristics with Nazism; and finally – as I hope to argue in later chapters – provides in itself a quite unsatisfactory explanation of the dynamic radicalization of politics within the Third Reich itself.

This evaluation of the concepts of totalitarianism and fascism in relation to Nazism's alleged uniqueness as a phenomenon has suggested the following conclusions:

1 The concept of fascism is more satisfactory and applicable than that of totalitarianism in explaining the character of Nazism, the circumstances of its growth, the nature of its rule, and its place in a European context in the inter-war period. The similarities with other brands of fascism are profound, not peripheral. Nazism's features place the phenomenon squarely within the European-wide context of radical anti-socialist national-integrationist movements, which also rejected the forms though not the economic substance of bourgeois society, derived from the era of open imperialist conflict and emerged to prominence in the upheavals following the First World War.

2 This is not incompatible with the retention of the concept of totalitarianism, though this latter concept is much less usable and its value is strictly limited. Nazism undoubtedly did have a 'total' (or 'totalitarian') claim, which had consequences both for its mechanics of rule and for the behaviour – acclamatory and oppositional – of its subjects. Consequences for the mechanics of rule were reflected especially in new forms of plebiscitary mass mobilization through new technologies of rule combined with an exclusive dynamic ideology and monopolistic demands on society. On the basis of these features, it is legitimate to compare the forms of rule in Germany under Hitler and the Soviet Union under Stalin, even if, for the reasons adduced earlier, this comparison is doomed from the outset to be superficial and unsatisfactory. Moreover, 'totalitarianism' according to our analysis, if to be used at all, would have to be restricted to passing phases of extreme instability reflected in the paranoid sense of insecurity of the regimes, rather than being seen as a lasting structure of rule. From a long-range perspective, the entire period of the Third Reich and the bulk of Stalin's rule could be said to fall within such a categorization. This would be a reason additional to those mentioned earlier to exclude the application of the comparative totalitarianism concept to post-Stalinist communist system, where it rapidly approaches futility if not outright absurdity.[65]

3 The peculiar features which distinguish Nazism from other leading manifestations of fascism are only to be fully comprehended within the structures and conditions of German socio-economic and ideological–political developments in the industrial-bourgeois era. The person, ideology, and function of Hitler have to be located in and related to these structures. Without question, Hitler played personally a vital part both in the rise of Nazism and in the character of Nazi rule. But the significance of his role can only be assessed by relating his input to the conditions which produced and shaped him, and which he could not

autonomously control even at the height of his power. Nazism was in many respects indeed a unique phenomenon.[66] But its uniqueness cannot – except in a superficial sense – be solely attributed to the uniqueness of its leader.

Notes

1. Representative of this line of argument is Jürgen Kocka, 'Ursachen des Nationalsozialismus', *APZ* (21 June 1980), pp. 3–15.
2. See David Blackbourn and Geoff Eley, *Mythen deutscher Geschichtsschreibung* (Frankfurt am Main/Berlin/Vienna, 1980), Engl. trans., *The Peculiarities of German History* (Oxford, 1984). For the sharp and polemical debate unleashed by this book, see e.g. the reviews by Hans-Ulrich Wehler, ' "Deutscher Sonderweg" oder allgemeine Probleme des westlichen Kapitalismus?', *Merkur* 5 (1981), pp. 478–87; Hans-Jürgen Puhle, 'Deutscher Sonderweg. Kontroverse um eine vermeintliche Legende', *Journal für Geschichte*, Heft 4 (1981), pp. 44–5; Wolfgang J. Mommsen, in *Bulletin of the German Historical Institute*, London 4 (1980), pp. 19–26; and the discussion forum *Deutscher Sonderweg – Mythos oder Realität* (Kolloquien des Instituts für Zeitgeschichte, Munich/Vienna, 1982). Directly relating to the causes of fascism, and partly in reply to Kocka's article (see note 1), see also Geoff Eley, 'What produces Fascism: Preindustrial Traditions or a Crisis of the Capitalist State?', *Politics and Society* 12 (1983), pp. 53–82. Jürgen Kocka, 'German History before Hitler'. The Debate about the German *Sonderweg*', *JCH* 23 (1988), pp. 3–16, provides an excellent critique of the pros and cons of the *Sonderweg* argument. He concludes that while the term '*Sonderweg*' is itself misleading and dispensable, the notion of a divergence from the pattern of development of other 'advanced' western countries retains its value in explaining why Germany offered so few barriers to the fascist challenge.
3. See the essays by Karl Dietrich Bracher in his *Zeitg. Kontrov.*, Part I, and his 'The Role of Hitler: Perspectives on Interpretations', in Walter Laqueur, ed., *Fascism. A Reader's Guide* (Harmondsworth, 1979), pp. 193–212; Hildebrand, *Das Dritte Reich*, pp. 132 ff., 187 ff.; and Hillgruber. *Endlich genug?*, pp. 38–42.
4. For the developing usage of the 'totalitarianism' concept, see Walter Schlangen, *Die Totalitarismus-Theorie. Entwicklung und Probleme* (Stuttgart/Berlin/Cologne/Mainz, 1976), chs. 1–3. For guidance on the early Italian usage, I am indebted to Professor Meir Michaelis (Hebrew Univ. of Jerusalem). See his informative paper: 'Anmerkungen zum italienischen Totalitarismusbegriff. Zur Kritik der Thesen Hannah Arendts und Renzo de Felices', *Quellen und Forschungen aus italienischen Archiven und Bibliotheken* (published by the German Historical Institute in Rome), 62 (1982), pp. 270–302, esp. pp. 292–7.
5. Franz Neumann, *Behemoth. The Structure and Practice of National Socialism* (London, 1942). The German edition (Cologne/Frankfurt am Main, 1977, based on the extended 1944 English edition) has a valuable 'Nachwort' by the editor, Gert Schäfer. See also Richard Saage, 'Das sozio-politische Herrschaftssystem des Nationalsozialismus. Reflexionen zu Franz Neumanns "Behemoth" ', *Jahrbuch des Instituts für Deutsche Geschichte, Tel Aviv* 10 (1981), pp. 342–62.
6. Arendt, *Origins* (see ch. 1 note 33). See the remarks of Klaus Hildebrand, 'Stufen der Totalitarismus-Forschung', *PVS 9* (1968), pp. 406–8; Martin Kitchen, *Fascism* (London, 1976), pp. 30–1; and Ayçoberry, pp. 130–3.
7. Friedrich first advanced his model in his essay, 'The Unique Character of Totalitarian Society' in the volume he edited, *Totalitarianism* (Cambridge, Mass., 1954),

and extended it in Friedrich and Brzezinski, *Totalitarian Dictatorship and Autocracy*. For criticism from within the 'totalitarianism' approach and a revised model, see Leonard Schapiro, *Totalitarianism* (London, 1973).
8 See Schlangen, ch. 4.
9 For a succinct statement of his position of 'totalitarianism', see *Totalitarismus und Faschismus. Eine wissenschaftliche und politische Begriffskontroverse* (Munich/Vienna, 1980), pp. 10–17, 53–4, 69–70.
10 Karl Dietrich Bracher, *Schlüsselwörter in der Geschichte* (Düsseldorf, 1978), pp. 109–10, 121–3.
11 Ernst Nolte, *Der Faschismus in seiner Epoche* (Munich, 1963), Engl. trans., *The Three Faces of Fascism* (London, 1965, subsequent references to Mentor edn., New York/Toronto, 1969).
12 E.g. Eugene Weber, *Varieties of Fascism* (New York, 1964); 'International Fascism, 1920–1945', *JCH* 1 (1) (1966); Ernst Nolte, *Die faschistischen Bewegungen* (Munich, 1966); Francis L. Carsten, *The Rise of Fascism* (London, 1967); Stuart J. Woolf, ed., *European Fascism* (London, 1968), and *The Nature of Fascism* (London, 1968); Wolfgang Schieder, 'Faschismus', in C.D. Hernig, ed., *Sowjetsystem und demokratische Gesellschaft. Eine vergleichende Enzyklopädie* (7 vols., Freiburg/Basel/Vienna, 1966–72), vol. 2 (1968), columns 438–77; Renzo de Felice, *Interpretations of Fascism* (Cambridge, Mass., 1977, first Italian edn. 1969). For useful later anthologies and surveys of the literature, see Wolfgang Wippermann, *Faschismustheorien* (Darmstadt, 1972); Wolfgang Schieder, ed., *Faschismus als soziale Bewegung* (Hamburg, 1976); Hans-Ulrich Thamer and Wolfgang Wippermann, *Faschistische und neofaschistische Bewegungen* (Darmstadt, 1977); Walter Laqueur, ed., *Fascism. A Reader's Guide* (Harmondsworth, 1979); Stanley Payne, *Fascism: Comparison and Definition* (Madison, Wisconsin, 1980); Stein Ugelvik Larsen *et al.*, *Who were the Fascists? Social Roots of European Fascism* (Bergen, 1980); Wolfgang Wippermann, *Europäischer Faschismus im Vergleich, 1922–1982* (Frankfurt am Main, 1983) and Detlef Mühlberger, ed., *The Social Basis of European Fascist Movements* (London/Sydney, 1987). More recent valuable studies include: Roger Griffin, *The Nature of Fascism* (London, 1991); Roger Eatwell, *Fascism: A History* (London, 1995); and Stanley G. Payne, *A History of Fascism, 1914–45* (London, 1995).
13 E.g. Ernst Noltre, ed., *Theorien über den Faschismus* (Cologne, 1967); Wolfgang Abendroth, ed., *Faschismus und Kapitalismus. Theorien über die sozialen Ursprünge und die Funktion des Faschismus* (Frankfurt am Main/Vienna, 1967); Reinhart Kühnl, ed., *Texte zur Faschismusdiskussion I. Positionen und Kontroversen* (Reinbek bei Hamburg, 1974); Reinhard Kühnl, *Formen bürgerlicher Herrschaft* (Reinbek bei Hamburg, 1971); Manfred Clemenz, *Gesellschaftliche Ursprünge des Faschismus* (Frankfurt am Main, 1972). A cross-section of 'New Left' work of the 1960s can be seen in *Das Argument* 1–6 (1964–70). For a sharp critique, see Heinrich August Winkler, *Revolution, Staat, Faschismus* (Göttingen, 1978), ch. 3.
14 For a summary of GDR research by some of its foremost historians, see Eichholtz and Gossweiler, *Faschismusforschung* (see ch. 1 note 28).
15 On Thalheimer, Bauer, and 'Bonapartism', see esp. Gerhard Botz, 'Austro-Marxist Interpretations of Fascism', in 'Theories of Fascism', *JCH* 11 (4) (1976), pp. 129–56, esp. pp. 131–47; Jost Dülffer, 'Bonapartism, Fascism, and National Socialism', in *JCH* 11 (1976), pp. 109–28; and Hans-Gerd Jaschke, *Soziale Basis und soziale Funktion des Nationalsozialismus. Studien zur Bonapartismustheorie* (Opladen, 1982). See also Kitchen, ch. 7; Ayçoberry, pp. 57–64; and Hildebrand, *Das Dritte Reich*, pp. 125–6. Winkler, *Revolution*, ch. 2 and pp. 83 ff. offers a

critique. And for an excellent evaluation of interwar marxist analyses of fascism ('orthodox' and 'deviant'), together with a selection of the most important texts, see David Beetham, *Marxism in Face of Fascism* (Manchester, 1983).
16. Leon Trotsky, *The Struggle against Fascism* (New York, 1971). Trotsky regarded the presidential cabinets of Brüning, von Papen, and von Schleicher, not Fascism itself, as 'Bonapartism'. See Robert S. Wistrich, 'Leon Trotsky's Theory of Fascism', *JCH* 11 (1976), pp. 170–1.
17. Nicos Poulantzas, *Fascism and Dictatorship* (London, 1974).
18. See Talcott Parsons, 'Democracy and Social Structure in Pre-Nazi Germany', and 'Some Sociological Aspects of the Fascist Movements', in his *Essays in Sociological Theory* (London/Toronto, 1949). The quotation is from Geoff Eley, 'The Wilhelmine Right: How it Changed', in Richard J. Evans, ed., *Society and Politics in Wilhelmine Germany* (London, 1978), p. 115.
19. Sauer, p. 414 (see ch. 1 note 41); Kitchen, p. 40.
20. Nolte, *Three Faces*, pp. 529, 537 ff., 566–7. The quotation is from Ernst Nolte, 'The Problem of Fascism in Recent Scholarship', in Henry A. Turner, ed., *Reappraisals of Fascism* (New York, 1975), p. 30.
21. Weber, *Varieties*, p. 139.
22. Hildebrand, *Das Dritte Reich*, p. 136.
23. Wolfgang J. Mommsen, 'Gesellschaftliche Bedingtheit und gesellschaftliche Relevanz historischer Aussagen', in Eberhard Jäckel and Ernst Weymar, eds., *Die Funktion der Geschichte in unserer Zeit* (Stuttgart, 1975), pp. 219–20; Hildebrand, *Das Dritte Reich*, p. 136.
24. A.J. Gregor, *The Ideology of Fascism* (New York, 1969); A.F.K. Organski, 'Fascism and Modernization', in Woolf, ed., *The Nature of Fascism*, pp. 19–41; Barrington Moore Jr., *Social Origins of Dictatorship and Democracy* (London, 1967).
25. Pointed out in Hildebrand, *Das Dritte Reich*, pp. 137–8.
26. Ralf Dahrendorf, *Society and Democracy in Germany* (London, 1968); David Schoenbaum, *Hitler's Social Revolution* (London, 1966; all subsequent references to Anchor Books edn., New York, 1967).
27. Seymour Martin Lipset, *Political Man. The Social Bases of Politics* (New York, 1960), ch. 5.
28. See Heinrich August Winkler, 'Extremismus de Mitte? Sozialgeschichtliche Aspekte der nationalsozialistischen Machtergreifung', *VfZ* 20 (1972), pp. 175–91; and Thomas Childers, *The Nazi Voter. The Social Foundations of Fascism in Germany, 1919–1933* (Chapel Hill/London, 1983). On voter support for Nazism see the sophisticated study of Jürgen W. Falter, *Hitler's Wähler* (Munich, 1991).
29. For the big city vote, see Richard F. Hamilton, *Who voted for Hitler?* (Princeton, 1981). The wide social spectrum of Nazi support is emphasized by Childers, Jürgen W. Falter, 'Wer verhalf der NSDAP zum Sieg?', *APZ* (14 July 1979), pp. 3–21, and Heinrich August Winkler, 'Mittelstandsbewegung oder Volkspartei? Zur sozialen Basis der NSDAP', in Schieder, ed., *Faschismus als soziale Bewegung*, pp. 97–118. For the social structure of the party membership, see Michael Kater, *The Nazi Party. A Social Profile of Members and Leaders, 1919–1945* (Oxford, 1983). A good survey of the literature on the social composition of Nazi support, in particular the vexed questions of the nature and extent of working-class backing for Nazism and whether the SA had a more 'middle-class' or 'proletarian' character, can be found in Mathilde Jamin, *Zwischen den Klassen. Zur Sozialstruktur der SA-Führerschaft* (Wuppertal, 1984), pp. 11–45. New evidence on the structure of Party membership is presented by Detlef Mühlberger, *Hitler's Followers. Studies in the Sociology of the Nazi Movement* (London, 1991). The most fundamental study of electoral support for National Socialism is now Falter, *Hitler's Wähler*.

30 Bernt Hagtvet and Reinhard Kühnl, 'Contemporary Approaches to Fascism: A Survey of Paradigms', in Larsen *et al.*, pp. 26–51, here p. 31. This is a perceptive analysis of the problems of comparative fascism. From a different perspective, see also Juan J. Linz, 'Some Notes towards a Comparative Study of Fascism in Sociological Historical Perspectives', in Laqueur, pp. 13–78.
31 See Karl Dietrich Bracher, 'Betrachtung: Terrorismus und Totalitarismus', in his *Schlüsselwörter*, pp. 103–23 (a lecture given in 1977 at a CDU conference on the causes of terrorism), and the comments of Bracher and Martin Broszat in *Total. und Fasch.*, pp. 10–11, 32–3.
32 Uwe Dietrich Adam, 'Anmerkungen zu methodischen Fragen in den Sozialwissenschaften: Das Beispiel Faschismus und Totalitarismus', *PVS* 16 (1975), pp. 55–88, here esp. pp. 75–6.
33 Examples for fascism are the books of Clemenz (note 13), Richard Saage, *Faschismus-theorien* (Munich, 1976), and Niels Kadritzke, *Faschismus und Krise* (Frankfurt am Main/New York, 1976), and, for totalitarianism, Hans Buchheim, *Totalitäre Herrschaft. Wesen und Merkmale* (Munich, 1962).
34 There is an excellent summary of up-to-date findings in Larsen *et al.* (note 12).
35 The striking differences in the state of research and historiographical development are clearly brought out in the contributions by Mark von Hagen and Mary Nolan in Ian Kershaw and Moshe Lewin (eds.), *Stalinism and Nazism: Dictatorships in Comparison* (Cambridge, 1997).
36 Kocka, 'Ursachen', pp. 14–15, and the comments of Kocka, Broszat, Schieder, and Nolte, in *Total. und Fasch.*, pp. 32–53.
37 Kitchen, ch. 2, comes close to this position.
38 Adam, 'Anmerkungen', pp. 64–7.
39 Kitchen, p. 31
40 Martin Broszat, *Der Staat Hitlers* (Munich, 1969), p. 9, not included in the Engl. trans., *The Hitler State* (London, 1981).
41 Hans Mommsen, in *Total. und Fasch.*, pp. 18–27.
42 Jürgen Kocka, in *Total. und Fasch.*, pp. 39–44.
43 Kitchen, p. 31.
44 Martin Broszat, in *Total. und Fasch.*, pp. 32–8.
45 See Ian Kershaw, *Popular Opinion and Political Dissent in the Third Reich. Bavaria 1933–1945* (Oxford, 1983), esp. pp. 374 ff.
46 For a perceptive assessment of the impact of Nazism on German society, see Detlev Peukert, *Volksgenossen und Gemeinschaftsfremde* (Cologne, 1982). Engl. trans., *Inside Nazi Germany. Conformity and Opposition in Everyday Life* (London, 1987).
47 Broszat, *The Hitler State*, pp. ix–xiv, 346 ff. In his later work, Franz Neumann came to deploy the 'totalitarianism' concept in its conventional 'Cold War' usage. See his *The Democratic and the Authoritarian State* (New York, 1957).
48 E.g. Hans Mommsen, in *Total. und Fasch.*, p. 65, where he states: 'The totalitarianism theory is the myth which stands in the way of any *real* social historical explanation [of Nazism]', particularly because of its teleological tendency to take the end product for granted before examining the conditions of its growth.
49 A wide variety of interpretations – supportive and critical – of the totalitarianism model can now be found in Eckard Jesse (ed.), *Totalitarismus im 20. Jahrhundert. Eine Bilanz der internationalen Forschung* (2nd edn., Bonn, 1999).
50 E.g. Manfred Weißbecker, 'Der Faschismus in der Gegenwart', in Eichholtz and Gossweiler, pp. 217 ff.; Kurt Gossweiler, *Faschismus und antifaschistischer Kampf* (Antifaschistische Arbeitshefte, Röderberg Verlag, Frankfurt am Main, 1978), pp. 18–23.

51 Kurt Gossweiler, *Kapital, Reichswehr und NSDAP, 1919–1924* (East Berlin, 1982), ch. 1 provides a thoughtful discussion.
52 See the theoretical remarks of Adam, 'Anmerkungen', pp. 70–6; and Winkler, *Revolution*, pp. 108 ff.
53 See the comments of Schieder, in *Total. und Fasch.*, pp. 45–9. MacGregor Knox, 'Conquest, Foreign and Domestic, in Fascist Italy and Nazi Germany', *JMH* 56 (1984), pp. 1–57 provides an interesting comparative essay on the Mussolini and Hitler regimes.
54 Hildebrand, *Das Dritte Reich*, pp. 139–42; Hillgruber, *Endlich genug?*, pp. 17, 38, 42; Bracher, *Zeitg. Kontrov.*, chs. 1–4, and in *Total. und Fasch.*, pp. 14–17; Henry A. Turner, 'Fascism and Modernization', in Turner, *Reappraisals*, pp. 132–3; see also De Felice, p. ix (introductory comments of Charles F. Delzell) and pp. 10–12, 180.
55 For modern traits in Nazism, see e.g. Peukert, pp. 42–7; Tim W. Mason, 'Zur Entstehung des Gesetzes zur Ordnung der nationalen Arbeit vom 20. Januar 1934: Ein Versuch über das Verhältnis "archaischer" und "moderner" Momente in der neuesten deutschen Geschichte', in Hans Mommsen *et al.*, eds., *Industrielles System und politische Entwicklung in der Weimarer Republik* (Düsseldorf, 1974), pp. 322–51; Horst Matzerath and Heinrich Volkmann, 'Modernisierungstheorie und Nationalsozialismus', in Jürgen Kocka, ed., *Theorien in der Praxis des Historikers* (Göttingen, 1977), pp. 95–7; Hans-Dieter Schäfer, *Das gespaltene Bewußtsein. Deutsche Kultur und Lebenswirklichkeit 1933–1945* (Munich/Vienna, 1981), pp. 114–62; Martin Broszat, 'Zur Struktur des NS-Massenbewegung', *VfZ* 31 (1983), pp. 52–76.
56 Nolte, in *Total. und Fasch.*, pp. 77–8, and in *Three Faces*, pp. 529, 569–77.
57 Winkler, *Revolution*, p. 66.
58 Linz (note 30), p. 24.
59 Kocka, 'Ursachen', esp. p. 15.
60 See Kocka, 'Ursachen', p. 15, and in *Total. und Fasch.*, pp. 39, 44. See also Winkler, *Revolution*, p. 66. Recent analyses by the British scholars Roger Griffin and Roger Eatwell, though applying different definitions, have no difficulty in including Nazism as an integral part of their comparative studies of fascism. See Roger Griffin, *The Nature of Fascism* (London, 1991) and Roger Eatwell, 'Towards a New Model of Generic Fascism', *Journal of Theoretical Politics* 4 (1992), pp. 161–94. In particular, Griffin's emphasis on 'palingenetic ultranationalism' – extreme populist nationalism focused upon national 'rebirth' and the eradication of presumed national decadence – as the core of fascist ideology, self-evidently embraces Nazism.
61 The importance of this simultaneous three-fold transition is stressed by Schieder, in *Total. und Fasch.*, pp. 45–9.
62 See Bracher, 'The Role of Hitler', in Laqueur, pp. 209–10, fully developed in Karl Dietrich Bracher, *The German Dictatorship* (Harmondsworth, 1973), esp. ch. 1; Andreas Hillgruber, 'Kontinuität und Diskontinuität in der deutschen Außenpolitik von Bismarck bis Hitler', in his *Großmachtpolitik und Militarismus im 20. Jahrhundert* (Düsseldorf, 1974), pp. 11–36, and *Endlich genug?*, pp. 48 ff.; Klaus Hildebrand, 'Hitlers Ort in der Geschichte des preußisch-deutschen Nationalstaates', *HZ* 217 (1973), pp. 584–632, and his *Foreign Policy* (see ch. 1 note 17), esp. Introdn. and Concl.
63 E.g. Wehler, *Kaiserreich* (see ch. 1 note 16); Jürgen Kocka, *Angestellte zwischen Faschismus und Demokratie* (Göttingen, 1977); Hans-Jürgen Puhle, *Von der Agrarkrise zum Präfaschismus* (Wiesbaden, 1972); Heinrich August Winkler, *Mittelstand, Demokratie und Nationalsozialismus* (Cologne, 1972).

64 See Bracher, *Zeitg. Kontrov.*, pp. 30, 88–9, 99; Hillgruber, *Endlich genug?*, pp. 40–2; and Klaus Hildebrand, 'Nationalsozialismus oder Hitlerismus?', in Michael Bosch, ed., *Persönlichkeit und Struktur in der Geschichte* (Düsseldorf, 1977), pp. 55–61, here esp. pp. 56–7.
65 For a critical assessment of the much-disputed application of the term 'totalitarianism' to the political system of the German Democratic Republic, see Mary Fulbrook, 'The Limits of Totalitarianism: God, State, and Society in the GDR', *Transactions of the Royal Historical Society*, 6th series, 7 (1997).
66 In their *The Racial State, Germany 1933–1945* (Cambridge, 1991), Michael Burleigh and Wolfgang Wippermann emphasize the 'specific and singular character' of Nazism (p. 306). I agree with their interpretation of the Third Reich 'as a singular regime without precedent or parallel'. In order to uphold this claim, nevertheless, systematic comparison of the regime with other modern state systems and not simply a description – however compelling – of Nazi race policies is necessary. To contend that theories based upon totalitarianism or global theories of fascism are 'poor heuristic devices' (p. 307) for understanding Nazism is, in my view, therefore, going too far. The extent to which Burleigh and Wippermann stress the quest for racial purification as the core of Nazism is, in my opinion, valid. But this does not rule out as conclusively as they appear to presume other valid perspectives and questions about Nazism's comparability with other forms of fascism and/or totalitarianism. (For a comment on their criticism of the application of modernization theory to Nazism, see ch. 7 note 62.)

9.2

Fascisms under authoritarian conservatism

57

NATIONAL SYNDICALISM AND INTERNATIONAL FASCISM

António Costa Pinto

Source: António Costa Pinto, *The Blue Shirts: Portuguese Fascists and the New State*, New York: Columbia University Press, Boulder Social Science Monographs, 2000, pp. 225–43.

It is difficult to speak of an 'international family' of fascist movements. Despite attempts to create 'internationals' along the lines of the Italian CAUR, the ideology and political strategy of the fascist movements did not transcend national boundaries. Nonetheless, both the German and Italian dictatorships set up international relations institutions that supported movements in the Balkans and Eastern Europe. The CAUR, for instance, were set up to counter-balance the growing influence of Nazism.[1] Political institutions associated with the Nazi Party developed parallel diplomatic structures, which also happened, albeit on a smaller scale, in the Italian case. This parallel diplomacy occurred mainly in countries that the fascist regimes considered strategically important, or where there were significant numbers of German or Italian emigrants, essentially in Central and Eastern Europe and Latin America.[2] Portugal was not important for either reason.

The diplomatic strategy of the fascist powers did not initially involve support for political parties. It was only during the Second World War that a network of parties was used for propaganda purposes, although this was not the most important form of fascist diplomacy. The rise of the Nazis, however, made fascism an international political phenomenon, as the party became a point of reference for the political activities of other movements.

An "International Family"

NS propaganda was marked by its identification with European fascism. It was at the heart of the movement's identity and distinguished it from Salazarism and other political ideologies and forces. International developments were followed closely and became a point of reference for NS political activity and propaganda. Reference to international events was particularly important given that Portugal was progressing towards the consolidation of a still contested authoritarian order.

When asked about NS identification with Italian Fascism in a United Press interview, Preto prudently replied: "they are evidently similar movements, sons of the same social anguish, of the same collective necessity. In each country, however, the revolutionary wave breaks and extends in a different way and has unique characteristics and rhythms. Fascism, Hitlerism are totalitarianisms that deify the Ceasarist State, others seek to find in the Christian traditions of the Portuguese people the formula that permits the harmonisation of the Portuguese people the formula that permits the harmonisation of the undisputed sovereignty of national interest with our dignity as free men, as living spiritual beings".[3] This interview was often cited when other authoritarian groups, particularly the catholics, accused him of being a mere follower of international phenomena.

Despite this demarcation, fascist conquests in Europe were a central element of NS propaganda. Identification with fascism was a structural component of NS political activity, helping to mobilise sectors of the political and cultural elite, which identified with it and lacked organisational expression. There were two key aspects to NS references to international events. The movement identified with regimes where fascism had won the day. These were upheld as positive examples of "revolution". It also noted the solidarity among fascist movements, particularly those ideologically close to NS, or those that emphasised "social" and "corporatist" concerns. Almost all NS leaders wrote articles and participated in debates about fascism. Attitudes to National Socialism ranged from reserved to unconditional support, but Italian Fascism and movements close to it were identified with completely.

NS saw itself as an integral part of the fascist wave that seemed ready to dominate the political fortunes of Europe after Hitler's rise to power. NS newspapers, and Preto's editorials in particular, followed Hitler's rise and his initial state reforms with enthusiasm. Thus, part of the conservative press, particularly the catholics, criticised Nazism. NS responded to all attacks by excessively defending nazification measures and was only more moderate regarding racist policies, although the persecution of the Jews was excused by many writing for the fascist press.

For Preto, Hitler's ascendancy represented "the new cadence of the National Revolution in progress" embodying the "strong edifice of the New State" throughout Europe. He supported Hitler's "revolutionary" strategy and expressed doubts regarding the German dictator's surrender to electoral principles, a move that could "compromise his position". He preferred to see Hitler "free of political compromises, armed, vigilant and determined" to redeem Germany.[4] Preto was certain that neither the "*Centrum* nor the violence of liberal reaction, nothing, could detain the breaking wave of Germany's national instinct" and he felt that Hitler "owned the era".[5]

Younger NS leaders were even more unconditional in their support for Hitler. They expressed fewer reservations regarding National Socialism than Preto. They saw it as the great ideological movement of their generation. Hence the following statement in the first edition of *O Nacional Sindicalista*: "Hitler, great animator of the multitudes [is the] perfect incarnation of a generation that loves and wants to fight, that ardently seeks to destroy the myths and sophisms of the past and to replace them with the magnificent realities of nationalism".[6]

The instrumental nature of Preto's editorials on Nazi Germany was particularly evident when he commented on the tensions between conservative authoritarians and fascists resolved in favour of the latter. Preto always stressed the similarities between Salazarism and the Dolfuss regime, and criticised the conservative authoritarian mistrust of fascist movements.[7] Nazism's 'social' and 'anti-plutocratic' tendencies were held up as a model to follow. The racist dimension was ignored. The fascist press criticised those who saw the persecution of the Jews as the dominant issue. It stressed "the Nazi's slow and methodical battle to conquer the State, the liquidation of the opposition parties, the absorption of similar currents of opinion, and the extermination of the only two forces that seriously oppose them – Jewish capitalism and marxism".[8] Although closer to Italian Fascism, NS portrayed the Nazi dictatorship as heroic, ignoring initial tensions between Italian Fascism and Nazism. NS criticised the "conservative" non-fascist dictatorship in Lisbon, and promoted itself as the alternative force that would create and consolidate a real "New State".

Solidarity with sister movements was greater when the framework was closer to NS ideologically and culturally. This was the case with the JONS and the Falange in Spain. The activities of Brazilian Fascists like Severino Sombra's Labour League (*Legião do Trabalho*, LT) and Plínio Salgado's Brazilian Integralist Action (*Acção Integralista Brazileira*, AIB) were followed with enthusiasm. Severino Sombra spent two years in exile in Lisbon between 1932 and 1934 and participated in some NS rallies.[9] After the foundation of AIB, which incorporated Sombra's movement, the Portuguese fascists supported Salgado, who was also in exile in Portugal.[10] As noted in an article of January 1933: "our Brazilian comrades also want our principles, adapted more or less to suit their circumstances, to proliferate exuberantly on the other side of the Atlantic".[11] Relations with the Falange were intense and became particularly important when Preto was exiled to Spain. These were the movements and "comrades" to which NS was most closely associated. To a lesser extent, the NS also identified with O'Duffy's Irish "Blue Shirts" and Mosley's "Labour" fascists, who once sent compliments to their Portuguese counterparts.[12]

The activities of fascist movements and the support they received from fascist regimes contrasted with Salazar's "prudence" and his "lack of combativeness and modernism".[13] However, NS condemned the extremist myths and violence of some Eastern European movements such as the Iron Guard.[14] In response to a murder perpetrated by the Romanian fascists, for example, NS noted that although they regarded "with sympathy the Nazi 'Iron Guard' movement", they could not "but deplore the excesses that it commits, which bring no prestige to the movement".[15]

Foreign fascist movements were often referred to in internal correspondence, particularly after tensions with the Lisbon government had intensified. In the summer of 1933, an NS leader wrote to Preto about the possibility of responding with violence to government attacks. He referred to the Irish Blue Shirts "who beat their chests to threaten De Valera, saying that if he wants violence he's going to get violence", concluding that "Hitler suffered great persecution and many propaganda disasters before he won. Nothing will convince us that we will not win".[16]

Contacts with the German and Italian embassies were also used to boost domestic political legitimacy. PNF and NSDAP delegations regularly attended NS rallies.[17] Visits by Fascist dignitaries were also exploited for propaganda purposes. When Italo Balbo arrived in Lisbon in September 1933, a delegation of uniformed NS leaders hired a tugboat to receive him.[18] This ambassadorial search for legitimacy did not prevent NS from demonstrating its extreme nationalism whenever possible. In March 1933, for example, when rumours circulated that Mussolini had porposed to Britain the 'internationalisation' of Portuguese colonies, NS immediately organised a demonstration in front of the British Embassy that was prohibited by the government.[19] Despite ideological differences and a greater identification with Latin fascism, Hitler's rise to power and identification with an international "fascist family" constituted an important element in showing the distinct nature of NS political activity and propaganda.

Iberian national syndicalism

Programmatically, culturally and politically there were many affinities between the Portuguese and Spanish Fascists. There were numerous exiles on both sides of the border, and there were ideological similarities and friendships binding radical right-wing leaders from both countries. This permitted a mutual understanding and very rapid cross-fertilisation. At the beginning of the century, contacts between Portuguese and Spanish cultural élites were closer than they were fifty years later, when *Action Française*, dominated the renovation of the Iberian radical right, particularly within traditional monarchist circles.[20] The 1910 Republican Revolution in Portugal led to the emergence of IL as a doctrine and pressure group, much earlier than the emergence of its Spanish equivalent, Spanish Action (*Acción Española*, AE), but their programmes were very similar. Created in 1931 after the fall of Primo de Rivera, AE was immediately supported by Integralists.

Both inspired by AF, IL and AE were traditionalist, corporatist and monarchist alternatives to Liberal Republicanism, supported by similar elitist and aristocratic social networks. Although they admired Italian Fascism, the founders of both movements were quite reactionary and railed against economic, social and political modernisation. Both Portugal and Spain had experienced dictatorships under Sidónio Pais and Primo de Rivera, respectively.[21] Although relations between the founders of Portuguese and Spanish National Syndicalism had been overshadowed by the Galician question and Portuguese fear of Spanish expansionism, ideological and political beliefs were almost identical.[22] The youths that founded *Revolução* had an identical programme to Ledesma Ramos's Conquest of the State (*Conquista del Estado*).[23] Although Ledesma considered Integralist support for the restoration of the monarchy as being "anachronistic", ideological and programmatic similarities were strong. Morodo notes that Preto's 'Twelve Principles of Production' had a "clear influence on nascent Spanish Fascism".[24] When NS was founded its texts were well received by AE.

Iberian National Syndicalists had the same cultural base. The reactionary element was perhaps more evident in the Portuguese case, as monarchism was more important than in Spain. However, as Javier Tusell notes, imperial nationalism, corporatism, traditional catholicism and the rural-industrial dichotomy shaped both movements in equal measure.[25] Both had social catholic influences and saw the "New State" as an organic structure that would replace liberalism.[26] Both supported "vertical syndicalism" to unite producers, opposed communist labour politics and had a 'revolutionary' discourse in which a despised 'modernism' clashed with an undisguised ruralism.

The rural-industrial cleavage was common to both fascist movements. Despite the attempt by both movements to appeal to the proletariat and the urban middle classes, ruralism remained an important ideological component. In Portugal this was visible in Preto's speeches, and in Spain it was apparent in "the image of the small rural landowner" and the peasantry, a class "free from political disputes" and thus the "carrier of the 'essence of the nation' ".[27] They projected a mythical image of a society of small-scale producers that would inspire the proletariat to integrate with the 'national community' through a corporatist system.

Religion was a more complex issue. Catholic traditionalism was important in both movements. They differed, however, due to the existence of other political parties closer to the catholics. The existence of parties and organisations inspired by social catholicism constituted powerful barriers to fascist political activity in Portugal and Spain.[28] Furthermore, their 'anti-bourgeois' and 'anti-conservative' radicalism reflected a predominantly secular urban social reality. The Fascists were conscious that large segments of society "were already secularised and that efforts at national integration, particularly of the labouring classes, on a religious basis would be impossible".[29]

The two parties were also similar organisationally and sociologically.[30] Both were small movements that never became mass parties. Both were based on the support of students and intellectuals and did not move beyond urban middle-class circles. The adherence of workers to NS was a result of the clandestine situation of left-wing parties, as well as the capacity of NS to mobilise workers unattached to independent unions. In Spain, right-wing organisations that competed with the Falange were more successful in this arena under the Second Republic, although their following was reduced.[31]

The Portuguese movement had more Army officers than the Spanish Falange. The Spanish fascists and other right wing forces appealed for military intervention, but had much less influence on the military than their Portuguese counterparts. Spain's neutrality during the First World War, as well as the Primo de Rivera dictatorship partly explain this difference; both helped to prevent the emergence of significant breaches within the military, making it more difficult for fascists to penetrate junior officer ranks.[32] By contrast, in Portugal the Army had been divided and politicised, such that civilian radical right-wing organisations had a greater influence over the military. It is possible to say that the 1936 coup in Spain was more praetorian than the intervention leading to the 1926 Coup in Portugal. As Ricardo Chueca notes about the military rebellion that led to the Spanish Civil War: "of the many interpretations ventured, one thing is certain: there was a genuine and strict military *pronunciamiento*".[33]

NS was closer to the JONS led by Ledesma Ramos than to Primo de Rivera, at least in its final years. After the split in the movement, the group that remained with Preto emphasised their differences with traditional reactionary positions and moved closer to a "Social Fascism" that distanced it from the Falange.

It was only during his Spanish exile, that Preto met the leader of the Spanish fascists. According to Preto, José Antonio was working on the Falange programme, which appeared to him to make many of the "concessions to capitalism" that had already brought Portugal "within sight of revolt".[34] During the Civil War, the small Falange was brought into a new party under Francoist control. Preto expressed his lack of confidence in their ability to decisively influence the new regime. Shortly before Franco's victory, Preto noted that "if the Falange manage to defeat the resistance of certain reactionary sectors, as I hope, it will have to undertake the great task of the National Syndicalist Revolution".[35] The outbreak of the Spanish Civil War led Preto to declare a political truce with Salazar and to unconditionally support the nationalist front. He met Franco in Salamanca, and was not impressed. In 1937, Preto spoke as NS leader on Radio Seville, leading Salazar and the Portuguese government to successfully appeal to Francoist authorities to prohibit "any propaganda" by the National Syndicalists.[36]

After his return to Portugal, NS contacts with FET-JONS were sporadic. According to internal reports, Preto's delegates maintained regular contact with the Galician Fascists. During the Civil War, one of these delegations visited the offices of the Galician People (*Pueblo Galego*). The director of this newspaper, Jesus Suevos, was a member of the old JONS (by this time a part of FET y de las JONS) and agreed with Preto.[37] These contacts were marginal and of little significance, however, and were stifled by co-operation between Salazarist and the Nationalist authorities when FET-JONS was incorporated into Spain's single party.

National syndicalism and Brazilian integralist action (AIB)

AIB was the most successful of all the Latin American fascist movements and followed a path identical to NS. After a period of growing tension with the Vargas regime, it was forced to disband.[38] Following several failed attempts to bring down the dictator, AIB leaders were sent into exile, some to Italy, and others, their leader Plínio Salgado among them, to Portugal.[39]

The transition from oligarchic liberalism to democracy, and the overthrow of liberalism in 1930s Brazil cannot be analysed here, but the process led the fascists to develop a political discourse and mobilisation strategy was very similar to that of the Portuguese organisation.[40] AIB was the product of the unification of several fascistic groups created at the beginning of the 1930s. The cultural influence of IL had been important for Brazilian monarchist movements like Brazilian Imperial National Renovation Action (*Acção Imperial Patrionovista Brasileira*, AIPB) created in 1928 and Portuguese authoritarian literature had some impact in Brazil from the 1920s onwards. Plínio Salgado was closely influenced by Portuguese Integralism.[41] This is obvious in his constant references to their theorists, particularly Hipólito Raposo and Rolão Preto. Although National Socialism and republicanism influenced Brazilian leaders such as Gustavo Barroso, Salgado was a catholic and identified more with the traditionalist and spiritual corporatism of IL. Indeed, social catholicism had an important influence on AIB élites in contrast with National Syndicalism, whose élite was more secular.

Like other fascist movements, AIB sought to create an original nationalist programme. However, its 'Integral State' was very similar to the 'National Syndicalist State' proposed by Portuguese fascists. Integralist and National Syndicalist theories of corporatism significantly influenced the Brazilian fascists. Salgado in particular synthesised Italian thought with António Sardinha's corporatism. AIB's political programme regarding 'municipal autonomy', for example, was lifted straight out of Integralist theory and adapted to Brazilian reality.[42]

The nature of Portuguese fascism

The fascists were divided and merely junior partners in the large coalition that brought down Portuguese liberalism. They represented a minority among the groups most affected by radical republicanism. The independent organisations founded during the 1920s were not strong, merely a few among the many groups appealing for a military coup. NS was only a small and lately formed part of the fascist current within the vast anti-liberal coalition that sustained the Military Dictatorship. It was deeply influenced by the cultural forces shaping Integralism. NS was programmatically committed to an ideology of reaction against modernisation. It evolved in an authoritarian political context in which its main enemies already lacked a wide margin for manoeuvre. The Portuguese fascists were a by-product of the institutionalisation of the Military Dictatorship. They gained strength because they were able to mobilise and garner the support of junior officers at a time when the republican parties were suspended and the dictatorship hesitated over the creation of new institutions.

The fascist élite originated with the radical right, emerging from a youthful group that challenged the reactionary traditionalism and pro-restoration dogma of IL. The emergence of this fascist élite under an authoritarian political order allowed them to use IL provincial network as well as those of other fascistic parties created at the end of the 1920s.

Socially, NS had two particularly notable characteristics. First, its influence among young army officers and, second, a high number of working class members. The support of a significant number of junior officers gave NS the capacity to mobilise the actors who had played a central role in bringing down the Republic in the 1920s, particularly during the unstable years of the Military Dictatorship. NS upset the chain of command, as lower ranking officers took up government and local administration posts, and the top brass found it very difficult to restore the hierarchy the first years of the dictatorship.

The fascists organised themselves as a political party, which claimed to be the faithful repository of the spirit of the 'revolution of 28 May'. They supported military values and a radical turnover in the conservative political élite to allow for the rise of the young civilians and military officers who had participated in the 1926 coup. The fascists exalted the '*tenentismo*' of the 28 May League for some years, as it expressed resistance to stabilisation and the concomitant re-establishment of the chain of command.

The high number of working class supporters should be assessed in context, as it is not indicative of a particularly significant fascist 'working class' success or of a fascist alternative within the union movement. The fascist movement developed under a dictatorial regime that severely limited the scope of action of free unions. The movement aimed to create an embryo corporatist system while remaining flexible in terms of its ability to mobilise and form support groups in the unions of the service sector in particular, which later became a part of Salazar's corporatist 'national unions'.

The fascist strategy, however, was overtaken by the 'constitutional pacts' between the military élite and Salazar, which joined conservative groups within the UN, and put down fascist groups through violent and administrative repression. The conflict between the fascists and other authoritarian pressure groups that dominated Salazarism were expressive of a conflict that its typical of the majority of transitions to authoritarianism undertaken in the presence of weak fascist movements.[43] Its rapid resolution in favour of Salazarism and the concomitant defeat of the recalcitrant fascists can be summarily explained as follows.

Since 1910, there had been competing political movements and ideologies able to work with the military chiefs of the dictatorship, which did not threaten the position and values of the military. Juan Linz points out that even if its younger members sympathised with the fascists, in a transition to authoritarian rule the military tends to seek out bureaucratic élites and conservative parties rather than fascists.[44] This was certainly the case with the Military Dictatorship established in 1926.

The 'constitutionalisation' and gradual civilianisation of the dictatorship was negotiated according to a government initiative involving part of the civilian élite, mostly law professors, led by the then young Finance Minister, António de Oliveira Salazar. The fascists had a 'negligible influence' over these processes, as they were blocked by the existence of an authoritarian right, which was supported by powerful institutions such as the Church, most military officers, as well as landowning and industrial groups.

The Spanish fascists were numerically and sociologically comparable to their Portuguese counterparts. In Spain, however, the military coup led to a prolonged civil war, which permitted the fascists to leave a strong mark on the Franco regime. By contrast, in Portugal the military coup led to the establishment of a 'preventative' dictatorship under which the fascists only had scope for action when there were crises over the creation of institutions. Further, there were no other domestic and foreign factors that came to the aid of the fascists in Portugal.

In other cases, external factors have been significant. In Vichy France, for example, and some Eastern and Northern European countries, the outbreak of the Second World War influenced many right-wing dictators not to eliminate or swiftly dissolve native fascist movements. In countries where democracy survived, as in Belgium, Norway, and Denmark, the fascist movements were negligible phenomena right up until the eve of the German occupation. By contrast, in Portugal, as in Brazil, international variables did not shape what was a spontaneous decision by governing elites to eliminate contending native fascist movements.

Some inter-war dictatorships used the fascists for propaganda purposes.[45] In Portugal, however, the 'integration' of fascists into the Salazar regime was timid due to the bureaucratic prudence of the New State élite, which placed former fascists in secondary regime institutions. Consequently, the fascists influenced neither the configuration of the political élite, nor the main institutions of Salazarism.

Those who resisted incorporation got involved in the 1935 coup and gradually evolved towards a 'social' and 'left-wing' fascism, which led some, albeit only a small number, to become oppositionists to the Salazar regime after 1945. The majority became New State converts, however, particularly in the wake of the Spanish Civil War. By 1939, the Salazar regime was consolidated, replacing the unstable Military Dictatorship.

The most important genetic characteristic of the New State is that it was born out of a military intervention. For many years, the President of the Republic was the guarantor of the interests of the Armed Forces. The party of the New State was weak, non-mobilising, serving only as a complement to the bureaucratic-administrative machine. The state apparatus was only de-militarised very slowly, as evidenced by Salazar's prudence in removing officers who exercised political functions. Some of these officers were sent to the single party. Others worked in government services, such as the censorship board, which retained a strong military presence, or the political police, which was led by army officers. When Salazar permitted the creation of a militia in 1936, its leaders and top echelons were always army officers.

The New State meant the hegemony of a traditionalist, catholic, and anti-democratic right. Social catholicism and the Church hierarchy constituted important instruments limiting the fascistisation of the Salazar regime. In other words, these elements constituted the axis of a 'functional alternative' to the role that fascism played in other countries in consolidating a new authoritarian order in the 1930s.

Clearly, the New State, like most other dictatorships of the time, imported ideas and institutions from the two existing fascist models. Parts of the corporatist legislation, the propaganda apparatus, the Legion and the youth organisation were based on the fascist example. But they were swiftly abandoned when the Spanish Civil War ended.

A variant of European fascism

Some studies have identified NS as sharing strong ideological traits with a so-called "Latin fascism". Although not particularly apt, this expression reflects the attempt to identify cultural traits common to what were sometimes very different inter-war fascist movements in the Iberian Peninsula, France, Belgium and Latin America. It is useful nonetheless to highlight some NS traits and compare it with other contemporary fascist movements. Those who argue in favour of the concept of 'generic fascism' agree upon the existence of two variants. The National Socialist model, whose influence was greatest within the fascist movements in Northern and Central Europe, and the Italian model that, along with AF, was the one favoured by fascist movements in western and southern Europe. This does not mean that NS, the Spanish Falange, *Le Faisceau*, or even Belgian Rexism were not affected by the rise of Nazism, particularly its organisation, ideology and 'social' aspects. Nonetheless, other more durable cultural influences characterised the majority of fascist movements in countries where a strong authoritarian right conditioned fascist political activity.

The association of fascist movements with groups and ideologies that reacted against modernisation during the first half of the twentieth century was not always easy. Almost all claimed to have a 'revolutionary myth,' distinguished themselves from traditional reactionaries and advocated anti-bourgeois and anti-capitalist 'social' strategies. Nonetheless, their cultural origins and political practices did not transcend traditional left-right political dichotomies[46].

Without actually discussing the validity of theories of modernisation, it is important to acknowledge that movements like NS were very marked by Latin reactionary politics. Radical right-wing movements in Portugal and Spain identified with restorationism, integral corporatism and traditional catholicism. In each of these countries, movements inspired by these principles formed the basis of national fascism and were fascistised to varying degrees. AF in France, and AE, Spanish Renewal (*Renovación Española*, RE), Popular Action (*Acción Popular*), as well as the Carlists in Spain were organisationally more significant than IL and the PCC in Portugal. They all emerged in conjunction with the rise of 'mass politics', which Portugal experienced only on a much smaller scale.[47] From this perspective, the movement that most closely resembled NS was Georges Valois's *Faisceaux*.

More so than in other countries, in Portugal the emergence of fascist movements were created by radical right-wing dissidents, mainly the younger élites who were disillusioned by the inability of older leaders to adapt to the post-war situation. These old élites proved to be prisoners of an elitist reaction and could not adapt to mass politics and accept the mobilisation of urban industrial workers in particular. As noted by Payne "the historical importance of fascism has tended to obscure what were two important new authoritarian anti-leftist forces in inter war Europe: radical fascism proper and what, for lack of a better definition, may be called the 'new right' (or modern, 20th century authoritarian right)".[48] Tensions between fascists and Integralists were not as exacerbated as those between AF and the French fascist movements, but this was only because Integralism never became a political party and had collapsed by the end of the 1920s.

These fascist movements were thus born on the margins of the radical right. They represented a generation's revolt against the right's inability to confront the fundamental problems posed by the new urban and industrial centres of Western Europe and the galvanising threat of communism. Valois's criticism of AF anticipated many of the writings of the young Iberian fascists, from Ledesma Ramos and José António Primo de Rivera to Rolão Preto at the beginning of the 1930s.[49] Nationalism and integral corporatism were integrated into a 'modern' context, secularised and even 'proletarianised'. These movements supported a 'Totalitarian State' that could integrate a national community divided and polarised by democracy and communism. The populist strategy, the primacy of 'workers,' para-military ideology and symbolism and the agitation of the masses all distinguished them from those who had originally inspired them, leading to the birth of new fascist centres. Different levels of economic and social development notwithstanding, in countries like Spain, and Portugal, fascism was from the outset an urban youth movement that emerged as a 'revolutionary' response to a left-wing threat.

Operating in the presence of a strong radical right, movements like the Portuguese and Spanish National Syndicalists radicalised the 'social' and 'popular' dimensions and distinguished themselves from the right less by ideological principles and more by their political practice. By contrast, in Belgium traditionalist integralist Catholic elements co-existed with the ideal of a popular decentralised monarchy. Leon Degrelle's Rexism was an example of a movement with the same origins although balanced by catholicism.[50] Like Preto, Degrelle shared similar cultural influences and was doubly affected by the French radical right and Italian Fascism. It was only after the occupation that the Rexists proceeded with 'nazification' like other movements in 'German Europe'.[51]

The political culture within which fascist movements developed in Spain and Portugal did not lead to the elaboration of original theories of government. Mussolini's dictatorship was the regime model for the Latin cultural universe in the 1930s. It was a mobilising regime seeking mass support and supposedly capable of eliminating class war. It introduced 'syndicalist corporatism' and was able to 'nationalise' the working classes, combining the values of a traditional 'Latin imperialism' with the mystique of modernity. Mussolini's fascism, rather than National Socialism, was National Syndicalism's most important international reference, despite its different origins.

Notes

1 Ledeen, M. A., *Universal Fascism*, (New York: 1972); Borejsza, J. W., *Il fascismo e l'Europa Orientale. Dalla propaganda all' aggressione*, (Rome and Bari: 1981).
2 The bibliography on this theme is enormous. For an introduction see Larsen, S.U., (ed), *Fascism Outside Europe*, (New York: Forthc.).
3 *Revolução*, 10 January 1933, p. 2.
4 Preto, R., 'A hora de Hitler', *Revolução*, 23 March 1932, p. 1 and 4.
5 Preto, R., 'Não!' *Revolução*, 26 April 1932, p. 1.
6 *O Nacional Sindicalista*, Fato, N⁰ 1, 18 December 1932.
7 *União Nacional*, Leiria, 14 January 1934, p. 1.
8 *Alcácer*, 21 May 1933, p. 2.
9 *Revolução*, 19 January 1933.
10 *Revolução*, 5 January 1933, p. 5.
11 *União Nacional*, Leiria, 14 January 1934.
12 Public reports of these contacts were censored at the end of 1933, such that Mosley's letter was not published. See: Processo 466-box 19, AGMI/ANTT. For

more on Mosley see: Thurlow, R., *Fascism in Britain*, (Oxford: 1987). For the Irish Blue Shirts see: Manning, M., *The Blueshirts*, (Dublin: 1971) and Cronin, M., *The Blueshirts and Irish Politics*, (Dublin: 1997).
13. *União Nacional*, Leiria, 28 January 1934.
14. For more on the Romanian Iron Guard see: Weber, E., 'The Man of Archangel', *Journal of Contemporary History*, 1 (April 1966), pp. 101–126; Ioanid, R., *The Sword of the Archangel: Fascist Ideology in Romania*, (Boulder: 1990).
15. *União Nacional*, Leiria, 14 January 1934.
16. Letter from an unidentified NS leader to Rolão Preto, n. d. [1933], ARP.
17. See, for example, reports of Preto's regular presence at Italian Embassy receptions. *Revolução*, 24 July 1933.
18. *União Nacional*, Leiria, 10 September 1933, p. 1.
19. *Revolução*, 26 March 1933.
20. See: Cuevas, P. C. G., *Acción Española*, (Madrid: 1998), pp. 88–96.
21. See: Preston, P. *Las derechas españolas en el siglo XX: autoritarismo, fascismo y golpismo*, (Madrid: 1986); Meneses, F. R., "Sidónio Pais: The Portuguese 'New Republic' and the Challenge to Liberalism in Southern Europe", *European History Quarterly*, Vol. 28 (1), 1998, 109–130.
22. An example of this mistrust can be found in the article "Los 'Nazis' de Portugal" which was written by Ramiro Ledesma Ramos, and published in May 1933 in the first edition of the magazine *J.O.N.S.* See: Ledesma Ramos, R., *Escritos politicos, 1933–1934*, (Madrid: 1985), pp. 71–72. There are several examples of promptly denounced verbal excesses of both sides. At the beginning of 1931, Ledestna referred to Portugal's 'embezzled independence'. When Ralão Preto published his study of Portuguese National Syndicalism in *Acción Española*, Onésimo Redondo attacked the magazine in his regional paper for airing the views of a movement that defended the integration of Galicia into Portugal, citing Preto's phrase 'the Portuguese of the other side of the Minho River'. Redondo's complaint was probably the product of his personal observations of Portuguese National Syndicalism during his brief exile in Lisbon in 1933. In fact, the Portuguese National Syndicalists referred to the Galician question only occasionally and never made any official territorial claims. Preto himself immediately denied any 'expansionism'. See: *Acción Española*, Nº 45, 16 January 1934, pp. 881–882. On the Galician question, see: Nuñez Seixàs, X. M., 'Portugal e o galeguismo até 1936: algumas considerações históricas', *Penélope*, Nº 11, 1993, pp. 67–81.
23. The adoption of the name National Syndicalism by the Portuguese fascists was based on Ledesma Ramos's JONS. See: Ledesma Ramos, R., *Fascismo en España? La Patria libre, Nuestra Revolución*, (Madrid: 1988), p. 69.
24. Morodo, R., *op. cit.*, p. 189.
25. Tusell, J., *La dictadura de Franco*, (Madrid: 1988), pp. 287–289; Payne, S., *op. cit.*, pp. 135–240.
26. As Primo de Rivera wrote to the Portuguese journalist Oscar Paxeco. See: Jiménez Campo, J., *El fascismo en la crisis de la II República*, (Madrid: 1979), pp. 53–154.
27. Jiménez Campo, J., *op. cit.*, pp. 149–150.
28. Montero, J. R., *La CEDA: el catolicismo social y politico en la II Republica*, 2 vols., (Madrid: 1977).
29. Linz, J. J., 'Some notes toward . . .' *op. cit.*, p. 19.
30. The only attempt to compare the social bases of the two Iberian fascist movements is M. Blinkhorn, 'The Iberian states', in Mühlberger, (ed) *op. cit.*, (London: 1987), pp. 320–348.
31. Montero, J. R., *op. cit.*, pp. 747–779.
32. Linz, J.J., *Fascism, Breakdown of Democracy, Authoritarian and Totalitarian Regimes: Coincidences and Distinctions*, mimeo, 1986.

33 Chueca, R., *op. cit.*, (Madrid: 1983), p. 140.
34 Medina, J., *op. cit.*, p. 171.
35 Barboso, J. P. M., *op. cit.*, p. 184.
36 AOS/CO/PC-3F, ANTT.
37 Letter from José Francisco da Silva to Rolão Preto, n.d., [1937?], Archive PIDE/DGS, ANTT.
38 See: Deutsch, S. M., *Las Derechas. The Extreme Right in Argentina, Brazil, and Chile, 1890–1939*, (Stanford: 1999); Trindade, H., 'Integralismo: Teoria e práxis política nos anos 30' in: *História geral da civilização brasileira.* Vol. III *Brazil republicano*, (São Paulo: 1981), pp. 297–335.
39 Salgado, P., *Minha segunda prisão e meu exílio*, (São Paulo: 1980).
40 On the evolution of the Brazilian political system during the first half of the 20th century see: Trindade, H., 'Bases da demoracia brasileira: lógical liberal e práxis autoritária (1822–1945)' in: Rouquie, A., Lamounier, B., and Schvarzer, J. (eds), *Como renascem as democracias*, (São Paulo: 1985), pp. 46–72. For an introduction to the formation of the Vargas regime, see: Levine, R., *The Vargas Regime: The Critical Years, 1934–1938*, (New York: 1970).
41 Trindade, H., *op. cit.*, p. 251.
42 *Ibid.*
43 Griffin, R., *op. cit.*, pp. 116–145.
44 Linz, J.J., *op. cit.*, p. 71.
45 Linz, J. J., *op. cit.*, p. 71.
46 Paxton, R. O., "The Five Stages of Fascism", *The Journal of Modern History*, 70 (March 1998), pp. 1–23.
47 On Carlism see: Blinkhorn, M., *Carlism and Crisis in Spain, 1931–1939*, (Cambridge: 1975).
48 Payne, S. G., 'Introduction,' in: Larsen, S.U. et al. (eds), *op. cit.*, p. 421. See also, Levy, C., "Fascism, National Socialism and Conservatives in Europe, 1914–1945", *Contemporary European History*, 8, 1999, pp. 97–126.
49 In addition to the works already cited, see: Stemhell, Z., *Ni droite ni gauche: l'ideologie fasciste en France*, (Paris: 1983).
50 Schepens, L., 'Fascists and Nationalists in Belgium, 1919–1940' in: Larsen, S.U. et. al (eds), *op. cit.*, pp. 512–513.
51 On Dagrelle's political and intellectual development, see Chertok, R.H., *Belgian Fascism*, unpublished dissertation, Washington University, 1972. On the evolution of Rexism during the war, see: Conway, M., *Collaboration in Belgium: Léon Degrelle and the Rexist Movement*, (New Haven and London: 1993).

58

Conclusion to
FASCISM IN SPAIN 1923–1977

Stanley G. Payne

Source: Stanley G. Payne, *Fascism in Spain 1923–1977*, Madison: University of Wisconsin Press, 1999, pp. 469–79.

The fascist party in Spain was the longest-lived political organization of its type, surviving in one form or another for forty-six years, from the formation of the JONS in 1931 to the dissolution of the Movement in 1977. By comparison, the Italian party survived for only twenty-six years, and the German party a total of twenty-seven. This longevity stands in inverse proportion to the original strength of the movement, however, for under conditions of normal electoral politics the Italian and German parties became mass movements, and in the German case, particularly, generated a huge following, whereas the Falange was insignificant. In Austria, Hungary, and Romania, fascist parties also gained a large share of the popular vote during the 1930s, whereas the original Falange registered only 0.7 percent of the ballots in Spain in February 1936. Even in neighboring Portugal the National Syndicalist movement enjoyed higher support: given the size of the respective national populations, the Portuguese party at one point in the early 1930s was proportionately nearly eight times as large as its Spanish counterpart.[1] Conditions of mere political crisis, however, were inadequate to win a significant following for the Falange in Spain, where only the incipient collapse of the political system—a collapse that the Falange itself at least in small measure helped to bring about—followed immediately by an intensively mobilized revolutionary civil war, sufficed to expand the Falange into a mass movement.

Some of the reasons for the weakness of fascism in Spain—a weakness that at first persisted even under conditions of crisis—are fairly obvious, being similar to those which underlay the general weakness of nationalism in the country, and were analyzed by Marxist writers such as Luis Araquistain and Joaquín Maurín in 1934 and 1935. In his article in *Foreign Affairs* in

April 1934, Araquistain referred to a series of factors missing in Spain: a demobilized mass army, large-scale urban unemployment, a Jewish question, or a recent history of nationalist resentment or imperial ambitions. This analysis was accurate enough as far as it went, though Araquistain himself was disingenuous, for it would be he and his colleagues in the violent, revolutionary sector of socialism who would soon be providing much of the rationale for a Spanish fascism.

His Marxist-Leninist rival Joaquín Maurín would be even more explicit in the following year. Despite having committed the egregious errors inevitable in any form of orthodox Marxist-Leninist analysis, Maurín has continued to hold a deserved reputation as the outstanding Marxist theorist in Spain during the Republican years. In his book *Hacia la segund revolución* published in Barcelona in 1935,[2] he expressed doubt that any genuine fascism was possible in Spain. Maurín pointed out that the recent experience of the Primo de Rivera dictatorship had inoculated much of the country against any new form of rightist authoritarianism, that in Spain a large part of the lower middle class was politically democratic that Spanish workers (unlike their counterparts in Italy and Germany were generally impervious to such appeals, and that the small industrial bourgeoisie seemed to be oriented toward the conventional rightist forces rather than toward a radical fascism. The tiny fascistic elements were themselves somewhat divided, whereas the only mass party of the right the CEDA, was Catholic and not really fascist (despite all the leftist propaganda about the CEDA's representing "fascism on the march"), and its leader, Gil Robles, was in fact frightened by fascism. Thus in Spain, as in eastern Europe, the counterrevolution would be rightist and military, not fascist, in character.

With the benefit of comparative historical hindsight, it is possible to extend these contemporary analyses. Elsewhere I have suggested that any "retrodictive theory" seeking to account for the relative strength or weakness of fascism in any given country or milieu must consider a series of fundamental cultural, political, social, economic, and international variables.[3] In the case of Spain, for example, none of the cultural factors that would inform a retrodictive theory of fascism was particularly strong or influential. The cultural elites had not experienced a comparatively strong, influence from the cultural crisis of the end of the century, which was rather weaker in Spain than in central Europe, France, and Italy; nor were there preexisting, comparatively strong currents of nationalism. The artistic world in Spain provided very little assistance to fascism; whereas in Italy avant-garde culture had nourished nationalism and proto-fascism, in Spain Giménez Caballero was left virtually isolated by the close of the 1920s.

A certain perceived crisis of values existed, but before it would become predominant in Spain there quickly developed a tendency toward polarization between the new values of leftist materialism and the old values of Catholic neotraditionalism, leaving less space in Spain than in some other countries for an alternative radical modernism. Secularization was a strong force by the 1930s, but the sectors who experienced this were largely monopolized by the left, once more leaving little space for a radical, non- or anticlerical fascism of the sort originally preached by Ramiro Ledesma. The dominant historical role of religion had always presented an obstacle to any form of modern secular nationalism in Spain, and when fascism belatedly achieved significance, it would inevitably be mutated and syncretized into a more hybrid "fascismo frailuno" a la española.

Strictly political factors at first seemed more favorable, at least in the abstract, even though the Spanish state was not one of the inexperienced "new states" of central and eastern Europe. In Spain, however, as in most of the latter countries, political democracy was a novel experience, totally unconsolidated, and under the Republic there existed a system of parties that was at one and the same time badly fragmented and, increasingly, gravely polarized. Though the prospects for fascism were weakened by the absence of any previous strongly developed form of nationalism, the threat from the revolutionary left was more real than in most other countries. Conversely, fascist leadership in Spain failed to find new ways to generate support and was unable to find political allies. Ultimately, the party was simply suppressed by a government that no longer maintained civil rights. One of the paradoxes of the historic fascist movements was that their broad cross-class nationalism could only be developed in European countries that had undergone considerable political development, and by the same token they required the relative maintenance of civil liberties in order to become strong enough to gain the strength to triumph. They could not come to power independently in countries that failed to guarantee them civil liberties, either because of a sectarian government of the left (as in Spain on the eve of the Civil War) or because of a rightist or military authoritarianism (as in Austria, Hungary, and Romania, or in Spain after the Civil War began).

One of the main social factors specified by any retrodictive theory of fascism—the existence of grave social tensions—certainly existed in Spain by 1934. Yet other key social factors were lacking. There was, for example, little opportunity for mobilization of workers, who had become strongly organized by leftist groups, and there was scarcely any greater opening among the middle classes as a whole, already mobilized by the liberal and Catholic parties. Neither of these large social sectors substantially altered their political orientation until after the Republic had begun to break down, but the breakdown would produce the imminent onset of civil war, rather than the rise of a dominant fascist movement. Contrary to the situations in Italy, Germany, Hungary, or Romania, prior to the Civil War no new social or political space was available for the mobilization of a broader fascist force. The left remained strong, while the middle classes felt little need to move beyond the established left-liberal, liberal, and Catholic parties. Thus the Spanish party system—however fragmented and ultimately destructive—was nonetheless more sophisticated and developed than in many other European countries and yielded no new space; in Spain the political system broke down, but up to that point the party system proved relatively impervious.

Even the peculiarly intermediate structure of the Spanish economy had an effect, for a system not heavily linked to exports softened the impact of the Depression of 1930, limiting urban unemployment and reducing the pressure on both the middle classes and urban workers. Another factor that reduced the potential of fascist demagogy in Spain was the fact that even though the Depression caused stress and suffering, there was little sense that its causes were purely "exogenous" or that it was a national rather than a class problem. No "proletarian national" theory thus proved attractive in Spain. It was fairly clear that Spain's problems had not been brought on by foreign defeat or even especially by foreign discrimination, and a nationalistic discourse for economic solutions had less appeal than in central or east-central Europe.

Even Spain's modern "pretorian tradition" played a role. Though the Republic had hoped to overcome it altogether, its effect was to create expectations in many quarters that an authoritarian nationalism, to be effective, would almost inevitably have to be led by the military (as indeed proved to be the case in July 1936). Conversely, in countries such as Italy and Germany, the combined level of development was such that the military had generally been superseded as a major variable, and certainly as an independent variable. The situation in Spain was therefore more analogous to that in eastern Europe and in Portugal, where the military remained a significant political power factor, ultimately helping to limit the possibilities of any independent fascist mobilization.

Nothing was more important, as Araquistain pointed out, than neutrality in World War I, which had obviated any wartime mobilization of nationalism as well as such postwar problems as unemployed veterans prolonged economic costs, or national frustration and irredentism. Given the absence of international and military competition, there could be little in the way of a perceived foreign threat or menace, and no sense that Spain had been overtly humiliated or exploited during the past generation. Resentments about foreign relations certainly existed but never became a predominant factor in political competition. Given the combination of all these factors, no lever existed with which to "nationalize" part of the left. The predominant sense of nationalism that did begin to emerge on the right was not a revolutionary fascist nationalism (in which, by definition, the right would not be interested) but a rightist reaction against the internal threat of the left to the established Spanish structure of nation and society, and against the perceived threat of what was generally called "communism." This strengthened the right and made polarization more acute, but provided no independent opening to fascism until the right finally fell into disarray in the spring of 1936 and civil war loomed on the horizon. But that situation in turn increasingly placed all initiative and power in the hands of the military.

Fascism came to Spain as an import. It was initially embraced by members of the radical intelligentsia, as in other countries, but lacked the cultural and social support to develop. Giménez Caballero made the first major effort to affirm a Spanish fascism, and responded not simply to the original revolutionary national syndicalism of Italian Fascism but to the tentative Italian synthesis of 1928–1932, with its rightist and semi-Catholic compromises, which he tried to Hispanize as the "new Catholicity." "Gece" did not focus on pristine revolutionary fascism, in which he had comparatively little interest. What he did intuit was the greater appropriateness of a hybrid fascism merged with rightism and religion, and to that extent he became the initial prophet not of the more revolutionary Falange but of the hybrid "fascismo frailuno" of the Franco regime.

A full or genuine fascism was thus first articulated by Ramiro Ledesma Ramos, who may be considered a paradigm of the radical intellectual. For Ledesma, fascism was *only* revolutionary, and he sought to draw out the fullest logical consequence of fascist ideas, all the easier for him in that he never had to lead a significant political force of any size. Ledesma recognized that the ideal type of generic fascism existed, abstracted from the common features of the new European revolutionary anticommunist movements, but he also quickly grasped the danger of mimicry, and the need to avoid simply imitating the Italians.

By contrast, the point of departure of José Antonio Primo de Rivera was different, as he sought to vindicate the work of his father and develop the formula for an effective modern nationalist and authoritarian regime. In his case, fascism was less the motivation than the solution, and thus his initial mimetism of 1933 and 1934 became logical and obvious, though ultimately embarrassing. By 1935 he was trying to create a sort of "differentiated fascism" that was less dependent on the Italian model, but while a free man José Antonio never renounced the fundamental fascist principles of extremist nationalism, an authoritarian state, radical national syndicalism, and the three fascist negations—opposition to the collectivist left, the liberal center, and the conservative or reactionary right; no did he reject fascistic militarism and the preferred orientation toward violence, even though in practice he had sometimes resisted the latter.[4]

The differentiation of or from fascism in the later thinking of José Antonio Primo de Rivera involved the increasing avoidance of the term on concept of totalitarianism and the corporate state as a slogan or formula though the state remained a "totalitarian instrument" in the Falangist program. Cynics might point out that Adolf Hitler avoided the term "totalitarian" more scrupulously than did José Antonio. Moreover, the attempt to create a sort of fascist humanism with an abstract stress on "man the bearer of eternal values" and the recognition of human personality might have been more promising had this vein of rhetoric enjoyed the slightest development in political theory. But like nearly all of José Antonio's concepts, these remained vague, abstract, and merely formulaic, and were never developed concretely in conjunction with a precise political program or theory. The few scattered critical or negative references to fascism found in his writings expressed little concern over the tyrannical aspects of fascism, but much more over the danger of its being "false" of "inauthentic" as a revolution or transformation.

The main differentiation—incomplete and disconnected—lay in the areas of religion and traditional culture. There was a natural need for fascists everywhere to come to terms with national culture and tradition but the incorporation of traditional religion and culture was in some sense important for José Antonio, for Redondo, and for many other Falangists even though largely rejected by the uncompromising revolutionary Ledesma.[5] Yet if José Antonio had been primarily a traditionalist, he would have been a Carlist, whereas in fact he rejected Carlism as inadequate for the twentieth century. Neither was he any sort of neo-Thomist. José Antonio's vaguely invoked concepts never developed into a clear doctrine in which religion and traditional moral and cultural values specifically differentiated Falangism from generic fascism; although he may have wished to do so, this effort remained inchoate and formless, a potential idea, not a developed doctrine. He rejected Giménez Caballero's notion of "the new Catholicity" because its formulation was too rightist, too reminiscent of the compromises and limitations of the Mussolini regime. This orientation nonetheless became very strongly developed under the Franco regime. What José Antonio would have rejected about *franquismo* was not its religiosity so much as its lack of revolutionary content, but he would also probably have been uncomfortable with the extreme clerical quality of its cultural and educational policies as well. There is no doubt that religion and cultural traditionalism were important to him, but he failed to integrate them clearly into political doctrine, or to use the former to control or differentiate the latter in any specific manner.

Since fascist movements so strongly emphasized the roles of elites and of leadership—characteristics fully reflected in the Falange—one must ask whether the leadership of fascism in Spain was inherently deficient. By 1935 José Antonio had established almost uncontested personal dominance within the Falange, but he was never able to exert that leadership effectively in Spanish politics. Given, however, the limited number of "fascistogenic" factors affecting Spanish affairs prior to the outbreak of the Civil War, it is doubtful that a more skilled leadership would have accomplished very much more. The most serious breakdown in José Antonio's political leadership occurred in the negotiations for the elections of 1936, when he proved unable to persuade the other leaders of the party to accept the very limited terms of alliance offered by the CEDA. The resultant Falangist electoral strategy of total independence appealed to revolutionary fascist intransigence and a certain kind of political romanticism dear to the hearts of José Antonio and his associates, but it proved disastrous. It deprived José Antonio of the parliamentary immunity that might have made possible a more effective and continuous leadership of the movement, and that might have guaranteed his own physical survival (though it is likely that, had he not been in prison, José Antonio would have been the primary target of the insubordinate Assault Guards on the night of 12 July).

The poor quality of Falangist leadership during the first year of the Civil War is something about which nearly all commentators agree, and yet again it is not clear that more able directors would have accomplished a great deal more, given the basic realities of total civil war and the complete military and political dictatorship of Franco. The character of Spanish public affairs did not permit a fascist movement the space for mobilization and independent action that would have been required to develop earlier or to triumph politically later. With regard to the possibilities for fascist politics, Spain was more similar to Romania than to Italy or Germany, but even this comparison is inadequate, for by 1937–1938 the Legion of the Archangel Michael had developed a mass following and become the second-largest popular force in the country, something of which the Falange had been totally incapable during peacetime. Its expansion was due exclusively to complete national political breakdown, not to the inherent mobilizing potential of Falangism in other circumstances. Though Falangism was dependent on total crisis, only the military could act decisively to resolve the crisis, and thus the Falange could be subordinated much more easily and effectively under the Franco regime than the Legionnaire movement under Antonescu in Romania, where direct viollent conflict was required. At first a weak fascism in a land of weak nationalism, Falangism always remained a dependent, rather than an independent, variable—dependent first on external financing, second on total external crisis to accelerate mobilization, third on the Franco regime, and fourth and finally on the course of World War II.

At first glance this would seem to substantiate Azaña's observations in his diary on 6 October 1937:

> When they talked of fascism in Spain, my opinion was this: in Spain there are or can be all the fascisms you want. But a fascist regime there will not be. If a movement of force should triumph against the Republic, we would fall into a military and ecclesiastical dictatorship of a traditional type. However many slogans might be translated and however many mottoes might be used. Sabers, chasubles, military parades, and homages to the Virgen del Pilar. In that direction, this country does not offer anything else. Now they are seeing it. Late. And with a difficult adjustment.[6]

But Azaña's political analyses, though superficially plausible, were usually mistaken in one or more major respects. In this case, he seems to be defining the Franco regime as "a military and ecclesiastical dictatorship of a traditional type." To exactly what "traditional type" would this refer. The only possible candidate would be the Primo de Rivera regime. Franco certainly drew inspiration from the first Spanish dictatorship, but to conceive of Franco as a second Primo de Rivera is profoundly mistaken. Franco was much more radical, much more sanguinary, and much more authoritarian, determined to create a lasting regime of the twentieth century. He incarnated a new Spanish radical right that was more innovative and vigorous than Azaña gave it credit for. The Franco regime would not seek to embrace tradition fully until after a gigantic world war had been fought and lost by its preferred allies.

This does not mean that Franco was ever a generic fascist *sensu strictu* More than twenty years after his death, Franco has still eluded precise definition save in the vague and general categories of "dictator" and "authoritarian." Thus scarcely any of the serious historians and analysis of Franco consider the Generalissimo to have been a core fascist. Paul Preston, never known to give Franco the benefit of the doubt, once observed at a scholarly conference in Madrid, "Franco no era un fascista sino algo mucho peor" (Franco was not a fascist but something much worse). Compared, for example, with paradigmatic Italian Fascism, the Franco of the first ten years of the regime, having come to power by means of a ruthless civil war, was much more violent, autocratic, and repressive in every respect—politically, culturally, socially, and economically.

Franco's political style, though always retaining fundamental principles of authoritarianism, nationalism, traditionalism, and Catholicism, was always eclectic. He demonstrated no interest in Falangism before the Civil War, but devoted his political attention to the CEDA and was raised to the highest military posts by Radicals and the CEDA. Soon after the beginning of the Civil War, he picked up the language of "totalitarianism" and an ad hoc model of charismatic leadership to develop an authoritarian new system with its own partido único. The nearest thing to a paradigm was Mussolini's Italy; but while retaining the Twenty-Six Points as the doctrine of the FET in 1937, he explicitly recognized the goal of a more broadly syncretistic amalgam of Falangism and other doctrines of the right, flanked by and to a completely ambiguous degree mediated by a strongly traditional and authoritarian form of Catholicism. In comparative political analysis, all this was no more than "semifascist."[7]

Somewhat paradoxically, the weakness and subordination of Falangism, with the peculiar syncretism and compromises decreed by Franco—those very factors most vituperated by radical camisas viejas—were the qualities required for its longevity. A truly revolutionary and independent fascism might have undermined Franco's war effort, producing the triumph of the Republic and the end of fascism in Spain,[8] or else it could have resulted in a subsequent rebellion that might have required the total suppression of the movement by Franco, much as Antonescu had to eliminate the Legion in Romania completely after its armed revolt of January 1941.

The one FET institution that became better developed than its Italian counterpart was the Sección Femenina. Though the girls' organization was never as extensive as its counterpart in Italy, the adult Sección Femenina was more extensive and more active. Thus it merits the attention it has received from historians in recent years, generating more new bibliography than any other Falangist institution. Yet the relative success of the Sección Femenina was not due to its fascism, for ideologically and politically it was distinctly less fascist than either the Italian Fasci Femminili or the much larger National Socialist Frauenschaft. More than the male party, the Sección Femenina exhibited a culture of Catholic traditionalism even though expressed in original forms of mobilization.

Franco was never a "core fascist" or a genuine Falangist, and never personally espoused or gave any priority to all the goals of the Falangists and their Twenty-Six Points, but his political orientation was definitely pro-fascist. During the second half of the Civil War, perhaps partly under the influence of Serrano Súñer, his thinking and language moved farther in the direction of fascism,[9] a trend only encouraged by the outcome of the first phases of World War II and also by the tensions and frustrations encountered in negotiations with the Papacy between 1939 and 1941. A process had thus been begun whose result would be determined not merely by the outcome of the Spanish conflict but also by the results of the world war in Europe.

Moreover, the core Falangists largely dominated the FET, and the chief opportunity for the triumph of Falangism came not during the Civil War but during the three years that followed—the high water mark of fascist domination in Europe. Nearly all the activist Falangists during World War II were fully identified with the Axis powers, even though many of them sought in certain respects to differentiate Falangism from National Socialism. Though the regime did not go beyond nonbelligerence, its basic position was, in Tusell's words, "much more for the Axis than was Finland,"[10] a country that had openly entered the war on the German side against the Soviet Union. Even during this period, however, Franco's personal authority and power were so great that any complete Falangist take over per se remained only the most remote of possibilities, for the anti-Falangist military always remained loyal to Franco. Thus only the basically exogenous factor of a complete triumph by the Axis in World War II could have brought about a more genuine and thorough process of fascistization in Spain.

The creation of the FET in 1937 had first established the inherently contradictory goal of syncretism between a form of fascism and Catholic traditionalism, though the complete transition to a watered-down fascismo frailuno was only carried forward in the later phases of the world war. For the remainder of the long history of the FET, the latent contradiction within the doctrines of founders such as José Antonio and Onésimo Redondo was resolved—to the extent that it could be resolved—more and more in favor of an authoritarian form of Catholic corporatism and cultural neotraditionalism.

The National Movement that survived for more than three decades after the end of the world war is most accurately described as an increasingly postfascist partido único. It kept one foot anchored in historic fascism, did not receive a fully postfascist program until 1958, and scarcely completed its full defascistization until the very last years of Franco's life, if then. Yet it had been forced by the unalterable consequences of world history to abandon any effort to realize a genuinely fascist program after 1943, and served merely the political and bureaucratic convenience obanaging dictator, determined to avoid "el error Primo de Rivera" (perhaps the main root similarity between José Antonio and Franco), and ever hoping to leave a structured system behind him. Falangism lived on as no more than an ambiguous residue, a consequence of the idiosyncrasies of national history, as contrasted with world history, and of the longevity of a dictator from an increasingly distant era. Even more than the regime itself, the Movement had lost its cultural and social basis long before the physical death of Franco. All this has tended historically and historiographically to obscure the fact that native fascism was extremely weak in Spain, whose political culture and historical development prior to the Civil War had generated fewer fascistogenic qualities than most other European countries.

Notes

1 See the statistics in A. Costa Pinto, *Os Camisas Azuis: Ideologias, elites e movimentos fascistas em Portugal 1914–1945* (Lisbon, 1994).
2 This work was reprinted much later as *Revolución y contrarevolución en España* (Paris, 1966).
3 In my *A History of Fascism* (Madison, 1995), 487–95.
4 The most recent attempt to deal with José Antonio's "fascisticity" is M. Argaya Roca, *Entre lo espontáneo y lo difícil* (Oviedo, 1996), especially 107–29. On this problem, see also J. L. Jerez-Riesco, *La Falange, partido fascista* (Barcelona, 1997); and the final chapter of J. del Aguila Tejerina, *Ideología y fascismo* (Madrid, 1982), even though the ideal types used in these works leave something to be desired.
5 Ledesma was quite firm on religion. While admitting on occasion that it could not be altogether avoided in a Spanish nationalist movement, he insisted that "the enterprise of building a national doctrine, a plan of historical resurgence, a strategy of combat, effective political institutions, etc. . . . is something that can be done without appealing to the Catholic emblem of the Spanish." *Discurso a las juventudes de España* (Barcelona, 1935 ed.), 94.
6 *Obras completas* (Mexico City, 1968), IV, 813.
7 On the comparative analysis of the Franco regime, together with its similarities to and differences from Fascist Italy, see J. Tusell, *La dictadura de Franco* (Madrid, 1988); E. Ucelay da Cal, "Problemas en la comparación de las dictaduras española

e italiana en los años treinta y cuarenta," in *El Estado moderno en Italia y España*, ed. E. D'Auria and J. Casassas (Barcelona, 1993), 155–74; and the final chapter of my *The Franco Regime 1936–1975* (Madison, 1987).
8 This was, of course, the opportunity, however tenuous, that the Republican authorities had foregone with the execution of José Antonio.
9 This is brought out most clearly in J. Tusell, *Franco en la Guerra Civil: Una biografía política* (Barcelona, 1992).
10 Tusell, *Franco, España y la II Guerra Mundial* (Madrid 1995), 648.

59

Extract from
'HUNGARY'

Igor Déak

Source: Igor Déak, *The European Right*, Berkeley and Los Angeles: University of California Press, 1965, pp. 383–405.

The Gömbös conspiracy of 1923 was by no means the only extreme rightist undertaking of the Bethlen period. It has been mentioned here only because it was characteristic of the "gentleman era" of the radical Right, with its secret, conspiratorial activities and its lack of popular appeal—for the *putschist* of the 1920's was just as reluctant to appeal to the masses and thus stir up dangerous waters as was Bethlen himself. The first popular agitator, Zoltán Böszörmény, emerged during the great depression. His political party, although awkward and helpless, was also National Socialism's most original, most characteristically Hungarian version.

Böszörmény, born in 1893, was the son of a bankrupt landowner. His youth was a succession of odd jobs that turned him, successively, into an apprentice, a messenger, a worker, and a porter. In 1919 he joined the counterrevolution; later he dabbled in journalism and managed to enter the University of Budapest, where he was elected leader of the patriotic student fraternities. Böszörmény was also a poet, and to peddle his patriotic verses he employed a couple of agents who later became his party's organizers.

In 1931, if his confessions are to be believed, Böszörmény visited Germany, where he met Hitler and was instantly converted by him. On his return, he published a manifesto and announced the birth of the Hungarian National Socialist Workers' party, the first of a great many undertakings bearing the same or similar names. As his party's emblem, Böszörmény chose the crossed scythes. He never doubted his destiny. In 1932, he wrote:

> Even among the giants of intellect I am a giant, a great Hungarian poet with a prophetic mission. . . . My heart shudders at the cry of pain of Hungarian mothers. . . . I have listened to the call of the

> sweetest mother of all, Mother Hungary, and—answering it—I started off on the road, abandoning all worldly goods and happiness.... I knew well that my fight, begun without arms, would be ruthless: a fight to the teeth-gnawing bitter end.

To this, he later added: "This is the fullness of time, and the lonely poet, the Man, who always stood alone, departs to oppose the destructive forces of Money.... One Man against the whole world."

For the time being, the "tribune," who—in his own words—was ready "to caress but also to have hundreds of thousands executed without batting an eyelash," became the favorite target of the Budapest satirical newspapers. Yet, among the peasants of Eastern Hungary, his message spread fast. In these arid regions beyond the Tisza River, where villages were strangled by large estates, the "agrarian proletariat escaped into sectarianism to get away from misery," wrote Imre Kovács, one of the famed "village explorers" who in 1937, in his book *A néma forradalom* ("The Mute Revolution"), recorded the plight of the Hungarian peasants. Kovács describes how the hopeless life of these peasants forced them to seek salvation in religious ecstasies and in pursuit of fanatical "ideas." When the Scythe Cross movement became their savior, he writes, they inscribed on their banners: "We have had enough!" Kovács met some members of the Scythe Cross in 1934: "It was on a large estate beyond the Tisza; they were seasonal workers and very poor. They all wore the Scythe Cross armband and a badge: two crossed scythes on green background, in a red circle, with a skull in the center. 'We fight for the Idea'—they repeated when I questioned them, but were unable to tell what the 'Idea' was about. They hated the Communists and the Gentlemen."

In Gömbös' Hungary, the Scythe Cross did not have a chance. By the end of 1932, Böszörmény boasted of twenty thousand party members and, supported by some boisterous storm troopers, he made several attempts to run as candidate at parliamentary by-elections, but the customary vigilance of the local authorities prevented him from collecting the necessary number of "recommendations" for candidacy. Only once did he manage to stand for election and then he won only a few hundred votes. The party's weekly was occasionally suppressed and the Leader himself condemned to short prison terms which, however, he never served.

Böszörmény's ideology is not easy to define. He was against Jews, Bolsheviks, and liberals, and for his own dictatorship, land reform, and "justice for the poor." In the "Ten Commandments of the Storm Troopers," published in 1935, he exhorted his followers to violence, in language enriched by Hitlerite slogans and magic Turanian terms. He described his comrades as "Gardeners of the Hungarian race, fateful Death Reapers of the Jewish swine and their hirelings ... opponents of all Habsburg aspirations," but history records no serious evidence of Scythe Cross violence, and its one attempt to act failed miserably.

A regular peasant rebellion was planned for May 1, 1936, when three million peasants were to march on "sinful" Budapest and raze it to the ground. In one peasant town of the great Hungarian plains a few thousand peasants actually met on the appointed day, but they were easily dispersed by the ubiquitous gendarmes. Several trials ensued. Böszörmény and his principal codefendants were given relatively light sentences, varying from a few months to two and a half years in prison; none of them was placed in custody, and Böszörmény was allowed to escape to Germany in the spring of 1938. He was the first of many Hungarian National Socialists to seek asylum from the Horthy authorities in Hitler's Germany.

The mass trial of the Scythe Cross rank and file presented a disheartening spectacle. Altogether 700 peasants were arrested, and 113 of them judged at a single trial. All declared themselves ready to die for the "Idea," but were unable to provide the judge with further elucidation. "Out of a hundred defendants," wrote Kovács, "98 owned neither house nor land.... They wore torn trousers, miserable short overcoats or old sheepskin vests; none of them wore a shirt." The judge permitted most of the defendants to return to their poverty.

By the time Böszörmény's movement was suppressed, he was no longer in the forefront. National Socialism had shifted to the cities, especially to Budapest, where socially acceptable leaders turned it into a more consequential political force.

It was during the premiership of Gömbös that Zoltán Meskó, an independent deputy, announced in parliament on June 16, 1932, that he had formed a "Hungarian Hitlerite movement." As the *Budapesti Hirlap* reported on June 17, 1932, Meskó, whose appearance in parliament in a brown shirt caused great hilarity on both sides of the House, expounded the demands of his National Socialist Peasants' and Workers' Party as follows:

> Emphasis on public, rather than on private interest; prevention of religious persecution; restoration of Hungary's historic frontiers; safeguarding of Hungary's independence; universal, secret suffrage.... Naturalization restricted to people of clearly established Turanian descent.... Forced labor sentence or death for profiteers, embezzlers, perjurers and swindlers.... Abolition of all entailed estates; universal military service; compulsory premarital medical examination....

At the close of his oration, Meskó "attached the Swastika to his jacket." His National Socialism brought little that was new to the parliamentarians. The demands he voiced were those of all rightist splinter groups. A year later brown shirt and swastika were forbidden by the Minister of Interior as "official emblems of a foreign power." Meskó then exchanged his brown shirt for a green one, adopted the *nyilaskereszt* (arrow cross) as his party's emblem, and trimmed his Hitler-type moustache in the Hungarian style. The green shirt and the Arrow Cross subsequently became the symbols of most Hungarian National Socialist movements.

Now that the ice was broken, scores of new National Socialist parties sprang up. Their programs repeated that of Meskó, or rather of the German Nazi party, with more or less servility. Some were brutally anti-Semitic, others were more precise on the issue of land reform; still others were more generous than Meskó in defining membership in the Magyar race. Thus Aryans were added to Turanians, presumably to the relief of Meskó himself who was of pure Slovak descent. By 1933, several Hungarian aristocrats had each founded his own Arrow Cross movement. This made National Socialism somewhat more palatable to good society, and provided the Arrow Cross with desperately needed cash. Count Sándor Festetics—Leader of the Hungarian National Socialist party and a candidate, in 1935, for parliament, in one of the rural open-ballot districts which he practically owned—simply ordered his employees to vote for him rather than for the government's candidate. Faced with the agonizing dilemma of disappointing either the gendarmes or the count's stewards, the electors voted their lord into parliament with a comfortable majority.

At this time the National Socialists had two representatives in parliament, a fact which annoyed Gömbös. For the moment, however, there was little to worry about, as the National Socialist parties were engaged in the complex strife so characteristic of this movement outside of Germany. Leaders negotiated, amalgamated their parties, expelled each other, or proceeded to tearful reconciliations, all to the great delight of the satirical press. Not until the emergence of the Prophet, Ferenc Szálasi, did the Arrow Cross achieve at least spiritual unity, and then only because Szálasi elevated himself to such philosophic heights as to remain undisturbed by mean factional quarrels or practical political considerations.

In Hungary's troubled history, perhaps no politician was subjected to such extremes of abuse and of idolatry as Ferenc Szálasi. In C. A. Macartney's *History of Hungary, 1929–1945*, the author describes Szálasi as one of the strangest and most interesting characters of contemporary Hungarian history. While his many enemies spared no invective in denouncing him, Macartney writes that he inspired a personal devotion among his followers "such as no other Hungarian of his age could equal, and after his death they carried on the cult of him, passing his words from hand to hand, speaking of him as early Christians spoke of the Messiah."

As for Szálasi's personality, Professor Macartney provides us with the following description:

> ...an original, for whose mental processes the word eccentric would be a strong meiosis; but not... a brute, a traitor or a stupid

man.... Incidentally, had he been a brute, and above all had he been a traitor, he could have achieved power before he did. It was precisely his refusal to compromise on matters of principle which kept the Germans from giving him support and led time and again to less scrupulous followers deserting him. His responsibility for the many sins committed under the aegis of his name lies in his unwillingness or inability even to see, much less to guard against, the dangers of the spirits which he conjured up. For himself, he was a man of the most unyielding principles, on which he insisted with a maddening monotony and a rigidity which rejected the slightest compromise.

Although this is too tolerant a judgment, it is certain that Szálasi was no hireling of Hitler. In his childish conceit, he considered Hungary Germany's equal partner in a new Europe. He was convinced that the Hungarians, "this little people," could reorganize Europe if only they would follow him. "I have been selected by a higher Divine authority to redeem the Magyar people—he who does not understand me or loses confidence—let him go! At most I shall remain alone, but even alone I shall create the Hungarist State with the help of the secret force that is within me." Szálasi coined the word "Hungarist" (Hungarista) to designate his principles and program. It indicated that his National Socialism was different from that of the Germans. It also made Szálasi's movement invincible for, while his Arrow Cross party could be and often was suppressed, the "Hungarist Movement" would continue to live in the hearts of his followers.

It must come as no surprise that this superpatriot was also of foreign descent. Szálasi's father was of Armenian, and his mother of mixed Slovak-Magyar, stock. His father was an NCO in the Austro-Hungarian army. Like so many other sons of noncommissioned officers, Szálasi chose an officer's career. He served on the front during the late years of World War I; in postwar Hungary he was permitted to enter the General Staff College from which he graduated with highest honors. It was in the General Staff College, where such activity was encouraged, that Szálasi began to write on political and economic subjects. But he was already a major on the General Staff when, in 1933, he published, without permission of his superiors, his "Plan for the Construction of the Hungarian State." As the plan seemed to do injustice to Magyar aspirations, he was severely reprimanded for insubordination. He then addressed a memorandum to Prime Minister Gömbös, criticizing the government's policy. This angered Gömbös, who had no use for officers—besides himself—in politics. Apparently, the Prime Minister nevertheless attempted to win Szálasi over, offering him a mandate in the coming elections, but Szálasi put forward impossible conditions. In March, 1935, he resigned his army commission and founded his first political movement, the Party of National Will. He was then thirty-eight years of age. He stood twice for election, but was handsomely defeated. He then decided (1936) never again to run as a candidate.

On April 16, 1937, he was for the first time arrested and the party headquarters, comprising two rooms, were sealed. The police found a total of 420 *pengös* ($84) in the party treasury. The court sentenced him to three months in honorable confinement for anti-Semitic agitation, but he was never called to serve the sentence, although it did bring his name before the public. The nebulous statements on social reform he made at the trial won him many sympathizers. Soon after that he visited Germany, which caused the Budapest liberal press to credit him with Germany's favor. Membership in his party, renamed the Arrow Cross Party-Hungarist Movement, grew rapidly to twenty thousand by the summer of 1937. In October of the same year, he effected a merger of most National Socialist parties in an impressive demonstration held in Budapest. The merger lasted only a few weeks, but no one now doubted Szálasi's political importance. Yet his sudden popularity was hard to explain. He was neither a good speaker, nor a good organizer; but his sincerity and undoubted honesty kindled admiration, perhaps because such qualities were rare in contemporary Hungarian politics. He was fond of visiting, à la Hitler, in every corner of the country, where he amazed and charmed his followers by remembering their names. His popularity among women was one of his great assets. More important were his connections in the officer corps. Indeed, the younger officers who formed the bulk of the General Staff were impatient for political and social reform, which, they felt, was mandatory in view of the coming war. They besieged the regent with warnings against the leftist and Jewish agitation, and insisted that he implement a "new, determined, uncompromisingly Christian, national and popular policy." This meant in essence that the regent should curtail parliament and impose further restrictions on socialists and Jews. The officers negotiated with Szálasi and counted on him, but most of them were still reluctant to entrust him with political power.

The regent himself was aware of Szálasi's activity and, although he consistently refused to give an audience to his factious officer, he allowed the chief of his military cabinet to seek out Szálasi and inquire into his intentions. Szálasi made his views clear: the regent should "take charge of the country," that is, he should stage a *putsch* with the help of the army, and nominate Szálasi prime minister. But the regent refused to listen.

The year 1938 promised to be stormy. Rumors of a coming rightist coup were circulating and were played up enormously by a near-hysterical liberal press; the Arrow Cross flooded the streets of Budapest with leaflets, announcing Szálasi's impending triumph. The regent himself was booed by students and officers at a gala performance in the Budapest Opera. At parliamentary by-elections, some of Szálasi's younger lieutenants ran successfully against the candidates of the Government Party and half a dozen Smallholder deputies left their party to join the National Socialist movement. In addition, the

Arrow Cross now seemed to have almost unlimited funds. Through some Hungarian agents and through the German minority in Hungary, German money flowed into the coffers of the radical Right. Some influential Budapest newspapers changed hands and endorsed a National Socialist program. Szálasi knew nothing of these transactions, but then he was above such petty considerations.

Finally, the regent took matters in hand. In May, 1938, he dismissed the hesitant Darányi, Gömbös' immediate successor, and appointed Béla Imrédy prime minister. Imrédy was a financial expert and had the reputation of being a liberal and an Anglophile. He subsequently disappointed the regent because of his violent anti-Semitism and his aspirations to dictatorship, but for the Arrow Cross his appointment was a great blow. Imrédy, like Gömbös, had no use for other leaders and least of all for the unruly Arrow Cross. A week after his appointment he forbade all employees of the state to be members of political parties; as there were very few civil servants with leftist sympathies, this was designed as a measure against the Right.

Next, Szálasi was arrested. This time the government meant business; he was indicted for subversive activity, and sentenced to three years' hard labor. On August 27, 1938, he was taken to Szeged prison from where he was not to emerge for over two years. From then on, until the German occupation in March, 1944, the Arrow Cross was subjected to almost continual harassment. Its newspapers were suspended, its meetings forbidden, some of its leaders imprisoned, hundreds put in internment camps, there to outnumber by far the Communist prisoners. The German press reacted with violence to such persecution and hailed Szálasi as a martyr. At home, the Arrow Cross went into the new elections with his name on its banner. The parliamentary elections of May, 1939 (the first since 1935), were held with secret balloting in accordance with a law adopted a year earlier. The National Socialists scored a great success. Out of 259 seats the Government Party won a comfortable 183, but the National Socialists increased the number of their mandates to 49 (Szálasi's Arrow Cross alone received 31 mandates). The Social Democrats and the Smallholders were defeated. They won 5 and 14 seats respectively. Worse still, the majority of the Government Party had clearly rightist sympathies.

The popular vote was even more favorable to the Arrow Cross: out of a total of approximately 2,000,000 votes, they scored 750,000. In Budapest the National Socialists obtained 72,385 votes, as opposed to 95,468 for the Government Party and 34,500 for the Socialists. "Red" Csepel, Budapest's most industrialized suburb, elected two National Socialist deputies.

In the new parliament the Arrow Cross deputies became the government's first true opposition. They remained, of course, completely impotent but they posed as the people's champions; between 1939 and 1944 their parliamentary speeches repeatedly harped on the plight of Hungary's poor. The extreme Right spoke with fire and conviction. No longer did it have to parrot the Horthy Right's slogans; it had its own ideology, formulated by Ferenc Szálasi.

Judging by the exhilarating effect of Szálasi's ideas upon the mass of his followers, one would expect some rational or emotional appeal in his many speeches and writings. Nothing could be further from the fact. Not only do these pieces of wisdom make dull reading, they are also infuriatingly garbled. Szálasi was fond of the newly coined word, of the juxtaposed phrase, and the involuted sentence. His magnum opus, *Ut és Cél* ("Road and Goal"), was published in 1936 and is as incomprehensible in the original as it is in translation:

> ... Social Nationalism is life's only genuine physics and biology. The true individual forms matter with his soul; his hand is but an instrument. And since this is so, the formed matter is a value and not a ware. Social Nationalism is therefore the nation's biological physics and not its historical materialism. Its biology: the nation; its physics: socialism fulfilled in the nation. It is life-community and matter-community in partner-community and fate-community, with a basis in the nation and Fatherland, pure and true in its moral and its spirit.

Or again from the same chapter:

> The ideological foundation of Hungarism's national economy and work-order is Social Nationalism and its conscious practice. Only through the ideology and practice of Social Nationalism can the individual become a true national socialist. . . . National Socialism means nationalist order in socialism, Social Nationalism means socialist order in nationalism, therefore: spiritual order in matter, material order in the spirit. The soul's order in the body, the body's order in the soul.

Although these and similar pronouncements make the reader wonder about the intellectual climate of a General Staff College from which such a writer could emerge with distinction, it must be admitted that not all Szálasi's writings betray equal depth and confusion. On the question of Hungary's territorial aspirations, his major field of interest, Szálasi is almost precise. His aim was to restore Hungary's historic boundaries. That he gave to his resurrected Great Hungary the name Carpatho-Danubian Great Fatherland, or The United Lands and the March of Hungaria, was not without its justification. For Szálasi was intent upon establishing a happy community of nationalities in the Carpathian basin. The national minorities were to have their autonomy, while submitting, of course, to the authority of the Hungarian state. To the Magyars, he allotted the plains, to the Germans the hills, to the Romanians the "Alpine" regions, and to the Slavs the rest of the mountain areas.

It is true that on his maps Magyar autonomy far exceeded the limits of the plains and incorporated a good many areas inhabited by Slavs and Romanians, but then he was certain that such favoritism would meet with the approval of those concerned. Indeed, the Magyars alone had been able in the past to form an "organic state system" and it was therefore natural that they should occupy the largest areas and assume a commanding position in the new Hungarist state.

The unity of the Carpatho-Danubian Great Fatherland was to be created by the Hungarian army. To this army would belong a commanding position in the state, and to its needs all the material and moral resources of the nation would have to be surrendered. "When the Army sees that in the nation the three pillars of Religion, Patriotism and Discipline have been shaken"—wrote Szálasi in his party daily—"then it is the Army's duty to force the nation back on these pillars."

This time, he said, the "stab in the back" tragedy of 1918 would not be repeated: "The war of the future will be total; from it only those nations will emerge successfully where the masses stand united behind the fighting army." Thus the army needed the domestic peace that neither Marxism nor liberalism could secure. The solution was "national capitalism." In that system, labor peace would reign; there would be no privileged classes; work would be both a right and a duty. Strikes and idleness would be outlawed, the tyranny of money abolished, the National Bank expropriated, and a General Council of Corporations formed to direct the national economy. As for agriculture, the agricultural proletariat would be transformed into a smallholders' class, a system of co-operatives set up, and the "planning of agricultural production" introduced. He failed, however, to announce which lands he intended for distribution or where, in his view, the upper limits of land ownership lay.

Szálasi was a devout Catholic; his vaguely Turanian Christ was the King of all Hungarians. The Hungarist state was to be based on a "Christian moral order" where atheism and nondenominationalism would not be tolerated. On the other hand, Church and state would be separated, and education taken out of the hands of the religious orders. A "political Church" had no place in the "Hungarist order." His religious orthodoxy was not necessarily shared by his followers. The party intellectual, Dr. Pál Vágo, for instance, was violently anticlerical; he accused the Church of propagating a Jewish version of Christianity. Dr. Vágo considered himself an expert in biblical studies and was able to prove that Christ was a Scythian (and thus a Turanian), and so were all the early Christians.

In Szálasi's opinion women and children were two of the "seven pillars of the nation." The concept of illegitimate birth was to be abolished, and divorces restricted to cases of "national interest." Church weddings were to constitute the only legal act of marriage, civil marriages were to be forbidden. Women were to remain at the hearth. "The basis of Hungarism is the family . . . the head of the family is its warrior, the mother its soul, the child its weapon, and the youth its symbol." As for the Jews, alien to Hungarians in both spirit and physique, they were to find themselves a new home. Szálasi insisted he was no anti-Semite, but an "a-Semite," a fact that did not prevent him from publicly referring to the Jews as a pestilence, and believing in the existence of an anti-Christian Jewish world conspiracy as formulated in the "Protocols of the Elders of Zion."

Macartney maintains that Szálasi was no brute. Indeed, very few of his speeches or writings contain expressions of hatred. He loved his people and had no such low opinion of the credulous masses as Hitler did. He did not attempt to coërce, but rather to persuade. But in his obsession with ideology and with his utopia, he allowed his subordinates to bring human sacrifices to the altar of his "Idea."

There are no studies or reliable statistics concerning the organization or membership of the Arrow Cross party. Sources of information are limited to contemporary reports, newspaper accounts, or interviews with former Arrow Cross leaders now in exile. The task is not made easier by the fact that the Arrow Cross, many times suspended, established a secret network alongside its regular organization, nor by its mania for archaic terminology in designating its officers and subdivisions. A few facts, however, can be cited.

At the top of the Arrow Cross pyramid, authority was divided: Szálasi, the National Leader, reserved for himself the party's spiritual direction and left a Party President, the young journalist Kálmán Hubay, in charge of politics and organization. Below the national leadership functioned a set of various central departments, among them the Councils for Land-Building, Party-Building, Recruitment, Industrial Recruitment, Propaganda, Social Problems, and Ideology. The different social classes and sectors were represented in headquarters by so-called Grand Councils, and congresses of these groups were held at regular intervals. Parallel to these organizations functioned several secret groups to which this writer's informants attach a great deal of importance. Thus, the Land-Building Council, in addition to its officially recognizable members, gathered about fifteen hundred or two thousand non-party intellectuals, professionals, engineers, army officers, and so on, allegedly engaged in drafting bills and planning social, political, and economic reforms for the period after Szálasi's assumption of power. Another secret group consisted of civil servants and employees of large private enterprises whom Imrédy's decree had excluded from official membership. These secret members formed the so-called Clan Organizations where they were registered by number rather than by name. Membership in these groups seems to have reached fifty-eight thousand by April, 1944.

As for storm troops or a National Socialist militia, these could not exist as long as Horthy was in power. Although there were some incidents, like beatings of Jews and isolated acts of terror, on the whole the Minister of Interior, Keresztes-Fischer, kept order, and the street scenes of the Weimar era had no parallel in Horthy Hungary.

Regarding membership, the data are contradictory but, according to one source, it rose from an original 8,000 in September, 1935 (Party of National Will), to approximately 19,000 in April, 1937, 116,000 at the end of 1940, and, finally, 500,000 in September, 1944. These figures, however, cannot be guaranteed. Membership fluctuated wildly. In December, 1943, for example, Szálasi noted in his diary that membership sank well below 100,000. Apparently he himself could not keep up with the changes. If these calculations, furnished mainly by former National Socialists, are correct, national membership rose from 0.3 per cent in the summer of 1938 to 4.0 per cent of the total population by September, 1944, not counting about another hundred thousand members of National Socialist groups not under Szálasi's authority.

The former President of the Supreme Audit Office in the Szálasi government provided me with information on the occupational distribution of Arrow Cross party members. According to him, industrial workers made up one-half of the party's membership in April, 1937, and even at the end of 1940 their proportion was as high as 41 per cent. During the same time, the proportion of peasant members rose from 8 to 13 per cent, and that of professionals, self-employed people, and so on, from 12 to 19 per cent. Army officers in 1937 constituted 17 per cent of the membership! This was at a time when over 52 per cent of the working population was engaged in agriculture and only 23 per cent in industry and mining. The reasons for the preponderance of workers are not far to seek. The Socialist trade unions included only skilled workers, and those chiefly from heavy industry and the large plants; the Christian unions, or the government-sponsored yellow unions, had never achieved serious proportions. For unskilled or unemployed workers, and for small artisans and their journeymen, the Arrow Cross was their first friend. Contemporary Arrow Cross newspapers are crowded with reports of convivial dinners, excursions, varied social contacts of workers' groups, requests for mutual help, and announcements begging aid for some unfortunate, unemployed "Brother." The Arrow Cross performed a function that the socialists were unable to fulfill.

The release of Szálasi from prison in September, 1940, did not mean the beginning of a triumphant rise to power. On the contrary, his party's strength appeared to have passed its zenith. Factional struggle became more violent and several of Szálasi's lieutenants deserted him, charging him with insanity or embezzlement of party funds. Furthermore, the government was more firmly in the saddle than ever. The territorial gains made between 1938 and 1941, and Hungary's involvement in the war, commanded national unity and order; this the government was resolved to enforce.

Hungary took up arms on Germany's side in June, 1941. But although she intended to profit from this alliance, she was also intent upon making few sacrifices, and it was not before late 1942 that substantial numbers of Hungarian troops were sent to the Russian front. These units were all but annihilated in the Russian offensive in the winter of 1942–1943; the remaining soldiers were thereupon ordered back to Hungary and only some light units were left in the Ukraine, well behind the front lines. By this time, Hungary was engaged in an ambiguous policy. Horthy, who never surrendered his belief in an Allied victory, dismissed the over-eager Bárdossy and in March, 1942, appointed Miklós Kállay prime minister. Kállay was a country gentleman of pure Magyar stock with relatively little political experience and a great deal of hatred for everything Russian or German. He and Horthy planned a "purely Magyar" policy. Convinced that the Western Allies would never permit the Red army to penetrate into the heart of Europe, they decided to defend the eastern borders of Hungary against the inevitable Russian onslaught and, meanwhile, to make Hungary ready for an eventual surrender to the Anglo-Saxons.

Under Kállay's premiership, between March, 1942, and March, 1944, Hungary underwent a remarkable transformation. She became a safe haven for many victims of German National Socialism, harboring close to a million Hungarian and foreign Jews, refugee Polish soldiers, and French, English, and American prisoners of war who had escaped from German camps. Contacts were established with the Western Allies who were given repeated assurances of Hungary's friendly intentions. Government-sponsored newspapers were ordered to comment with moderation on German triumphs; the Arrow Cross was kept under strict control, and the "Left" was advised to attack the government. Indeed, Kállay encouraged the formation of an "Independence Front," composed mainly of Smallholders, Social Democrats, and bourgeois Democrats, and their leaders were asked to demand an "independent Hungarian policy" in parliament. By 1943 Hungary was, for all practical purposes, a neutral country. English, American, or Russian planes flying overhead were not fired upon; contacts were established with Tito; enemy agents were received and some hidden in, of all places, the regent's residence. On December 31, 1943, the semiofficial *Magyarország* ("Hungary") published a government-inspired editorial that said in essence that Hungary would gladly surrender but could not, in the absence of an enemy.

The Germans, well aware of what was going on, finally lost patience when, in the spring of 1944, the Russian front moved dangerously close to Hungary. In March, Horthy was ordered to visit the Führer in Germany, where he was blackmailed into co-operation by the threat of a joint German-Romanian-Croatian-Slovak attack on Hungary. On March 19, German troops entered the country and Horthy was forced to appoint the pro-German General Döme Sztójay, former Hungarian minister to Berlin, as prime minister.

*

The cabinet of Sztójay, at least in appearance, did not differ greatly from previous counterrevolutionary governments. While Kállay hid from the Gestapo in the Turkish legation, and Minister of Interior Keresztes-Fischer was imprisoned, other more coöperative members of the Kállay government remained in office where they were joined by rightist members of the Party of Government. Later in the spring, Béla Imrédy, now head of the Party of National Renewal, joined the cabinet. A few non-Arrow Cross National Socialists were also given important positions but not on the ministerial level.

Under Sztójay, the essential duality of the Horthy Right was once again proven. Wavering constantly between the old aristocracy's parliamentary traditions and the fascist ideology of the "young" counterrevolution, most of the deputies and the nationalist press eagerly accepted the latest turn of events. The new government was feted as Hungary's savior by the same deputies of the Party of Government who, a few days earlier, had celebrated Kállay for similar endeavors. The government announced a "new, rightist, Christian and national" policy, the same announced by all governments in the past but, this time, with determination to put at least part of it into practice. Of course, there could be no question of social reforms—the war would have made these impossible anyway—but at least Hungary could rid itself once and for all of Jews and of their hirelings. A flood of restrictive measures descended on the Jews. First "Jewish" telephones were cut and "Jewish" horses confiscated; eventually distinctive badges were made compulsory, Jews were excluded from all skilled employment, and their rations were greatly reduced. Finally, they were concentrated in ghettos and deported to extermination camps. This was achieved in negotiations between Eichmann and two National Socialist secretaries of state in the Hungarian Ministry of Interior, and carried out by the SS with the enthusiastic coöperation of the notoriously brutal Hungarian gendarmes. The deportations began on May 14, 1944, and, as far as the Jews in the provinces were concerned, they were completed within two months. In this short interval, 434,000 Jews were taken to Auschwitz, there to be gassed or—a minority—to be transferred to concentration camps.

Yet, as usual during the Horthy regime, the Left was far from silenced. The deportations and even the gassings remained no secret, and, for the first time in Nazi Europe, a storm of protests arose. The leaders of the Budapest Jewish community and conservative politicians in hiding addressed Horthy, and so did the Hungarian churches. When the papal nuncio, neutral governments, and President Roosevelt added their protests, Horthy finally roused himself and, in July, 1944, decided to put an end to the deportations. In the provinces not a single Jew remained, but in Budapest there were still at least 200,000. Fearing a coup against his person, Horthy stopped the gendarmes from coming to Budapest and deporting the Budapest Jews. The last two or three trainloads of deportees had to be literally smuggled out of the country by Eichmann and his SS. Further, on August 27, 1944, Horthy dismissed Sztójay and appointed General Géza Lakatos as prime minister. The latter was ordered to make preparations for Hungary's surrender to the Russians who now, after Romania's volte-face, entered Hungarian territory.

In all these events, Szálasi and his Arrow Cross played no part. In May, 1944, Szálasi had had his much-sought-for audience with the regent, but there had been no agreement between them. Upon the appointment of Lakatos, the Arrow Cross had finally decided on action. Abandoning his previous loyalty to the regent, Szálasi began negotiations with the Germans, offering his services and warning them of Horthy's surrender plans. Veesenmayer, the German plenipotentiary, who had a very low opinion of Szálasi, was slow to come around to the Arrow Cross point of view; but even he gave in when the SS Command in Hungary decided that Szálasi alone, of all Hungarians, remained a true friend of Germany. Clearly, the surrender of the Hungarian troops, now fully involved in operations against the Russians, would have caused the collapse of German defenses. Szálasi was therefore groomed for a take-over, and preparations were made for the day when Horthy would announce his surrender. This came when Horthy, following an agreement concluded in Moscow, made the armistice public in a radio address on October 15.

Perhaps no political turnabout was more poorly prepared. There were no troops in Budapest to defend the regent; the Hungarian generals were taken by surprise; the socialist workers and the resistance movement had not been given the promised arms. The armistice was literally the undertaking of Horthy and his immediate family with the help of a few trusted officers and a few conservative politicians. (The latter, like Bethlen, emerged from their hiding places for that occasion.) The exclusiveness of Horthy's undertaking was motivated not only by a very justified fear of betrayal, but by the clique character of the whole Horthy system. The true Left, particularly the Social Democrats, had always been regarded as instruments, never as serious partners. On the decisive day, Horthy remained isolated. The great majority of the officers disobeyed Horthy's orders; commanders loyal to the regent were arrested. The Germans acted rapidly: the radio station and the royal palace were seized by a few tanks; Horthy was placed in custody and forced to withdraw his orders. German arms were distributed to the Arrow Cross and, before the people of Budapest could recover from their surprise, the formation of an Arrow Cross government under Szálasi was announced. In his first order of the day, Szálasi exhorted the nation to a final effort against the Russian invaders.

Szálasi's reign was a sad epilogue to a tragic story. Insisting on legal sanctification of his coup, and using his enforced appointment by the regent, Szálasi had himself accepted as prime minister by a rump parliament, and, subsequently, proclaimed himself National Leader. On November 3 he took a solemn oath to the Holy Crown in the Royal Palace.

Szálasi was not entirely without support among the "historic classes." Although liberals, conservatives, socialists, and royalists were sent to German concentration camps, he was enthusiastically accepted by some members of the Upper House—including the head of the House of Habsburg in Hungary—and by the right wing of the former Government Party, which had formed a "National Alliance" with the National Socialist deputies in the parliament. The majority of the civil servants and the army officers took their oath to Szálasi, and so did the National Socialist splinter groups, now finally united with Szálasi's party.

The social composition of Szálasi's cabinet did not completely differ from that of the Horthy governments. It contained, beside Szálasi, other pensioned officers, two generals in active service, and a former White terrorist officer who had spent the war years in German exile as a member of the SS. There were also some aristocrats and three civil servants; the latter had served in Horthy's cabinets. But there was also a journalist, a physician, a pharmacist, and finally, a former left socialist who liked to boast that he had known Lenin. Arrow Cross appointees took over the important positions in the ministries and in private business. They were almost without exception of lower-middle-class origin.

Elated, Szálasi published a working program that announced, among other things, the transformation of Hungary into a Hungarist state, and the creation of a prosperous peasant class before January 1, 1945. Szálasi's subordinates proceeded with equal enthusiasm. Total mobilization of the nation's human and material resources was again and again proclaimed; the formation of representative corporations was announced, and parliament drew up plans for the coming years. But as the Russians approached and reached the outskirts of Budapest in November, contradictory orders were issued. Workers who had been ordered to stay put and work hard were now asked to pack and leave with their dismantled factories. Several classes of recruits were mobilized and then sent home, as they could be provided neither uniforms nor arms. These orders were generally disregarded; in some factories the workers engaged in sabotage; the underground movement, now largely Communist, began to make life difficult for the Nazis. Nevertheless, in the final days of their reign, the Germans and the Arrow Cross managed to transport to Germany practically all the movable goods of Hungary.

Meanwhile, Eichmann reappeared in Hungary, and, following an agreement concluded with Szálasi, about 50,000 Jews were driven, during the winter, from Budapest to the Austrian border, there to build fortifications and to perish in the process. The rest of the Jews (unless they were in hiding, or under the more or less effective protection of neutral legations) lived in a ghetto in misery and starvation. The Red army found 124,000 Jews in Budapest. Altogether 200,000 Jews survived within the boundaries of pre-1938 Hungary.

By December, the situation was completely out of hand. The wholesale disposal of stocks of former Jewish stores turned into regular looting. National Socialist terror commandos hunted down army deserters and Jews. On December 24, 1944, the Red army surrounded Budapest. By that time, the government, the ministries, and the high army command had abandoned the capital for western Hungary. The city was left in charge of the SS and of self-appointed Arrow Cross commanders. The latter sent policemen, mailmen, streetcar conductors, and children to the front, which usually lay only a few blocks away. There, German and Hungarian troops resisted until February 13, when the 800,000 civilians of Budapest were finally liberated from the horrors of the siege.

The fighting in western Hungary, bolstered by some powerful German Panzer attacks, continued for two more months. A few Hungarian divisions were engaged in this struggle. This, however, was no longer the work of the Arrow Cross but of Hungarian officers who wanted to save themselves and their soldiers from Russian captivity. Arrow Cross activity was restricted to the execution of underground leaders captured in Budapest, and to some propaganda speeches. Szálasi was busy writing his copious memoirs and could seldom be disturbed. On January 20, 1945, he made his last speech in a small village near the Austrian border. He promised the liberation of the country within a year, threatened death to those who would doubt his words, and assured his peasant audience that "everyone in Hungary will be compensated down to the last red farthing for his losses."

On April 4, 1945, the last German and Hungarian troops left Hungary, preceded by the two houses of parliament and Szálasi's cabinet. These institutions continued to meet in German exile until they were picked up by the Americans and sent back to Hungary at the request of the new Hungarian government. There was not one among the Arrow Cross leaders who obeyed Szálasi's orders: "Better be a hero for a moment than a slave for life." None of them died a hero's death.

After December, 1944, Hungary had a new government. Appointed by the Russians, it was composed of such members of the "Left" as could be found in eastern Hungary and was headed by a former Horthy general. It concluded an armistice with the Russians and declared war on the German Reich.

The trials of the Horthyite and Arrow Cross war criminals were conducted during 1945 and 1946 in Budapest by a People's Court composed of a professional judge and delegates of the four parties assembled in the National Independence Front (Smallholders, Peasants, Social Democrats, and Communists). This was avowedly a political court, acting under revolutionary conditions. Capital sentences were passed in 264 cases, and 122 of these were carried out. Among the executed were five former prime ministers (Imrédy, Bárdossy, Sztójay, Szálasi, and Szöllösi, Szálasi's later prime minister), several army commanders, all the members of the Arrow Cross cabinet, and those accused of the deportation or murder of Jews and of resistants. Szálasi faced his trial with equanimity; he denied all knowledge of the Jewish persecutions, refused to admit that his acts on October 15 had constituted treason, but upheld his Hungarist ideas with unflinching conviction. He marched quietly to his execution.

The majority of the "small Nazis" were permitted—after a brief period of internment—to join the democratic parties. Most of them seemed to favor the Communist Party. As for the more important National Socialists whose lives were spared by the courts, they were, after 1948, joined in prison by their former democratic opponents. Indeed, it was a common sight to see, in the concentration camps of the Stalinist Rákosi era, the torturer working alongside his former victim, and both watched by a Communist political police officer who was himself often a former member of the Arrow Cross movement.

The political history of Horthy Hungary was characterized by a conflict between different segments of a counterrevolutionary movement. Its moderate element constituted a "Left" in contemporary Hungarian parlance but not in its political practices. The Left was conservative; it thrived on noble Hungary's parliamentary tradition, and had neither democratic nor socialist aspirations. Yet, inevitably, it came to enjoy the support of the country's weak liberal and socialist forces. Curiously enough, it was the Right that opened the way to social upheaval.

In the final reckoning, the Horthy regime represented the successful extension of a traditional system, while the Szálasi experiment was both an epilogue to the history of traditional Hungary and the beginning of the emancipation of Hungary's lower classes.

60

Extract from
'CHARACTERISTICS OF RUMANIAN FASCISM'

Radu Ioanid

Source: Radu Ioanid, *The Sword of the Archangel: Fascist Ideology in Romania*, New York: Columbia University Press, Boulder East European Monographs, 1990, pp. 126–48. Translated by Peter Heinegg.

I Anti-semitism and racism

... There is no essential difference between Nazi anti-Semitism and the legionary variety, contrary to the affirmations of Andreas Hillgruber, who maintains that "legionary anti-Semitism had a religious and national character, and was not based on racism. Codreanu had no ties with Professor Cuza, the real promoter of anti-Semitic propaganda in Rumania."[1] The Couzists as well as the legionnaires demonstrated a violent anti-Semitism, using the same arsenal of arguments, while the links between Codreanu and his mentor Cuza are well known. The difference between the two fascist leaders occurred, as Ernst Nolte shows, on the level of tactics. While Cuza envisaged the movement as a rather lax formation, Codreanu wanted to impose a rigid organization and a severe discipline, something he succeeded in doing, by the way . . .: "The new method that he inaugurated in Rumanian politics consisted in individual terror."[2] Individual terror aimed at adversaries of the legionary movement, individual terror aimed at Jews.

The anti-Semitic violence and crimes of the legionnaires have been denied by some former members of the movement who try to advance the exclusively anticommunist image of the legionary movement.

In this vein Mihai Sturdza noted: "The truth is that the Captain's whole life proclaimed that physical violence against the Jews represents a stupid error. He would have expelled from the movement even those who had been guilty of so much as breaking a window."[3] Although there is no text by

Codreanu containing ideas to support his affirmation, although the Legion's politics proved the contrary, Sturdza insists on the fact that in Rumania, outside the legionnaires there were ... other anti-Semitic organizations: "There existed in the country parties and organizations whose anti-Semitic character was manifested even more palpably than in the case of Corneliu Codreanu's Legion...."[4]

Sturdza's claims are partially true, to the degree that Rumanian anti-Semitism between the World Wars was not exclusively the business of the legionnaires. But that is not worth much, considering the waves of anti-Semitic crimes committed by the legionnaires.

Rumanian anti-Semitism in the 1930s and 1940s was evidently influenced by German racism, despite such positions, such as Georgescu Delfaras', who (on economic, not humanitarian grounds) called for a gradual solution of "the Jewish problem" under the aegis of "a permanent committee constituted by manufacturers and merchants, who will recommend to the government the measures it must take and the moment when it must take them."[5] "Let us avoid the economic disturbances ... an abrupt elimination of the Jews from our economic life can do no one any good, and above all it cannot be desired by the State,"[6] Delafaras wrote, while reproaching the Goga-Cuza government for "the error of hastening to liquidate the Jews without any prior preparation, which has led to needless incidents, compromising the good intentions of the principal leaders."[7] Delafaras' position was that "The Jewish problem takes on a specifically Rumanian character in our country, and it must be treated as such: by Rumanian solutions."[8] This was also the declared position of Antonescu's fascist group. The proponents of "gradual elimination," of so-called "Rumanian" methods, bear the grave responsibility of the massacre of the Jews in Jassy in the summer of 1941 as well as for other crimes. Having approved the massacre of Jassy, Ilie Radulescu, the director of *Porunca Vremii*, wrote on July 4, 1941: "The 500 kike-communists executed at Jassy, as well as the sanction of killing 50 kikes, who will pay with the cadavers for the life of every brave Rumanian or German cowardly cut down, constitutes a hard lesson and a sharp notice with regard to all the hare-brained Galician provocations."[9]

In 1945, to the question from the president of the tribunal, "Is it true that by your articles you supported the extermination of Rumanian citizens and of the civilian population for racial and political reasons, through collective and individual excesses,"[10] Radulescu answered that, "If you are alluding to the Jewish problem–because that is the only instigation you can talk about—I always argued, before and after 1941, in favor of solving the Jewish problem through elimination. The only support I gave was the mass executions in Jassy."[11] This is how anti-Semitic practice blurred the boundaries between the advocates of "gradual solutions" and those of "radical solutions."

After Hitler's rise to power, there appeared in Rumanian fascist journalism apologists for German racism as well as partisans for methods of total extermination of the Jewish population. In 1935 Nicolae Bogdan published an article in which we can see the influence of the Nazis and Arthur de Gobineau: "The crude but pure truth is this: All those Yellow, Blacks, Reds, or other colors see in us, the Whites, mortal enemies, whose submission and defeat they desire with unanimous ardor and with common accord."[12] In his book, *Conceptia eroica asupra rasei* ("The Heroic Conception of Race"), legionnaire Ion Foti claims as his sources of inspiration Adolf Hitler, Alfred Rosenberg, and Benito Mussolini. He accepts the definition that Rosenberg gives of race ("Seen from within, the soul means race, and conversely, race is the external clothing of the soul," p. 17), while affirming that the Aryan principle constitutes the foundation of the State, that "the legionary State has in its structure, as its backbone, the steel block of the Rumanian race and all the privileges that flow from it."[13] Foti tries to promote the idea of the unity of the blood of the Rumanian people, arguing that the Rumanian race is characterized by "clarity and precision of expression, seriousness, devotion to God and to the nation, nostalgia for life to the point of enjoying the pleasure of death, the pride of an imperial people whose race has been kept pure, the safeguard of the light of Christ, the pious preservation of tradition."[14]

We meet with spiritualist subterfuges in the attempt to characterize the Rumanian people through ideological, legionary elements. The arguments in favor of "racial unity" were inadequate, even from the standpoint of the "methodology" proposed by Gobineau, Chamberlain, and the German school of racism.

Nicolae Rosu said that "the nationalist (legionary) ideal is a myth that presupposes a permanent psychic and biological perfecting of the Rumanian nation beyond the limits of an epoch, heading toward eternity by way of imperialism."[15] For his part Dan Botta asked rhetorically, "Aren't the reactions of these young people the expression of an impulse coming from far off, of an order of blood, of ancestors to whom only the pure are sensitive?"[16] Let us see what this "psychic and biological perfecting of the nation" was supposed to mean and what it really did mean for the legionnaires. Theoretically it was a reaffirmation of aberrant fascist ideas: "Race in consequently the basic phenomenon of social structure. . . . The soul of a race is simply the perfected expression of the ancestral residues of unconscious and irational states, of a collective anthropological substratum. . . . A race affirms itself in culture by its conception of authentic life, while eliminating the heterogeneous and bastard elements. . . ."[17]

In the eyes of the legionnaires the main enemy, apart from communism, was the Jews, who were presented, obviously with the goal of diversion in mind, as nothing less than ". . . in their totality the ruling class in our State, in the economic domain."[18] The logical consequence of this gross falsification, which was repeated many times by fascist theoreticians and journalists, was that the solution of all society's problems called for the elimination of the Jews and, in general, of all "foreign elements": "For every nation that wishes to live free in its own country, the foreigner, whether superior or inferior, is a pagan and polluted."[19] The practical solution for this problem consisted in "state anti-Semitism, a phenomenon that marks a new era in history."[20]

In 1938 Alexandru Razmerita,[21] while criticizing the position of a priest who wanted to drown the Jews in the Black Sea, described with great abundance of details "a plan for the total elimination of the Jews in the cities and their deportation to the countryside to do forced labor. According to Razmerita, the Jews ought to be deprived of the right to have recourse to the justice system. Attempts to escape the work camps ought to be punished by execution. He proposed installing little village camps containing 24 to 40 men, with forced labor applying also to children older than ten. These children were to be separated from their parents and their identity papers were to contain only the name of the boss to whom they were assigned. Practically speaking, this was organized slavery, of the Nazi type, quite close to the reality of the Nazi concentration camps, although the internment of the Jews in the latter was not yet known. During the same year of 1938, Mihail Polhroniade, another legionary journalist, justified the necessity of state anti-Semitism by the "example" of Nazism, arguing that "the victory of national socialism with respect to the Jewish problem is particularly important for Germany, but it acquires at the same time a still greater importance, as it represents an event that reverberates in world history."[22]

Traian Herseni was one of the legionnaires who pressed their belief in racism to its ultimate theoretical consequences. He maintained that "The reality of racism is based on solid scientific foundations, and represents one of the most stable political ideals. . . . Science proves that men are not equal, that their characters vary as a function of the race to which they belong. There are races ill suited for culture, there are also races that barely manage to profit from the culture of others. Only very few races are endowed with the gift of creating culture. The results of studies done up to the present moment seem to prove that of all the races on earth, the Nordic race is the most gifted, and that it is to them that the most noble Rumanian cultural productions are due. Once the race lost its purity, and the bloodlines were crossed, the culture fell off little by little until it completely disappeared from history. . . . The doctrine of inequality is completed by the doctrine of the betterment of the human races."[23]

Along with other legionnaires, Herseni became the ideological vassal of national socialism through his convictions about the superiority of the Aryan race, the Nordic origin of the values of Rumanian culture, as well as through his justifications for the expansionism of Nazi Germany. Thus he conceived the perfecting of human society as an operation to improve livestock. Declaring his agreement with the slogan of the legionnaire C. Papanace, who aimed at "purification from Judaic, Phanariot, and Gypsy influences," which appeared in the journal *Cuvintul*, Herseni wrote: "We are in complete agreement with these conclusions. The racial purification of the Rumanian people is a question of life and death. There are a number of ways to solve this problem. To begin with, it must be precisely determined what are the racial characteristics to which the Rumanian people owe their present-day creations and their periods of historical flowering, as well as their moral and political defeats, their periods of decadence and of historical shame.... We must struggle against everything that is foreign to our nation and against everything that constitutes a baneful influence, and encourage, in exchange, everything that is authentically Rumanian...."[24]

Accordingly, Herseni demanded "a rigorous social selection based on particular racial qualities,"[25] to favor the supremacy of legionnaires made up of "the purest, most gifted examples of our race."[26] What did this selection consist in? It consisted in the application of eugenics, one of the most essential components of criminal Nazi politics. Herseni maintained that "through the intermediary of eugenicism every nation becomes master of its destiny. It can systematically improve its characteristics and attain the highest stages of betterment and of human creation: and the genius of Adolf Hitler lies in his clear vision of this possibility."[27]

The master was acknowledged, declared, and assimilated in detail: "We need eugenic laws and a eugenic practice. Reproduction can no longer be left to chance ... dys-genics must be eliminated from reproduction, the inferior races completely separated from the ethnic group. The sterilization of certain categories of men is to be envisaged, not in a stupid manner, as a violation of human dignity, but as a tribute to beauty, to morality, and in general to perfection."[28] Here we have an example of a typically fascist mentality by virtue of which the incitement to crime clothes itself in fanciful language.

Another Rumanian fascist and a supporter of eugenics was P. Tiparescu, who was influenced by N. C. Paulescu, and spoke of "racial maladies" as well as of "the necessity of a rapid and intense eugenic activity."[29] He maintained that the Jews "are the most dangerous bearers of infectious diseases because of their dirtiness,"[30] without being, for all that, too infested themselves. As we can see, this is the myth of the Jewish poisoner all over again.

Alexandru Randa, equally racist, thought that "Rumanianness today represents the rearguard of the great Aryan mass that descended 4,000 years ago into Greece, Asia Minor, into Persia, and into India,"[31] that "the land of Thrace is the most important racial reservoir of the Aryan world."[32] Such affirmations, running contrary to the most elementary historical evidence, could have had two motivations, the first grounded in the fanatical outcome of typically Nazi indoctrination, the second in the desire to please the Nazi leaders, in whose eyes everyone except Nordies were considered inferior.

II The myth of the state, the cult of the hierarchical authority of one's own elites

Theories about elites and their practices go back much further than fascism, with which they share some arguments and motives for action: "Since the epoch of the Asiatic despots, the Pharohs, the Greek oligarchs, up til the time of the merchant princes, the Renaissance condottieri and fascist leaders of today, the value of the individual has been exalted by those who had the possibility of developing their own individuality to the detriment of others."[33] Nevertheless, up until fascism the theory of elites has never been expressed in forms so brutal, often reduced to the simple affirmation of the supremacy of the stronger and the more aggressive. Fascism has made use of terror (psychic and physical) with a view to reducing human beings to the state of mere social atoms, out of fear of human personality and its possibilities, and fear of the capacity of the human individual for critical analysis. Along these lines C. Z. Codreanu noted that "criticism is a dangerous disease, for it cuts off the wings of great impulses."[34] By "great impulses" he meant . . . his own orders.

The boundless contempt for the individual, for mass democratic movements, as well as the affirmation of the necessity of a providential man – this is what characterizes A. C. Cuza, Octavian Goga, Mihail Manoilescu, Nichifor Crainic, as well as a whole series of legionary journalists and others.

The division of society into three classes (ruling, middle, and rural) and the recognition of the social role of each one among them, do not seem to mark A. C. Cuza as a theoretician of elites. But his precocious racism, the way he conceived, organized, and ran the L.A.N.C., the maintaining of his own cult, the amendments he wished to bring to the bourgeois constitution, do place him among the spokesmen for the fascist theory of elites.

Just like Octavian Goga,[35] who raised the "need for authority" to the level of the pregnant characteristic of the Rumanian soul, Mihail Manoilescu also sang the praises of the fascist elites and leaders. He was convinced that the fascist movements "have succeeded in creating a ruling elite that has not been transformed into a ruling class and that . . . revives the ancient institution of the chivalric or monastic order, drawing it from the idea of a State as a disinterested instrument in the service of the collectivity."[36] The fascist party, Manoilescu continues, "represents an order and an army. It is an order by its faith, and an army by the unlimited rights that it has over man."[37]

Thus we should keep in mind the theme of an ascetical elite, an originally medieval theme that will also return in the writings of other Ruman fascist theoreticians. The desire to return to certain medieval social structures, to the "natural elites," is likewise confirmed by the following claim of Manoilescu: "Since the role of the boyars has been minimized, one might say that the art of commanding as a natural, spontaneous, and almost unconscious attribute of the soul has disappeared."[38] Consequently, "the quality of leadership is not the result of accumulating certain merits, one is a leader because one is a leader."[39] At the risk of destroying the consistency he usually displayed, Manoilescu did not want the authority of the supreme fascist chief to be questioned or questionable. The leader was supposed to enjoy a maximal personal power. This vision of Manoilescu's with regard to the fascist hierarchy fits in perfectly with that of all the fascist theoreticians.

As for Nichifor Crainic, he initiated the cult of the elites and the supreme chief, which adulated in turn A. C. Cuza, Octavian Goga, Carol II, C. Z. Codreanu, Ion Antonescu, and . . . himself. The cult of the monarchy was imposed as a trait common to various Rumanian fascist ideologues. In that sense, Traian Braileanu stressed that "for the legionnaires, the monarch represents the supreme principle of order and the political hierarchy,[40] while Ilie Radulescu exclaimed: "Ah yes, we must have a Fuehrer. And this Fuehrer can only be the king."[41] Radu Gyr[42] and Nicolae Crevedia[43] also supported the fascist cult of the monarchy. This cult had to be maintained because, from the perspective of the Ruman fascists, the monarchy represented a crowning of the elite: "At the head of the nations, above the elites we find the monarchy."[44]

The legionary theory of the elites was based in principle on the notions of order, discipline, and hierarchy, on absolute submission to the chief, as well as on a boundless contempt for the masses. As in the case of the other fascist movements, one of the sources of this theory lay in the militarist spirit. On this score, C. Z. Codreanu mentioned the years he spent in the military lycee "Manastirea Dealului": "The order, the discipline, the hierarchy inculcated into my blood at a tender age, constituted, alongside the feeling of soliderly dignity, the guideline for my whole existence."[45] Codreanu declared that a nation cannot be run by itself, it must follow the direction laid out for it by its elite: ". . . The opinions of the crowd proved to be the most capricious and the most unstable."[46] Considering the so-called caprices of the people, they ought not to have the right to choose their elite because "soldiers don't choose their best general either."[47]

"At first it was the Phanariots who gradually replaced the aristocracy of blood with a false ruling aristocracy, liberal in politics. They let the kikes invade our country, becoming the tools of the Freemason organization, which has its headquarters in England. *The legionary revolution, a revolution of racial elites* (my emphases), several times over millenial, of the Dacian nation, has aimed at uprooting all those noxious weeds from this country, like that king of our ancient times who destroyed the vine in order to fortify the combative virtues of the nation."[48]

Vasile Marin, another legionary leader, also insisted on the role of the Guard's elite, on its obligation not to leave the initiative in politics to the masses: "The initiative of the foundation of the new State, which the nation demands of us these days, cannot and must not be left to the care of the street. The masses are not in a position to participate in the movements to inaugurate a new order on their own initiative, but only by their conscious adherence. The masses have a role that is anything but dynamic in the currents of fundamental transformation. In what concerns us, the initiative must belong to the elite of our generation, to those few men who have been chosen on the strength of their bold character and their spirit of solidarity. The minority that has been selected and disciplined becomes the instrument for the concrete realization of all the aspirations that the masses, in their vague and confused way, have nourished."[49] In refusing the masses "any dynamic role," Marin was giving free sway to the legionnaires' desire to reduce them to mere tools to be manipulated.

By accepting the supposed distance separating the masses from the elites, the legionnaires went so far as to affirm the necessity of the existence of two cultures, one destined for the masses, the other for the elites.[50] Under the acknowledged influence of Vilfredo Pareto, Nicolae Rosu showed his contempt for the role of the masses and his cult of the elites, when he wrote in praise of the sum of the "hereditary and military virtues" of the old aristocracy: "The lower classes are by definition amorphous and diffuse,"[51] "the lower classes are incapable of leading, first of all because by their essence they do not have the virtues necessary to become a ruling force of good quality, and then because they are inclined, by the very laws of their nature, to amputate their biological substance by mixing with the upper classes. Blood circulates from the bottom up. The skeletal structure of societies depends upon the circulation of the elites."[52]

Traian Braileanu followed the same tack in recognizing still more explicitly the real role played by fascist social selection: "And so universal and individual suffrage does not solve the problem of selecting the political elite. The legionary movement, like fascism and national socialism, has solved that problem by virtue of an education corresponding to this goal.... By this system, we avoid the emergence of revolutionary currents, of groups of malcontents."[53] Three years later Braileanu presented the result of fascist "selection" as follows: "By their deeds and by their example, they have proved that they are destined forever to the role of rulers whom the people obey and follow, and whose right to rule is acknowledged without a murmur."[54]

In Braileanu's eyes this legionary "elite" has been called to replace the old Rumanian elite that had been "... in decline, was no longer capable of governing and leading the Rumanian community toward its historical destinies, an elite separated from the masses, corrupted and spiritually deformed by internationalist ideas, and serving the Jewish community. This elite then, was corrupted and sold to Freemasonry and Judaism...."[55]

Nicolae Patrascu provided explanations as to the methods of selection used within the legionary movement: "The selection of the legionary movement has taken place in combat, during the 15 years of persecution. It has developed naturally because the only ones engaged in this combat are those who had something to give. The virtuosi of the different professions do not belong to the elites."[56]

As a legionary theoretician of elites, Constantin Noica argued that, "Since within the Legion education has taken place through elites, it follows that the Rumanian world too will be transformed by the influence of the legionary elites that are already in existence or in the course of being born within its ranks."[57] Noica also provided statistics on the legionary elites, which "... will have to be so powerful that the Captain has forbidden their number to exceed 10,000."[58] Noica likewise insisted on the supposed asceticism of the legionary elites, while misogynistically excluding women from their ranks: "The Captain has always dreamed of an ascetical elite in his entourage. Every spiritual movement perfects itself along the lines of an ascetical elite. Is that a pitiless concept with regard to women? Possibly. But that is how the mind shows itself when it reaches the highest summit: without pity."[59]

According to C. Z. Codreanu, the legionary elite would have to show the following qualities: "purity of soul, capacity for work and creation, courage, ability to lead a hard life and engage in permanent combat against the shackless binding the nation, poverty, that is, voluntary renunciation of the accumulation of riches, belief in God, love."[60]

The theme of the ascetical elite with monkish and warlike qualities, return in an obsessive fashion in the texts of the legionnaires. Thus a legionary journalist arguing against Mihai Ralea, who opposed the fascist attacks on democracy, wrote that, "The political leaders of an authentic right wing regime will not be parasites and will not live on lies, on shameful complicity and Jewish publicity. On the contrary, they will be models of wisdom, of character, of abnegation and voluntary renunciation of earthly things for the moral transfiguration of their fellows and of their brothers who are less gifted than they in this aspect."[61] In the same spirit, a fascist journalist who exalted absolute submission toward the supreme chief, expressed himself this way: "Obedience is a law of the Captain . . . the legionnaires – monks of love for the fatherland – will not violate this law. The country needs submission, a monastic submission."[62]

As for Mircea Eliade, he defined in the clearest possible fashion the Legion's "new elites": "We are the fortunate contemporaries of the most significant transformation in the thousands of years of Rumanian history, i.e., the appearance of a new aristocracy . . . our old aristocracy, so attached to the soil and to peasant civilization . . . has been thrown into confusion by a whole series of hapless regimes . . . the new legionary aristocracy resurrects the Rumanian Middle Ages."[63] The legionary "elite" thus described itself as a new political class with totally different characteristics as compared with the "classic" capitalist elite. The legionary government, along with the Antonescu government, would demonstrate the falsity of such claims.

The legionary theory of elites did not limit itself to singing the praises of its own organization. It also proceeded to an unbounded adulation of its own leaders, trying to identify them with the aspirations of the Rumanian nation. As C. Z. Codreanu saw it, the head of the Legion had to have all the following qualities: "Let him be wise, gentle, joyful, just, courageous, and firm, let him take part in joys and pains, let him be skillful, let him give clear orders, let him not calumniate his comrades, let him maintain harmony, let him be polite, measured, let him keep his word, let him be honest, intrepid (the chief of the legionnaires is an intrepid man)."[64]

A man incarnating all these qualities looks more like a Renaissance ideal than the head of a criminal, terrorist, fascist organization. This is how Nae Ionescu explained the relationship between the leader and the masses within the fascist system: "In addition there must be a creative element in history that is neither the man against the masses (dictatorship) nor the masses against the man (the degenerate democracy of our times), but the man whom the masses have found. It is evident that a geometrical way of judging has a hard time getting used to such forms within the framework of which mystical (i.e., hidden) relations make and unmake the hazards. What sort of man is this? On this topic there is no room for guessing games. The man of the masses is the man who is. He whom the masses recognize as such. By what method do they recognize him? By their faith in him. There are also votes, of course . . . But beyond the votes, there is the act of faith, of faith and not of confidence."[65]

Ion Mota emphasizes that since the appearance of the Legion there was an indissoluble bond between the principle of the leader with an incontestable authority and the very existence of the Legion: "The organization cannot be born and develop in a healthy way without discipline, without a hierarchy, and above all without a leader. Thus our organization has a leader whom no one elected but who has the consent of all those who, drawn by a mysterious force, have come to set up, under the leader's direction, the ordered and disciplined cells of the organization. *Our* leader is Corneliu Zelea Codreanu."[66]

Later on Traian Herseni also insisted on this same idea when he wrote that "the legionary movement has a commandant who guarantees its unity and who leads it to victory. Deprived of its commandant the Movement would become an amorphous mass and would be lost in the immense mass of the country. It follows that the commandant represents the very principle of existence and action in the Movement. Without a commandant, the Movement would not be possible."[67]

The mystical obedience, the non-elective status of the legionary chief, like the obligation to absolute submission to him, were argued for by Herseni in the following manner: "The ruler is not the one nominated or elected but the one naturally recognized as such, by the position that he adopts all by himself with regard to the necessities of life and of the victory of the Movement. The rulers who have been selected in this way must be followed with unbounded devotion."[68]

During the selection of the supreme chief it was not an issue, practically speaking, of any selection but of the brutal intimidation not only of political adversaries, but also of one's own partisans. The latter were called upon to contribute to the cult of the supreme chief.

Many publications presented the legionary leaders as demigods. Mihai Manoilescu[69] compared Ion Mota to . . . Byron. Other texts praised Zizi Cantacuzino-Granicerul or Horia Sima, but most of them dealt with C. Z. Codreanu. P. P. Panaitescu described him as "the greatest prophet of our nation. Those who looked him at least once in the eye have felt, without knowing him, that he saw beyond the age,"[70] like a "founder of the country."[71] With respect to the same person, Traian Herseni affirmed that "hundreds and thousands of years have prepared his birth, other hundreds and thousands of years will be necessary for the accomplishment of his commandments, but the presence of the Captain in history constitutes, from now on, an unshakable guarantee that at the end of the path he is traversing will be found the eternal city of the redemption of the Rumanians."[72]

Dozens of numbers from the legionary press presented immense photographs of Codreanu taken in different poses (giving speeches, visiting work camps, skiing with General Antonescu, etc.). In the eyes of his disciples he passed for "a hero, in both the legendary and the historical sense of the term. Wisdom and courage, dream and empiricism, power and corporal beauty of a demigod, evangelical simplicity and clarity, and above all, a serene radiation from his marble forehead and his burning look in those moments that were dangerous to the soul, the past, and the land of Rumania."[73]

Nicolae Crevedia likewise associated himself with this excessive praise: "Nevertheless, it is still true that everything that is newest in the ideas and organization of this mission is due to the Captain of the Legion, Corneliu Zelea Codreanu, to that man of fire who, by the example of his very life, which is made up of virility, faith, and sacrifice, has managed to make us believe that this Nation has not disappeared."[74] The cult offered to Codreanu was maintained even after his death, taking on a powerful mystical coloring.

General Antonescu should not be forgotten either. He was not overly afflicted by modesty, and presided himself over the cult of his own person. In the eyes of his adulators, the general was identified "with the ideals of the Rumanian people to the point of total fusion . . . truly (representing) the soul of the Rumanian Nation."[75]

The same sources that presented the man who was leading Rumania into disaster as a "genius, an eminent man with noble principles, just, honest, a remarkable creator, capable of a penetrating comprehension of history,"[76] also took him for the founder of a new epoch: "a man with an energetic character, an iron will, animated by the most ardent nationalism and patriotism, a noble mind, dominated by the sense of justice, the fundamental law of his life, correct, honest, and magnanimous, the Leader lays the foundations of a new epoch of our history."[77]

III Mysticism

"Fascism prefers to stir up faith rather than to address itself to the intelligence."[78] It is true that fascism strove to win faithful, submissive followers, ready to carry out any order from above, and this by appealing to pagan or Christian mysticism, to the cult of the providential leader, of youth, of the old warrior or else to the glorification of instinct. Writers who have analyzed the problem of fascist mysticism, such as Franz Neumann, Daniel Guerin, Serge Tchakhotin have shown many points of similarity between the mysticism of Italian or Nazi fascism and the mysticism of the Church. As for Rumania, there is no need to prove this, given the fact that the legionnaires incorporated orthodox mysticism into their doctrine. As the continuation of the link-up between fascist ideology and orthodox mysticism, Rumanian fascism and in particular the legionary movement used a series of rites that took the form of collective prayers, chants, processions, etc. in order to channel the states of soul of the members or sympathizers of the organization into the direction that the leaders wanted. The color contrasts, the lights and darks used during the legionary ceremonies, were also intended to induce a state of mystical receptivity into the mass of adherents.

"God is a fascist!"[79] This cry of the legionary journalist, I. P. Prundeni, succinctly captures the place of mysticism as a distinctive quality of Rumanian fascism. Like all fascist movements, the Legion addressed faith rather than reason, employing an intentionally vague and grandiloquent mystique as a bond between the most different sorts of men. As I have emphasized, legionary mysticism took on an orthodox shading, not a pagan one, as in the case of Nazism. Legionary mysticism, which presupposed "the insertion of Orthodox Christianity into the movement's political doctrine,"[80] represented, according to Lucretiu Patrascanu, a specific trait of the Iron Guard.

Thus the legionary movement is one of the rare modern European political movements with a religious structure. Legionary mysticism did not set itself up as an orthodox mysticism in the pure state. On the contrary, the latter underwent alterations owing to the attempts to canonize certain saints chosen from among the "legionary martyrs," to the intense cult of death, of instinct, of the providential leader, along the lines of the creation of the myth of youth and of the old warriors. Of all these cults that of death served especially for the psychological formation of the executors of the policy of physical liquidation for the Legion's adversaries.

This brings us to what Lucretiu Patrascanu called the mystico-criminal aspect of the Guard's ideology. Patrascanu also stressed that the symbiosis between the legionary movement and orthodoxy was simply the subordination of certain religious elements to the commandments of politics: "The incorporation and subordination of orthodoxy to political ends pursued by the Legionary movement are more specific to the Iron Guard than the recognition of a Christian spirituality as a behavioral norm or a source of ethical and social directives."[81] With an eye toward winning over the rural population, which made up the majority in Rumania and within which religious beliefs were the strongest, the legionnaires made use of the "core of primitivism, the lack of culture, and the superstitions with which the Rumanian peasantry was imbued."[82]

While mysticism was zealously propagated by the State the legionnaires had recourse to forms of religious propaganda that were even more fanatical. The legionnaires went around the villages, organized special masses, kissed the soil, filled little bags with earth and hung them around their necks, asked the peasants to swear fidelity to them, but they profited especially from miracles, such as the one in Maglavit. In 1935 Petrache Lupu, "a wealthy syphilitic ... tongue-tied and a cretin ... weak in the head"[83] saw ... God. As a result, "tens of thousands of peasants from the most remote corners of the country and thousands of people from the city took the road to Maglavit to see and hear Petrache Lupu ... A wave of religious exaltation swept over the whole country, from one end to the other."[84] That same year a fascist newspaper spoke of a visionary from the shores of Lake Herastrau: "Maria Rusu spoke five times to the Holy Virgin. The first sick persons to be cured sleep by the side of the lake and pray every day ... The crowd drinks the water ... the women was with blessed water from the lake."[85] Such sensational events were heavily exploited by the legionnaires and their supporters, among whom Nichifor Crainic and partisans of Cuza such as Nicolae Crevedia were conspicuous.

In 1935 Crevedia told how he had suffered from uncontrollable blinking and how Petrache Lupu cured him.[86] A year later Dan Botta "explained" that "What happens in Maglavit sheds light on the irresistible desire for the ideal, for abnegation, for self-renunciation, the belief in the value of the human soul, the infinite fear of losing it in the vicissitudes that all the Rumanian people confront at this moment."[87] Nichifor Crainic, considered by some of his fascist confreres the author of the new saint's birth certificate – "Petrache Lupu now has a birth certificate, furnished by Nichifor Crainic"[88] – said of him: "This shepherd, gentle as a child ... his solution was simple and practical ... His good sense is faultless."[89] Even much later, in April 1941, the newspaper *Sfarma Pistra* was still talking about the "genius of Petrache Lupu."

The legionary movement used for its propaganda a part of the Orthodox clergy that was devoted to it. This became evident at the burial of Mota and Marin, as well as when the legionaries and General Antonescu, their ally, took power: "... During the first days of his ascent to power the general made extensive use of the Church in order to impose upon public opinion and especially on the lower strata of the population. Some of his appeals and convocations were ostentatiously broadcast through the churches, publicly read by the priests ..."[90]

The fact that some priests lent their support to the legionary movement also emerges from a book by Ilie Imbrescu entitled *Biserica si miscarea legionara* ("The Church and the Legionary Movement"), where he maintains: "A true priest will therefore be a legionnaire by the nature of things, just as a legionnaire will be in his turn, and again by the nature of things, a legionnaire, the best son of the Church."[91] At the same time the amount of support given the legionary movement by some of the orthodox clergy must not be overestimated, "For Codreanu himself who was closer to the Church than the other founders of the fascist movements, and whose ideas were greatly valued by the orthodox Rumanian traditionalists, bitterly complained that the immense majority of the priests had been hostile to the Iron Guard."[92] But we should also recall that in the elections of 1937 of 103 candidates from the "All For the Country" Party, 33 were priests.

The immense efforts at religious propaganda made by the legionnaires, the torrents of ink they spilled, the symbolic white horses, the masses in the street, ceremonies that tens of thousands of people participated in, did not enjoy the expected success, perhaps because, among other reasons, Eastern Orthodoxy, unlike other Christian or non-Christian religions, was impregnated by a more tolerant spirit, which was incompatible with the fanaticism of the legionnaires.

The legionary movement was at first called "The Legion of the Archangel Michael," precisely to justify its religious legitimacy. According to Nae Ionescu, the Legion never made mistakes: "The victory of the Legion advances as a necessity of Destiny," and this because it is "under the sign of the archangel."[93] The idea of the predestined character of the legionary movement can be seen in the remarks of Ion Veverca, who wrote: "We are going to overcome, not because we dominate life by our youth and our will, but because we are predestined,"[94] or in the writings of Ion Foti, who declared that, "The idea of the Legion constitutes our sole hope of salvation and our unshakable belief in a better world."[95]

Foti also spoke about the role played by mystique in the actions of the legionnaires: "By its beneficient mystique, by the triumph of the supreme faith of the Cross, by the rebirth of piety in souls, of the desire for sacrifice, of the will to illuminate the spirit beneath the heavenly banner of the Archangel Michael, God's envoy to earth, the Iron Guard, leads our race toward new destinies. It leads it not only to redemption but it makes it rediscover the great path of magnificent national and cultural achievements."[96]

Embracing the same type of "arguments" favorable to the Legion, Ion Gavanescu claimed that its guiding principle was "... the force containing animal impulses, the force of elevation, thanks to sacrifice, up to the ideal of divine Justice, which attains its apogee by the luminous love of the Nation, a concrete form of love for God."[97]

Mircea Eliade described "the legionary ideal (as) a rude Christian spirituality,"[98] while stressing the place of mystique in the legionary ideology. "Our commentary on the legionary oath tries to shed light on the Christian structure of the life of Rumanian youth today. A terrible Christian will dominates the soul of the young elites nowadays. This mystique is not new. . . ."[99]

According to P. P. Panaitescu, "the legionary movement signifies in itself a religious resurrection of the nation both by the moral purification of man and by putting faith back in the place that it merits."[100] Mihail Polihroniade, less exalted and more lucid, explained exactly what the efficiency of the mystical legionary propaganda consisted in: "Let us point out that it is capable of manipulating with a formidable master hand the elements that touch the masses, the skillfully composed and broadcast popular songs, the impressive marches, the theatrical but impressive cavalcades, a whole cortege of means that induce a quasi-religious impression in the masses, and are not limited to repeating the borrowed tactical cliches, but are adapted to Rumanian conditions."[101]

Among the legionnaires there were also individuals who could be characterized as great mystics, in the eyes of whom the orthodox religion was capable of exploiting all the features of the legionary movement. One example of this kind was furnished by Ion Mota, who justified C. Z. Codreanu's position as leader by citing "divine" reasons: "Thus we wish to found (and by the grace of God we shall found) a cell gleaming with light that will act, that is, will illuminate and so bring salvation. We are not creators of light. That belongs only to God. . . . This little house naturally constitutes a system. At present it is already built. And every living system is moved by a force. In the system of human societies force is acquired only by movement. Thus our system must have an organization, and it has one already. But the organization will certainly not manage to be born in a healthy manner without a hierarchy, without a director. That is why our organization has a chief whom no one elected, but to whom all those who have been drawn by a mysterious force have consented, those who have come to found, under the direction of a chief, the ordered and disciplined cells of our organization. *Our* chief is named Corneliu Zelia Codreanu."[102]

The cell or little house, therefore, represents, the legionary organization that will be built but . . . that already exists! Then, the cell becomes . . . an individual drawn by a secret force that accepts the authority of Codreanu. This sort of incoherent considerations were used to justify the structure of the Legion. From Mota's perspective the Legion was not a political, but a religious, organization: "We don't do politics and at no time have we done politics. . . . We have a religion, we are the slaves of faith. Its flame consumes us."[103]

Another zealot for the legionary mystique was Constantin Noica. In his eyes the soul of the Rumanian nation was represented by . . . the legionary movement: "He who does not believe that nations too have a soul, does not see, does not touch this extraordinary beginning that constitutes the legionary movement."[104] For those who allowed themselves to have doubts Noica pointed out during the first days of the legionary-Antonescu dictatorship: "You are not permitted to doubt. Believe in the resurrection of legendary Rumania."[105]

According to Noica, Nae Ionescu was "the man who had paid so that God and Life might descend upon our nation,"[106] and Codreanu was a reincarnation of Joan of Arc.[107] Even the insignificant intriguer, Horia Sima, took on special virtues in Noica's eyes: "At this moment when the divine breath is upon us, Horia Sima does not demand taxes on salaries, he gets souls moving."[108]

Similarly, Noica claimed that the Legion, through "the sufferings it has endured, has stirred up, for two and a half years now, in every pure conscience in the country, a feeling of shame for not being in prison."[109] And further on: "There is something incorruptible in the Legion's heritage that has brought to our nation for today or for tomorrow the gift of the marvelous story: perpetual youth."[110] Constantin Noica judged that the Legion was "... in perpetual crisis and suffering,"[111] since it was not contemporary with society owing to its supposed qualities.

Just as with other fascist journalists, the legionnaires' cult of the dead occupied a privileged place in Noica's writings: "And what if one night the 47 legionnaires who have fallen should rise from their tombs to embark on a terrible voyage?"[112] he wondered – and he found the answer in Mota's prophecy: "The day of the terrifying domination of the ghosts approaches."[113] Referring to the legionary dead, Noica cried out: How great ought the value of the dead to have been, so that the arm of the living should still take action."[114] In his eyes legionary Rumania represented a Rumania . . . of the spirit: "You do not see that it is also a question of a Rumania of the spirit, a Rumania of the spirit before all things!"[115]

Mircea Eliade also believed that "the ghosts of Ion Mota are going to reign for a time," until Rumanians "make a country like the worthy sun of the sky,"[116] the latter formula being a very familiar watchword of the Legion.

The theme of "spirit" similarly recurs in Traian Herseni, who argued that, "The spirit of the Captain leads the nation to victory."[117] The cult of the dead, common to several fascist movements, occupied a privileged position in the legionary mystique. Another example of this is the opinion of Mircea Vulcanescu: "However tragic and paradoxical it may appear, it must be acknowledged that the prospect of war is what gives the young people a certain hope in life. . . . And even if the "prudent" should cry out, lifting their arms to heaven, 'We don't want to die!' todays youth hopes to be able to sacrifice something itself, at least by death, to be able to find at last its own face, which cannot be found elsewhere."[118]

Envisaging the legionary cult of death as inspired by the Nazis, Lucretiu Patrascanu provides us with several instances in his book, *Sub trei dictaturis*: "The legionnaire loves death, because his blood will serve to prepare the bond of union for legionary Rumania, thus he who renounces tombs renounces the resurrection: . . . Death is the only means capable of ennobling poor human turpitude: I preach the voice of love in order to develop your taste for eternity."[119] Along the same lines of the legionary cult of death were the songs of the Iron Guard, where death was known as an end in itself or else as a sign of absolute obedience to the Captain: "Death, only death in the Legion/Is the dearest wedding of all/If we all fail, struck in the forehead/We love death for the Captain"[120] or else: "We form part of the Death Squad: From Moldavia we come today/The die of death is cast/It is conquer or die. . . . Alongside the Captain/We shall sacrifice ourselves with joy/On the bodies of the enemy/We shall build a new country."[121]

Often it is rather hard to distinguish, within the framework of legionary ideology, between the cult of the supreme leader (and his kindred) and mysticism. In this vein there was a significant attempt made to complete the orthodox calendar by adding new legionary "saints" or "prophets." As if to contradict Emil Cioran, who affirmed that "Rumania is a country without prophets,"[122] P. P. Panaitescu wrote: "The greatest prophet of the nation, however, has been the Captain."[123]

Alexandre Cantacuzino judged that "The nation that gave birth to Ionel Mota and Vasile Marin will be the elect of God for a noble and imperial mission in the world of men."[124] In the eyes of Traian Braileanu the same two men were "the conquerors of death (who) today hold between their hands the destinies of the Rumanian nation."[125] With regard to the arguments for raising Mota and Marin to the rank of martyrs and saints of the nation, Mircea Eliade came straight out and called the death of the two legionnaires the birth of a Christian revolution: "Those who had dedicated their youth to the Legion, i.e., to prisons and persecution, did not hesitate to sacrifice their life in order to hasten the redemption of the whole nation. This death has borne fruit. It has set the seal on the meaning of life and of creation for our generation. The climate of the spirit against the climate of the temporal, in which the preceding generations have believed. And they have indicated to us what remained to be made of this ephemeral human life. A Christian revolution."[126]

Mircea Eliade likewise denied the political nature of the legionary movement, while claiming that "the legionary movement has a spiritual and Christian meaning. If all the contemporary revolutions have as their goal the conquest of power by a social class or by a man, the legionary revolution aims, on the contrary, at the supreme redemption of the nation, the reconciliation of the Rumanian nation with God, as the Captain said. That is why the legionary movement has a different meaning with regard to everything that has been done up till now in history; and the victory of the Legion will lead not only to the restoration of the virtues of our nation, of a hardworking Rumania, worthy and powerful, but also to the birth of a man who is in harmony with the new kind of European life."[127] While emphasizing the "spiritual force" of the Legion, Eliade wrote: "The tide of love that the legionnaires pour out is so strong that it would suffice to make us hope for the triumph of the legionary movement."[128] Praising the "legionary spirituality," which he claimed was separate from the terrestrial world of politics, Eliade thought that, "he who does not doubt the destiny of our nation cannot doubt the victory of the legionary movement either"[129] and hence believed in the triumph of the legionary movement: "I believe in the victory of the legionary movement because I believe in freedom, in the force of the soul as opposed to biological and economic determinism."[130]

Eliade was impressed by the idea of Codreanu's wishing to mediate between Rumania and God: "A political leader of youth said that the goal of his movement was 'to reconcile Rumania with God.' Here was a messianic formula that did not appeal to the class struggle, nor to political interests, nor to economic interest, nor the bestial instinct in man."[131] This interview with Eliade did not go unnoticed by the top men in the Legion. During his trial, Codreanu mentioned it as eloquent proof of the specific nature of the legionary movement, stressing the exemplary fashion in which Eliade had distinguished between the legionary movement, founded on "The Grace of God," Italian fascism, and national socialism.

Codreanu also focussed on "the New Legionary Man," whom Eliade loaded with praise.[132] In an article with the same title, "De ce cred in biruinta miscarii legionare" ("Why I Believe in the Victory of the Legionary Movement") another famous intellectual, Sextil Puscariu, noted: "The sympathy that I felt for the legionnaires has grown since I became aware of their profound and sincere religious faith. I began to love the legionnaires from the moment that I read the Captain's book, a moving epic on the most humiliating persecution, a work guided by the most pure idealism."[133]

One should keep in mind the idea of death "bearing fruit," giving a meaning to life, because it marked a whole generation of the Legion. In accordance with the legionary thinking, by dying in Spain Mota and Marin became no less than ... archangels: "Vasile Marin, the Archangel of Christ"[134] or "The bolshevik demon has torn two archangels from us."[135] Along the same lines of inciting to the legionary "sacrifice," a necessary condition for taking up a place among the new "archangels," Nicolae Crevedia also attracted notice, writing by way of exhortation, "Legionnaires, at the right side of the Captain two shirts have been left free. The men who once wore them have raised themselves by the spirit into the Pantheon ever more crowded with the heroes of the Legion. Each one of you can put on these two shirts belonging to the iron phalanx of the Rumania of tomorrow. Under only one condition: dying."[136]

Many Legion songs reflected the efforts to canonize the legendary dead: "Wearing his fur cap/Decked with silver, which suits him so well / There is my little Captain/So handsome, from the icon of yesteryear."[137] Other songs express the legionary notion that "the dead are the living,"[138] as a text by Radu Gyr shows: "... So many dead, so many dear tombs/By their souls come to us from the gardens/And kiss our burning foreheads/Like an evening wind scented with lily/ . . . / We forge a destiny, a mountain of holy walls/We build with the help not of lime but of stone/And we make roughcast with the bones of the dead/We build with the bricks of wounds."[139] The same idea is presented by Horatiu Comaniciu, who writes: "And above our heads, from the Dniester to the Tisza our Captain passes in flight. Tears of joy gleam in his steely eyes, while his holy lips murmur all atremble: the Fatherland! the Fatherland! the Fatherland!"[140]

Despite its pronounced orthodox character, legionary mysticism did not simply mean the total assimilation of orthodox theology by a fascist political movement, but on the contrary an attempt at subordinating and transforming that theology into a political instrument. By an abusive extrapolation all the Legion's adversaries became at the same time adversaries of the Church, Christ, God, etc.[141]

The legionnaires took the mystique of orthodoxy for a fundamental element of the historical continuity of the Rumanian people"[142] and notably for an efficient means of propaganda. Dumitru Micu claimed with regard to Nichifor Crainic that he "was not expressly aiming for theoretical clarifications but he wanted to justify his political activity on the level of thought. Everything that fit in with such politics . . . was used to meet the needs of strategy and tactics . . ."[143]

This is also perfectly valid for the Legion's propagandists and for their relations with the mystique of orthodoxy. First of all, the people involved were politicians, and not theologians, despite their much-flaunted mysticism. These remarks remain equally valid for the partisans of A. C. Cuza: ". . . since the league of Cuza's followers used the same propaganda methods as the Iron Guard,"[144] even though those methods were never as widely employed as the Legion's propaganda.

Notes

1 Andreas Hillgruber, *Hitler, Regele Carol is Maresalul Antonescu, relatiile germano-romane (1938–1944)*, tr. from the German (Bucharest, 1971), p. 34.
2 Ernst Nolte, *Les mouvements fascistes* (Paris: Calmann-Levy), pp. 241–242.
3 Mihai Sturdza, *Romania si sfirsitul Europei. Aminturi din tare pierduta* (Rio de Janeiro, Madrid: Ed. Dacio 1966), p. 222.
4 Ibid., p. 44.
5 P. Georgescu Delafras, *Problema evreiasca in Romania, Cum poate fi ea definitiv rezolvata* (Bucharest: Ed. Cugetarea, 1940), p. 16.
6 Ibid., p. 23.
7 Ibid., p. 12.
8 Ibid., p. 23.
9 Ilie Radulescu, in *Porunca Vremii*, July 4, 1941.
10 "Ziaristii fascisti in fata Tribunaleului Suprem," in *Scinteia*, June 2, 1945.
11 Ibid.
12 Nicolae Bogdan, "Problemele demografice ale rasei albe," in *Porunca Vremii*, May 12, 1935.

13 Ion Foti, *Conceptia eroica asupra rasei* (Bucharest: Biblioteca eroica "Generatia noua," 1936), p. 133.
14 Ibid., pp. 153–155.
15 Nicolae Rosu, "De ce cred in biruinta miscarii legionare," in *Buna Vestire*, December 11, 1937.
16 Dan Botta in *Sfarma Piatra*, No. 31, 1936.
17 Nicolae Rosu, "Biologia culturii," in *Cuvintul*, January 10, 1941.
18 Traian Braileanu, *Sociologia si arta guvernarii politice* (Cernauti: Editura "Insennari Sociologice," 1937), p. 82.
19 Ibid., p. 67.
20 Mihail Polihroniade, "National-socialismul si problemajidoveasca," in *Buna Vestire*, February 11, 1938.
21 Prof. Alexandru Razmerita, *Cum sa ne aparam de evrei, Un plan de eliminare totala* (Turnu Severin: Tipografia Minerva, 1938), pp. 65–69.
22 Mihail Polihroniade, op. cit.
23 Traian Herseni, "Mitul singelui," in *Cuvintul*, November 23, 1940.
24 Traian Herseni, "Rasa si destin national," in *Cuvintul*, January 16, 1941.
25 Ibid.
26 Ibid.
27 Traian Herseni, "Mitul singelui."
28 Traian Herseni, "Rasa si destin national."
29 P. Tiparescu, *Rasa si degenerare* (Bucharest: Tipografia Bucovina, I. R. Toroutiu, 1941), p. 8.
30 Ibid., p. 49.
31 Alexandru Randa, *Rasism romanesc* (Bucharest: Ed. Bucovina, I. E. Toroutiu, 1941), p. 6.
32 Ibid., p. 17.
33 Max Horkheimer, *Eclipse de la raison* (Paris: Payot, 1974), p. 184.
34 C. Z. Codreanu, *Carticica sefului de cuib*, 5th ed. (Bucharest, 1937), pp. 29–30.
35 Octavian Goga, in *Porunca Vremii*, October 1, 1933.
36 Mihail Manoilescu, *Revolutia nationala, sensul ei antiburghez* (Bucharest: Tipografia ziarului "Universul," n.d.), p. 10.
37 Mihail Manoilescu, *Partidul unic* (Bucharest: Ed. Cartea Romanesca, 1937), p. 50.
38 Mihail Manoilescu, *Revolutia nationala, sensul ei antiburghez*, p. 24.
39 Mihail Manoilescu, *Partidul unic*, p. 205.
40 Traian Braileanu, "Legiunea si Parlamentul," in *Buna Vestire*, January 1, 1938.
41 Ilie Radulescu, "Avem un Fuhrer," in *Porunca Vremii*, October 3, 1935.
42 Radu Gyr, "Biruinta huliganilor," in *Sfarma Piatra*, June 30, 1940 and "Calatoria regelui," in *Porunca Vremii*, July 4, 1937.
43 Nicolae Crevedia, "Mihai I Fat-Frumos de Alba Iulia," in *Porunca Vremii*, November 9, 1936, and "Ecuata internationala pe care o rezolva regele," in *Porunca Vremii*, July 4, 1937.
44 C. Z. Codreanu, *Pentru legionari* (Sibiu: Ed. Total pentru tara, 1936), p. 426.
45 Ibid., p. 11.
46 Ibid., pp. 413–414.
47 Ibid., p. 416.
48 Horia Stamatu, "Pozitia noastra," in *Buna Vestire*, January 22, 1941.
49 Vasile Marin, *Crez de generatie* (Bucharest: Cartea Romanesca, 3rd edition, 1940), p. 21.
50 P. P. Panaitescu, "Profetii neamului," in *Cuvintul*, December 1, 1940.
51 Nicolae Rosu, *Dialectica nationalismului*, p. 318.

52 Ibid., p. 322.
53 Traian Braileanu, "Legiunea si Parlamentul."
54 Traian Braileanu, "Problema elitelor in statul national-legionar," in *Universul*, January 11, 1941.
55 Ibid.
56 Nicolae Patrascu, "Pozitia nelegionarilor fata de miscarea legionara," in *Universul*, January 16, 1941.
57 Constantin Noica, "10.001," in *Buna Vestire*, September 20, 1940.
58 Ibid.
59 Constantin Noica, "Electra sau femeia legionara," in *Buna Vestire*, October 9, 1940.
60 C. Z. Codreanu, *Pentru legionari*, p. 420.
61 Anonymous, "Doctrina stingei," in *Porunca Vremii*, September 14, 1935.
62 G. Racoveanu, "Ascultarea, lege a Capitanului," in *Cuvintul*, December 4, 1940.
63 Mircea Eliade, "Noua aristocratie legionara," in *Vremea*, January 23, 1938.
64 C. Z. Codreanu, *Carticica sefului de cuib*, p. 28.
65 Nae Ionescu in *Cuvintul*, January 27, 1938.
66 Ion I. Mota, *Pamintul stramosesc* (Jassy: August 1927).
67 Traian Herseni, "Noua rinduiala a tarii," in *Cuvintul*, Friday, December 20, 1940.
68 Traian Herseni, "Tilcul disciplinei legionare," in *Cuvintul*, December 30, 1940.
69 Mihail Manoilescu, "De la Lord Byron la Ion Mota," in *Buna Vestire*, February 24, 1937.
70 P. P. Panaitescu, "Profetti neamului," in *Cuvintul*, December 1, 1940.
71 P. P. Panaitescu, "Descalecator de tara," in *Buna Vestire*, September 14, 1940.
72 Traian Herseni, "Duhul Capitanului," in *Cuvintul*, December 5, 1940.
73 Mihai Sturdza, *Romania si sfirsitul Europei*, p. 99.
74 Nicolae Crevedia, "Zece ani de legionarism," in *Porunca Vremii*, June 9, 1937.
75 I. Popa, *Geniul si personalitatea Maresalului Antonescu, conducatorul Statului roman* (Bucharest: no publisher given, 1943), p. 13.
76 Ibid., pp. 93–95.
77 Ibid., p. 14.
78 Daniel Guerin, *Fascisme et grand capital* (Paris: Ed. Maspero, 1971), vol. II, p. 63.
79 I. P. Prundeni, "Dumnezu e fascist," in *Porunca Vremii*, July 20, 1937.
80 Lucretiu Patrascanu, *Problemele de baza ale Romaniei* (Bucharest: Editura Socec, 1945), p. 242.
81 Ibid., p. 243.
82 Ibid., p. 242.
83 Lucretiu Patrascanu, *Sub trei dictaturi* (Bucharest: Editura Politica, 1970), p. 51.
84 Ibid., p. 50.
85 "Sfinta de la Herastrau," in *Porunca Vremii*, September 27 and October 1, 1935.
86 Nicolae Crevedia, "Maglavit," in *Porunca Vremii*, August 2, 1935.
87 Dan Botta in *Sfarma Piatra*, Year II, No. 8, 1936.
88 *Sfarma Piatra*, February 27, 1937.
89 Nichifor Crainic, "Vizita la Maglavit," in *Sfarma Piatra*, Year I, Nr. 8, 1936.
90 A. Simion, *Regimul politic din Romania in perioada septembrie 1940-ianuarie 1941* (Cluj-Napoca: Ed. Dacia, 1976), p. 48.
91 Ilie Imbrescu, *Biserica si miscrea legionara* (Bucharest: Editura Cartea Romaneasca, 1939), p. 201.
92 Ernst Nolte, *Le fascisme dans son epoque* (Paris: Juillard, 1970), p. 60.
93 Nae Ionescu, "Sub semnul Arhanghelului," in *Buna Vestire*, June 27, 1937.

94 Ion Veverca, *Suflet si gind legionar*, ed. by Serviciul propagandei legionare, Bucharest, 1937–1940, p. 29.
95 Ion Foti, *Conceptia eroica asupra rasei*, p. 167.
96 Ibid., p. 163.
97 Ion Gavanescu in *Buna Vestire*, September 12, 1940.
98 Mircea Eliade, "Provincia si legionarismul," *Vremea*, 13, February 1938.
99 Mircea Eliade, "De unde incepe misiunea Romaniei," *Vremea*, 28, February 1937.
100 P. P. Panaitescu, "Nae Ionescu si Universitatea din Bucuresti," in *Cuvintul*, December 7, 1940.
101 Mihail Polihroniade, "Garda de Fier," in *Calendarul*, November 17, 1932, reproduced in *Pamintul stramosesc*, January 1, 1933.
102 Ion Mota, *Cranii de lemn, articole, 1922–1936* (Sibiu: Editura "Totul pentru tara," 1936), p. 53.
103 Ibid., p. 57.
104 Constantin Noica, "Sufletul cetatii," in *Buna Vestire*, September 24, 1940.
105 Constantin Noica, "Crede," in *Buna Vestire*, September 8, 1940.
106 Constantin Noica, in *Buna Vestire*, September 21, 1940.
107 Constantin Noica, "Procesul Ionaei d'Arc," in *Buna Vestire*, September 26, 1940.
108 Constantin Noica, "Sinteti sub har," in *Buna Vestire*, October 4, 1940.
109 Constantin Noica, "Esti necinstit sufleteste," in *Buna Vestire*, 11 September 11, 1940.
110 Constantin Noica, ". . . Si viata fara de moarte," in *Buna Vestire*, September 11, 1940.
111 Constantin Noica, "Nu sintem contemporani," in *Buna Vestire*, September 26, 1940.
112 Constantin Noica, "Cumplita lor calatorie," in *Buna Vestire*, September 12, 1940.
113 Ibid.
114 Constantin Noica, "Fiti infricaosatori de buni," in *Buna Vestire*, September 10, 1940.
115 Ibid.
116 Mircea Eliade, "Strigoii," in *Cuvintul*, January 21, 1938.
117 Traian Herseni, "Duhul Capitanului," in *Cuvintul*, September 1940.
118 Mircea Vulcanescu, Mihail Manoilescu, *Tendintele tinerei generatii-doua conferinte* (Bucharest: Tipografia ziarului "Universul," 1934), p. 21.
119 Lucretiu Patrascanu, *Sub trei dictaturi*, p. 56.
120 "Sfinta tinerete legionara," in *Buna Vestire*, February 8, 1938.
121 Nic. Iancu, "Marsul legionarilor din echip Mortii," in *Cintece legionare*, p. 9.
122 Emil Cioran, *Schimbarea la fata a Romaniei* (Bucharest: Ed. "Vremea," 1941), p. 8.
123 P. P. Panaitescu, "Profetii neamului," in op. cit.
124 Alexandru Cantacuzino, *Pentru Cristos* (Bucharest: publisher not given, 1937).
125 Traian Braileanu in *Buna Vestire*, January 14, 1938, p. 29.
126 Mircea Eliade in *Buna Vestire*, January 14, 1938.
127 Ibid.
128 Mircea Eliade, "De ce cred in biruinta miscarii legionare," *Buna Vestire*, December 17, 1937.
129 Ibid.
130 Ibid.
131 Mircea Eliade, "Un popor fara misiune," *Vremea*, December 1, 1935. See also, "Cele doua Romanii," *Vremea*, October 4, 1936.
132 *Adevarul in procesul C. Z. Codreanu*, May 1938, Serviciul de propaganda legionara, p. 73.

133 Sextil Puscariu, "De ce cred in biruinta miscarii legionare," in *Buna Vestire*, December 7, 1937.
134 "Vasile Marin, arhanghel al lui Hristos," in *Porunca Vremii*, January 25, 1937.
135 Ilie Radulescu, "Editorial," in *Porunca Vremii*, January 17, 1937.
136 Nicolae Crevedia, "Morti pentru Hristos si latinitate," in *Porunca Vremii*, January 17, 1937.
137 "Visul unui legionar," in *Cintece legionare*, p. 20.
138 *Cuvintul*, December 19, 1940.
139 Radu Gyr, "Atitia morti, atitea oseminte," in *Buna Vestire*, February 19, 1938.
140 Horatiu Comaniciu, "Se reface sufletul tarii," in *Buna Vestire*, September 18, 1940.
141 See Nichifor Crainic, *Ortodoxia, conceptia noastra de viata* (Sibiu: T.T.S., 1937), and Alexandru Cantacuzino, *Intre lumea legionara si lumea comunista*, Serviciul de propaganda legionara, 2nd ed., Bucharest, 1940.
142 Vasile Marin, *Crez de generatie*, p. 158.
143 Dumitru Micu, *Gindirea si gindirismul* (Bucharest: Editura Politica, 1975), p. 232.
144 Lucretiu Patrascanu, *Sub trei dictaturi*, p. 244.

9.3

Fascisms under liberalism

61

THE BLACKSHIRTED UTOPIANS

Philip M. Coupland[1]

Source: *Journal of Contemporary History*, 33(2) (1998): 255–72.

By coining the word 'Utopia', Thomas More bequeathed to scholarship the means to describe the gaze of desire which looks at life as it is and then projects a picture of how it could be, resolved of its defects. This was a vision which was *ou*topia, *no*-where in reality but potentially a powerful spur to action because it suggested what *could* be. More's island was also an *eu*topia, a *good* place. In contrast, fascism is synonymous with the dystopian hallmarks of oppression and misery. Nonetheless, it is the contention of this article that examining the British Union of Fascists (1932–40) as a utopian movement provides a valid and valuable insight into the ideology and motivations of Blackshirts.[2]

The promiscuous life that the concept of 'utopia' has led means that for it to be useful, it must first be reclaimed. In summary, 'utopianism' is understood here to be intellectual, cultural and political activities centred around the union of a critical gaze which takes in life *as it is*, a speculative and imaginative faculty which prompts a vision of how life *could be*, and a desire which may beget the hope, or maximally the will, that utopia *should be* realized. Hence, the commonplace use of 'utopian' to delegitimize others' ideas as fanciful is put to one side; they may be, but what is of interest here is that they are perceived to be practical by their bearers. Respecting subjective reality also requires that the commentator accepts the relativism of values and that utopia is not defined by a specific content, but is, as Levitas suggests, a common 'repository of desire'.[3]

Although previous studies of BUF ideology have recognized 'a fascist utopia' and a 'new fascist man', the Blackshirts have not previously been analysed as a utopian movement in any depth. Similarly, studies of BUF membership have not yet fully investigated the role of the fascist utopia as a motivational factor.[4] By examining BUF ideology as a species of utopianism, and the vision of 'The Greater Britain' – the blueprint for which Oswald Mosley laid out in his first major fascist text of that name – as an object of desire, new light is thrown on both the nature of the movement and the appeal of fascism. The following analysis is divided in two: first, the blueprint and vision of the BUF's utopia is examined. The BUF's policy and ideology have been analysed in depth elsewhere. In this context the major stress is on the effects and qualities claimed for the Greater Britain rather than its fine detail.[5] On that basis the attractions of the fascist utopia to Blackshirts are then investigated.

Access to the BUF's thinking is relatively unproblematic. It produced a plethora of material dealing with questions of the day from, in Nugent's terms, both 'authoritative' and 'non-authoritative' fascists.[6] Mosley dominated the movement, was an effective communicator, enjoyed privileged access to the means of propaganda and the legitimating stamp of status. Mosley also endorsed the writings of other leading fascists. Therefore, it is necessary to concentrate on Mosley and, to a lesser extent, his lieutenants as the canonical source of the BUF blueprint for utopia.

The political blueprint, for reasons of expediency, often cloaks its utopianism in no-nonsense tones. However, 'non-authoritative' Blackshirt writers whip this insubstantial shroud away with their 'word pictures' of the new order realized. Florence Hayes imagined the 'Nightmare? — Vision?' of Sam Hibbs 'in the new Greater Britain' and Michael Goulding pictured Christmas 'in the New Age'. Henry Gibbs, after quoting Omar Khayyam's classic evocation of utopianism, imagined *his* heart's desire as a 'Fascist in Wonderland'. Utopia always exists in relation to its other – dystopia, and in F.A.S. Smith's 'Rude Awakening: A Story with a Warning', Britain has been transformed into 'Abby's dream' the 'land flowing with milk and honey' of the fascist anti-man, the Jew/communist.[7]

Although the BUF has often been separated from the mainstream, it can only be understood as part of the wider utopian politics and culture of the 1930s – a period when belief that the current order of things was unsustainable was widespread and confidence in the ability of science to manage society and inaugurate an 'age of plenty' made the claim of Nicolas Berdyaev, that 'Les utopies sont réalisables', a joy for some and a horror for others, but at that time realistic. The entrance of the BUF into British life was a part of this utopian moment, the 'revolution' which Julian Huxley characterized as tending 'toward the subordination of economic to non-economic motives; toward more planning and central control; toward greater social integration and cultural unity'.[8]

Through slogans, parties seek to communicate the central essence of their ideology. The BUF communicated its ideological core by declaring that 'if our policy could be summarised in two words, they would be "Britain First" '. The interpretation of the slump premised by this ultra-nationalism was that it demonstrated the bankruptcy of a system which condemned the cherished nation to decay. Fascists agreed with Spengler's prophesied 'decline of the west' but believed they could intervene in history. The BUF was 'revolutionary or it is nothing', because the 'corporate state' would not reform the current system but create a new society. Fascism, rather than communism, would be the 'end of history' as 'the final system of the modern age'. Claiming a venerable symbol with a blinding utopian message and also an archetypal image of the period appearing on suburban garden gates, set into stained glass windows and cut into fretwork wireless speakers, the sunrise of the 'Coming Corporate State' was depicted on the cover of a pamphlet of that name to cast the glow of its promise over the land.[9]

Although the BUF proclaimed itself *the* 'modern movement' this was not the modernism of a Wellsian future. National identity, based on what Benedict Anderson calls an 'imagined community', is built on the myth of shared culture and heritage which cannot live with aggressive iconoclasm. But neither could a modern revolution return to a golden age. The BUF sought a 'third way' which recognized that, although 'a new machine is required to meet modern fact', the BUF would never 'destroy for the sake of destroying, or uproot existing institutions merely because they now exist' but 'preserve and adapt' 'whatever is good ... to a new synthesis and harmony of the nation, while ruthlessly cutting away the dead wood of obsolescence'.[10]

However, the aspect of BUF ideology which required that it would have to, in Mannheim's phrase, 'shatter ... the order of things' was the central axiom of fascist collectivism that 'the interests of the nation transcend the interest of every faction'. In place of liberal individualism would come:

> ... a nation ... organised in the divine parallel of the human body, as the Corporate name implies. Every organ plays a part in relation to the whole and in harmony with the whole. The warfare of sections and interests gives way to a co-operative synthesis.

This society would be 'like a healthy organism' which 'reacts decisively and like one man'. Class and other factions would be obliterated and the individual would have the opportunity to 'attain his highest potentiality', for high status could only come from service to the nation rather than accident of birth.[11]

Mosley's argument before 1932 was essentially an economic one, and economics continued to be at the centre of his thinking. His thesis was premised on the observations that, while 'Science, invention, technique have recently increased the power to produce out of the range of all previous experience', at the same time essential export markets were being denied to Britain by protection and the increase of indigenous manufactures which also threatened the home market with cheap imports. This was 'the major question of the age' and 'to it the Corporate system alone provides the answer'.[12]

Capitalism would remain, but tamed, and ultimately subordinated to the national interest as interpreted by the fascist government. Instead of the conventional response to falling profitability caused by market saturation and price competition of cutting wages, the Corporate economic system would be a system of 'economic self-government', protected from internal and external shock by the subordination of finance capital to the national interest, 'scientific protection' and imperial autarchy. Each corporation would have elected representatives of labour and capital and consumer representatives would provide arbitration. With the interests of all parties represented, 'industrial peace and stability' would be achieved and 'strike action' and 'political action' through the Labour Party would become obsolete.[13]

In place of the boom-slump cycle would come 'national equilibrium'. The world of strikes and lock-outs, unemployment and poverty, expensive and shoddy goods, national decline and the frustration of science would be replaced by the El Dorado of abundant quality goods at low prices, high wages and shorter hours, industrial harmony and the fullest growth that technology would permit. 'Fascist in Wonderland' Gibbs found that 'now there's plenty of work, they all have sufficient money and security to have a good time', 'shop windows ... crammed full with clothes, toys, mysterious parcels, turkeys, sweetmeats – all very tempting in coloured paper and ribbons' and 'everyone ... buying'. 'Sam Hibbs' concluded: 'Yes, England, not Russia was the paradise for the worker.'

As a fascist ideology, the BUF's was distinctive in its synthesis of two principal streams of political thought. Romantic elements drawn from fascism abroad merged with the ideas of economic planning and technocracy descended from Mosley's earlier *Revolution by Reason*. Thus, Mosley did not evince the anti-scientific and anti-industrial thinking often identified with fascism and, on occasion, his rhetoric became almost Wellsian – 'Science shall rule Great Britain' and afford 'not only the means with which to conquer material environment ... but ... probably also the means of controlling even the physical rhythm of civilisations.' However, despite claiming to be able to fuse the best of old and new, synthesis was probably syncretism. Other fascist authors believed that Huxley's dystopia had indeed been 'brought in to the region of practical politics' and feared Britain's 'ancient culture' would be replaced by 'Brave New World machine-fantasies'. The best answer that the fascist imagination could produce was that they did 'not hope to escape from the Machine, they do not want to smash it, but they are determined to master it'.[14]

The claim of every utopia to be the best possible world naturally tends to restrict the scope for disagreement, and like utopias from the time of Plato's *The Republic*, the corporate state would see the end of politics as conventionally understood.

The BUF was 'not a political party because we do not believe in politics', and, in the wish-dreams of Hayes and others, politics is significant by its complete absence. The rebirth of Britain as an organic nation would mean that, instead of politics driven by the selfish 'I', there would be technical discussion in the service of the corporate 'We'. Parties would be banned, and in place of a parliament elected on a territorial basis there would be an occupational franchise. This reflected the transcendence of class and faction in that people would instead vote and be elected on the basis of their role in the corporate whole. Electors and their representatives would vote and speak as 'experts' in their own field; 'in this way even the most insignificant individual will be able to contribute to the planning of the state'. Fascist government would be elected directly by the people, would only be able to be dismissed by a plebiscite and would not be dependent on the ultimately advisory new House of Commons and 'House of Notables'. The real power would rest with Mosley, who would replace the 'futility and cowardice' of committees with rule according to the 'leadership principle'.[15]

These new 'politics' were also predicated on a belief similar to that of the American technocrats that due to the 'increasingly technical nature of all problems', 'the task of Government [was] to keep the ring for the technician, and to protect him from the forces of chaos, while he solves the problem of human liberty'. The demands of modernity were such that the BUF would 'bring to an end the party game' because 'there is no time in the modern world'.[16]

Radical new economic and political institutions were only two parts of a wider project which, it was envisaged, would also see new land- and cityscapes, a better material, physical, cultural and spiritual life and a different relationship between the individual and the state.

Despite subsequent attempts to retell the story of the 1930s which emphasize prosperous suburbs and new industries, it was also a time of 'distressed areas' and demands for state measures to end poverty and unemployment. However, almost as prevalent was concern about unrestricted capitalism producing an England 'littered with the fungoid growths of the machine age' which either prompted nostalgia or demands for state intervention.[17] The BUF combined all three elements.

'The might of the nation' would 'be mobilised to obliterate the disgrace of the slums, to place electric power at the disposal of all, to build vast roads, to reclaim land from the sea, to do the hundreds of jobs that cry aloud to be done'. Fascism promised 'sun and air, decent surroundings and wholesome nourishment for all'. ' "Ribbon" development' would no longer 'disfigure' the countryside.[18] Gibbs imagined a London with 'no terrifying plate-glass and steel confectionery invented by Mr Wells. Yet the buildings were cleaner, more personal and better planned. . . . The drab buildings had gone. In their place were fine white blocks of shops and offices.' In Goulding's utopia, 'slum' was a 'word that has no meaning in our language. We have built . . . habitations fit for the workers of the greatest living race.'

In place of the problems of the first age of mass motoring, the author of *Motor-Ways for Britain* painted what he believed would 'seem a utopian dream' to 'many motorists' with 'nine motor-ways' to 'connect all the main centres of population' and 'special tracks . . . for cyclists, . . . to enable them to . . . traverse the more beautiful stretches of countryside'. 'Sam Hibbs' found himself on a 'highway' which was 'very wide and even. . . . The lorry sped smoothly along at a good fifty'. Problems of road safety would require 'streets in the sky' 'connected at intervals by bridges, giving marvellous opportunities for our engineers and architects to show their skill, and transforming our drab cities into modern Venices'.[19]

Surveys of the health of the nation at this time depict localized awfulness amid relative improvement. For an aesthetic which idealized the body beautiful, relative improvement was immaterial, and the BUF aimed to revitalize Britons physically. Although a nationalized health service was not envisaged, 'Strength through Health' promised state support for medicine and free health care for the poor. 'Everyone looked fit and healthy; none had worried lines creasing their foreheads or souring their lips' in Gibbs's dream; 'Sam Hibbs' had a vision of 'a thousand or more young factory workers doing physical jerks in their grounds', whom he admitted to be 'a credit to any race'. Mosley not only found youth with 'a physique impaired' but with 'an intelligence undeveloped' and promised, 'whether a man starts in a castle or a cottage' 'a straight road from cradle to university', 'to use his talent if he possesses the capacity'. Instead of 'machine replac[ing] man' causing the 'problem of leisure', in the fascist 'age of plenty', mechanization would instead yield an 'opportunity' to 'develop . . . the cultural standards of the masses by recreational activity' in state-provided facilities.[20]

The physical rebirth of Britons had a metaphysical dimension also. The BUF believed that 'no people can live that is uprooted from the soil'. The 'dream of an England renewed and reawakened' in William Morris's *News from Nowhere* was, 'allowing for differences in the technique of production', an anticipation of the values of the fascist utopia, because, in contrast to Marx, who

> . . . was a man of the study, Morris was a man of the open air and the workshop. Marx hugged the city, Morris dreamed of a countryside purged of 'the snorting steam and piston stroke' and a London 'small and white and clean'. Marx was a machine-enthusiast, Morris desired to revive the individual craftsmanship which had made England beautiful.

The combination of 'blood and soil' mysticism and modernism resulted in an unstable combination of a pledge to 'repeople the land' by encouraging the 'yeoman, or small working farmer' while making 'every method of modern science . . . available to British agriculture'.[21] Fascist wish-dreams for the future found that 'thousands have gone back to the land. . . . Farming districts all have their own big schools and nurseries, cinemas and theatres.

Their slums have gone – just like the industrial parts' and 'fields . . . whitening for the harvest . . . farm buildings . . . very clean, very modern in line'.

The new Briton, in return for 'public obligation' to the corporate nation, was promised 'private freedom' to enjoy 'the things which really matter to people': 'good wages, good houses, short hours of labour, opportunity for culture, recreation, and self-development, a chance for the children of the family equal to the chance of any children in the land'. However, liberty in the private sphere would, it appeared, go even further as fascists took a distinctly robust attitude to restrictions on British pleasures. Licensing laws would be liberalized and lotteries would be legal as long as their profits went to 'public purposes approved by the state'. However, this was not licence for hedonism, as the ideal was 'a morality of the Spartan pattern . . . tempered with the Elizabethan atmosphere of Merrie England'.[22]

So far, this summary has sought to present the 'constructive' side of the society which fascism aimed to bring about. However, it was either explicit or implicit that 'ruthless force' would be employed if necessary. The human implications of such vague threats would only become apparent if power was achieved. Then the violence of the last resort would, in all probability, become a daily necessity in the struggle to overcome obstructions which the utopian blueprint did not anticipate. Remoulding an individualistic, liberal democracy into an organic society would have put many beyond the pale because of how they behaved, or who they were. Mosley made clear that 'there will be no room in Britain for those who do not accept the principle "all for the State and the State for all" '. The tendency is for such vague axioms to expand and mutate into an Orwellian totalitarian cage.[23]

A person's inclusion in the BUF's organic nation required at least a minimal conformity to a standard of conduct and would be experienced as 'liberty' for those who had internalized the fascist worldview. This distinguishes the BUF model of the nation from concepts based on what a person 'was' according to 'racial' criteria, as in nazi ideology. Mosley, in his earliest fascist text, ignored 'race' and the 'Jewish question' altogether and later commented that, as the Empire was comprised of 'many different races . . . it would be bad . . . to stigmatise by law other races within it as inferior or outcast'. However, this was predicated on the belief that the Empire had been created 'without race mixture or pollution, by reason of the British social sense and pride of race' and hence legislation to prevent miscegenation was not necessary. If it should become so, 'fascism would not hesitate to introduce it'.[24] That the Greater Britain would be 'pure' white required no discussion.

Similarly, the BUF treatment of the Jewish 'question' was premised by different assumptions from those of the nazis. Jewry was not attacked on account of 'race' or 'religion' it was claimed, but because Jews 'set the interests of their co-racialists, at home and abroad, above the interests of the British state'. However, it must be stressed that in the shadow of this official line existed a very unpleasant antisemitic culture. Although this antisemitism was, except in the cases of men like William Joyce, premised by xenophobia and/or economic fears rather than nazi racial 'science', fascism in Britain also shared the desire for a 'final solution', albeit a territorial one. Mosley wrote: 'Jews, who have placed the interests of Jewry before those of Britain, must leave Great Britain. . . . Those against whom no such charge rests will not be persecuted, but will be treated as the majority of their people have elected to be treated.'[25]

The outsiders of the Greater Britain are absent from the fascist utopia. The 'black-uniformed men' whose marching feet interrupt 'Abby's dream' have averted its realization. There is no statue of Karl Marx in place of the Cenotaph or Jewry living like 'a race of Gods'. Instead of 'tradition' being 'stamped out' and 'history' 'burnt' in the Greater Britain, the 'culture' of 'our people' 'flower[s] . . . for here it is not subject to the alien influences of other races'.

'No greater mistake' Blackshirts believed could be made than to ignore the role of the 'new fascist man' in the Greater Britain.[26] This new man was the embodiment of the 'antimaterialistic and antirationalistic revision of Marxism' of Georges Sorel. Sorel had observed the failure of historical materialism and concluded that mass action flowed not from reason but from 'myths'; that emotions, dreams and symbols motivated people to act. Sorel's name appears only rarely in British fascist writings, although one prescient reviewer noted the affinities of *The Greater Britain* to the 'philosophic violence of M. Georges Sorel'. However, through observation of the Sorelian heritage in Italy, via the catalyst of the personality of Mosley and others, the fascist man was born at the centre of BUF ideology. Mosley wrote in *The Greater Britain*:

> The case advanced in these pages covers, not only a new political policy, but also a new conception of life. In our view, these purposes can only be achieved by the creation of a modern movement invading every sphere of national life.

From the outset, Mosley made clear that the fascist utopia would not come via the politics of 'old women, tea fights and committees'.[27]

The 'modern movement' was to be built from 'new men . . . free from the trammels of the past'. Unlike the inhabitant of the materialist utopias who would be made good by a new environment, the fascist, 'before transforming society transformed his own life'. The fascist would listen to 'the voice of the blood' and be 'shocking to the pedant . . . raw and ruthless', possessing 'a mastering contempt for . . . theories and formulas'. The Blackshirt was depicted as tall and muscular, square-jawed and straight-backed – signifying discipline, courage and vitality. Drawn without softening curves, he was a product of an industrial society, an 'instrument of steel' for an 'iron age'. In the cartoons of 'Bowie', this aesthetic was emphasized by its juxtaposition to the fascist's 'anti-man': the BUF's vicious stereotype of the Jew. Many of these ideal attributes would give credence to the anti-fascist stereotype of the Blackshirt as barbarian. However, fascist syncretism hoped for the 'virility of the Elizabethan combined with the intellect and method of the modern technician'.[28]

But most important of all, the fascist had only one joy: The Cause. 'They who lead the people to a higher civilisation are ever those who are capable of supreme self-dedication', Mosley wrote. Fascist man was to recapture the spirit of the front, the 'dedication ... to a cause that transcends self and faction'. Fascism required 'men and women who will build up their corporate life with sweat and agony of labour, and interpret that building as the cardinal purpose of their lives'. The only compensation for 'abuse, misunderstanding, bitter animosity, and possibly the ferocity of anger and danger' the BUF could offer was 'the deep belief that they are fighting that a great land may live'.[29]

These attributes would allow fascism to transcend society and history, and achieve utopia. However, the characteristics of this utopian man would also need to permeate society to act as the keystone of utopia. 'The political and economic implications of fascism are not so significant as the ... moral and spiritual reactions which derive inevitably from the fascist faith', Allen believed, and building the fascist utopia was 'not merely a matter' of substituting a different 'formal arrangement and technique' but rather it was 'the ideals and gods of the present order ... with which Fascism as a spiritual movement must do battle'.[30]

As such, British fascism took its place in the wider search for a fusion of the materialistic and the idealistic in an increasingly secularized society. Exploring this, Orwell articulated the problem that although 'faith vanishes, ... the need for faith remains the same as before' and had no doubt that a 'pseudo-religion' of 'progress' with 'visions of glittering utopias and ant-heaps of steel and concrete' was no substitute. Unlike the materialistic utopias which left humanity alone in a cold and silent universe, fascism claimed it would 'respiritualise the daily life and thought of the people ... until the basic principles of religion return to their hearts – service and love; the militant service and mystical love'.[31] If the people were so infused with these fundamental Christian values translated into fascism, everything could be overcome.

The fascist man was to stand at the centre of all points of synthesis and syncretism, 'in the whole of our national life', and 'by the force of the spirit alone' overcome every obstacle on the road to utopia. Science had offered the 'weapons' whereby he could 'conquer even destiny ... But one compelling necessity remained, that he shall win within himself the will to struggle and to conquer.' The outcome of that personal struggle would dictate 'whether man at last will grasp the stars'.[32] In a Blackshirt wish-dream, that struggle has been won and the narrator looks back on those

... who, seeking no reward, scaled the greatest heights of human endeavour; who by their spiritual courage broke through the shackles of materialism. Their nation is once more united in common accord. Freedom, Justice and Comradeship have replaced the artificial liberties of the past. They have stretched out their hand and from the heavens brought to earth the finest ideals which can possess mankind. For they believe in sacrifice and not in profit. They believe in souls untrammelled and unfettered and not in mean spirits enslaved in greed.

The movement is now not in society, but society itself. Gibbs rejoiced that 'wherever I looked I saw it. In shops, on flags, cut into bas-relief on buildings, outside cinemas and cafés, on cars and in stations . . . on papers and magazines . . . It was a flash within a circle.' In the streets, people 'greeted their friends with a strange salute' and the fascist ' "Song of Revolution" was on everyone's lips'.

The institutions of the Greater Britain and the spirituality of the fascist man seemed to offer something for everyone. A new national society at once harmonious and abundant, spiritual and scientific, modern and traditional, 'democratic' but dynamic. As such, the fascist utopia appeared to overcome the 'strategic value conflicts' – industrialism vs anti-industrialism, private property vs common ownership, religion vs secularization, revolution vs gradualism, statism vs communitarianism and democracy vs authoritarianism – which the utopian imagination had long struggled over. Although the attempt to realize this utopia would have in all probability brought an Orwellian dystopia of 'a world of rabbits ruled by stoats', the Greater Britain could still be attractive, if only to a few.[33] The belief among fascists, in common with members of other radical movements, was that they were the elect. Beverly Nichols believed that the BUF was 'welded by a religious faith' and that for 'rank and file' fascists 'this creed is a matter of life and death'. The young Blackshirt Olive Hawks remembered a 'desire to merge into the greater unit of nation or faith' which came from the 'spiritual instinct of self-sacrifice' which set fascists apart from 'most people [who] drifted along'. The novelist Henry Williamson, who joined the BUF in 1936, believed that fascists saw themselves as 'heralds of a great destiny, the pioneers of a Greater Britain'.[34] Utopias do not only exist on paper and imagination is not the preserve of the literary mind. By seeking out such visions, it is possible to move further toward understanding how the revolutionary can be satisfied by their endeavour and how an organization like the BUF managed to build up a core of dedicated activists.

In the chiliastic euphoria of the early days in which 'enthusiasts confidently predicted that Mosley would be in power within twelve months', Raven Thomson identified a group which he named the 'Post-Fascists', because they were 'asking what is to come *after* Fascism comes to power'.

Although 'every Fascist is interested in what the Corporate State is going to be like', Thomson recognized that the 'Post-Fascists' were distinctive because their 'fear' was the 'very success of the Corporate State'. A 'materialist paradise' they regarded as 'by no means an unmixed blessing'. These men, including the fascist poet E.D. Randell, formed a

> ... group ... characterised by a profound dissatisfaction with all modern standards of values ... [which] requires a complete revolution in our outlook upon life. In particular, the Post-Fascists demand the liberation of the race from the burden of modern materialism and from the repression of natural tendencies.

The 'Post-Fascists' looked forward to a revolt from 'anaemic intellectualism' and 'musty libraries' to a 'New England' of the 'things of life – virility, movement and youth'. Instead of the 'limit of bourgeois ambition' in 'artificial garden suburbs', Randall called for 'youth to leave the unreality of cities for the reality of cosmic harmony ... for the truths of Blood and Spirit; to return ... to the life of the soil and sun'.[35]

The 'Post-Fascists' were typical of those who saw fascism as a cultural revolution to transcend the 'decadent' values of the age. Baker's study of A.K. Chesterton explores a similar ideological attachment in detail. Chesterton tended to evaluate the nation primarily in terms of its artistic and cultural aspects, and his own cultural ideals led to his alienation from contemporary British culture. Instead of the idealized image of the homeland he had internalized as a colonial, he found, on his return from the war, his 'native land transformed ... into a sort of monstrous *palais de danse*, with every species of commercial "ramp" '. He came to believe that he was in 'a mean, tawdry, rapacious, cut-throat incompetent age' and blamed the 'aliens ... who ... supply the films with their slop and slush' and thought that the Jews were 'bent on destroying his dream of a unified nation'.[36]

His wife remembered him before his plunge into fascism as a 'prophet in search of a creed' and he became the most zealous of fascists. His agnosticism had earlier led him to reject providence and believe that humanity had to blaze 'its own trail from the slime' and he came to believe fervently that 'will' could enable fascism to transcend the 'commercial civilisation *de luxe*' with 'an order of civilisation never before approached by mankind'. In this rebirth, economic and political reconstruction was the first step which would 'set free the human personality for all the adventures that the spirit of man has still to take'. In this heroic world Blackshirts, the apotheosis of this new spirit, would 'maintain their posts in the watch-towers of mankind, eternally devoted, eternally vigilant – the sentries who maintain watch and ward over the nation's soul'.[37]

In contrast to Chesterton's utopia of an essentially secular new spiritual age, for B.D.E. Donovan, one of the many Catholics in the BUF, the Greater

Britain would be the new Jerusalem. Fascist revolutionaries were the apostles whose 'group outlook', he believed, was one of 'almost religious zeal' and the BUF 'ten point leaflet' contained 'all that is necessary to create an ideal society', his utopia: a 'religious and Christian conception of the state'. He continued:

> They provide for an aristocracy of talent and a new hierarchical principle applied to social organisation. They guarantee strong and stable central government ... they give honest and honourable administration ... They inculcate a social sentiment founded on the love of one's neighbour and respect for all honourable work ... a feeling of unity and solidarity free from all class prejudice.

After the war, Donovan's Catholicism drew him towards one of the original ingredients of the utopian tradition, the 'heaven on earth' of the monastic community, in his case at Aylesford Priory.[38]

In relation to Lewis's taxonomy of 'socialist', 'reactionary' and 'fascist' Blackshirts Chesterton, Donovan and others like them can be placed on the 'reactionary' wing of the party.[39] However, they were not 'reactionaries' in the normal sense of the term because their new society could only be achieved by revolution. Among those whose dreams centred instead on the physical and material nature of the Greater Britain, matters are somewhat more complex, with a variety of 'socialist' and 'reactionary' traits in evidence.

The author Francis Yeats-Brown was an early enthusiast for the BUF whom Griffiths describes as a 'High Tor[y]'. However, such an appellation is perhaps questionable. Not only did Yeats-Brown prefer the 'utopia of sharply-contrasted peoples' to the 'deadening peace of an insect-like industrialism', but he believed that 'England needs a purging, a systemic cleansing' even at the cost of 'the collapse of our ancient institutions'. A corporate state would be 'a body whose units were at harmony', 'where the yeoman and peasant and craftsman will again enjoy their ancient status, and through an intelligent application of science to industry and agriculture be assured of a place of dignity in our social system'. In common with the fascists of Mandle's survey, Yeats-Brown's life had a 'restless' searching quality, 'quiet comfort has no attraction' he believed. His time in India he depicted as an unsatisfied attempt to transmutate from 'the straying atom that I am' by 'merging into the glory and beauty of life' to become one with the 'creator'. In the fascist utopia Yeats-Brown perhaps sought the greater social unit into which he could so 'merge'.[40]

Henry Williamson's wife recalled him as a man who 'lived in the future, never happy with the present' and he saw himself as someone 'intent on his vision of perfection' who 'could not rest until it was achieved'. Williamson shared the dissatisfactions of fascists of the front generation, but distinctively believed in the power of social 'redemption through Nature'. Perhaps because this love of nature had been learnt from a child's perspective in unspoilt Devon countryside, his dismay at the condition of Britain was all the more acute. From the cities spilled out a 'civilisation' of

> ... big business, fornication, and death ... chromium fittings, radio, love with pessary, rubber girdles, perms, BBC gentility and the sterilising of truth, cubic international-type concrete architecture ... white sepulchral bread, gin, and homosexual jokes in the Shaftesbury Avenue theatres ... world leadership and freedom from tradition ... Hoardings, brittle houses, flashiness posing as beauty, mongrel living and cosmopolitan modernism, no planning, all higgledy-piggledy ...

While the healing countryside lay 'desolate, abominable: strewn with the bones of animals, and the broken hopes of men', the policies of the BUF would provide 'a classless, unified nation inspired to build ... a fine new co-operative Socialism' where farming would 'take its rightful place'.[41]

Both his membership of the BUF and farming in Norfolk were expressions of his will-to-utopia. Thus, while he imagined 'sun shining through the clearings of the old industrial jungle' where 'bronzed youths ... from the classless education camps of a Greater Britain of the future' worked the land, he also sought to 'help create a Greater Britain' by his attempt 'to do on a small scale' what Mosley was 'attempting to do on a national scale', such that 'our farmhouse and our land should become part of Merrie England once more'. However, while Williamson's utopian dreams are marked by a deep veneration of tradition – he 'dreamed of a new village of skilled and happy people, ... of laughter and strength of harmonious living, of a true balance between country and town' – he was not a reactionary. Rather, on his farm as in the country, 'old disorder had to be replaced with new order. He was determined to have no compromise with the old.'[42]

As a recent biography of Williamson observes, 'he was obsessed with his vision of ... "a new world, a Utopia" '. However, Anne Williamson argues that 'he was not a fascist in the normally understood sense of the world' but rather 'a twentieth-century romantic'. This conclusion perhaps follows from a definition of fascism as typified by 'authoritarianism and a closed feudal order'. If, instead, the central thread of utopianism in fascism is recognized, then a 'twentieth-century romantic' can also be a fascist.[43]

Moving 'left', the utopianism of fascists demonstrates a more distinctively socialist and industrial aspect, reflecting the life-world of urban and working-class Blackshirts. However, this ideological wing, despite its more utilitarian flavour, shared the same emotions as the dreamers of 'Merrie England'. One ex-East End fascist recalled the 'feeling that you could help to build a "Greater Britain".... That you could achieve it. You just had a vision.' For another, working for the movement 'was like paying in to something to get a goal, . . . like getting to heaven'. Fascist 'HM' 'looked forward to a National Socialist Britain . . . to see Britain great again. . . . It just meant something you would have given your life to achieve . . . something to work for . . . to look forward to.' Charlie Watts believed that 'if only we could get our message over . . . this country could have been made as near to a Utopia as possible'.[44]

A young school teacher, Louise Irvine, seemed to straddle the boundary between 'reactionary' and 'socialist' fascists. She remembered having a 'leaning toward a vague kind of Utopian Socialism' and being 'appalled by the economic conditions that I found in Birmingham'. The BUF, she believed, held that

> . . . 'small is beautiful'. It was hostile not only to dark satanic mills and soulless factories . . . but to the very cities which contained them. After the festering city slums had been destroyed . . . their inhabitants would be rehoused in small and largely self-sufficient communities, in rural environments.

Fascism, for Irvine, stood for the 'human Socialism' which was opposed to the 'Marxist "scientific socialism" ' which 'would lead through blood and fire "to a new Utopia where there will be neither law, nor Government, nor Religion" '. In contrast to Irvine, Arthur Beavan, the son of a Fabian Socialist, left the communists to work 'seven days a week' for what he saw as 'a revolutionary patriotic movement' purposed to inaugurate a 'scientifically managed society under efficient leadership, in which expert executives replaced amateur legislators'. Leonard Wise believed the corporate state would bring 'a system of government . . . to put the ideas of the American technocrats into practice and solve the awesome problems caused by the growing replacement of man by machine'.[45]

Alexander Raven Thomson, another former communist who was the BUF's leading theorist of the corporate state, believed that he had discovered, in Kolnai's terms, 'a hidden key . . . which opens the door to the solution of many problems at once'. This led him to argue that the termite mound was the highest stage of a series of 'integrations' of matter because the formicary transcended the individual organisms of which it was composed. This pattern, he believed, was paralleled in the cycles of social history which reached their highest point when society itself became a 'superbeing' because its corporate abilities transcended those of the individual people of which it was made. This super-organism was 'the highest expression of the cosmic scheme' and as such was 'not the servant of man' but 'his master and tyrant' because this higher existence could only be obtained by 'abandoning . . . freedom of action to the higher aims of the communal spirit'.[46]

Religion, Thomson believed, represented the 'dim ... apprehension' that only through the super-organism 'can we attain the highest expression of our possibilities' and that 'self-sacrifice is greater and finer than self-indulgence'. Having 'found ... [a] conception of history' which 'seemed to shed a flood of illumination over so much that was obscure and inexplicable' and having had his belief in 'the moral value and efficacy of religion' restored and its 'true meaning' exposed, fascism provided both a utopia which came close to his ideal, but also a cause which entirely fulfilled his understanding of the human purpose of life.[47]

These individuals represent only a tiny proportion of the membership of the BUF. The degree to which their utopianism was shared by fascists who have left no trace is not known. However, we cannot infer from their silence that their motivations were, therefore, more mundane. The case of Dorset farmer, Robert Saunders, is suggestive in this respect. Although Saunders lacked the skills of Chesterton or Williamson to articulate his vision, his commitment was no less utopian. Recognition often comes more readily than description and when questioned on what he was 'really doing this for' Saunders referred his correspondent to part of Mosley's *The Alternative* which 'expresses what I have long felt – before I even joined the B.U.'. Before Saunders lay the

> ... duty ... to build a world worthy of the new genius of man's mind. ... It is to evoke from the womb of the future a race of men fit to live in that new age. We must deliberately accelerate evolution. ... [Man] must transcend himself; this deed will contain both the glory of sacrifice and the triumph of fulfilment. ... From the dust we rise to see a vision that came not before. All things are now possible; and all will be achieved.

Saunders, who lost any meaningful belief in God in his 'late teens', filled that gap by finding a purpose in the cause and vision of the BUF.[48]

The study of utopianism can illuminate that which may be less visible to other modes of enquiry and opens a window on how men and women saw the world, their dearest hopes and worst fears. By looking at the ideology of the BUF as utopian, one sees how Blackshirts translated the wider cultural will-to-utopia into their own version of the European fascist myth of 'national rebirth'.[49] As is almost always the case, detailed investigation reveals the uncomfortable complexity of real life. In the ideas and motivations of the Blackshirts, evil or dangerous means often stand next to honourable ends and the zeal and self-sacrifice without which nothing great can be achieved were devoted to a purpose which, in other lands, thrust peoples into the inferno instead of bringing them heaven on earth. Perhaps by better understanding the dangers of utopianism, we will be able to keep utopia on the map but humanity off the road to serfdom.

Notes

1 I should like to thank John Bourne, Scott Lucas, Martin Durham, Steve Cullen and James Hinton, who read and commented on earlier versions of this article. All conclusions and any errors or omissions are, of course, my own.
2 In order to distinguish the terms 'utopia' and 'fascism' as generic concepts their first letters are not capitalized except in cases where quotations do so. The interwar Fascist Party led by Sir Oswald Mosley went through a number of changes of name during its life. However, for the sake of consistency it is referred to by its original acronym (BUF) except when quotations do otherwise.
3 Ruth Levitas, *The Concept of Utopia* (Hemel Hempstead 1990), 199.
4 Richard Thurlow, *Fascism in Britain: A History, 1918–1985* (Oxford 1987), 143–62; Stephen Cullen, 'The Development of the Ideas and Policy of the British Union of Fascists, 1932–40'; *Journal of Contemporary History*, 22, 1 (January 1987), 115–36; Robert Skidelsky, *Oswald Mosley* (London 1990), 312–15. On the membership of the BUF see: Stuart Rawnsley. 'The Membership of the British Union of Fascists' in Kenneth Lunn and Richard Thurlow (eds), *British Fascism* (London 1980), 150–65; John Brewer, 'The British Union of Fascists: Some Tentative Conclusions on its Membership' in S.U. Larsen, B. Hagtvet and J.P. Myklebust (eds), *Who were the Fascists?: Social Roots of European Fascism* (Bergen 1980), 542–56; John Brewer, *Mosley's Men* (Aldershot 1984); Gary Webber, 'Patterns of Membership and Support for the British Union of Fascists', *Journal of Contemporary History*, 19, 4 (October 1984), 575–606; Gary Webber, 'The British Isles' in Detlev Mühlberger (ed.), *The Social Basis of Fascist Movements* (London 1987), 140–54; Martin Durham, 'Women and the British Union of Fascists, 1932–1940' in Tony Kushner and Kenneth Lunn (eds), *The Politics of Marginality* (London 1990), 3–18; Thomas Linehan, 'The British Union of Fascists in East London and South-West Essex, 1933–40. A Study of the District Branches, their Memberships, and the Local Context of Branch Recruitment' (PhD thesis, University of London 1992) published as *East London for Mosley: The British Union of Fascists in East London and South-West Essex 1933–40* (London 1996); Stephen Cullen, 'Four Women for Mosley: Women in the British Union of Fascists, 1932–1940', *Oral History*, 24,1 (Spring 1996), 49–59.
5 Oswald Mosley, *The Greater Britain* (London 1932). On the ideology and policy of the BUF see: Neil Nugent, 'The Ideas of the British Union of Fascists' in Neil Nugent and Roger King (eds), *The British Right* (Farnborough 1977), 133–64; Gary Webber, *The Ideology of the British Right* (Beckenham 1986); Cullen, op. cit.; Thurlow, op. cit.; D.S. Lewis, *Illusions of Grandeur: Mosley, Fascism and British Society, 1931–81* (Manchester 1987); Martin Durham, 'Gender and the British Union of Fascists', *Journal of Contemporary History*, 27, 3 (July 1992), 513–29.
6 Nugent, op. cit., 134–5.
7 *Action*, 3 September, 17 October 1936; *Blackshirt*, 26 December 1936, 24 December 1937.
8 Nicolas Berdyaev quoted by Aldous Huxley, *Brave New World* (Harmondsworth 1974; first published 1932); Julian Huxley, *On Living in a Revolution* (London 1946; first published 1942), 1.
9 Mosley, *The Greater Britain*, op. cit., 13, 15; Oswald Mosley, *Tomorrow We Live* (London 1938), 77, 75; Alexander Raven Thomson, *The Coming Corporate State* (London 1937).
10 Mosley, *The Greater Britain*, op. cit., 13; Benedict Anderson, *Imagined Communities* (London 1991); Mosley, *Tomorrow We Live*, op. cit., 40.

11 Karl Mannheim, *Ideology and Utopia: An Introduction to the Sociology of Knowledge* (New York, no date; first published 1936), 192; Mosley, *Tomorrow We Live*, op. cit., 40, 54, 57–9; Arthur Reade, 'William Morris – Nordic', *The British Union Quarterly*, 2, 4 (October-December 1938), 62; Thomson, op. cit., 47.
12 Mosley, *The Greater Britain*, op. cit., 47 (italicized in original), 84–5.
13 Thomson, op. cit., 6–9; Mosley, *The Greater Britain*, op. cit., 86. Mosley, *Tomorrow We Live* op. cit., 54–5; William Risdon, *Strike Action or Power Action* (London 1938?).
14 Oswald Mosley, *Revolution by Reason* (Leicester 1925); *Blackshirt*, 4 February 1933; Mosley, *Tomorrow We Live*, op. cit., 79; P. Bloomfield, *Imaginary Worlds or the Evolution of Utopia* (London 1932), 40; *Action*, 12 December 1938; W.E.D. Allen, 'The Fascist Idea in Britain', *The Quarterly Review*, 261 (1933), 223–38.
15 Bernhard Talbot, *To the Electors of St George's Ward* (Manchester, no date). Reproduced in Stuart Rawnsley, 'Fascism and Fascists in Britain in the 1930s: A Case Study of Fascism in the North of England in a Period of Economic and Political Change' (unpublished PhD thesis, University of Bradford 1983), 389; Mosley, *Tomorrow We Live*, op. cit., 10–20; A.K. Chesterton, *Creed of a Fascist Revolutionary* (London 1936?), 16.
16 W. Warren Wagar, 'The Steel-Gray Saviour: Technocracy as Utopia and Ideology', *Alternative Futures*, 2, 2 (1979), 38–54; Mosley, *The Greater Britain*, op. cit., 34; Mosley, *Tomorrow We Live*, op. cit., 6, 17.
17 John Stevenson and Christopher Cook, *The Slump* (London 1979); John Baxendale and Chris Pawling, *Narrating the Thirties: A Decade in the Making: 1930 to the Present* (Basingstoke 1996), 1–16, 140–67; Hugh Massingham, *London Scene* (London 1933), 98.
18 A.K. Chesterton, *Oswald Mosley: Portrait of a Leader* (London 1937), 148; *Blackshirt*, 11 July 1936; Oswald Mosley, *Fascism: 100 Questions Asked and Answered* (London 1936?), question 66.
19 Alexander Raven Thomson, *Motor-Ways for Britain* (London 1938?), 3–5.
20 BUF, *Medical Policy* (London 193?); Oswald Mosley, *Education Not Conscription: A Real National Militia* (1938?); Mosley, *Tomorrow We Live*, op. cit., 60; Thomson, *The Coming Corporate State*, op. cit., 43–4.
21 Mosley, *Tomorrow We Live*, op. cit., 50; *Fascist Week*, 3 March-5 April 1934; Arthur Reade, 'William Morris, National Socialist', *The British Union Quarterly*, 2, 3 (1938), 61–8; Jorian Jenks, *The Land and the People* (London 1938?).
22 Mosley, *Tomorrow We Live*, op. cit., 3, 6; 'A Freeman', *We Fight for Freedom* (London 1936), 54–7; Mosley, *The Greater Britain*, op. cit., 38.
23 Ibid., 124.
24 Mosley, *Fascism*, op. cit., question 93.
25 Mosley, *Tomorrow We Live*, op. cit., 63–6.
26 Thomson, *The Coming Corporate State*, op. cit., 47.
27 Zeev Sternhell, *The Birth of Fascist Ideology* (Princeton 1994), 3–35; C.F. Melville, 'The Greater Britain', *The Fortnightly Review*, 132 (December 1932), 792; Mosley, *The Greater Britain*, op. cit., 147, 25.
28 Ibid., 153, 16; Chesterton, *Creed of a Fascist Revolutionary*, op. cit., 17. Allen, op. cit., 224, 226. For the graphical depiction of the new fascist man, see the cover of Oswald Mosley, *Blackshirt Policy* (London 1934?); Mosley, *Tomorrow We Live*, op. cit., 10, 79.
29 Ibid., 11, 76; Chesterton, *Creed of a Fascist Revolutionary*, op. cit., 9; Mosley, *The Greater Britain*, op. cit., 160.
30 Allen, op. cit., 237; R. Blackwater, 'Man in Revolt', *The British Union Quarterly*, 2, 1 (January–March 1938), 49–58.

31 George Orwell, *A Clergyman's Daughter* (Harmondsworth 1964; first published 1935), 258–9; R. Gordon-Canning, *The Inward Strength of a National Socialist* (London 1938?), 3.
32 Mosley, *The Greater Britain*, op. cit., 13; Mosley, *Tomorrow We Live*, op. cit., 10, 79–80.
33 Barbara Goodwin and Keith Taylor, *The Politics of Utopia: A Study in Theory and Practice* (London 1982), 129–37; George Orwell, *The Road to Wigan Pier* (London, 1937), 248.
34 Beverly Nichols, *News of England or A Country Without a Hero* (London 1937), 292; Olive Hawks, *Time is My Debtor* (London 194?), 110–11; Henry Williamson, 'A Chronicle Writ in Darkness', *The European*, 8 (9 October 1953), 28; cited in J.W. Blench, 'Henry Williamson and the Romantic Appeal of Fascism', *Durham University Journal*, LXXXI (1988–1989), 123–39, 289–305.
35 Richard Reynell Bellamy, 'We Marched with Mosley: A British Fascist's View of the Twentieth Century' (unpublished typescript, no date), 81; *Fascist Week*, 2 March-8 March, 16 March-22 March, 30 March-5 April 1934, emphasis in original.
36 David Baker, *Ideology of Obsession: A.K. Chesterton and British Fascism* (London 1996); Chesterton, *Creed of a Fascist Revolutionary*, op. cit., 24, 15; *Shakespeare Review* (September 1928), 307–11 in Baker, op. cit., 71.
37 Doris Chesterton, 'Lowest Albert' (unpublished manuscript, 1938–9) in Baker, op. cit., 123; *Torquay Directory*, 3 July 1931 in Baker, op. cit., 78; Chesterton, *Creed of a Fascist Revolutionary*, op. cit., 21, 17; *Fascist Week*, 19–22 January 1934; cited in Baker, op. cit., 207; Chesterton, *Oswald Mosley*, op. cit., 163.
38 *Blackshirt*, July, August 1938; A.W.B. Simpson, *In the Highest Degree Odious: Detention Without Trial in Wartime Britain* (Oxford 1994).
39 Lewis, op. cit., 7–8.
40 Richard Griffiths, *Fellow Travellers of the Right: British Enthusiasts for Nazi Germany 1933–9* (London 1980), 15–16; Francis Yeats-Brown, *Golden Horn* (London 1932), 282–3, 287; *Everyman*, 29 September 1933; Evelyn Wrench, *Francis Yeats-Brown 1886–1944* (London 1948), 166–77; Francis Yeats-Brown, *Bengal Lancer* (Harmondsworth 1947, first published 1930), 200; W.F. Mandle, 'The Leadership of the British Union of Fascists', *The Australian Journal of Politics and History*, 12 (1966), 360–83.
41 Daniel Farson, *Henry: An Appreciation of Henry Williamson* (London 1982), 120; Henry Williamson, *The Phasian Bird* (London 1948), 192, 203; Blench, op. cit., 128; Henry Williamson, *The Phoenix Generation* (London 1965), 205, 373–4; Henry Williamson, *The Story of a Norfolk Farm* (London 1941), 343, 353.
42 Henry Williamson, *Goodbye West Country* (London 1937), 251; Williamson, *The Story of a Norfolk Farm*, op. cit., 285, 346; Williamson, *The Phasian Bird*, op. cit., 146, 225; Williamson, *The Phoenix Generation*, op. cit., 323.
43 Ann Williamson, *Henry Williamson: Tarka and the Last Romantic* (Stroud 1995), 195–9.
44 Taped interview with 'KM' Limehouse BUF member, Linehan, 'The British Union of Fascists in East London and South-West Essex', op. cit., 488; taped interview with Mrs. 'H', BUF Women's District Leader for Epping 1938–1940, ibid.; taped interview with 'HM' Limehouse District Leader 1940, ibid., 415; Charlie Watts, 'It Has Happened Here: The Experiences of a Political Prisoner in British Prisons and Concentration Camps during the Fifth Column Panic of 1940/41' (unpublished typescript 1948? and 1966?), 89.
45 Louise Irvine, 'The Birmingham School Teacher', *Mosley's Blackshirts: The Inside Story of The British Union of Fascists 1932–1940* (London 1986), 46, 49–50; taped interview with Arthur Beavan, West Ham BUF District Leader, Linehan, op. cit.,

437–9; Arthur Beavan, 'The Welsh Security Officer', *Mosley's Blackshirts*, op. cit., 57; Leonard Wise, 'The East London Shopkeeper', ibid., 2–3.
46 Aurel Kolnai, *The Utopian Mind and Other Papers: A Critical Study in Moral and Political Philosophy* (London 1995), 156; Alexander Raven, *Civilisation as Divine Superman: A Super-organic Philosophy of History* (London 1932), 27–40.
47 Raven, op. cit., 225–34.
48 Robert Saunders, 'A Tiller of Several Soils' (unpublished typescript 1987), unpaginated document; letter from Robert Saunders to Rafe Cotton, 1 January 1948 in ibid.; Oswald Mosley, *The Alternative* (Ramsbury 1947), 309–14.
49 Roger Griffin, *The Nature of Fascism* (London 1993), passim.

62

Extract from
'FROM WHITE TO BLUE-AND-BLACK: FINNISH FASCISM IN THE INTER-WAR ERA'

Lauri Karvonen

Source: *Commentationes Scientiarum Socialium* 36 (1988): 18–29.

Fascist movements in Finland

As we have seen above, the political, social and economic conditions throughout the 1920s made for a considerable turbulence within the Finnish right wing. In fact, impulses from Italy were manifested in political debates fairly early in the 1920s.[1] By the same token, organizations were formed shortly after the Civil War which held great potential for fascist activity. The foremost of these was the Academic Karelia Society (AKS), founded in 1922 after the unsuccessful expedition to East Karelia. "Border nationalism" was its chief issue, but it soon became engaged in the internal linguistic strife, where it emerged as the main vehicle for extreme Finnish chauvinism. Clearly, the AKS harbored ideas which were both anti-Marxist and anti-parliamentary at the same time. Nevertheless, this organization was basically a single-issue group, ultranationalism being its trademark. Furthermore, since the AKS was an organization of students and young academics at the University of Helsinki, it could never really become a genuine mass movement. This was even more true of the smaller extreme rightist organizations of the 1920s.[2]

The beginning of the mass movement can be dated to late November, 1929; the site was *Lapua*, a rural community in Southern Ostrobothnia about sixty miles from the Finnish West Coast. The incident that sparked it off was in itself fairly insignificant. A Communist youth meeting had been arranged in Lapua. It was clearly no ordinary meeting: the Communists can hardly have been unaware of the provocative effect of such a meeting in a community characterized by a clear-cut rightist political tradition parallel with profound religiosity. The area was the heartland of the White Army of 1918. The Lapuans indeed let themselves be provoked! A group of men marched to the Workers's lounge where the meeting was held. They dissolved the meeting and ripped the reds shirts off the backs of the participants. Some minor violence occurred. The Communists were escorted to the railway station and warned for ever returning to Lapua.[3]

The news about the incident was met with enthusiasm throughout the country. Packs of letters and telegrams flooded Lapua. Not only the right wing press, but entire non-Socialist Finland seemed to condone the action of the Lapuans. A week after the incident a meeting was held in Lapua with the aim of discussing ways to put an end to Communist activity. It turned out to be no small local gathering: approximately two thousand persons from all over the country took part in it. It immediately gave inspiration to similar meetings in other parts of Finland. These meetings adopted resolutions containing demands to the Government about tougher measures in order to eradicate Communism. They also sent delegations to Helsinki to present their demands for Cabinet and Parliament. By the turn of the year and the decade it was apparent that there was a new popular mass movement in the country, with nation-wide potential to affect the course of Finnish politics.[4]

To begin with, the Lapua Movement explicitly backed the Cabinet and the legal form of Government of the Republic. Consequently, it received the unequivocal support of the President, *Lauri Kr. Relander* as well as the Prime Minister *Kyösti Kallio*, both Agrarian Party members. As early as March, 1930, the Cabinet was prepared to introduce its first anti-Communist bill to the Parliament. This bill, known as the "Close-the-Printing-Works Act", aimed at rendering Communist newspaper activity impossible. However, since questions having to do with the liberty of the press have constitutional status in Finnish legislation, a two-thirds majority would have been necessary in Parliament. This failed to materialize. This failure proved to have decisive consequences for the future course of the Lapua Movement.[5]

Just a few days before the bill fell in Parliament, the Lapua Movement received a nation-wide organizational structure. This national organization, called *Suomen Lukko* (the Lock of Finland) declared officially its support for the Government and the political system of Finland. The principle of legality had, however, strong critics within the movement from the very start. Already at the first meetings, opinions were voiced demanding that the entire system of parliamentary democracy be toppled. For a while, these demands lost their appeal due to the enthusiastic reaction the movement encountered throughout the nation and the positive attitude shown by government authorities towards its aspirations. With the failure of the Printing Works Bill, the idea of direct extra-parliamentary action rapidly regained support within the movement. On the night of March 28, 1930, a group of Lapua

Movement members, most of them from Lapua and adjacent communities, broke into the printing shop of *Työn Ääni*, a Communist newspaper in the city of Vaasa. They completely demolished the printing works of the newspaper. Eventually, the suspects were tried at the local court in Vaasa. Outside the courthouse, hundreds of indignant Lapua men gathered. When the attorney of the Communists, *Asser Salo* appeared, he was suddenly seized by a group of men who threw him into a car. He was knocked about to some extent and, of course, threatened with considerably worse things. He was released in Viitasaari in Central Finland after having made a promise never to return to Ostrobothnia.

This undertaking provided a model for what became known as *"rides"*: persons displeasing to the activist wing of the Lapua Movement were seized and transported by car eastward, frequently all the way to the Russian border. Physical violence and varying threats were part of the pattern; in a few cases, rides ended in murder. Typically, the victims were alleged Communists; in some cases, even Social Democrats qualified for a ride. Soon enough, small-time local Communists were not enough. A band of car-borne Lapua men broke into a session of the Constitutional Committee of the Parliament. The Committee's two Communist members were "taken for a ride". At another occasion *Väinö Hakkila*, the Social Democratic Vice Speaker of the Parliament, received a similar treatment. The by far most spectacular of these incidents occured in mid-October, 1930. *K. J. Ståhlberg*, the first President (1919–1925) of independent Finland, and his wife became the object of a Lapua ride. Ståhlberg was Finland's most distinguished Liberal politician, and he had consistently renounced the activities of the Lapua Movement. All told, the balance of the wild "Lapua Summer" of 1930 was some 250 "rides" or attempts to that end.[6]

These summer months signified, despite numerous assurances to the contrary by official *Suomen Lukko* representatives, a shift to direct extra-parliamentary actions within the Lapua Movement. The "Peasant March" in Helsinki in July, 1930 (cf. Mussolini's "March on Rome"!) was, to be sure, a dignified peaceful demonstration. Nevertheless, its 12,000 disciplined troops left no-one uncertain of the sheer physical power potential of the movement.[7]

The acts of violence during the summer of 1930 gave rise to an increasingly critical attitude towards the Lapua Movement also outside the left wing. The fact that the Agrarian Party gradually turned against it was to be of great importance. Nevertheless, it was during this period that the movement accomplished its most significant political victories. In June, the Kallio Cabinet introduced a series of bills known as the Communist Laws to the Parliament. When implemented, these laws would in practice render all Communist activity impossible. Once again, the Cabinet feared that the stipulations about qualified majorities would get in the way in Parliament. Under constant pressure from the movement Kallio filed in the resignation of his Cabinet. A new Cabinet, headed by P.E. Svinhufvud, took office in July. Svinhufvud had become legendary for his struggle for Finland's position in the face of escalated attempts at russification towards the end of the autonomy period. Together with Mannerheim he was one of the few Finnish notables who enjoyed the full support of the Lapua Movement. His allbourgeois coalition was formed under exceptional circumstances. The party caucuses of the Parliament were not heard at all. Instead, direct negotiations between Svinhufvud, the Lapua Movement, President Relander and some other central persons in Finnish politics were carried out. Originally, it was intended that the Movement would have seats of its own in the Cabinet. However, problems concerning personal relations made this impossible to achieve. Nevertheless, *Suomen Lukko* declared that the Svinhufvud cabinet had the full support of the movement.[8] When the Communist Laws eventually fell in Parliament, President Relander utilized his right to dissolve it and proclaimed new parliamentary elections to take place at the beginning of October. At these elections, most Communists were prevented from voting. Both national measures taken by the Government and local activity on the part of the Lapua Movement contributed to this. Those Communists who took the considerable risk of showing up at the polling-place normally found that their names had simply been deleted from the electoral register. It is no wonder that this "Lapua Election" finally produced a sufficient parliamentary majority for the enactment of the Communist Bills; in fact, this election was a spectacular success for the Conservative National Coalition Party. This party had endeavored to stand out as the "Lapua Party" above all others, and it had consistently refrained from criticism of even the most spectacular acts of violence performed by the movement.[9]

The Lapua Movement had now reached the goal it had set out in its initial declarations. The Communist Laws, modelled after the German *Reichsschutzgesetz*, were enacted by Parliament. This legislation, unique in Finnish legal history, put an end to all Communist activity. Many people expected that the Lapua Movement would refrain from further actions.[10]

Such optimism rarely comes true. Quite the contrary: the achievements of 1930 represented an Open Sesame! for the activist phalanx of the movement. It was *after* the violence had begun that the authorities started taking effective measures in accordance with Lapua's demands. This was clearly the way to get things done. At the same time, this violent activity was fomented by another factor. Although the Government demonstrated considerable tolerance towards most actions of the movement, the authorities could not help but investigate and, at least to some extent, prosecute "rides" and other forms of violence. After all, they regularly involved serious breaches of the peace, flagrant personal harrassment, sometimes even murder. This meant that there were constant interferences – formally if not more – on the part of the authorities in the "patriotic work" of the movement. Social Democrats in Parliament and in their party press saw to it that these processes received constant publicity and shed unfavorable light on the Lapua Movement.[11] The result was that Lapua Movement turned increasingly against the system of government as a whole. Social Democracy was more and more seen as part and parcel of the same Marxist conspiracy as Communism. Towards the end of November, 1930, the organizational structure of the Lapua Movement was reformed. The new national organization was simply called *the Lapua Movement*. *Suomen Lukko* was amalgamated into it, and in practice this maneuver meant that the official facade of legality and its spokesmen disappeared from the movement. Interestingly enough, the new district division of the movement matched that of the Civil Guard system. In his comprehensive study of the Lapua Movement in 1930 *Juha Siltala* writes:" ... for it was through an unofficial mobilization of Civil Guard members into extraparliamentary political action that the Lapua Movement had gathered its strength".[12] The new organization was, therefore, a codification of existing practice as well as a symptom of where the movement expected to find military muscle if need be.

It was thus no longer a question of whether or not the movement officially condoned direct action. For all practical purposes, the Lapua Movement *was* direct action. Simultaneously, the ideas advocated in the name of the movement bore an increasingly apparent fascist stamp. Anti-Communism and nationalism were accompanied with anti-parliamentarism, a glorification of the leader principle, and so on. In fact, one of the mouthpieces of the movement called itself *Fascisti*. The concept of the *Law of Lapua* became a central device in the debate about justice and legality. The principle was simple. Legal action and procedures were all right as long as they served the objectives of the movement. If legality was, however, perceived to be incompatible with "the good of the Fatherland", there was always a higher form of justice to turn to: the Law of Lapua, which justified even ever so extreme actions. Or as *Vihtori Kosola*, sometimes (rather misleadingly) characterized as the Finnish Führer, put it: "We do what we please, others do what they can".[13]

The result of the 1931 Presidential Election definitely convinced the Lapua Movement that nothing could stop it, no matter how far it wished to go. The Finnish President was previously elected through an indirect procedure, which at various occasions left maneuvering space to varying kinds of political coalitions.[14] In 1931, the Lapua Movement had declared that Svinhufvud was its choice for the Presidency. In the first ballot he was, however, but one of four fairly equal candidates. In the decisive ballot, however, he defeated his main opponent Ståhlberg by 151 votes against 149. Those who had rallied behind Svinhufvud after having first supported another candidate openly declared that they had apprehensions about extreme Lapua reactions should Ståhlberg, the leading bourgeois critic of Lapua, be elected. Many Lapua men seem to have thought that the First Finnish Leader had been chosen. Svinhufvud received the following telegraph message from the movement: "Command or forbid – we shall obey you".[15]

For a while, Svinhufvud seemed to do neither. He continued the policy vis-à-vis the movement he had adopted as Prime Minister. He emphatically renounced all forms of illegal action. At the same time, he publicly characterized the Lapua Movement as a welcomed reaction against the treacherous activities of the Communists; a sign of moral health on the part of the Finnish people. He thus adhered to what has become known as the "*fringe theory*": the Lapua Movement was a fully legal, patriotic reaction against Communism: the illegal actions were carried out by irresponsible individuals on the margin of the mass movement. For them, the movement as a whole could not be held responsible.[16] At all times, Svinhufvud kept intimate contact with representatives of the movement. One might say that there was a continuous process of consultation between these two main actors in Finnish politics.

Nevertheless, the war against the Social Democrats had been declared once and for all, and there seemed to be no way of stopping it. In fact, especially the local level of organization of the movement was so loose and undisciplined that it is uncertain whether a central control could have been successful had it been attempted. It was now that the political tide definitely turned. Most bourgeois parties and politicians had, to be sure, welcomed the movement as a necessary crusade against Communism. Most of them, however, opposed Communism because they thought that Finnish democracy needed to be *defended*. No-one save the right wing of the Conservative Party regarded the Social Democrats as anything but a self-evident part of democratic Finnish politics. Tannerian Social Democracy had little in common with the movement that had started the war of 1918. The Lapua pledge to crush Social Democracy as well represented, in this view, an *attack* against democracy.[17]

Svinhufvud's position was not enviable. He was the "Lapua President", brought to power by the pressures exerted by the movement. At the same time, his name was inseparably associated with the principle of legality; he had become legendary for his defense of Finnish law in the face of Russian chauvinism towards the end of the autonomy period. Furthermore, the radicalization of the Lapua Movement threatened the unity of bourgeois Finland, another thing dear to him. The Minister of the Interior of the Sunila Cabinet, *Ernst von Born*, became the key person in this predicament. von Born was a leading conservative member of the Swedish Party; at the same time, he was a staunch defender of the principle of legality and a well-known critic of the Lapua Movement. The cabinet in which he held a seat was an all-bourgeois coalition and the first one Svinhufvud had appointed as President. Being the minister in charge of the police force, von Born started to actively investigate the illegal activities of the movement. The movement attacked him vehemently and appealed to Svinhufvud to get von Born removed from the Cabinet. Svinhufvud refused to contribute to this end.[18]

There seems to be considerable unclarity and disagreement in the literature about the extent to which the idea of a *coup d'etat* had been adopted within the Lapua Movement. This has to do with the lack of reliable sources and with the unclarity of the lines of authority and command within the movement. The movement at all times spoke with a multitude of voices. To be sure, from the very start Lapua meetings witnessed opinions urging a revolt against the entire system; the step from such outcries to orchestrated action is, naturally, long. Nevertheless, many things seem to indicate that plans of a coup d'etat received increasing attention among the leading circles of the movement during 1931.[19]

Although there was a growing opinion for an open revolt against the Government among Lapua members, the incident in Mäntsälä in February, 1932, showed the movement's inability to mobilize its troops into a militarily significant force against Government authorities. Just as the initial scuffle in Lapua in late 1929, the "*Mäntsälä Revolt*" started with what might be called a touch of left wing provocation. *Mikko Erich*, a defector from the Conservative Party to Social Democracy had been invited as a speaker to the local workers' lodge. Local Civil Guard and Lapua members had demanded that the authorities stop the meeting. The authorities had no legal right to do so, but they advised Erich against going there. Situated northeast of Helsinki, Mäntsälä had witnessed ruthless "red terror" in 1918, and there was a strong aversion against the political left in the community. Erich would not listen to this advice. Armed Lapua men started to assemble in Mäntsälä. A rumor of a coup d'etat under way spread throughout the country, and Lapua as well as Civil Guard units started to prepare for combat. The hour of truth had finally come for President Svinhufvud. He went on national radio and in a resolute manner told the Lapua men in Mäntsälä to lay down their weapons and obey the police. Hinting at his four years in Siberia because of his defense of legality during the autonomy period, he declared that he would not allow the lawful system of the country to be crushed. As it became apparent that he was prepared to send the Army against them – and, equally important that he had the defense forces under his control – the Lapua men decided to give in. Of major importance was the role of the national Civil Guard System. After considerable internal disagreement, the Civil Guards decided to remain outside the revolt. The "Mäntsälä Revolt" was officially interpreted as a subversive act. Consequently, the Lapua Movement was outlawed and a large proportion of its leaders arrested. The movement was stopped by the "Lapua President". The irony of history was complete when the new and more severe laws on the liberty of the press and the freedom of association – that is, the "Communist Laws" – were used against the press and organizations of the Lapua Movement.[20]

With the benefit of hindsight, one might say that democratic, bourgeois Finland had played high stakes and won. It wanted the Communists out of the way, and the Lapua Movement was needed to do the job. After that, the main thing was to make the country safe for parliamentary democracy, which meant that the Lapua Movement had to stumble and fall. It is difficult to determine how near a Lapua-led fascist dictatorship the country had been at Mäntsälä during those February days in 1932. What is clear is that from then on, Lapua would no longer be able to dictate anything in Finnish politics. Act two of the Civil War was over. Politically, it was once again a victory for the democratic bourgeois parties rather than for the extreme right wing.

The shift from the all-bourgeois anti-Communist front to an increasingly fascist-oriented subversive force had naturally weakened Lapua's popular support. Nevertheless, it was still a nation-wide movement in 1932. Clearly, one could not expect these people to go home and forget the movement altogether. Quite the contrary: only a few months after Mäntsälä, the *IKL (Isänmaallinen Kansanliike* = Patriotic People's movement) was founded. Its explicit aim was to carry on the work of the Lapua Movement.[21]

In spite of this objective and despite the fact that many prominent Lapua leaders became dominant in the IKL as well, the new movement came to deviate from the Lapua Movement in several respects. The IKL became strong in those respects that had been Lapua's chief weaknesses, and vice versa. Lapua never managed to create a functioning organizational apparatus; the IKL built up, with models from Germany, the hitherto most modern and efficient party organization and political press in Finland. Lapua had possessed a wide network of informal contacts to all power centers in Finnish politics, which made for a strong and pervasive influence throughout the political system. For the IKL, such channels did not exist. Only the conservative National Coalition Party was willing to cooperate with it, and even it turned against the IKL in 1934 after *J. K. Paasikivi* had gained the upper hand of the Lapua wing of the Conservative camp.

Nevertheless, the efficiency of the IKL's organization and the dedication of its members made it a conspicuous feature in Finnish politics in the 1930s. According to a frequently cited but somewhat uncertain figure the membership of the IKL once reached the 80,000 mark. This is quite remarkable in view of the fact that the largest Finnish parties at that time had less than half that membership. Besides, the IKL had a large, semi-autonomous youth organization called *Sinimustat* (the Blue-and-Black) and a close relationship with the Academic Karelia Society. For the organizational structure of the IKL, see Appendix 1.

A special feature, which further distinguished the IKL from Lapua was economy. The Lapua Movement had received ample financing from the Finnish industrial and business communities, particularly those branches that had been affected by the Communist-led strikes of the late 1920s. The IKL lost almost all of this financial support. Instead, it engaged in direct business activities of its own. Not without commercial success, the IKL ran a large number of restaurants (called Bear Restaurants after the symbol of the party, the Black Bear), newspaper companies and wholesale stores. The fact that this business could be started with fairly limited backing from external sources tells a good deal about the dedication of IKL activists.

The IKL had a strong bent for ceremonies and symbols which enhanced internal solidarity and cohesion. The foremost of these symbols was the party uniform, a black shirt with a blue tie. It can hardly be denied that this outfit had been inspired by models from central and southern Europe. It contributed strongly to the impression, which has been particularly wide-spread after the Second World War, that the IKL was primarily an imitation of Italian Fascism and German Nazism. Eventually, however, the IKL uniform was outlawed by a decree which forbade the use of political uniforms in public.

Ideologically, the IKL naturally inherited much from the Lapua Movement. While Lapua had a fairly dim ideological profile and lacked a clear program, however, the IKL had an extensive and detailed program covering general theoretical perspectives as well as more practical aspects of politics. In many respects the IKL program explicitly defined ideological components that had been implicit in the actions of the Lapua activists. The program was not, however, a mere codification of Lapua ideas. On several points, the IKL added to the ideological arsenal of Finnish fascism.

Anti-Communism was naturally the central heritage of the Lapua Movement. Just as the Lapua Movement during most of its existence, the IKL extended its struggle against Communism to include "international Socialism, which is equally dangerous to the country, which propagates class hatred, shuns patriotism and contempts the national and religious spirit".[22] The *anti-parliamentarism* of the Lapua Movement, increasingly apparent as the movement was gradually radicalized, led the IKL to rally behind an idea which had not been a central issue in Lapua rhetoric. A *corporative system*, organized along occupational divisions was to replace the system based on political parties. It is hardly necessary to point out that this idea was an imported one, originating from Mussolini's Italy. Having adopted corporatism as an important ideological guideline the party proceeded to organize anti-Communist labor unions of its own. The IKL took an increasing interest in the Finnish working class. The main problem was to convince the working man that a nationalistic, anti-Socialist ideology would help him improve his conditions better than anything else. This interest led the IKL to adopt a degree of *anti-capitalist* rhetoric, which of course made the party rather suspect in the eyes of industry and business.

Nationalism continued to be an ideological component of paramount importance. In external affairs, Finland was to pursue an *ultra-nationalist foreign policy*. Above all, this policy was directed against the Soviet Union. Basically, the IKL urged Finland to seek alliances with all powers hostile to the Soviet Union. To this end, Finland's own defense forces should also be radically strengthened. The idea of a "Greater Finland" including East Karelia enjoyed strong support within the IKL. Since the IKL also took a negative attitude to an expanded cooperation with the rest of Scandinavia, this foreign policy line in practice meant an active pro-German orientation.

In internal Finnish politics, IKL nationalism turned *against the Swedish-speaking population* of the country. This represented a rather radical deviation from Lapua's language policy. The Lapua Movement had remained neutral in the linguistic strife raging in interwar Finland. In fact, it had made successful attempts to bridge the linguistic gap by actively recruiting Swedish-speaking persons to the movement. The change on this point was due to the strong influence that AKS members had gained over the IKL in 1932. This anti-Swedish stand is probably a much better explanation of the IKL's poor contacts to business and industry than the rather vague anti-capitalism of the party. The ownership and management of commercial and industrial enterprise in the 1930s still lay to a large extent in Swedish hands.

The *leader principle* represented still another import from continental Europe. This idea was, however, never really practised within the IKL. It simply lacked a person with the necessary charisma and personal ability; after Mäntsälä, the choice of available leadership for Finnish fascism was strongly limited.

Religiosity was equally important for both Lapua and the IKL. The fundamental role of Christian values in Finnish traditions was strongly underlined. This created a certain friction in the relations between the IKL and German Nazism; the Nazis were engaged in a campaign to turn the German Lutheran Church into an instrument of their political propaganda. The IKL never questioned the autonomy of the Church. Since theologians formed a highly important part of the IKL intelligentsia, the "pagan Germanic" elements of Nazi mythology must necessarily remain alien to the IKL.[23]

Furthermore, the IKL to some extent engaged in propaganda against *Freemasonry* and *Jews*. These issues had never been considered of any importance in Finnish politics. In fact, the Jewish population of Finland at that time numbered something like fifteen hundred (0.04 per cent of total population). These issues were not at the very core of IKL ideology, either, but the attention paid to them illustrates the impulses the party received from Nazi Germany.

The IKL loathed the concept of partisan politics, and orginally it endeavored to stand out as a "popular movement" rather than a political party. There was considerable debate within the movement about whether or not the IKL should seek representation in Parliament. Nevertheless, in 1933 the IKL formed an electoral alliance with the Conservatives. The outcome of the election can be characterized as a disappointment. The alliance conquered fewer seats than what the National Coalition had won in 1930, when this Conservative Party throve on the popular support of the Lapua Movement. The parliamentary cooperation between Fascism and Conservatism lasted a little over a year. After that, 14 MPs formed a separate IKL caucus.

In 1936 the IKL ran for Parliament as an independent party. It polled 8.3 per cent of the vote, which was the highest figure it was ever to gain; it managed to hold its fourteen seats. In the 1937 Presidential Election it received 23 of the 300 electors. In the 1939 Parliamentary Elections its share of the vote fell to 6.6 per cent, and the number of seats dropped to merely eight. All in all, the IKL never managed to become one of the major parties in Finland. Compared to many other European countries, particularly the rest of Scandinavia, the Finnish fascist party can nevertheless be characterized as sizeable.

In the parliamentary arena the IKL was more or less isolated. Its ideological message was, after Mäntsälä, no longer *comme il faut*. The inflexible and uncompromising line characteristic of the IKL made it a poor partner for other parties. After the breach with the Conservatives in 1934 it had few means to effective political influence. However, with the war against the Soviet Union the IKL's idea of national unity became somewhat more topical. Between 1941 and 1943, the party chairman *Vilho Annala* held a seat in *J. W. Rangell*'s grand coalition cabinet.

The main importance of the IKL lay in the ideological arena, where it sometimes held the initiative through an active participation in the public debate. Its strong position in the academic community, especially among students, was an important means in this respect. The other bourgeois parties probably feared the ideological competition the IKL represented. The abortive attempt in 1938 to outlaw the fascist party – an undertaking initiated by *Urho Kekkonen*, the Minister of the Interior at that time – should at least to a part be seen in this light. This cabinet decision was, however, upheld by the court; the IKL's policy to refrain from all illegal or extra-parliamentary activity had born fruit. The IKL continued to exist until 1944, when it was outlawed through the provisions of the Finnish-Soviet Armistice.

The basic current of Finnish fascism represented by the Lapua Movement and the IKL can be summerized in the following manner. The Lapua Movement started out as a general bourgeois front against Communism. For all practical purposes its aims were compatible with those of the Government during the first months of its existence. Consequently, it could maintain an official facade of legality. Soon, however, the activist wing hostile to party government gained the upper hand. In practice, it was already during the summer months of 1930 that the movement's activities crossed the border to clear-cut fascist policies. All in all, the Lapua Movement had an impressive list of achievements, and it can be characterized as one of the more influential fascist movements in Europe.

The IKL, by contrast, never reached the same kind of influential position as Lapua. It was a political party with a nearly classical fascist program bearing clear marks of impulses from the "fascist core countries" in continental Europe.

Notes

1 Hyvämäki (1971), pp. 178–205.
2 For a comprehensive study on the AKS, see Alapuro (1973).
3 Siltala (1985), pp. 51–54, Rintala (1962), pp. 164–165.
4 Upton (1981), pp. 203–204.
5 Ibid., pp. 204–205.
6 Siltala's comprehensive study (1985) focuses specially on "rides" and their background.
7 Alapuro and Allardt (1978), pp. 131–133.
8 Jääskeläinen (1977), pp. 471–474.
9 Upton (1981), p. 209.
10 For the blueprint of the law, see Finlands författningssamling (Finnish Legislative Record) 1930/336.
11 Siltala (1985) offers a detailed analysis of the official action taken due to "rides", see especially pp. 369–430.
12 Ibid., p. 195.
13 Ibid.
14 The people first elected 300 electors, who were formally not bound to any particular candidate; they were simply supposed to "act according to their conscience". The electors took a maximum of three ballots so that one candidate received more than fifty per cent of the vote.
15 Rosengren (1973), pp. 176–192, Kalela (1976), p. 117.
16 For the concept, see Siltala (1985), p. 24.
17 Cf. Rintala (1962), p. 187.
18 Stjernschantz (1984), pp. 171–186.
19 Rintala (1962), pp. 189–190.
20 Alapuro and Allardt (1978), pp. 133–134. For a special study, see Hyvämäki (1971), pp. 233–271.
21 Our account of the IKL draws heavily on the comprehensive study by Uola (1982).
22 Ibid., p. 60.
23 Murtorinne (1982).

References

Alapuro, Risto (1973): *Akateeminen Karjala-Seura*. Porvoo-Helsinki: WSOY.
Alapuro, Risto and Erik Allardt (1978): The Lapua Movement: The threat of Rightist Takeover in Finland, 1930–32. In Juan J. Linz and Alfred Stepan (eds.): *The Breakdown of Democratic Regimes. Europe*. Baltimore: The Johns Hopkins University Press.
Hyvämäki, Lauri (1971): *Sinistä ja mustaa. Tutkielmia Suomen oikeistoradikalismista*. Helsinki: Otava.
Jääskeläinen, Mauno (1977 a): Demokratian kriisi. In *Valtioneuvoston historia 1917–1966 I*. Helsinki: Valtioneuvoston historiatoimikunta.
Jääskeläinen, Mauno (1977 b): Vähemmistöhallitukset. In *Valtioneuvoston historia 1917–1966 I*. Helsinki: Valtioneuvoston historiatoimikunta.
Kalela, Jorma (1976): Right-Wing Radicalism in Finland during the Interwar period. *Scandinavian Journal of History 1*, 105–124.
Lindman, Sven (1951): Notes on the Presidential Elections in Finland. *Acta Academiae Aboensis, Humaniora*, Vol. XIX. Åbo.

Murtorinne, Eino (1982): Den finska kyrkans inställning till högerradikala rörelser och till den tyska kyrkokampen under 1930-talet. In Ingun Montgomery and Stein Ugelvik Larsen (eds.): *Kirken, krisen og krigen*. Bergen-Oslo-Tromsø: Universitetsforlaget.

Rintala, Marvin (1962): *Three Generations. The Extreme Right Wing in Finnish Politics*. Bloomington: Indiana University Press.

Rosengren, Christer (1973): *Lapporörelsens utomparlamentariska verksamhet och påtryckningspolitik gentemot statsmakten till och med presidentvalet år 1931*. Åbo Academy: unpublished "licentiat" thesis.

Siltala, Juha (1985): *Lapuan liike ja kyyditykset 1930*. Helsinki: Otava.

Stjernschantz, Göran (1984): *Ernst von Born. Den siste hövdingen*. Lovisa: Söderströms.

Uola, Mikko (1982): *Sinimusta veljeskunta. Isänmaallinen kansanliike 1932–1944*. Helsinki: Otava.

Upton, A.F. (1981): Finland, In S.J. Woolf (ed.): *Fascism in Europe*. London-New York: Methuen.

63

SWEDISH FASCISM – WHY BOTHER?

Lena Berggren

Source: *Journal of Contemporary History* 37(3) (2002): 395–418.

Traditionally, Swedish interwar fascism[1] has been perceived of as a mishmash of ridiculous NSDAP-lookalikes and Hitler-wannabes constantly fighting each other, never gaining influence of any kind on Swedish politics, and failing spectacularly. The failure of Swedish fascism on a large scale is indisputable, but the idea that it simply attempted to copy the NSDAP can be called into question, as can the assumption of its insignificance in Swedish interwar history. The purpose of this article is to discuss what we know about Swedish interwar fascism and why it failed, but also to try to put Swedish fascism and the study of it in a new light; in short, to argue that we should actually bother about it, because of its ideological kinship with more successful varieties of inter-war fascism.

In 1980, Bernt Hagtvet published an over-view article on interwar Swedish fascism in the voluminous anthology *Who were the fascists*.[2] This article, the first scholarly account of Swedish fascism in English, was mostly based on a book written on the subject in Swedish by Eric Wärenstam in 1970.[3] Both Wärenstam's book and Hagtvet's article follow a rather traditional pattern, where focus is put on the organisation and support of different fascist organisations, rather than on how fascist ideology expressed itself in a Swedish context. More than twenty years have now elapsed since Hagtvet's article appeared and more than thirty since Wärenstam's survey was written, and one would expect that a great deal of new and illuminating research has been done on Swedish fascism since. Unfortunately, this is not the case. With one exception,[4] the 1980s can be characterised as a decade of silence on the topic. The silence was temporarily broken in 1990, when Heléne Lööw's dissertation *Hakkorset och Wasakärven* was published.[5] Offering a thorough, detailed and reliable survey of the structure and actions of the largest fascist party in Sweden, this was a truly groundbreaking book.

It was only in the late 1990s that the silence was broken once again, this time by a number of books on different aspects of the history and contemporary context of Swedish fascism.[6] Unfortunately for scholars of international and especially interwar fascism, very little of this research has been made available in languages other than Swedish yet. Despite the domestic inwardness of the publication of results, this newly awakened scholarly interest in Swedish fascism actually, though not outspokenly, fits into the broad theoretical framework that Roger Griffin has labelled 'the New Consensus' of fascist studies.[7]

There has been a disturbing tendency in most of what little pre-1990 research there is on Swedish fascism to regard generic fascism, as well as adjacent phenomena as racism and antisemitism, as something very unfamiliar to Swedish mentality and culture. This research usually ends up with the mistaken and simplified conclusion that Swedish fascism and more or less all that accompanied it in the interwar period was essentially due to the importation of predominantly German ideas. Besides the assumption of the 'un-Swedishness' of fascism, there is yet another misconception that has surfaced distressingly often. This is the assumption that a 'common-sense' definition of fascism as nothing but an irrational hotchpotch of disparate ideas, paranoid mythmaking and racist violence, is quite sufficient. Taken together, these two misconceptions have been used to imply that the study of Swedish fascism is actually of little scholarly value, but instead some kind of underhand activity which respectable scholars should give a wide berth.[8]

In the light of this rather gloomy historiography, it is refreshing and very promising for the future of fascist studies in Sweden that perspectives are now beginning to shift towards the 'New Consensus' theory. But to understand this, we must first look at what encompasses this theory. In short, the 'New Consensus' is a loose 'agreement' between scholars that has emerged especially in the 1990s on how fascism should be conceptualised. First, and most importantly, the consensus' basic postulate is that fascism should be treated as a coherent and positive ideology with its own utopian core myth, equivalent to those of socialism, liberalism, conservatism and so on. Second, it proposes an ideal-type concept of generic fascism, in order to arrive at a heuristically useful tool for fascist analysis instead of constructing a 'real-type' concept using one of the existing fascist movements as a role-model. Third, it contains a general agreement that fascism, in Roger Griffin's words 'draws its internal cohesion and driving force from a core myth that a period of perceived national decline and decadence is giving way to one of rebirth and renewal in a post-liberal new order'. This leads Griffin to a bold one-sentence definition of ideal-type generic fascism as 'palingenetic populist ultra-nationalism'.[9] In other words, there is a general consensus that fascism should be seen as a revolutionary and modern political force, searching to create a fundamentally new society.[10]

Studies of Swedish fascism from the late 1990s do not explicitly link themselves to the theoretical framework of the New Consensus.[11] In fact, there is not much talk of theory and dwelling upon definitions at all.[12] For instance in his book *Lunds universitet under andra världskriget* (The University of Lund during the Second World War), Sverker Oredsson promptly defines a nazi as someone whom was a member of a nazi party. There is not one word to define the ideology as such, apart from an incomplete list of parties.[13] In contrast, the point of these new books on Swedish fascism, and the reason why they can be said to link up to the 'New Consensus', is that *they actually end up taking fascism seriously as a coherent ideology with its own logic*.

This is a step in a more useful direction for the as yet embryonic fascist studies in Sweden as well as for the study of Swedish fascism. But it also poses problems. Given this new approach, how much previous research on Swedish fascism can actually be considered trustworthy? If we take Wärenstam's survey from 1970 as an example, this book is not so much an analysis of fascist thought, but instead rests on implicit theoretical assumptions about which organisations are to be considered fascist, who the leading figures were, why parties split, and so on. In other words, even surveys claiming a purely delineating purpose are actually written from a specific perspective, one needing to be re-examined in the light of new theoretical frameworks.

This leads to the rather discouraging conclusion that much of the scarce research on Swedish fascism that is available must be re-examined. On the other hand, scholars now have the opportunity to link the study of Swedish fascism to the international field of Fascist Studies, not only by doing 'traditional' comparative studies but also by using the same tools that are increasingly being used for other countries. It may also be the case that some features of fascist ideology can be more clearly elucidated by studying its manifestations in neutral Sweden – and for that matter Switzerland as well, given the very special conditions in these countries during the 1930s and World War II. But to be able to determine if this is the case, we need to know more about the development and growth of fascism in Sweden without compromising assumptions.

As a consequence of the unstable foundations of research, the following survey of Swedish fascism in the years 1925–50 is tentative and in need of thorough expansion.[14] Nevertheless it is an effort to trace the main currents and features of Swedish fascism, hopefully filling some of the gaps. Ideally, it will also arouse some interest in further pursuit of scholarly work on Swedish fascism and the context in which it arose.

Sweden's first fascist party, the Swedish National Socialist Freedom Federation (Nationalsocialistiska Frihetsförbundet) was founded in 1924. Through a number of transformations and changes of the party name, this party was to constitute the core of the Newswedish National Socialist Party (Nysvenska Nationalsocialistiska Partiet, NSNP) which was founded in 1930 under the leadership of Birger Furugård. This party could at the time of its founding boast that it had managed to unite more or less all of the fascist groupings in Sweden, who at this time were predominantly national socialist in outlook. In 1931, the party changed its name to the Swedish National Socialist Party (Svenska Nationalsocialistiska Partiet, SNSP).

One of the groupings that merged in the NSNP in 1930 was what remained of the Sweden's Fascist People's Party (Sveriges Fascistiska Folkparti), which was founded in 1926. The name was soon changed to Sweden's Fascist Combat Organisation (Sveriges Fascistiska Kamporganisation, SFKO), which initially constituted the militia of Sweden's Fascist People's Party and was modelled on the Italian *squadrismo*, but in reality constituted the whole of the party. SFKO was from the beginning heavily influenced by Italian Fascism, an influence that in part was mediated by the antisemitic writer Elof Eriksson through his paper *The Nation* (Nationen). Conflicts on a more personal level soon evolved between Eriksson and the leading figures of the SFKO such as Konrad Hallgren, Sven Hedengren and Sven-Olov Lindholm, and the SFKO soon founded its own paper, *The Fasces* (Spöknippet).[15] During 1928 and 1929 the party leadership started developing contacts with the German NSDAP, which resulted in a change of role-model from Italy to Germany culminating with a change of the party name to Sweden's National Socialist People's Party (Sveriges Nationalsocialistiska Folkparti, SNFP).

This virtually ended the use of Fascist Italy as a role model for Swedish fascists, who now became generally national socialist in outlook. This is not very surprising, since Germany was closer to Sweden than Italy not only geographically but also culturally, and there was a long tradition of cultural, scientific and other exchanges between the two countries. But if there is one exception from this change of role model, it can be found in the different groups and movements headed by the political scientist Per Engdahl. Engdahl initially joined the SFKO, but when the party turned towards nazism in 1929, Engdahl and a few other members left the organisation and started the Newswedish Federation (Nysvenska Förbundet), an organisation more faithful to the Italian version of fascism.

When the NSNP was founded in 1930, both the SNFP and the Newswedish Federation joined the new formation. Engdahl wanted to have nothing to do with the new party however, forming instead the Association of the New Sweden (Föreningen det Nya Sverige). This was later renamed the National Federation of the New Sweden (Riksförbundet det Nya Sverige, RNS). Neither of the organisations mentioned above nor the Swedish Opposition (Svensk Opposition) which Engdahl started in 1942 were intended to function as proper political parties. The intent was rather to organise what Engdahl himself called 'idea movements'; groupings intent on ideological and intellectual exchange of ideas rather than on formulating party programmes for electoral use. Since these formations never entered general elections, it is hard to determine how much popular support these ideas actually received. After the war, Swedish Opposition was renamed the Newswedish Movement (Nysvenska Rörelsen, NSR), and this movement continued to exist until the 1990s.

Throughout his life – he died in 1994 at the age of 85 – Engdahl fiercely opposed any attempt to label him a nazi. At some points in his life he reluctantly succumbed to being called a fascist, even if there is no doubt where his general ideological abode was. Instead of calling himself a fascist, he maintained that he was the advocate of 'Newswedishness' or 'Newswedish Socialism'. This was an attempt to create a coherent policy based on the idea of a national rebirth consciously adapted for the special conditions of Sweden. If by any foreign movement, it was influenced by Italian Fascism rather than German nazism.[16] During the war, Engdahl maintained a very critical standpoint toward Nazi Germany, which partly set him on a collision course with most Swedish nazis.[17] At present, there is no exhaustive study of Per Engdahl, who should be considered as a fascist ideologue and intellectual well of the same class as for instance many of his better known French contemporaries.[18]

After the war, Engdahl also became quite influential within what was left of the fascist movement in Europe. In the 1950s, he functioned as director of the international office of the Europäische Soziale Bewegung (ESB), also known as the Malmö Movement, since its headquarters were situated in Engdahl's home town Malmö in the south of Sweden. This movement was founded during a conference entitled 'For Europe – Against Communism!' which Engdahl and NSR organised in Malmö during Whitsun 1951. The conference was attended by for instance the French revisionist Maurice Barèche, the leader of the Italian MSI, Arturo Michelini, and the former head of propaganda for the Hitlerjugend, Karl-Heinz Priester. In the mid-1950s the ESB consisted of groups from all over Europe. Engdahl also edited the movement's paper *Nation Europa*, a paper still in circulation.[19]

The consolidation of Swedish fascism that was established through the NSNP/SNSP in 1930 was not going to last. Birger Furugård managed to keep the party together until January 1933, when the ideological and personal antagonisms that had been built in to the party from the start, became decisive. On January 13 Sven-Olov Lindholm and a number of his closest followers were excluded from the SNSP. This was countered the next day by the formation of the National Socialist Labour Party (Nationalsocialistiska Arbetarepartiet, NSAP) under the leadership of Lindholm.

Sweden now had two major fascist parties, both outspokenly national socialist in outlook, and even if the main reason for the split was disagreements on a personal level, there is also an ideological split discernible. Bluntly put, the SNSP can be said to have put a stronger emphasis on 'National' in national socialism and the NSAP on 'Socialism', thus dividing the two parties along a left-right scale within the fascist framework.[20] These two were soon to be accompanied by yet another party claiming to be national socialist, the National Socialist Bloc (Nationalsocialistiska Blocket, NSB), also founded in 1933 and led by the decorated Colonel Martin Ekström.

This party was organised as the initiative of a number of industry magnates and other highly influential people, and was commonly perceived as the upper class nazi party of Sweden. Since the party could count quite a number of wealthy people among its members and supporters, financing the activities and propaganda was initially unproblematic. More troublesome was the fact that the party leader, Colonel Ekström was in total want of charisma, a quality rather vital for an inter-war fascist leader. In January 1934 the party held a large party rally in Stockholm to launch the new party. The 'Auditorium' in Stockholm was packed full by an audience of about 1500 people, eagerly waiting for Sweden's new Führer to set matters straight with liberal decadence, the marxist menace and the threat to the Nordic race. The result was complete disaster, since Ekström's appearance was as far from the expected vigour as can be imagined. The party nevertheless managed to maintain some kind of activity, and even managed to gain some representation in the local elections of 1934. But the grand visions that preceded the party's formation never became more than grand visions.[21]

The Furugård party of SNSP was debilitated by even more conflicts after the split in 1933, in which it lost many of its younger and most energetic leading figures. Even so, estimations made by the Security Service in the spring of 1934 put the membership at 8,000 members. Simultaneously, the NSAP was estimated as having 12,000 members. In the local elections of 1934–35, the party gained in all about 16,800 votes resulting in about 80 seats. This result shows that the party, despite the chaos within the leadership, had a remarkably loyal body of members and sympathisers. The general elections of 1936, however, were disasterous. The SNSP formed an election coalition with the NSB, gaining a mere 3,025 votes. In the same elections, the NSAP got 17,483 votes, and it was clear who had won the struggle for the pronazi electorate.[22] This disaster made Furugård decide to terminate the party, and the party leadership encouraged the members to join the NSAP instead, which most of them probably did.

Also in 1936, the NSB more or less vanished, even if the party never was officially put to rest, leaving the NSAP as the only Swedish fascist party of any significant size. During the mid-30s, which was the heyday of Swedish fascism in general, the NSAP managed to uphold a significant level of organisation, including women's and youth organisations, a uniformed militia and a trade union. The party also had its own publishing branch, which besides the publication of the party paper *Den Svenske Nationalsocialisten* (The Swedish National Socialist) and a varying number of journals, booksand pamphlets also produced records in a number of different genres.[23]

Ideologically, the NSAP maintained its 'socialist' demands for the improvement of working conditions and social policies, nationalisation of

to the conservative establishment necessarily had repercussions beyond the political sphere, even before the league's social programme had been given special emphasis in 1935. On the one hand, it is impossible in any society to separate the people-state opposition from other sources of contradiction (class, gender, religion). On the other hand, particular groups became involved in the Croix de Feu where they had previously been involved in conflicts with conservative elites.

Croix de Feu discourse was suffused with anti-capitalism. La Rocque held that international capitalism, behind which could be found the City of London, was part of a conspiracy which also included Freemasons and the Third International. This unholy alliance of London and Moscow sought European war, civil war in France and ultimately the collapse of western civilization. To this end international capitalism distributed cheques to the leaders of the Popular Front.[74] The classic myth of a secret alliance between international capitalism and Marxism has been put to many uses by the extreme Right in France and elsewhere. In this case what is most important is that the social establishment was condemned, as were political leaders, for the rise of Marxism. Thus La Rocque denounced 'ceux dont l'improductivité ou la crainte, ont causé, en grande partie, la confusion actuelle'.[75] Of course, anti-capitalism of this nature had its limits and was as contradictory as any other aspect of the league. In effect big capitalists were being blamed for the emergence of a threat to property. Anti-capitalism was prevented from spilling over into a general attack on the social order by the very language in which it was expressed. Good capitalism was implicitly distinguished from bad by the use of qualifications such as 'international' and 'unproductive', which rendered capitalism acceptable as long as it was national and productive. Yet Croix de Feu anti-capitalism was connected with real sources of tension within the Right.

For this reason its social programme cannot be seen as a traditional social Catholic paternalism, as Pierre Milza argues it should.[76] It is true that La Rocque drew on ideas long familiar to the Catholic Right. He spoke favourably of the need to rebuild a sense of tradition, referred routinely to the French nation as an 'organism' and wanted to revive such *ancien régime* curiosities as the right of 'remonstrance'.[77] The influence of such ideas upon La Rocque could perhaps be traced back to his royalist father's association with Albert de Mun. Yet on closer inspection La Rocque's social ideas turn out to have been as ambiguous as other aspects of the league. The central problem of the Milza thesis is that by the 1930s the social Catholic tradition itself had become subdivided. It now included elements which opposed traditional paternalism, such as the various specialist branches of Catholic Action and the CFTC.[78] Some within these movements combined radicalism and anti-Communism in such a way as to create affinities with the populist radical Right. François Mitterrand, for example, seems to have regarded involvement in the Croix de Feu as the logical extension of his activity in the

Jeunesse étudiante chrétienne.[79] Furthermore, some social Catholics were, paradoxically, prepared to compromise on aspects of Catholic observance in order to reach dechristianized sections of the population. Starting from an integrist conception of Catholicism they therefore ended up defending a quasi-secular position.[80] The same kind of considerations were perhaps behind La Rocque's attempts to connect with the Revolutionary tradition, as is evident in the Jacobin resonances of the 'Volontaires Nationaux'.[81] This in turn explains why there was surprisingly little explicit mention of religion in *Service public*, and still less in *Le flambeau*. In Lyon at least these views earned the Croix de Feu the distrust of some in the Church.[82]

The ambiguity of the social Catholic heritage can be seen too in La Rocque's views on social hierarchy. He spoke in terms which superficially resembled the Legitimists. Excessive ambition combined with unemployment had created an anarchic battle for material existence which fomented class struggle and damaged the health of the social organism. But the Legitimists had used the organic metaphor to sustain a world-view in which the well-being of society depended on constituent elements sticking to their allotted spheres.[83] La Rocque on the contrary saw the social organism as naturally unstable, resembling a mixture of liquids of different densities and agitated by contradictory currents in which some elements were rising and others falling. The task of the state was to keep this natural struggle for existence from damaging the well-being of the whole. And whereas the Legitimists believed in a natural hierarchy renewed only by the best elements of the bourgeoisie, La Rocque held that differences in rank could be justified only by services rendered to the collectivity. A position based on inheritance, speculation or unproductiveness was illegitimate. Particularly revealing in this respect is La Rocque's view that the purpose of the education system was both to inculcate a sense of tradition and to produce 'leaders', who would in turn renew our 'popular reflexes'.[84] In other words, La Rocque's ideas emerged from a melting pot of traditionalist ideas about order and hierarchy, and liberal and social Darwinist ideas of competition and struggle. The result was a synthesis which reinforced the paradoxical nature of the movement.

The same blend of radicalism and reaction can be seen in the league's commitment to corporatism. The accusation of 'unproductiveness' connected the league with a tradition of populist social radicalism. But whereas this tradition had originated in the nineteenth century as a liberal critique of the old order, the radical Right of the 1930s was fundamentally hostile to liberalism. At the centre of the Croix de Feu's social programme was the *profession organisée*, a brand of corporatism designed to supersede the liberal state. The league's ideas were certainly constructed partly out of traditionalist materials, but the ideas of the Socialist revisionist Henri de Man were also quoted with approval. Moreover, the league was responding to a real crisis, for in the 1930s there was a widespread perception that parliamentary sovereignty had been undermined by the growth of corporate bodies, from the CGT and the new Chambers of Agriculture to the veterans' associations and National Catholic Federation (FNC). The conflicting aims of these associations were held to be responsible for the failure of a weak Parliament to provide a coherent response to the economic crisis.[85] La Rocque's aim was to reconcile these competing bodies with the general interest, and thereby to permit them to play the determining role in regenerating deficient institutions.[86] He therefore called for the creation of a network of corporations. On the regional level, these would group existing bodies such as the CGT and Chamber of Commerce, once they had been purged of political and selfish elements. The existing *Conseil national économique* would be endowed with the right to examine and request redrafting of legislation concerning the economy. But tinkering with this body could not be expected miraculously to bring about social harmony. A preliminary moral reform was essential.[87]

As with the constitutional projects of the Croix de Feu it is not easy to say what the practical impact of the *profession organisée* would have been. It is nevertheless essential to examine the role of state, for historians have sometimes argued that the supposed opposition of the Croix de Feu to state intervention in the economic and social spheres distanced it from Fascism.[88] A fundamental problem with this view is the identification of Fascism with a maximalist view of state power implicitly based on the totalitarian theory. In fact the question of where and how the state should intervene was a matter of controversy among Fascists in Germany and Italy. Interestingly, in Italy it was the radicals who opposed excessive state control of corporatist bodies.[89] Neither were the Croix de Feu's ideas fully formed. La Rocque called for strengthening of the state in the political sphere, but declared that the economic 'organism' was refractory to regulation. His ideal was a middle course in which the state would co-ordinate interests and initiatives without absorbing them. The state would be neither a fiction nor a religion (which he took to be the case in Fascism).[90] But even La Rocque rejected liberal doctrines as permitting the development of an irresponsible and parasitic capitalism. He called for the state to take upon itself the task of arbitration, inspection and punishment, and expected that it would 'distribute production in an appropriate framework'.[91] Another writer in *Le flambeau* defined his opposition to 'étatism' even more paradoxically as the subjection of the state to private interests, permitted by manipulation of the masses through 'electoralism'. Defined thus 'étatism' meant *weakening* of the state. So in order to fight 'étatism' it would be necessary to restore the primacy of the state over individual interests! This task would be carried out by men independent of short-term considerations, animated by the desire to serve the general interest.[92]

Furthermore, if these ambiguities are related to the context in which corporatism emerged it is possible to recognize the centrality of state intervention.[93] The crisis of the 1930s was, as we have already seen, experienced by many on the Right as a breakdown of social cohesion in which interest groups and individuals conducted a war of all against all to the detriment both of the general and individual good. The advantage of corporatism was that it seemed to reconcile pursuit of private interest with the welfare of society as a whole: professions would govern themselves, but it was also assumed that the state would reassume the task of arbitration it had supposedly neglected. Given the extent of interest group competition in the 1930s such arbitration would certainly have been extensive. This was acceptable in principle to business people schooled in the freedom of enterprise partly because they believed that the general interest was identical to their own concerns. Furthermore, it was assumed that if the general interest had for the moment been undermined, it was because of the presence within the profession of 'alien elements'. For the Croix de Feu the elimination of such elements, whether foreign artisans or Communists, was an indispensable precondition for the re-establishment of harmony. Here, too, the state would have a role to play, not least because the CGT would have to be released from the grip of the Communists.

In view of these considerations it is not surprising that the Croix de Feu programme of 1936 recognized that the state would have initially to take a leading, if indirect, role in the establishment of the *profession organisée*. La Rocque took care to stress that even when fully established the organized profession would not have a direct legislative role, for this would permit special interests to carve out a sphere of influence.[94] The state would always in the last resort decide contentious issues. The league also envisaged state control over the Bank of France and measures to reduce the influence of financial institutions over private enterprise. The most important point, however, is that the Croix de Feu envisaged a decisive break with the institutions of the liberal parliamentary system. This implied reinforcement of intervention in the economic and social spheres on the part of a state that was truly independent and representative of the people.

V

This does not, of course, mean that the state could ever really have been independent. Rather we are dealing with what historically situated individuals *thought* a neutral state would look like. This means that the social dimension of Croix de Feu populism must also be analysed from the perspective of those who joined the movement. The most reliable information regarding the social composition of the Croix de Feu is that of Janine Bourdin, according to whom the movement was largely bourgeois and lower middle class, with managers, businessmen, technicians and white collar workers all over-represented. Industrial workers and farmers were numerous neither in relative nor absolute terms. Individuals from the social elites were also relatively rare.[95] For Milza these statistics are evidence that the Croix de

Feu were not Fascist, for Fascism in his view was more plebeian. We can leave aside the debatable view of the social base of Nazism and Italian Fascism. More important in the present context is the assumption of a necessary relationship between social composition and the nature of a political movement.[96] The league cannot be reduced to an expression of middle-class discontent, even though it was not well supported either by industrial workers or by the social elites.[97] If we look at the league in the light of the concept of populism it is possible to see that the Croix de Feu swept together broad groups who had in common only hostility to the Communists, the government and the leadership of the Right. They included more marginal sections of the elites and conservatively inclined workers. Elements of the lower middle class formed a part of this coalition but even then their motivation cannot be seen exclusively in terms of supposedly objective material interests.

Take, for example, the league's effort to penetrate rural constituencies, which was under way from the autumn of 1935. The Croix de Feu promised to restore to the land the spiritual value which had been corrupted by international capital, parasitical political committees and revolutionaries. In more practical terms the basis of Croix de Feu agricultural policy was, inevitably, the *profession organisée*. In order to construct this new order the Croix de Feu would penetrate existing agricultural syndicates, whose leaders would be expelled since their so-called disinterestedness was merely a cover for selfishness. It was also stated that these professional bodies could not themselves provide the framework needed to protect the nation from the dangers which confronted it. *Encadrement* by the disciplined force of the Croix de Feu was the essential precondition of success.[98] Two contrasting regional examples reveal the different ways in which this programme was put to use.

The first comes from the Soissons region in the department of Aisne.[99] Like the rest of Picardy this was an area where large-scale farms run by wealthy tenant farmers predominated. These were worked by landless labourers, often immigrants. Wages had been reduced and there was much unemployment. A considerable number of peasant proprietors also inhabited the Soissons region. They farmed increasingly subdivided properties and were especially vulnerable to falling grain prices because of their inability to spread sales over the year. Politically the region was dominated by Socialists, led by the future Minister of Agriculture Georges Monnet. To agricultural labourers he promised public works, limits on employment of foreign labour, raising of the school-leaving age and obligatory family allowances for farm labourers. To peasants he offered a national wheat office.

As for the Croix de Feu, they represented mainly the middle class and lower middle class of Soissons and other smaller towns. Their aim was to combat Monnet and at the same time to bid for leadership of the Right in the countryside. To this end they began to pressurize tenant farmers. The Croix de Feu evoked the spectre of collectivization, appealed to memories of the war, called for class collaboration and urged tenants to limit sackings. But it also spoke of practical measures. Croix de Feu members in each commune would constitute themselves as agricultural syndics. These would endeavour to raise the wages of agricultural workers and seek a tax on big proprietors in order to protect peasants from falling grain prices. During and after the strikes of June 1936 the Croix de Feu and later the PSF took these policies a stage further. On the one hand, they helped to organize the breaking of strikes. On the other hand, they continued to call for legally enforceable collective contracts and attempted to organize labourers into 'professional' unions. Aside from the greater violence, there is much here to recall role played by small town Italian Fascists in the Po valley in the winter of 1921–2.[100]

In this example populism was evident in the attempt to mobilize, from outside, the peasantry against the Left, and in the simultaneous remaking of the Right by elements of the urban middle class. In the second example there was a more self-contained populist mobilization of the peasantry. In the southern part of the department of the Rhône, most farmers were either small proprietors (on the plateau in the east of the department) or small tenant farmers (in the mountainous west). In both cases the Church provided the main link between relatively isolated peasant families, most were relatively prosperous and most were conservative. Peasants generally accepted the leadership of liberal notables, who dominated both the main political party of the Right, the Fédération républicaine and the powerful agricultural syndicate, the Union du sud-est (USE).

In the 1920s, however, a combination of factors began to strengthen a class of self-conscious Catholic medium peasant proprietors. The exodus from the countryside of smaller proprietors helped them to consolidate their farms. Veterans' associations grew in the smallest of communes. Expansion of milk and fruit production brought greater exposure to the market. At the same time the Church began to modify its social programme. A series of specialist peasant groups were created, chief among them the Jeunesse agricole chrétienne (JAC) in 1928, which expressed peasant fear of the market ecónomy. This organization expanded among the young male peasants who in the course of the 1930s began to win positions in the USE. Their relations with the leaders of this latter body were ambiguous. On the one hand, the elites promoted the JAC as an alternative to Socialism. On the other the peasant militants sought to convert the USE into a genuinely peasant organization by transforming it from a lobby operating within the liberal parliamentary system to a corporatist body. In 1935, many of these peasant militants (along with supporters of other social Catholic organizations) turned to the Croix de Feu.[101] Thus in the politically polarized circumstances of the mid-1930s a group with a long standing hostility to the leadership of the Right turned to the populist and authoritarian radical Right. Three general comments can be made on this example. Firstly, the passage from social Catholicism to the Croix de Feu was facilitated by the fact that both shared anti-Communism, hostility to the establishment, anti-liberalism, the belief in the creation of a new elite drawn from the people and corporatism. Secondly, this movement cannot be defined uniquely in terms of class conflict between peasant proprietors and the social elites. The peasant militants also felt that the tolerant liberalism of the elites was an obstacle to the rechristianization of the nation. Their aim was therefore to reach the masses by demonstrating the efficacy of Catholic solutions to social problems.[102] Finally, the same tendency for groups already opposed to right-wing elites to join the Croix de Feu was repeated elsewhere in France. In Côte-d'Or, for example, peasants rejected the leadership of conservative notables and turned from the Parti agraire to La Rocque's movement.[103]

In the present state of research it is impossible to give similarly detailed examples to illustrate the approach of the Croix de Feu to the industrial proletariat. In any case, before the upheaval of June 1936 the Croix de Feu paid rather less attention to the specific grievances of workers than it did to the peasantry. It is therefore possible only to give the broad outlines of its approach. If paternalism means the distribution of charity to a privileged group of workers then there is some truth in Pierre Milza's view of the social programme of the Croix de Feu.[104] The league organized donations of clothing to the poor. Businessmen such as André Citroën were asked to protect veterans from lay-offs.[105] But La Rocque also spoke of the limitations of private charity and thought in terms of winning over the working class as a whole to the movement. This was evident even in apparently classic charitable activities such as the *soupe populaire* in the working-class district. These were accompanied by a bodyguard of Croix de Feu and VN, whose function was not only to provide protection but also a physical reminder to the unemployed of the fraternity of Verdun and the Somme.[106]

In other words, La Rocque sought mobilization of the proletariat in a new national community. In practical terms this meant acceptance of the 'legitimate anger' of the workers. Suffering as they did from unemployment and harsh exploitation, the workers were said to be rightly distrustful of international capitalism, committees and *salons*.[107] Some of the measures envisaged were the common property of right-wing movements – profit-sharing, paid holidays for faithful employees. Others, such as the regional minimum wage, were somewhat more novel. Of much greater importance were the league's corporatist projects, of which there was no equivalent in the constitutional Right. Whereas the response of the latter to working-class unrest had usually been to point out the illegality of the CGT, the aim of the Croix de Feu was to take it over and to incorporate it into the *profession organisée*, once it had been depoliticized and regionalized.[108] In the meantime the Croix de Feu created a series of professional groups. These were most successful among white collar workers in department stores, banks, the stock exchange and insurance. But undoubtedly a minority of workers were attracted, in the aero industry for example.[109] The same groups provided the core of the Syndicats professionels francçais (SPF) set up by the Croix de Feu during the strikes of June 1936, just before the movement was dissolved. Formation of the SPF was the logical outcome of the Croix de Feu's strategy, especially as it was explicitly connected to the league's belief in the need for compulsory collective contracts.

The SPF was, of course militantly anti-Communist. But it was also connected to the populism of the movement. The Croix de Feu's response to June 1936 was not simply to call for repression, but to make a bid for leadership of the labour movement. As to the motives of the rank and file we can, in the present state of research, do little more than speculate. But it is plausible that the Croix de Feu appealed to conservative workers partly because it appeared better able to protect them from increasingly selfconfident Communists than were the established authorities. Furthermore, under the impact of the economic crisis the parliamentary Right had become increasingly reactionary on social matters, often calling for the abolition of social security measures introduced only a few years previously. So conservative workers, like other sections of the right-wing constituency, had reason to feel neglected by the parliamentary Right. There is evidence that some Croix de Feu workers participated in the strikes of June 1936.[110] And it is not surprising that the SPF developed in some areas a certain dynamism of its own, going beyond the official programme of the parent organization.[111]

The emphasis in the present article on the populism of the Croix de Feu should not be allowed to obscure the fact that the league possessed links to the political establishment. The support of figures such as the forgemaster de Wendel and the electricity magnate Ernest Mercier is well known.[112] Shipping magnates in Marseille and bankers in Lyon also supported the movement.[113] Such links were not merely tactical. Rather they were intrinsic in the very origins of the league's populism: a movement of revolt against conservatives who had failed as conservatives and which therefore combined the mass mobilization more usually associated with the Left with efforts to form alliances with the establishment. Nevertheless, the support of figures such as de Wendel and Mercier for the league was never whole-hearted. Both were reported to distrust the anti-capitalism of the league.[114] The opposition of other wealthy businessmen was more thorough-going. In Lyon, Humbert Isaac, a leading figure in the veterans' movement and a member of the wealthy silk-manufacturing family, denounced La Rocque for stirring up civil war.[115] There was within the Croix de Feu an on-going dialectic of manipulation from above and mobilization from below.

VI

Few would contest the authoritarianism of the Croix de Feu. Research also reveals the populism of the movement. But was it Fascist or national-populist? The answer depends on the extent of the league's hostility to democracy and pluralism. The argument of this article is that attention cannot be confined to La Rocque himself, to his constitutional projects, or to the undoubtedly conservative implications of many of his ideas. The Croix de Feu's project was inseparable from the radical activism of a mass movement which regarded itself as a new elite drawn from the people, mandated by the fallen of the Great War, invested with the task of national regeneration and guided by a leader with heroic qualities. Croix de Feu members were convinced that the existing system was anti-national, and that the agents of corruption were Communists, politicians and Freemasons all united in a bloody conspiracy. The league expected to win power by semi-legal means in circumstances of extreme crisis and knew that its first task would be purge of the administration and trade unions and suppression of the Communist party. Crucially, members would have expected this repression to be carried out not simply by the agencies of the state, but by their own movement, and must have believed that this was what they had been training for in their paramilitary mobilizations. Once these preliminary tasks had been achieved the league would set about the task of reforming the constitution and holding elections. Above all it would establish a corporate system in which antagonistic interests would be subordinated to the needs of the nation. In Griffin's terms it is possible to see in the Croix de Feu a populist 'palingenetic' ultra-nationalism, engaged in a crusade to regenerate a decadent nation. It is in this combination of radical populism with reaction and the use of force by a mass movement that totalitarianism, in the sense used in this article, is to be detected. By this standard, members of the Croix de Feu, at least in 1934 to 1936, were Fascist.

The Croix de Feu was clearly not as extreme as were the Nazis, though judged by the standard of Hitler and the NSDAP none of the paramilitary mass movements which flourished in interwar Europe would have been Fascist. All the same, a principal reason for the relative moderation of the Croix de Feu was that La Rocque both encouraged and restrained radicalism. Also the movement went through several changes. It was radicalized in 1934 and 1935, then from the winter of 1935–6 it moved in a more moderate direction. The PSF gradually abandoned paramilitarism, one of the defining features of Fascism. One cannot therefore conclude that La Rocque's movement was intrinsically Fascist – this would be to fall victim to the essentialism criticized in this article. Rather it operated on the boundary of the Fascist and non-Fascist (perhaps Bonapartist) radical Right, sometimes crossing to one side or the other.

Notes

1 R. Paxton, *Vichy France: old guard, new order* (New York, 1972), pp. 232–3.
2 Z. Sternhell, *Ni droite ni gauche: l'idéologie fasciste en France* (1983).

3 R. Soucy, 'French Fascism and the Croix de Feu: a dissenting interpretation', *J Cont Hist*, 26 (1991), 159–88, and W. Irvine, 'Fascism in France. The strange case of the Croix de Feu', *J Mod Hist*, 63 (1991), 271–95. See also R. Soucy, *French Fascism: the first wave, 1924–1933* (Cambridge, Mass., 1986); M. Margairaz, 'La droite et l'État en France dans les années trente', *Cahiers d'Histoire de l'Institut Maurice Thorez*, 20–1 (1977), 69–88. For the traditional view see R. Rémond, *Les droites en France* (1982); P. Milza, *Fascisme français, passé et présent* (1987); P. Milza 'L'ultra droite des années trente', *Histoire de l'extrême droite en France*, ed. Michel Winock (1992), pp. 165–71; G. Howlett, 'La Rocque, the Croix de Feu and the Parti social français', unpub. D.Phil. thesis (University of Oxford, 1986).
4 P. Péan, *Une jeunesse française: François Mitterrand, 1934–1947* (1994), pp. 25–42.
5 Rémond, *Les droites en France*, pp. 200–2, 213–14. For similar views of the Croix de Feu: P. Burrin, 'Le fascisme', *Histoire des droites en France* ed. J-F. Sirinelli (1992), especially p. 634; P. Milza, *Fascisme français*, p. 137; Z. Sternhell, *Ni droite ni gauche*, p. 20; 'Strands of French Fascism', *Who were the Fascists?*, ed. B. Hagtvet, S. Ugelvik and J. P. Myklebust (Oslo, 1980). For a penetrating critique of Rémond's use of the concept of Bonapartism see Irvine, 'Fascism in France'. See also J. Rothney, *Bonapartism after Sedan* (New York, 1969), conclusion.
6 Soucy, 'French Fascism and the Croix de Feu', p. 163.
7 Irvine, 'Fascism in France', pp. 279, 287, 294–5; Soucy, 'The Croix de Feu', pp. 163–4; Paxton, *Vichy France*, pp. 228–32, offers a more nuanced view, but has something in common with Irvine and Soucy.
8 Rémond, *Les droites en France*, pp. 201–2.
9 By far the most suggestive analysis of this concept is contained in two essays by Ernesto Laclau, 'Fascism and ideology' and 'Towards a theory of populism', both in Laclau, *Politics and ideology in Marxist theory* (1977).
10 Irvine, 'Fascism in France', pp. 287–8, sees in the Croix de Feu an 'essentially petty bourgeois resentment'. Another underlying assumption here is that because populism is petty bourgeois it can have no real substance.
11 This is not to say that there is a single path to the emergence of right-wing populist movements. Dissidents of the Left have often turned to the radical Right. In such cases they are perhaps attracted by the fact that populist movements enable them to indulge simultaneously their hostility to Marxism and to the political establishment. But in the period in question such journeys from Left to far Right were relatively rare, even in Italy. It should also be remembered that the leftist origins of some Fascists does not mean that Fascism ceases to be right wing.
12 This is to modify the interpretation of C. S. Maier, *Recasting bourgeois Europe: stabilization in France, Germany and Italy after World War One* (Princeton, N.J., 1975).
13 These arguments are explained more fully in K. Passmore, 'The French Third Republic: stalemate society or cradle of Fascism?', *Fr Hist*, 7 (1993), 417–49. This article, however, deliberately left aside the question of whether or not the Croix de Feu were Fascist or national-populist, for it is difficult to draw a direct link between a particular type of social crisis and the nature of a political movement. On the one hand, one set of social and political conditions may produce a variety of political responses. On the other, the circumstances which produce Fascist movements may vary. On these questions, see M. Dobry, 'Février 1934 et la découverte de l'allergie de la société française à la "Révolution fasciste" ', *Rev Fr Soc*, 30 (1989), 511–33; K-J. Müller, 'French Fascism and modernisation', *J Cont Hist*, 11 (1976), 75–107.

14 Burrin, 'Le fascisme', pp. 631–2. For a similar argument: P. Milza 'L'ultra droite des années trente', p. 167.
15 Burrin, 'Le fascisme', pp. 631–6.
16 R. Griffin, *The nature of Fascism* (1991), ch. 2, especially pp. 44–6. Note however that Griffin, like some of the authors mentioned above, exaggerates the revolutionary side of Fascism and dismisses compromises with conservatives as 'tactical'.
17 La Rocque's editorial in *Le flambeau* on 1 January 1934 had been on the army.
18 P. Chopine, *Six ans chez les Croix de Feu* (1935), p. 95.
19 Passmore, 'The Right and the extreme Right in the department of the Rhône', unpub. Ph.D. thesis (University of Warwick, 1992), pp. 306–9.
20 It is significant that Pierre Milza's account of the programme of the Croix de Feu comes from *Le flambeau* of October 1933, the only issue of the journal he cites: 'L'ultra-droite des années trente', p. 167.
21 In Lyon, *Le flambeau du sud-est* appeared only five times from 1934 to June 1936.
22 A[rchives] N[ationales] 451 AP 85 (Fonds La Rocque), minutes of the meetings of the subsection of Grasse; AN F^7 13 241, reports of 13 June 1935, 11 July 1935, 30 Nov. 1935.
23 Lt-Col. de La Rocque, *Service public* (1934), pp. 14–19; AN 451 AP 81, circular of 5 Feb. 1934; *Le flambeau*, 1 Apr. 1934.
24 W. D. Irvine, *French conservatism in crisis: the Republican Federation of France in the 1930s* (Baton Rouge, La and London, 1979), p. 114; Chopine, *Six ans chez les Croix de Feu*, pp. 80–6.
25 *Le flambeau*, 7 Sept. 1935.
26 AN 451 AP 81, circular of 22 May 1933.
27 *Le flambeau*, 1 Jan. 12 Oct. 1935.
28 Ibid., 1 Nov. 1934.
29 Ibid., 1 Jan. 1935. 'Un normalien' stated: 'C'est dans cette lutte quotidienne contre l'insécurité, menée avec l'esprit d'équipe, que se réalisera l'oeuvre de votre génération. Vous aurez enrichi notre patrimoine d'idées d'une philosophie nouvelle traduisant les nécessités et les grandeurs de l'action collective et coordonnée.'
30 Ibid., 1 Jan. 1935, 11 May 1935 (signed 'Un normalien').
31 La Rocque, *Service public*, p. 226: La Rocque described the Croix de Feu as a meeting point of Left and Right – an idea, central to Sternhell's view of Fascism.
32 Sternhell, *Ni droite ni gauche: l'idéologie fasciste en France* (1982). For the influence of de Man and Drieu on the Croix de Feu: *Le flambeau*, 2 Mar., 13 Apr. 1935.
33 For Mussolini's commitment to liberal *laissez-faire* doctrines: M. Robson, *Italy: liberalism and Fascism, 1870–1945* (1992), p. 53.
34 Broszat, *The Nazi dictatorship* (1974); I. Kershaw, ' "Working towards the Führer". Reflections on the nature of the Hitler dictatorship', *Cont Eur Hist*, 2 (1993), 103–18; P. Melograni, 'The myth of the Duce in Fascist Italy', *J Cont Hist*, 12 (1976), 221–37.
35 La Rocque, *Service public*, pp. 96–7.
36 Chopine, *Six ans chez les Croix de Feu*, pp. 89–91, 143. AN 451 AP 81, undated circular, impressed on propagandists that they were delegated by the leader himself.
37 AN 451 AP 81, regulations for a *Bureau de propagande*. Propagandists at all levels were enjoined to emphasize a few simple themes in order to create a mystique within the audience, and to distrust *démonstrations savantes*. Another circular of 9 September 1935 laid down guidelines for a propaganda speech and ended with a eulogy of La Rocque.

38 *Le flambeau*, 5 Oct., 16 Nov. 1935.
39 Ibid., 16 Nov. 1935.
40 Ibid., 1 Nov. 1934. See also AN 451 AP 81, national circular of 25 April 1933. A circular of XII section, 20 September 1935, spoke of the imminence of the hour of French renovation.
41 Sometimes even Hitler denied hostility to existing institutions. Introducing the Enabling Act in March 1933 he stated: 'The existence of neither the Reichstag nor the Reichsrat is threatened': quoted in J. Fest, *Hitler* (1977), p. 604.
42 La Rocque, *Service public*, pp. 254–8; *Le flambeau*, 1 Jan. 1935.
43 La Rocque's constitutional projects were not much different either from those of his supposedly more radical opponents within the VN: *La république*, 29 Sept. 1935.
44 *Le flambeau*, 1 Oct. 1933; La Rocque, *Service public*, pp. 196–216.
45 *Le flambeau*, 25 Nov. 1935: 'Dans une époque normale, avec un gouvernement conscient de sa puissance et de ses droits, l'interdit serait d'ores et déjà jeté sur l'officine de trahison qui organise l'émeute dans l'Afrique du Nord, déclenche des agressions préméditées sur la voie publique, impose à des magistrats municipaux des actes de forfaiture et fait bafouer les décrèts lois par ceux-là mêmes qui sont chargés de les appliquer . . . Le mouvement Croix de Feu se montr[e] seul capable de s'opposer à sa volonté destructrice'. On 14 December 1935, *Le flambeau* called for prison sentences for the leaders of the Popular Front.
46 Rémond, *Les droites en France*, pp. 213–14; Milza, *Fascisme français*, p. 137.
47 *Le flambeau*, 2 Mar. 1935.
48 Ibid., 1 Jan. 1935.
49 In *Le flambeau*, 25 May 1935, La Rocque commented on the ability of Hitler, Pilsudski and Mussolini to capture the deep feelings of the masses.
50 La Rocque, *Service public*, pp. 91–3, 197.
51 Ibid. pp. 78–92; *Le flambeau*, 1 Feb., 13 Mar. 1935.
52 Ibid., 1 Feb. 1934. This had been La Rocque's view just before the 6 February riots.
53 Ibid., 2 Nov. 1935.
54 Ibid., 11 Nov. 1935. In *Le flambeau*, 1 March 1935, Francis Georges defined democracy as spontaneously expressed public outrage against corrupt leaders, and refused to identify it with occult and quarrelsome committees.
55 Ibid., 18 May 1935. See also ibid., 1 Oct. 1934 (report on Marne demonstration), for an appeal to the Croix de Feu to unite its efforts in order to establish a new social and national order, in conformity with the wishes of those who had fallen for the defence of liberty.
56 Ibid., 1 Sept. 1934; AN 451 AP 81, special instruction of 25 April 1933, which stated: 'Notre intervention initiale consistera à réduire au silence les fauteurs de désordre – parlementaires ou autres – et à imposer un rassemblement général sur la base des institutions présentes.'
57 *Le flambeau*, 1 Sept. 1934
58 La Rocque, *Service public*, p. 260.
59 *Le flambeau*, 10 Dec. 1935.
60 Ibid., 12 Oct. 1935.
61 Ibid., 1 Mar. 1934. La Rocque argued that such an assault would lead to confrontation with the army.
62 Ibid., 1 Jan. 1935 (La Rocque's editorial and an interview reprinted from *Candide*); ibid., 16 Mar. 1935.
63 Extract from *Le Figaro*, reprinted in *Le flambeau*, 5 Oct. 1935.
64 *Le flambeau*, 1 Jan. 1935, article reprinted from *Candide*.

65 Milza, *Fascisme français*, pp. 135–6.
66 Chopine, *Six ans chez les Croix de Feu*, pp. 161–8.
67 AN F^7 13 241, reports of 13 June 1935, 11 July 1935, 30 Nov. 1935; Fonds La Rocque, 451 AP 85, minutes of the meetings of the subsection of Grasse.
68 Howlett, 'La Rocque', pp. 157–62. For the manifesto of the dissidents: *La république*, 29 Sept. 1935.
69 P. Jankowski, *Communism and collaboration: Simon Sabiani and politics in Marseille, 1919–1944* (New Haven, Conn., 1989), pp. 50–1.
70 This document is quoted in Howlett, 'La Rocque', pp. 171–8.
71 This issue is discussed more fully in K. Passmore, ' "Boy-scouting for grown-ups?" Paramilitarism in the Croix de Feu and PSF', *Fr Hist Stu* (forthcoming, 1995).
72 Interview with La Rocque in *Candide*, reprinted in *Le flambeau*, 1 Jan. 1935.
73 *Le flambeau*, 1 Jan., 6 Apr., 12 Oct. 1935.
74 Ibid., 13 Apr., 21 Sept. 1935.
75 Interview with La Rocque in *Candide*, reprinted in *Le flambeau*, 1 Jan. 1935.
76 This is the view of Milza, *Fascisme français*, p. 137.
77 La Rocque, *Service public*, pp. 129, 208–10.
78 M. Launey, *La CFTC: origines et développement, 1919–1940* (1986).
79 Péan, *Une jeunesse française*, pp. 25–42. This question is dealt with at greater length in Passmore, 'Stalemate society or cradle of Fascism?'.
80 For a stimulating discussion of the changing nature of social Catholicism: J-M. Mayeur, 'Catholicisme intransigeant, catholicisme social, démocratie chrétienne', *Annales ESC*, 27 (1972), 483–99.
81 K. Passmore, 'Une contre-mobilisation: la droite et l'extrême droite lyonnaises en 1939', *Le geste commémoratif*, ed. J. Duvallon, P. Dujardin and G. Sabatier (Lyon, 1994), pp. 445–65.
82 For the hostility of the Church: letter of abbé Michoud, chaplain of the Jeunesse agricole chrétienne in the Rhône, quoted in G. Gayet 'L'Union du sud-est des syndicats agricoles', unpub. DES d'histoire (Lyon II, 1969), pp. 73–4.
83 R. R. Locke, *French Legitimists and the politics of moral order* (Princeton, N.J., 1974), pp. 154–69. Most Legitimists agreed that education was not for the masses.
84 La Rocque, *Service public*, pp. 117–22, 124–8.
85 Passmore, 'The French Third Republic', pp. 427–33.
86 La Rocque, *Service public*, pp. 81–3.
87 Ibid. pp. 142–8, 211; *Le flambeau*, 1 Sept. 1934 ('Un normalien').
88 Milza, *Fascisme français*, p. 137.
89 D. Roberts, *Italian Fascism and the syndicalist tradition* (Manchester, 1979), pp. 304–5. In September 1922, Mussolini stated: 'we want to remove from the state all its economic attributes. We have had enough of the state railwaymen, the State postman and the State insurance official. We have had enough of the State administration at the expense of Italian tax-payers, which has done nothing but aggravate the exhausted financial situation of the country': quoted in Robson, *Italy: liberalism and Fascism*, pp. 43–4. Hitler cited the Italian precedent in arguing against Strasser's plans for nationalization: J. Noakes and G. Pridham, *Nazism 1919–1945. I. The rise to power 1919–1934* (Exeter, 1983), pp. 66–7.
90 La Rocque, *Service public*, pp. 139, 197–8.
91 Ibid. pp. 139–40, 148. See also *Le flambeau*, 1 Jan. 1935, for his view on regulation of the arms industry.
92 *Le flambeau*, 2 Mar. 1935.
93 K. Passmore, 'Business, corporatism and the crisis of the French Third republic. The example of the silk industry in Lyon', *Hist J* (forthcoming, 1995) for further development of these arguments.

94 La Rocque, *Service public*, pp. 211–12.
95 Quoted from an unpublished paper by Janine Bourdin, in Milza, *Fascisme français*, p. 138. These figures derive from unpublished party sources and are more reliable than those used by Irvine, 'Fascism in France', p. 284.
96 For example, P. Machefer, 'Les Croix de Feu', *Inf Historique*, 34 (1972), 28–34.
97 In other words, the fact that industrial workers did not generally join the Croix de Feu can be explained in terms of historical context. There is nothing intrinsic to right-wing radical populism which means that it cannot have a working-class base, as the experience of Argentina shows.
98 *Le flambeau*, 7 Sept. 1935.
99 AN 451 AP 85, letter of André Ferté to Mlle Feraud of the Croix de Feu Foyer agricole, undated, written during the electoral campaign of 1936.
100 Snowden. 'The social origins of agrarian Fascism in Italy', *Arch Eur Sociol*, (1972), 268–95.
101 Gayet, 'L'Union du sud-est', pp. 73–4; Passmore, 'The Right and the extreme Right', p. 353.
102 *Croix du Rhône*, 31 Mar. 1935, 12 Apr. 1936.
103 T. Hohl, 'Le Parti agraire et paysan français. Une tentative agrairienne en Côte d'Or (1929–1939)', *Ann Bourgogne*, 59 (1988), 140–50.
104 Milza, *Fascisme français*, pp. 137–8.
105 Howlett, 'La Rocque', p. 94.
106 *Le flambeau*, 23 Mar. 1935.
107 Ibid., 29 June 1935.
108 La Rocque, *Service public*, pp. 145–8.
109 AN BB^{18}3048^2, history of the Croix de Feu, 31 June 1936.
110 *Lyon républicain*, 18 June 1936; Jankowski, *Communism and collaboration*, pp. 50–1.
111 Passmore, 'The Right and the extreme Right', pp. 503–4. Some SPF unionists were involved in agitation for implementation of forty-hour legislation, for index linked wages and for collective contracts.
112 R. F. Kuisel, *Ernest Mercier: French technocrat* (Los Angeles, 1967); J-N. Jeaneney, *François de Wendel en république* (1979), pp. 485–90.
113 Jankowski, *Communism and collaboration*, p. 47.
114 AN F^7 13 241, report of 20 July 1935.
115 A. Prost, *Les anciens combattants et la société française*, 3 vols. (1977), ii. 170–1.

9.4

'Parafascism'

65

VICHY AND FASCISM

Julian Jackson

Source: Edward Arnold (ed.) *The Development of the Radical Right in France 1890–1995*, London: Routledge, 2000, pp. 153–71.

In the summer of 1940, the normally decorous and sleepy spa town of Vichy was seething with activity. Politicians, pundits and prophets arrived to peddle their solutions to France's problems and offer their services to the newly installed government of Marshal Pétain. Among them was Marcel Déat, a former Socialist, who now believed that France must learn from the example of the fascist powers. On 8 July 1940 he wrote: 'We need, like other peoples who have carried out their revolution, whether Italy, Germany or Russia, a party, a single party, which establishes and orients the shared aspirations of the people.'[1]

Déat approached Pétain and Laval to propose the establishment of a single party, and he set up a committee to work out the details. Most members of the committee had previously signed a declaration on 7 July, calling for an 'authoritarian new order' in France. The author of this declaration was Gaston Bergery, another former leftist politician who had progressively moved into the orbit of fascism after 1934. Although wishing the 'new order' not to be a 'servile copy' of Nazism, Bergery's declaration insisted that it be compatible with the new regimes of 'continental Europe'.[2] By 27 July Déat's committee had produced its report. It advocated the establishment of a single party, acting as the sole mediator between state and society. The Party would forge a national community and create 'an activist élite, almost an activist order'. Jews would not be admitted to join it.[3]

Déat's idea was that all existing parties and interest groups would allow themselves to be absorbed into the single party. In fact the members of his committee could not even agree among themselves. Bergery wanted to be sent on a mission to study the single parties of Italy, Germany, Spain and Portugal; the prewar fascist leader Jacques Doriot, who sent a representative to the committee, was angling to ensure a predominant rôle for his party the PPF; Colonel de la Rocque, whose PSF was the most successful party of the extreme right, put it about that Doriot was in receipt of German funds, and withdrew his support from the committee on 11 August. Even if the organisers had agreed among themselves, the scheme would never had got off the ground because Pétain, although not openly discouraging, was not keen on parties of any kind. General Weygand and Charles Maurras, the leader of Action Française, intervened to express their opposition to this 'totalitarian' solution. As for Pierre Laval, Pétain's deputy premier, he was suspicious of anything which he did not control.

Pétain suggested that the supporters of a single party should be sent on a mission around France to sound out opinion and prepare the ground. The eternally credulous Déat was pleasantly surprised, failing to see that this was a manoeuvre to get the protagonists of this single party out of the way. The committee's discussions continued during August in an increasingly unrealistic way – one session even considered the uniforms – but even Déat knew the game was lost when it was announced on 29 August that Vichy was uniting the existing war veterans' associations into a single Légion Française des Combattants (LFC). This was not a single party, but Vichy's alternative to it.

At the start of September, Déat left in disgust for Paris. He was not the only fascist to have despaired of Vichy in the summer of 1940. Lucien Rebatet, journalist on the extreme right newspaper, *Je suis partout*, was another fascist sympathiser who had unsuccessfully tried to gain a foothold in Vichy. He and a group of friends tried to secure key positions in the regime's propaganda services, but they were quickly seen off by Pétain's more traditionalist advisers.[4] Like Déat, Rebatet headed for Paris. As he later wrote: 'everyone who possessed real fascist and anti-Jewish convictions returned to Paris'.[5] Or, to quote another prominent fascist writer, Pierre Drieu La Rochelle: 'we were stupidly expelled from Vichy by all those who plotted against the salutary but fascist idea of the single party'.[6]

I

Was that the end of fascism at Vichy? With the exception of the Communist historian Roger Bourderon, most historians have judged that it was, at least until the final days of the regime in 1944.[7] The fascists were confined to Paris from where they hurled imprecations upon what they judged to be the conservative and reactionary Vichy regime. Paris was the home of the 'collaborationists' – the word was first used by Déat in November 1940 – who were ideologically committed to collaboration. This distinguished their attitude from the policy of the Vichy government whose collaboration was motivated by pragmatic or geo-political calculations. Not all collaborationists were fascist – some of them were pro-German because they were pacifist – but all fascists were collaborationist. Of course the boundaries between Paris and Vichy, collaboration and collaborationism, were always porous.

Doriot received some subsidies from Vichy; the Légion des Volontaires Français contre le Bolchevisme (LVF), which recruited volunteers to fight with the Germans against the Soviet Union, obtained discreet Vichy approval; and no one was more committed to the collaborationist position than Vichy's official representative in the Occupied Zone, Fernand de Brinon.

In general, however, the dichotomy between Paris and Vichy was absolute. It mirrored the situation prevailing in the rest of occupied Europe where Hitler backed conservative leaders over fascist ones. In Rumania, Antonescu was preferred to the Iron Guard, and in Hungary Admiral Horthy was preferred to Szalasi's Arrow Cross. In Holland, Anton Mussert was kept at arm's length, as was Léon Degrelle in Belgium. Similarly in France, Drieu, Doriot, Déat and others waited impatiently for their moment to arrive, plotting and counter-plotting, trying to exploit to their benefit the rivalries of the different German authorities – the Abwehr, the SS or the German Ambassador Otto Abetz. In 1941, Déat, who had founded a fascist movement (the RNP), seemed to be in the ascendant. In 1942, the coming man seemed to be Doriot who began to talk of Laval as the Kerensky to his Lenin (Doriot had once been a Communist). But in September 1942, Hitler made it clear that he was still backing Laval. Until the end of 1943, Hitler's main use for the French fascists was as a sword of Damocles suspended over the Vichy regime.

If Vichy was not fascist, what kind of regime was it? One comparison often made by historians is with Salazar's Portugal. This is given credence by the fact that the comparison was explicitly drawn by Vichy supporters at the time. Salazar's regime was styled the New State. Vichy was L'Etat Français.[8] Pétain's aide Henri Dumoulin de Labarthète tells us that Pétain, not excessively bookish, kept on his bedside-table a copy of Salazar's collection of speeches which had appeared in France under the title *Comment on relève un Etat* (1937).[9] The third edition of the speeches in 1942 contained a preface which explicitly noted the similarities with France: 'Like Salazar, the declared enemy of destructive communism, [Pétain] clearly distances himself from Nazism and Fascism, rightly believing that this totalitarian system ... does not correspond to the French character and temperament.... Like Salazar, Marshal Pétain does not want a single party, which on the pretext of supporting the State in fact dominates it. That is why he has organised the Legion of Veterans.'[10]

Even if it is true that the Portuguese model is the most appropriate comparison with Vichy, this still begs the question of the nature of Salazarism, and its relationship to fascism. After all, Portugal did have a single party, the União Nacional (UN, National Union), from 1930. This does not make the regime fascist, but it does at least distinguish it from Vichy, where the single-party solution had been rejected in 1940. Before proceeding further, therefore, it is necessary to offer some comparative typology of interwar fascist and authoritarian regimes. One classic distinction is that made by

Juan Linz between totalitarian and authoritarian systems. In authoritarian regimes, according to Linz, the single party, when it exists, is not interested in mass mobilisation and it does not have a monopoly of access to office: its role is to prevent dissidence not to organise consensus.[11]

It is possible to distinguish three types of regime which resort to the use of single parties:

1. Italy and Germany where a fascist party captured power (with help from conservative élite), and more or less speedily moved to outlaw all other parties.
2. Regimes where there was an existing fascist movement of some importance which played little part in the overthrow of democracy but was significant enough to need to be accommodated in some way. This was the case of Spain where the fascist party, the Falange, was amalgamated with various other movements and became in theory the official support of the new regime. In fact many Falangists felt frustrated by the force of traditional conservatism and there was a shifting triangle of power between army, the élite (Church, landowners) and the party.
3. Regimes with no fascist movement of any importance prior to the collapse of democracy where single parties were created from above as a means of retaining power. This was the case, for example, of Primo de Rivera's Spain or Salazar's Portugal where the *coup d'état* occurred in 1926, but the UN was not created until 1933. The UN's role, however, was highly circumscribed. It existed to channel the support of the notables rather than to harness the support of the masses.[12]

This tripartite typology can only be used very approximately. Even in Salazar's Portugal, despite the fictitiousness of the UN and despite the fact that the only pre-existing fascist movement, Francisco Preto's National Syndicalists, was destroyed, there were other organisations with a more mobilising purpose than the UN. There was a National Secretariat for Propaganda run by Antonio Ferro who was an admirer of fascism; there was a paramilitary Portuguese Legion; there were state sponsored youth movements.[13] Roger Griffin, who has recently offered a very interesting 'ideal-type' definition of fascism, argues that these devices were only a 'facade' and that the elimination of Preto shows the difference between 'parafascism' and 'the real thing'.[14] Such a distinction, however, seems to fall into the trap of essentialism which Griffin in general tries to avoid. Even in Italy, after all – and surely Italy must be 'the real thing' – the old structures of clientelism still operated in the South, and the party was never more than a decor on the old notables.

The main problem with any kind of essentialism is that it fails to consider fascism dynamically.[15] Even in Germany and Italy the arrival to power of the fascists was followed by tensions in the relationship between the party, the state apparatus and the traditional élite (Churches, army, business leaders).

These struggles for power were complex – it is a major over-simplification to consider the traditional élite as homogeneous in their interests and strategies – and the differences were never resolved.[16] Nazi rule, as Martin Broszat long ago pointed out, was 'polycratic'.[17] Broadly speaking, as time went on, in Germany the party and its annexes absorbed the state apparatus and weakened the élite; in Italy the party was less successful at securing its hegemony. In both cases there was a totalitarian aspiration – the word was invented in Italy, after all – but it came nearer to being achieved in Germany. So striking are the differences between the regimes that, as the late Tim Mason lamented, the concept of generic fascism has come to be downplayed in the recent historiography of Nazi Germany.[18] The Nazi regime is now often viewed *sui generis* as a racial state.

Authoritarian regimes should be studied dynamically, in terms of a shifting balance of forces and unresolved tension between different groups. There is a sense in which no regime, not even Italy or Germany, was ever fully 'fascist', but equally no interwar authoritarian regime was not affected in some respect by the new kind of politics which fascism represented. Essentialism is particularly inappropriate in the case of the Vichy regime, which displayed one fundamental difference from the other regimes mentioned above. The regime was a product of external defeat and did not emerge out of an internal political crisis in which one faction, as it were, triumphed over others. There had of course been a profound crisis of liberal democracy in interwar France, but a resolution of that crisis seemed to have been achieved by the arrival to power of Daladier in 1938. Daladier provided an authoritarian style of government which reassured conservatives who had been terrified by the Popular Front. The defeat of 1940 reopened France's internal crisis without preconditioning its outcome. Of course even in Germany, Italy or Portugal, power struggles continued after the collapse of democracy, but some options were closed off by the way in which democracy had collapsed. In France in 1940, the situation, without being a *tabula rasa*, was comparatively open-ended. The political battles lay ahead.

Any discussion of Vichy must bear in mind that the regime was not a bloc. In the four years of its existence, the regime went through several political upheavals – the dismissal of Laval on 13 December 1940, the short interlude of Flandin's premiership between December 1940 and February 1941, the premiership of Darlan from February 1941 to April 1942, the return of Laval in April 1942 – and at any one moment there were always several factions contending for influence. Having said this, two general observations can be made about the regime. First, there was no Vichy *Gleichschaltung*, and no attempt to carry one out. The regime believed in handing back power to 'natural communities', although the severe shortages of food and raw materials forced the state to intervene much more in the running of economic and social life than was compatible with such an aspiration.

In many areas of policy, the regime did not so much set up its own organisations and institutions as encourage initiatives which were believed to be in the right spirit. These included the cultural youth organisation Jeune France founded by Pierre Schaeffer, the cadre training school at Uriage founded by Pierre Dunoyer de Segonzac, and the Compagnons youth movement founded by Henri Dhavernas. The existence of these semi-independent bodies created extensive 'spaces of liberty' between the regime and civil society.[19] There was a lesser degree of cultural uniformity than might have been expected. It is the case that the spaces of liberty shrank over time. When heterodoxy became too blatant, the regime was ready to intervene – Jeune France was closed down in April 1942 and Uriage in November 1942 – yet some areas of cultural life remained seemingly impervious to official propaganda. Most films produced in France during the Vichy period seem curiously timeless. It may well be that the values of the regime were subtly represented on the cinema screen, but it also remains true that there was probably less anti-Semitism and Anglophobia in the Vichy cinema than there had been in the cinema of the 1930s.[20]

One area where Vichy was explicitly committed to pluralism was youth policy. In September 1940 the regime set up the Secrétariat Général à la Jeunesse (SGJ, General Secretariat for Youth) which was headed by Georges Lamirand, and engineer with a strong social Catholic affinities and a belief in the morally elevating virtue of scouting. Originally Lamirand had intended to promulgate a Youth Charter requiring every young person to join a youth movement, but he backed down in the face of Church opposition. Even so Lamirand had never intended to create a single youth movement. This was ruled out by Pétain in a speech of 13 August 1940: 'all youth movements will be maintained, their originality will be respected, their action encouraged'. Vichy required pre-existing youth movements – mainly Catholic – to apply for official accreditation (*agrément*), but this was granted quite liberally. In June 1941, it was extended to all six scouting movements – including the Eclaireurs Israélites de France, the Jewish scouts (until January 1943). The regime's youth policy was that defined by the Church in July 1941: 'A united youth? Yes. . . . A single youth? No.'[21] The only obligation which Vichy imposed on the young was the requirement that all 22-year-olds carry out six (later eight) months of civic training in so-called Chantiers de Jeunesse (Youth Work Sites). Originally conceived as a measure against unemployment, this was effectively a replacement for military service which was no longer possible given the restrictions on the size of the army.

The second preliminary observation which needs to be made about Vichy is that the regime proposed a radical project for the restructuring of the political and social order. It aimed to break with the Third Republic, the '*ancien régime*', as it was dubbed. This project for renewal, which Vichy called the National Revolution, involved, among other things, re-casting the relations between workers and employers, establishing a new pattern of gender relations (or rather returning to one which it was believed had been disrupted), reinvigorating the country's youth and purging France of its supposed internal enemies (anti-France, as Pétain put it). These enemies – foreigners, freemasons, communists and Jews (both French and foreign) – were the subject of repression, persecution and exclusion from the earliest days of the regime. The idea of 'palingenesis', of rebirth, which Roger Griffin sees as one of the characteristics of a fascist caste of mind, was an ingredient of Vichy. There was much talk of creating an *'homme nouveau'*, and there was a distinctively new style of politics.[22] The humanist writer Jean Guehenno wrote of his first visit to the unoccupied zone in 1942: 'we were in a strange world where everyone, from the children of six regimented in Youth groups right up to War Veterans wearing francisques or insignia of the Legion [of war Veterans] seems to be in uniform. Where is France in all this?'[23]

II

Vichy, then, was a curious mixture of tolerance and repression, of cultural pluralism and ambitious state projects for cultural regeneration. The configurations were constantly shifting as the factions struggled for power. The forces in contention included *fonctionnaires*, the military, large business interests, small businessmen and technocrats. They represented a wide range of political positions: Maurrassianism, conservative liberalism, syndicalism, social Catholicism, personalism and fascism. In the first months of the regime – the moment when the 'fascist' option was rejected – the most important influences were the traditional élite – the Church and army – and the state administration. These were the forces which had remained most intact during the *débâcle* of 1940. One of General Weygand's main reasons for demanding an armistice had been, like Ludendorff in Germany in 1918, to prevent the total disintegration of the army. The military were all-pervasive in the first days of the regime. In the government formed by Pétain on 12 July 1940 there were more military men than in any other government since Marshal Soult's in 1832.[24] The first months of the regime were also a high-watermark of Catholic influence, culminating in the reforms of Jacques Chevalier, Minister of Education between December 1940 and February 1941. These gave the Church more influence over education than it had enjoyed for a century. Most of Chevalier's reforms were to be abandoned by his successors. As for the influence of the state apparatus, Yves Bouthillier, Vichy Minister of Finance, but also a member of the high administrative caste of Inspecteurs des Finances, remarked that Vichy was the 'triumph of administration over politics'.[25] Indeed, under Vichy the line between government and administration became very blurred. In each ministry the regime created the new administrative post of Secretary-General (somewhat on the model of British permanent secretaries) who often became as powerful as their ministers, if not more so. In some cases when the minister was sacked he was replaced by his Secretary-General (for example, Chevalier who became Minister of Education in December, Marcel Peyrouton who became Minister of the Interior in September 1940).[26]

With the advent of Darlan in February 1941 there was a shift in the balance of forces within the regime. More than ever Vichy became a government of 'experts'. To the Inspector of Finance Yves Bouthillier, the engineer Jean Berthelot as Minister of Communications and the agricultural economist Pierre Caziot as Minister of Agriculture were added the classicist Jérôme Carcopino as Minister of Education and the respected law professor Joseph Barthélemy as Minister of Justice. Vichy was in that sense a realisation of the Orleanist dream of a government of *compétences*. But under Darlan a new and different kind of 'expert' also came to prominence: the 'technocrats'. These were mostly around 40 years old – which in Vichy terms made them very young – often with backgrounds in industry or finance, and with ambitions to modernise the French economy. The most powerful figure among them was Pierre Pucheu, formerly an international sales director for the French steel industry, who became Minister of Industrial Production, February 1941–July 1941, and Minister of the Interior, July 1941–April 1942. Other technocrats included Jacques Barnaud, who was in charge of the economic relations with the Germans from February 1941 to November 1942, and François Lehideux (b.1904), who was Minister of Industrial Production from July 1941 to April 1942. Barnaud had worked for the Worms Bank and been involved in discussion groups of modernising businessmen in the 1930s; Lehideux had been a manager at Renault.

These Young Turks aroused much suspicion. It was rumoured that they were members of a secret organisation known as the Synarchy which was allegedly linked to the Worms Bank. Their influence was seen as the result of a sinister conspiracy. The Synarchy had no basis in fact, but Jacques Benoist-Méchin (1901–83), who was one of the group who came to prominence under Darlan, admitted in his memoirs that, although the notion of a conspiracy was far-fetched, there was a 'team' which shared similar views and met regularly to discuss them. Many of them had known each other since the 1930s through groups such as X-Crise or the *Nouveaux Cahiers*.[27] They shared a sympathy towards fascist-style politics, if not indeed a fully-fledged commitment to fascism. In 1941, fascist solutions were under discussion again.

The two important fascist presences at Vichy in 1941 were Benoist-Méchin and Paul Marion, both of whom were appointed as Secretary-Generals to the President of the Council (Benoist-Méchin became Minister of State in June 1941). Their titles sound fairly anodyne, but they exercised considerable power, Marion over propaganda – he was in effect Minister of Propaganda – and Benoist-Méchin over relations with Germany. Benoist-Méchin had been a journalist in the 1930s and an active member of the Comité

France-Allemagne. The passion of his life was the need for Franco-German reconciliation. This meant, as he put it in his memoirs, that France should 'align her institutions on those of the totalitarian powers', and carry out a 'boldly Socialist policy' and a 'racist policy'.[28] Paul Marion (b.1899) was a quintessential representative of that generation whose political anchors had been forever destroyed by the Great War. He had been a communist until 1929, after which he passed through a number of stages in Jacques Doriot's PPF which he left in 1938. The only consistency in this trajectory was the rejection of liberalism and conservatism, and a restless search for an energetic politics. Marion was fascinated by totalitarian methods of propaganda on which he wrote a book in 1939 entitled *Leur combat: Lénine, Mussolini, Hitler, Franco*. Déat said of Marion: 'he was a true fascist . . . he had this mixture of love and irreducible hatred which characterises true revolutionaries'.[29]

If there was a mafia at Vichy in 1941, it was to be found less in the imaginary Synarchy than in the presence of former members of the PPF which is one of the few right-wing movements of the 1930s which historians agree to identify as fascist. Apart from the presence of Marion and Pucheu in the government, former PPF members were also prominent among the advisers of the new team: Robert Loustau and Yves Paringaux in Pucheu's *cabinet*; Claude Popelin in Lehideux's *cabinet*; Maurice Touzé, as an aide to Marion.

There was, then, at Vichy in 1941 a group which had fascist affinities. What was the nature and extent of their influence? Darlan's priority, and that of the technocrats, was that France should be able to hold her own economically in the new Europe. Where his predecessor, Laval, had only been interested in collaboration and cared little about domestic reform providing it did not annoy the Germans – leaving the field clear for the traditionalists on the domestic front – under Darlan there was a greater congruence between domestic and foreign policy. Pucheu pushed for a greater politicisation of the administration. He wanted to give a more political training to the Perfects, and he undertook major reforms of the police. In October 1941, he created three new police services: the Anti-Communist Police (SPAC), the Jewish Police (PQJ) and the Secret Societies' Police [i.e. freemasons] (SSS). These were not staffed by police professionals but by professional anti-Semites and members of the PPF who made up in zeal what they lacked in professionalism.

This was part of the more repressive turn taken by the regime in the summer of 1941. But repression was also accompanied by increased concern with propaganda, and a return to the idea of a single party. This occurred because the regime had so far failed to create any organisations or institutions to able to mediate successfully between State and society. The Légion des Combattants, which had been Vichy's substitute for a single party, proved unsatisfactory. Its exact role had never been well-defined – the veterans were told that they were to be the 'ears and eyes' of the Marshal throughout France – and there was a lot of tension between local Légion leaders and the Prefects. Darlan, who was primarily interested in efficient government, tried to resolve the issue by issuing official guidelines in February 1941 which stipulated that the legionnaires were to assist the government's legal representatives – the Prefects – not supplant them. But ambiguity remained, and a further instruction was issued in April demarcating the limits between the Légion and the administration. This allowed them the 'right and even the duty' to enlighten the authorities on any matter which contradicted the spirit of the National Revolution. Another problem with the Légion was that it was limited to one category of the population, and an ageing one at that (rules of admission for veterans of 1939–40 were much tighter than for their First World War elders). Thus it excluded by definition many potentially dynamic supporters of the regime.[30]

Given the inadequacies of the Légion, other means were sought to construct links between state and society. One such attempt was Flandin's Conseil National, founded in February 1941, which was intended to provide some representation for traditional notables. But it was never given an important role to play. Another was the Amicale de France, founded in November 1940, by members of Pétain's entourage, among them his doctor Bernard Ménétrel. The Amicale had a network of Equipes du Maréchal who were supposed to spread the gospel of the National Revolution. Rather than being an avatar of a single party the Amicale was a struggle in the battle of influence between Pétain's entourage and Laval. Technically it was an independent organisation which put itself at the service of the National Revolution.

More ambitious was the Comité du Rassemblement pour la Révolution Nationale set up in January 1941. Vichy intrigues were always so complicated that it is impossible to be sure exactly who was behind this initiative and why. It seems to have been an attempt by Pétain's traditionalist adviser, Dumoulin de Labarthète, to outflank the efforts of the ultra-collaborationist groups in Paris, and it may have got the support of Darlan because he saw it as a way of undercutting 'Flandin's' Conseil national. The Comité contained representatives of the LFC, the PSF and the PPF, but it never got off the ground because these groups could not agree. The LFC in particular had no intention of being absorbed into any other organisation. By the spring the Comité had ceased to meet.[31]

The protagonists of a more fascist-style solution received a boost when Marion took over responsibility for propaganda in January 1941. He set about organising a network of propaganda delegates in each department as the embryo of a future single party. As a step in this direction Marion absorbed the Amicale de France into his own propaganda organisation. He talked à la Goebbels of his ambition to remould the population: 'a government inspired by the revolutionary spirit must act towards France like a sculptor with his clay'. In October 1941 Marion set up a special school at Mayet de la Montagne to train his propaganda cadres.[32]

Marion found an ally in Pucheu, and in the summer of 1941 there was renewed talk of a Single Party. One route to this was to get the cooperation of La Rocque whose PSF still represented a considerable potential force. But La Rocque proved uncooperative when Pucheu saw him on 18 September. Instead Pucheu and Marion turned their attention to toughening up the LFC and pushing it further towards being a dynamic fascist-style party. In November 1941 the Légion's statutes were changed: it was now opened to non-veterans and its name changed to Légion Française des Combattants et des Volontaires de la Révolution Nationale. Yet another circular in February 1942 put the Légion much more directly under the control of the government. But this result fell far short of Pucheu's ambitions. François Valentin, the leader of the Légion, clung on to his independence, and at the moment that the Légion was supposedly given a wider role, its influence was declining. Recruitment fell, and the most dynamic members were siphoned off by the Service d'Ordre Légionnaire (SOL), which was to become in 1943 the Milice.[33]

Marion and Pucheu also had designs on youth policy. They viewed Lamirand's SGJ as too pluralistic, too Catholic, and insufficiently political. In May 1941 Marion tried to get his protégé Armand Petitjean appointed to head the supposedly independent Compagnons de France youth movement. This was unsuccessful and instead Marion tried to build up another youth movement, the Jeunesse de France et d'Outre-Mer (JFOM), which was more overtly political than the Compagnons. Lamirand was successful in keeping youth policy under his control, but even within the SGJ there remained differences of view about this. His immediate subordinate, Louis Garrone – the main architect of the policy of *agréments* – was in sympathy with his outlook, but another SGJ official, Georges Pelorson, in charge of propaganda in the Occupied Zone, was closer to Marion's position.

At the start of 1942 the fascists turned their attention again to youth policy. There was an important debate on youth policy in the Youth Commission of the Conseil National between 5 and 12 March 1942. Representatives of the Churches, both Catholic and Protestant, continued to defend pluralism. Lamirand, while admitting disappointments, defended what he had achieved so far. Pucheu attacked the 'boy scout' and 'churchy' (*calotin*) spirit of the government's youth policies and claimed that the Church had too much influence over youth movements, and was too marked by the past to be able to offer the necessary cadres and vigorous leadership which the new France required. Pelorson spoke in the same spirit, and even more outspoken was Bergery who explicitly called for a single youth movement to create in France the classless and egalitarian society he believed to exist in Germany. In the middle were the spokesmen of Pétain's cabinet – Massis, Dumoulin – who agreed that the SGJ had been too lax, but rejected any move towards what they called totalitarianism. Pétain's opening remarks had reiterated his rejection of any single youth movement – 'there is no question of creating a State youth movement' – but went on: 'Could we not, if we perceived a determined political vocation among some of the young, group them together and mobilise them in the service of the National Revolution?' In the end the compromise reached envisaged the creation of a new non-confessional movement which would absorb the Compagnons and JFOM. This certainly seems to have been a considerable step in the direction of Pucheu, but whether it might, as Pucheu hoped, have developed into a single movement we cannot know since the return of Laval a month later removed from power many of the protagonists in the debate (Pucheu, Dumoulin), and changed the political situation entirely.[34]

III

Laval's government, although containing unconditional collaborationists like his Minister of Education Abel Bonnard, represented a shift away from any experimentation with, even discussion of, fascist-style methods. Marion remained in the government, but lost influence; Pucheu was removed. The new head of the LFC did announce in October 1942 that there should one day be a single party based around the Legion,[35] but in the immediate term, at least, Laval preferred to attempt a return to the clientelist practices of the Third Republic. At local level the regime abandoned the appointive Commissions Administratives with which Vichy had replaced the elective Conseils Généraux of the Republic. Instead Laval set up new 'Conseils départementaux'. The members were to be designated by the Prefects, but Laval asked for preference to be given to traditional notables, especially people who had held elected office under the Republic. Paul Creyssel, whom Laval had appointed to look after propaganda, told the propaganda delegates in May 1943 that the single party had been abandoned: 'French society can only be led by its natural cadres, by the intermediary of the political notables'.[36]

This superficial 'republicanisation' does not mean that Laval intended any return to democracy. On the contrary, in this period Vichy became ever more repressive. Laval, however, was interested in using whatever means might be most effective at selling collaboration and keeping order. His promotion of officials like Jean Bichelonne, who became Minister of Production, and René Bousquet, who was put in charge of the police, was inspired by the same logic. Bousquet was un-ideological and had started his Prefectoral career in the Third Republic as a protégé of the powerful Radical politicians, the brothers Sarraut. Bousquet, who had no time for para-political police forces, immediately tried to wind up or absorb the politicised police forces which Pucheu had created. Although his name is associated above all with the round-ups of Jews in the summer of 1942, his primary motive was to prevent the Germans interfering in French policing. Bousquet acted more in a spirit of administrative tidiness than ideological commitment.[37]

One area in which the fascist temptation was not entirely abandoned was youth policy. Bonnard brought in a team of advisers who were, like him, committed to collaborationism: Maurice Gait, a Maurrassian increasingly attracted to National Socialism and believing in a single youth movement, and Jacques Bousquet (no relation of René), who shocked ministry officials by giving the fascist salute when he took over as director of Bonnard's *cabinet*.[38] Although Lamirand remained nominally at the head of the SGJ, Pelorson now became his deputy. The pluralistic policy of the Youth commissariat was not abandoned, but accreditation was now conferred on politicised movements close to the collaborationists – JFOM and the Jeunesses Francistes. Pelorson was clear that his conception of the SGJ was to provide the 'political and revolutionary formation necessary for the New French State'.[39] The instrument of this transformation were to be the Equipes Nationales, founded in 1941 in the Occupied Zone, to clear bomb damage. In August 1942, Pelorson summoned the leaders of the Youth Movements and told them that the Equipes were to be the core of a single youth movement swearing total obedience to the Marshal. But the resistance of the youth leaders, especially those of the Catholic movements, prevented anything coming of this. In the autumn of 1943 the SGJ agreed that the Equipes would after all be confined to social tasks.[40]

In 1943 the regime became increasingly repressive as its authority was undermined by the massive movement of civil disobedience sparked off by the introduction of compulsory labour service (STO). The main instrument of repression was the Milice set up in January 1943. The Milice had grown out of the most activist members of the LFC. Its leader Darnand, who had something of the *baroudeur* mentality of Ernest Rohm or the members of the German Freikorps, was one of those First World War veterans who never entirely re-adapted to civilian life after 1919, and had dabbled in right-wing politics ever since, seeking in it the masculine comradeship he had found in the trenches. Laval wanted the Milice as a sort of praetorian guard protecting the regime against its enemies. It did become increasingly important during the course of 1943 as the Resistance became increasingly threatening and the regime less and less able to rely on the loyalty of the police.

But Darnand envisaged a much more extensive role for the Milice than this. It was divided into several sections with the majority members continuing a normal professional life and devoting a few hours a week to their Milice activities. In addition, there was a special section – the Avant-Garde – for boys and girls; a fully militarised section – the Franc-Garde – whose members would be permanently mobilised and live in barracks; a propaganda service; and a weekly newspaper, *Combats*. Darnand's ultimate objective was to create a political movement on the model of a fascist single party. The Milice cultivated the image of a chivalric élite with something of the spirit of the Rumanian fascist movement the Legion of the Archangel

243

Michael. The Miliciens swore an oath of 21 points condemning democracy, individualism, international capitalism, bolshevism, freemasonry and 'Jewish leprosy' and vowing to defend 'Christian civilisation'.

The recruitment to the Milice was far below Darnand's expectations, probably between around 25 000 and 30 000. Its members were a mixture of virulent anti-communists, former Légionnaires who still believed they were being faithful to the Marshal, and a number of young men, of no fixed political opinion, who used it as an opportunity to escape from STO. It never became a mass movement or one which succeeded in mobilising any support for the regime.

In January 1944, the Germans had nothing to lose by allowing the ultra-collaborationists to take power. Darnand was given control over policing, the violently anti-Bolshevik Philippe Henriot over propaganda; and finally in March Marcel Déat took over the Ministry of Labour. The fascists were now in power, but Vichy had become a police state, not a fascist State. It existed only to repress dissent and carry out German policies. There was no longer any attempt to mobilise support except in the broadcasts of Philippe Henriot whose dark, apocalyptic predictions of civil war, anarchy and communist terror played only on fear and despair, not on any exalting fascist vision of a New France.

IV

In the balance of forces at play within the Vichy regime, then, fascism never played more than a subsidiary role. But it remained on the agenda even after the rejection of the single party in August 1940, and never more so perhaps than in 1941. In 1942 Laval had preferred to return to Third Republic clientelism although he did not interfere with the unsuccessful efforts of Pelorson to politicise youth policy. In 1943 the Milice was responsible for an accentuation of repression and state violence, but it never became the political movement of mass mobilisation that Darnand, but not Laval, had wanted.

Even in 1941, however, the influence of fascist lobbies within the regime must not be overestimated. In the first place, it would be wrong to take the issue of the single party as the defining criterion of fascism. Speaking to the propaganda delegates at Mayet de Montagne in October 1941, Dumoulin de Labarthète, while warning against any simple imitation of Germany or Italy, denied that there were fundamental differences between himself and Marion: 'M. Marion is perhaps, more totalitarian than I am in some respects, but these are nuances.' He was sceptical about Pucheu and Marion's idea of turning the LFC into a single party, but accepted that if they failed 'it will be necessary to create, outside the Legion, a construction which approximates to the one you want, and which must correspond to the desires of the country'.[41] As for Pucheu, he told one interlocutor in December 1941 that his conception of the single party did not require it to be compulsory for everyone: 'they say I am totalitarian, but nothing could be less true'.[42] The conservative authoritarianism of Dumoulin, the muscular authoritarianism of Pucheu and the dynamic fascism of Marion, could all accommodate the idea of the single party in some form or other.

It was also the case that Marion's propaganda delegates came nowhere near to playing the ambitious role that he had conceived for them. If they approximated to the embryo of a single party it was only in his head. The interference of the Propaganda Delegates was resented by the Prefects who remained the main representatives of the government in the departments, as they had always been. One canny observer of the Vichy scene noted of the monthly meeting of the Propaganda Delegates in July 1942: 'I was present at one of the meetings when they report on the Departments which they represent, watch over and are supposed to invigorate politically. What strikes me is that they feel themselves still to be in opposition.' If in 1941 the fascists had achieved some influence at Vichy, they were never more than strangers in their own country.

Notes

1 M. Cointet, *Vichy et le fascisme*, Brussels, 1987, p. 97.
2 P. Burrin, *La Dérive fasciste. Doriot, Déat, Bergery*, Paris, 1986, pp. 332–5.
3 See J.-P Cointet, *La Légion française des combattants 1940–1944* (Paris, 1995), pp. 30–46; 'Marcel Déat et le Parti unique (été 1940)', *Revue d'histoire de la deuxième guerre mondiale*, 91 (1973), pp. 1–22; A. Prost, 'Le Rapport de Déat en faveur d'un parti unique, essai d'analyse lexicale', *Revue française de science politique*, 23, 5 (1973), pp. 933–72'; Cointet, *Legion*, pp. 30–46; Burrin, *La Dérive fasciste*, pp. 346–59.
4 H. Dumoulin de Labarthète, *Le Temps des illusions. Souvenirs (juillet 1940–avril 1942)* (Geneva, 1946), pp. 29–30; L. Rebatet, *Les Décombres*, Paris, Denoël, 1942.
5 L. Rebatet, *Les Décombres*, pp. 574, 588.
6 P. Drieu La Rochelle, *Fragments de mémoire*, Paris, 1982, p. 47.
7 R. Bourderon, 'Le Regime de Vichy était-il fasciste? Essai d'approche de la question', *Revue d'histoire de la deuxième guerre mondiale* (1973), pp. 22–45; A. Slama, 'Vichy était-il fasciste?, *Vingtième siecle*, 11 (1986), pp. 41–54; Michèle Cointet-Labrousse, *Vichy et le fascisme*, pp. 241–48; R. Paxton, *Vichy France. Old Guard New Order*, London, 1972, pp. 228–33.
8 A. Costa Pinto, "L'Etat Nouveau' de Salazar et le Regime de Vichy', in J-P.Azéma and F. Bédarida, *Vichy et les Français*, Paris, 1992, pp. 670–84.
9 H. Dumoulin de Labarthète, *Le Temps*.
10 M. Ferro, *Pétain*, Paris, 1987, p. 216.
11 J. Linz, 'An Authoritarian Regime: Spain', in E. Allard and S. Rokkan (ed.), *Mass Politics: Studies in Political Sociology*, New York, 1970, pp. 251–83.
12 A. Costa Pinto, *Salazar's Dictatorship and European Fascism*, New York, 1995, pp. 171–81.
13 Costa Pinto, *Salazar's Dictatorship*, pp. 187–90.
14 R. Griffin, *The Nature of Fascism*, pp. 122–3.
15 R. Paxton, 'The Four Stages of Fascism', *Journal of Modern History*, 70, 1(1998), pp. 1–23.

16 P. Burrin, 'Politique et société: les structures du pouvoir dans l'Italie fasciste et l'Allemagne nazie', *Annales: Economies, sociétés, civilisations*, 43 (1985), pp. 615–37.
17 M. Broszat, *The Hitler State*, London, 1981.
18 T. Mason, 'Whatever happened to "Fascism"? in T. Childers and J. Caplan, *Reevaluating the Third Reich*, New York/London, 1993, pp. 253–61.
19 H. Rousso, 'L'Impact du régime sur la société' in J-P. Azéma and F. Bédarida, *Vichy et les Francais*, pp. 670–84; J-P. Rioux, *La Vie culturelle sous Vichy*, Brussels, 1990.
20 F. Garçon, *De Blum à Pétain. Cinéma et société française 1936–1944*, Paris, 1984.
21 W. Halls, *The Youth of Vichy France*, Oxford, 1981, pp. 132–57; B. Comte, *Une Utopie combattante. L'Ecole des cadres d'Uriage*, Paris, 1991, pp. 155–62, 311–69.
22 L. Yagil, *'L'Homme nouveau' et la révolution nationale de Vichy 1940–1944*, Paris, 1997. This book contains some interesting material, but it should be used with care since the author seems unwittingly to have adopted the assumptions of the sources she uses. There is no critical distance.
23 J. Guehenno, *Journal des années noires*, Paris, 1947, p. 30.
24 R. Paxton, *Parades and Politics at Vichy*, Princeton, New Jersey, 1966, p. 147.
25 Y. Bouthillier, *Le Drame de l'Armistice I*, Paris, 1950, p. 13.
26 M-O. Baruch, *Servir l'Etat français*, Paris, 1997, pp. 176–81.
27 J. Benoist-Mechin, *De la Défaite au désastre*, Paris, 1984, pp. 51–63.
28 J. Benoist-Mechin, *De la Défaite*, pp. 37, 337–8.
29 Drieu, *Fragments*, pp. 85–6.
30 On the Legion, see J-P. Cointet, *La Légion française des combattants*.
31 Cointet, *La Légion*, pp. 102–111; P. Nicolle, pp. 168–201; P. Aumary, *Les Deux expériences d'un 'Ministère de l'Information' en France*, Paris, 1969, pp. 115–23.
32 D. Peschanski, 'Encadrer ou contrôler. Information ou propagande sous Vichy', in D. Peschanski, *Contrôle et exclusion*, Brussels, 1997, pp. 39–58 and 'Vichy au singulier, Vichy au pluriel', *Annales ESC*, 3 (1988), pp. 632–61; P. Aumary, *Les deux premières expériences*, pp. 140–236.
33 J-P. Cointet, *La Légion*, pp. 132–73.
34 Comte, *Une Utopie*, pp. 400–19; Halls, *The Youth of Vichy*, pp. 143–57; P. Giolitti, *Histoire de la Jeunesse sous Vichy*, Paris, 1991, pp. 466–8.
35 D. Peschanski (ed.), *Vichy 1940–1944. Archives de Guerre d'Angelo Tasca*, Paris, pp. 416–7.
36 Peschanski, *Vichy 1940–1944. Contrôle et exclusion*, p. 50.
37 J. M. Berlière, *Le Monde des polices et policiers en France, XIXème and XXème siècles*, Brussels, 1996, pp. 163–202; P. Froment, *René Bousquet*, Paris, 1994, pp. 190–7; M-O. Baruch, *Servir l'Etat*, pp. 333–50.
38 Baruch, pp. 417–22.
39 Austin, 'The Educational and Youth Policies of the Vichy Government in the Départment of the Hérault', PhD, Manchester, 1981, p. 368.
40 Duquesne, pp. 233–4; Austin, p. 390; 458–9., ed. *Les catholiques francais sous l'Occupation*, Paris, 1996.
41 M. Berges, *Vichy contre Mounier. Les nonconformistes face aux années 40*, 1997, pp. 188–92.
42 M. Berges, *Vichy contre Mounier*, Paris, p. 185.

66

Extract from
'CONNECTIONS WITH FASCISM'

Mike Cronin

Source: Mike Cronin, *The Blueshirts and Irish Politics*, Dublin: Four Courts Press, 1997, pp. 49–68.

The fascist policies of the Blueshirts

It will be shown in the next chapter that the policies of the Blueshirts were based around the ideological adherence to, and eventual adoption of a corporate and vocational state. Despite the usual correlation between the adoption of such ideas and fascism, it will be shown that the impetus for the corporate and vocational state came largely from the Vatican and not from fascist Italy. Despite such arguments, the existence of fascist ideals within the Blueshirts policies should not be dismissed. In explaining the links between the Blueshirts and fascism, I am exploring the traits of fascism within the movement. Although it is clear that the intellectuals and political thinkers of the movement looked towards the Vatican for their ideology, the interpretation of those ideas by certain Blueshirts, especially O'Duffy, showed the vestiges of fascistised thought. Dealing with the adoption of such ideas as a definitional component of fascism does require care. It is often presumed that there is a correlation between corporatist policies and fascism. The importance of such ideas is that they can point to the desire to create a new order on fascist lines – as happened in Italy, and was planned by the British Union of Fascists – though this is not actually necessary. Salazar and Franco corporatised their economies, yet are not defined as fascists, whereas the Nazis, a true fascist regime, remained ambivalent to the whole theory. Corporate policy points to a degree of probable fascistisation, yet is not a pre-requisite.

The Blueshirt intellectuals adhered strongly to the view that Ireland needed a radical restructuring of the social, economic and political mechanics of the state. This was to be achieved through the adoption of various corporate and vocational ideals. It was never argued that to achieve such restructuring would require the destruction of parliamentary democracy. The Dáil and the Senate were always seen as central to the new way forward.[1] True fascism is, in its very character, anti-democratic. Griffin, in his 'Discursive Characterization of the Nature of Fascism' states, 'though they (the fascists) may well make some concessions to parliamentary democracy in order to gain power, the pluralism of opinion and party politics upon which it rests is anathema to their concept of national unity, which implies in practice the maximum totalitarian control over all areas of social, economic, political, and cultural life.'[2] The intellectuals view of the Blueshirt policies, which did not condemn democracy, were not therefore fascist. The presentation and interpretation of the policies of corporatism and vocationalism by certain senior Blueshirts did on occasions demonstrate that there was a commitment to destroy democracy and by doing so accomplish an authentic fascist revolution. Admittedly these Blueshirts were few in number and their references to the destruction of democracy rare. It does demonstrate the undercurrent of fascist thinking in the movement, if not a hidden agenda amongst certain members and leaders.

O'Duffy's political views are difficult to fathom, as little remains of his personal archive from the early 1930s. His speeches do remain and before they were censored by the Party after August 1934, they are the key to understanding the man's ideas. O'Duffy's speeches were prepared for him by Blythe, Tierney and others, and always put forward the accepted views of the Blueshirts/Fine Gael which had been agreed at various Ard Fheis. It is in these speeches that O'Duffy presents an image of a traditional and constitutional politician who has no affinity with fascism. By reading from prepared speeches O'Duffy was being stage managed by the traditional conservative right in the organisation. O'Duffy was, however, beyond complete control. There are numerous occasions when O'Duffy chose to either ignore his script or add his own views to a speech. It is at this point that O'Duffy's own views come to the fore. James Dillon once said to O'Duffy, 'When you stick to your notes, General, you're the greatest speaker there is. But let some old women in the audience shout "Up Dev" and God knows what you will say next.'[3] When O'Duffy turned his speeches towards his own interests and his own political views, the ideas that were presented were quite different from those of Fine Gael. He was highly controversial and confrontational and presented a brand of fascism which Manning sums up as, 'emotional and instinctive rather than intellectual.'[4] The nature of O'Duffy's unscheduled pronouncements can be gauged from the following.

> Party politics has served their period of usefulness, and the sooner a change is effected the better.[5]
>
> As sure as we are here we shall be Masters of Ireland in three years. We do not want party politics and politicians; we want a disciplined and well governed country. This evolution is inevitable.[6]

> When we think of the striking similarity of the Italy to which Mussolini came as leader and our own present day Ireland, we realise that this book [Mussolini's *The Political and Social Doctrine of Fascism*] will have more than a passing value to those who are interested in rescuing our country from weak government, civil unrest and the encroachment of Communism. This is not to say that Ireland can be rescued only by Fascism, but we would be fools were we to shut our eyes to the fact that behind fascism in Italy, and responsible for its phenomenal success is the same spirit which is now making the Blueshirt movement the biggest political movement that Ireland has ever known.[7]

As well as the traits of fascism and anti-democratic sentiments which were appearing in O'Duffy's speeches, the company he was keeping, especially towards the latter stages of his Fine Gael leadership, was increasingly fascistic. In August 1934 *An Phoblacht* claimed that O'Duffy was in contact with Oswald Mosley and was scheduled to meet the Norwegian fascist leader Terje Ballsrud (leader of the Greyshirts).[8]

Once he had resigned from the Presidency of Fine Gael, O'Duffy gave full reign to his fascist ideas. The National Corporate Party, the Greenshirts, was openly fascist.[9] He attended the December 1934 conference of International Action of Nationalisms. This was a neo-Nazi organisation meeting in Zurich. O'Duffy's fellow representatives at the conference were Mosley from Britain, General Pouderoux from France and J.F. Hurst from America. The conference was funded by the Nazis and promoted the ideas of international National Socialism and a universal racist doctrine.[10] He also attended the December 1934 International Fascist Congress at Montreux and was elected to the international committee of seven to plot the future course for European fascism. The Congress was Italian-inspired, and aimed to woo foreign fascist movements into an international movement by guaranteeing their independence and integrity. Its aim was to promote a theory of the Corporate State which provided a unique solution to the European economic crisis and to establish a universal, Christian, yet tolerant doctrine which resisted any claims to racial superiority or regional dominance. The Congress was attended by representatives from the Austrian Heimwehr, the Belgian Legion Nationale Belge and Ligue Corporative du Travail, the Danish National Corpset and Nationalist Socialist Party, the French Francistes, the Greek National Socialists, the Norwegian Nasjonal Samling, the Dutch Front Noir, the Portuguese Salazar government, the Romanian Iron Guard, the Swedish National Union of Youth, the Spanish Falange, the Swiss Fascist Federation, and the Lithuanian Nationalist Party. In Montreux O'Duffy, without a movement of any numerical strength, was mixing and plotting with the big guns of European fascism, most of whom would either form independent or collaborative regimes during the 1930s and 1940s.[11] O'Duffy's major contribution to the Congress was to fully support an ideological commitment to anti-semitism.[12] In January 1935 O'Duffy's work at the Congress led to his election in Rome to the newly established International Centre for Corporate Studies. O'Duffy's political career eventually ended with the comical excursion to fight for the nationalist cause in Spain.

Bew's belief that O'Duffy was a fascist is correct. Although he adopted the conservative and constitutionalist ideas put forward by the intellectuals of the Blueshirts/Fine Gael, this is a move of common sense. O'Duffy can be seen as a highly inept politician, but he was not stupid. He realised that a traditional grouping in politics such as Fine Gael offered a greater chance of success than a marginalised fascist group which in the climate of the early 1930s de Valera would have attacked with all his political weaponry. Behind the respectability of O'Duffy's Presidency of Fine Gael was a political mind which was aiming for complete power and a fascist styled State. Dillon noted in January 1935 that O'Duffy 'has returned from his interview with Mussolini definitely fascist'.[13] MacDermot had written to O'Duffy in July 1934 that 'the time has come when I feel obliged to make a more formal protest than I have yet done against the tendency of certain speakers and writers of our Party to attack the Parliamentary system of Government, and to imply that it is our official policy to replace it by a Blue shirt ascendancy modelled on fascism'.[14] From the comments of Dillon and MacDermot it is clear that these two leading members of the Fine Gael hierarchy had realised that O'Duffy's political direction was different to their own. The Blueshirts in general were careful to avoid direct comparisons between their own organisation and the fascist regimes in Germany and Italy. There was widespread support for Dollfuss and Salazar, while in hindsight most of the ex-Blueshirts I have interviewed are supportive of Franco. Thomas Kelly made a worthwhile point when completing his questionnaire, and subsequently in his interview. He makes clear the distinction between the impressive years of fascism in Europe (i.e. the economic reconstruction of Hitler and Mussolini up to 1934), and the poor image of fascism after the Night of the Long Knives and the Second World War atrocities. He said: 'There was a similarity to the fascists of Germany at that time in that they were a disciplined body who wore a uniform to parades, meetings etc. That organisation then portrayed the rebirth of a nation that had been brought to its knees less than twenty years previously and as such were to be admired. It is understandable when a writer or anyone tries to discredit the Blueshirts they refer to the athrosaties [sic] that Hitler later led his army to commit. Making a parallel of the Blueshirts to the fascists of the forties has no logic.'[15] If Kelly's view is common among Blueshirts, then there is a definite admiration for fascist policies in the Blueshirts. Phrases such as the re-birth of the nation in this context belong to the language of fascism, not to the concepts of traditional Irish nationalist re-birth which are common in Irish politics.

This section has not shown the policies of the Blueshirt movement to be fascist. What it has attempted to do is to show the traits of fascist thought within the Blueshirt movement. These were largely suppressed by the conservative alliance with the Blueshirts and the controlling influence of the Fine Gael politicians who would play no part in a fascist movement. Once O'Duffy moved closer to a complete embracing of fascist identity in 1934 he was unceremoniously dumped by Fine Gael. Equally, the admiration of fascist forms by men such as Thomas Kelly was largely suppressed by Fine Gael, as they directed the Blueshirts towards the more important domestic role of defeating Fianna Fáil. There was definitely a strand of fascist thought, policy, and admiration in the Blueshirt psyche, but this was successfully muffled and marginalised.

Violent fascist activities of the Blueshirts

In implementing fascism as a political ideal numerous regimes and movements turned to violence. This violence was usually directed at the enemies of the State or the Party. The range of violence in Europe of the 1930s stretched from street battles to incidents involving weapons.

The cult and use of violence is in many ways central to the psychological base of fascism and counters the lack of firm ideology in fascist thought. Violence against perceived enemies was the embodiment of the vital energy and life-force of fascism. Roger Scruton states: 'In other words, the ultimate doctrine (fascism) contains little that is specific, beyond an appeal to energy, and action: it is, one might say the form of an ideology, but without specific content. This perhaps explains some of its appeal; it seemed to make no demand other than those which the individual himself would make had he the energy.'[16] The specific use of violence as a political necessity was championed by Primo de Rivera, amongst others, when he said, 'Finally, we desire that if on some occasion this must be achieved by violence, there be no shrinking from violence. Because who has said – while speaking of "everything save violence" – that the supreme value in the hierarchy of values is amiability? Who has said that when our sentiments are insulted we are obliged to be accommodating instead of reacting like men? It is very correct indeed that dialectic is the first instrument of communication. But no other dialectic is admissible to save the dialectic of fists and pistols when justice or the Patria are offended.'[17] The Blueshirts did not shy away from using and espousing the use of violence to achieve their aims. There is an obvious non-fascist tradition of violence within Irish political life. The activities of the IRB and the IRA had been violent, and the War of Independence and the Civil War had seen the use of violence as a justifiable means of gaining victory and liberty. It is my belief that the violence connected with the Blueshirt cause did not belong in its entirety to this Irish tradition. Members of Cumann na nGaedheal and the Army Comrades Association had been banned from possessing firearms in the early months of 1933, and both the Party and the movement went out of their way to portray the Blueshirts as an unarmed and non-violent organisation. The main targets of Blueshirt violence were the IRA, the Communists and the government officials who were implementing the collection of annuities and other legal processes connected with the Economic War. These targets were all political, and the atmosphere of violent conflict which the Blueshirt attacks produced were aimed to heighten the sense of emergency in the Free State and to reinforce the belief that the Blueshirts were the only trustworthy and legitimate grouping in the country.

The Blueshirts had their basis in an ex-Servicemen's organisation, the Army Comrades Association. These men were armed and well versed in the mentalities of comradeship, military operations and the use of violence. Woolf observed, 'the future fascist parties in almost all the countries of Europe traced their origins back to the numerous groupings of patriotic associations which emerged or re-emerged in strength after the war'.[18] The Blueshirts had at its core a group of men with the mentality and experience that could, with the right encouragement and nourishment of their grievances, be moulded into a violent political, if not fascist, force. The Blueshirt leaders who predated O'Duffy's involvement were the greatest believers in violence as a justifiable political weapon Cronin, Quish, and Quinlan were foremost in this group. Manning believes that there were speeches by Cronin and Quish 'which could be construed as inciting civil war' and that 'there is the undoubted military aspect of Blueshirtism'.[19] Cronin demanded in 1933 that members should 'exchange ten blows for every one received' and 'break gobs if necessary'.[20]

The rhetoric of violence was reinforced by reality. These acts took place at Blueshirt meetings where hecklers became the victims, or were premeditated attacks on the public meetings of their opponents. The atmosphere of fear provoked by certain activities of the Blueshirts is summed up in a letter to the Minister of Justice in March 1934.

> About 7.30 three I.O.C. buses full of blue shirts pulled in at no.3 Merrion Square. They were of the rough ex-soldier type. After a lot of demonstrating and singing they planned to march past government buildings. This they actually did singing 'blue shirts blue'. These incidents appear, perhaps trivial, but with the note of terror struck, and the panic to women and ordinary citizens, the whole affair took on a tone of strength, and the bringing of the Government into contempt.[21]

This kind of display of power was rare in Dublin. The real shows of Blueshirt strength and violence took place at smaller rural meetings.[22] An example of Blueshirt violence can be seen in the Government files relating to a meeting in Castlerea in February 1934. The Justice Minister was sent endless testimonies from members of the public who had been caught up in the violence. John Moore's account of the violence reads as follows,

> The meeting was generally orderly but there were some interruptions, mainly from a woman in the vicinity of the meeting and outside the blue shirts. Outside the Guards were members of the general public. The first disturbance arose when James Dowling, Patrick Street, saw a blue shirt with a revolver. Some men in the crowd protested and an argument with the blue shirt followed. A blue shirt leader was then seen to give an order and afterwards an attack was made by the blue shirts on men in the crowd. The attack was made by batons previously concealed under their coats and in some cases by walking sticks or what appeared to be. Superintendent O'Hara was present and no attempt was made to save defenceless members of the public. I had my two hands in my pocket when I was struck by batons, but no attempt was made to disarm the imported blue shirts who began the row. There were fights in various places over the Square and through the town.[23]

The violence in Castlerea was re-enacted at countless political meetings over the country. Despite the Blueshirts adherence to free speech, that privilege, did not cover their opponents. The violence, and the Blueshirts open flaunting of the uniform and firearms legislation, raised the political temperature. The Blueshirts use of violence in support of their own political views reached a peak in the struggle over land annuities. The shooting of the young Blueshirt Michael Lynch at Marsh's Yard in Cork was vitally influential. It provided the Blueshirts with a young hero, a martyr who had fallen in action (part of the pantheon of fascist heroism). Lynch was given a full Blueshirt burial, and many of the 4,000 mourners were uniformed. The incident brought into sharp focus the problem of the Blueshirts adherence to violence and lawlessness, and forced the government to begin taking concrete steps against the Blueshirts. For the Blueshirts the killing of Lynch gave great impetus to their increasingly violent anti-annuities campaign. Countless cattle seizures became flashpoints between the Blueshirts and the government, and members of the movement were imprisoned in ever increasing numbers for numerous offences.

As with elements of fascism in the Blueshirt ideology, these incidents of politically oriented violence are not the whole story. They are selected incidents which demonstrate that the movement's use of violence indicated certain characteristics of fascism. The bulk of members and leaders, although involving themselves in fights at meetings, did not see violence as a means to a political end. They stayed within the movement's official bounds as to the use of force.

The perception of the Blueshirts as fascist

One of the major reasons for the past and current identification in the popular mind of the Blueshirts as a fascist force lies in the perception of the movement in the 1930s. The de Valera government, the IRA and the various wings of the socialist/communist movement constantly denounced the Blueshirts as a fascist force which was attempting to bring about a dictatorship. The widespread condemnations of the Blueshirts by highly influential groups entered the public mentality, and the word fascist was freely and openly connected with the Blueshirts. The denouncements ranged from the hysterical class war condemnation of the Socialist *Irish Worker's Voice*, to considered and guarded attacks from Ministers. At the formation of the National Guard the *Irish Worker's Voice* brought the attention of the workers to the threat of the fascist guard. It stated

> the organisation of this new 'civil and unarmed' force is a challenge to the working masses of Ireland by the bankers, ranchers and big capitalists. The purpose of the Guard is openly stated to be against the struggle of the Irish workers and working farmers for national and social freedom. It is essential that every working man and woman realise the menace of the fascist imperialists. The blue shirted band are directed against every section of the working class movement. Every section must unite against them. Form the united front of the Irish working class against the fascist class and their anti-communist allies.[24]

The analysis of the *Irish Worker's View* was backed up in a similar class war vein by the *Republican Congress*. That organ attempted to bring about a greater awareness of the dangers of under-estimating the threat posed by the Blueshirts. 'The danger is not that fascism could get the backing of a deep section of the Irish people: its naked imperialism prevents that. The danger is that fascism might slip past before Republicans have been roused to a sense of their danger.'[25] These hysterical condemnations of the Blueshirts indicate the atmosphere of mutual paranoia that existed in the Free State during the 1930s. The anti-fascist consciousness which denounced the Blueshirts in the period 1932–5, resurfaced in 1936 when O'Duffy formed a Blueshirt Brigade to go to Spain. Despite the portrayal of the Brigade by sections of the Church and the Press as saviours of Catholicism against the forces of Communism, the links between the Blueshirts and fascism had been well learnt in the preceding years. The brigade was condemned as fascist. Patrick Galvin remembers a neighbour protesting. 'When the Spanish Civil War broke out, Mr Goldman stood at the corner of Washington Street and protested against the Fascists. My Mother supported him and, in the evenings, she painted slogans on our tenement wall urging the natives of Cork to aid the Republicans and join the International Brigades'.[26] The Ministers of Fianna Fáil were more subtle when expressing their doubts about the Blueshirts political background. In the debate on the Wearing of Uniforms Bill in 1934 Ruttledge said: 'the wearing of uniforms in this country, as in other European countries has resulted in the creation of disorder, and a strain that the authorities cannot adequately deal with'.[27] Ruttledge also charged the Blueshirts with attempting to create a fascist state.

Internationally the Blueshirts were identified as fascist. The most important journal within Italian Fascist circles, that which contributed to the formation of the regime's interpretation of the spread of fascism, was *Ottobre*. It declared that the Irish Blueshirts under the leadership of General O'Duffy were a true fascist movement.[28] This would have had little effect on the perception of the Blueshirts in Ireland, but is interesting none the less.

With the constant and widespread reiteration of the links between the Blueshirts and fascism by numerous bodies within the State, the belief that the movement was indeed fascist became a truth in many peoples minds.

Fascist elements in Ireland during the 1930s

The work of previous historians has largely concentrated on the Blueshirts as the only candidate for the mantle of Ireland's fascists. The aim here is to briefly demonstrate that others in Irish society looked towards fascism, or at least far right ideas, as a way of taking Ireland forward.

In Europe during the early 1930s there were countless organisations established to study, encourage, and promote fascism. A major group of this type was the Centre International d'Etudes sur la Fascisme (CINEF) based in Lausanne, Switzerland. This group was led by an Englishman, James Strachey Barnes, and constituted a principal means of circulating fascist propaganda across Europe in the 1930s. The governing body, which was truly international, included the Irish representative, Walter Starkie, Professor of Romance Languages at Trinity College Dublin. The governing body was made up largely of University intellectuals. The official purpose of the group, outlined in its 1928 Yearbook by H. De Vries De Heekelingen (Professor at the University of Nijmegen), was to 'furnish the means by which the student may be enabled to lay his hands on anything of importance that has been published on the subject'.[29] The official reason for existence is fairly innocuous. Behind the veneer lay a far greater emphasis on the positive nature of fascism. CINEF published endless articles in its journal, of which Starkie was an editor. The articles covered numerous subjects including Edmundo Rossoni's 'The significance of the Fascist Syndicalist movement in Italy', Gioacchino Volpe's 'The Civil Strife in Italy, 1919–22', Augusto Turati's 'The Labour Charter', and James Strachey Barnes' 'The Universal Aspects of Fascism'. The journal constantly stressed the uniqueness of Italian Fascism as a way for other nations to solve their own problems. The experience in

Italy should convince other nations to abandon the outmoded principles of Western Civilisation: laissez-faire economics, liberalism, socialism and communism. Barnes concluded that fascism was the political system of the future 'the present Weltanschauung of Fascism may be summed in one word: Youth'.[30] Starkie had involved himself in, and became the leading Irish advocate for the import of Italian Fascism. This happened three years prior to the establishment of the ACA. Starkie's ideas received little attention in Ireland. There is no evidence that he ever wrote in an Irish journal or newspaper promoting the ideas of CINEF. His only successful converts may have come from within Trinity, but even this seems unlikely as within the College he was a somewhat frivolous figure, known for his obsession with Spanish gypsy life and fiddle playing, and not taken very seriously.[31] The promotion of his ideas amongst his personal friends had more effect.

Starkie's post as Professor of Romance languages (specifically Spanish after 1926), and his constant travels to Spain and Portugal studying Gypsy culture, resulted in a wide understanding and experience of the climate in Europe in the 1920s and 1930s. During the Second World War he was appointed to head the British Council Office in Madrid, where he successfully established a sort of alternative Irish Embassy. He never returned to Ireland after the War, preferring to live in Spain, where it is probable that he would have come into contact with O'Duffy's ex-second in command, Thomas Gunning. Starkie's importance lies in his position as a wider symptom of the attraction of fascism. His fascination pre-dated the emergence of the Blueshirts, and he demonstrates the existence of an awareness of such issues, albeit in a highly marginalised way, in Ireland. Interestingly, Stark was a Director of the Abbey Theatre. Here his colleagues included W.J. Yeats and Ernest Blythe. Yeats was fascinated by the ideas connected with fascism, and would have been an intent listener to Starkie's views, either reinforcing or developing Yeats' ideas of the time. Blythe, one of the Blueshirt foremost thinkers, and a great advocate of the Italian system, was likely to be highly attentive to Starkie's direct involvement with ideas connected to the Fascist regime.

Another figure who involved himself with the thinking of fascism yet never became involved in the Blueshirts was the novelist Francis Stuart. He had married the daughter of Maud Gonne, and was intrigued by events of the Continent in the early 1930s, especially in Germany. As with Starkie, Stuart's open support and advocation of the fascist way in Ireland at the time was a largely private affair. In his autobiographical work *Things to live for*, published in 1928,[32] he pursues lines of thought which follow the arguments put forward by fascist writers in Italy at that time. It was not until the late 1930s he revealed his true colours. He accepted a lectureship at Berlin University and witnessed a meeting addressed by Hitler. He recalled, 'there was a blue light on his Mercedes as it came down the Unter den Linden. He [Hitler] was small, stocky, very wooden-like figure in a comparatively simple uniform surrounded by ostentatious Foreign Ministry dignitaries and SS men. No reaction to Hitler could be objective. I felt that somehow the system in Europe needed completely destroying and for me Hitler was a kind of Samson pulling everything down.[33] During 1942 Stuart's belief in the Nazi regime led him to broadcast to Ireland from Berlin as an Irish Lord Haw-Haw. Stuart's support of the Nazis has little direct relevance to the Blueshirts, but it demonstrates the transition which he had gone through since he was first attracted to fascist ideas during the 1920s and 1930s. It shows how he, like Starkie and countless other more anonymous figures, although not attracted by the Blueshirt message, were immersed in the positive debate surrounding fascism as the Blueshirts came into prominence.

The existence of a small group of people preoccupied with fascism, both practically and ideologically, illustrates the atmosphere of the 1930s. The specific Blueshirts who believed in fascism, and the fascistised trappings of the movement did not stand in isolation. It was minimal, but there was a wider debate surrounding the merits of fascism. Lee believes that Fianna Fáil in the early 1930s demonstrated some of the traits of fascist action and ideology.

> In electoral terms, therefore, Ireland seemed to promise a potentially fruitful harvest for fascism. Ironically it was Fianna Fáil that most effectively harnessed this potential. Circumstances conspired to align forces, frequently sympathetic to fascism elsewhere, on the side of the party that came to be considered, because of the apparent Blueshirt association with fascism, peculiarly anti-fascist. Some isolated resemblances can certainly be detected between fascist and Fianna Fáil rhetoric. The more strident forms of integral nationalism favoured on some Fianna Fáil platforms could veer close to the fascist variant. Aspects of Fianna Fáil's autarkic economic policy were reminiscent of fascist panaceas. Some Fianna Fáil spokesmen clung to the idea of an agrarian utopia as insistently as any fascist rhetorician. And Fianna Fáil certainly possessed the type of charismatic leader cherished by fascist ideologists.[34]

Elements of fascism certainly pervaded the political climate in Ireland during the 1930s, yet only the Blueshirts are remembered as Ireland's fascists. This is symptomatic of the whole problem of the lack of a definition of the term fascist within Irish History.

Any of the traits of fascism within the Blueshirts were heightened, and put under microscopic consideration during the 1930s. The combination of fascist traits present in the movement, and the increased perception of the movement as fascist, led to the condemnation in popular history of the Blueshirts as fascist. Historians, in contrast, have chosen to dismiss the notion of the Blueshirts as a fascist force. The aim of the preceding section was to demonstrate that certain areas of Blueshirt thought and action and of Irish life generally could be interpreted as fascist. By being aware of the elements of fascism within the Blueshirts, their proper place within the various definitions and experiences of European fascism can be decided on, as can their relationship with the traditional politics of the Free State.

Definitions and experiences of fascism

The amount of written work which attempts to define fascism is huge, and it would be impossible to cover the plethora of different definitions here. The definitions that will be used are generalised and do not allow for discussion of the points of disagreement between historians, and social and political scientists. The aim is to broadly define different varieties of fascism with the aim of understanding where, if at all, the Blueshirts fit.

Fascism

Stanley Payne's typological description of fascism in 1980 listed three areas thought and activity which a movement or regime must follow to be consiered fascist. These were the fascist negations (anti-liberalism, anti-communism, and anti-conservatism); the ideology and goals (creation of a new nationalist authoritarian state, a new type of regulated, multi-class, integrated national economic structure, a goal of empire, and the espousal of an idealist, voluntarist creed attempting to realise a new modern, self determined secular culture); and the style and organisation (an emphasis on the aesthetic structure of meetings, symbols, etc., mass mobilization with militarization of political relationships and style, positive evaluation and use of violence, stress of masculine principle, exaltation of youth emphasising conflict of generations, and tendency towards charismatic and authoritarian personal style of leadership).[35] Payne's definition is in line with those put forward by Scruton,[36] Sternhall,[37] Robinson,[38] and others. Griffin's concise definition of fascism states 'fascism is a genus of political ideology whose mythic core in its various permutations is a palingenetic [i.e. rebirth, regenerationist] form of populist ultra-nationalism'.[39] This definition breaks down into a fascist belief and use of: its own style of politics, a revolutionary aspect while out of power and a reactionary stance once in power, an affective power rooted in myth, a total commitment to a new order but with the foundations of that belief lying in the past, and the use of political force in the pursuit of 'integral' or 'radical' nationalism.

These definitions are complex, and derive from many different approaches to the whole study of fascism. Payne attempts to mould his definition around specific examples of fascism in inter-war Europe, whereas Griffin is suggesting an 'ideal type'. Payne classifies movements from each country in Europe as fascist in the light of his definition. Those possessing the required components include the NSDAP in Germany, the PNF in Italy, the Faisceau in France, the Iron Guard in Romania and the Falanga in Spain. Griffin, by comparison, only views the regimes in Italy and Germany as fascist, choosing to list several other examples of fascism under the heading 'aborative fascist movements'. He is making the worthwhile distinction between a regime, a movement and an artificially created fascist regime which emerged as a result of invasion by Germany and Italy. This distinction is important in relation to the Blueshirts. They were only ever a movement and never achieved control of the country. By failing to become a regime, the Blueshirts' links to true fascism are weakened. Whatever fascist views the movement may have held it was never in a position to implement them. Without power, any dreams of an ultra-nationalist single party state which O'Duffy and others may have harboured came to nothing. This idea reverts back to a point made by Payne. In listing anti-conservatism as a constituent of fascism he added: 'though with the understanding that fascist groups were willing to undertake temporary alliances with groups from any other sector, most commonly with the right'.[40] In such an alliance fascist beliefs were suppressed in the pursuit of political power. This is a common experience of fascist movements within Europe. The Blueshirts, if the fascist traits which were demonstrated earlier are to be believed, followed this experience when entering the alliance which formed Fine Gael. In terms of being a fascist movement the Blueshirts as a whole undoubtedly fall wide of the mark: this despite the obvious commitment to fascism by O'Duffy and other organisers and ideologues. This select group did include men who held genuine (if nebulous) palingenetic goals, but the Blueshirts, as will be explained below, should not be condemned for their beliefs. The definitions put forward by Payne, Griffin, etc., do not apply to the Blueshirts. Although the movement possessed certain attributes which are listed in the definitions, the attributes were largely marginalised and inspired the political beliefs of only a small number of Blueshirts.

Para-fascism

Para-fascism is a concept put forward by Griffin and is in some ways similar to Payne's idea of a Radical Right. Griffin argues that 'a para-fascist regime, however ritualistic its style of politics, well-orchestrated its leader cult, palingenetic its rhetoric, ruthless its terror apparatus, fearsome its official para-military league, dynamic its youth organisation or monolithic its state party, will react to genuine fascism as a threat'.[41] The examples of para-fascist regimes are Salazar in Portugal (threatened by Preto's National Syndicalists), Franco in Spain (threatened by Falange), Vichy France (threatened by Deat's Rassemblement National Français) and Horthy in Hungary (threatened by the Arrow Cross). Similar regimes existed in Greece, Austria and Romania. The problem of differentiating between regimes such as those listed above and a movement such as the Blueshirts is once more present.

The solution I would suggest is that the Blueshirts should be viewed as 'potential' para-fascists. So much of the movement's rhetoric and ideology attempted to distance themselves from true fascism, the denials of dictatorship, constant stressing of their belief in democracy and so on, that they obviously viewed genuine fascism as a threat. The attributes listed by Griffin as present in a para-fascist regime were existent in the Blueshirt movement, albeit highly underdeveloped, as they were not in a position of power. By adopting many of the trappings of fascism (however badly) the Blueshirts were attempting to become a populist movement and their ultimate aim was to gain power. It is difficult to say what form of power the Blueshirts would have taken if they had ever been successful and the problem of defining a clear taxonomy for a movement only magnifies the difficulties. It will be shown below how carefully Fine Gael controlled the party. On the evidence of this level of control it seems likely that had the Blueshirt/Fine Gael coalition ever deposed de Valera, the Fine Gael interpretation of politics would have been in the ascendancy. Against this needs to be weighed the unknown quantities evident in the Blueshirts. O'Duffy's pronouncements as leader of the National Corporate Party show him as tailor-made for a would-be fascist regime leader. Had he controlled the Blueshirts for longer would these views have emerged there? Also, the fact that the Blueshirts wanted to gain power, and not merely influence policies, points to the possible existence of some kind of revolutionary thrust – tendentially a fascist one. The populist nature of the Blueshirts also poses problems. Para-fascist regimes as defined by Griffin stem, as in the case of Salazar and Franco, from the conservative elite (Salazar as Finance Minister of a military regime, and Franco as an army general). The Blueshirts were not themselves the conservative elite (though their relationship with Fine Gael moves them in that direction), but were attempting to build on a populist basis in the same way as Hitler and Mussolini. In defining the Blueshirts and their relationship to fascism their short lifespan and their existence as a movement prevents the difficulty of dealing with countless unknowns, and numerous deviations from models of fascism's progress to power.

Reverting to the potential para-fascist definition and its attempts to neutralise fascism's revolutionary impetus, we have to look back to Lee's view that de Valera should be seen as more of a potential fascist than the Blueshirts. Revolutionary politics belonged in 1930s Ireland to the IRA's political wings and the impetus for change to de Valera. The Blueshirts, in acting as 'potential' para-fascists, continually attacked the policies of the IRA and de Valera, while attempting to exploit those groups populism for their own purposes'.[42] The para-fascism of Salazar and Franco is especially worthy of comparison to the Blueshirts. The Blueshirts did not have control of the army or the police in the way which Salazar and Franco managed, but they were not in power. The politics of those regimes were similar to the Blueshirts. In neither Portugal nor Spain was the position of the Catholic Church attacked, indeed, it was preserved. The inspiration for the development of a corporate state was always seen as Catholic, not fascist. The power within the State, outside of the sphere of government, was left in the hands of those who had traditionally held power – large farmers, big business, etc. Neither of these regimes, although radically restructuring their countries, relied on the support of the dislocated middle class and the discontented working class. They relied on the support of the established and traditional centres of power. All these attributes are similar to the experience of the Blueshirts. By failing to gain power they could not fully implement their ideas, but the experience of the period 1932–5, and the rhetoric of certain Blueshirts demonstrates what might have happened. Seen in terms of the pursuit of a traditional course in relations with the powerful in the state aimed at the preservation of key institutions, but with a radical restructuring of the economic, social, and political life of the state, and the trappings of fascism, the Blueshirts' place in the political spectrum becomes clearer. They were not fascists, but neither should their potential be lightly dismissed, as sometimes in the past.

Within the Blueshirt movement and wider Fine Gael coalition, potential para-fascism is also in existence. Fine Gael (including the Blueshirt wing) supported the elites, and relied on those elites for the bulk of its support: many leading Fine Gael politicians constituted the elite as they controlled large businesses and farms. The potential para-fascism within the movement emerges as a result of its recent history of political misfortune and defeat, and its need to maintain a non-threatening stance and close support of the elites. The Blueshirts were a definite reaction to the political ineptitude of Cumann na nGaedheal. Twice defeated by Fianna Fáil, with no natural new direction, and lacking a glamorous unifying leader, Cumann na nGaedheal had nowhere to turn. With the establishment of the Blueshirts, and the ever increasing cross-over of Cumann na nGaedheal membership and Blueshirt membership the two movements were destined to become allied. The Blueshirts initially offered Cumann na nGaedheal everything they were lacking: a populist and dynamic answer to the excesses of Fianna Fáil, yet tempered by a seeming adherence to the traditional political values which Cumann na nGaedheal held dear. With the arrival of O'Duffy, the involvement of the intellectuals, and the advent of the Fine Gael coalition which gave the Blueshirts real power all this changed. As has been demonstrated, certain sections within the Blueshirts, especially O'Duffy, moved ever nearer a redefinition of the Blueshirts (and hence Fine Gael) as a fascist movement. Certain sections within Fine Gael, such as Cosgrave, recoiled from these developments with horror. They had no desire to see Fine Gael transformed into a fascist party willing to use any degree of violence or anti-democratic activity to win power. At the other end of the scale were the Blueshirts, such as O'Duffy and

Gunning, who were content to see Fine Gael, led by the Blueshirts, transformed in this way. In the middle of these two factions were the largest section, the internal potential para-fascists. This group, which straddled both Blueshirts and the Cumann na nGaedheal traditionalists, were the ones who had backed the dynamic twist the Blueshirts had brought to politics – and to Fine Gael politics in particular. During 1934, they did not see the position in black and white as the two extremes did. They believed whole-heartedly in the normal functions of the state, the preservation of the elites, the shirted, ritualistic, and youthful nature of the Blueshirts. They were utterly committed to ousting de Valera. But they opposed anything that could be condemned as fascist. Thus this group fits into Griffin's definition. It composed men like Blythe, FitzGerald, Tierney, and Minch. Internally they recoiled from a commitment to total fascism of the type backed by O'Duffy, and were instrumental in his removal. They still believed, however, that there was a place for the Blueshirts, and all that their ideology and style of politics stood for.

The Blueshirts clearly deserve the label of potential para-fascists. Externally they react against the perceived threats of an autocratic de Valera/IRA regime, and internally they react against the threat of an openly fascist regime led by O'Duffy. What they are fundamentally attempting is a Salazaresque transformation of power. The Blueshirts can lead the mythical battle fought in the heart against the evils of society, while Fine Gael can establish the regime which the mind demanded, that which preserved the status quo, yet banished the sibboleths of liberalism, socialist republicanism, and de Valera's nationalist economic system.

The Blueshirts: 'potential' para-fascists and Fine Gael: the traditional conservative right

Despite suggesting during this chapter that the Blueshirts possessed certain fascist traits, and can be viewed as 'potential' para-fascists, this does not answer the complete question surrounding the movement and its relationship with fascism.

Previous historians have largely dismissed any links between the Blueshirts and fascism. This is a result of the confused interpretation of the relationship between Fine Gael and the Blueshirts. If these two are viewed as separate entities who entered an uneasy coalition for the mutual good, the Blueshirts can be interpreted far more clearly. Fine Gael came together as an anti-Fianna Fáil coalition, forced together by the banning of the National Guard. As with any coalition each component had its own agenda. The Centre Party were the smallest and weakest group, and such a coalition could only improve its profile and that of its leader Frank MacDermot. From the outset MacDermot was unhappy with the activities of the Blueshirts and the antics of O'Duffy. Cumann na nGaedheal were undoubtedly the strongest group, but after their recent record in elections were a discredited force. Despite these failings Cumann na nGaedheal were part of a tradition of legitimate and constitutional politics, and had countless experienced and well respected ex-Ministers in its ranks. The Blueshirts were the misfits in the coalition. They were an avowedly extra-, if not anti-parliamentary group up to August 1933. They were brought into the coalition to provide a new dynamic life-force for the greying ranks of Cumann na nGaedheal. Although presenting a unified image, Fine Gael was torn by internal disputes as to the best way forward. The old Cumann na nGaedheal grouping in particular wanted to recapture its previous dominance of Irish politics, not only on a personal basis, but also to re-establish the validity of their political ideas. With the split in the Fine Gael leadership in 1934 and the resignation of O'Duffy as President, Cosgrave and Cumann na nGaedheal became pre-dominant, and the Blueshirts became a minor organ of the party, which would be jettisoned completely by 1936 following a gradual running down of its operations.

The experience of the Blueshirts in the coalition with Fine Gael echoes numerous fascist, or potentially fascist movements in Europe in the inter-war years.[43] Under threat from, or banned by (a usually) Left dominated government, fledgling fascist movements would seek a coalition with the traditional Conservative Right. The fascists would be seeking to take over the traditional grouping and by gaining respectability be better placed to use democratic means to launch the fascist revolution. The traditional Conservative Right by comparison would be seeking to use the fledgling fascists to provide populism and dynamism for its own ends. The use of fascists to gain popular support would result in a return to power for the traditional Conservative Right, at which point (if not earlier), the fascists would be dumped. This happened in Germany where the Conservative Party attempted to use Hitler and the NSDAP as their little drummer boy. The Party mistakenly believed that they were always in control of Hitler, but were outwitted by him, allowing him to establish his dictatorship. In Spain the Falange fought with the Generals in the Civil War in the hope that a fascist agenda would emerge after the victory, but Franco, repelled by the Falangist beliefs, absorbed them into the Falange Espanola de las Juntas Nacional-Sindicalista. After absorption the Falange had no role. In the Blueshirt equation the part of the traditional Conservative Right was played by the Cumann na nGaedheal dominated Fine Gael.

Free of the restraints of party politics the Army Comrades Association and the National Guard had been able to build up their own support base with original policies and organisational methods previously unseen in Ireland. It is at this point that the movement was universally showing most of its fascist traits. Manning noted that 'the Blueshirts, as they were developing during the National Guard days, were on the way to becoming a Fascist movement'.[44] With the advent of respectable party politics under the Fine Gael coalition the Blueshirts were dominated by the practical demands of the Cumann na nGaedheal and Centre Party factions. In the later months of the coalition the Blueshirts were controlled by the other factions and their own brand of political belief increasingly suppressed. Effectively what had happened was similar to the situations in Germany and Spain, but with a peculiarly Irish outcome. In an attempt to secure a future in de Valera's Ireland, the coalition had been forced into existence to ensure survival. The presence of O'Duffy and the Blueshirts were Fine Gael's safety gauge; their own drummer boy. The coalition not only had an impressive array of Dáil-bred political talent, it also had an extra-parliamentary force to protect meetings, bully opponents and bring about populist support. There are crude parallels with the relationship between German Conservatives and the NSDAP. For the Blueshirts, especially O'Duffy, the formation of the coalition and the movement's huge but unwarranted importance within it (few Blueshirts held seats in the Dáil), gave the signal that the time of their political ascendancy had arrived. The relationship was fraught with difficulties; the traditionalists within Fine Gael concerned were at the new direction which the party was taking, with O'Duffy and the other fascistised leaders and intellectuals pushing ever harder for a new agenda. The concerns of the traditionalists were voiced by Dillon, who stated, 'We've got to get rid of this man [O'Duffy] – he could be dangerous. I remembered Hitler.'[45] With the eventual expulsion/resignation of O'Duffy in 1934, Fine Gael returned to an entirely traditional form of politics. The route to power presented to O'Duffy by Cumann na nGaedheal and the Centre Party on the formation of Fine Gael was blocked by those same groups and the Blueshirts joined the ranks of failed movements like the Falange. This was a result of the danger which the extreme views of O'Duffy presented to Fine Gael, and the inadequacy of O'Duffy's own hand. Unlike Hitler and others who had used the coalition route to power successfully, O'Duffy failed to win over enough support to his vision of politics within the coalition. When he left he could take only eighty men with him. The remainder, including many of his intellectuals, stayed loyal to Fine Gael.

The progression of events within the Blueshirt/Fine Gael coalition demonstrates the weakness of the Blueshirts fascism. Only a small knot of supporters shared O'Duffy's vision. Although fascism was evident within the Blueshirts, it was backed by a minority. The remainder, like Blythe, were either potential para-fascists, or totally traditionalist democrats. The jettisoning of O'Duffy and later the Blueshirts as a whole, illustrates two points. Fine Gael perceived in 1934 that the O'Duffy faction was fascist and in 1936 decided that anything but constitutional politics was not worthwhile.

The Blueshirts undoubtedly possessed certain fascist traits, but they were not fascists in the German or Italian sense. The movement should be viewed as an attempt at an original interpretation of Irish politics. Certain sections of the movement struggled to put forward their own brand of fascism, 'potential' para-fascism. Against the strong government of de Valera such a movement with extreme views had little chance of success. By being forced to seek political respectability in Fine Gael, the Blueshirts were in turn suppressed by their coalition partners. Any movement with even minor traces of fascism in their beliefs had little chance of success, especially in a coalition with the traditional Conservative Right whose aim was to manipulate their popularity, but ultimately distance themselves from such political ideas. The rejection by the membership of the values of fascism is instructive. Certain leaders and intellectuals held fascist or fascistised views, and developed their ideology accordingly. Members of fascist movements in inter-war Europe have rarely held views which have the ideological self-awareness and complexity of the leaders, yet members of the PNI and NSDAP were assured in their revolutionary principles. The Blueshirt members were not at all clear in their conviction of their leadership's revolutionary ideas; indeed most rejected those ideas. The whole question of the Blueshirts and fascism needs to be revised along these lines; simple contradiction of the view that the Blueshirts were fascists needs to broaden out into a wider debate that actually attempts to understand fascism, the relationship between the potential para-fascists and the traditional Conservative Right, and the differences in the ideological commitment of the members and the movement.

Notes

1. For full details of the Blueshirt intellectuals' ideas for a radical restructuring of the social, economic and political mechanics of the state (and hence the possible presence of a hard-core palin-genetic myth) see chapter four.
2. Griffin, R., *The Nature of Fascism* (London 1991), p. 44.
3. Quoted by Manning, M., *The Blueshirts* (London, 1971), p. 160.
4. Ibid., p. 229.
5. *Irish Times*, 9 August 1933, p. 3.
6. *Irish Times*, 14 August 1933, p. 7.
7. *United Ireland*, 25 November 1933, p. 7.
8. *An Phoblacht*, 18 August 1934, p. 8.
9. For full details of the ideas and activities of the National Corporate Party B46/34, B1/35 and B9/35, Department of Justice, NAI.
10. See Ledeen, M.A., *Universal fascism. The Theory and Practice of the Fascist International, 1928–36* (New York, 1972), p. 113.
11. Ibid., p. 115.
12. Ibid., p. 120.
13. Letter from James Dillon to Frank MacDermot, 1065/2/7, MacDermot Papers, NAI, 1 January 1935, p. 2.
14. Letter from Frank MacDermot to General O'Duffy, 1065/3/1, MacDermot Papers, NAI, 9 July 1934, p. 1.
15. Questionnaire received from Thomas Kelly, Co. Leitrim, September 1991.
16. Scruton, R., *A Dictionary of Political Thought* (London, 1982).
17. Primo de Rivera, J.A., 'What the Falange wants' in Weber, E., *Varieties of Fascism* (London, 1964).
18. Woolf, S.J. *European Fascism* (London, 1968), p. 6.
19. Manning, *The Blueshirts*, p. 238.

20 Ibid.
21 Letter from E. Corcoran to the Minister of Justice, Blueshirt complaints, 62/1, Department of Justice, NAI, 20 March 1934.
22 See 62/1 and H306/23, Department of Justice, NAI, for numerous examples.
23 62/1, Department of Justice, NAI . . .
24 *Irish Worker's Voice*, 5 August 1933, p. 2.
25 Gilmore, G., *The 1934 Republican Congress* (Dublin, 1969), p. 33.
26 Galvin, P., *Song for a Poor Boy. A Cork Childhood* (Dublin, 1990), p. 25.
27 *Dáil Debates*, vol. 50., col. 2120.
28 *Ottobre*, 28 October 1933.
29 Quoted by Ledeen, *Universal Fascism*, p. 87.
30 Barnes, J.S., *The Universal Aspects of Fascism* (London, 1928), p. 138.
31 See Webb, D.A., *History of Trinity College Dublin, 1590–1952* (Cambridge, 1954), p. 226.
32 Stuart, F., *Things to live for* (Dublin, 1928).
33 Quoted in Fisk, R., *In Time of War: Ireland, Ulster, and the Price of Neutrality, 1939–45* (London, 1983), p. 381. See also, Elborn, G., *Francis Stuart – a life* (Dublin, 1990).
34 Lee, J.J., *Ireland 1912–85* (Cambridge, 1990), p. 182.
35 Payne, S.G., *Fascism. Comparison and Definition* (New York, 1980).
36 Scruton, *Dictionary of Political Thought*.
37 Sternhell, Z., *Blackwell's Dictionary of Political Thought* (Oxford, 1987).
38 Robinson, R. A. H., *Fascism in Europe, 1919*, p. 1.
39 Griffin, *Nature of Fascism*, p. 26.
40 Payne, *Fascism*.
41 Griffin, *Nature of Fascism*, p. 122.
42 Ibid., p. 124.
43 See the example of Doirot's Parti Populaire Français in joining the Federation Republicane dominated Front de la Liberté in Austin, R., 'The conservative right and the far right in France: the search for power, 1934–44' in Blinkhorn, M. (ed.), *Fascists and Conservatives* (London, 1990), pp. 176–99.
44 Manning, *The Blueshirts*, pp. 243–4.
45 See Fisk, *In Time of War*, p. 427.

Part 10

FASCISM IN LATIN AMERICA

67

Extract from
'FASCISM AND AUTHORITARIANISM IN BRAZIL UNDER VARGAS (1930–1945)'

Helgio Trindade

Source: Stein Ugelvik Larsen (ed.) *Fascism outside Europe: The European Impulse against Domestic Conditions in the Diffusion of Global Fascism*, New York: Columbia University Press, Boulder Social Science Monographs, 2001, pp. 491–528. Translated from French by Dag Hellesund.

Introduction

The debate on the concept of fascism in Latin America dates back to the nineteen thirties. At the time when fascism was rising in Europe, the appearance of political movements of a fascist kind was visible in several countries (in particular Brazil, Argentina, Chile, Bolivia and Mexico), and they did inspire a climate of ideological radicalization in the intellectual and political spheres. Thus the question we will pose is less related to the presence of fascism in this area as such, than to the impact of its various manifestations. During this epoch, there certainly were some conditions favourable to the blooming of fascist-inspired movements or parties: The type of the economic transition in the most developed countries, the important influence of European ideologies on the political and intellectual elite, and the presence of significant ethnic minorities from several waves of European immigration (especially of Italians, and of a smaller number Germans), were favourable factors for the political-ideological imitation from and the arrival of fascist movements. From these facts it follows that the debate on the Latin American experiences, and especially the Brazilian one, illuminates two main problems: How can we distinguish, among these various manifestations, those which came from a pure and simple imitation of European fascism, and therefore had a limited signification on the domestic political level, and those which, because of their character of mass phenomena, did become authentic, national, political movements.

a) The political path of the leader and the foundation of the AIB

The intellectual training and the political apprenticeship of Plínio Salgado developed in a society which in the twenties was in a period of rapid transition. His father was a local political leader, and he was a part of the old Republic's political system. Salgado himself also served this system until the Revolution of 1930. The rupture away from the dominant republican policy and his new ideological engagement were influenced by the ideas of the modernist movement. Before 1930 he had at the same time been member of a traditional political party and actively participated in the 'aesthetic revolution'. His political past seemed to pressure him towards integration within the oligarchic circles, but his literary activity incited him to pass outside these established frames. As many other 'Young Turks', Salgado decided slowly and reluctantly, and after having tried without any success to renew the Paulist Republican Party, he went on to try out a new experience.

The most important influence on Salgado's intellectual training came from the modernist group. His participation during the modernist literary revolution in 1922 imbued him with the national problems and reinforced his nationalist inclinations. Although his political engagement was affirmed in the '*Partido Municipalista*', the modernist experience would bring him to a break with his former political activities as they were a compromise towards the First Republic. He was becoming aware of the necessity to create a political movement independent of the traditional forces.

Salgado joined those who wanted to renew the old PRP from the inside. This movement called itself 'National Action' in order to reconcile the old republican party with the ideas of the current situation: "It was a matter of revival of the power and the youthfulness from the past of the Party".[1]

Despite the failure of the endeavour to renew the Party, Salgado stayed within the PRP until the Revolution of 1930. Thanks to the success of 'The Stranger' in 1926, he was invited to run in the general election. He was elected representative for the Assembly of São Paulo together with Menotti del Picchia. Then he saw another opportunity for renewal, and he followed the newly elected president of the State of São Paulo, Júlio Prestes. But once again he was misled. However, Salgado's evolution towards ideological action and break with the traditional parties was more guided by the literary revolution and aesthetical evolution than by his political activities. Salgado also recognized the effects modernism had on his political views:

> The literary and artistic revolution of 1922–23 lightened a blazing spirit of rebellion with which we have started to overturn the old defenders of form, and broke the political rhythm of the country.[2]

Disappointed by the traditional republican policy and stimulated by the modernist literary revolution, Salgado decided in April 1930 to leave for Europe and the Orient as a private tutor for the son of a São Paulo lawyer.[3] This journey should play an important role in his decision to launch an autonomous ideologically movement.

From then on, two elements could be seen which indicated the birth of the Brazilian Integralist Action: Firstly, the concern in elaborating new ideas that were to be adapted to the reality of the country. Secondly, the existence of a predisposition for 'áction'. Yet, he did not see the fascist option as the right choice. Two ideas are expressed with force when he defines the role his generation has to play:

> As it is more a movement of action than of thought, it will certainly be the great awakening of a final national idea, which will have a less important place than it has deserved in the political and social development of Brazil.[4]

The 'pre-integralist' phase started when Salgado integrated the dominating nationalist themes of modernism into his vision of political action. This phase, after Salgado's break with the Republican party, was characterized by elaborating a new political doctrine. His conceptions were shaped during his journey to Europe and to the Orient, from late April until October 1930. While studying the European political experiences and being disappointed with his old party, Salgado was thinking of the future of Brazilian politics. Then the ideas of fascism as a possible solution came to his mind.

From that moment, he started to incorporate new themes into his political visions. He finished his book *The Hope*, and he sketched out a political manifesto which later could be the basic doctrine of the Revolutionary Legion of São Paulo in its first phase.[5] When he returned to Brazil, as he was the chief editor of *A Razão* (The Reason), he wanted to create a political movement as his principal goal. The writing of a daily 'political note' allowed him the opportunity and hope to build up a political consciousness within public opinion. In 1932, with a group of intellectuals under his influence, he founded the Society of Political Studies (SEP).

The visions of integralist leader thus emerged from conflicts in his inner, personal contradictions. Nationalist, catholic and republican from his youth, Salgado later found himself caught in these social-political tensions and ideological worries. Disappointed by the Liberal republic, he offered his energy to the literary revolution that had urged him into political action. Fascinated by the European fascist experience and the rise of the far-right in Brazil, Salgado felt stimulated to create the Integralist Action and to try to give it an ideological basis close to the Revolution of 1930. The rapid rise of integralism and its ideological penetration into the middle class, but also among segments of the working classes, made this movement influential enough to become the main mass organization of Brazil.

Salgado knew about fascism in Europe, and in one of his letters he told about his conversation with 'Il Duce':

> I told Mussolini what I was planning to do: he found reason to admire my proposals, given the different situations of our two countries. He thought as I do, that *before the organization of a party, a movement of ideas is necessary.*

He finished his letter with the affirmation of nationalism which aims at hegemony:

> I have thought of the necessity of giving the Brazilian people an ideal which will lead them to their historical position. A goal that can arouse the enthusiasm of the people consisting of nationalism, order and discipline in the country and *our hegemony in South America.*[6]

Four days later, after he had been to three biennial expositions that 'honoured Italy and the fascist government', he wrote a letter from Venice where he repeated the project of forming a 'movement of ideas':

> I leave Italy with a program of action. This holy light will not burn out even in this magnificent France which otherwise absorbs all strange characters. I will bring it to Brazil. I will come back full of enthusiasm to start working for our country.[7]

The journal *The Reason* was created in the middle of 1931. It was founded by Alfredo Egydio de Souza Aranha, a lawyer and banker from São Paulo and also an admirer of Salgado for whom he had already paid a voyage to Europe as the private tutor of his son. *The Reason* was to play a decisive role for the formation of the Integralist Action.

During a talk with the Minister of Justice of the Revolutionary Government, the founder of *The Reason* did not hesitate to say about Salgado: "This man can be the ideological founder of the Revolution".[8]

The political orientation of the journal was then entrusted to Plínio Salgado and Santiago Dantas. On May 23. 1932 the premises of the journal were sat on fire by followers of the Paulist Revolution. However, his goals had been reached: Thanks to the publication of approximately 300 articles, Salgado had established contact with a diversified group of intellectuals and persons 'of action' all over the country.

Salgado began to formulate the political basis of his autonomous 'political action', apparently in complete freedom from interference from the political establishment. This was the beginning of *pre-integralism* which became manifesto within the Society of Political Studies (SEP) in March 1932.

The first 'political note' was written on May 5. 1931 with the title "Mistakes of Today, Dangers of Tomorrow" and clarified the program of Salgado:

> In Brazil, there is still no common feeling of national interest. It is our responsibility to declare from the beginning, in the discussion of the problems that this period creates, that there exists no interest above the supreme national interests. From this integral and nationalistic point of view, we shall start our journalistic action in these difficult moments in the life of Brazil. In this daily note we will outline our political thoughts and try to indicate the objectives that seem to us to be of the outmost necessity and our basic needs.[9]

To direct the actions of the young people, he presented some basic criteria. He appealed and he made some affirmative statements about the future: "This paralyzed and deaf Brazil will wake up one day, with weapons in hands, thanks to the strong consciousness of the new generations".[10] What was the nucleus of this new doctrine? It was a philosophical vision of the society directed towards a higher morality and based on a new conception of the State:

> The Modern State, which is a synthesis of all the material, moral, intellectual and spiritual energy of the people, cannot stay indifferent towards the struggle between the two apocalyptic monsters (capitalism and communism). We must define a new conception of the State, an organization and a propaganda based upon the superior aim of Man.[11]

From April 1932 Salgado did not communicate with the Provisional Government any more. Before that he published a series of articles in February on the 'Orders to the Dictatorship'. His language revealed a disillusionment vis-à-vis the dictatorship and about his intention of creating an autonomous political movement. Moreover, from the end of February 1932, the organization of the Society of Political Studies (SEP), which was a real waiting-room for the Integralist Action, came into being.

In a new series of articles entitled "National Construction" beginning on April 20. 1932, he announced the necessity of a *revolution within the Revolution*. He stated that if the Revolution meant a return to the past, it had failed. He declared that a "new revolution was being born". Brazil would not return into the past because "if it is not the one of 1932, it will be the one of a future date: it is as unavoidable as was the movement of 1930".[12] Therefore his plan was to establish the ideological basis for the new revolution.

b) Fascism

Salgado's now favourable position towards fascism makes it easier to capture the development of his thought.

Analyzing the international political situation, and especially the case of Germany, his first observation was that in a moment of crisis, there is no place for indecisive persons. "The crowd is not interested in those who want reconciliation and delay. It is the courageous ones that should lead the masses".[13]

In 1932, he wrote that the modern world was facing two interpretations of society, thus he envisaged a polarization of two extremes:

> Either we stay with Marx' thesis and adapt the principle of historical materialism, as well as the process of social revolution, or we stay with the far-right thus maintaining that man and society will live through economic contingent changes led by the superiority of ideals and with intellectual, moral and spiritual standards.[14]

This choice in favour of the far-right did however put him in a specific dilemma. He had a more distinct sympathy for fascism than before, but at the same time, he wanted to invent a genuine regime for Brazil. Salgado therefore considered that:

> Italian fascism is the *state synthesis* where the state in particular carries in itself all the national features and realizes all the desires of the nation in its harmonic structure.[15]

However, Salgado wrote in a later article that:

> what exists of essentials in the fascist doctrine is directly acceptable, as an absolute conception of the state . . ., what's formal in this regime cannot be used in Brazil.

It is therefore proper to follow the thinking of Alberto Torres who:

> already in 1924, before the appearance of the fascist concept of the state had advocated a form of republican government that included the doctrines today accepted by Rocco and Gentile.[16]

Salgado's position, despite all his efforts of making distinctions, therefore integrated into the fascist stream. He tried desperately to take Brazilian specificities into account, because he believed that:

only strong governments with a position of a genuine authority, could realize a policy of imposing their rhythm on the world of today.[17]

Salgado's journalistic work in *The Reason* and his organization of the *Society of Political Studies* (*Sociedade de Estudos Políticos*) offered him the opportunity of integrating all these factors into his emerging ideological organization. The journal was the instrument that spread his ideas, and the SEP became an arena of ideological reflection, from where the Integralist Manifesto arose.

Salgado himself recognized the role of the journal as his instrument, and his articles attracted the attention of intellectuals and leaders who refused the return to the liberalism of the 1891-constitution.

The first meeting of the *Society of Political Studies* was held on the initiative of Salgado on October 24. 1932 in the headquarters of the journal in São Paulo. Among the group of young intellectuals from the city who came to this meeting were: Candido Motta Filho, Ataliba Nogueira, Mario Graciotti, João Leãres Sobrinho, Fernando Calage and several students from the Faculty of Law.

The founding assembly of the *SEP* took place on March 1932, and was presided by Salgado. In his introductory statement, he defined the role of the association:

> Gentlemen, everywhere I hear the word 'revolution'. From every place we receive echoes of complaints which, in the middle of the confusion that dominates the country since October 1930, call for *a revolutionary spirit*. Actually, everything indicates that Brazil wants renewal, wants to regain its self-control, and wants to march firmly into history. We call for better social justice and a more human redistribution of material necessities, in order to readjust the abuses of ardent individualism. At this moment, I convene you in order to examine the national problems so that we can point out the correct way to a sound political solution . . .[18]

After this event Salgado started to melt the fragmented movements and the scattered intellectuals of the far-right into one unit. In his eyes, the pioneering role of São Paulo should reappear and thus save the nation. He took contact with the former known group of intellectuals from Rio through his old friend the poet Augusto Frederico Schmidt and Santiago Dantas who edited *The Reason* together. One of the members of this group of young intellectuals from the *Journal of Law and Social Studies* was the director of *Hierarchy*, Lourival Fontes, and he was later joined by two future integralist leaders, Raimundo Padilha and Madeira de Freitas.[19]

Salgado was able to reach, with the organization, into the north of the country and to the state of Minas Gerais and to Ceará. A few days after the first meeting of the SEP, Salgado sent a letter to Olbiano de Mello who had dreamt of creating a *National Syndicalist Party*. After expressing thanks for the book *The Syndicalist Republic of the United States of Brazil*, Salgado informed him of his activities in the journal and the foundation of the SEP.

When the SEP organized its third session in São Paulo on May 6. 1932, Salgado, supported by the majority, suggested they should create a "new technical council called Brazilian Integralist Action".[20] Its goal was to "transmit to the people, in a comprehensive language", the results of the studies and the basic doctrines of the SEP.

Even though the decision of creating the AIB was made in May, it did not begin to function until five months later, visibly with the publication of the *October Manifesto* of 1932.

The SEP organized two meetings in June in order to debate the outline of the Manifesto as it had been presented by Salgado. During its first meeting, Salgado explained his proposal to the assembly, and inspection copies were given to the members of the SEP for possible modifications. At the next meeting, the Manifesto was approved without serious modifications. However, the contemporary launching of the 'Constitutionalista' Revolution of 1932 in São Paulo, forced Salgado by caution or by political strategy, to publish the document a few weeks later than intended.

Salgado thus benefited from the foundation of the integralist movement: The AIB was to become the main far-right movement during the thirties.

Integralism as a fascist mass party

1. A bureaucratic and totalitarian organization

Fascist parties are generally organized hierarchically with an emphasis on the training and efficiency of its militants. The aim of the integralist organization went even further than this instrumental function. Beyond the vertical and strict structure and under the influence of the bodies of training and ideological socialisation, integralism added a new element of ideological integration and organization: The structure of the AIB portrays the Integral State. By conceiving the organization on this model, the relationship between the leader, the functions and the different organs constituted a pre-state structure. The organization provided not only a functional means for the political action, or a frame for the ideological training of leaders and members, it was also an instrument for development and experimentation, on a limited scale, towards the Integralist State.

The integralist organization had a triple function: It offered the leader the power to control the entire movement, it was intended to realize a pre-state experience designed after the theoretical model of the Integralist State, and finally it was an instrument for political-ideological socialization of the members.

These aspects defined its fascist contents: The leader was the source of legitimacy in the system, its pre-state structure and its means of ideological socialization characterized its bureaucratic and totalitarian nature.

Inspired by the fascist model of the thirties, the integralist organization was controlled by a 'national leader'. All the written founding material entrusted to him the total and unchallenged leadership of the movement. His power was at the same time *centralized, total and permanent. The centralization of the power of the leader* was so pivotal that all the bodies and functions of the movement were out-lined as delegations from his absolute power. Finally they always depended upon his decision. The statutes of 1934, which created the national departments (1), specified that "the national leader will direct and command the entire movement in all the provinces through the national departments". In each department, the leader will "name a national secretary under his direct control to assist him" (Estatutos 1934: art. 9 and rules of the departments).

The power of the leader ('chef') was total, since he was present in all the important spheres of the movement. The *power to define the doctrine*, the *political decision-making* and the *control of the action* laid in his hands. When needed, he defined and clarified the integralist idea. "He had the sole right of resolution in any ideological and practical matters" (ibid.: art. 3, § h and § m). He had "all the rights" of nomination to positions, the governing of the movement and he had the exclusive power to name the secretaries of the national departments, the leaders in the provinces and the members of the National Council. Finally, he decided the political-ideological direction among the integralists because he was "the commander-in-chief of the integralist forces" (ibid.: art. 3, §6).

The nature of his power is best defined by its permanent character. Nobody can, without the risk of exclusion, "comment upon any action done by the leader in his functions", neither question him on any subject without soliciting him first, nor intervene on the range of his exclusive powers (ibid.: art. 4 to 8). During the interpretation of the *Protocols and Rituals of the AIB* in 1936, the nature of the powers of the leader had not changed compared to the initial documents, but the text was designed to depersonalize the basis for this form of unlimited power. The legitimacy of the power of the leader was due to the fact that "he was the synthesis of the aspirations of all the integralists, the supreme exponent and defender of the doctrine", and, more than a person, he was "the idea within it" (Protocols 1937: art. 11).

Despite this change in terminology, the submission to the personalized leader remained, giving unconditional loyalty to Plínio Salgado. Faithfulness to the chief was therefore a consequence of his unlimited power. All new militant integralists had solemnly to take this oath in front of the portrait of the national leader: "I swear by God and my honour to work for the Brazilian Integralist Action and execute the orders of the national leader and my superiors in the hierarchy without arguments".

Always when the leader went on an assignment, the integralists had to be present at his departure. In accordance with the ritual, after singing the integralist hymn, they had to greet the chief: "Up with Brazil! Up with the Integralist State! Faithful in life and death to our national leader, Plínio Salgado!" Then they raised their right arm and shouted out three times the word of greeting, which originally was Indian: "Anauê! Anauê! Anauê!" (Protocolos 1937).

The basis for the power of the leader can be found in four different elements. Firstly, nobody had the right to question his authority. A leader who tolerated any questioning of his authority would experience a crisis of power, and give signs of weakness. Secondly, and linked to the first: There can not exist any contradiction between the leader and the political doctrine. This principle was absolute in integralism, since the chief was at the same time the founder and the interpreter of the political principles. Thirdly the logic of the concept of the leader and the two corollaries of his authority was perfect, and fourthly the charisma of Salgado can largely be explained from his rhetorical capacity: In his conception, the leader needed a 'liturgy' for external communication. If it is true that presentation does not replace eloquence, it did, however, create an auspicious atmosphere for the transmission of messages and symbolic attachment to the leader. Salgado shaped the outward appearance and the contents of rituals, and this explains the entire 'protocols and rituals' assigned to the ceremonies of the integralists.

a) The pre-state structure

The general power-principle of the organization was derived from the position of the leader and went in his name. The hierarchically organized structure was designed to accomplish the system of delegation from the leader and under his direct responsibility. At the same time, it was a bureaucratic entity protected against the challenges of practical decisions and matters of detail. Thus, the organization was an instrument of action for the leader and also functional as a protective screen. The history of the movement shows, however, that Salgado's temperament and the ambiguity of his commands proved him less able to steer and control the machinery than envisaged. On the other hand, the impact of bureaucratization was reinforced when the machinery was in crisis. Therefore, the screening function predominated and Salgado became more and more an isolated leader. His speeches, articles and works were the only direct means of communication between the members and himself.

The integralist congress at Vítoria established the organizational structure of the AIB which lasted until the reorganization in 1936. Its basic structure was the leader, the national council and the national departments which constituted the executive body. These organizational elements became the embryo of the pre-state structure.

As in any government, the leader had a civil and a military council at his disposal. The council was divided into several branches. One of the most important ones was 'the Military Department and the Commander of the Special Services Troops', which was responsible for Salgado's protection. It was made up by four aides-de-camp at the leader's service and two more from the Military Department and the Special Services Troops. The other branches of the Council were the Secretary, the Official paper (*Monitor Integralista*), the Press department and the Department of foreign affairs. The latter established contacts with authorities and political movements abroad, more precisely "the organizations in the world which had affinities with the integralism", "the consular and diplomatic authorities". They also got the responsibility for "the propaganda among Brazilians abroad".[21] The competence and responsibility of the leader resembled that of governmental functions. It permitted him to institute 'honorary orders' for integralist personalities giving them a distinction of high 'moral, intellectual and civic' standards.[22]

The National Council had an advisory role, with no autonomous power of decision. It was a secondary organ composed of secretaries to the national departments, the provincial leaders, and members appointed by the national leader.

The executive organs were led by a national secretary, and the national departments were under the direct control of the national leader. The first model of the AIB organization was divided into six departments: Political Organization, Ideology, Propaganda, Culture and Arts, Militia and Finances. The leader headed himself the Department of Justice.

In 1936, the entire model was reorganized. New bodies were added to the formerly mentioned. Resolution 165 (January 1936) created two new bodies of representation: The Chamber of Forty and the Supreme Council. It also instituted one of the most important units of the AIB: the Court of Sigma (*Côrtes do Sigma*).

The *Chamber of Forty* was an advisory body comprising 'individuals of high moral and intellectual standards' of the AIB (*Monitor Integralista* October 36). It was subdivided into specialized committers which gave their opinion on problems raised by the national leader. The Supreme Council was defined as an 'auxiliary body' of the national leader, and replaced the National Council. The latter had a more advisory than executive role because it was composed of the national secretaries and the provincial leaders. But the composition made it difficult to assemble because of the geographical distance between the states. Salgado also needed a consultative body close to him, composed of important integralist leaders. That is why he created the Supreme Council and then nominated ten members among the old secretaries of the national departments.[23]

The most important body of representation was the *Court of Sigma*. It comprised the highest leaders of the hierarchy: The members of the Supreme Council, the national secretaries, the Chamber of Forty, the provincial leaders (later the Chamber of Four Hundred), and individual co-opted members. Its first meeting was held on October 15. 1936.

The reorganization in 1936 had increased the number of executive bodies and widened their functions. Thus the old departments strengthened their staff of secretaries. In June 1936 the leader created new divisions: Division for Moral, Physical and Civic Education (*Militia*), Division for Feminale and Youth organization (*Plinianos*) and Division for Foreign Affairs (*Monitor Integralista*, October 1936, Resolution 168).

This change marked the beginning of a strategic transformation of integralism and the beginning of a process of negotiation with the Brazilian establishment. The movement left the 'revolutionary' line and pretended to become a regular political force. The Department of Militia changed name to the Office of Education (moral, civic and physical); the composition of the Chamber of Forty changed and expressed willingness to legitimate the economic elites, thus to gain prestige and respectability for themselves. However, this transition from confrontation to negotiation proved fatal for the movement. President Vargas utilised his machiavellian insight given by this change in the AIB,[24] and obtained, if not the co-operation of the integralists, then at least their proven complicity in the coup of November 1937, which he launched before the end of his mandate. By this manoeuvre and in line with the Cohen plan, the AIB provided him, consciously or not, the opportunity to implant the *Estado Novo* ('the New State'). It was a faked staging of so-called communist subversion in Brazil, and according to the integralists it was presented as a document of an 'internal study' by the leader of the Militia staff. He was at the same time a member of the Secret services of the army, Captain Mouãro Filho. This plan was given by a friend to the Minister of War, General Goes Monteiro. The government made it public and pretended it was a real plan disclosed by the army. Salgado recognised it when he heard it over a national radio station. However, he did not deny it publicly in order not to make people believe a document disclosed under the authority of the staff of the army was a fake: I could not demoralize the only organized force we still had available in our fight against communism."[25]

b) *The militia and ideological socialization*

The *Department of the Militia* directed 'all the integralist forces (F.I.)' (Regulamento 10: art. 1) and imposed a paramilitary organization on the movement. It was inspired by the organization of the regular Army, according to its architect, Captain Mourão Filho.[26] The Militia was organized in a 'top command' and with 'troops'. The first was the steering body and the second the executive. The supreme command of the Militia belonged to the national leader who was head of the "Integralist Forces of the Army, the Navy and the Air force", assisted by a national secretary from the integralist Militia and the Protection Troops. The chief of the military staff, who was

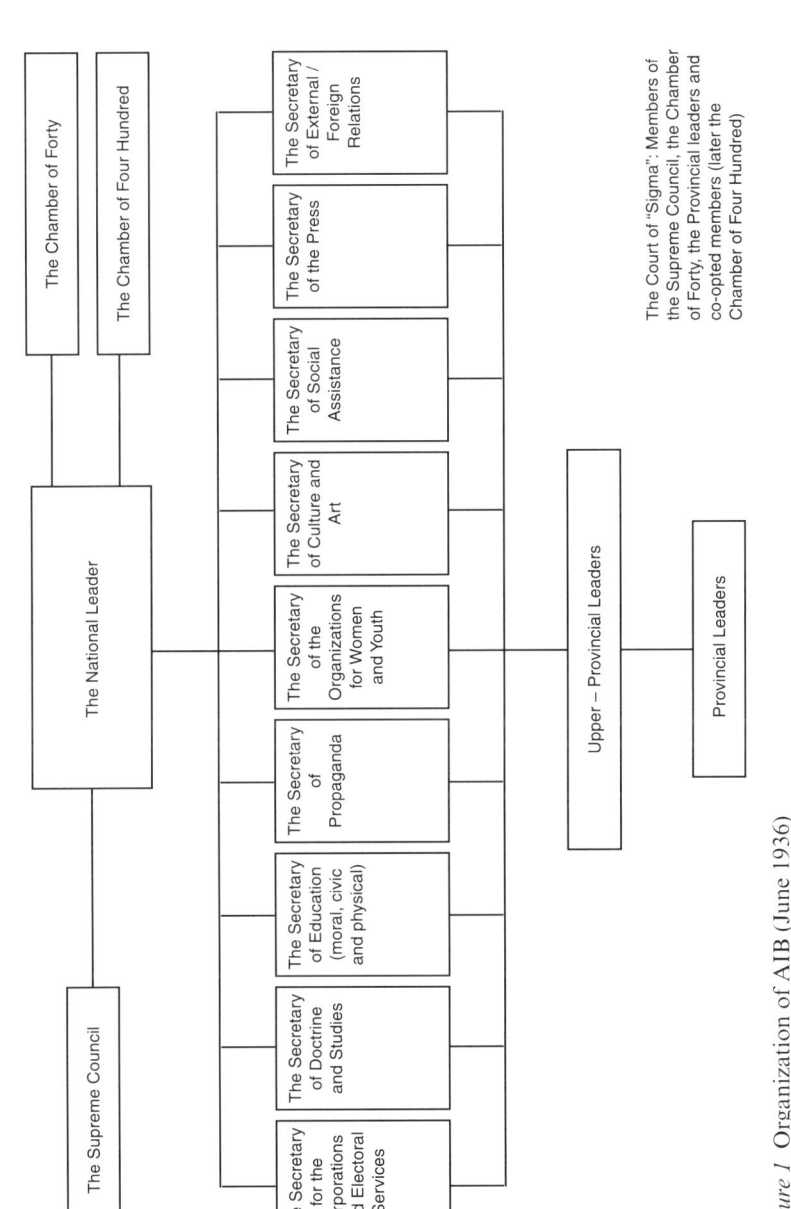

Figure 1 Organization of AIB (June 1936)

nominated by Salgado, was responsible for 'the preparation and the execution of the decisions made by the High command" (Regulamento 10: art. 11). The same structure was applied to the regional level with local branches.

The Militia was organized into four sections: The first took care of correspondence, control of the organization (statistics, members), of discipline, and of justice (inquiries and promotions). The second was responsible for information, and the third of equipment and other services. Finally, the fourth section was in charge of military instruction and preparation of plans for military operations.

The role of the last section was not only to prepare the integralists for parades and physical education, but also to ensure that they got a relevant military training. The education was "technical, tactical and moral", and it ranged from physical education to elaboration of combat plans. Moreover, this training corresponded to the five armed sections of the 'Troops': Infantry, cavalry, pioneers, artillery and air force.

The Troops were structured in three categories: Militia of the first front line, militiamen of the second line, and youngsters. The Hierarchy of the Militia included three grades: The Guard (*Second Decurion*, the *Decurion* and the *Second Instructor*), the Non-commissioned officers (the *Instructor*, the *Bandeirante* and the *Camp Chief*) and the Officers (the *Brigadier*, the *Lieutenant-General* and the *National Chief*). The command lines in each unit were exercised directly within the local groups of militiamen. In the first system created in 1934, the different groups were organized as follows: The *decuria* was composed of six militiamen and a commander (*decurion*), the *terço* was made up of three *decurias* under the command of an *Instructor*, the *bandeira* comprised four *terços* and was directed by a *Bandeirante* who carried the integralist flag. Finally, the most important unit, the *Legião* consisted of four *bandeiras* and was lead by a *Camp Leader*. This was the only one permitted to carry the national flag (See fig. 2).

It was obligatory for the militiamen to wear uniform: A green shirt, a black tie, black and white trousers, a green cap and black shoes. The AIB symbol: The Greek letter 'sigma', surrounded by a black circle which symbolized the will of union of all Brazilians, was placed on the right arm and on the cap. The different format of the symbols showed the ranks within the hierarchy.[27]

2. *Structure of the integralist militia*

Every integralist aged from sixteen to forty-two, after having chosen which militia category he wanted to participate in, was obliged to join the Integralist Forces. If he chose to be a 'front line militiaman', he was enrolled in a training program for sixty days, after which he was integrated into a *decuria*. At the beginning of the training he would fill out a form with all his personal data. Afterwards, in front of the Militia command and a group of witnesses, he took the following oath:

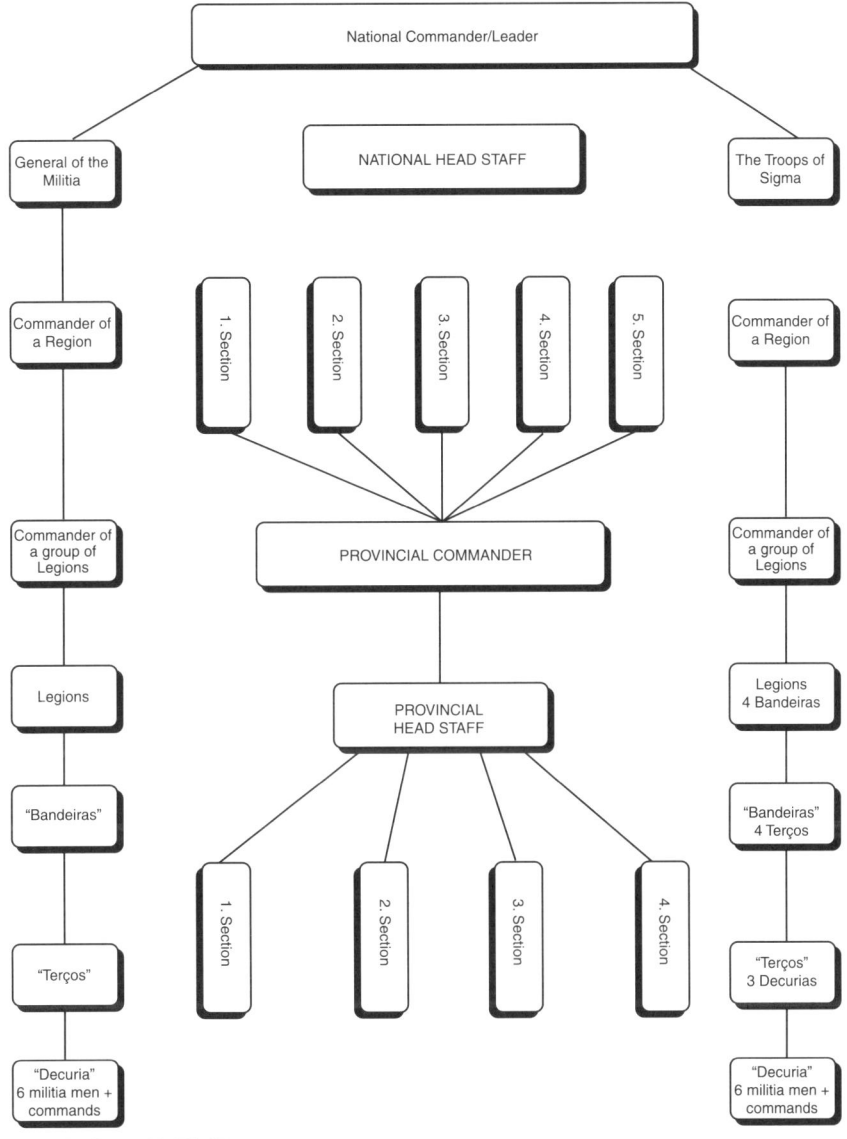

Figure 2 Structure of the integralist militia

As I now become engaged in the Militia, I swear in the name of God and by my honour to obey in absolute discipline my leaders and commit myself to total solidarity with my comrades. I swear to give my life, if necessary, for the Integralist Revolution, to love, respect and make respected the national leader (Regualmento 10).

When the training of the militiaman was over, he had to participate in the ceremony of the 'oath to the flags'; a public and solemn event in front of the AIB headquarters. On this occasion a new statement of loyalty was given, collectively. Even though it was called the 'oath to the flags', it was an oath of absolute submission under the discipline and the leader. After a military ritual, the militiamen proclaimed:

> In the name of God, our country, our family and by our honour, we swear to give our life, if necessary, for the Brazilian Integralist Revolution. We swear to love, respect and defined the national flag and the integralist flag, the symbols of our glorious country. We swear loyalty to the integralist doctrine and absolute, submission without any argument, to the leader (ibid.).

The integralist organization thus became an instrument of political-ideological socialization of the militants in accordance with the internal needs of the organization. It also served as a basis for moulding the citizens of the future Integralist State. Apart from its role of classical ideological education, which mainly was the responsibility for the bodies in charge of doctrine, press and propaganda, the AIB structure allowed for several activities directed towards the transmission of values, symbols and behaviour compatible with its conception of the society and the state. These means of socialization were linked from birth to maturity, through rituals and means of intellectual, moral, civic and physical education, in order to assure the relevant political-ideological training. The integralist leaders were undoubtedly aware of the importance of these 'totalitarian' means of forming the personality, and inspired by European fascists they had meticulously developed such instruments. They found that similar means were necessary to teach obedience to the leader and submission to the authoritarian structures. It was not only, as some integralist leaders pretended, a blueprint of 'some superficial frames of fascism', but the adoption of mechanisms suitable for fascist totalitarianism.

Integralism often underlined the importance of symbols. The supreme mark was the Greek capital letter Σ: 'sigma'. This was chosen because it symbolized 'the whole', 'the sun', and because: "It reminds us that our movement will integrate all the social forces of the country into the supreme expression of our nationality". For the integralists it also signalized that: 'The first Christians used it to symbolize God', and this mark also represented 'the polar star in the Southern hemisphere' (Protocols 25: art. 12).

This Greek symbol was placed in the center of their flag and in all integralist emblems. The flag itself was blue with a white section in the mid point, encircling a black capital sigma. All the militants should wear an emblem with a small black sigma in the center of a silver-coloured circle painted on a blue map of Brazil. The obligation during meetings and official ceremonies to display the symbols was very strict. The AIB motto itself demonstrated attachment to the specific values of: "God, Country, Family", and the integralist greeting was done with the right arm raised shouting "Anauê"!.

The shouting "Anauê!" could also be used "during the parades to stimulate the integralist's enthusiasm, in the wagons during transportation, or as a horn of combat and victory in serious moments of fighting," (ibid.: art. 56). In collective greetings, the national leader had to be saluted with three "anauês". The Supreme Council members, the Chamber of Forty, the national secretaries, the archprovincial leaders and the provincial leaders got two, and the regional and local authorities one single "anauê". During important ceremonies it was also foreseen that "God, the creator of the Universe, should be greeted by the national leader with four 'anauês'" (ibid.: art. 76).

The first oaths were taken within the Youth organization, the *plinianos*, to inculcate the worship of the national leader. The socialization process started when the child was four years old, and went on until he, at the age of fifteen, was accepted in the militia. During this period, the *plinianos* were recruited into four different groups, depending on their age: From 4 to 6 years they were in the category of *infantis*, from 6 to 9 *currupiras*, from 10 to 12 in the group of *vanguardeiros* and at last from 13 to 15 the *plinianos* became pioneers.[28]

Typical for an authoritarian training program the 'integral' method of socialization of children was its intentions to cover their total set of activities. The instruction aimed at developing the civic feeling among the pupils, to strengthen their personality, to stimulate their physical activity (sports, hiking and walks) as well as giving them intellectual education (primarily, moral and professional education) (Regulamento 17: art. 38). The *plinianos* organization was split into divisions: The division of schooling (nursery schools, to read and write, and technical schools), the training division (special integralist education with the 'pliniano alphabet primer', moral and civic education, integralist law, health training and sports), the holiday division and finally the scout division ('paramilitary' training with a technical section for the development of strategy, 'operations' and a 'camp-school' to learn how to become a leader (ibid.).

The authoritarian submission was secured by the rigid hierarchy which was established in all categories, and by the obedience to the leader. The worship of and the loyalty to the national leader was initiated with the oath they had to take at the age of seven! The *infantis* (4 to 7 years) were received according to the scout rituals, but the *currupiras* (7 to 9 years) were obliged to take this oath:

> I promise to be a little soldier of God, my country and my family. I promise to obey my parents, to be a good friend to my brothers, my colleagues and my comrades and to study hard in order to become useful to God, my country and my family (ibid.: art. 34).

A new oath was to be taken when the child became a *vanguardeiro*. It was an oath to the national flag, which demanded the child at ten to be prepared to make sacrifices:

> My country's flag! I swear to serve Brazil, in time of joy and in time of suffering, and in days of sacrifices . . . (ibid.: art. 33).

After two months in the ranks of the *vanguardeiros*, the youth would take the same oath as the militiamen to the national leader and the flag.

2. The social and ideological origins of the militants

The analysis of a fascist party cannot be limited to the study of its organization. It would in addition be necessary to answer two main questions: Which was the social origin of its militants, and what were their motivations to join?

a) The social basis of the militant leaders

The conceptualization of the Integralist Action as a fascist movement may also indicate a similarity of social structure compared to the European fascist models. Data on the social basis of the European movements reveal that at least Italian fascism and German national socialism were dominated by certain social groups comparable to integralism.

Information collected through a survey among former integralists and through the official documents of the AIB gives us the opportunity to reconstruct, in approximation, the social origin of the leaders and the militant integralists.[29]

On the national and regional level, the Integralist Action was composed of upper middle class persons (liberal professions and officers). At the local level the leaders and militants comprised two social categories: The majority came from the lower middle class (small landowners, employees and civil servants), but also some from the working class (workers, mostly from small and medium-sized enterprises), farmers and farm workers (generally in zones with small farms), and some craftsmen.

This general profile seems to come rather close to European fascism. Seymour Lipset concluded from information on fascism in different countries that 'fascism, in its original form, was a movement of the middle class, mostly former followers of liberalism and who as such were opposed to conservative milieus".[30] These findings are especially valid for Italy and Germany.[31] An over-all analysis of movements of a fascist kind shows, however, many deviant examples with different social bases. The most paradoxical case is called by Lipset "fascism of the left". The most typical examples were 'peronism' in Argentina and 'vargism' in Brazil both of which were heavily supported by the lower classes.

The general social basis of the AIB was, as in the European fascist movements, dominated by the middle class, although with a strong recruitment from the working class. But what about the structure of the social strata during the thirties in Brazil compared to Europe?

For Nazi Germany Lipset formulated the hypothesis, based on three sociological analyses on electoral behaviour, that "fascism was particularly attractive to the middle classes, and among them primarily to those in liberal professions" (Lipset 1960: 163, 182). The middle classes were also the basis for the Belgian Rexism:

> It was the middle class that was going through a rather difficult period, and they had the impression that the regime wanted them to disappear. By voting for a new party which promised to defend them against Communism and hyper-capitalism, they thought they could avoid it. This is probably why the lower middle class and particularly the shopkeepers came to fascism.[32]

In Europe the middle classes felt threatened by the crisis of the economy, they were afraid to lose their status, and they felt oppressed by the aggressivity of the working class. In Brazil, on the contrary, they constituted a climbing social class aiming at political power. The same middle class, however, opted both for the right (AIB) and the left (ANL – National Liberating Alliance).

Their main goal, however, was to strengthen their social position which was blocked by the grip from the traditional classes. This situation of not having their own political movement, combined with the influences from the European ideological climate of the period, put them in the dilemma: Fascism or Communism? Therefore, the middle classes began to join either the right wing or the left wing. Both seemed to represent valid political options, being autonomous from the dominating system. Those who felt Communism as a threat were fascinated by nationalistic themes. They looked at the rise of fascism with interest and went to integralism.

The social structure of the AIB as a whole can be seen as a pyramid in three layers with recruitment to the organization conforming to the national, regional and local divisions. The upper layer, the national leaders, came exclusively from the bourgeoisie and the middle classes, with the intellectual elite as the majority. The middle layer comprising the regional leaders was also dominated by the intellectual middle class. Three quarters of the leading positions were held by the upper middle and the middle classes. Integralists from the lower middle class, and some representatives of the working class comprised the last quarter, most of them in advisory positions. Finally, on the lowest layer, three quarters of the militants came from the lower middle and the working classes. Seen as a whole, this stratification corresponded with the scheme of the militia in the para-military organization: The

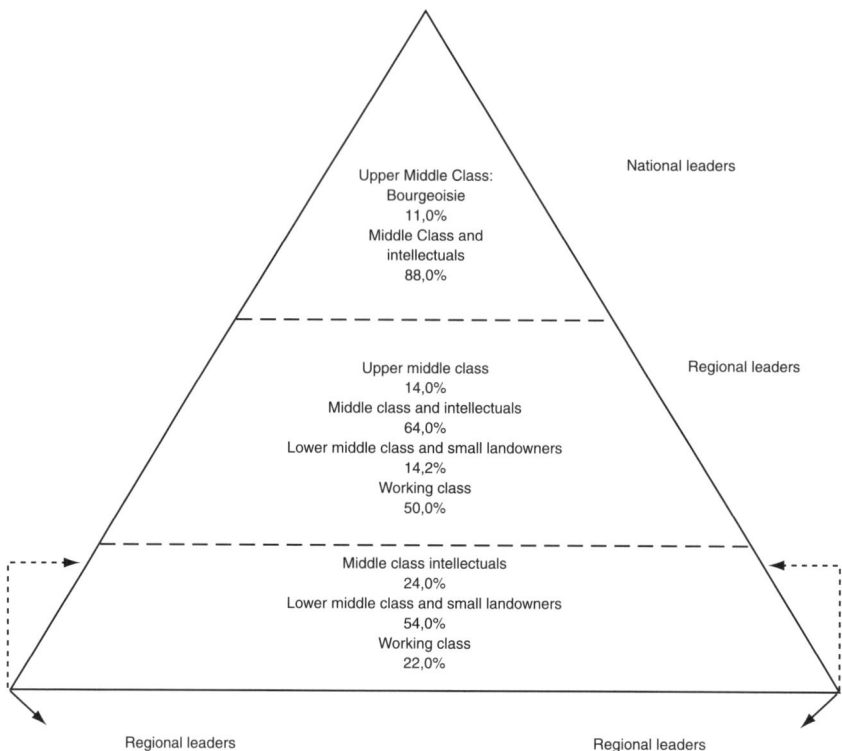

Figure 3 The Pyramid of the social structure of the AIB

intellectual elites were in command, and the non-intellectual middle and working classes were at the bottom: they were 'the troops'.

b) Identification of fascist ideology

The analyses of fascism are in general confined to the study of the ideology and the organization of the movements. This classical approach may be sufficient for movements whose nature is indisputable. Nevertheless, to determine the nature of a party of the fascist type, its seems necessary to introduce a new dimension: The study of the ideological beliefs of the militants. An inquiry among the national, regional and local leaders and the ordinary militants has given us the opportunity to disclose their attitudes on some ideological issues.

The aim of this inquiry was to verify if attitudes of a fascist type were present in Brazil during the inter-war years: Did the integralists identify themselves with fascism? Was there a high correspondence between the main beliefs of the militants and the principal elements in fascist ideology?

We worked out a set of propositions in order to evaluate the integralist attitudes. The measures were based on ideological propositions while attempting to reduce the Italian model of fascism to its principal elements, and adding some elements from National socialism. Consequently, the fascist attitude was not treated as done in the studies directed by Adorno on the 'authoritarian personality', but it tried to grasp the attitudes of the integralists, and to compare them with a control group.[33]

The degree of identification by the integralist with fascist ideologies does not imply a moral judgment on the relationships between integralism and European fascism. We only tried to find out how these two ideological universes were related. By using an ideological profile which integrates the principal fascist themes and values, we can use it in order to establish the degree of comparative similarity.[34]

The first dimension is *nationalism*, included in all fascist movements. Often nationalism is not explicitly mentioned in the basic texts, but we know that fascism mobilizes essentially on exaggerated national sentiments.

The results revealed a very high degree of identification with nationalism among the integralists. The idea that Brazil had to accomplish a historical mission was more than a belief. It became a myth mover in the sorelian meaning of the concept. The ideological nucleus of this nationalism was organized around a worship of the past, by the independence of and the future of the nation. The origin of these feelings was the wish to rediscover the past of the nation, and the glorifying of the primitive inhabitants, the Indians, who were there before the Portugese colonization.

Even though some fascists claimed some adherence to socialism (Mussolini was a former militant socialist), one common element in this ideology was the rejection of socialism in any form. During the period when fascism was born in Italy, the struggle of the working class was very violent, and anti-socialism had a concrete content. For the second generation of these movements, it became first and foremost a rallying theme or a source of inspiration for 'preventive' actions. Under the threat of the Soviet revolution the struggle of the working class was met with a general expression of *anti-communism*. When this threat did not prove real, fascist propaganda created and exaggerated it. One of the functions of anti-communism was therefore to invent an external enemy and to intensify a willingness to fight.

The answers confirmed the intense anti-communism among the integralists. The depreciation of the Cuban revolution and the defense of the private property against socialization, revealed an anti-socialist attitude both on the historical and on the theoretical level. Three quarters of the answers were favourable to struggle against the socialist movements, to resist them, or to defeat them with violent means, which proves the strength of anti-socialism. The combination of these two elements, ideological anti-socialism and anti-communist mobilization, provides the basis of fascist anti-socialism. The first attitude was common among the liberal and conservative right and fascism. The second supposed a predis-position for direct action which generally did not exist in the first group. Despite the anti-communist actions of the Italian 'black shirts', who were examples to other fascist or nationalist movements, we cannot consider Italian fascism as an exclusively anti-communist movement. Still, this violent mobilization distinguished the classical right and the nationalist or fascist far right.

The question "Is there no substantial difference between Socialism and Communism?" wanted to measure the degree of distinction that the integralists made between the two ideologies. Even though socialism after the Second World War had developed towards Social Reformism, more than two thirds of the integralists asserted that socialism and communism were identical, and that the 'democratic socialism' had to be defeated by all means.

The third dimension common to all fascist movements was *anti-liberalism*. The authoritarian conception of the fascist state represented an antithesis to the classical non-interventionist, liberal state. Two aspects can be distinguished in fascist anti-liberalism: The first one came from their analysis of history and emerged from the ideals of the French revolution and the neutrality of the liberal state. The second refused, in the name of the unity of the nation, to accept the liberal and democratic mechanisms being responsible for this separation.

The questions formulated to evaluate the attitude of the integralists towards liberalism had two dimensions: The integralists asserted their disagreement with liberalism, which they thought of as "one of the most noxious elements of our civilization", and they considered that the liberal state was responsible for the disorder in the world of today. Furthermore, most of the integralists found that political parties and elections divided the nation, and they approved to sacrifice democratic procedures as elections in order to realize the 'aims of the nation'.

The *anti-plutocratism* and the international *anti-capitalism* were included in the fourth dimension. These two aspects are related since a study of the fascist ideology compared to historical experience clearly revealed such a contradiction. If the role of fascism was to revive liberal capitalism in crisis, by using national capitalism controlled by the corporative state, the ideological language still often had an anti-capitalistic tone. When going deeper into the nuances in the ideology, we discovered once again its internal logic. Behind the anti-bourgeoise and anti-plutocratic attitude, fascism was aware of the strategy that in order to save the weakened capitalism, it had to get rid of liberalism and try to control capitalism by a strong state.

The result became a mixture combining an anti-plutocratic attitude hostile towards international capitalism, with the exaltation of the strong corporative state, which should be capable of bringing capitalism out of the economic crisis and prevent the social revolution.

The answers almost unanimously condemned oligarchic domination and bourgeois ideas of the role of elites. Two thirds considered the capitalistic plutocracy to be the most favoured class in history. Almost all responses showed an anti-capitalistic attitude well linked to their nationalism.

The fifth ideological dimension integrated the *myth of social transformation*, symbolized by the idea of a 'fascist revolution'. Despite its general conservative position, the fascist action accepted social reformism. The implicit hypothesis was that fascism was a movement of social conservation, but not necessarily reactionary, since it permitted some changes. If the corporative solution and the exaltation of the ideas of the past are traditionalist ideas, then a return to the roots of the nation signified a search for energy to construct a mythical future. Even though it did not go further than Social reformism, the transformation of the state was one of the characteristics which distinguished fascism from traditional nationalism of the far right, as for instance the *Action Française* in France.

The answers from almost all the integralists brought out a belief in social change. We noticed that the large majority of interviewed did not oppose state intervention in the economy at the expense of the interests of private initiative, neither did they oppose agrarian reforms with expropriation of land. A certain resistance against the 'nationalization' came from the fact that this measure originally 'tapped' socialism. Still, what is striking was that though almost all the answers were in favour of a total change in society, there was a certain polarization when it came to measures of social reform: That was the myth confronted by reality.

The sixth dimension was *spiritualism*. Even if it cannot be considered as an essential ideological aspect of fascism (National Socialism did not claim to be attached to any specific spiritual values), spiritualism often appeared in the ideological texts of Italian fascism, and especially in Spanish Falangism and Belgian Rexism. The references to spiritualism in fascism were vague, but its importance in the history of religious values and moral principles were recognized. On this theme Falangism and Rexism were more explicit. These two movements believed in a society based upon Christian principles and the spiritual transformation of man. In integralism, the Catholic tradition of the Brazilian people and the Catholicism of Salgado led to the incorporation of spiritualism within the doctrine.

The seventh dimension was at the centre of the 'fascist revolution': The *transformation of the state*. In fascism, the state was not only a means to realize Social reformism, but also an end in itself. Fascism declared that if there was no transformation of the State, there was no revolution. We also had to consider the different reform plans of the fascist State in order to compare it with the attitudes of the integralists.

Almost all the integralists agreed that a strong state, a new elite and a corporative organization were necessary. The ambiguity in two other questions, which mixed the leader with an essentially messianic personality, explained why a part of the interviewed rejected the idea of a 'providential man'. It explained at the same time the polarization among the integralists when they were confronted with the false dilemma in the contradiction between the State and the Nation, conceptualized in abstract terms. In Italy more than in Germany, the organization of the nation was the responsibility of the State, but according to the fascist conception, the State was created in the name of the Nation.

We had to add one more question concerning the ideological dimension. We tried to find a connection between the integralists' perception of their ideology and the idea that fascism finally was a form of National Socialism which went beyond Marxism and internationalism. Inasmuch as the integralists feared to be qualified as 'National Socialists', the question tried indirectly to discover if they accepted that the right ideology was a combination of the *concern for social justice and the nationalist spirit*. The positive weight in the answers showed that the use of the term 'socialism' combined with the idea of 'social justice' did not lead to a refusal of the content of the question. National Socialism therefore seemed legitimate in this context.

Another dimension in the ideology was related to some prejudices in the fascist ideological universe. They were systematically incorporated into the ideology, particularly in National Socialism: The *anti-semitic* and *anti-masonic* attitudes, and the idea that men from nature are not equal. The fight against masonry was clearly demonstrated in Italian fascism: Mussolini was anti-masonic from his socialist period. Anti-semitism was one of the principal elements of Nazism. These two prejudices had existed latent or manifest and in various degrees within the majority of fascist ideologies. The same was true for the hierarchical vision founded on the inequality between people, and upon which National Socialists based their racist world view.

The results proved that anti-semitism and anti-masonry were very deeply implanted in the old integralists, even though the fear of Jews was not too strong. As regards the hierarchial vision and the natural inequality of men, this was rejected by one third of the integralists when the question of inequality implied a right of domination over other people. This demonstrated, however, that there was a certain National Socialist influence among some of the integralists.

Another dimension comparable to European fascism was the *pessimistic vision of history*. As the contradictory position to the liberal philosophy of history, fascism was not imbued with the optimism founded on the classical liberal feeling of happiness and progress. Their positions were determined by a heroic and at the same time a tragic conception of history. (According to Manicheism, the historic process is the result of a permanent struggle against the elements of disintegration challenging our societies continuously, since this phenomenon is rooted in the nature of man.)

Two thirds of the integralists did not believe in an indefinite moral or technical development, and almost all of them rejected the hypothesis that political development based on the democratic idea or that of social development would be capable of eliminating conflicts and wars.

After having taken an inventory of the main dimensions of the ideological fascism and its prejudices that were current among the integralists, their degree of attachment to some values that were exalted by fascism must again be taken into consideration. This set of values were not always explicit in their ideological texts, but they were part of some sort of a moral code for fascist behaviour. Therefore, we cannot dissociate the ideological aspects out of a bundle of particular values.

The first issue is the *exaltation of authoritarian values*. Not only did fascism support the restoration of authority by the state. The fascist organization was a school of individual leaders, and at the same time predisposed individuals for submission to authority. The three dimensions needed for the acceptance of the authoritarian values are: the pre-eminence of the role of the leader, the importance given to the hierarchy, and the acceptance of the submission to the authority. The homogeneity in the answers to these three questions proved the degree of support to authoritarian values.

Nevertheless, other values were incorporated in the fascist ideology. One of the most important was *faithfulness*. The importance given to oaths in the integralist rituals proved this. Another, which was directly linked to the first, is what we could call the *ethics of friendship*. If the faithfulness to the leader was essential to the effective functioning of the organization, the spirit of comradeship was, according to Brasillach, the founding value of life in community and of the feeling of loyalty among individuals. Therefore the youth organizations had an important role in community life by stimulating friendships and group spirit. In this same sphere, it also fostered enthusiasm for intellectual- and physical discipline, and the taste for adventure and a risky life in order to realize their ideals. The answers from the integralists were almost all in favour of these three elements, which finally were the basis for the worship among fascist youth.

One of the paradoxes of fascism was that it represented an attempt of rebirth, and at the same time a nostalgia to the past. Besides the exaltation of the youth and the myth of the new society, there was a willingness to *worship the traditional values*. This traditionalism was not necessarily reactionary: Fascism did not simply want to return to the past, but tried to conserve parts of the traditional values making them relevant for today. Fascism wanted to realize a symbiosis between a traditional element, which was corporatism, and a modern element, the Interventionist state.

The last dimension was founded on a fundamental suggestion decisive to conclude on the fascist nature of integralism. We have to understand the Brazilian character of the AIB, in deciding whether or not there was a feeling of affinity to the fascist movements in Europe. To call a movement fascist, it is not sufficient that there were traits similar to European fascism. The militants themselves must also be subjectively aware of the affinity. The previous analysis showed that the integralist theorists and their partisan press, as well as the 'motivations' of adherence, did not conceal this feeling of direct contact. But we also had to measure the degree of moral 'connectedness' among the integralists towards the movements that fought similar battles in Europe at the time. This is not only a question of having a purely intellectual or affective attitude. It is also necessary that there are common aims beyond the national particularities of every movement, which unites them in a sort of 'fascist internationalism'. The answers to our questions seemed to confirm this hypothesis.

We can therefore conclude, by using a psychosociological approach, that the analysis of the integralist ideology has made us able to verify the hypothesis of its fascist content. In the first place, an analysis of the texts showed fundamental elements of typical fascist ideology, especially on themes as the definition of the 'enemies' and the social and political model which was proposed. Furthermore, the attitudes reveal a high degree of fascist inclinations. However, if we can affirm that the AIB ideologically belonged to the fascist family, this does not mean that other ideological aspects of the traditional right or of the social Catholicism were not part of the integralist ideology. Yet, this does not change the overall judgment of its fascist nature.

3. *The integralist political project*

The composite, integralist ideology spread in three different directions. It is therefore appropriate to study its doctrinal basis, from which it developed a certain conception of man, society and history, and also to understand how the social and political organization of the movement was based upon the perception of the transformation of the state. At last, it is important to examine its antagonistic positions: Against liberalism, socialism, international capitalism, and the Jews.

a) The doctrinal foundings

In Italian fascism, 'the fact preceded the doctrine'. Integralism was an ideology which pretended to lean on a conception of the Universe and of man. The integralist theorists made a systematic effort to define the philosophical basis of the movement, which, despite its eclecticism, helps us today to understand their ideology.

Integralist ideology was built on a conception of man and of society which was outlined in the *October Manifesto* edited by Salgado. This conception was based on two postulates: Spiritualistic humanism and social harmony.

The first sentence of the *Manifesto* asserted that "God guides the destiny of the peoples" (Manifesto 1932: 1). This conception of history implied a belief in the moral progress of human beings: "on the Earth, human beings must practice the virtues which raise them to a higher level and lead them to perfection" (ibid.). As a consequence, integralist ethics, inspired by Christianity, evaluated the value of a man "by his work and his sacrifice in favour of the Family, the Country and the Society" (ibid.).

This conception of social life, which consisted of a dream of return to medieval ideals of social harmony, was conceptualized on the basis of spiritualist humanism:

> The individuals and the classes can and must live in harmony (. . .)
> All their dignity comes from a superiority which exists above the human beings: Their common and superior aim (ibid.).

Social harmony was thus a result of the hierarchic organization of society, according to the natural differences between people. In the social structure, harmony and hierarchy merged. Consequently, the spiritualist foundation of integralist ideology was inspired by the traditional conception of the Catholic social doctrine. This ideological foundation brought integralism much closer to Portuguese- ('salazarism'), Spanish- ('Spanish Falange') and Belgian- ('rexism') conservative and Catholic fascism, than to the vague spiritualism of Italian fascism, or to German National Socialist agnosticism.

The integralist *Manifesto of October 1932* gave an important position to nationalism. It wanted to "affirm the value of Brazil" and unite all the Brazilians into one single 'mind' and to build an "organized, united, indivisible, strong, powerful, rich and happy" nation (Manifesto 1932: 1).[35] This confession of faith indicated an ambitious project: That integralism intended to create "a true Brazilian culture, civilization and a way of living" (ibid.:3).

The principal ideological statement which emerged from the Manifesto was nationalism, and the weight of the contents was more on culture than on economics. The nationalistic idea was thus essentially a call for national consciousness: "Up with the nation!".[36] This integralist slogan, founded on the understanding of the basic needs of the nation and on the imperialist exploitation of all the resources on the earth, represented the transition from the sentimental nationalism of Salgado and the coming of the more aggressive expressions of integralist nationalism.

It is interesting to compare the nationalism defined by Salgado in the *Manifesto* ("the deep awareness of our needs, the character of the 'tendencies', the aspirations of the nation and the value of the race") and the nationalism of later integralist theorists with their emphasis on economic and anti-semitic issues. The nationalism of Salgado was attached to the national roots in the thinking of the twenties, and despite his growing politization, he stayed faithful to the same themes: The exaltation of man and of the Earth, the birth of the new race and the search in the past for the foundations of the Brazilian society.

The dream of an empire was a new dimension of his nationalism. It was based on the myths of the disappeared civilization of Atlantis. In the

Brazilian context, the idea of an imperialistic expansion was meaningless because of the great size of the national territory. Nevertheless, we have to see how the idea of an empire developed, considered as an essential feature of fascism.[37] This theme existed in Salgado's works in the form of the idea of an expansion of the integralist views on the Latin-American continent:[38]

> I will not be content with the establishment of the Integralist State in Brazil. I want this idea to spread all over South America (...). When all the countries of South America will be pulsing with the same rhythm, the time has come to realize this vision. The integralist revolution is the revolution of the entire continent.[39]

The integralist nationalism also had an anti-imperialistic economic dimension. This dimension was not the most dominating one in the writings of Salgado, but it appeared clearly in the books of Reale and Barroso. The difference was that in Barroso's work economic nationalism took an anti-semitic flavour, while in that of Reals, who was marked by being a former Marxist, it took an essentially economic materialist flavour.

b) The social and political model

The integralist theorists all agreed that the aim of the movement was to establish the Integral State. The basic idea was that an integralist revolution should aim at a transformation of the state. Mussolini had defined the central concept of the state in fascism as follows:

> the force of fascism, he said, consists of this: It takes the vital parts of all the programs, and it has the power to realize them. The central idea of our movement is the state: The state is the political and legal organization of the national societies, and it is reflected in a series of different institutions. Our slogan is as follows: Everything within the state, nothing outside the state, nothing against the state.[40]

However, the Integral State may have been 'strong' in the Italian meaning of the word, but it wanted to be a spiritualistic state in the Spanish meaning:

> It is a totalitarian and missionary state, asserted a text of the Falange. Totalitarian in its structure and missionary in its Catholic inspiration and its work of education and orientation.[41]

If we compare the *Manifesto of 1932* and the *Alphabet Primer of 1933*, which were the two first official ideological documents, the gap is evident. In

Salgado's Manifesto the Integralist State had a secondary position, and was described in a rather obscure way. In the *Alphabet Primer*, of which Reale was the author, the state was the key element of ideological reasoning, and its content was drawn in more detailed legal terms.

The comparison of the two documents brings face to face two different conceptions. The idea of the state which emerged in the *Manifesto* was one of authoritarian suprastructure. This idea became the spiritualistic nationalistic conception and was the nucleus within the ideological reasoning. The state was only a regulator of the social balance necessary for the accomplishment of man in society. On the other hand, *The Alphabet Primer* considered "the co-operation of the national producing forces for the progressive realization of the Integralist State" to be the fundamental principle of integralism.[42] This finally became the forming principle of the integralist ideological universe.

But how was the Integralist State to be organized? The representative state organs were the President of the Union, the National Corporative Chamber and the National Council or the Senate. The general principle of the system was based on a restricted and hierarchical suffrage at all levels, apart from the local level.

At the local level (município), every profession should form a union, since only a union was to be recognized by the integralist government. The elections were to be made within every union, which all had one representative in the Town Council. Then the representatives of all the unions indirectly elected the mayor.

In the provinces, the union federations were made up by all the union representatives for one profession, who then chose their provincial representatives. All the representatives of every federation formed the Provincial Council, which elected the governor of the province.

All the federations of the same profession formed the unionist confederations. The corporations were organized at the same level, which were made up by representatives of different professions constituting one important, national task-area.[43] The corporations were the most important sources of the Corporative integral state. Every corporation elected representatives to the National Corporative Chamber.

Also a National Council or Senate existed in the integralist state. This comprised the non-economic corporations (social and cultural) and controlled and emphasized their specific problems, so that the National Corporative Chamber could give priority to them as national problems. The National Corporative Chamber together with the Senate formed the National Congress, which elected the national leader. In this state, the political parties were abolished because they could not be justified in a "nation where all the economic and cultural forces were organized within the state".[44]

Integralism intended to fight liberalism, socialism, international capitalism and the secret societies connected to the Jews and to masonry. The lack of concern for the development of the society in the liberal state created favourable conditions for international capitalism and the growth of socialism. Therefore, the integralists did not think of socialism as an antithesis to capitalism, as the natural result of its evolution, but not in the Marxist meaning. Socialism was not necessary because of the internal contradictions within the capitalistic system, but because they both were based upon the same materialistic base. An important part of the integralists believed that all these enemies were united under Jewish domination. This anti-semitic stream was not dominant among the integralist theorists, for reasons of principles or tactics, but because of the simplicity of the idea it was very widespread among the average militants. Everything from the international finances to the Soviet Revolution was controlled by the Jews' conspiracy and they tried to hold the whole world in their hands.

Conclusion

To decide on the fascist nature of the integralist movement (and this could also be inferred to other Latin-American movements of similar type), we have to analyze it on three typical components of European fascism: The ideology, its social basis and the organization. The presence of these three elements, even with some national peculiarities, is a necessary condition outside Europe to firmly establish the fascist character of a political movement. In the case of the Integralism, we have analyzed the ideology on different levels: the theoretical formulation of the ideology, the publications of propaganda and ideological popularization, and the ideological attitudes of the leaders and the militants. We have underlined the various aspects of the ideology in order to better understand the contents of an ideological reasoning mainly elaborated in a different historical context. Furthermore, how the manifestation of the ideology of a political movement can vary depending on the position of its adherents in the 'ideological pyramid' (the ideology of the theorists, the leaders, the militants, etc.). The internal cohesion of the ideology has empirically been confirmed and tested by the hypotheses developed on the basis of the theoretical model of European fascism.

With regard to the social origin of the militants, comparison of the social structure of the Integralism with European fascism was the main criterion to decide on its fascist nature. Information obtained from old militants, by our survey, or thanks to official documents of the AIB, has allowed us to make a rather precise reconstruction of the social basis of the movement. The profile of the social composition of Integralism demonstrated that it was quite similar to the European model. It compared especially well to both Italian fascism and German National Socialism. This also corresponds to the analyses made by Juan Linz.[45]

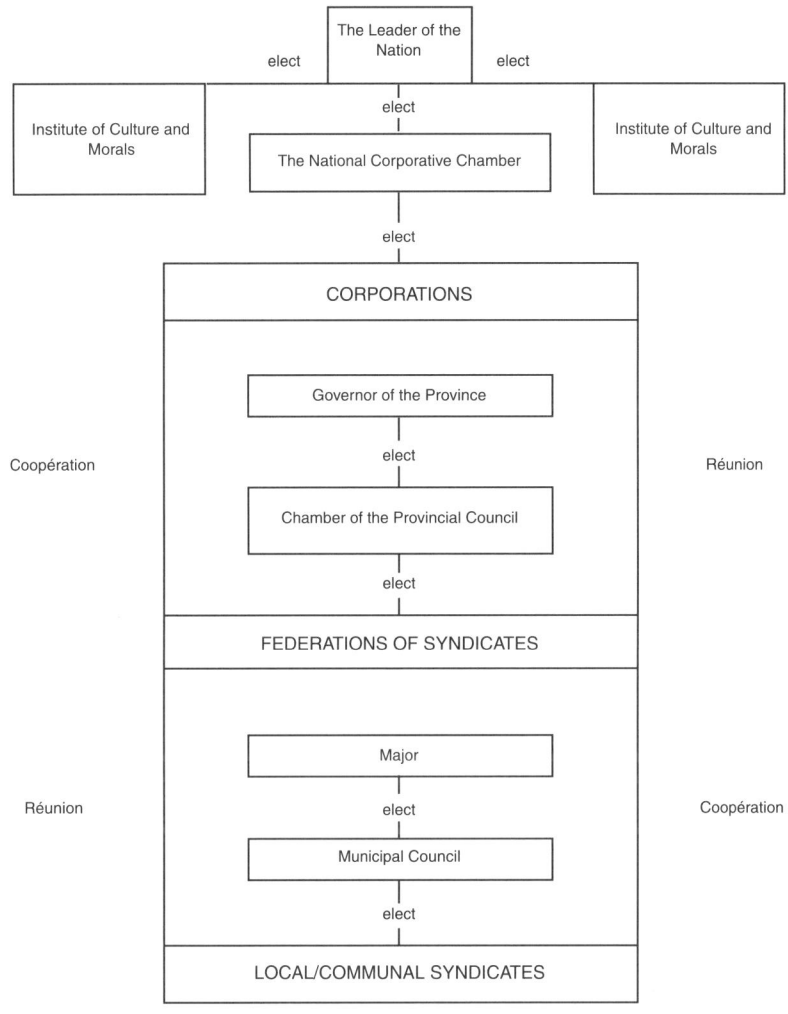

Figure 4 The Corporate Organization of the State

The type of organization of the Integralism was another important characteristic to define the nature of this movement. In a fascist movement, ideology and organization cannot be separated, since there is an explicit connection between the structure of the latter and the contents of the former. Authoritarian political organizations are hierarchically structured in order to efficiently educate and supervise their militants. However, the *integralista* movement played a double role both as an instrument of mobilization, training, supervising and ideological socialization, and as the possible forerunner of the Integralist state. The structure of the AIB, from its leader down to its militants, formed a bureaucratic and totalitarian organization. The bureaucratic structure of the organization appeared through a system of bodies, functions, roles and behaviours which in minute details had been written down in rules, been manifest in the commands of the leader and prescribed in the rituals. Totalitarianism appeared through the strict relations between the bodies of training of the militants (from the youth organizations to the militia), and in the unconditional submission and the faithfulness to the superiors in the hierarchy.

The range of authoritarian movements in Europe during the inter-war years makes integralism an eclectic ideology. With roots in an earth-bound nationalism and founded on the mythical messianism of the historic destiny of the new cross-breeded race, it integrated into a new synthesis the social and religious traditionalism of Lusitanian integralism and Salazarism, the Roman state control and corporatism of Italian fascism, as well as anti-semitism of National Socialist inspiration.

Two convergent doctrinal elements, nationalism and spiritualism, associated towards a common enemy, permitted the coexistence of two juxtaposed ideological tendencies into one single movement. The conciliatory role of the integralist leader saved the unity of the integralism from its birth to its dissolution.

However, integralism, which was believed to be the answer to the aspirations of a young country open to outside influences, was finally rejected by Brazilian history as a part of the nightmares of the thirties.

The analysis of the Brazilian case could be the answer to the objections of Renzo De Felice, who insisted upon the European limit to the fascist phenomenon.[46] Integralismo reproduced the characteristic features of the European fascist movements without being a plain imitation of them. The situation in Brazil during the inter-war years favoured the development of Integralism as a mass movement, and made it a threat to the traditional political establishment. Because of its importance at the time and its effects on the development of the Brazilian society, this fascist political experience probably constituted a special case. Only by a continued effort of research and analysis on fascism in Latin America, particularly by monograph studies and by comparison of the various cases of fascism in Latin America, will we manage to obtain a final answer regarding the true limits of the phenomenon.[47]

Notes

1 Motta Filho, C., *Témoignage sur l'AIB*, Rio, 1970.
2 Salgado, P., *Despertemos à Nação*, Rio, José Olympio, 1935, p. 7.
3 Alfredo Egydio de Souza Aranha with whom he worked during 1926–27 and who in 1932 did finance the establishment of the journal A *Razão* (the Reason).
4 Salgado, P., *Literatura e Política*, São Paulo, Edit. das Américas, 1927, p. XIII.

5 The Revolutionary Legions were the political movements which, in some States and after 1930, organized themselves and kept alive the ideas of the future Revolution.
6 Collectif, *Plínio Salgado*, São Paulo, Edição da Revista Panorama, 1936, p. 21.
7 Callage, F., "Alguns aspectos da vida de Plínio Salgado" in Collectif, *Plínio Salgado*, São Paulo, Edição da Revista Panorama, 1936, p. 174.
8 Silvia, H., *Os tenentes no poder*, Rio, Civilização Brasileira, 1966, p. 76.
9 Salgado P., "Erros de hoje perigos de amanhã", *A Razão*, 5 juin 1931.
10 Salgado P., "O Baile de Máscaras", *A Razão*, 25 novembre, 1931.
11 Salgado P., "Rumos à Ditadura (VIII)", *A Razão*, 14 février, 1932.
12 Salgado P., "Construção Nacional", *A Razão*, 20 avril, 1932.
13 Salgado P., "A Marcha para os extremos", *A Razão*, 16 décembre, 1931.
14 Salgado P., "Federação e Sufrágio (XXVII)", *A Razão*, 3 février, 1932.
15 Salgado, P., "Regimens políticos", *A Razão*, 21 octobre, 1931.
16 Salgado, P., idem.
17 Salgado, P., "Democracia e Nacionalismo", *A Razão*, 12 décembre, 1931.
18 Salgado, P., *O Integralismo na vida brasileira*, Rio, Livr. Clássica Brasileira, 1958, p. 143.
19 They were the coming chefs of the integralist in the State of Rio and in the federal District, and also members of the Supreme Council and the National Secretariat of the l'AIB.
20 Salgado, P., *O Integralismo na vida brasileira*, Rio, Livr. Clássica Brasileira, 1958, p.17.
21 Resolution no 19 of the statutes for the internal Cabinet of the national Chef. (*Monitor Integralista* no 6, May 1934). The development of these international reports gave later, in 1936, birth to the Secretariat for External Relations.
22 Resolution no 2, creation of Orders of honor (*Monitor Integralista*, 1(6) May 1934). The orders were the following: 1. The Cross of 'Ancieta', 2. The Star of 'Guararapes', 3. The Order of 'Cacador de Esmereldas', and 4. the Order of 'Sigma'.
23 The national departments were lead by: Everaldo Leite (Political organization), Miguel Reale (Doctrine), Madeira de Freitas (Propaganda), Rodolfo Jesetri (Culture and Arts), Gustavo Barroso (Militia), Maciel Ramos (Finance), and Jehovah Motto (Justice). All the secretaries were appointed to the Supreme Council. The only one who belonged to the former National Council was Raimundo Padilha.
24 Getulio Vargas became the 'chef' of the provisional Government, set up by the Revolutions of 1930 and 1934, and he also wanted to become president of the Republic under the new constitution.
25 Salgado, P., Conversations with *H. Trindade*, Brasília, 1969.
26 General Olympio Mourãa Filho was the main responsible for the military operations leading to the coup d'etat against the government of president Goulart in 1964. In the pre-war period he was 'Chef for the l'etat-major of the intégralist Militia', under the command of (the historian?) Gustavo Barroso.
27 The duty to wear uniform was very rigourously written into the Manifesto of the Integralista. In article 32 of 'The Protocol of Rituals' it was stated that "all integralists are obliged to have a green shirt ready to wear in any moment of importance". Even if he was on a private voyage he was obliged to carry "the green shirt with him in his suitcase". The respect for the shirt demanded every one, in the event when an integralist was arrested, that he shall ask the authority arresting him to get the opportunity to take off his shirt before he entered the prison, except when it concerned an arrest for political reasons.
28 This organization resembled very much the fascist one in Italy: 'From 4 to 8 years, all young Italians form the *Fils de la Louve* (established in 1931). A 8-year child

begins with more serious things. The boys enter *the Balilla*. They receive a uniform, artificial weapons and participate in parades. One tries to give them the feeling of how to live in communal contexts and being involved in military activities. During this period the girls receive physical and civic education in the *Small Italians*. From 14 years of age the boys enter *Avanguardisti*, and the girls *Young Italians*, until they reach 18 years of age, when all of them are integrated into the *Young fascists*. (Berstein, S and Milza, P: *L'Italie fasciste*, Paris, Arman Colin, 1970 p. 213–14).

29 A distinction must be made between the social origins of the national and regional leaders, and those of the other leaders and militants. It is justified to treat the two latter ones together, because in smaller societies, recruited leaders and militants were, in general, from the same social groups.

30 Lipset, S. M. "Some social requisites of democracy: economic development and political legitimacy", *American Political Science Review*, 53, 1960, p. 193.

31 Concerning Italian fascism, Lipset noticed that it strongly maintained the alliance between the anti-democratic traditionalism and the populist authoritarianism of the middle class. These were opposed to the left-wing milieus in the cities and in the countryside. Many specialists believe that fascism was born in the lower middle class (see Tasca 1964: chap. VIII; and Paris 1968).

32 Etienne, J.-M., *Le mouvement rexiste jusqu'en 1940*, Paris Armand Colin, 1968, p. 66.

33 The themes we focused on were nationalism, anti-socialism, anti-liberalism, anti-plutocratism, international anti-capitalism, corporatism, national socialism, anti-semitism, the hierarchic visions, anti-freemasonry, the pessimist vision of history, exaltation of the authoritarian, spiritual and traditional values, increasing of the value of ethnic groups, of military arts, the fascist code of ethics (loyalty, discipline, friendship, sacrifices), the mystic of the social transformation and solidarity with European fascism.

34 Our analysis used a comparison between the persentages of answers given to each question, constructed as an ideological subset on purely theoretical criterions. Although the analysis of this part is a comparison of the marginal distributions, we tried to construct scales of attitudes in the section of ideological radicalism.

35 The concept of the greatness of the nation was clearly inspired from Mussolini: "What does the concept of the greatness of the country mean to us, this word which impassionate us when we pronounce it? It consists of the feeling of well-being, prestige, and power of the Italian nation". (Benito Mussolini: *O Euvres Completes*, Paris, Flammarion 1935–1938, p. 113).

36 "*The celebrations of the Nation!*" is the title of a collection of articles published during this period which is marked by a more defensive nationalism than an aggressive one.

37 During a speech in June 1925 Mussolini declared that "the concept of the empire is the base for our doctrine" (Benito Mussolini: *O Euvres Completes*, Paris, Flammarion, p 98). This idea as considered by H. R. Southworth in his analysis of the essential aspect of fascism in general: "The fascist movement in Spain – the Falange – aimed at successively achieving three goals for their activity in Spain. First to organize a fascist movement. Secondly to conquer the State with this movement, and third to – the final goal – conquer the Empire". (Soutworth, H. R.: "What is fascism?", *Esprit*, 1969, p 423–426).

38 Barroso also refers to the idea of the Empire: "The Brazilian Integralism wants to create a large imperial Republic, a large christian Empire and its integral doctrine will influence the overall fate of the humanity". (Barroso, G.: *O Quarto Imperio*, Rio de Janeiro, Livr. José Olympio, 1935, p. 175).

39 Salgado, Plínio *O que é o Integralismo*, São Paulo, Edit. Star, 1933, p. 143.
40 Mussolini, B. *O Euvres Complétes*, Paris, Flammarion, 1935–1938, p. 129–130.
41 Pré de Saint-Maur, J. *La Phalange espagnole*, thèse IEP, Paris, 1951, p. 50.
42 Salgado, p., Reale, M., Mendes de Almeida, J. C., Leires Sobrinho, J., "A cartilha do Integralismo Brasileiro", São Paulo, 8 mars 1933, p. 8, in *A Doutrina Integralista*, Porto Alegre, AIB, Provinica do Rio Grande do Sul, s.d., 8–14.
43 The corporation of the coffee branch, does for example unite the representatives from the producers' and the worker's associations in the sector of coffee business: export as well as production.
44 Salgado, p., Reale, M., Mendes de Almeida, J. C., Leires Sobrinho, J., "A cartilha do Integralismo Brasileiro", São Paulo, 8 mars 1933, p. 10, in *A Doutrina Integralista*, Porto Alegre, AIB, Provinica do Rio Grande do Sul, s.d., 8–14.
45 Linz, J. "Some notes toward a comparative study of fascism in sociological historical perspective', in Laqueur, W. ed., *Fascism: a reader's guide*, New York, Free Press, 1976, 1976, p. 59–87.
46 De Felice, R. *Clefs pour comprendre le fascisme*, Paris, Seghers, 1975.
47 Meyer, J., *Le sinarquisme: un mouvement fasciste mexicain (1937–1947)*, Paris, Hachette, 1977; Potashnik, M. *Nacismo: national socialism in Chile (1932–1938)*, Los Angeles, University of California, 1974; Campbell, H., *The radical right in Mexico (1929–1939)*, Los Angeles, University of California, 1968; Trindade H. *L'Action intégraliste brésilienne: un mouvement de type fasciste des années 30*, 1971, thèse de doctorat, Paris I. Translated in Portugese: *Integralismo: o fascismo brasileiro na década de 30*, São Paulo, Difel, 1974.

68

A CASE OF NON-EUROPEAN FASCISM

Chilean National Socialism in the 1930s

Mario Sznajder

Source: *Journal of Contemporary History* 28(1) (1993): 269–96.

The Chilean version of National Socialism – MNS (*Movimiento Nacional Socialista de Chile*) – developed between 1932 and 1938, and its political activity culminated in the attempted coup of 5 September 1938. It is on this period of Chile's political history, and on the role played by Chilean National Socialism that this work will concentrate. Through an analysis of MNS's ideology, its political development and organizational structure we will try to define its relationship to the European varieties of fascism, and to what extent it was original.

First, we shall examine the political development of the MNS and its connection with the re-establishment of democracy in Chile. This will be followed by an analysis of the ideological components of Chilean Nacism (written with a 'c', as did the MNS in order to stress the Creole character of the movement in contrast to German Nazism). We shall then deal with the organizational structure of the MNS and its relationship to ideology and political practice in the light of the 5 September 1938 putsch and its consequences. Finally, we shall try to define to what extent the MNS imitated its European counterparts and to describe its original qualities as a fascist movement.

The *Movimiento Nacional Socialista de Chile* was founded in Santiago on 5 April 1932, at a meeting held in the office of 'el Jefe' (the Chief), Jorge González von Marées, who declared that he would lead the movement.[1] The MNS was founded a day after González's thirty-second birthday. A Chilean-born lawyer of German extraction, during his university years he had organized a workers' evening school and was President of the Rafael Sotomayor

League for Popular Education.² González's public career began in the municipality of Ñuñoa – one of Santiago's communes – after he graduated from law school in 1923. In 1932 he was appointed mayor of Ñuñoa, but after a few months was fired following the socialist *coup d'état* led by Marmaduke Grove in June 1932. From then on 'el Jefe' dedicated all his time and energies to the MNS.

1932 was a year of profound crises in Chile. The world economic depression had a tremendous impact on Chile's capacity to export, especially nitrates and copper, but also agricultural products. In 1931 Chile's export income in dollars had been reduced to a third of the level reached before 1929. A decline in production, a rise in unemployment, a large increase in the fiscal deficit and internal migration from the most affected mining areas in the north of the country to Santiago and other urban centres, characterized the period prior to the appearance of the MNS on the Chilean political scene. According to the League of Nations' *World Economic Survey 1923–1933*, Chile was the country most affected by the world economic depression of 1929.³ Political unrest led to the resignation and exile of Carlos Ibáñez del Campo, whose authoritarian government was regarded by many of his opponents as a dictatorship. Ibáñez crossed the Argentinian border on 27 July 1931, leaving Chile in a state of political turmoil for the next fifteen months.⁴ During this period, nine different governments failed to cope with the serious economic and political crises, and harsh economic measures taken in August 1931 caused a revolt among NCOs and sailors in the Chilean navy, whose pay was reduced by the government. The revolt was crushed by the army, loyal to the civilian government, after eleven days. On 4 June 1932, a *coup d'état* brought in a Socialist Republic that lasted for one month and four days. As a result of divisions among its leaders, this republic was governed by four successive civilian-military juntas. In September, the President of the Supreme Court, as acting president of the country, called a national presidential election, in which Arturo Alessandri Palma, who had governed Chile between 1920 and 1925, was re-elected president.⁵ Alessandri assumed office on 24 December 1932, beginning a period of return to liberal democracy – the period in which the *Movimiento Nacional Socialista de Chile* became a small but important actor in the political development of the country.

Chilean Nacism grew rapidly. The group of nine who founded the movement in April 1932 was joined by another thirty in the first two months of its existence. In October 1932 the MNS participated in the general elections and received almost one thousand votes in the Santiago electoral area, nearly enough to put one of its candidates in parliament. This was the result of a recruitment campaign and much publicity. In July 1932 the MNS started publishing a weekly page in *El Imparcial* and in April 1933 it began to produce a weekly newspaper, *Trabajo*, which became a bi-weekly in April 1935 and a daily in April 1936.⁶

In 1933 the *Tropas Nacistas de Asalto* (Nacist Assault Troops, TNA) made their appearance in clashes with communists and socialists. These occurred during two public meetings of the MNS in August 1933, the first in the Teatro Providencia and the second in the Teatro Iris. From then on, the presence of the MNS uniformed militia came to be felt, not only because of its paramilitary character, but also because of the increasing political violence. Party militias were common in Chile at the time. The most numerous was the Milicia Republicana, without any clear political ideology but dedicated to the defence of liberal democracy. In 1935 this group, which had nearly fifty thousand members, dissolved itself, believing that the Republic was already sufficiently strong. The government prohibited the use of uniforms by the TNA at the end of the same year, but political violence still increased. In 1933 the MNS had already expanded its activities outside Santiago. In October 1933 it held an assembly in Chillán and on 8 and 9 December 1934 the MNS held its National Convention in Concepción, the third largest city in the country. More than one thousand uniformed MNS members, from different parts of the country but mainly from Santiago, attended this meeting. The widening of the MNS's activities in the country was reflected in the municipal elections of May 1935. In Santiago the MNS list received more than 2,300 votes but did not succeed in getting any of its members elected to the municipality. However, in Temuco and Angol, two provincial cities in the south, the MNS was successful in getting one of its candidates in each city elected to the local municipal council.[7] In the 1935 municipal elections, the Chilean National Socialists received 6,000 votes in the whole country. In the parliamentarian elections of March 1937, 14,235 people voted for the MNS, and three National Socialist representatives entered the Chilean parliament. Jorge González von Marées was elected in Santiago, Fernando Guarello Fitz-Henry in Valparaiso and Gustavo Vargas Molinare in Temuco.[8] Together they polled 3.5 per cent of the vote while, in the same election, the Communist Party received 17,162 votes, 4.2 per cent of the total.[9]

In the municipal elections of April 1938, the last in which the MNS participated before attempting to overthrow the government by violent means on 5 September 1938, the Nacistas polled about 4.6 per cent of the total, with some 22,500 votes out of a national total of 488,904. This brought about the election of 29 Nacist *regidores*, city council members, out of a total of 1,485, in different parts of the country but mainly in the main cities, where the MNS electoral strength was concentrated.[10] In six years, Chilean National Socialism became a political force to be taken into account, not only because of its electoral competitiveness but also because of its activism and violence which were similar to those of the contemporary fascist parties in Europe. The MNS simultaneously played the democratic parliamentarian game and used direct action and extra-parliamentary methods, thus helping to create a feeling of instability that could further its political ambitions. Being a strongly authoritarian and disciplined movement willing to use force, it could claim to be the only group able to impose order.

The violence of the MNS went beyond the actions of its militia and its militaristic tendencies. The language used by its leaders and the titles and contents of many of the articles published in *Trabajo* and *Acción Chilena* – the ideological publication edited by Carlos Keller, one of the co-founders of the MNS and its main ideologue and intellectual figure – not only revealed a lack of will to compromise necessary for political dialogue but also a doctrine of total sacrifice and a cult of heroism which served as a basis for the coup attempt of September 1938.

The most notorious of the violent incidents in which Chilean Nacists participated took place on 15 November 1936 at the railway station of Rancagua, an agricultural city some fifty miles south of Santiago. An MNS group, travelling on a train, responded to a hostile demonstration against its members by shooting into the crowd. This act of violence produced a strong parliamentary reaction, as a result of which the Chilean Congress enacted the 'Ley de Seguridad Interior del Estado' – Law for the Internal Security of the State – and forbade the circulation of *Trabajo*. Law number 6,026, promulgated on 12 January 1937, prohibited political parties which sought to enforce an anti-democratic ideology by the use of force. The long list of prohibitions mentioned in the Ley de Seguridad Interior del Estado included the use of uniforms, flags and symbols bearing a revolutionary character, publications inciting the disruption of public order, the importation and distribution of weapons and explosives, insults against and disobedience to public functionaries, and the formenting or propagation of ideas aimed at the destruction of the state's legal framework.[11] By passing this law, the democratic liberal government of Chile was able to act at any moment against what it saw as the anti-democratic fringes – the MNS, and the Communist Party. And by reducing the political space in which Chilean Nacism could operate, Alessandri's government drove it into an unsatisfactory parliamentary future, in which the basic contradiction between an ideology of direct action and parliamentary representation would hamper its activities, while at the same time forcing it to make the difficult decision to adopt a one-sided violent solution that could change the destiny of the country.[12]

At the opening session of parliament on 21 May 1938, an MNS member threw a bomb that exploded in the garden of the Chilean Congress. Later, in the tumult provoked by left-wing members of the parliament who opposed the presence of President Alessandri at the inauguration ceremony, González von Marées and his colleagues were insulted by the deputies of the left while they were leaving in protest against Alessandri's presence. Provoked by his political enemies, González drew his revolver and fired a shot, an act without parliamentary precedent that led to his arrest and a prison sentence of one and half years. 'El Jefe's' appeal was accepted at the end of August 1938.[13]

Verbal and physical violence was a characteristic of the MNS not only in theory but also in practice.

The character of the MNS was clearly revealed in three fundamental features: (1) an anti-liberal and anti-communist nationalism; (2) the primacy of politics reflected in a desire to change the political structure; and (3) a desire to improve the socio-economic system.[14] These features were transformed, within the ideological context of the MNS, into aims that gave the movement its fascist character. The ideology of the MNS, rejecting the left and the right simultaneously, adopted a 'third way' characteristic of European fascisms. The parallel rejection of liberal and communist values was indicative of the anti-materialistic nature of the MNS, especially when coupled with its preference for politics rather than economics as a means of achieving real change in any given society. The third feature links the MNS to a particular brand of socialism, leading it further away from the ideals of the democratic-liberal vision, a socialism of an anti-Marxist kind, in which a new authoritarian corporative political structure provides for the needs of the masses. The revolution Nacism sought to carry out in Chile in the 1930s was a moral revolution of an anti-materialist and anti-rationalist kind similar to those aimed at by European fascists. Like its European counterparts, the MNS rejected the political principles established by the French Revolution as guiding parameters of modern political structures. The MNS opposed both liberalism and Marxism, propounding a new kind of socialism for Chile: a national socialism. 'While Marxism is a prolongation "*ad absurdum*" of rationalism and liberal materialism, socialism, according to the new conception of it that is conquering the world today, becomes, while replacing Marxism, a rehabilitation of the eternal spiritual values of humanity.'[15] In this context, González von Marées mentioned the higher forces of the spirit, unconditioned by economic realities but able to dominate them. The individual, he said, is not the subject of history, and therefore individual well-being is not the chief goal of humanity. It is the social group that is of central importance, an organic whole whose moral and material improvement should become the aim of all true socialists, according to Chilean Nacism. The subject of history is the nation, which serves as the cultural, moral and socio-economic framework of the social group; it is never the individual or the social class, seen by the MNS ideologues as artificial subjects of a materialistic and rationalistic nature, detached from reality. In Chile as elsewhere, the national socialist alternative to Marxist socialism was 'a co-operation between social groups as against the absolutely theoretical, hateful and fatal "class war" propagated by international Marxism'.[16]

Carlos Keller, the ideologue of the MNS, placed Marxism in the same category as liberal ideology:

> Both are essentially materialistic, for both the only real preoccupation is the economic situation of the individual, both are amoral and

both deny, in theory and in practice, the basic values on which Western culture is based: religion, the family, the fatherland and property.[17]

Nacism wished to replace the materialistic values of its despised political opponents with 'a new conception of life which magnifies heroic values . . .', '. . . a doctrine for the strong, the healthy, the virile, rejecting all weakness and feminism'.[18]

The ideological model of the MNS redefined the relationship between the individual and society in accordance with fascist conceptions. The individualist criteria associated with the philosophical and political tradition of the French Revolution, were rejected.

The adoption of the socialist title by Chilean Nacism reflected its use of the social function as a criterion of differentiation between the good and the bad. Thus, the MNS strove to overcome the conflict of interests between the individual and society without eliminating private property, which would continue to exist as long as it benefited society as a whole. The different forms of property to be adopted – whether private or public – were to depend on the measure of social benefit which each of them produced. Here, criteria of social service replaced criteria of personal utility or profit, without eliminating private property. According to the MNS, the aim was to curtail the dominance of one class and to promote

> the moral and material elevation of the whole people. . . . The individual, besides labouring for himself, must work for the good of the community, and in the conflict between his personal interests and the common interest, the latter must predominate over the former.[19]

Keller wanted to diminish parliament's authority, favouring the political representation of what he saw as the productive sectors of society. 'It will probably be necessary to limit voting rights to those that carry a responsibility towards society and to adopt a system that will allow for a genuine representation of those that produce our wealth.'[20] This ideological approach led to a proposed reorganization of society according to sectorial-productionist criteria, endowing the state with a new double system of representation. In this system, the different productive sectors were to be represented in a corporative house of parliament which would function parallel to the house of political representation.[21]

This scheme necessitated a productionist model which brought together all the positive economic forces of the country – as seen by the MNS – into a corporative political model under the tutelage of a strong state.[22] In the ideology of Chilean Nacism, the state was given a central position where it exercised a function of socio-economic regulation, directing private initiative in order to make it work with a maximum of efficiency for the benefit of society.[23] This kind of political-economic model aimed at harnessing all productive forces for the benefit of the nation, led by an authoritarian, highly centralized government and based on social mobilization, was another fascist characteristic of the MNS.

The kind of political-economic model envisioned by Chilean national socialism also required a high measure of discipline, social solidarity and a definite hierarchy led by the figure of 'el Jefe'. The centrality of the leader was expressed by Keller when describing the way to solve Chile's problems: 'As usual, the solution will depend on finding a strong personality, conscious of his mission, a fiercely energetic person who will succeed in bringing together a group of select individuals with whom he will be able to work efficiently.'[24] Ideologically, the leader was to be willing to commit himself totally to the cause and make the required personal sacrifices in order to promote the ideals of the MNS and put them into practice. In the ideal MNS state, a total identification between it and 'el Jefe' would be required. Keller stated that:

> For us, the greatness of the State does not derive from the theoretical perfection of the constitution and the laws but from the intensity with which the idea of the State is embodied in the leader, the mutual combination of the idea and the person being so extreme that their separation becomes impossible.[25]

'El Jefe' had to be a person able to impose his will, with a high moral sense, knowledge of reality and possession of a clear vision of the future – all qualities that Chilean Nacists ascribed to González von Marées.[26] The *Führerprinzip* was clearly expressed in the movement's regulations stating that 'El Jefe is solely responsible for the economic, social and spiritual orientation of the MNS. In consequence of this, his command over the movement is exercised in a personal and absolute manner.'[27]

González von Marées and Keller sought to set up in Chile a governmental system based on the political model that Diego Portales had created with the 1833 constitution. This ideal and the admiration of the MNS for national leaders of the last century such as Portales himself, Manuel Montt and José Manuel Balmaceda, demonstrated the national roots of Chilean Nacism.

The ideal political structure, according to MNS ideology, would be an authoritarian presidential republic. A neutral and abstract entity, it would be embodied in the figure of the president. Government would be strong and above political divisions and considerations of personal prestige, under the aegis of the president, the leader of the country. This formula, according to the MNS, had made Chile a strong and prosperous country during most of the nineteenth century. It was subsequently abandoned in favour of a parliamentary republic dominated by an oligarchy and political parties after the defeat of President Balmaceda in the Battle of Placilla in August 1891. In the view of the MNS, this was the cause of Chile's decline. The ideology of Chilean Nacism was far from reactionary. Its leaders did not want Chile to return to nineteenth-century practices but to adapt the spirit of the model that had ensured Chilean greatness in the last century to the socio-economic realities of the twentieth century. They admired the public spirit, austerity, will to fight and heroism of the founders and leaders of the authoritarian republic and wished to re-establish them in Chilean public life. In order to do so, the influence of parliament and the power of the political parties had to be curtailed, government had to be centralized and more authority had to be invested in the president. Legislative faculties were to be given to the president, as well as control over the nomination of judges and the head of the government. The latter was politically responsible for the functioning of the government and could be removed from his post by the president.

The unification of most of the legislative function with the executive, and the power to appoint the judiciary, would make the president the leader of the country both symbolically and in practice. The diminution of parliamentary power was an idea in accordance with the motto of Chilean Nacism: 'Chileno a la acción!' (Chilean, to action!), which signified the replacement of political dialogue – embodied in the parliamentary institutions – by direct action, represented in the governmental model of the MNS by a strong executive, with almost unlimited powers. Parliamentarianism was considered anachronistic, and the principle of deliberating assemblies contrary to that of authority based on a selected and disciplined hierarchy able to suppress political opportunism and place public affairs in the most competent hands.[28] Basically, the political structure proposed by the MNS required a strongly authoritarian type of regime, willing to intervene directly in every area of life where necessary, and thus possessing partially totalitarian tendencies. The Chilean national socialist vision of the state included a corporatist dimension to be realized under the guidance of the state.[29]

Other aspects of this model, present in the political programmes of the MNS, are the strengthening and maintenance of the value of the national currency; the nationalization of copper, saltpetre and petroleum; the stimulation of growth in the birthrate; a national plan for sanitary improvement (*cruzada sanitaria*), and the creation, under the guidance of the army, of an obligatory Labour Service for the young. The latter was meant to educate Chilean youth.

> in a spirit of discipline and the dignity of manual labour, and at the same time to perform social and public tasks of great value that, because of the high cost, cannot be done through public or private initiative, such as clearing woods and cleaning uncultivated land, planting forests, building dams, roads and channels of irrigation, building houses for industrial and agricultural workers, sanitary programmes in poor neighbourhoods, etc.[30]

The centrality of the leader in relation to the movement, the élitist, hierarchic, organic and disciplinary vision of society, the anti-communism, anti-liberalism and the corporatist model of the state combined with an authoritarian étatism, the violent political style, the principle of direct action, the use of a political militia and the consequent militarization of the movement, the totalitarian tendencies and the general ideology, all lead to the conclusion that the MNS intended to apply a fascist solution, developed in Europe both in theory and practice, to the problems of Chile. 'El Jefe' proposed putting into practice the ideas of Chilean Nacism by creating 'a mystique of sacrifice and solidarity on behalf of the cause of national *risorgimento*' that would replace individual appetites as well as 'the materialist deformation of the spirit ... caused in the upper strata of society by the corrupting action of capitalism and in the proletarian masses by the vilifying doctrines of Marxism'.[31]

The national socialism of the MNS was one of two elements which cause this movement to be defined as fascist. The other was a modern and radical variety of nationalism which, combining with the anti-Marxist socialism of the MNS, created a fascist model similar to those which anticipated Chilean fascism in Europe.[32]

In the spiritual world of Chilean Nacism, the nation was a superior entity which determined social limits. Thus, the movement acted only within those limits and so declared itself to be nationalist. For the MNS the nation, as a natural entity, was the unit within which socioeconomic problems were discussed and solved. No foreign elements had the right to interfere in this process. Nevertheless, the reliance of Chilean Nacism on the nation did not preclude the recognition of a superior Western cultural unity, or of an Ibero-American vision and community of interests, nor the possibility of living together with other nations.[33] Within this framework, Nacism did not oppose Christianity. On the contrary, it saw it as the foundation of Western culture, whose restoration constituted one of the main aims of the MNS.[34] This is an important difference between the Chilean MNS and German National Socialism. The MNS rejected nazism's pagan ideals and even the possibility of replacing Christianity with a modern political religion. In this sense, the MNS was nearer to the Falange of José Antonio Primo de Rivera in Spain than to the Nazi Party in Germany.[35] Chilean Nacists pointed out that liberalism and communism, their principal enemies, were also the main enemies of religion.[36] Other common denominators of Chilean Nacism and Christianity were the defence of the family as an essential social institution and the defence of private property. As most Chileans were Catholic, the Church, from the point of view of the MNS, played a very positive unifying role, since its activities, as those of an institution of high moral calibre, contributed to social solidarity and thereby to national solidarity, another goal of the MNS. Chilean Nacism objected only to the fact that the Church was perceived as being associated with conservative political elements which formed the mainstream of the country's oligarchy, and demanded, therefore, the dissociation of the Church from political conservatism.[37]

Jorge González saw in the fascist-nationalist *risorgimento* an expression of the race's soul. According to this view, the aim was to liberate the spirit from the tyranny of materialism through a revival of the people's heroic virtues. It is in this context that institutions such as the fatherland, religion and the family – institutions on which, according to the MNS, Western culture had been based – played an essential role and had to be strengthened. 'Chile could not be left out of this process of spiritual reconstruction. Its heroic and austere past, the centenarian national virtues, could not die buried under a wave of materialism.'[38]

The nationalism of the MNS was impregnated with the pessimism of Oswald Spengler as expressed in *The Decline of the West*. González von Marées and Keller considered Spengler almost a prophet in relation to the destiny of the West. They regarded the fascist regimes in Europe and elsewhere as positive evidence of the profound truth contained in Spengler's writings.[39] From Spengler they learned to distinguish between culture and civilization, associating soul and spirit with the former and regarding the latter as the most external and artificial state which the human race could achieve. It reached its full development in materialism, implying the loss of the soul and spirit on which culture is based.[40] Influenced by intellectual theories of this kind, Chilean Nacism declared that: 'To base politics and life on Jewish historical materialism is to create thereupon the ruin of our civilization, whose formidable historical pedestal is the spirit.'[41] Spengler's thought had influenced not only the MNS leadership but also major Chilean intellectuals of the 1920s and 1930s, such as Alberto Edwards and Francisco Encina, whose revisionist line of historical interpretation had many points in common with the one developed into a political ideology by the MNS.[42] Not only did the historical interpretation confer originality on Chilean Nacism but there were three characteristics which clearly distinguished the MNS from nineteenth-century nationalism. These were its attitudes to anti-semitism, imperialism and Ibero-Americanism.

The anti-semitism of the MNS was not and could not be of a racial, biological character because of the nature of Chilean society, which was a conglomerate of different waves of immigrants of diverse origins who mixed with the local population and with each other. Nevertheless, Chilean Nacism assimilated other elements of German National Socialism, and was also strongly influenced by the Spenglerian vision of history. In the eyes of the MNS leadership, 'the Jew' embodied the essential materialism present in liberalism as well as in communism. Starting from this point, it was relatively easy to relate the problems of Chile to a mythical Jewish World Conspiracy. Thus, the MNS believed that the Chilean nation was being simultaneously attacked by communist Jews from the left and capitalist Jews from the right. In the eyes of Chilean Nacism, Soviet communism was totally controlled by Jews.

'It may be clearly observed that communism is simply the product of corrupting and mischievous International Judaism.'[43] Soviet communism, an ideology which, according to the MNS, imposed itself through the imperialistic activities of the Comintern, had to be fought not only because it presented the danger of ideological contamination, due to its materialistic and amoral essence, but because it constituted a direct threat to the integrity of the Chilean nation.[44]

From the point of view of the MNS, Jewish communist imperialism represented an imminent danger, but Jewish capitalist imperialism had already penetrated Chile and dominated part of the country's wealth. This 'has transformed Chile into an appendix of the North American economic system', increasing the already existing level of dependency and contributing to the deterioration of the country's economic situation.[45] The argument was based on the supposed Jewish international financial control of the saltpetre industry which 'agonizes under the claws of international Judaism' referring, in this case, to the control that the Guggenheim family at the time exercised over the financial aspects of this industry.[46]

In this way, anti-semitism and anti-imperialism were united in Chilean Nacism to form a mobilizing social myth, to use Sorel's and Pareto's terminology. In this case, anti-semitism served as a bridging concept between day-to-day reality, in which Jews were present, at least in the main cities of the country, and a less immediate international imperialism in which the 'Jew' was present mythically. The descriptions and fantasies about a menacing Jewish presence in spheres beyond most people's reach were meant to arouse the masses emotionally and bring them to support the MNS. But the anti-semitic press campaign of the first years of the MNS had very little effect in Chile, due to a number of factors, the most important being the small numbers and limited influence of the local Jews. The idea of the mobilizing myth was consistent with the anti-intellectualism and anti-positivism characteristic of the different fascisms and of Chilean Nacism as well. Its main purpose was the creation of a myth to help overcome class differences, social cleavages and conflicting interests.[47] The Jew, in his role of capitalist, was made responsible for working-class poverty and misery, while viewed as a communist, he was presented as the inventor of the revolution that destroyed the basis of a tranquil society characterized by class harmony.[48]

Imperialism was not only a theoretical problem or menace, and it was analysed by the MNS in relation to the main source of foreign income in Chile at the time, the exploitation of the copper and saltpetre deposits in the north of the country. If the problem of communist imperialism had theoretical, ideological and even practical political connotations in the confrontation with the Communist Party of Chile, the problem of economic imperialism was seen by the MNS as urgent and vital for the survival of Chile as a nation. Keller accused the 'all-powerful alliance between Yankee capitalism (saltpetre, copper, iron) and the oligarchy of our landowners' of trying to destroy the Chilean monetary system.[49] The solution lay in the organization of the national economic forces and the nationalization of the principal sources of wealth according to the already-mentioned principle of social functionality.

The problem of America's cultural unity brought the MNS to discuss the Indo-American thesis of the Peruvian APRA. Chilean Nacism claimed that this thesis was not applicable to Chile because of the lack of an indigenous cultural tradition in that country. The Chilean 'roto' – the man of the people in the poorest sectors of the population – could not be regarded as an Indian, while concerning the Chilean Indians the MNS stated: 'We will preserve a romantic and respectful memory of our Araucanian ancestors, but from the point of view of our social institutions and habits of life, we have no ties to them.'[50] The MNS saw the idea of forging a continental unity on the basis of an autochthonic culture as an impossible fantasy. Each nation had to create a socio-economic model on the basis of its particular characteristics. In the case of Chile, according to the author, society had been moulded almost entirely in accordance with the Western cultural model. Thus, 'Our Chilean reality tells us that the actual collective problem that Chile has to solve has much more in common with analogous problems that have arisen in Europe than with those that preoccupy other nations in America.'[51] This vision did not exclude the creation of a common front of Latin-American nations against Yankee economic and political imperialism, or other imperialisms, and it accepted the possibility of economic and spiritual union between the different peoples of the continent, as long as each nation first made a serious effort to resolve its internal problems.

Chilean historical particularism was undoubtedly related to the writings of the Chilean nationalist, Nicolás Palacios. The ethnic vision that Palacios expounded in his book, *La Raza Chilena*, described the intermingling of two warrior races, Chile's Spanish conquerors, coming from the north of Spain, of Gothic-Germanic origin and forged in the long *Reconquista* against the Arabs, and the Araucanians, the warrior Indians who confronted the Spaniards from the *Conquista* onwards and throughout the colonial period.[52] Without totally incorporating Palacios's theory, Chilean Nacism adopted a position of cultural and social particularism which drove it towards differentiation and a concentration on its own nationalism. González von Marées saw in Chile 'a unique mixed racial entity with a net predominance of European blood. This social combination supported the development of a depersonalized, relatively stable political structure in Chile and Argentina, different from that of the rest of the American republics.'[53] Thus, in 'el Jefe's' view, only the self-definition and resolution of the particular problems of the different Latin American nations could create a common ground for mutual understanding.[54]

This type of nationalism was the second element in the ideological and political claims of the MNS in Chile in the 1930s. Without being racist in biological terms, this nationalism understood the logic of ethnic differentiation as the basis for a particular kind of socio-economic development. Defining itself as a product of Western culture, it saw many affinities between the problems of Chile and those of Europe – affinities that legitimated the presence of fascism, an ideology originating in Europe but of universal validity, according to the MNS, which could be adapted to a particular reality, providing a deep understanding of its parameters and the limits of the local situation was shown by the national fascist movement. Thus Chilean Nacism used fascist techniques and theorized in fascist terms, as in the case of the use of the mobilizing myth or political violence and the elaboration of corporativist socio-economic solutions or the advocacy of a strong monistic state in the pursuit of its anti-imperialistic ideals.

The organization of the MNS as a political movement was very similar to that of its counterparts in Europe and Brazil. The characteristic fascist structures derived directly from the ideological principles of hierarchy, discipline, solidarity and the absolute centrality of command and obedience. In this kind of political model 'el Jefe' – in this case Jorge González von Marées – became not only the absolute leader of the movement but also its axis. His power over the MNS was total and he took full responsibility for the 'political, economic, social and spiritual direction of the MNS'.[55] The executive branches of the movement were subordinate to the leader and consisted of six departments, each headed by a director directly responsible to 'el Jefe'. The departments were: (1) the Preparation Department (PR), which dealt with doctrinal problems and proposed solutions in cooperation with the Propaganda Department; (2) the Provincial Department (P), which directed the various Nacist Party groups around the country; (3) the Propaganda Department (PRO), which issued publications and provided information about the MNS, and organized conferences and meetings; (4) the Administration Department (A), which mainly dealt with the finances of the MNS; (5) the Department of the Nacist Assault Troops (TNA) which directed the movement's militia; and (6) the Department of Nacist Youth (JNS), which organized all those sympathizers not yet old enough for full membership in the movement. The leader himself retained direct control over *Trabajo*, the publication of the MNS, and also over the Nacist University Group (*Grupo Nacista Universitario*), one of the most active sections of the movement, and over the MNS sections in the city and province of Santiago.[56] Parallel to this horizontal executive national structure of the MNS there was a vertical structure of command, ordering the territorial division of the movement. This structure was parallel to the administrative division of the country and was made up of commissariats for provinces, departments and communes. The territorial division was also strictly subordinate to the leader of the MNS, each commissary – head of a Nacist Group (*Núcleo Nacista*) – being a direct representative of 'el Jefe', nominated by him personally, down to the level of the department, while the Nacist leaders of the communes were nominated by the provincial or departmental commissary.[57] 'El Jefe' could designate each year ten members of the *Consejo Nacista* – an advisory council – and renew or discontinue their membership at will.

The organizational structure of the MNS precluded any possibility of discussion, concentrating the decision-making process and all authority in one person, Jorge González von Marées, the founder and leader of the movement. This made the MNS an organization of a bureaucratic rather than political character for most of its members. The combination of absolute authority, strict discipline and a rigid hierarchy controlled from above, encouraged the kind of totalitarian conduct which characterized fascism elsewhere, within both the movements and the countries where it succeeded in taking over the government.[58]

To a certain extent, the structural-organizational characteristics of the MNS and its ideological substructure help us understand the nature of the violent coup carried out by a part of Chilean Nacism under the direct instructions of Jorge González von Marées on 5 September 1938. The *coup d'état* by Chilean Nacism was the climax of the activities of the MNS which had never abandoned violence as a means of action. The TNA — the political militia of the Chilean Nacists – were used almost from the foundation of the movement at public gatherings, to defend its members and fight the corresponding socialist and communist militias.[59]

In 1938 the MNS joined the presidential campaign of Carlos Ibáñez del Campo, the authoritarian military ex-president (1927–31), who had returned to Chile from exile. The General had a heterogeneous band of followers composed of the Organization Ibáñista, the Union Socialista and the MNS. Ibáñez's supporters grouped together in the Alianza Popular Libertadora, forming a third force, competing against the candidate of the liberal right and the government, Gustavo Ross Santa María, and the candidate of the leftist Popular Front, the main opposition to Arturo Alessandri's government, Pedro Aguirre Cerda. Undoubtedly the presence of the third candidate, with a populist authoritarian platform and his MNS following, worked electorally against the left, as was reflected in the political caricatures of the time. On 4 September 1938, a mass meeting of the Alianza Popular Libertadora, at which Ibáñez's candidacy was announced, was held in Santiago, with the organized participation of the MNS and many of the General's followers who had come from near and far.[60] It was probably the success of this gathering which made González von Marées decide to launch an anti-governmental putsch the next day. The MNS coup, limited in scope to a small area of the capital, was meant to trigger off a wider military coup with the participation of the Buin batallion and the Army School of Infantry, which were both near Santiago.

The violent attempt of the MNS to provoke the intervention of the army against the democratic government was carried out by a selected group of unquestioning TNA militiamen, blindly obedient to the orders of 'el Jefe'. The operational groups were commanded by the leader of the MNS university students' section, Cesar Parada, who before noon took over the central building of the University of Chile in downtown Santiago. The commander of the Santiago TNA, Ricardo White, led the Nacists who occupied the Workers' Social Security Building, within a stone's throw of the presidential palace, La Moneda, killing a carabinero and taking some of the clerks as hostages.[61] Afterwards, TNA members, commanded by Orlando Latorre, blew up two high-tension electrical pylons in Pataguillas and La Florida, thus completing the operational programme of the coup.

The government's reaction was quick and harsh. The buildings occupied by the TNA were taken back by the carabineros, Chile's militarized police. First, the main building of the University of Chile was taken, after two cannon rounds were fired at close range into its doors, by a battery of the Tacna batallion. Six TNA members died as a result. The rest surrendered and were taken prisoner by the police. The prisoners were taken to the Workers' Social Security Building where the police were still firing against the second Nacist group, which responded in kind. On the orders of the commander of Carabineros de Chile, General Humberto Arriagada Valdivieso, all the captured TNA members who surrendered in the second building were summarily executed by the police, together with their comrades who had surrendered previously. Six Nacists had died fighting in the university building, and one in the Workers' Social Security Building. Another fifty-four were summarily killed in what is known in the political history of Chile as the 'Matanza del Seguro Obrero'.[62]

The attempted putsch was made possible by the same characteristics that define the MNS as a fascist movement. Total subordination to the authority of the leader and blind discipline made the TNA follow González von Marées's instructions without question. The political echelon of the MNS was not consulted nor even told about the coup. The use of violence for political purposes — in this case provoking a wider military coup to install Ibáñez as president, circumventing the despised liberal democratic electoral process — was perceived as completely legitimate by the TNA fomentors of the coup. The heroic vision of life as war, and the belief that one was acting on behalf of 'higher ideals', facilitated the decision to participate in the hopeless adventure. Thus, a combination of fascistic warlike ideals and a completely vertical political command-structure, demanding total obedience and rejecting the principle of decision by deliberation and agreement, made possible the violent coup, changing the course of Chilean political history.

The consequences were immediate. Chilean Nacism had liquidated its future chances by committing suicide. The acts of violence associated with the coup made Ibáñez withdraw his candidacy for the presidency, bipolarizing the electoral process of 1938. The forceful repression of the MNS coup on the orders of president Alessandri worked against his presidential candidate, Gustavo Ross Santa María, especially as Chilean public opinion could not accept the fact that the response of the government to MNS violence was of an even more violent character, ending in the massacre of the Chilean Nacists.

Another extraordinary consequence of the events of 5 September was that the MNS vote helped the Popular Front to win the presidential election of 25 October 1938. A few days before the election Jorge González von Marées, still the unquestioned leader of the MNS, ordered his followers and branches of the Nacist Party all over the country to vote for Pedro Aguirre Cerda, the candidate of the Popular Front. Taking into consideration that there was a difference of only 4,181 votes between the 222,790 received by Pedro Aguirre Cerda and the 218,609 votes for Gustavo Ross Santa María, and that the MNS had polled some 22,500 votes six months before in the municipal elections of 1938, it is safe to conclude that the Nacist vote brought to power the candidate of the Popular Front.[63]

González von Marées had to choose between two enemies, and it was his hatred of the liberal right in Chile that brought him to cooperate with the left. Historical circumstances caused more stress to be laid on the anti-oligarchic side of the MNS than on its nationalistic anti-Marxism. There were precedents. In 1937, when three MNS parliamentarians were elected to the Chilean Congress, 'el Jefe' explained his adherence to the opposition by declaring that

> having to side with one of the two currents, we cannot but see that the left pursues an ideal that is also ours, this ideal being the attainment by the people of the social justice that the regime denies it.[64]

'El Jefe' explained the electoral triumph of the Popular Front not as the victory of a tactical combination of political parties reflecting the influence of the Comintern on national politics but as 'a triumph of the Chilean people. As a result of the sacrifice of the [Workers' Social — M.S.] Security martyrs, a totally Chilean mystique, drawn from the pages of the nation's history, superimposed itself upon the imported and anti-national mystique of frontism.'[65]

When Pedro Aguirre Cerda assumed the presidency of the country at the end of 1938, he pardoned González von Marées as a reward for the political support the MNS gave him in the election. As a result, González von Marées was allowed to continue as leader of the MNS, which later became the Vanguardia Popular Socialista. In the 1941 parliamentarian election, González von Marées was again elected deputy, but the political strength and potential of national socialism in Chile were already spent.[66]

Strangely enough, the MNS's cult of violence promoted the cause of liberal democracy in Chile in the 1930s. The political vision the MNS tried to impose resulted in restrictive legislation to protect the state against the anti-democratic political fringes, as explained above. Within the competitive electoral framework of 1938, the MNS putsch provoked the kind of violent repression on the part of the government which, in liberal democratic terms, helped to delegitimize its candidate, Ross Santa María. When the system became bi-polar through Ibáñez's withdrawal of his candidacy, the only political group that still played by the rules of the liberal democratic political game in avoiding violence, the Popular Front, won the elections. This victory of legitimacy, in terms of popular sovereignty reflected in the polls, brought the previously anti-system left nearer to the centre of power, thus providing Chile's democratic-liberal political system with a broad base and greater stability. The dangerous fringes had not entirely disappeared but were much less of a threat than before, and the Chilean political system was able to carry on peacefully the pluralistic democratic process by which the former partly anti-system opposition became the new government and the former government went into opposition. To use Sartori's terminology, Chile was on its way from being a polarized pluralism to becoming a moderate multiparty pluralism.[67]

In answering the question whether the MNS constituted a simple imitation of European fascist movements or contained original features, it is misleading to consider to what extent Chilean Nacism became a mass movement, since this confuses two different elements, or at least contains the hidden assumption that only an original political ideology can serve as the basis for the creation of a mass movement, or that only mass movements are based on original ideological foundations. This assumption may not necessarily be true, especially if, like Linz, we consider the problem of fascism as a latecomer and of the political space for development which the new movement finds in the society where it operated.[68] In Chile, as in Europe at the time, large segments of the population had identified themselves, in one way or another, with already existing political parties, including the communists, who by the time of the MNS's foundation had already been operating for twenty years, first under the name of Partido Obrero Revolucionario and, from 1922, as the Partido Comunista. Furthermore, the Socialist Party of Chile, founded in 1933 and ideologically Marxist but opposed to the Comintern, competed not only with the communists but also with the MNS as the mobilizing party on the left that in political campaigns preached a certain brand of populistic nationalism as well as Marxism.[69] The traditional right was divided between conservatives and liberals who collaborated in the second Alessandri government (1932–38). Thus, one can understand the relatively low percentage of electoral support achieved by the MNS between 1932 and 1938, though its growth curve may seem quite impressive.

If we examine the MNS according to the typological description of generic fascism used by Payne, we will find that Chilean Nacism possesses most but not all of the characteristics of a fascist movement.[70] The MNS was certainly anti-liberal, anti-communist and willing to compromise with rightist groups and principles on certain ideological issues. Its anti-conservatism was doubtful, not only because of its idealization of the statesmanship of Diego Portales and of the authoritarian republic of 1833, but also because of its acceptance of family and Church as the basic pillars of Western culture. The MNS wished to create a new nationalist authoritarian state based not only on traditional principles or models, although these still played an essential mythical role in its ideology. The socio-economic structure envisaged by Chilean Nacism was national-corporatist and geared to transform existing socio-economic relations, thus fitting Payne's typology. The idealistic voluntaristic creed was also present, but without denying the basic values of Catholic culture. The style and organization of the MNS exactly fitted the above-mentioned typology, including the symbolic elements, which stressed the mystical character of Nacism, the attempted mass mobilization with a militarization of political relations within the movement, and the creation of a political militia. Violence was seen as a legitimate political means and was used, although the MNS would claim that this was done in self-defence. The violent coup of 1938 is the clearest example of Nacism's positive evaluation of the political function of violence. Social organicism and male chauvinism were accepted features of MNS ideology, as well as the cult of youth, but without emphasizing the generational conflict, probably as a result of the acceptance of Catholic and family values as basic. The preference of the MNS for charismatic authoritarian leadership has been made sufficiently clear, and was reflected in the non-elective principle by which González von Marées designated himself 'el Jefe'.

In most respects the MNS fits the typology which Payne created on the basis of Linz's suggestion about differentiating between (1) the fascists' negations or 'anti' attitudes; (2) the fascist ideology and goals; and (3) the common features of political style and organization.

Chilean Nacism, aware of the problem of artificiality and originality, expressed its views on the similarity between its ideology, style and organization and those of European fascisms. Javier Cox, the author of an article on this subject, claimed that Chilean Nacism was not an imitation of Mussolini's fascism or German Hitlerism but that they were 'three diverse expressions of the same idea'.[71] Cox claimed that fascism was a universal political idea which served as the basis for similar national political movements, differentiated by the particularism of the history and problems of each society. Since it was an idea, no one could claim ownership over it except those that put it into practice. Chilean Nacism asserted that fascism was to be found as a latent idea among all the peoples of Western culture, because it represented the possibility of stopping what MNS saw as the materialist decadence embodied in the traditional right as well as the Marxist left. In addition to the elements common to the different fascisms, it was pointed out that national unity, as a prerequisite for the application of any kind of fascism, had to be founded in positive elements. These were to be found in the different racial, cultural and historical characteristics of various peoples, thus producing the diverse national varieties of fascism. The term fascism, adopted by the movement in Italy, became generic, since Italian fascism was the first of these movements to achieve power. Cox argued that if one were to confer on these movements a scientific name, 'it could only be national-socialism'.[72]

Chilean Nacism stood somewhere between fascism and the radical right. This evaluation is largely based on the fact that respect for Catholic values, the family and the view of the Portales political model as a nineteenth-century predecessor of Nacism do not harmonize well with the totalitarian fascist conception of the relationship between the state and civil society.[73]

Another feature that differentiates the MNS from European fascist movements is the anti-imperialism of the MNS. This was a direct derivative of the analysis of the socio-economic situation in Chile. Despite the relatively high level of political development and the existence of a political culture similar to that of its European counterparts at the time, Chile suffered from extreme levels of poverty, aggravated by the impact of the world crisis, and was an underdeveloped country dependent on foreign investment and trade. Awareness of these problems, together with the nationalist ideology, characteristic of fascism, helped to produce the anti-imperialistic element in Chilean Nacism. The problems of poverty and underdevelopment also influenced the MNS goals with regard to social justice, inclining the movement more to the left than to the right, with corresponding ideological and practical results.[74]

There is no doubt that the MNS formed part of the anti-parliamentarian currents existent in Chile at the time, as was pointed out by Hugh Bicheno.[75] But the MNS was not anti-political or extraneous to the political system. On the contrary, in spite of its fascist style and organization and its anti-establishment ideology, it played according to the rules of liberal democracy by participating in elections, issuing political publications and organizing public meetings, without resorting to the kind of underground organization or terrorist practices which would have qualified it as anti-political.[76]

Although the socio-economic and political conditions which favoured the appearance of fascism in Europe were clearly not identical with the conditions in Chile at the beginning of the 1930s, the political terminology was nevertheless very similar. A Popular Front was formed against fascism and war, despite the fact that its main political enemy was the traditional right, neither fascistic nor warlike. The application of European political concepts to Chile did not make the MNS more or less authentically fascist or more original in its ideology and practice. It is interesting to note that although a high percentage of the MNS activists were of German extraction, the movement relied on Chilean nationalism and distanced itself from the German NSDAP which operated within the German immigrant community in Chile, led by Karl Hubner, the local representative of Goebbels, Minister of Propaganda in the Third Reich.[77] Basically, as Javier Cox himself recognized, the inspiration came from Europe, but the adaptation was Chilean.[78]

The MNS is more interesting on account of the impact it had on Chile's political life in the 1930s than because of its contributions to fascist political theory or its size. The violent action of the MNS in September 1938 had the same effect on the political system of Chile as the fascist riots of February 1934 had on the political system in France, or the Lapua movement's attempt to seize power in Finland in 1932.[79] In all three cases, the political system of each respective country was able to overcome the fascist attempt at destabilization. In the particular case of Chile, the MNS, unwillingly and indirectly, contributed to the strengthening of a liberal democratic system that enjoyed stability for many decades.

Notes

1 The co-founders of the MNS were Gustavo Vargas, Carlos Keller, Felipe Laso, Eduardo Undurraga, Emilio Aldunate, Francisco Infante, Mauricio Mena and Raul Valdivieso. Two of the founders — González von Marées and Keller — and later many members and sympathizers of the MNS were of German extraction. See Mauricio Mena Mena, 'Génesis y desarrollo del Nacismo', *Acción Chilena*, vol. IV. no. 2, 1935, 80–1. A later version of the foundation of the movement places it at the home of González von Marées. See Carlos Keller, 'El 5 de Abril de 1932', *Trabajo*, suplemento, 5.4.1938.
2 For biographical details on Jorge González von Marées in English see George F.W. Young, 'Jorge González von Marées: Chief of Chilean Nacism', *Jahrbuch für Geschichte von Staat, Wirtschaft und Gesellschaft Lateinamerikas*, Band 11, 1974, 311–14. In Spanish see Rodrigo Alliende González, *El Jefe, La vida de Jorge González von Marées* (Santiago 1990). Rafael Sotomayor was a famous Chilean politician who, as Minister of War, successfully co-ordinated the campaign against Peru in the Pacific War. He died from overwork on the eve of the battle of Tacna on 20 May 1880. On Rafael Sotomayor see Jordi Fuentes, Lia Cortes, Fernando Castillo Infante and Arturo Valdés Phillips, *Diccionario Histórico de Chile* (Santiago 1984), 568. It was probably the nationalism and patriotism represented by the figure of Sotomayor which attracted the attention of Jorge González.
3 Federico G. Gil, *The Political System of Chile* (Boston 1966), 61.
4 See Luis Correa Prieto, *El presidente Ibáñez. La politica y los politicos* (Santiago 1962) 151–5.
5 About the July 1931-December 1932 period in the political history of Chile see Federico G. Gil, *The Political System of Chile*, op. cit., 61–5, and Jordi Fuentes et al., *Diccionario Histórico de Chile*, op. cit.; on Juan Esteban Montero, see 366–7, on the Socialist Republic Juntas, 293–4, on Carlos Davila Espinoza, see 172, on Bartolomé Espejo Blanche, see 84 and on Abraham Oyanedel Urrutia, see 404–5.
6 For a short story of the MNS by one of its founders see Mauricio Mena Mena, 'Génesis y desarrollo del Nacismo', loc. cit., 80–9, and also Lía Cortés, Jordi Fuentes, *Diccionario Político de Chile* (Santiago), 331–5.
7 Mauricio Mena Mena, 'Génesis y desarrollo del Nacismo', loc. cit., 88.
8 Lía Cortés, Jordi Fuentes, *Diccionario Político de Chile*, op. cit., 334.
9 Erwin Robertson, *El Nacismo Chileno* (Santiago n.d.), 8.
10 George F. W. Young, 'Jorge González von Marées', loc. cit., 321.
11 On this point see Mario Sznajder, 'El Movimiento Nacional Socialista: Nacismo a la Chilena', *Estudios Interdisciplinarios de America Latina y el Caribe*, 1 (1),

Enero–Junio 1990, 45, and Ricardo Donoso, *Alessandri, agitador y demoledor. Cincuenta años de historia política de Chile* (Buenos Aires/Mexico 1954), vol. II, 198–201.
12 To reinforce this point with a comparison with Europe, we may recall the recurrent phenomenon of a strong traditional right saving a democratic regime by closing the political space which permitted a fascist movement to lead a civil war through its activist and uncompromising attitudes. This point is stressed in Juan J. Linz, 'Some Notes Towards a Comparative Study of Fascism in Sociological Historical Perspective' in Walter Laqueur (ed.), *Fascism. A Reader's Guide* (Berkeley and Los Angeles 1976), 101.
13 George F. W. Young, 'Jorge González von Marées', loc. cit., 324.
14 *El Movimiento Nacional Socialista de Chile* (Santiago 1932), 5, 8–9.
15 Jorge González von Marées, *El mal de Chile (Sus causas y remedios)* (Santiago 1940), 82.
16 *Trabajo*, 5.5.1933, 2.
17 Carlos Keller, 'Ideología y Programa Nacistas', *Acción Chilena*, vol. IV, no. 2 (1935), 96.
18 Ibid.
19 *Ideario Nacista* (Santiago 1932), 5. This is part of a collection of articles published in *El Imparcial*. The article in question is 'Qué es el Nacismo?', *El Imparcial*, 12.7.1932, on the MNS page, published weekly in that daily between July 1932 and February 1933.
20 Carlos Keller, *Un país al garete. Contribución a la seismología social de Chile* (Santiago 1932), 31.
21 The corporative political structure envisaged by the MNS was described in Jorge González von Marées, *El mal de Chile*, op. cit., 216–33.
22 'Plan de acción', *Acción Chilena* vol. IV, no. 2 (1935), 110.
23 'Qué es el Nacismo?', loc. cit., 5.
24 Carlos Keller, *Un pais al garete*, op. cit., 29.
25 Idem, 'El Jefe', *Acción Chilena*, vol. IV, no. 2 (1935), 76.
26 On the personality of González von Marées, see George F. W. Young, 'Jorge González von Marées', loc. cit. It is interesting to note that Young discusses the possibility that 'el Jefe's' behaviour could be interpreted in the light of a mental illness resulting from a brain tumour which caused his death in 1962. Due to the anachronistic character of the explanation, Young rejects it, when dealing with the attempted MNS coup of September 1938, in favour of the thesis of political failure leading to violence. Another work that deals with the thesis of González von Marées ordering his subordinates to make the suicidal attempt of the coup is a novel written by Carlos Keller, *La locura de Juan Bernales* (Santiago 1949). This fictional work describes the history of a political movement of the extreme right that tries to take power through a *coup d'état*. The movement is led by an absolute leader who suffers from a mental illness that leads him towards violence. Keller insisted that this was a work of fiction, despite all the analogies with the history of the MNS in Chile in the 1930s.
27 'Qué es el Nacismo?', *Acción Chilena*, vol. IV, no. 2 (1935), 113.
28 *El Movimiento Nacional-Socialista de Chile* (Santiago 1932), no. 1, 8.
29 'Plan de acción', *Acción Chilena*, vol. IV, no. 2 (1935), 110.
30 Ibid., 110–12.
31 Jorge González von Marées, *El mal de Chile*, op. cit., 89–90.
32 The theoretical development of this model has been described in Zeev Sternhell, 'Fascist Ideology', *Fascism. A Reader's Guide*, op. cit., 325–406, and especially 338ff (here we refer to the Pelican Books edition of 1982). In the same volume, a

brief reference to the MNS may be found in Alistair Hennesy, 'Fascism and Populism in Latin America', op. cit., 287–8.
33 Carlos Keller, 'Ideologia y Programa Nacista', loc. cit., 99.
34 'Nacismo y civilización', *Trabajo*, 6.7.1933.
35 On this point see Stanley Payne, *Fascism. Comparison and Definition* (Madison 1980), 149.
36 Diego Lira, 'Nacismo y religión', *Acción Chilena*, vol. IV, no. 2 (1935), 122.
37 Ibid., 27.
38 Jorge González von Marées, 'El alma de la raza', *Acción Chilena*, vol. IV, no. 2 (1935), 74.
39 Idem, 'Spengler, filósofo del fascismo', *Trabajo*, 25.1.1934.
40 On this point see George L. Mosse, *The Crisis of German Ideology. Intellectual Origins of the Third Reich* (New York 1984), 6 and 283; also H. Stuart Hughes, *Consciousness and Society. The Reorientation of European Social Thought 1890–1930* (Sussex 1986), 375–8. George F. W. Young stressed the fact that González von Marées had read Spengler's *The Decline of the West* in German. See George F. W. Young, 'Jorge González von Marées', loc.cit., 314–15. In the same place he also points out that Carlos Keller was educated in Germany between 1914 and 1921, just in time to know about the publication of the first volume of Spengler's book in mid-1918, which won for the author immediate acclaim from the general public if not from professional historians and philosophers.
41 'Nacismo y civilización', loc. cit., 6.7.1933.
42 The interest in Spengler was common among these intellectuals. Carlos Keller had lectured in 1927 on Spengler and the politico-cultural situation in Latin America, a fact quoted in Erwin Robertson, 'Las ideas nacional-socialistas en Chile 1932–1938', *Dimensión Histórica de Chile*, no. 1 (1984), 92–3, especially note 7. The same author mentions the influence of Spengler on Francisco Encina, especially in his work on Portales, much commended by Keller himself. Alberto Edwards, the author of *La fronda aristocrática en Chile* (Santiago 1928) had published in *Atenea* in 1925 an article on Spengler's work under the title 'La sociología de Oswald Spengler'.
43 *Trabajo*, 20.4.1933, 7.
44 On this subject, see Mario Sznajder, 'El Movimiento Nacional Socialista: Antisemitismo y movilización politica en Chile en la década del treinta', *Coloquio*, no. 21 (1989), 61–70.
45 Carlos Keller, *Un país al garete*, op. cit., 39.
46 *Trabajo*, 27.7.1933, 1.
47 See the description of the Jew as a personage incarnating the 'mythic evil in France' in Zeev Sternhell, *Maurice Barrès et le nationalisme français* (Bruxelles 1985), 243.
48 Ibid., 241.
49 Carlos Keller, *Un pais al garete*, op. cit., 147.
50 Civis, 'Nacismo y Americanismo', *Acción Chilena*, vol. IV, no. 2 (1935), 142.
51 Ibid., 144.
52 Nicolás Palacios, *La Raza Chilena* (Santiago 1918; 1st edition 1904). Influenced by Gustave LeBon and other anti-positivist European thinkers, Palacios attacked utilitarian and materialistic doctrines which, in his view, arrived in Chile through unrestricted immigration. See Nicolás Palacios, 'Decadencia del espíritu de la nacionalidad' in Enrique Campos Menéndez (ed.), *Pensamiento Nacionalista* (Santiago 1974), 164 ff.
53 Jorge González von Marées, 'El porvenir de nuestra América', *Acción Chilena*, vol. IV, no. 2 (1935), 148.

54 Ibid., 157.
55 'Organización Nacista', loc. cit., 113.
56 Ibid., 113–14.
57 Ibid., 115.
58 An interesting comparison can be made between the organizational structure of the MNS in Chile, of the NSDAP in Germany, the PNF in Italy and the Açao Integralista Brasileira. We shall find that although the number of Executive Departments and the levels of territorial divisions differ due to the particularities of each country and the diverse character of the main leaders and ideologues, the basic principle of the totalitarian-bureaucratic, political, non-deliberative, mass-mobilizing structure is common to all of them. Undoubtedly, this is a consequence of the ideological principles common to all fascisms, beyond their national differences. One section or department is obviously absent in the MNS – also for ideological reasons – the Department for the Mobilization of Emigrants. This is not because there was no Chilean emigration – historically there are large nucleii of Chilean emigrants in Argentina, a country much richer, in that period, and able to provide work for part of the unemployed labour force of its neighbouring countries – but because of the anti-imperialistic character of Chilean Nacism. On the organization of the NSDAP see Karl Dietrich Bracher, *The German Dictatorship* (Middlesex 1985), 178–83; on the PNF see Alberto Aquarone, *L'organizzazione dello Stato totalitario* (Torino 1978), vol. 2, 315–29 and the new work by Emilio Gentile, *Storia del Partito Fascista. 1919–1922. Movimento e Milizia* (Roma-Bari 1989), vol I, 25–37; and on the Açao Integralista Brasileira (AIB) see Helgio Trindade, *Integralismo. O fascismo brasileiro na década de 30* (São Paulo-Rio de Janeiro 1979), 164–88.
59 Mauricio Mena, 'Génesis y desarrollo del Nacismo', loc. cit., 84.
60 Ricardo Donoso, *Alessandri, agitador y demoledor*, op. cit., 256–7.
61 'Nazi insurrection put down in Chile after 4-hours fight', the *New York Times*, 6 September 1938, 1 and 12.
62 The most complete description of the episode is to be found in Ricardo Donoso, *Alessandri, agitador y demoledor*, op. cit., 258–68. A partial list of the killed 'nacistas' was published in *La Senda del Sacrificio. 5 de Septiembre 1938* (Santiago 1940), 191–2. This list contains 58 names, including three pairs of brothers. A very detailed account of the coup, in a version that implicates General Ibáñez, is found in Rodrigo Alliende González, *El Jefe*, op. cit., chap. 9. The author was a nephew of Jorge González von Marées and his work explains and defends 'El Jefe's' attitude on many occasions. Despite the apologetic tone, the richness of the sources, many of which come from family archieves, and the seriousness of the writing make it obligatory reading for those interested in González von Marées and the MNS.
63 Electoral results in Lía Cortés, Jordi Fuentes, *Diccionario Político de Chile*, op. cit., 202.
64 González von Marées in Congress, cited by Ricardo Donoso, *Alessandri, agitador y demoledor*, op. cit., 211.
65 Jorge González von Marées, *El mal de Chile*, op. cit., 56–7.
66 Lía Cortés, Jordi Fuentes, *Diccionario Político de Chile*, op. cit., 219.
67 Giovanni Sartori, *Parties and Party Systems. A Framework of Analysis* (London/New York/Cambridge 1976), vol. 1, 131 ff.
68 Juan J. Linz, 'Political Space and Fascism as a Late-Comer: Conditions Conducive to the Success or Failure of Fascism as a Class Movement in Inter-War Europe' in Stein Ugelvik Larsen, Bernt Hagtvet and Jan Petter Myklebust (eds), *Who Were the Fascists. Social Roots of European Fascism* (Bergen/Oslo/Tromso 1980), 153–6.

69 On the Partido Socialista see Paul W. Drake, *Socialism and Populism in Chile 1932–1952* (Urbana/Chicago/London 1978), 140 ff. See especially the references to the Nueva Acción Publica led by Eugenio Matte and Marmaduke Grove, one of the main socialist groups, which propounded a doctrine of spiritual renewal and greater state control of the principal means of production without abolishing private property, preferring social solidarity to class conflict and envisioning a 'functional corporative regime'. Ibid.
70 Stanley G. Payne, 'The Concept of Fascism' in Stein Ugelvik et al., *Who Were the Fascists*, op. cit., 20–1.
71 Javier Cox, 'Nacismo, Fascismo e Hitlerismo. Semejanzas y diferencias', *Acción Chilena*, vol. IV, no. 2 (1935), 138.
72 Ibid., 141.
73 Here we refer to the classification made by Stanley G. Payne in *Fascism*, op. cit., 14–18.
74 Both Keller and González von Marées stressed the problems of poverty and underdevelopment. 'El Jefe's' graduation thesis as a lawyer was entitled 'The Worker Problem in Chile'. It was presented in 1923 (Jorge González von Marées, *El problema obrero en Chile* [Santiago 1923]); see Rodrigo Alliende González, *El Jefe*, op. cit., 214. See also Jorge González von Marées, *El problema del hambre (Sus causas y solución)* (Santiago 1937).
75 Hugh E. Bicheno, 'Anti-Parliamentary Themes in Chilean History', *Government and Opposition*, 7 (3), 1972, 373–4.
76 The thesis about the anti-political nature of the MNS was put forward by Michael Potashnik, 'Nacismo: National Socialism in Chile 1932–1938', PhD dissertation, University of California, Los Angeles, 1974 (unpublished), 55. This work of great descriptive scope, rich in primary sources, stresses the mobilizing aspect of the MNS but does not deal with the problem of the relationship between Chilean Nacism and European fascism from a theoretical perspective.
77 See the article on the consequences of the MNS coup, 'South American Snub Fascism', the *New York Times*, 11 September 1938, section 4, p. 5.
78 Ernst Halperin in his *Nationalism and Communism in Chile* (Cambridge, MA 1965), 44, points out the confusion of political terminology caused by the extrapolation of European political terms and their application to different Chilean realities. Erwin Robertson in his 'Las Ideas Nacional Socialistas en Chile 1932–1938', op. cit., tries to stress the originality of the ideology of Chilean Nacism in its interpretation of Chilean history and the solutions to the socio-economic and political evils which affected the country in the 1930s. Robertson's theory is clearly apologetical, a fact proved not only by the contents of his writings but by the ideological and political position of the author today. When Erwin Robertson was asked: 'Since when have you been a Nazi?' he responded: 'Some ideas, a certain vision of the world is always professed, even before their rational formulation'. See 'Erwin Roberson: Nazi "desde siempre" ', *Análisis*, 23.11.1987, 34.
79 On the second and third generation of French fascists see Zeev Sternhell, 'Strands of French Fascism' in Stein Ugelvik Larsen et al., *Who Were the Fascists*, op. cit., 489–92. On the dissolution of the Lapua Movement as a result of the attempted rebellion of Mantsala in 1932, and the foundation of the IKL in Finland, see Reijo H. Heinonen, 'From People's Movement to Minor Party: The People's Patriotic Movement (IKL) in Finland 1932–1944' in ibid., especially 689–92.

69

THE FASCIST AND POPULIST SYNDROMES IN THE ARGENTINE REVOLUTION OF THE RIGHT

Alberto Spektorowski

Source: Stein Ugelvik Larsen, *Fascism outside Europe: The European Impulse against Domestic Conditions in the Diffusion of Global Fascism*, New York: Columbia University Press, Boulder Social Science Monographs, 2001, pp. 529–60.

Introduction

On June 4, 1943, the armed forces led by General Rawson assumed power in Argentina. Although the coup surprised the Argentine public, it was in the words of the nationalist intellectual Marcelo Sanchez Sorondo, the "revolution we announced"[1]. This comment indicates that the military upheaval represented the consummation of an ideal expected by nationalists of the right and left. Interpretations of the revolution's fundamental goals differed, since officials with democratic ideals participated in the coup, but one thing was clear from the outset: this was not merely an authoritarian military coup d'etat intended to eradicate political liberalism, but rather an attempt to introduce a new order in Argentina. Based on a new, regenerative ideal, a political model synthesizing state corporatism, social justice, and anti-imperialist politics was presented as the alternative to what the nationalists saw as a decadent society rotted by liberal politics and cosmopolitan culture.

In contrast to Felix de Uriburu's abortive revolt in 1930, the military upheaval of 1943 produced a radical change in the political and economic development of Argentina. The basis for this change, however, was largely, if not solely, the ideological development of right wing and left wing nationalism during the 1930s. Indeed, for more than a decade both the Argentine constitutional order and the ideology of the conservative liberal and reformist socialist parties had been delegitimized in the intellectual laboratories of left wing and right wing nationalism, which dominated the intellectual and ideological climate of the thirties.

Consequently, at the end of that decade the revolution's military leaders viewed the political and social situation through the ideological prism of growing radical nationalism. In their eyes, only a strong, industrialized and nationalist state could maintain Argentine neutrality during the Second World War. Only an autonomous state independent of the parties of the political oligarchy could develop a full program of social reform that would mitigate social unrest. Thus, the new military regime initiated a period of populist authoritarianism in Argentina by synthesizing the most important ideological elements of right wing nationalism – political authoritarianism – economic autarky, and traditional Catholicism – with the 'left-wing' national-populist ideology which centered on economic and cultural anti-imperialism. The result was an Argentine brand of integrationalist, mobilizing fascist ideology that inclined towards autarky, industrialization and emphasized issues of social justice. This ideological formula, adopted by the military revolution of 1943 and by Peron during his first administration, effected a radical change in Argentina's socio-economic development[2]. In this article, I will trace the intellectual sources of what can be defined as a local fascist ideology, confirming thereby that the fascist phenomenon was universal rather than merely European.

Some aspects of the theoretical discussion of modernization and fascism in Latin America

In Europe, fascism was the product of an ideological synthesis between a new socialism stripped of Marx's economic and rationalist basis, and a new concept of radical nationalism based on cultural- and blood ties rather than rational self-determination[3]. In 1911, writing for *Les Cahiers du Cercle Proudhon* in France and *La Lupa* in Italy, Edouard Berth and other followers of Georges Sorel found themselves in agreement with intellectuals like Georges Valois, who belonged to the left wing of *Action Francaise*, that democracy had been the greatest mistake of the last century[4]. From this ideological synthesis, between antiliberal nationalism and the anti-Marxist socialism derived from Sorel's revision of Marxism, was to come a new, national, syndicalist formula. As an alternative to liberalism and Marxist socialism, fascism proposed another solution to the problems the technical and intellectual revolution presented to European society at the turn of the century.

The appeal of fascist ideology was not limited to Europe, however. As Jose Antonio Primo de Rivera said: "Fascism is a universal attitude to return to one's [national] essence . . ."[5] The spiritual revolt embodied in fascism influenced intellectuals of different parts of the world who adapted the new message to their local problems. This is why strong fascist movements emerged even in countries with no significant left wing revolutionary movements and where the working classes were not organized, as in Romania and Hungary.

There, however, they served a different function from similar movements in the West. They were able to act freely as national revolutionary movements, a threshold of political action never reached in the West[6]. In Argentina such movements combined a demand for national emancipation with the concept of fascism as the ideological framework for a New world order. For them, dependence was a direct function of liberalism, while a new authoritarian order would be the base for real emancipation.

Some scholars, however, have used the concept of Latin American fascism to describe what they perceive as the authoritarian and exclusionary corporatist characteristics of 'dependent fascism,' the term they use to define the authoritarian regimes of the 1960s[7]. Social scientists like Theotonio dos Santos, Celso Furtado, and Marcos Kaplan have argued that the military dictatorships of the sixties and seventies represented a new type of fascism, one based on a hegemonic crisis and an authoritarian form of response to the tensions of modernization.

Whatever its validity, this approach fits within an established tradition – one which, although not necessarily Marxist – often uses Marxist insights based on the premise of Latin America's peripheral, dependent position in the global economy and its consequent condition of permanent underdevelopment. By using the concept of 'dependent', or 'atypical' fascism, these scholars try to link the demobilization of the working classes by the military rulers of the sixties and seventies to the monopolistic interests of US capitalism. In their view, the essential element of fascism is its 'class nature,' while its unique political style and ideological synthesis are of secondary interest. This analysis also overlooks the possibility of achieving a high level of industrialization despite the limitations 'imposed' by the dependent character of peripheral countries, a possibility that Guillermo O'Donnell perceived and analyzed in his model of the bureaucratic authoritarian state[8].

In any event, the term 'fascism' is not appropriate in the cases cited by proponents of the dependency theory. Fascism sought to establish an autarkic economy, while its political style – its vitalistic spirit and reliance on mass mobilization and proletarian rhetoric – made it something very different from a political system based merely on the need for efficiency, or one bent on ensuring the country a role in the modern transnational capitalist system.

Some scholars are reluctant to apply the term 'fascism' to any authoritarian political development in Latin America, and they are especially cautious when analyzing the populist movements of the 1930s. In fact, they use the terms 'authoritarianism' and 'populism' in an effort to differentiate the sociohistorical process of Latin America from that of Europe[9], observing that Latin America did not share with Europe the moral crisis and mass mobilization of World War I. Thus, they reject the fascist label applied to Vargas's regime in Brazil and Peron's regime in Argentina.

In my analysis, however, which in the Argentine case is clearly substantiated, fascism was a new cultural and ideological synthesis providing an innovative solution to the tensions created by political and social modernization. Neither right-wing nor left-wing, the fascist orientation appealed to a new generation of nationalist intellectuals who, unwittingly, were part of this deep cultural and political revolution. In short, the Argentine regime was based on a local variant of fascist ideology, directly related to nationalist populism.

Roger Griffin defines fascism as a palingenetic form of populist ultranationalism[10], while Roger Eatwell sees it as a spectral-syncretic ideology that synthesizes what could be seen as a wide range of opposing issues[11]. Both definitions, however, emphasize the appearance of a new populist nationalism and the myth of rebirth and renewal. As Eatwell suggests, this rebirth could have a conservative or reactionary dimension, or it could be a radical revolutionary symbol of the need to create something new[12].

To sum up, during the 1930s Argentine leftist and rightist intellectuals raised fundamental issues that defined the contours of a new national ideal: an innovative nationalism that stood in opposition to liberal conservatism, socialist Marxism, and bourgeois politics, and which promoted a new regenerative myth and a synthesis between tradition and modernity. In contrast to other works on Argentine nationalism, I suggest that Argentine nationalism was neither antimodernist nor nostalgic. It was revolutionary, and propounded an alternative formula for national modernization. Far from being unrelated to Peronism, it began a process of ideological development that would reach its apex under the government of Juan Peron.[13]

Cultural nationalism and the emergence of a regenerative myth

Argentina's progress towards modernization was guided by the utopian views of the 'generation of 1837.' Alberdi, Sarmiento, and Echevarria, influenced by the positivist philosophical and sociological thought of the time, tried to fit their own reality into an analytical framework reflecting their faith in linear economic and political progress, in conformity with the European experience[14].

That generation's political thought was summed up in Sarmiento's book *Civilization or Barbarism*. Civilization meant the import of Western liberal values through education, foreign immigration and economic development, while the barbaric heritage that was to be eradicated was represented by Juan Manuel de Rosas's tyrannical regime and its populist *caudillo* mentality. Political liberalism and the free flow of capitalist investment did indeed prople Argentina into rapid economic growth at the beginning of the century. However, the practical result of the ideology of modernization as defined by the liberal elites was a disintegrated society, an unbridgeable gap between the state and the people, and an economic development dependent upon foreign demand for agricultural export products.

The production system was the basis for a sociopolitical organization intended to serve the singular combination of British interests and their Argentine 'liberal partners.' This system was supported by an ideal of civilization shared by both the European-oriented oligarchy and the immigrant working class and their social movements. In fact, although the anarchist and socialist movements that arose at the beginning of the century disturbed the liberal elites' utopian dream, they proposed no fundamentally different project of national development.

From the beginning of the century, Argentine syndicalism had been influenced by foreign ideas, represented as it was by immigrant newcomers who attempted to revolutionize society rather than being absorbed by it. The anarchists catered to the subjective needs of the 'labor aristocracy' of craftsmen, simultaneously establishing a profound division between skilled 'European' workers and unskilled 'creole' workers. Their vision of a utopian, progress-oriented and internationalist working class was suited to the needs of the highly politicized proletariat then existing in Argentina. It could not, however, satisfy the requirements of the mass mobilization that began during the thirties and reached its height under Peron in the forties[15].

The Socialist party, founded by J.B. Justo, proposed another analytical insight, although within the same cultural parameters. In his book *Theory and Practice*, Justo describes a process of development by stages in Argentina in which the capitalist stage and the formation of a national bourgeoisie are preconditions for the development of a socialist society. For Justo, the Bernstein hypothesis of socialist evolution was valid for agro-export as well as industrialized countries. More important in this context, however, Justo, like other socialist leaders, attached no special value to anti-imperialist politics. For them, in fact, a dependent economy was a temporary stage, a step in the process of modernization.[16]

In short, neither the socialists nor the anarchists challenged the liberal elites' positivist philosophy of progress. There was no real attempt to delegitimize the elites' model of political modernization until a new nationalist concept based on different cultural parameters appeared at the beginning of the century. It was around that time that, influenced by new philosophical trends in Spain and France, and by indigenous Latin American sources, new magazines, literary clubs, and study groups formulated the antipositivist critique that was to be the basis for a new nationalism with two faces: a European-influenced, integralist one and an authentic populist one. Although opposed to each other in certain ways, both trends contributed to the development of a single concept of radical, antiliberal nationalism during the thirties.

The best Argentine interpreters of this nationalist cultural renaissance were Ricardo Rojas and Manuel Galvez, whose books *La Restauracion Nacionalista* (The nationalist Restoration) (1909) and *El Solar de la Raza* (1913), respectively, became cornerstones of an authentic Argentine nationalism. Ricardo Rojas's book, *La Restauracion Nacionalista*, was commissioned by the Argentine government to present an educational plan for Argentine schools. Its publication in 1909 elicited considerable public response, putting the book at the center of an ideological discussion that was in some ways the local equivalent of similar discussions in Europe.

Not surprisingly, the first reactions to the book came from the Spanish intellectuals Miguel de Unamuno and Ramiro de Maeztu. A series of articles by Unamuno appeared in *La Nacion* in 1910, expressing warm approval of the book: "how could I not applaud [Rojas's] nationalism, since I, like him, ... have tried to prove all the egoistic contents of humanism"[17]. The book's basic message was a devastating critique of the liberal elites' project of national modernization and its cosmopolitan consequences. Rojas protested against the excessive liberalism that since the beginning of the century had led Argentina to adopt the principle of freedom of education from countries entirely different from Argentina in both situation and destiny: "an adaptation of the same [political and ideological] system would help 'the commerce of adventurers without homeland ... and the invasion of imperialist powers".[18]

The connection between immigrants and economic and cultural imperialism was a classic formula guaranteed to motivate integralist as well as populist nationalists in Argentina. In fact, Rojas's attitude towards immigrants reflected the radical stance of most nationalist thinkers at the beginning of the century. The novelist Manuel Gálvez, one of the most important intellectual figures at the time of the 'centenary' in Argentina, confirmed this point. His own central theme was the antagonism between the traditional village and the cosmopolitan city, or, in other words, between culture and civilization. According to Gálvez, the national spirit was not dead, but merely hidden under a cosmopolitan veneer.[19] In fact, he claimed, it was local provincialism, with its love of tradition, its rejection of anything foreign, its American spirit, that inspired the resistance to denationalization[20].

This assumption inspired a whole generation of nationalists who understood that the Argentine nationality was spoiled by the materialist spirit of the liberal generation, whose interpretation of national history bore the stamp of its cultural and economic world conception. That generation:

> seemed to be marching ... towards universal happiness, without suspecting the future conflicts that would derive from the industrial revolution, and from the expansion of capitalism. ... Given this universal faith, the liberal interpretation of national history was the antecedent and justification of the political action of our oligarchies ... in other words of the party of "civilization"[21].

For the new generation of nationalist intellectuals, however, the utopia espoused by the party of 'civilization' was to be replaced with the revolutionary mobilization myth.

Thus, in contraposition to the enlightened utopia of the liberal elites, a new regenerative myth appeared, inspired by the heroic, energetic life of the *gaucho*, who represented the preliberal past. According to Georges Sorel, the "revolutionary myths of our days are almost pure; they allow us to understand the acts, the feelings and the thoughts of the masses that prepare themselves for the definitive struggle"[22]. Although it was the myth of the general strike that mobilized the proletariat to revolutionary action, the power of tradition – the mother of the social instinct – also played a decisive political role. It was the historical myth, the myth of the Argentine pre-liberal tradition with its social and cultural configurations, which became the new mobilizing myth that accompanied the economic denunciation of Argentine liberalism.

In fact, the revisionist interpretation of Rosas's era became the cornerstone of the ideological and political rebellion against the liberal state, and served as a comprehensive denunciation of the Argentine political culture and economic process. The reconstruction of Argentina's self-identity, based as it was on the Rosas myth of resistance to the great imperial powers, France and England, in the first half of the eighteenth century, also symbolized national unification under a violent, authoritarian, traditionalist regime.

The identification of liberal political culture with economic dependence was most clearly expressed in a book by the brothers Irazusta – *La Argentina y el imperio britanico* (Argentina and the British Empire) – published in 1934 at the time of the Roca-Runciman pact – which constituted the most direct intellectual attack on the Argentine liberal oligarchy's version of history. This book analyzed the reasons for Argentine dependence on Great Britain throughout the political and economic development of the oligarchy. In fact:

> the mistakes committed by Roca's mission ... are so huge that they cannot be explained by a simple personal formula... Personalities which the universal consensus [defines] ... as skillful could not have represented the country so badly, were it not because of a transcendental reason. That reason is the history of the oligarchy[23].

This historical approach was indeed a purely ideological and political one. "Making politics is almost unavoidable when doing history"[24], commented Julio Irazusta. Coming to terms with the Rosas period meant much more than doing proper historical research. Although, unlike other nationalist interpreters of history, J. Irazusta did not claim to be "using the example of Rosas in order to dream of dictatorships based on the Rosas precedent"[25], he sought the historical antecedents of the new concept of antiliberal and antirationalist populist democracy, which was based on social justice and the heroic revolutionary power of tradition in Argentine nationalism. In short, he represented the communion between traditional populism, social justice, and anti-imperialism which linked the populist and integralist versions of nationalism.

Two concepts of radical nationalism: the populist 'left' and the integralist 'right'

The first political expression of the intellectual rebellion against the liberal oligarchy's modernization project was the populist Radical movement, which from its inception in 1890 changed the rules of the game of the conservative establishment. The Unión Cívica Radical took as its ideological cause the need to open the political system to the new native middle classes that were evolving in tandem with the process of economic development. Advocating a violent, intransigent struggle for democratization and the rescue of the Argentine 'authentic' national identity, Radicalism was synonymous with rebellion and a new morality, opposed to bourgeois materialism and the cosmopolitan spirit of the oligarchy.

By granting universal male suffrage in 1912, the oligarchy had made some concession to the new reality of the 'native middle classes' – children of immigrants, young, urban professionals and the urban proletariat. At the same time, the conservative politicians believed that only by participating in political elections could the Radical movement be 'civilized'. This view allowed the Radical party to attain power in 1916 under the leadership of Hipolito Yrigoyen.

What set Yrigoyen apart in liberal conservatives circles was his political style and innovative view of nationalism. Yrigoyen, heir to the rebellious tradition of the *caudillos*, attempted to integrate the politics of regional federalism with the constitutional order. His penchant for operating through party committees produced a new direct democratic style that challenged his own party bureaucracy as well as the alienated conservative parties of the oligarchy. This, however, proved to be his downfall, for he challenged the political culture of the oligarchy without trying to change the agrarian-based economy that supported it.

Yrigoyen, in fact, had no intention of promoting any essential structural change in the economy. But his political message was rejected by both the oligarchy – who despised his political style – and the corporatist national right – who felt that his brand of constitutional populism was not a valid answer to the current economical and political challenges[26]. At the end of the 1920s, during the height of the widespread economic depression that was devastating agricultural interests, these diverse elements formed a broad coalition to promote Felix de Uriburu's 1930 coup d'etat. It must be emphasized, however, that, apart from the desire to bring down Yrigoyen's regime, the members of this coalition had almost nothing in common, and the alternative regimes they favoured were conflicting: the conservatives demanded a return to the old liberal system, without the populist rhetoric, while the national corporatists aspired to a corporatist state in line with the new integralist revolutionary currents in the world. Although Yrigoyenist nationalism had antipositivist, antiliberal, and antimaterialist roots, the new generation of nationalist intellectuals who contributed to the journal *La Nueva Republica* believed that this sort of populism was anarchical and disintegrationist. The nationalist intellectuals of *La Nueva Republica*, disillusioned with the old conservative parties, found their main local source of inspiration in the poet Leopoldo Lugones. Lugones, one of the main proponents of military nationalism, had since 1925 been heralding the "hour of the sword." This was a reference to the Argentine army, which had fought for independence and, in Lugones's view, was the only reliable organism that could serve as an example of hierarchy and order. For Lugones the army did not represent the means of preserving the current bourgeois order. Only the army could insure the future of the nation, since it synthesized tradition with technical advancement. Lugones's teachings to the new nationalist generation can be summed up by the concept that "[l]ife does not triumph by means of reason and truth, but by means of force."[27]

When the newspaper *La Nueva Republica* was founded in 1927, it became a focal point for a group of intellectuals who, under Lugones's influence, were to elaborate an integralist political program as an alternative to "inorganic democracy." Ernesto Palacio, Cesar Pico, the brothers Rodolfo and Julio Irazusta, Roberto de Leferrere, and Juan Carulla edited the paper. Their political alternative was termed

> nationalism, that would represent the organized and corporatized collectivity, in which individual interests are subordinated to the Nation. The common good of the people, which is the end of all government, is contrary to these abstract principles of popular sovereignty, freedom, equality or proletariat redemption[28].

Those ideals were the intellectual base for the unsuccessful revolutionary attempt led by General Felix de Uriburu in September 1930. Although that attempt did not lead to a corporatist state as the nationalist intellectuals had expected, it opened a new era of ideological struggle that delegitimized the liberal democratic order. In fact, although the oligarchical establishment remained in power, supported by the government of General Agustin Justo, the intellectual preparation for a second round began immediately[29].

From Uriburu's corporatist project to a new synthesis of populist and integral nationalism

The Justo era, although characterized by a certain industrial modernization, was in fact a period in which the dependence of the Argentine economy and society was greatly felt. It was during this "infamous decade," as it was defined by the nationalist Jose Luis Torres, that the government entered into controversial commercial agreements with England that favoured the interests of the wealthiest ranchers[30].

The thirties provided an objective opportunity to unify the values of the 'authentic' and the 'foreign,' the modern corporatist system of mass control proposed by the integralists and the populist rebel tradition manifested in Yrigoyen's movement. For the integral nationalists of the right, the concepts of anti-imperialism, industrialization, and social justice were interrelated. They also had a clear ideological conviction that the revolutionary political style of fascism could well be integrated with the concepts of economic and cultural emancipation. That was the reason that a new fascist style of politics and a new anti-imperialist rhetoric characterized the nationalist groups that proliferated during the thirties. In fact, quasi-military leagues like the Legion de Mayo, the Legion Civica, the Liga Republicana, and the Accion Nacionalista Argentina were the proofs that a new, hitherto unknown political style had developed in Argentina.

La Liga Republicana and the *Legion Civica* were the Argentine promoters of the new fascist trend. Before Uriburu's military revolt, the *Liga Republicana* had pursued its new style of revolutionary activist politics against Yrigoyen's regime. Founded by Roberto de Laferrere and Rodolfo Irazusta in 1929, this organization was responsible for preparing the public to accept the necessity of a revolution through direct street confrontations with *the Radical party* militias called the *Klan Radical*[31].

The Liga was the first nationalist movement to apply a revolutionary terminology more significant than a mere appeal for a coup d'etat against Yrigoyen's constitutional government. The basic goal was "to promote the revolution of spirits ..."[32], and to announce the "imperious urgency of opposing the actual government and its system ..."[33]. The main feature of *La Liga Republicana*, however, was its insistence on ideological purity. Contrary to the *Legion Civica*, which was created by the provisional government after the military coup, the *Liga Republicana* understood ideological purity to mean that it should not compromise with the military government, should the latter abandon the basic revolutionary ideas.

The *Legion Civica*, on the other hand, had been created as a paramilitary group directly attached to the government when General Felix de Uriburu realized that his corporatist plans had entered a blind alley. Its goal was to propagate the ideology of the revolution. Less dogmatic than the *Liga Republicana*, "the *Legion Civica* [was] an a-political force" that would collaborate in carrying out the program of the revolution, although remaining under the control of the military government[34].

In spite of their different approaches, both organizations presented a radical message and a political style which challenged the very political establishment that had called for the end of Yrigoyenism – but had not bargained for its replacement by fascism. This new style represented a new ideological wave based on the assumption that war "more than a function of armies was a function of peoples, and no component of the nation . . . could (afford) not to participate in it"[35].

In keeping with its paramilitary status, the *Legion Civica* was organized on military lines, in brigades and divisions that paraded in columns of eight. The Legion also mobilized women and children, and gave them military training[36]. But beyond its military activities, the *Legion Civica* sought an ideological and social role based on a new concept of solidarity. This solidarity symbolized the spirit of the organic concept of nationalism in Argentine society. In August 1932, for example, the Legion used the fascist model to organize its own syndicalist movement, the *FONA* (*Federacion Obrera Nacionalista*: Nationalist Workers Union). At the same time, it provided free food and housing to unemployed workers in various parts of the capital, an activity in which the women's branch of the Legion was particularly prominent. Nevertheless, the *Legion Civica's* welfare activities should not obscure its more important political functions, described by the police as follows: "diverse commissions of the organization tour the city in order to push members to . . . maintain surveillance over worker centers and the domiciles of the principal Radical (party) leaders . . ."[37]. Although occasionally the police collaborated with the government-supported militia, it detected and disapproved of what it wrongly considered to be the organization's "putschist" characteristics, fearing that it could be transformed from a civil auxiliary group supporting the provisional government into an uncontrolled revolutionary force. In fact, since the nationalists questioned the legitimacy of the liberal constitution, the legionaries' function of helping the security forces to maintain order in the cities could well be viewed as maintaining a revolutionary order rather than the actual legal one.[38]

The legionaries demonstrated their new political path by means of street confrontations and vandalism. These acts were reported by the national press, and it was clear that a spirit of violence was taking over Buenos Aires and the provinces. In the province of Cordoba, the legionaries collaborated with the local police to close down the newspapers *El Dia* and *Cordoba* because of the papers' criticism of the legionaries' vandalism[39]. Such actions were tacitly supported by the government.

Accordingly, Felix de Uriburu's resignation in 1931 initially seemed likely to deal a mortal blow to the Legion's activities. That it did not was due to the permissive attitude of Augustin Justo, Uriburu's successor, towards the *Legion Civica* and the activities of other proponents of nationalism. In order to minimize the nationalists' resistance to the restoration of constitutionalism, Justo persuaded the members of the *Legion Civica* that the most important goal was the struggle against leftist communism which loomed behind the imminent social revolution.

This created a dilemma for the nationalist movement of the time: was the final goal of the nationalist struggle the fall of Yrigoyenism, or was it in fact an all-out assault on the entire liberal state? The answer to this question was found amid the ideological developments of Argentine nationalism in the aftermath of *Uriburismo*, and it was reflected in the initial reactions against what appeared to be the Legion's appeasement of the liberal state. The conviction that began to take hold of the rank and file of the nationalist groups was that the end of Yrigoyenism was not enough. It was evident to the nationalists that "after the September revolution, . . . another revolution is unavoidable . . ."[40]. That conviction, of course, demanded a more decisive revolutionary action in which all the political and economic institutions of the liberal establishment would be destroyed. The new revolution, however, should be led by a popular movement; this appeared to be the new conception of Argentine nationalism.

Although the *Legion Civica* had succeeded in attracting many recruits by mid-1931 – there were between 10.000 and 30.000 brigade members scattered throughout the capital, eleven provinces, and one territory – it never constituted a mass movement. The search for a mass movement would represent a radical change in the political style and ideological message of Argentine nationalism. While the militarily oriented movement represented a new set of values that promoted the militarization of society as the necessary remedy for a decadent, bourgeois society, it had a long way to go to establish itself as a popular movement.

For Argentine nationalism, becoming a popular movement signified the sacrifice of ideological doctrinarism. That ideological process, which would reach culmination under the next military government in 1943, was begun during the 1930s, when, in a new socio-economic framework, the nationalists of *La Nueva Republica* decided to 'nationlize' the counter-revolutionary movement. Accepting the masses into the political game was an additional step towards synthesizing the ideological elements of the fascist revolution with the indigenous republican tradition of the Yrigoyenist movement.

As noted by Galvez, fascism had a social, modernizing aspect: "fascism [in Italy] is a doctrine of the right, which opposes democracy and socialism; but socially it belongs to the left . . ."[41]. The fact that, in Argentina, the people responded to Yrigoyen's radical party, a populist and nationalist movement, led him to conclude that "an authentic radical could not be far from fascism . . ."[42]. Galvez's reconciliation with the Yrigoyenist tradition had important ideological consequences for Argentine nationalism. Up to that point, the nationalist integralist revolutionaries had been able to visualize a corporate authoritarian society, antiliberal and anti-oligarchic, brimming with youthful vitality; but they were unable to envision the people's function in that schema, since everything connected with the people would be understood as Yrigoyenism, anarchy, and disorder. Galvez, in effect, projected an ideological reconciliation permitting a synthesis between two brands of nationalism that were considered antagonistic until the 1930s.

The emphasis on economic emancipation and the revision of the historical role of Juan Manuel de Rosas, as well their deep-seated anti liberalism, was to become the link between the integralists' thinking and that of FORJA (*Fuerza de Orientacion Radical de la Joven Argentina* – Radical Force of Young Argentina), the new left wing of the Yrigoyenist movement. The FORJA group promoted a new brand of economic nationalism that was to have great influence on the former integral nationalists. Although they did not share common philosophical roots and they related differently to the specific results of liberal modernization, both nationalist wings added complementary components to the 'third way' of development.

FORJA members like Arturo Jauretche and Luis Dellepiane did not speak in terms of class struggle but addressed themselves to the Argentine people at large. As the left wing of the Yrigoyen populist movement, they understood better than the integralists that giving the masses political expression was the only route to integration, especially since this new wave of leftist nationalism came at a time when the masses were not represented by the Communist or Socialist parties. The integration process was to be accompanied by economic anti-imperialism, basically directed towards Great Britain in their case, and virulent in character.

They did not consider the Argentine economic crisis to be a structural one – that is to say the result of free market forces. Rather, it was a political crisis resulting from the dealings between a non-nationalist elite and British interests. Breaking off this disadvantageous relationship was a precondition for national industrialization and integration. Here again the similarities to Irazusta's analysis are clear. Going against the comfortable agro-export economic order would require a social contract based on the so-called 'third way' of development, one differing from both the liberal democratic system and the socialist proletarian revolution. This alternative was to be a populist, corporatized society that would push for social integration and industrialization. In the eyes of FORJA members, this was the only formula for national dignity and survival in the competitive modern world.

Both nationalist movements believed Argentina should maintain its neutrality in the confrontation between the Axis and the Allies. It must be emphasized that FORJA members were not pro-Axis and did not share the philosophical roots of the integral nationalists. Nevertheless, both nationalist wings perceived liberal democracy and its supporters around the world as enemies of Argentine nationalism.

Scalabrini Ortiz, an intellectual closely linked with FORJA and one of the most prominent defenders of neutrality at the time, did not hide his fierce opposition to British imperialism and liberalism. This opposition led him to accept contributions from integral nationalists such as the brothers Irazusta and Ernesto Palacio for the daily newspaper *Reconquista*, which he had founded in 1939. He used the paper to promote the idea of Argentine neutrality in World War II, an idea not far removed from Argentine support for the Axis. Scalabrini himself was not, in fact, pro-Axis but, at the height of the world ideological crisis, he found he had more in common with the defenders of the New order than he did with liberals.

Despite the differences between the two strains of nationalism, however, a political synthesis was possible. To FORJA, liberal modernization meant dependence and underdevelopment, and for the integral nationalists it meant cultural dependence and a loss of the native Hispanic heritage. Anti-imperialist politics, which to FORJA members signified economic emancipation and mass participation in the political process, was a precondition for the development of an authentic national program of industrial modernization and social welfare – views shared by former integral nationalists like R. Irazusta, E. Palacio, and M. Galvez, who perceived that elitism and exclusivism were incompatible with the new gospel of mass politics. The practical conclusions of both nationalist wings resulted in the same political order: a corporatist, antiliberal, antibourgeois, anti-imperialist state in which the people would be organically organized. Such a state in fact represented a practical synthesis between radical integral nationalism and populist anti-imperialism.

One of the nationalist groups that best expressed this proposition was the *Alianza de la Juventud Nacionalista*, founded by Queralto in 1937, which postulated economic intervention by the state and which, even before Peron appeared, had already spoken of social justice and anti-imperialism. The Alianza's program provided that "production would rest on the principle of being at the service of the country and not at the service of liberal, capitalistic accumulation . . ."[43]. Furthermore, it commented, "until now any social policy was based on reforms conceded by the liberal system," but "our national revolution will transform the main concept of labor . . . Labor is going to be associated as a partner in the production of wealth . . ."[44].

In some ways this rhetoric resembled that of the *Legion Civica Argentina*. The Legion's political program for a "representative and popular democracy" was full of economic and social reforms for the New world it envisaged. The Legion's members were convinced that the evils of capitalism and industrialization could be overcome by a strong syndicalist state, to the benefit of the workers. "We are not enemies of the workers." Solutions to the workers' problems had not yet been provided by "socialism and could not be given in the future." The only road left was "class syndicalism . . . that can mediate between workers and employers, . . . [and] that would certainly develop into a corporatist state that binds and harmonizes . . ."[45].

In fact, it was clearly necessary to transform the liberal democratic state into a class state that could preserve harmony and social justice at the same time. "The unjust capitalist regime should be transformed," declared the Legion Civica's propagandist organ *Combate*[46]. The nationalists of the right saw plainly that nationalism had to be popular or it would be nothing at all.

The *Alianza de la Juventud Nacionalista* had a less military style than the *Legion Civica*. It synthesized more clearly than any other nationalist group the new populist, worker-oriented approach and the struggle for economic independence with the traditional concepts of corporatist organization. The Alianza's basic stance was defined thus:

> Against capitalism that has imposed its . . . tyranny over the working masses! Against super capitalism and marxism! For the moral and material significance of the Argentinean proletariat! For the economical freedom of the nation! We demand social justice![47]

The Alianza advocated the syndicalist state that was later to be established by Peron, and was, in fact, the first nationalist group to succeed in holding mass May Day meetings in the Plaza San Martin in Buenos Aires, in a clear attempt to transform the international workers' day into a national celebration of the Argentine worker. In general, the organization boosted the participation of workers and the unemployed, precursors to Peron's *descamisados*.

The Alianza synthesized both wings of Argentine nationalism better than did any other nationalist group; but like the other groups, and in spite of the revolutionary and populist rhetoric adopted during the 1930s, it never became a real political force. Furthermore, neither Argentine nationalist movements nor other nationalist movements worldwide managed to reach the masses during the period between the world wars. The practical implementation of the nationalist ideology did not take place in Argentina until the military revolution of 1943; and, in fact, the Argentine nationalists trusted the army much more than they did themselves. This time, in contrast to Uriburu's revolutionary attempt in 1930, a new group of officers were to launch the political revolution so long awaited by the nationalists. Thus it was in 1943 that a new, fascist authoritarian era began for Argentina.

The military revolution of 1943 and the nationalists

No single explanation can be offered for the army leaders' decision to act against Ramon Castillo's conservative government in 1943. On the domestic front, of course, there was growing dissatisfaction with the government's economic strategy, which, along with certain administrative abuses, provoked army leaders to express their moral censure in certain revolutionary proclamations.

The greatest goal to the proponents of revolutionary change, however, was Castillo's support for the candidacy of Robustion Patron Costa, an aristocratic conservative with clear pro-Allied tendencies. By supporting Costa,

Castillo meant to reaffirm the political power of a united front between conservatives and the anti-Yrigoyenist wing of the Radical party. However, important sectors of the army doubted the ability of a conservative government to defend the country's sovereignty in the face of Brazil's growing strength[48]. They also suspected that no conservative liberal government would defend Argentina's proud tradition of neutrality in the world war. All these factors played a role in the ultimate decision to overthrow Castillo's government.

The revolution also had some more comprehensive aims which went beyond these pragmatic factors. One of the revolutionary leaders, General Pedro Pablo Ramirez, a former war minister under President Castillo, declared in a speech that the aim of the military government was to "renovate the national spirit" of the country by giving an "Argentine ideological content to the whole country"[49]. The moral and nationalist content of Ramirez's speech raised the nationalists' expectations. Marcelo Sanchez Sorondo, in his speech to the military, commented:

> Since 4th June there has been a break in continuity, but it seems as though one has reached a sort of apolitical oasis. The military movement ousted a government that had the appearance of being the end of a regime ... You, the military, who make your lives a profession of honor, on 4 June made a profession of faith[50].

Sorondo's view was confirmed by the fact that although the revolution was carried out by officers of different political views, it was held together by a group of military men who had participated as secondary figures in Uriburu's revolution in 1930, and who in 1943 decided to reverse Argentine political development. Among them were Generals P.P. Ramirez, Emilio Ramirez, and Juan Peron, who, together with Colonels Avalos and Enrique Gonzales, were the most influential among the group of conspirators known as the G.O.U. (*Grupo de Oficiales Unidos*: United Officers Command). They were convinced that they would not repeat Uriburu's experience[51].

The rebels' immediate goals were to establish a new morality and discipline in the army and in the country as a whole, and to launch a crusade against communism[52]. After June 4th leaders and militants of the *Communist party* were arrested. The C.G.T. 2 – the majority sector of the C.G.T. *Confederacion General del Trabajo* – General Workers' Confederation) – was banned for coordinating the most important socialist and communist unions. Other unions – like the *Union Ferroviaria* (Railway Workers' Union) – were harassed as well. Thus, initially it seemed that the new government's anti-communist convictions and economic program would favour the economic interests of the oligarchy.

Jorge Santamarina, the minister of the economy, won the capitalists over with his policy of austerity and budget balancing. At the same time, there were clear indications that the government would not support a policy that imposed economic hardship on the people. The nationalists were not displeased with this line. The most important innovation from the nationalists' point of view, however, was that the new nationalist government intended to develop an autonomous state that would not depend exclusively on the dominant economic classes.

It seemed to convince the nationalists that their ideology had penetrated into Argentine mentality, particularly in the army. The nationalist press comprehended the social character of this nationalist 'de facto' government: "One of the [military] movement's basic points, set out in the revolutionary proclamation, was to outlaw foreign capital maneuvers [in the country] . . ."[53]. The journal *Crisol* published Ramirez's standpoint on the social question: 'The army has moved, not in order to make a revolution, but to give a solution to the problems of the people, especially the problems of the working masses."[54]

The revolution produced a similar reaction in the left-wing Yrigoyenists of FORJA. A declaration by FORJA's National Executive on June 4, 1942 stated:

> 1. The overthrow of the regime constitutes the first stage of every policy of national reconstruction and of an authentic expression of sovereignty.
> 2. The implantation of a moral system that will lead the institutional development of the country . . . is an essential principle on which any possibility of national creation should be based . . .[55].

The conclusion was that FORJA would follow the developments with reserved optimism.

Integral and populist nationalists were certain that this revolution was a moral one that provided answers to social problems and to the question of economic emancipation. More than that, the revolution seemed to be the real expression of the Argentine national identity. "If the liberal democracy we have suffered under [until now) . . . had originally been Argentine, nationalism would not have borne the fruits it has"[56].

Thus, both left wing and right wing nationalists focused their expectations on the Argentine army. By guarding Argentina's neutrality in the world conflict, by threatening the liberal democratic order and the bourgeois and socialist establishments, and by offering a social and political alternative, the GOU reflected the ideological evolution of Argentine nationalism. Indeed, the military revolution of 1943 surpassed military 'Uriburism' with a new integralist-populist formula synthesized by the national right and left.

The military government's short-term industrial policies were directed towards aiding national industry. Mixed industrial complexes were created with the goal of exploiting national resources, and long-term loans were offered to national industry. At the same time, the productive policies inspired by Lugones's thesis of national strength were accompanied by a limited social policy that attempted to achieve a certain degree of the social justice advocated by most of the nationalist intellectuals.

The Syndical Statute formulated by the military government in 1943 was intended to achieve corporatist authoritarian control of the workers' organizations. The latter were to be subject to government approval and supervision, while certain benefits were guaranteed for the working class: housing rents were reduced and higher wages were established for the lowest paid public-administration workers. This trend was reinforced in November 1943, when the *Secretaria de Trabajo y Prevision*, headed by Juan D. Peron and previously a minor arm of the Interior Ministry, became the *Departamento Nacional del Trabajo*, an autonomous department. Decree 156.074 of November 27, 1943, assigned Peron the duty of taking the measures necessary to establish harmony between the country's productive forces[57]. This office was to be the first step in the young GOU general's meteoric rise to power. The nationalist press responded enthusiastically to his new appointment and to what was seen as an effort to establish a productive economic system with a clear commitment to social justice:

> Peron's statements to the press . . . accorded with what we have been maintaining in these pages for ten years. The problems of labor and its relations with capital have overcome the provisions of legislators and statesmen of the early century . . . [Now] the state will abandon its passivity . . . and that cold, repressive attitude of early times, which merely favoured . . . those who abuse the weaknesses of others . . .[58]

While the task of social pacification was given to Peron, many nationalists were given important posts in the public administration. In fact, the government actively sought the intellectual support of the nationalists, especially the Catholic right, when the conflict with the United States over the question of Argentine neutrality intensified.

Still more important was the ideological function performed by the nationalists in the universities and other intellectual institutions. They were strongly convinced that the military revolution should express clearly the concept that "the nation is a military reality." They saw no contradiction between real freedom and the military regime[59].

These assumptions, which pleased the military rulers, were reflected in practical administrative measures. Political parties were banned, freedom of the press was extraordinarily limited, the autonomy of higher education was abolished, and on December 31 a government decree imposed religious education in all public schools. Martinez Zubiria (Hugo Wast), the well known anti-Semitic writer who had recently been appointed minister of justice, declared:

> We must Christianize the country, ... we must encourage the birth rate instead of immigration, we must ensure the benefits of work, ... we must extirpate those hateful and atheist [liberal] doctrines ...[60].

At the same time, however, the international situation was causing many difficulties for the new military government, forcing it to reshape its ideological positions, particularly with respect to foreign policy. In 1944 the Allies powers' ultimate victory in World War II was generally anticipated. From 1943 Argentina attempted to create a rational, comprehensible framework for its neutrality. The Argentine leaders tried to convince the United States that they would be able and willing to break off diplomatic relations with Germany in exchange for American military support. Cordell Hull rejected the Argentine petition. Moreover, the Americans attempted to publicize Argentina's alleged involvement in the fascist military revolution of the *Movimiento Nacionalista Revolucionario* in Bolivia, and threatened to freeze Argentine accounts in the United States. Capitulating to American pressure, President Ramirez finally agreed to sever diplomatic relations with the Axis – a step that precipitated his ouster, since nationalist ministers like Martinez Zubiria and Colonel Enrique P. Gonzalez defined this governmental act as a betrayal of the nation, and demanded Ramirez's resignation[61].

Ramirez was replaced by another hard-line nationalist, General Edelmiro J. Farrell, who reinstituted the intransigent-nationalist line within the government. General Farrell's administration was characterized by a renewed nationalist, militaristic message. The vitality and heroism of the army that had saved the country's traditional Hispanic nature, the praise of God, sovereignty, and the nation's combative morality – all the old myths were recycled by the government.

The blackboard in every Argentine school classroom read "Each additional son is a new guard of sovereignty," and "The new Argentina wants healthy, strong, and heroic women"[62].

The nationalists' direct influence on the government can be said to have ended when Peron was appointed vice-president of the nation and began to consolidate the political power he had achieved as secretary of labor and social planning. Peron understood the new rules of the game, that certain sacrifices would have to be made on the international level so that the internal reform of the state could be continued. In his role as labor secretary, he had realized the importance of the new working class made up of migrants mobilized in the industrial cities. Clearly, a nationalist revolution could not forget the support of the 'nationalist' masses, a concept promoted by the nationalists themselves since the mid-thirties. They had identified 'the new migrant working classes' as representative of the Argentine nation, while the unionized worker, the revolutionary working-class leadership, was influenced by foreign ideas and anti-nationalism. Peron, although rejecting the nationalist intellectuals' collaboration with the regime, was very clearly swayed by their convictions. Referring to the working class, he declared:

> I am personally a syndicalist ... and as such I am anti-communist, but I believe that labor must be organized in syndicates, so that workers, and not the leaders and agitators, would be the ones to take advantage of the benefits of their sacrifice ... I have advised the Department [of Labor], an organization that responds to the goals ... of improving the living conditions of the workers, although without tolerating any social conflict, ... [that] I won't tolerate the activities of agitators, ... most of whom are not even Argentines but foreigners who have not known how to respect the nationality of my homeland ....[63].

Peronism: authoritarian corporatism, social justice, and political mobilization

Juan Peron's meteoric ascent to power reflected the trend towards a New revolutionary order. The times called for a New order attentive to social realities. Thus the notion was conceived that "totalitarian movements of national and popular liberation are proletarian and democratic"[64]. The revolution had to be radical and social but not Marxist; Marxism was rejected on fundamental philosophical grounds. The thesis developed by the nationalist intellectuals and afterwards adopted by Peron was significant in that it included the Argentine revolution in the inevitable world revolution, which implied a new socialist order; one which was, "however, free of the Marxist materialist project".[65].

Peronism, in fact, expressed the new politics of mass mobilization in an inclusionary, corporatist framework; through it, Peron gave concrete expression to a synthesis of both ideological currents analyzed here, complementing it with his own charismatic leadership and his direct approach to the workers.

During the military government Peron established direct contact with the union leaders, aided by his colleague, Lieutenent Colonel Mercante, the son of a railway worker. Peron met with the syndicalists from the dissolved CGT, and in 1943 he intervened in favour of the workers in the Berisso Frigorificos' strike in La Plata. With Peron's support the first collective agreement was reached between labor and the government. Although the nationalists and the military were suspicious that Peron, with his corporatist ideas, would let the working classes into the political arena instead of controlling them, most of his military comrades agreed with Peron's social and political agenda.

Peron's visit to Italy in the period 1939–1941 had encouraged his admiration of Italian fascism, especially as a way to lead the working class[66]. In fact, Peron's approach to industrial relations resembled Mussolini's. As labor secretary in the military junta, he brought most of the unions under his control by means of the 1945 *Law of Professional Associations*, which provisions were almost identical with those of Mussolini's *Labor Code*. Under this law, only officially recognized unions and employers' associations could sign labor contracts, and only one employers' association and one labor union was to be permitted in each economic sector; strikes and lockouts were forbidden. Peron's syndicalist organization in fact did promote growing working-class organization – although subject to state control:

> because it suits the state to have organic forces it can control and lead rather than inorganic forces that escape its leadership . . . We do not want unions divided into political factions, because what is dangerous is, precisely, the political unions[67].

In other words, the welfare of the workers could be guaranteed only under the tutelage of the state.

While the working class was soon corporatized, it was only after Peron had taken charge of the government that he finally succeeded in bringing big business under control by setting up the *General Economic Confederation* in 1952. In tandem with the Peronist-controlled CGT, this confederation gave the state enormous regulatory power over the economy[68].

Concepts like economic emancipation, 'productionism', the formation of heavy industry, full employment, and social justice, were all elements of the government's economic and social plan. The government undertook to achieve a:

> just equilibrium among all the factors that take part in production, . . . collaboration between labor and employer organizations, and the humanization of the function of capital . . . and [to] improve the living conditions of the workers[69].

This 'productionist' program was based on the conviction that although Argentina was not a country with territorial ambitions, world politics demanded the development of a strong, autarkic nation. Juan D. Peron's own goal was the development of heavy industry under conditions of social justice[70].

All the instruments created by the state during Peron's administration were designed to further these aims. The IAPI (*Argentine Institute of Production and Trade*) in particular was the symbol of state economic regulatory power, and was created to promote the industrialization plan initiated in October 1946. The so-called '*Plan Quinquenal*' forced farmers to sell to the government at low, fixed prices; the government then made a good profit by selling those goods on the free market. The law that most frightened the rural oligarchy, however, was the '*Estatuto del Peron*,' which recognized rural laborers as workers with normal labor rights. Although this law was promoted by the right wing nationalist intellectual Enrique Oses in the pages of the right-wing journal *Crisol*, left-wing nationalists like A. Jauretche directly influenced Peron in the matter as well. While on the surface this measure would appear to have favoured the industrialized sectors, the latter still feared the regulatory power of the state and the labor legislation that supported the IAPI's industrial policies.

Meanwhile, the revision in 1949 of the federal constitution of 1853 provided a constitutional basis for the new ideological approach. The constitutional amendments proposed by Peron's close collaborators, Jose Figuerola (a Catalonian syndicalist during the dictatorship of Primo de Rivera who had immigrated to Argentina in 1930), the law professor Arturo Sampay, and Domingo Mercante, offered a new legal framework for social reform. A new chapter III enumerated a series of rights inspired by Catholic encyclicals that had spoken against abuses in the capitalist system and in favour of state intervention in the economic sector[71].

The new ideological system, however, which combined corporate, industrial, and social welfare goals in an integralist-populist synthesis, functioned only during 1949. In Argentina, 1949 was a year of watershed year for labor. Until then, without abandoning its policy of heavy industrialization, the government had allowed labor wages to rise, by as much as 40 per cent from 1946 to 1949. From 1949 on, however, production interests rather than principles of social justice guided Peron's policies. Wages declined by over 20 per cent, and a new discipline was imposed on the unions.[72] In fact, from 1949 until 1955 Peron's populist policies resembled fascist corporatist practices more than they did during pre-1949 social reformism. Peron was well aware of the new developments produced by mass politics, and understood that fascism was the only revolutionary movement that could synthesize a leftist social approach with a rightist form of political organization.

Peronism, however, offered a peripheral society a new style of national socialism based on the regenerative myth of the preliberal *caudillista* past, as well as on the political mobilization of the working classes. Yet, as this chapter shows, none of the Peronist ideas were entirely new, since the ideological elaboration of this synthesis between right-wing integralism, anti-imperialism, and social justice had already begun in the intellectual laboratories of the Argentine nationalist right and left during the thirties.

Argentina in fact provides a clear example of a fascist ideology adapted to the needs of a peripheral society, and proves that fascism abroad could also serve the purpose of national emancipation and social integration. Paradoxically, while it might be supposed that the new revolutionary trend would have introduced Argentina into the world of the developed nations, the opposite came to pass: Argentina sank into an economic, social, and political morass that has continued up to the present day.

Notes

1 See Marcelo Sanchez Sorondo, 1945: *La revolucion que anunciamos (The Revolution we anticipated)*, Ed. Nueva Politica, Buenos Aires.
2 See Carlos Waisman, 1987: *Reversal of development. Postwar counterrevolutionary policies and their structural consequences*, Princeton Universities Press, Princeton p. 256.
3 Zeev Sternhell, "Fascist Ideology," in W. Laqueur, ed., 1976: *Fascism: A Reader's Guide*, Pelican Books, London, p. 349.
4 Zeev Sternhell, Mario Sznajder, and Maia Asherri, 1988: *Naissance de l'ideologie fasciste (The birth of fascist ideology)*, Ed.Fayard, Paris, p. 11.
5 Stanley Payne, "The Falange," in N. Green, *Fascism, An Anthology*, (Illinois: H.M. Publishing Corporation, 1968), p. 273.
6 Eugene Weber; "The Men of the Archangel," *Journal of Contemporary History* Vol. 1 (1966), p. 103.
7 See Theotonio dos Santos, "Socialismo y fascismo en America Latina hoy" (Socialism and fascism in todays Latin America), *Revista Mexicana de Sociologia* (January – March 1977); Marcos Kaplan, "Hacia un fascismo Latino-americano (towards a Latin American fascism"), *Nueva Politica* [Mexico] (January-March 1976); Gunther Frank, *Capitalism and under development in Latin America* (New York, 1969). These scholars have written about the 'dependency theory,' which is a variant of general theories of imperialism. The dependency theory sees the social and economical development of underdeveloped countries as being conditioned by external factors. Underdevelopment can be explained in terms of relations of domination in exchange for an analysis of forces and relations of production.
8 On the bureaucratic-authoritarian state, see G. O'Donnell, *El Estado Burocratico Autoritario, 1966–1973* (The Bureaucratic-Authoritarian State, 1966–1973) Buenos Aires: Ed. de Belgrano, 1982). For a discussion of O'Donnell's typology, see David Collier, ed., *The New Authoritarianism in Latin America* (Princeton: Princeton University Press, 1979).
9 For a discussion of fascism in Latin America, see Alistair Hennesy, "Fascism and Populism in Latin America," in W. Laqueur, *op.cit.* Juan Linz has made a valid distinction between the authoritarian characteristics of certain regimes as opposed to the totalitarian characteristics of fascist regimes, with their mobilizing ability and ideological assets. Franco's Spain was a clear example of the authoritarian conservative regime. See Juan Linz, "The Party System of Spain: Past and Future," in Seymour Lipset and Stein Rokkan, eds., *Party System and Voter Alignments* (New York, 1967), and "An Authoritarian Regime: Spain," in E. Allardt and V. Littunen, eds. *Cleavages, Ideologies and Party Systems* (Helsinski, 1964).
10 See Roger Griffin, "The Nation Reborn, A New Ideal Type of Generic Fascism," discussion paper prepared for presentation to Special Session 22 of the XVth World Congress of the International Political Science Association held in Buenos Aires, July, 1991.
11 See R. Eatwell, "Towards a new model of generic fascism," *Journal of Theoretical Politics* 4, No. 2 (1992), p. 189.
12 Ibid., p. 173.
13 In contrast to most of the works on Argentine nationalism, the thesis I present here radically defies the perception of Argentine nationalism as nostalgic and reactionary. Among the works that sustain the thesis that Argentine nationalism was nostalgic and anti-modernist, the best is Cristian Buchrucker: *Nacionalismo y Peronismo, Argentina en la crisis ideologica mundial* (Nationalism and Peronism,

Argentina in the world ideological crisis (1927–1955)). (Buenos Aires: Ed. Sudamericana, 1987). Other works, such as J.J. Hernandez Arregui: *La Formacion de la Conciencia Nacional* (The formation of national consciousness) (Buenos Aires: Hachea, 1960), and Jorge Abelardo Ramos: *Revolucion y Contrarrevolucion en la Argentina: Las masas en nuestra historia* (Revolution and counterrevolution in Argentina. The masses in our history) (Buenos Aires: Amerindia, 1957) present integralist nationalism as a nostalgic movement associated with the liberal oligarchy. In their view, the populist nationalism developed by the left wing of the Radical party (FORJA) was the same populist nationalism that supported Peronism, which is perceived as left wing nationalism. Those works attempt to rehabilitate Peronism as an authentic revolutionary, anti-imperialist, nationalist movement, a precursor to the left wing anti-imperialist struggle in Latin America.

These two books were in fact an answer to other 'ideologically' minded books that appeared during the 1950s and 1960s, which were influenced by the modernization theories predominant in the United States during those years. Some of these works pointed to the direct connection between Argentine reactionary nationalism and Peronism, which they considered a reactionary fascist movement. Among these studies in John Johnson, *Political Change in Latin America: The Emergence of the Middle Sectors* (Stanford University Press, 1958). A slightly more sophisticated analysis is Kalman Silvert's *The Conflict Society: Reaction and Revolution in Latin America* (New Orleans: The Hausser Press, 1961). Similarly, James Scobie, in *Argentina: A City and a Nation* (New York: Oxford University Press, 1963), describes the Argentine nationalist uprising as the result of patriotic feeling against foreign economic penetration. A more important work reflecting this distinction between populist nationalism on one hand and the nostalgic, traditionalist trend of nationalism on the other is Arthur Whitaker's essay, "Argentina. Nostalgic and Dynamic Nationalism," in a book published with David Jordan, *Nationalism in Contemporary Latin America*, (New York, New Press 1966). Unlike other works, which point up the differences between the different strains of nationalism, this book identifies the ideological elements shared by both populist and integralist nationalism, which together produced an alternative, unified nationalist line. This thesis although based in an ideological political analysis, accepts the sociological explanation of Peronism developed by S. M. Lipset in his *L'Homme et la politique* (Paris Le Seuil, 1963, translated from *Political Man*). Lipset considered Peronism a 'fascism from the left'. While typical fascism is characterized by the support of the middle classes and could be considered a expression of the 'extremism of the centre', the peronist movement was a nationalist movement supported by the lower strata, similar to Brazil's G. Vargas one.

For the English reader, two other important works appeared lately. One is David Rock's *Authoritarian Argentina. The Nationalist Movement, its history and impact* (University of California Press, 1992) and Sandra Mcgee Deutsch and R. H. Dolkart ed. *The Argentine Right. Its history and intellectual origins* (Wilmington, Del. 1993). Both books deal with Argentine right nationalism over the *'longue duree' (up to the military regimes of the 1960's and 1970's)* As other books on Argentine nationalism they are focused on right wing nationalism and attempt to emphasize the limited relationship between Peronism and that rightist tradition. The thesis exposed in this article instead, relates Peronism to a right left synthesis, which resembles in some ways the fascist synthesis between an anti-conservative right and an anti-marxian left.

14 See Tulio Halperin Donghi, "Un nuevo clima de ideas." (A new climate of ideas) and Marcelo Montserrat, "Una ideologia del progreso" (An ideology of progress), in G. Ferrari and E. Gallo, eds.: *La Argentina del Ochenta al Centenario* (Argentina from the eighties to the centenary) (Buenos Aires: Ed.Sudamericana, 1980).

15 On the origins of the anarchist movement in Argentina, see Yaacov Oved, *El anarquismo y el movimiento obrero en Argentina* (Anarchism and the workers movement of Argentina) (Mexico:Ed.Siglo XXI, 1978).
16 On the history of the Argentine Socialist party, see J. Oddone, *Historia del socialismo argentino* (History of Argentina's socialism) (Buenos Aires: Ed. La Vanguardia, 1934).
17 Ricardo Rojas, *La Restauracion Nacionalista* (The nationalist Restoration) (Buenos Aires: Ed. Peña Lillio, 1971) [1st edition 1909], p. 18.
18 Ibid., p. 131.
19 Manuel Galvez, *El diario de Gabriel Quiroga – Opiniones de la vida argentina* (The diary of Gabriel Quiroga – opinions on Argentina's life) (Buenos Aires, 1910), p. 55.
20 Ibid, p. 153.
21 Ernesto Palacio, "La historia oficial y la historia," (The official history and the history) *Revista del Instituto de Investigaciones Historicas Juan M. de Rosas* Año 1, No. 1 (January 1939), p. 9.
22 G. Sorel, *Reflections sur la violence*, (Reflections on violence) in Z. Sternhell, *The Fascist Thought and Its Variations* [Hebrew] (Tel Aviv: Sifriat Hapoalim, 1988), p. 72.
23 Rodolfo y Julio Irazusta, "Historia de la oligarquia Argentina," (History of Argentina's oligarcy) *Nuevo Orden* (August 1, 1940). This essay was included in *La Argentina y el imperialismo britanico* (Buenos Aires: Ediciones Argentinas Condor, 1934).
24 J. Irazusta, *Ensayo sobre Rosas: En el centenario de la suma del poder, 1835–1935* (Essays on Rosas: On the centenary of the seizure of power, *1835–1935*) (Buenos Aires: Coleccion Megafono, 1935), pp. 28–29.
25 Ibid.
26 On the antipositivist roots of the Radical party and its theoretical debt to Frederich Krause, see Gabriel del Mazo, *El Radicalismo, Ensayo sobre su historia y doctrina* (Radicalism; Essay on its history and doctrine) (Buenos Aires: Ed. Gure, 1957), pp. 52–58.
27 Leopoldo Lugones, *La Patria Fuerte* (The mighty Homeland) (Buenos Aires: Ed. Circulo Militar, 1930), p.40. The poet Lugones was one of the most prominent Argentine nationalists, belonging to an older generation than the members of *La Nueva Republica (The new Republic)*. He grew up politically in the Socialist party, and turned from radical revolutionary socialism to radical nationalism. His famous Ayacucho speech, delivered in 1924 on the anniversary of the famous battle of Ayacucho celebrated in Lima, Peru, was known as "the hour of the sword." In it, he expressed his belief that the Argentine army was the only organism that could instill a new sense of life and order in Argentine society, which had been putrefied by liberal democracy.
28 *La Nueva Republica* (September 22, 1928). The Irazusta brothers belonged to a wealthy family of the province of Entre Rios which supported the antipersonalist wing of the Radical party. They began to study law in Buenos Aires in 1916, but did not pursue a legal career. In 1923 they went to France, where they were influenced by articles by Charles Maurras, published in the journal *L'Action Francaise*. The Irazustas, like Ernesto Palacio and other contemporaries who wrote for the journal *La Nueva Republica*, were part of the new generation of radical nationalists. Most of them grew up in well-established aristocratic families that were unable to cope with the modernization process in Argentina. The waves of immigration, the increasing materialism and technicality of Argentine society, and the social unrest left these intellectuals with no representation in the political system. The liberal conservatives represented the oligarchical elites that dominated

the political and economic processes in Argentina. It may be assumed from a sociological point of view that the new radical ideas of French nationalism suited the social status of both the members of *La Nueva Republica* and the participants in the *Cursos de Cultura Catolica* (Curses of Catholic Culture). Ernesto Palacio began his political career as an anarchist. Like other members of his generation, he was attracted to nationalism because the nationalist movement promised a new regenerative ideal. He was a founding member of the cultural magazine *Martin Fierro*, which represented a cultural breakthrough for Argentine intellectuals. From literary avantgardism he passed to fervent adherence to the Catholic faith, becoming a leading light among those ideologists who saw fascism and Catholicism as virtually united in a common struggle.

Like the Irazustas, Juan Carulla was a prominent contributor to *La Nueva Republica* (The New Republic), and also founded the journal *Bandera Argentina* (Argentine Flag). He, too, arrived in Europe during World War I. His gradual acceptance of the ideas of *L'Action Francaise* resulted from conversations with its principal members and from reading Charles Maurras.

29 On the political developments that led to the September Revolution, and on the role played by Felix de Uriburu, see J.J. Sarobe, *Memorias sobre la revolucion del 6 de Setiembre de 1930* (Memories of the 6th of September Revolution) (Buenos Aires: Gure, 1957), and Juan Orona, *La revolucion del 6 de Setiembre* (The 6th of September Revolution) (Buenos Aires, 1966).

30 The prominent nationalist Jose Luis Torres called the 1930s "the infamous decade." See also Arturo Jauretche, *FORJA y la decada infame* (FORJA and the infamous decade) (Buenos Aires: Ed. Pena Lillio, 1962). The era was marked by the bilateral pact between Great Britain wealth protectionism. The pact allowed for a stable but markedly reduced level of Argentine beef exports to Britain, and a loan to cover Argentine debts. In return, Argentina was to reserve 85 per cent of the reduced beef for British packing enterprises in Argentina.

31 The *Klan Radical* was a paramilitary shock troop organization of the Yrigoyenist wing of the Radical party, established in July 1929 to combat party dissidents. *Klan Radical* groups, composed by party committee members organized by Radical congressmen, clashed with *La Liga Republicana* in several street confrontations. However, in spite of the violent rhetoric used at some organizational meetings and isolated propagandistic political acts – such as the disruption of the speech of Agricultural Minister Juan B. Fleitas at the Sociedad Rural – no violent acts by the League were cited.

32 C. Ibarguren (hijo), *Roberto de Laferrere, periodismo, politica historia* (Roberto de Laferre; journalism, politics, history) (Buenos Aires: Ed. Coleccion Argentina, 1970), p. 41.

33 F. Ibarguren, *Origenes del nacionalismo Argentino, 1927–1937* (Origins of the Argentine Nationalism: Buenos Aires: Ed. Celcius, 1969), pp. 31–32.

34 F. de Uriburu addressed officers at a luncheon of the Armed Forces, July 7, 1931. See A. Rouquie, *Poder militar y sosiedad politica en Argentina*, (Military power and society in Argentina) vol.I, 7 edition (Buenos Aires, Emecé, 1983) p. 245.

35 Lautaro Montenegro, *Origen de la Legion Civica Argentina y la Doctrina de su constitucion* (Origins of Argentina's Legion Civica and the doctrine of its constitution) (Buenos Aires: no pub., 1931), p. 5.

36 As demonstrated by the research of Fernando Garcia Molina, Graciela Etchevest, Ana Maria Galibert, and Omar Cerdeira, "La Legion Civica Argentina (1931–1932)", Catedra de introduction al conocimiento de la sociedad a cargo del prof. Ruben Berenblum, Universidad Nacional de Buenos Aires, 1985, p. 14.

37 Policia Federal, "Prontuario Carulla", (Carulla's file) Legajo 1, Exp. 1, Folio 52, Leg. *Legion Civica*, June 15, 1931.

THE 'FASCIST EPOCH'

38 Policia Federal. "Prontuario Carulla", Leg.1, Exp.1, Folio 198, Leg. *Legion Civica*, June 12, 1932.
39 *La Prensa* (September 30, 1931), p.4. The motto declaring "With the revolution or against the homeland" was representative of the revolutionary totalitarian ambitions of the legionaries, which echoed the frustrated ambitions of General Uriburu.
40 *La Vanguardia* (September 16,), p. 1. F. Ibarguren, *Origenes del nacionalismo*, (Origins of nationalism) pp. 86–87.
41 Manuel Galvez, "Perspectivas de fascismo en Argentina," (Prospects of fascism in Argentina) in *Este Pueblo Necesita* (Buenos Aires, 1934), p. 119.
42 Ibid., p. 127.
43 *Tribuna* (December 20, 1945)
44 Ibid.
45 "Nacionalismo y sindicalismo," (Nationalism and syndicalism) *Bandera Argentina* (September 8, 1932).
46 "El nacionalismo aspira a una mayor justicia social," (Nationalism yearns for more social justice) *Combate* (May 15, 1935).
47 "Alianza de la Juventud Nacionalista" *Clarinada*, (March 1938).
48 See Alain Rouquie, *Poder militar y sociedad politica en Argentina*, vol. II (Buenos Aires: Hispanoamerica Ediciones Argentina, S.A., 1986), p. 14.
49 Speech by President Ramirez, *La Prensa* (June 16, 1943), in A. Rouquie, vol. II, p. 13.
50 Marcelo S. Sorondo, pp. 251 and 258–259, cited in A. Ciria, *Parties and Power*, p. 153.
51 See Juan Peron, "Discurso a los estudiantes" (Speech to the students) [December 21, 1945], in J. Peron, *Tres Revoluciones* (Three revolutions) (Buenos Aires: Ed. Escorpion), p. 93.
52 Authors like E. Diaz Araujo: *La conspiracion del 43* (The 43's conspiracy) (Buenos Aires: Ed. La Bastilla, 1971) downplayed the GOU's authoritarian and fascist orientation. However, the documents published by Roger A. Potash in: *Peron y el GOU: Los documentos de una logia secreta* (Peron and the GOU: Documents of a secret lodge) (Buenos Aires: Ed. Sudamericana, 1984) confirm the basic orientations that I have analyzed here. Moreover, it is clear that Peron, probably the most important member of the lodge, was most likely the ideological author of the programmatic documents.
53 "Los capitales extranjeros," (The foreign capital) *Crisol* (June 10, 1943).
54 *Crisol* (June 17, 1943).
55 A. Jauretche, pp. 149–150.
56 "Esto no lo borra nadie," (Nobody can erase this) *Crisol* (June 10, 1943).
57 See Alain Rouquie, vol. II, p. 32.
58 "El Estado regulara las fuerzas de la Production," (The state will manage the productive forces) *Crisol* (October 30, 1943). See also "La Secretaria de Trabajo y Prevision," *El Pampero* (December 1, 1943).
59 Bruno Genta, "La funcion militar en la existencia de la libertad," (The military role for the endurance of freedom) lecture delivered at the Circulo Militar, June 23, 1943, in *Revista Militar* (June 1943), cited in Rouquie, vol. II, p.31. See also Bruno Genta's remarks upon assuming the duties of an intervention at the Universidad del Litoral, Parana, on August 17, 1943, cited in Christian Buchrucker, *Nacionalismo y Peronismo: Argentina en la crisis ideological mundial 1927–1955* (Buenos Aires: Ed. Sudamericana), p. 282; and Bruno Genta, *Acerca de la libertad de enseñar y la enseñanza de la libertad*, (On freedom of teaching and the teaching of freedom) (Buenos Aires: Ed. Dictio, 1976).
60 *La Nacion* (November 8, 1943).

61 On the political conspiracy that brought about Ramirez's resignation, see Alain Rouquie, vol. II, pp. 38–54.
62 "Homenaje a la revolution del 4 de Junio," (Homage to the revolution of June 4th) *Revista Militar* (June 1944), pp. 1057–1114.
63 Interview given by Peron to *El Mercurio* [Chile], reprinted in *La Prensa* (November 12, 1943). See A. Rouquie, vol. II, pp. 39–40.
64 Bruno Jacovella, "Defensa de la Constitucion, la democracia y la ley Saenz Peña," (The defence of the constitution, democracy and the Saenz Peña law) *Nuevo Orden* (January 29, 1944).
65 E. Palacio, "Reaccion y revolucion, quienes representan el progreso politico?" (Reaction and revolution, which of them represents political progress?) *Nuevo Orden* (September 10, 1941).
66 Peron's admiration for fascism, is easily detected. In 1939, Peron was sent to Italy on a study mission by the Argentine army. He studied political economy at the Universities of Torino and Milan, and was impressed by the political and social practices of fascism. Peron never denied that "to guide people there is one technique, the technique of leadership. A technique, an art of military precision. During 1940, I have been taught that in Italy: that people really knew how to command." See the interview Peron gave to Eduardo Galeano, in Eduardo Galeano, *Reportajes* (Montevideo: Tauro, 1967), p. 74. During 1940 Peron visited Germany and the other countries occupied by Nazi Germany. Upon returning to Argentina, he became the ideological mentor of the GOU.
67 Juan Peron, *El pueblo quiere saber de que se trata* (The people want to know what it is all about) (Buenos Aires, 1944), p. 161.
68 Paul Lewis, "Was Peron a Fascist?", *The Journal of Politics*, vol.42, 1–2 (1980), p. 247–8
69 Vicepresidencia de la Nacion, Consejo Nacional de Postguerra, "Ordenamiento economico-social," (The social-economic order) Buenos Aires, Kraft, pp. 55–6 and 68.
70 See Presidencia de la Nacion, "El sindicalismo justicialista a traves del pensamiento de Peron" (A just syndicalism through Peron's thought) (Buenos Aires: Subsecretaria de Informaciones, 1951), pp. 71–86.
71 See Robert D. Crassweller, *Peron and the Enigmas of Argentina* (New York: W.W. Norton and Company, 1988), pp. 193–195.
72 See S. Baily, *Labor Nationalism and Politics in Argentina*, (New Brunswick, N.J.: Rutgers University, 1967), pp. 138, 142.

Part 11

FASCISM IN AFRICA, ASIA AND THE USA

70

THE BERLIN CONNECTION

Patrick J. Furlong

Source: Patrick J. Furlong, *Between Crown and Swastika: The Impact of the Radical Right on the Afrikaner Nationalist Movement in the Fascist Era*, Johannesburg: Witwatersrand University Press, 1991, pp. 70–96.

The historical background to Nazi activity

From the start of the Hitler regime, Germany considered South Africa an eminently suitable target for Nazi propaganda. Here was the weakest link in the chain of self-governing British dominions, with the possible exception of Ireland, which from 1937 on was, in any case, an independent republic with no remaining constitutional ties to the British Crown.[1] The longstanding ties of culture and common ancestry between Germany and the Afrikaners were considered particularly important in influential German circles.[2]

Apart from some French Huguenot background and a small but significant Afro-Asian admixture,[3] the seventeenth- and eighteenth-century settlers who were ancestors of the Afrikaners were as often German as Dutch; by 1700 one-sixth of Cape whites were of German origin. The Dutch East India Company regime encouraged this trend when it stipulated at the end of the seventeenth century that only Dutch or German married men, of good character, could receive land. Lutherans were the only denomination, other than the Dutch Reformed Church, that the Company tolerated (from 1784).[4]

Although, because of company policy to preserve an official Dutch cultural monopoly, the Dutch language and the Dutch Reformed Church emerged dominant in the cultural and religious spheres, the German component in the embryonic Afrikaner society remained a significant part of its heritage. One has only to consider the many prominent Afrikaner families of German origin to establish the importance of that strand simply from a genealogical perspective: alongside the many recognizably Dutch names, such as Van der Merwe or Van Deventer, and the French ones, like Du Plessis, Malan, and De Villiers, there were such notable names as Botha, Kruger, Muller, Hertzog, Vorster, Leibbrandt, and Meyer.

After the second British occupation of the Cape in 1806, German influences continued. A nearly three-thousand-strong contingent of German former soldiers, including some of their families, arrived in 1857. There was also a steady stream of German missionaries, first Protestant but later also Catholic, whose well-organized mission stations came to resemble German towns in their size and comprehensiveness. Some of the better known examples are Hermannsburg and Marrianhill in Natal. Both these missions and concentrated later German settlements such as New Germany, also in Natal, were to provide focal points for the later activities of the external wing of the German Nazi Party, the Auslandsorganisation (AO).[5]

In addition to the high proportion of German ancestry among Afrikaners and the impact of newer German immigrants, the history of Germany's relationship with the nineteenth-century Boer republics, and with Britain, the traditional Afrikaner foe, reinforced the potential for Nazi influence in South Africa. Thomas François Burgers, president of the Transvaal "South African Republic" from 1872 to 1877, and Jan Hendrik Brand, president of the Orange Free State Republic from 1864 to 1889, had both hoped to interest Germany in establishing a foothold at Delagoa Bay (now Maputo, capital of Mozambique), an old trading post held by Portugal, which had long ago ceased to show much concern about developing a more formidable presence in the area. Britain was genuinely concerned that the Germans might become involved in Southern Africa as Boer allies.[6] The German press showed considerable concern at Britain's annexation of the Transvaal in 1877, and after the restoration of independence in 1881, Transvaal president Paul Kruger led a deputation to Europe that met Bismarck and Kaiser Wilhelm II.[7]

By the mid-1890s Germany was becoming increasingly interested in South Africa,[8] spurred on not only by the great wealth of the new Witwatersrand gold mines, but also by the substantial German strategic and economic interest in the region created by the annexation of South-West Africa in 1884. When in January 1896 Leander Starr Jameson failed in his mission to seize the Transvaal for Britain, Kaiser Wilhelm sent his notoriously undiplomatic telegram congratulating Kruger on repulsing the raiders "without summoning the aid of friendly powers," a gesture that confirmed the worst British fears about German intentions in the region.[9] The kaiser's reference in the telegram to preserving Transvaal "independence" furthermore implied rejection of British claims to suzerainty under the 1884 Anglo-Boer London Convention.[10] The Boers took note of the kaiser's sympathy, and a massive arms trade ensued, including 73,000 modern Mauser rifles as well as German heavy artillery to protect the Transvaal against a possible British invasion.[11]

Germany's annexation of South-West Africa and its growing interest in the subcontinent as a whole, particularly St. Lucia Bay in Zululand on the east coast, was a major factor in promoting the British policy from the 1880s of encircling the landlocked Boer republics.[12] This policy could only cement long-term German-Afrikaner sympathies against a common enemy. Britain was not about to permit the turbulent republics to establish a physical link with German territory; the incipient Afrikaner nation in turn was not going to forget quickly this attempt to strangle its only chance of a non-British outlet to the wider world.

When war came in 1899 between Britain and the Boers, however, despite overwhelmingly anti-British sentiment in the European press as a whole, the kaiser's hands were tied for the moment by an alliance system that threatened a far greater conflict than Germany was as yet ready to fight,[13] and the republics were forced to stand alone against the British Empire. Short of actually going to war against Britain, Germany had been quite willing to take concrete steps to demonstrate its support of the Boers, as with the sending of a cruiser to Delago Bay in 1894 to emphasize to the British its interests, as the official German explanation put it, "both on the coast and in the Transvaal."[14]

A full-fledged war was something else, but there was now an historical basis for supporting Germany in the future when it in turn came to blows with Britain. This helps to explain the refusal of so many Afrikaners to support the South African war effort in 1914 and the widespread Afrikaner sympathy in the thirties and forties for Germany when the latter, humiliated at Versailles just as the Boers had been at the close of the Anglo-Boer War, sought to turn the tables on the victors of 1918. The Nazi leaders in Berlin recognized the possibility of such a sympathetic hearing among their distant African cousins, and also the potential for developing this sentiment with a view to undermining British interests in the region.

Within months of Hitler's accession to power, a strong anti-Semitic movement had taken hold in South Africa. Its Nazi source of inspiration was evident from the start. Swastikas began to adorn its uniforms, banners, and the title page of the Grey-shirts' official organ, *Die Waarheid*. The provenance of the literature with which the country was now swamped was equally unmistakable. Leslie Rubin, a longtime student of Nazi influence on Afrikaner nationalism, recalls reading one anti-Semitic pamphlet during the 1930s in Durban which, although in Afrikaans, had been printed in Erfurt, Germany.[15]

German interest in South Africa had a very personal point of focus, since the first leader of the South African Nazis, Hermann Bohle, had taught at the University of Cape Town before returning to Germany to take up an important consulting position for the Nazi Party. His South African-educated son, Ernst, had returned to Germany and rose to become head of the sprawling Auslandsorganisation in Berlin, which coordinated and led all party activities overseas.[16] Ernst Bohle's organization controlled the diplomatic representatives of Germany abroad, since the Foreign Office professionals themselves were considered by the Nazi Party bosses to be too independent-minded.[17] One consequence was that the official and the real hierarchies of power in the German diplomatic corps were by no means identical. For instance, the apparently lowly Lierau, the consul-general in the South-West African capital of Windhoek, was actually responsible for all Nazi interests in southern Africa.[18]

The Nazis's activities in the subcontinent had two dimensions. One was the creation of a power base among German nationals and naturalized Union citizens of German descent, many of whom, like the family of Hertzog's defense minister in the United Party government, Oswald Pirow, were now assimilated into the Afrikaner population. The second dimension of Nazi activity was the promotion of the Nazi cause among non-Germans, particularly Nationalists. In the first regard the Nazi campaign was most thoroughgoing, but their propaganda activities in promotion among non-Germans were by no means ineffective either. The growth of interest in the anti-Semitic issue was just the most visible example of the effectiveness of this effort.

The Nazis and the German-speaking community

The central focus of Nazi activity in South Africa was the German-speaking community. Hermann Bohle's South African wing of the Nazi Party was just the peak of a subterranean network of considerable dimensions, which went beyond the organizations typically associated with the Nazi movement, such as the Brownshirts and the SS. In Pretoria the Nazis rapidly gained control of the *Deutsch-Afrikaner*, the most important German-language newspaper in the country. Its editor, Wilhelm Stark, assissted the German legation as an agent of the Auslandsorganisation and reported to Berlin cases such as those of German pastors who refused to accept national socialist doctrines. According to Otto von Strahl, who had served as a German diplomat in South Africa in the late thirties, families in Germany were punished for their relatives' views.[19] The *Deutsch-Afrikaner* and several lesser German-language newspapers functioned both as key propaganda organs within the German-speaking community and as sorting houses for the flood of propaganda from Germany.[20]

Von Strahl's lengthy wartime report on Nazi press activities in South Africa, written for Interior Minister Harry Lawrence, describes in considerable detail the role and nature of the *Deutsch-Afrikaner* as a Nazi organ geared to the German-speaking immigrant community. This newspaper made regular use of semiofficial essays on Nazi foreign policy from the German Politico-Diplomatic Correspondence Service, an agency attached to the German Foreign Office which attempted to put Hitler's expansionist moves in the best light while attacking Britain and the Soviet Union.[21]

In addition to printed leaflets praising the accomplishments of the Third Reich in matters such as social welfare and technology, which the Auslandsorganisation sent from its National Socialist Service for Foreign Papers, the *Deutsch-Afrikaner* received numerous photographs of German personalities and events, as for example the 1936 Berlin Olympic Games, Hitler's involvement in the German "Winter Relief" fund, and functions held by the Nazi recreation organization, "Strength Through Joy." The *Deutsch-Afrikaner* was expected not only to publish these photographs, but also to distribute them among the South African press and among individuals sympathetic to Nazism or with potential for such sympathy.[22]

Besides publishing a wide variety of material from Berlin, Stark's newspaper gave extensive coverage to Nazi functions in South Africa: Nazi Party branch activities, Winter Relief Fund events, Nazi youth movement gatherings, Nazi fund-raising bazaars, and celebrations whenever German ships arrived in Union harbors. The financing of this key Nazi publicity organ was at least partly local: Von Strahl noted that companies owned by German-speakers were intimidated by local Nazi Party representatives into advertising in and subscribing to the paper.[23]

Another key role of the *Deutsch-Afrikaner* was to promote a militantly anti-British and anti-Smuts political attitude among German-speakers and Afrikaner nationalists who, if they could read German, would have found exhortations to look to Germany for friendship, to adopt anti-Semitism, and to support a pro-German policy in South-West Africa. On all these counts the newspaper questioned the policies of the Hertzog-Smuts government and the attitudes it seemed to represent among a majority of white South Africans. Thus an article in the 8 November 1934 issue, entitled "We Utter a Warning," contained the following passage (the translation is by Von Strahl):

> Isolation means becoming Anglicized to the Afrikaans nation. It would become stunted and demoralized and only that nation of Helots would remain of which General Sir Ian Hamilton spoke recently. If the Africander nation wants to preserve its originality against British culture, it cannot forego friendly relations with other nations, and who else would primarily deserve consideration in this respect as an unselfish friend, if not Germany? Sensible Africanders have therefore always set value on maintaining friendly relations with the German nation.[24]

On 22 November 1934 another article set forth similar ideas more bluntly:

> A country which through the mouths of its responsible statesmen pampers Jews and orientals [the latter reference, probably to Indians, is puzzling in light of the lack of any government attempts to improve their position] and eulogizes them as being the most valuable citizens, and at the same time ill-treats its German blood relations in South West Africa [a reference to the banning of the Nazi Party in that territory], is suffering from racial softening of its bones. . . . The teutonic culture whose champion in Africa the

Afrikaans nation proudly professes to be, can only be developed with Teutons. The task is so tremendous that it needs the collaboration of all the racially related teutonic nations whose colonial tradition is rooted in Africa.[25]

The German South African community was indoctrinated at every level: through not only newspapers but also the German-language schools, German pastors and priests, and front organizations such as "reading circles," through which Nazi literature was disseminated. Several teachers in the German schools, and at least two principals, belonged to the South African branch of the National Socialist Teachers' Organization (Nationalsozialistische Lehrerbund or NSLB), a Nazi professional organization.[26]

The Lehrerbund, which aimed at educating German-speaking youth according to the principles of national socialism, held regular conferences in the various regions of the Union, and its leaders and members who were school principals were expected to provide detailed reports to a central "Ausland Section" office of the Lehrebund in Berlin on matters such as the influence of German-language schools in the local German-speaking community, the percentage of German-speaking children attending these schools, and activities of alumni. In January 1939 the Ausland Section began its own magazine, *Der Deutsche Erzieher im Auslande* (The German Educator Abroad), to which all members were required to subscribe, and were encouraged to send contributions on themes like racial doctrines, world philosophy, character building, and national politics.[27]

Although, according to a Lehrerbund circular dated 8 March 1939 detailing a new membership fee structure, there were only fifteen active members in the Union, these members came from at least eight schools in diverse centers like Durban, Cape Town, Johannesburg, Hermannsburg, and East London. It is possible that, like the party, the Lehrerbund was intended to function as an elite body through which a few committed Nazis could exercise influence over other German-speakers in the workplace and in the local community.[28]

Professional groups such as the Lehrerbund fell under an umbrella organization, the Verband Deutsche Berufsgruppen (Association of German Vocational Groups), an arm of the German Labor Front (Deutsch Arbeitsfront or DAF).[29] The Labor Front was the largest of the Nazi front organizations operating in southern Africa. Such associations were crucial to Nazi activity, because German-speakers who were ineligible for or uninterested in party membership could be pressured into joining less overtly Nazi groups. According to Otto von Strahl, a tremendous effort was made to persuade all German-speakers in employment of any kind to join the DAF, which was ostensibly intended to provide a means of overcoming friction between the various classes of Germans, for instance in labor disputes in German-owned companies, through arbitration and discussion. Members paid a subscription fee in return for which they received benefits in the event of unemployment, illness, or death.

But, as the evidence collected by Von Strahl shows, the Labor Front had a much more important underlying function: it permitted the Nazis to enjoy some degree of influence over a much larger proportion of German-speakers in South Africa and South-West Africa than would have been possible through regular party structures. In each country where the Labor Front operated a reliable Nazi Party member was delegated to exercise disciplinary control over those belonging to the DAF,[30] and worked directly under the senior political official of the Nazi Auslandsorganisation in that territory.[31] At the local level, each individual Labor Front branch was headed by the leader of the Nazi Party branch in that area or by a deputy nominated by him. To complete the picture of efficient party control, Labor Front members were required to attend monthly meetings and other occasional gatherings, to cooperate with the front leadership, and to act "in a manner becoming of a German," in the words of a 1935 party directive.[32] Thus the Nazi policy of *Gleichschaltung* (roughly equivalent to "bringing into line") of German-speakers was effected at the southern tip of Africa just as in Germany itself.

Afrikaner leaders and German exchanges

A stream of visitors flowed back and forth between Germany and South Africa. The Deutsche Akademie of Munich, a key cultural organization for the promotion of the interchange of ideas between Germany and other countries, had twenty-three members on its South African committee in Germany, compared with twenty-one for the entire United States. Related organizations were the Goethe Institute, which held classes at Pretoria and Kingwilliamstown in the Eastern Cape, and the Kultuurraad (Cultural Council) in the Orange Free State capital, Bloemfontein.[33]

Trade between Germany and the Union was also a priority. Helmut Schacht, the powerful president of the Reichsbank in Germany and Hitler's top economist, stressed the "ties of blood" between the two countries in a 1936 speech at the launching of the new vessel of the Woermann shipping line, significantly named the *Pretoria*. He noted that Germany was South Africa's second-best customer, outranked only by Great Britain. Excluding gold exports, no less than 14 percent of Union exports went to Germany, 42 percent to Britain.[34] In order to encourage this practical relationship, a German economic delegation that toured South Africa in late 1937 and early 1938 provided five bursaries for young South Africans to pursue studies in Germany.[35]

Educational exchanges of this sort contributed to the intellectual formation of a generation of leading Nationalists. They helped to create a climate receptive to German propaganda in South Africa, and encouraged a new kind of Afrikaner youth culture, shaped by student leaders and teachers who had been exposed to fascist ideas abroad.

An important source of cultural cooperation and scholarly exchanges was the German-Afrikaans Cultural Union, under the presidency of J. F. J. ("Hans") van Rensburg,[36] an Afrikaner who served as secretary of justice under Minister Jan Smuts in the Fusion government and then administrator of the Orange Free State until the outbreak of war. Like Pirow, a powerful minister in the United Party government, Van Rensburg was both a devoted adherent of Prime Minister Hertzog and an admirer of the Hitler regime. His admiration for Hitler's new Germany is evident from the Nazi response when he visited Germany in 1936. A certain Herr Dieckhoff at the German Foreign Office wrote to General Smuts that his government had been glad to receive so important a guest: "All the more as in his case we have made the acquaintance of a personality of great value whose fundamental knowledge of the German character and lively interest in conditions in Germany we especially know how to appreciate."[37]

Van Rensburg was a Hertzogite of unusually Radical Rightist inclination. He was also the president of the Afrikaanse Nasionale Studentebond (Afrikaner National Student Union or ANS), founded by Piet Meyer in 1933 at Bloemfontein in order to provide an Afrikaner nationalist alternative to the "liberal" National Union of South African Students, which was dominated by English-speakers.[38] The Nazis watched Afrikaner student activities with interest, noting, for instance, their support for neutrality in the event of a war between Britain and Germany.[39] Bruno Stiller, the leader of the Nazi Party in South Africa, commented appreciatively on an address given in Stellenbosch in April 1937 by Van Rensburg to the Studentebond in which he discussed his impressions of Hitler's Reich:

> The Administrator particularly emphasized that national socialism meant a synthesis of nationalism and socialism and that through this synthesis Germany was being saved from the great danger of communism. The fact that Van Rensburg has frankly and freely upheld national socialism as an example to the Afrikaners, not only to the German-Afrikaans Cultural Union, but also before the student body of Stellenbosch, from which the future leader of Afrikanerdom will be drawn, shows how lasting are the impressions which he gained on his visit to Germany.[40]

Berlin retained an interest in several potential allies among Afrikaner nationalists, including Malan's party, but those connected with the ANS seemed to be among their most promising possibilities. Apart from Van Rensburg, the most important of these individuals were Piet Meyer and Nico Diederichs.

Meyer would become chairman of the influential secret and militantly pro-Afrikaner nationalist Afrikaner Broederbond (Afrikaner Union of Brothers, or AB) in 1960 and he headed the state-controlled South African Broadcasting Corporation (SABC) for most of the 1960s and 1970s. In the early 1930s he was offered a Rhodes scholarship to study at Oxford, but his uncompromising nationalism kept him from accepting it, electing to do a doctorate in philosophy and education at the Free University in Amsterdam instead, and to attend occasional courses in Germany as well.[41]

The other founding father of the ANS, Diederichs, studied at the graduate level in Germany in Munich, Cologne, and Berlin, apart from his main doctoral program in philosophy at Leiden in the Netherlands.[42] Diederichs, like Meyer, would later head the Broederbond, but he reached equally elevated heights in office as longtime finance minister under B. J. Vorster after 1966 and he crowned his career as state president of South Africa from 1975 to 1978.

Hendrik Verwoerd, prime minister from 1958 to 1966 and one of the most powerful figures in the Transvaal National Party from the late thirties, also studied in Germany, in Hamburg, Leipzig, and Berlin, preceding Meyer and Diederichs.[43]

There can be little doubt that these decades were of particular importance to the intellectual formation of these men. Professor Walter Markov, Emeritus, of Leipzig University, informed Leslie Rubin that the Nazi Party was beginning to gain a powerful hold over many students at this university as early as the mid-twenties.[44] Both Meyer and Diederichs were profoundly influenced by the antiliberal German Romantic mood, modeled after ideas of the early nineteenth-century philosopher Johann Fichte, the fashion at German universities at the time. It upheld the nation and Volk as the highest ideal of human existence. South African scholars have generally described the variant of this philosophy adopted by Afrikaner intellectuals such as Diederichs or Meyer as "neo-Fichteanism," a practice I follow in this study.[45]

At a much more practical level, the ANS leadership (Verwoerd did not belong, but many of his views were similar) was encouraged by Nazi cultural organizations to learn about national socialism at first hand. Meyer was invited in 1934 to lead the first Studentebond tour group to Europe, and he later recalled how excited he and his colleagues were to learn skiing in the Alps with none other than Rudolf Hess, Hitler's chief of staff, and to see Hitler himself close up.[46]

There was a more serious purpose to this tour, since the Studentebond took the opportunity to forge links between these South Africans and a number of German organizations, including the National Socialist Students' Association, the Colonial Society (which worked for the return of South-West Africa to Germany), Hitler Youth, and the German Academic Exchange Service.[47]

A series of Studentebond-sponsored tours of Germany followed. For young Afrikaners, with their parents' bitter memories of the devastation of the Anglo-Boer War, it must have been impressive to see how a nation in misery had succeeded in reclaiming its former eminence. In 1937–1938 no fewer than eighteen Studentebond members participated in the Berlin University celebrations honoring the fifth anniversary of Hitler's accession to power. Everywhere such groups were received warmly and feted by representatives of the various Reich departments.[48]

Senior ANS representatives received even more lavish treatment. Van Rensburg, of course, not only had the opportunity to meet top Nazis like Goering and Goebbels, but was also granted an interview with Hitler.[49] Diederichs, although strictly a private citizen, unlike Van Rensburg, gave a lecture in Goering's palatial "Aviation House" in Berlin. It was attended by many top Nazis, as reported in the *Deutsch-Afrikaner*. Diederichs's lecture must have been a rather dull affair, dealing as it did with the constitutional options open to the Union, but it was received with hearty applause. He did not use the opportunity to launch an attack on Britain or to advance his own political ideas.[50]

Diederichs was privately more forthright in expressing his views to Nazi officials. According to a transcript from captured Foreign Office records, in a two-hour discussion in May 1939 with Herr Kirschner, a Foreign Office official in Berlin, Diederichs confided his doubts about Malan's ability to transform the Purified National Party into an instrument for fundamental change. He was convinced that the old leader was burdened by traditional liberal-democratic institutions. A new party name was needed, as was a clear program resting on a broader policy than anti-Semitism. Diederichs felt that the problem with the National Party lay not only with Malan: "Very many of its currently leading members are still too extensively caught up in democratic ideas. Consequently, a far-reaching change of leadership becomes a prerequisite for a full-scale Nationalist takeover. Hope lies with the youth and all in the Nationalist camp are unanimous that every newborn Boer will one day become a Nationalist. Therefore nobody doubts the final victory."[51]

In addition to the promise of the youth, there was also the potential inherent in the Broederbond:

> ... the main concern should be the education of experts who would then be in a position to take over the government by virtue not only of their convictions but also of their professional training. The Broederbond will in the future devote itself to this task, starting with the smallest matters. With the request that I keep this strictly confidential, Prof. Diederichs then told me that he had recently taken over the leadership of the Broederbond. According to him, the Broederbond was a secret organization to which it was possible to be admitted only after a thorough investigation. He maintained that the goal of the organization was to infiltrate the whole country,

especially the leadership, and in this way to take over the whole state apparatus from within.[52]

Diederichs's own sympathies were made clear in the following passage from Kirschner's transcript of the interview: "... he did not believe that the inner strength of the National Party would suffice to form a government according to the model of the authoritarian states. But in the long run only such a government could ensure the position of South Africa south of the equator."[53]

Diederichs's doubts about the ability of the National Party to promote radical nationalism in South Africa were reflected still more broadly in the former South African Nazi leader Hermann Bohle's opinion of South Africans. Since his return to Germany in the mid-thirties, he had become the influential senior expert in Berlin on South African affairs. According to a German Foreign Office memorandum by Bohle, he noted that none other than Eric Louw, a South African diplomat in Paris and later a prominent Nationalist cabinet minister, "the so-called Streicher of South Africa," as Bohle put it in praise of his anti-Semitic stance, had returned to the Union to stand for Parliament in 1938 as a Malanite. Yet behind the scenes, Louw had written to Malan's archenemy, Hertzog, asking whether he could have his post back as "minister in Paris" in case he lost the election! Bohle wrote scathingly: "This lack of character is typically South African, hence in Germany one should have little faith in all South Africans and only allow oneself to be guided by absolute facts."[54]

The Nazis' propaganda network in South Africa

Distrust of this kind did not prevent the Nazis from pouring a fortune in propaganda material into South Africa. Two agencies were particularly important in this regard: the Hamburg Fichtebund (Fichte Union) and the Weltdienst (World Service), an agency that published a weekly bulletin in eight languages. The Fichtebund, founded in 1935 to disprove German "war guilt" in the First World War, sent more than five million leaflets abroad in its first year. Much of the material sent to South Africa was written in excellent Afrikaans, which suggests how important this audience was thought to be. The shipments were often sent into the country wrapped in other merchandise, or posted directly to individuals. Dutch Reformed clergymen received many of these pamphlets on the "Jew-Bolshevist" threat and the achievements of the Nazi regime.[55]

The Weltdienst specialized in what it regarded as Jewish machinations; it charged among other things that Jews killed Christian babies for ritual purposes. The bulletin had a still more useful purpose, the promotion of anti-Semitic organizations around the world. Advertisements from shirt movements everywhere were featured regularly; their activities in South

Africa received extensive coverage. Roosevelt and Smuts were referred to as Jews; the parliamentary system of government itself was also described as "Jewish."[56]

Such an avalanche of propaganda could well have had an influence, particularly on those with a limited educational background, those isolated in remote areas, the youth, and the poor. This may help to explain why there was so much pressure for action against the Jews from rank-and-file Nationalists. A grave crisis of faith in liberal-democratic institutions and values ensued. German propaganda fed on the discontent of whites least affected by the post-Depression recovery and on the anger of militant Afrikaner youth. The Nazis used Nationalist bogeys like Smuts and "Communism" for maximum effect.

Yet Hermann Bohle, three months before the war began, expressed an underlying unease about the Nationalists, although it was the largest rightwing political organization in South Africa: "In general no unity reigns in the camp of Malan. Malan is moreover a genuine democrat, who for egotistical reasons has adopted anti-Semitism. He is by vocation a Calvinist pastor."[57]

Since Malan himself seemed so unpromising a client leader, if the Nazis were to have any real impact on the Afrikaner nationalist movement, it seems to me, their only practical option was to subvert the sections of the grassroots Nationalist following most sympathetic to Radical Right ideas, and thus force the apparently softheaded elders of the party, like Malan, to make the necessary changes.

It is true that the Nazis did also have potential support among some of the Hertzogite ex-Nationalists in the United Party, but the coalition nature of that party, including so many English-speakers, limited its potential value for developing a "Berlin-Pretoria axis" on the lines of the relations Germany enjoyed with Mussolini's Italy, Imperial Japan, or right-wing regimes in Europe such as those in Hungary and Bulgaria. Nevertheless, there were a few striking cases of individual pro-German sentiment in the Hertzogite faction.

In addition to Hans van Rensburg's contact with Nazi officials during his 1936 trip to Germany, Oswald Pirow, Hertzog's minister of defense, who not only was the son of German immigrants but also had attended Kiel University in northern Germany,[58] made several visits to the fascist countries during the thirties. Pirow held discussions with Mussolini, Franco, and the Portuguese strongman, Salazar, and even met with Hitler at the Führer's private retreat at Berchtesgaden,[59] inciting unfavorable reaction about the purpose of such meetings.

For instance, in November 1938 the South African writer Sarah Gertrude Millin, a woman who enjoyed a wide range of contacts in political life, and a champion of her own Jewish community, noted in a letter to Smuts that the British politician Ramsay MacDonald had expressed his concern at Pirow's visit to Germany earlier that year; she added that in light of this visit England did not trust Pirow.[60] Jan Hendrik Hofmeyr, an unusually outspoken liberal United Party member of Parliament (for Johannesburg North) and until September 1938 a minister holding a variety of portfolios in Hertzog's cabinet, concurred with these sentiments in a letter written to her the next month: "I don't think Pirow has done himself much good in South Africa by his peregrinations through Europe. He is undoubtedly more distrusted than ever before."[61]

Hertzog himself, despite his own moderate attitude toward the British, refused to believe the stories of Nazi atrocities. Hofmeyr noted in a letter to Sarah Millin that Hertzog, who never had much patience with his strong opinions about racial prejudice, "steadfastly refuses to believe that the Germans, in whom he still has a pathetic confidence, really are ill-treating the Jews!"[62] Hofmeyr, whose anti-Nazi reputation was such that Berlin instructed the German consul in Johannesburg not to attend a banquet at which Hofmeyr was to speak,[63] was so convinced that Hertzog would pay no attention to any protest of his about Nazi Germany that he decided, against his own better judgment, not to speak to Hertzog about stopping Pirow's 1938 trip.[64] As he informed Sarah Millin in June 1938, when he was still a cabinet member, although he wanted desperately to express his outrage at Nazi treatment of the Jews, the response of the Hertzog government would be a foregone conclusion: "Sometimes I wonder whether I should not be gloriously indiscreet and say exactly what I think about Hitler's policy in this respect. Then no doubt the P.M. would send an apology to Germany and I would have to resign."[65]

But, despite Hertzog's sympathetic attitude to Germany, his advanced years must have limited his usefulness to the Nazis. If Hitler were to need an ally among the leading white political parties in South Africa, it seems that, even if Malan was an unlikely potential local führer, Malan's party, unfettered by the avowedly pro-British Smuts wing of Hertzog's United Party, and both openly anti-Semitic and anti-British in its rhetoric, must have been a far more promising candidate for a possible connection in the event of a war in Europe.

For such reasons, no doubt, Nationalist politics was carefully monitored from Berlin. Attempts at cooperation between the Greyshirts and the Malanites were considered natural. In October 1937 in a lengthy anonymous report from Cape Town to Berlin detailing the preparations for the 1938 general election, a local German agent did concede that "the fundamentals of both parties are radically different [*grundverschiedene*]."[66] But the report noted that, when considered in the light of a prospective electoral alliance between the equally dissimilar United Party and the small, left-wing Labor party, "the natural assumption of a rapprochement between the Malan Party and the Greyshirts is quite obvious. Both stand in honest and open opposition to the government, both retain the Jewish Question and Bolshevism as an essentially crucial element in their programs, and both want to secure the independence of the South African money market from international Jewry by establishing a purely South African National Bank."[67] The report showed that to the Nazi official mind the prospect of an arrangement between the Malanites and the Greyshirts was most reminiscent of the earlier similarly largely tactical alliance between Hitler and the more traditionally conservative nationalist, Alfred Hugenberg, in Germany: "While the National Party corresponds in essence with the earlier German National Party, the South African National Party (Grey-shirts) is thoroughly fascist in orientation."[68] Indeed the Nazi records on South Africa were littered with references to the Malanites as the "National Opposition," a term used in Germany to denote the Old Right of the Weimar Republic.[69]

The analogy could only evoke memories of how nationalists in Germany had assisted in bringing Hitler to power in a right-wing coalition, believing him to be easily manageable, only to find that they had been quietly removed from the political scene within the year.[70] That was a scenario of which the Afrikaner Nationalists of Malan were only too well aware, as their correspondence with the Greyshirts showed. As F. C. Erasmus noted in writing to Greyshirt secretary Willie Laubscher, Weichardt's aim of a "united volk state" (*eenheidsvolkstaat*) would mean the destruction of all parties, including its allies, because such a state could only come about "when all other parties either have willingly disbanded or have been forcibly compelled to do so. That it would happen voluntarily is unthinkable under the democratic system. Therefore only the second alternative remains." Nor did Erasmus accept the Greyshirts' position that they were not really a political party and that they also intended eventually to disappear as a separate political group: "That it in practice means the forced liquidation [*uitskakeling*] of all political parties besides your own is confirmed by your acknowledgment that in the five years of the existing German 'united volk state,' the National Socialists have always continued to exist."[71] Such a recurring nightmare dictated Malan's attitude to national socialism throughout the next few years, particularly in his often stormy wartime relationship with the Ossewabrandwag. It seems that the only practical response to such a threat was for the Nationalists to use the New Right without, in turn, becoming used.

The Nazis misjudged the true nature of the Purified Nationalists if they saw their relationship to the Greyshirts as mirroring that of Hugenberg's Nationalists to themselves. The ultranationalism, anti-Semitism, and anti-communism of the Hugenberg bloc was certainly shared by the Malanites, but while Hugenberg's support was drawn from the German upper classes,[72] Malan had no such constituency. The Purified Nationalist following itself more nearly coincided with that of the Nazis: young Afrikaners, some workers, small farmers and businessmen, schoolteachers, and other petit bourgeois elements. Only in the Cape did Malan have support of more affluent Afrikaans-speaking farmers.[73] If anything, South African Nationalists were more concerned than the Nazis themselves to reach out to the poor and oppressed of their own people, as "the champion of the worker and the farmer."[74]

Although the history of the Purified Nationalists shows an ability to build an ever-expanding support base that rapidly eclipsed the constituency of the pro-Nazi shirt movements in South Africa, the Hertzog-Smuts alliance drew a far larger proportion of support from wealthy capitalists, comparable in this regard to Hugenberg's Nationalists, than did the Malanites. The Hugenberg analogy is therefore quite inadequate, although useful for indicating what the Nazis *thought* the Nationalists in South Africa represented. As the future was to show, this was not the only instance in which Berlin misjudged Malan and his party.

The intellectual impact of fascism on Afrikaner nationalism

If the relationship of Afrikaner nationalism to the New Right was far more complicated than a simple analogy to that between traditional and radical nationalists in Germany, the influence of Radical Right thought on individual leading Afrikaner nationalists was nevertheless far more clearly identifiable. Those who had gone abroad for graduate studies, most notably Meyer and Diederichs, drank deeply of the intellectual waters available there.

But other important younger Afrikaner thinkers had had similar experiences, among these, Geoffrey Cronjé, professor of sociology at Pretoria University College and one of the architects of the apartheid ideology; J. Keyter, professor of sociology at Bloemfontein University College; and Albert Hertzog, son of the prime minister and a prominent Broederbond leader and rightwing labor organizer.[75] Hertzog, who mobilized Afrikaner workers for the Nationalist cause in the thirties and early forties, in the sixties was to become identified with the extreme nationalist wing in John Vorster's government.

The German Romantic philosophy espoused by these academics upheld an authoritarian and idealist type of nationalism, rooted in the thought of Johann Fichte (1762–1814), J. D. Herder (1744–1803), and Friedrich Schleiermacher (1768–1834). The key document in this tradition is Fichte's *Addresses to the German Nation* (1807–1808), an emotional series of appeals to the fragmented German people to unite in order to liberate themselves from Napoleon's rule. Fichte obviously struck a chord in the German-speaking world, because in 1809 the Prussian authorities appointed him a professor at the University of Berlin.[76] At the heart of his philosophy were the Volk (people—in the ethnic sense) and the nation. Hitler was far less concerned with statism and Volk-worship itself than with a cult that equated Volk and nation with himself;[77] thus Nazism, in this sense, was much more radical than any previous German philosophy, however ardently nationalist, and more radical than Afrikaner radical nationalism, in the main.

Yet Alfred Rosenberg (1893–1946), an important early influence on Hitler's thinking and the official Nazi Party "philosopher,"[78] made the Volk and its glorification a central concept in his ideological scheme. Rosenberg, whose *völkisch* nationalism was closely tied to his hatred of Jews as racial outsiders, was profoundly affected by the German Romantic tradition, with what historian Robert Pois calls its "glorification of the mysterious and the abstruse and its elevation of intuition, emotion and nationalism."[79] Fichte combined such emphases with the exaltation of German supremacy over other peoples and a marked dislike of the nobility and the Jews.[80]

Such ideas were appealing to many in the new generation of Afrikaner intellectuals. Excluded from access to the corridors of power by Hertzog's merger with the English-speaking elite, led by Smuts, they were suspicious of the established classes. And many shared a dislike of the Jews, perhaps because of the heavy representation of the latter in the professions and in business. Diederichs is a case in point, despite the sociologist Dunbar Moodie's denial that he was anti-Semitic.[81] In the interview with German Foreign Office representative Herr Kirschner discussed earlier, Diederichs responded to a question regarding government successes in recent by-elections by stating, in the words of this report, that "the United Party essentially had solely to thank the votes of the Jews for these seats."[82]

The ideas of Diederichs and of Piet Meyer are worthy of some elaboration, partly because of the positions of power both men ultimately held in the Afrikaner establishment, and partly because of the considerable influence they were already able to wield in the thirties through the ANS, the Broederbond, and other extraparliamentary groups.

Diederichs's doctoral dissertation, written in German at Leiden University, entitled *Vom Leiden und Dulden* (On Suffering and Patience), stressed the Romantic themes of pain, the irrational, and ways of overcoming suffering. In it he explicitly rejected liberal rationalism, which he hated passionately, focusing instead on the historical attitude toward suffering not only in Judaism and Christianity, as well as in ancient Greece, but rather more exotically in Brahmanism and Buddhism. He also treated these themes as they appeared in Schopenhauer and Nietzsche, philosophers whose work was diligently mined by Nazi academics.[83]

Such a palette of ideas inspired Diederichs's most famous work, published in 1936, *Nasionalisme as Lewensbeskouing en Sy Verhouding tot Internasionalisme* (Nationalism as a Worldview and Its Relationship to Internationalism). This work explicitly addressed the problem of a politically divided Afrikanerdom by an appeal to "a more lasting and noble terrain in which all of us, despite political division, can still be one."[84] This appeal to rise above the merely natural world of fratricidal intra-Afrikaner political strife attacked Bolshevist and liberal cosmopolitanism in favor of a nationalism that went much further than liberal-national aspirations to a common political heritage and institutions: "Only in the national as the most total, most inclusive human community can man realize himself fully. The nation is the fulfilment of the individual life." And further on: "To work for the realization of the national calling is to work for the realization of God's plan. Service to the nation is therefore part of my service to God."[85]

This is not the language of traditional Afrikaner Calvinist nationalism. Afrikaner heroes such as Paul Kruger would have found such views dangerously close to idolizing the state. H. G. ("Bram") Stoker, a leading Afrikaner philosopher at the University of Potchefstroom, expressed such a concern in reviewing Diederichs's book in *Die Volksblad* in April 1935, writing: "By placing my nation above me and God above the nation, [Diederichs] attributes to the nation at least in part that which belongs to God alone, and in so doing he deifies the nation."[86] Nor is it the language of the twentieth-century variety of neo-Calvinism, so influential among modern Afrikaner academics and first promoted by the conservative turn-of-the-century Dutch theologian and politician Abraham Kuyper, with its respect for traditional institutions and a clear sense of the boundaries among the various spheres of life, family, church, and state.[87] Here Diederichs was breaking away from the Calvinist intellectual heritage of the Afrikaner universities; his views were a distinct part of the worldview of the new Germany.

Such ideas of the Studentebond leadership were extremely controversial on Afrikaner campuses, and never accepted in unadulterated form by the broader Afrikaner public.[88] Yet the Studentebond leadership became increasingly powerful in the Afrikaner Broederbond, which did happily accommodate at least a modified form of Romantic neo-Fichteanism, blending its secular nationalism with a respect for Calvinist sensibilities.[89]

It is not surprising that the Broederbond did so. Its stronghold lay in the Transvaal, its original base in the twenties, where Afrikaner nationalism was most deeply fractured. After most Afrikaners, especially farmers, had gone over to the Hertzogite Fusionists in 1933 and 1934,[90] the Broederbond rapidly filled the political vacuum left there by the weak position of the Purified Nationalists. After the loss of the Vrededorp seat in 1938, there was only one Malanite member of Parliament in this province, J. G. Strijdom.[91] The Transvaal Purified Nationalist finances were in a desperate state until the late thirties, and the party there was riven by internal personality and policy differences.[92] Under these circumstances, the message of Diederichs, Meyer, and others proved a real boon to those who sought to fill the space left by the Purified Party and sought ultimately to bring Afrikaners together under the name, preferably, of the Purified Party itself. Staunch Potchefstroom neo-Calvinists who dominated the Broederbond Executive during the thirties, men like Professors L. J. du Plessis, J. C. van Rooy, and Bram Stoker,[93] therefore accommodated to a modified form of the Studentebond doctrines of Meyer and Diederichs.

Diederichs's message was addressed to specific concerns not unlike those facing the pre-Hitler German "National Opposition." Both countries confronted the fragmentation of the volk into hostile factions and classes, the poorest of which were increasingly vulnerable to the slogans of the internationalist left, which derided nationalism as a capitalist trick to divide the workers of the world. Diederichs attacked communism on the grounds of its antinationalism:

> Its striving is not to protect and strengthen the natural unity of a volk, but to break it down and destroy it; not to advance harmonious cooperation between groups and classes in the volk, but to drive these groups and classes against each other in a spirit of hate and enmity.... The highest task which according to Communism rests on the worker of every state, is to tear himself from his natural bond to other parts of his volk and to unite himself in a mythical world-proletariat in the struggle against his own fatherland and compatriots.[94]

Diederichs's message was promulgated not only to academics but also to Afrikaners; several chapters of his treatise against communism appeared in the popular journal *Die Huisgenoot*.[95]

Nor were the Nationalists entirely unconnected with the propaganda activities of the ANS leadership. Both of Diederichs's principal works were published by Nasionale Pers, the Malan-controlled company that produced the Cape Party's *Die Burger*. In collaboration with Van Rensburg and others, Diederichs brought out a short polemical account of current political movements, published by the other major Nationalist publishing house Voortrekkerpers, which was responsible for *Die Transvaler*.[96]

Piet Meyer, who spent much of his time as secretary of various Afrikaner nationalist organizations (see next chapter), produced even more complex theoretical systems. When Meyer first returned from his studies abroad at the beginning of 1936, he still displayed the concerns of a neo-Fichtean nationalist such as Diederichs, for instance working to mobilize Afrikaners against the dual threats of class conflict, which he, like most Afrikaner nationalists, saw as inspired by communism, and of the United Party philosophy of conciliation between Afrikaner and English-speaker. To achieve this end, he strove to unite, in a new Afrikaner Nasionale Kultuurraad (National Cultural Council) not only middle-class Afrikaners involved in cultural, educational, and church organizations, but also Afrikaner workers. Through such organizations Afrikaner workers would, he hoped, be detached from leftist labor groups and be organized into "Christian National" labor unions, financial backing for which would come from a National Council of Trustees (Nasionale Raad van Trustees), which he, Diederichs, and Albert Hertzog were instrumental in founding in October 1936 in Johannesburg.[97] Thus, as in Fascist-ruled Italy and Nazi-ruled Germany, where employer and employee belonged to a single umbrella body in the interest of national unity, the worker would be co-opted into the national movement and the class divide would be bridged by organizations stressing a common nationhood or ethnicity rather than class conflict.

Although Meyer's concerns were therefore more practical than those of the more academically oriented Diederichs, he did produce some theoretical work, primarily during the Second World War, when he moved closer to national socialism by stressing the roots of Afrikaner unity in the "organic" concepts of race and family.[98] Like Diederichs, he believed that the Afrikaner had a divine calling, which he attempted to explain in a highly convoluted argument stressing the organic, vital nature of the volk in his book *Die Afrikaner* (1941):

> The People as a faith-unit [*geloofseenheid*] fulfils its own calling on the one hand by realizing the value-whole [*waardegeheel*] and on the other the life-order [*lewensordening*] ordained by its faith.... The people is at the same time a social [*lewens*] and a cultural community. In the realization of its unique life-form the People creates its culture and in the creation of its culture it realizes its own life-form. These are the two sides of its unique calling as given in its faith.[99]

Ultimately Meyer attempted to combine national socialism and Kuyperian neo-Calvinism more explicitly than other Studentebond and Broederbond figures had done. The result was a curious transformation of Kuyper's theory of "sovereignty in own sphere" into one of "totalitarianism in each sphere":

> The totalitarianism of the *volksbeweging* [people's movement], which is subordinate to the Word of God, means on the one hand the struggle toward an organic community on the part of the estates of the People (*volksstande*) which are integrated into the *volksbeweging*, and on the other hand it means the independent existence alongside the People of other organizing human entities like the individual, the family and the church.[100]

Beneath this strange potpourri of ideas was a far more serious theme: the wedding of the new ideas of a fascist Europe to the old emphasis on church, family, and volk (used without any German Romantic connotations of ethnic superiority and purity) of traditional rural and small-town Afrikaner society. It was to bear fruit in the emerging political philosophy that increasingly underpinned the Nationalists on their road to power: "Christian Nationalism," a curious mixture of Nazi ideas, Kuyper's neo-Calvinism, and ideas inherited from the old Boer republics.

Diederichs had made it plain in his discussion with Kirschner in May 1939 that he desired some type of authoritarian state to replace the liberal-democratic parliamentary system, although he did not elaborate on what he meant by this.[101] Meyer was more forthright: his admiration for the new regimes abroad almost equaled the passionate expressions of Van Rensburg, his coleader of the Studentebond. On 3 October 1937 Meyer told a great crowd at the ANS annual congress on the subject of Italian-style Fascism: "Dictatorship is actually the real form of democracy.... The freedoms of the individual are not negative, as in liberal democracy, but positive. The volk rules itself through bringing to the fore its own leader and is not ruled by a little minority group."[102]

After expressing pleasure in Mussolini's belated acceptance of the role of religion, Meyer went on to discuss the importance of adapting Fascism, "the new thing in Western culture," to South African conditions. He suggested Kruger's Transvaal Republic as a model for such a hybrid state. He was particularly enthusiastic about the volk as "the real employer, and not the capitalist" in a fascist state, and advised his audience to pay serious attention to the practical work of effecting change in South Africa so that it would fit in with the volk life-style.[103]

With Afrikaner students exposed to such beliefs from their own leaders, it is perhaps comprehensible why the Greyshirts found such an easy appeal in the second point of their program (the first point supported "religious freedom," an important item in a Calvinist society): "We stand for the welfare of each member of the State where the National Interests of South Africa are placed before Self or Party Interests. The interests of the State must always precede the individual. We consider the present political democracy corrupt and exploded."[104] The worship of volk and state had, however, been adopted not only by the shirt movements, but increasingly by respected Afrikaner nationalist thinkers and the leaders of the youth.

The examples of Germany and Italy, along with the overt and clandestine propaganda work of the Nazis, had found a ready South African audience, from intellectuals like Diederichs to streetside orators like Weichardt. The great question was whether such views would be taken up, as anti-Semitism had been, by the largest and nationally the most organized voice of the Afrikaner right, the Purified National Party itself. Only in this way could the Nazis' propaganda network make a real difference to white South African politics. National socialist and broader fascist influences would otherwise be limited, as in so much of Europe and Latin America, to a small extremist fringe.

Notes

1 See editorial "Der Union von Südafrika zum 31. Mai 1935" in *Afrika-Rundschau* 1:2 (June 1935), p. 31, in which South Africa was described as enjoying the greatest German interest among the British dominions.
2 Ibid., p. 32. See also Werner Schmidt-Pretoria, *Der Kulturanteil des Deutschtums am Aufbau des Burenvolkes* (Hannover: Hahnsche Verlags-buchhandlung, 1938),

a highly propagandistic work, which deals in detail with the contribution of Germany to Afrikaner culture.
3. The best recent work on the racially mixed ancestry of the Afrikaner is H. F. Heese's *Groep Sonder Grense: Die Rol en Status van die Gemengde Bevolking aan die Kaap, 1652–1795* (Belville: Western Cape Institute for Historical Research, 1984).
4. See M. F. Katzen, "White Settlers and the Origin of the New Society, 1652–1778" in Monica Wilson and Leonard Thompson, eds., *A History of South Africa to 1870* (Cape Town: David Philip, 1982), pp. 174, 194, and 229; also E. H. Raidt, *Afrikaans en Sy Europese Verlede: Van Tacitus tot Van Wyk Louw* (Cape Town: Nasou, 2nd ed. 1982), pp. 83–85.
5. See, for instance, University of Cape Town, Jagger Library, Archives and Manuscripts Department, H. G. Lawrence Papers, E3.262, Otto von Strahl, "Protect Your Home Country," detailing prewar Nazi activities in South Africa.
6. F. A. van Jaarsveld, *The Awakening of Afrikaner Nationalism 1868–1881* (Cape Town: Human and Rousseau, 1961), pp. 70, 145–146, and 192.
7. J. S. du Plessis, "The South African Republic" in C. F. J. Muller, ed., *Five Hundred Years: A History of South Africa* (Cape Town and Pretoria: Academica Press, 2nd ed. 1975), pp. 266 and 275–276.
8. Ibid., p. 287.
9. Ibid., p. 289.
10. J. S. Marais, *The Fall of Kruger's Republic* (Oxford: Clarendon Press, 1961), p. 99.
11. Ibid., p. 291.
12. M. C. van Zyl, "States and Colonies in South Africa, 1854–1902" in Muller, ed., *Five Hundred Years*, pp. 309 and 312.
13. Ibid., p. 337.
14. Marais, *Fall of Kruger's Republic*, p. 47.
15. Leslie Rubin, "Afrikaner Nationalism and Nazi Germany: The Roots of Apartheid" (Unpub. paper, 1985), p. 2.
16. Donald M. McKale, *The Swastika Outside Germany* (Kent, Ohio: Kent State University Press, 1977), pp. 31 and 45ff.
17. Ibid., pp. 47–48.
18. Lawrence Papers, E3.9, "Very Confidential Memorandum Relating to Nazi Activities in the Union of South Africa," 28 October 1939, p. 6.
19. Lawrence Papers, E3.262, Otto von Strahl, Confidential Folder "Protect Your Home Country," 18 July 1941, p. 10.
20. See also the extensive discussion of the role of the *Deutsch-Afrikaner* in Lawrence Papers, E5.44, White Book on Nazi Activities in the Union of South Africa 1933–1939, Vol. 5, pp. 477–481, 544–548, and 567–578.
21. Ibid., pp. 546–547.
22. Ibid., pp. 554–555.
23. Ibid., p. 556.
24. Ibid., p. 570.
25. Ibid., p. 573.
26. Ibid., pp. 599–601. A detailed report on Nazi activity in one of the most famous German schools, that at Hermannsburg in Natal, can be found in H. G. Lawrence Papers, E3.221, "Nazi Activities and Propaganda in Schools in Natal," 22 February 1940.
27. Ibid., pp. I and II, and annexures A, B, and E.
28. Ibid., Annexure H.
29. See Lawrence Papers, E3.212–E3.215, Correspondence regarding Deutsche Berufsgruppen, 30 August 1939ff.

30 Lawrence Papers, E3.262, Von Strahl, "Protect Your Home Country," pp. 6 and 10.
31 Lawrence Papers, E3.213, Translated transcript of captured correspondence, "AA of the German Berufsgruppen," Hamburg, to all office bearers, 11 June 1935.
32 Lawrence Papers, E3.214, "Translation of Extracts from: Instructions for the Establishing of New *Stützpunkte* and *Zellen* Abroad," a mimeographed four-page report, part of correspondence seized at the outbreak of war, enclosed with a secret letter from the Secretary for South-West Africa in Windhoek to the Chief Control Officer, Department of Justice, Pretoria, 30 August 1940.
33 University of Cape Town, Archives and Manuscripts Department, Morris Alexander Papers, C. File 29, "German Nazis Organise in South Africa," reprinted from *Forward*, 1938.
34 Lawrence Papers, White Book on Nazi Activities in the Union of South Africa, 1933–1939, Vol. 2, p. 185.
35 Ibid., p. 232.
36 Lawrence Papers, White Book on Nazi Activities in the Union of South Africa, 1933–1939, Vol. 3, p. 293.
37 U.S. National Archives Microfilm Series, T-120, Captured German Foreign Office Records (hereafter USNAMS, T-120), Reel 3017/E491148, Dieckhoff to Smuts, 20 August 1936.
38 T. Dunbar Moodie, *The Rise of Afrikanerdom: Power, Apartheid and the Afrikaner Civil Religion* (Berkeley and Los Angeles: University of California Press, 1975), p. 155.
39 USNAMS, T-120, Reel 317/241170, Leitner to Foreign Office, 15 June 1939, p. 2.
40 USNAMS, T-120, Reel 3017/E491215, Stiller to Foreign Office, 28 April 1937.
41 P. J. Meyer, *Nog Nie Ver Genoeg Nie: 'n Persoonlike Rekenskap van Vyftig Jaar Georganiseerde Afrikanerskap* (Johannesburg and Cape Town: Perskor, 1984), pp. 10–11.
42 Rubin, "Afrikaner Nationalism and Nazi Germany," p. 5.
43 Ibid.
44 Interview with Leslie Rubin, 7 June 1985.
45 Fichte, the German nationalist philosopher, particularly admired the kingdom of Prussia as a model state. He would no doubt have been horrified to see some of the uses to which his ideas, like those of Nietzsche, Herder, and Schleiermacher, were put to use by pro-Nazi academics. The use of the term "neo-Fichteanism," following Moodie (*Rise of Afrikanerdom*, pp. 154ff.) and Rodney Davenport, *South Africa: A Modern History* (Toronto and Buffalo: University of Toronto Press, 1987), p. 318, does not imply that the ideas of Fichte, or indeed those of other nineteenth-century German philosophers, are in any way analogous to those of Hitler or other Nazi ideologues.
46 Meyer, *Nog Nie Ver Genoeg Nie*, pp. 11–12.
47 Lawrence Papers, White Book, Vol. 3, p. 314.
48 Ibid., pp. 303–304.
49 Ibid., p. 294.
50 Ibid., pp. 311–313.
51 USNAMS, T-120, Reel 317/241191–241192, "Unterredung mit Professor Diederichs, Suedafrika, am. 19. Mai 1939," pp. 1–2. The original German of this passage reads: "Sehr viele ihrer heute führenden Leute seien doch noch zu weitgehend befangen in demokratischen Ideen. Infolgedessen werde für eine völlige nationale Erhebung ein weitgehender Führerwechsel Voraussetzung sein. Die Hoffnung liege da bei der Jugend und man sei sich im nationalen Lager einig

darüber, dass jeder neugeborene Bure einmal Nationalist sein würde. Der Endsieg sei infolgedessen niemanden fraglich."

52 Ibid., pp. 2–3. This extract reads: ". . . habe die hauptsächlichste Sorge der Heranbildung von Fachleuten zu gelten, die hernach nicht nur gesinnungsmässig, sondern auch fachlich in der Lage seien, die Regierung zu übernehmen. Dieser Aufgabe werde sich in Zukunft mit kleinsten Anfängen beginnend, der "Broederbond" widmen. Mit der Bitte, dies als streng vertraulich zu betrachten, sagte mir Prof. Diederichs dann, dass er vor kurzem die Leitung des "Broederbonds" übernommen habe. Der "Broederbond" sei eine Geheimorganisation, in die eine Aufnahme erst nach eingehender Prüfung möglich sei. Ziel der Organisation sei, das ganze Land, vor allem auch die führenden Stellen, zu durchdringen und das gesamte Staatswesen auf diese Weise von innen her zu erobern."

53 Ibid., p. 4. ". . . er glaube nicht, dass die innere Stärke der Nationalen Partei dann schon genügen würde, eine Regierung zu bilden nach dem Muster der autoritären Staaten. Diese allein aber könne auf die Dauer seine Stellung südlich des Äquators sichern."

54 USNAMS, T-120, Reel 317/241190, "Bemerkungen von H. Bohle," 30 May 1939.

55 "It DID Happen Here! How the Nazis Conducted Propaganda in South Africa" in *Common Sense*, January 1940, pp. 9–10.

56 Ibid., p. 10.

57 USNAMS, T-120, Reel 317, "Bemerkungen von H. Bohle."

58 USNAMS, T-120, Reel 318/241238, Undated memorandum "Aufzeichnung für den Empfang des Wirtschafts- und Verteidigungsministers der Union von Südafrika Pirow," p. 1.

59 See copy of Pirow's letter of thanks to German Foreign Minister Ribbentrop in Stanford, 26 November 1938, Hoover Institution, German Foreign Office Collection, File 540/147841. On Pirow's visit to Germany and Italy, see also USNAMS, T-120, Reel 318/241235–241242, documents regarding Pirow's visit, 1938, including a discussion of Mussolini's impressions of Pirow, which were extremely uncomplimentary. See Telegram, Mackensen to Berlin, 28 November 1938.

60 Pretoria, State Archives, J. C. Smuts Papers, Vol. 56, S. G. Millin to Smuts, 12 November 1938.

61 Johannesburg, University of the Witwatersrand, Cullen Library, Manuscripts Department, S. G. Millin Papers, C1, Hofmeyr to Millin, 16 December 1938.

62 Ibid.

63 Ibid.

64 Ibid.

65 Millin Papers, C1, Hofmeyr to Millin, 19 June 1938.

66 USNAMS, T-120, Reel 3017/E491047, "Abschrift: Die Neuwahlen zum Unionsparlament im Juni kommenden Jahres, Kapstadt, ende Oktober 1937," p. 3.

67 Ibid. The text reads: ". . . sind sie natürlichen Voraussetzungen für ein Zusammengehen der Malan Partei und der Grauhemden durchaus vorhanden. Beide stehen sie in ehrlicher und offener Opposition zur Regierung, beide halten sie die Judenfrage und den Bolschewismus für einen wesentlichen Kernpunkt ihrer Programme, beide wollen die Unabhängig-keit des südakrikanischen Geldmarktes vom internationalen Judentum durch Errichtung einer rein südafrikanischen National Bank sicherstellen."

68 Ibid.

69 Alan Bullock, *Hitler: A Study in Tyranny* (New York: Harper and Row, 1964), p. 188.

70 A good account of the rise and fall of the German National People's Party can be found in John A. Leopold, *Alfred Hugenberg: The Radical Nationalist*

Campaign Against the Weimar Republic (New Haven and London: Yale University Press, 1977).
71. Bloemfontein, Instituut vir Eietydse Geskiedenis, Greyshirts (L. T. Weichardt) Records, File 3, F. C. Erasmus to W. R. Laubscher, 25 October 1937. See also Erasmus to Laubscher, 28 September 1937.
72. Bullock, *Hitler*, pp. 147–150.
73. See Peter Stachura, "The Nazis, the Bourgeoisie and the Workers during the *Kampfzeit*," in P. D. Stachura, ed., *The Nazi Machtergreifung* (London: George Allen and Unwin, 1983), pp. 15–32, and Dan O'Meara, *Volkskapitalisme: Class, Capital and Ideology in the Development of Afrikaner Nationalism, 1934–1948* (Johannesburg: Ravan, 1983), pp. 49ff. O'Meara points out that the large-scale Cape sheep farmers were particularly steadfast supporters of Malan, bound as they were by strong trade ties both to Germany and to Great Britain.
74. Ibid., p. 50.
75. Moodie, *Rise of Afrikanerdom*, p. 154.
76. E. W. F. Tomlin, *The Western Philosophers* (London et al: Hutchinson, 1968), p. 215.
77. Robert Waite, *The Psychopathic God: Adolf Hitler* (New York: Basic Books, 1977), pp. 98–102.
78. Ibid., p. 144.
79. Robert Pois, ed., *Alfred Rosenberg: Selected Writings* (London: Jonathan Cape, 1970), Introduction, pp. 17–18.
80. Ibid., p. 19.
81. Moodie, *Rise of Afrikanerdom*, p. 162.
82. USNAMS, T-120, Reel 217/241195, "Unterredung mit Professor Diederichs," p. 5. The text reads: ". . . die Vereinigte Partei ihre Sitze im Wesentlichen lediglich den Stimmen der Juden zu verdanken habe."
83. Nicolas Diederichs, *Vom Leiden und Dulden* (Bonn: Ferdinand Dümmlers Verlag, 1930).
84. N. Diederichs, *Nasionalisme as Lewensbeskouing en Sy Verhouding tot Internasionalisme* (Bloemfontein et al: Nasionale Pers, 1936), p. 3.
85. Ibid., pp. 17–18 and 63.
86. *Die Volksblad*, 25 April 1935, cited in Moodie's translation in *Rise of Afrikanerdom*, p. 160.
87. Moodie, *Rise of Afrikanerdom*, pp. 54–55.
88. Ibid., p. 155.
89. Ibid.
90. O'Meara, *Volkskapitalisme*, p. 51. Although by 1931 the Broederbond had begun to grow in the southern provinces, O'Meara's view that its base was the Transvaal is nowhere contradicted by the Broederbond materials I have used. Furthermore, for the first eleven years of the Bond's existence, branches were restricted to the Transvaal. Bond annual meetings were held in Johannesburg or Pretoria until 1938, when they were moved to the more centrally located Bloemfontein. See the Bond's official history by A. N. Pelzer, *Die Afrikaner-Broederbond: Eerste 50 Jaar* (Cape Town: Tafelberg, 1979), pp. 36–37 and 43. Furthermore, Transvalers held the chairmanship of the Bond until 1952 (Pelzer, p. 46). Of sixty candidates for the Bond Executive Council in 1941, at least thirty-six were Transvalers even at this relatively late date, when the Bond included branches in all provinces. See J. H. P. Serfontein, *Brotherhood of Power* (Bloomington: Indiana University Press, 1978), pp. 79–80.
91. O'Meara, *Volkskapitalisme*, p. 62.
92. C. J. H. de Wet led an agitation for a radical "Christian Nationalist" program during 1936–1937. This was only one of many crises reflected in the party

minutes of those years. See Pretoria, State Archives, J. G. Strijdom Papers, Vol. 36, C. J. H. de Wet to Secretary, Transvaal NP, 16 April 1937. As late as January 1939 the NP on the Witwatersrand had only been able to reduce its debt from 550 to 320 pounds, and the payment of constituency dues was being described as "a matter of seriousness." See Strijdom Papers, Vol. 36, Transvaal NP Executive, Minutes, 21 January 1939, p. 3.
93 O'Meara, *Volkskapitalisme*, p. 60.
94 N. Diederichs, *Die Kommunisme: Sy Teorie en Taktiek* (Bloemfontein et al: Nasionale Pers, 1938), pp. 162–163.
95 Foreword to ibid.
96 A. J. H. van der Walt, N. Diederichs, J. F. J. van Rensburg, and others, *Hedendaagse Politieke Strominge* (Johannesburg: Voortrekkerpers, n.d.).
97 Moodie, *Rise of Afrikanerdom*, pp. 169–170.
98 Ibid., p. 230.
99 *Die Afrikaner* (Bloemfontein: Nasionale Pers, 1941), pp. 55–56, cited by Moodie in his own translation in *Rise of Afrikanerdom*, p. 163.
100 P. J. Meyer, *Die Toekomstige Ordening van die Volksbeweging in Suid-Afrika* (Stellenbosch, ANSB, 1942), p. 12, cited in Moodie, *Rise of Afrikanerdom*, p. 230.
101 USNAMS, T-120, "Unterredung mit Professor Diederichs," p. 4.
102 *Die Transvaler*, 4 October 1937.
103 Ibid.
104 *Die Waarheid*, 23 February 1934.

71
BLUE SHIRTS, NATIONALISTS AND NATIONALISM FASCISM IN 1930S CHINA

Fan Hong

Source: J. A. Mangan (ed.) *Superman Supreme: Fascist Body as Global Icon – Global Fascism*, London: Frank Cass, 2000, pp. 205–26.

In the 1930s two political movements occurred in China: the Blue Shirts (Lanyishe) and the New Life movement (Xinshenghuo yundong). The Blue Shirts movement was an imitation of the Fascist youth movements in Italy and Germany. The New Life movement was an attempted 'social regeneration of China' through the revival of the ancient moral principles of Confucianism.[1] However, it was not a simple neo-Confucian revival. It was a Fascist movement with a Chinese character. These two movements were integrated and interrelated. This essay will trace the origins of both movements, examine how the Fascist ideology with its emphasis on total control, military power and male supremacy was implemented in China, and how the Nationalists used militarized physical exercise to promote male bodies as political metaphors symbolizing and ensuring a strong state.

Fascism is one of the less precise terms in the social science lexicon. Since it first appeared in Italian in the 1910s the meaning and definition has changed over time.[2] In 1992 Stephen Turner declared: 'The puzzle of Fascism remains, half a century after the conclusion of the war against the Fascist regimes... No sociology of the interior era grasped Fascism fully or produced an unambiguously 'correct' political receipt for dealing with it... The failure... indicates that the pretensions to political wisdom of social science are inappropriate...'[3] In this essay I follow Roger Griffin and Zeev Sternhell and define the political ideology of Fascism as 'a synthesis of organic nationalism and anti-Marxist socialism, a revolutionary movement based on rejection of liberalism and democracy...'[4] From this specific perspective, the subject under investigation here is the Fascist movement in China in the

1930s on two levels – political ideology and action. This will involve consideration of the creation of a single-party state, the founding of a mass youth movement and the training of male (and some female) bodies for 'national rebirth'. In Fascist studies the obsession with national rebirth and the need for a 'new man' has been frequently noted – in Europe. However, Fascism is not an exclusively European phenomenon. The Fascist movement in China in the 1930s illustrates the adaptability of Fascism to societies and cultures outside Europe as far distant as Asia.

The Nationalist party came to power in 1927. Led by Chiang Kai-shek, its Commander-in-Chief, the National Revolutionary Army drove the Communists from the cities into the countryside and attempted to unify China under one party rule. By 1928 the Nationalists had extended their territory north to the former capital of China–Beijing. From there their influence stretched on into Manchuria. The warlords in those areas were either destroyed or allied themselves with the Nationalists. In April 1927 Chiang and his supporters set up their own Nationalist Government in Nanjing. Chiang became President and remained the commander-in-chief of the Nationalist armed force. From 1928 to 1949, while challenging Western imperialist intrusion, facing up to Japanese aggression from the outside and waging war against the Communists from the inside, the Nationalists controlled about two-thirds of China's population and the greater part of China.

The Nationalists' ambition was to unite the whole country and create a new modern China. However, they were confronted with the challenge of reinvigorating a nation that had been declining at an accelerating pace for over a century, and with the further challenge of the Communists internally and Japanese imperialists externally. There was a brief period of optimism in the early years of the Nationalist government. Many thought that the new government would cope with the nation's problems, would restore political unity, economic prosperity, national pride and general security to the Chinese people. But the Nationalists failed. Its administration became increasingly ineffective and corrupt. The Nationalist Party was unable to impose any real unity upon the nation. It lost the popular support of some party members and most of the people.[5] Ludwig Rajchman reported in February 1930 that 'the Government . . . soon began to lose its original driving force; eventually, after two years of office, little remained of the early schemes of reconstruction'.[6] The Nationalist Party's Manifesto of the Fourth National Congress in November 1931 admitted: 'China was plunged into the abysses of national crisis. Our only chance of surviving this catastrophe is to . . . make the nation a genuine body of strength . . . by sacrificing personal freedom and interests for national reconstruction.'[7] Chiang confessed in 1932 that 'The Chinese revolution has failed. My one desire today is to restore the revolutionary spirit that the Chinese Nationalist Party had in 1924.'[8]

As the consequence of the Nationalist Party's determination to hold on to power Chiang and some young loyal party members and military officers looked to Italy and Germany. They admired European Fascism with its emphases on faith in the leader, a sense of national superiority and the militarization of the nation for its survival. Chiang proclaimed: 'Fascism is . . . a stimulant for a declining, stagnant society. Can Fascism save China? We answer: Yes! Fascism is what China now most needs. At the present stage of China's critical situation, Fascism is a wonderful medicine exactly suited to China, and the only tonic that can save it.'[9] Fascism came to be seen in China as the most advanced and efficient political ideology and system. It was considered a progressive doctrine and practice that was suited to China's restoration.

Fascism was not a new phenomenon to the Nationalist Party, which had a long and close relationship with the Germans. After he turned on his Communist allies in 1927, Chiang had brought in the Germans as advisors when the Russians pulled out. The German military mission, led by Colonel Max Bauer, came to China in 1928.[10] Bauer had close ties with Hitler and the German Nazi movement. Many of his subordinates in the mission had been selected at least partially because they shared his political predilections. Bauer died in May 1929 and he was succeeded by an extraordinarily ardent Nazi, Lieutenant-Colonel Herman Kriebel. Kriebel had marched in the front rank with Hitler during the famed Beer Hall Putsch of 1923. During his subsequent imprisonment, he had shared Hitler's prison cell. Bauer, Kriebel and other Nazis in the advisory mission virtually dominated military education in the military academies. They had, therefore, unique opportunities to propagate their political views among the army élite.[11] Furthermore, in 1933, after the failure of the four years of his First, Second, Third and Fourth campaigns against the Communists, Chiang, with the support of Hitler, imported the German Fascist General Von Seecket and some 70 German military advisers to plan the Fifth campaign. Von Seecket led the Fascist trained Nationalist armies and employed the military tactics used by foreign imperialist powers in the conquest of Africa and India and destroyed the Communist resistance. The Communists lost their Red Area and had to start the famous Long March in search of a new base.[12] The victory brought Chiang closer to the Germans. Meanwhile, after 1928 a large number of Chinese officers were sent to study in European countries, most of them went to Italy and Germany.[13] The youthful 'new Italy' arising from the collapse of the played-out liberal order in the Giolittian era, Hitler's rise to power and the Nazis' cry of 'Germany awake', the British Union of Fascists' campaign for a 'Greater Britain' and the Romanian Iron Guard's call for the appearance of the New Fascist Man gave further impetus to the Chinese military. They believed that liberalism was not suitable to their changing world. Fascism with its cogent and lucid idealism, in their view, could overcome the nation's sickness, decline, disintegration and collapse. More than this, it could restore the nation's hope, pride and glory.

Inspired by the Italian and German Fascist movements, in 1931, a young progressive party member Liu Jianqiong wrote a proposal called 'Suggestions of Reforming the Nationalist Party'. He suggested that the party should be transformed. The new party should imitate the ideals and forms of the Hitler Youth in Germany and the Black Shirts in Italy. The new party should be called the Blue Shirts, for the members would wear blue shirts as their symbol.[14] Liu's proposal met with an enthusiastic response from Chiang and some young officers of Huangpu Military Academy – China's equivalent to West Point of the United States, Sandhurst of Britain and St. Cyr of France. The Academy was founded in 1924 and Chiang was its first principal. Chiang retained the post even after he became commander-in-chief of the army and the President. The aim of the Academy was to train future military *and* political leaders. The graduates of the Academy became known as the 'Huangpu group'. They dominated the important positions of the Nationalist Party and army. The ties between Chiang and many of the Huangpu graduates involved the deep personal commitment and mutual loyalty of a Chinese master and his disciples. For the Huangpu group Chiang was Principal not President!

Supported by Chiang, in Autumn 1931, 12 young officers from Huangpu Military Academy and Liu, the writer of the Proposal, formed the Fascist Blue Shirts.[15] It was an élite organization. Membership was very selective. The recommendation of two Blue Shirts members and a thorough background investigation were essential. Once approved for membership, the candidate would face a portrait of Chiang Kai-shek and vowed to obey the leader and preserve the secrets and discipline of the organization or suffer the penalty of death. Although the Blue Shirts probably never exceeded 10,000 members, its power within the military and the party was pervasive.[16] It almost completely dominated the party's organization, political training in the army, government and schools. It also controlled the Nationalists' police force and public security organizations. The 13 founders were called 'the thirteen Taibao' (princes of the Nationalist élite). They were important figures in the Nationalist regime. For example, Dai Li and Zhen Jiemin became heads of the Chinese Special Service force (the Chinese SS). Dai's name became a symbol of terror and he was called 'China's Himmler'.[17]

The Blue Shirts claimed that their goal was national salvation through Fascism. They criticized the government as too soft, too liberal, too bureaucratic and too corrupt to continue the spirit of the reconstruction of China. They regarded Fascism as the only hope of saving China. They saw themselves not only as the embodiment of China's revolution, but indeed as its means of redemption.[18] An editorial article of *Shehui xinwen* (The Society Mercury), the Blue Shirts' mouthpiece, stated: 'Fascism is the only tool of self-salvation of nations on the brink of destruction. It saved Italy and Germany... Therefore, there is no other road than imitating the Fascist spirit of violent struggle as in Italy and Germany.'[19]

To imitate Italy and Germany was to assume total control. Obedience to a supreme leader was essential. Chiang stated:

> The most important point of Fascism is absolute trust in a sage, able leader . . . Now we in China do not have one leader. I believe that, unless everyone has absolute trust in one man, we cannot reconstruct the nation and we cannot complete the revolution . . . From the day we joined the revolutionary group, we completely entrusted our rights, life, liberty, and happiness to the group, and pledged them to the leader . . . Thus for the first time we can truly be called Fascists.[20]

The editorial of *Shehui xinwen* cried, 'We must not disguise that we demand a China Mussolini, demand China's Hitler.'[21] Chiang was regarded as the New Man for China. Therefore, faith in Chiang was the first principle of the Blue Shirts. 'Chiang Kai-shek is the only leader of the Nationalist Party and also the only great leader of China. Members, therefore, must absolutely support him, follow his order only, and make his will their own.'[22] Obedience to Chiang was unconditional. Members of the Blue Shirt were to live and die with him, sincerely and unwavering!'[23]

To the Blue Shirts, Western liberalism meant anarchy and individualism. This liberalism, in their view, had poisoned the Chinese since the May Fourth Movement (1915–19). It caused the people to yield to their personal whims and ignored the needs of society at large. Chiang stated: 'We have in vain become drunk with democracy and the advocacy of free thought. What has been the result? We have fallen into a chaotic and irretrievable situation.'[24] The Blue Shirts called for people to perform their duties not to speak of their rights. They should relinquish their freedom and even their lives for the nation. There was no room for individual freedom in the cause of national salvation.[25]

National salvation needed order and discipline. Paradoxically to achieve order and discipline violence was necessary. The Blue Shirts believed that the goal of restoration could only be achieved by 'fighting violence with violence'. An article in *Shehui xinwen* claimed: 'China today has no other road to restoration than to use an absolutely revolutionary body as a violent force that supports the principle of nation-first-ism.'[26] Chiang said in a speech to the Blue Shirts, 'all the comrades must unite their thoughts and beliefs. Party members . . . shall handle all matters in accordance with the principle of fighting violence with violence.'[27] The Blue Shirts directed this 'legitimate' violence not only against Communists, Japanese and political rivals, but also individual Blue Shirts who disobeyed orders. A *Shehui xinwen* editorial proclaimed: 'There must be a determination to shed blood – that is, there must be unprecedented violence to eliminate all enemies of the people.'[28] The Blue Shirts stated that all enemies must be punished and killed using extreme measures, so that the masses would be too frightened to disobey the laws.[29]

In summary, the Blue Shirts were a clear example of the Fascist movement in action in China. Its inspiration came directly from European Fascism. Liberalism in any form was equated with licence and personal indulgence. What was needed in China, they argued, was obedience to the leader, discipline and a new asceticism. Nationalism, exaltation of the state, glorification of the leader, subordination to the collective will and the glorification of violence and terror all had their place in this school of thought. Through the New Life Movement the credo of the Blue Shirts was widely spread across the whole country.

In February 1934 Chiang launched the New Life Movement from his Nanchang headquarters, Jiangxi province, where he served as commander-in-chief of the military operations for the suppression of Communism. As noted earlier, the leadership of the Nationalist Party held the view that the material and spiritual 'degeneration' of the people was responsible for China's continuing crisis. It was said when Chiang travelled through Nanchang city and saw a young boy in student's uniform with a cigarette in his mouth quarrelling and fighting in the street, he stopped to enquire why his family permitted such behaviour. He then found that such behaviour was common throughout the area. Chiang foresaw decline.[30] In his view the whole nation needed the spirit of the Blue Shirts. It was time to launch an indigenous moral crusade and restore social order in order to revitalize the country. Chiang intended to implant the Blue Shirts' spirit in the Chinese people and to turn the elite Blue Shirts movement into a national movement. Before the launch of the New Life Movement Chiang said to the Blue Shirts' conference of 1933: 'It is necessary to spread our revolutionary spirit to the masses of the entire nation, and to cause them to have faith in our group.'[31] A few months later, in February 1934, Chiang made a speech to a Nanchang mass meeting in which he called for 'a movement to achieve a new life'.[32] To the assembled citizens he cited the examples of Germany and Japan. He pointed out that such nations were strong because they had developed a proper way of life. What China needed in order to achieve strength was to *militarize* (my emphasis) the life of the people of the entire country.[33]

However, to make the Blue Shirts acceptable to the ordinary Chinese, Chiang attributed to them a moral code similar to that promulgated by Confucian thought. It was a Confucianism for the masses.[34] This is the reason that the essence of the Fascist movement has been overlooked by many scholars, who have viewed it simply as a neo-Confucian revival.[35]

The main purpose of the New Life Movement was to lead the Chinese people to a more rational life with three separate but interrelated aspects: the cultural, the productive, and the militarized modes of life. Through the cultural mode of life, it was hoped that rudeness and vulgarity could be eliminated. Through the productive mode of life, it was hoped that more people would contribute to the material welfare of the whole nation. Through the militarized mode of life, it was hoped that the people would become more disciplined and more able to defend the nation.[36] There were 96 specific rules issued to discipline the masses, including walk on the right side, stand straight, wash the face with cold water and drink water instead of tea or coffee.[37] Chiang believed that such strict rules would transform the 400 million 'scattered grains of sand' into disciplined citizens[38] guided by the four virtues *li, yi, lian, chi* (propriety, righteousness, integrity and a sense of shame), resulting ultimately in the creation of a new society and nation.[39] He stated that emphasis on the four virtues would make the people work harder, spend less, end corruption and make officials honest and patriotic – the secret of success of Italy and Germany.[40]

Chiang's call for a Chinese New Life, in February 1934, was followed by an immediate response by the population that exceeded his expectations. Following their disillusionment with democracy, partially because of China's recent experience with inefficient democratic institutions and partially because of political trends in the world at large, the Chinese became interested in dictatorship which they believed could effectively save the country from its deep crises. Since the military triumph of the democratic allies in the First World War, democracy as a system of government had everywhere come under attack for its seeming inability to cope with the mounting economic and political crises. In Italy, Mussolini's demand for a 'new Italy' had transformed a weak and humiliated nation into an international power. The achievements of Hitler left a deep impression on the Chinese people's political thinking The Chinese were well aware of ideological differences between Fascism and Confucianism, but they believed that both advocated the sacrifice of the individual to the state, both emphasized the stability of the society through the maintenance of the *status quo* and both praised the glory of the past. Fascism and Confucianism could deliver a future to the people. Therefore, with the endorsement of the government, within a matter of weeks, the movement had spread 'like wildfire' over most of China, encouraging some to believe that China's long-promised 'rebirth' was close at hand. Through March and April, New Life promotional associations were established in nine provinces as well as three municipal centres. By the first anniversary of the Movement in February 1935, 15 provinces, three municipalities and nine railway centres had New Life organizations. By the end of 1935, such organizations had spread to 19 provinces, five municipalities and 12 railway centres. At the lower administrative level, the organization had been extended to 1,132 counties by 1935.[41]

In May 1934 the Nationalist government sent a delegation of young officers to visit Italy and Germany to study Fascist military techniques. The correspondent in Berlin of the *New York Times* reported: 'Because of the revolutionary activities among the younger generation, the methods whereby the Chancellor Hitler has turned the revolutionary enemy in Germany to his own purpose are of particular interest to the Nanking authorities.'[42] The German Fascist techniques were applied to the New Life Movement.

The movement transmitted German principles through simple Chinese expressions. People were taught to accept Chiang as the only true leader of the country because he was a man of the people, who could look deep into the soul of the people and thereby bring the movement closer and closer to Chinese tradition.[43] To achieve this the people themselves were to be disciplined by a social moral order and trained to be new citizens. To be new citizens meant to 'sacrifice personal freedom and enjoyment'.[44] Puritanism held sway, including sanctioned physical attacks on people attending cinemas or dance halls or engaging in other forms of liberalism. Puritan violence was sanctioned also by the police and the New Life promotion organizations. It was reported that in Shanghai a woman was arrested because she wore shorts on a hot summer day – immoral behaviour and that she had died in prison.[45] Women with short hair were regarded as Communists or radicals and were arrested. In Wuhan city, all cabarets were forced to close at midnight. People were not allowed to dance, and music was to be only classical in nature. Furthermore, the Ministry of Education resorted to extreme methods: centres of radicalism were closed down, radical teachers arrested and radical students expelled. Meanwhile, the government attempted to dissolve progressive workers' organizations and shut liberal schools.[46] The 'White Terror', as it was called by leftist critics and Communists, swept over China. In the dormitories of Beijing, to a lesser extent in other areas, 1934 and 1935 were years marked by pre-dawn police raids, surprise searches and sudden arrests carried out by the secret police aided by the Blue Shirts and their allies.[47] It has been estimated that 300 students, professors, and intellectuals were arrested in North China in 1934.[48] Two hundred and thirty Beijing and Tianjin intellectuals were taken into custody between November 1934 and March 1935.[49] George Shepherd, a Christian missionary, observed, 'Radicalism and communism are dead.'[50]

Political indoctrination and military training were two crucial aspects of the Blue Shirts and the New Life Movement. Political indoctrination 'informed' people's minds and military training strengthened men's bodies – both essential for preparation for war and national rebirth. The Blue Shirts saw militarization as central to China's education and future. The ultimate goal of education was training future soldiers for the nation.[51] School should be organized like military regiments, and teachers and school administrators should receive compulsory military training and live the frugal, disciplined life of the army.[52] Military education should begin in the kindergarten, because the children belonged to the nation not the family. The children should be given toy guns, and pictures of battle scenes should be displayed on the walls so that they would develop an interest in military equipment and battle situations.[53] Middle school pupils should be enrolled in the Tongzijun ('Boy's Army' in Chinese, 'Boy Scouts' in English), which, like the Hitler Youth, would have a strong military emphasis. In schools, heavy stress was to be placed on physical training and team sports, group activities, group co-operation, and group discussion.[54] In this way, students would learn to identify first and foremost with the social group and then with the nation. In this way, the bookish students of the past would be replaced by the strong scholar-warriors of the future. Boys in high school and college would receive formal military training. Girls would receive training as nurses. Academic courses would be oriented towards militarization. Physics, chemistry and engineering would be oriented towards their wartime applications. Classes in chemistry, for example, would stress the study of such matters as poison gases and explosives.[55]

In September 1933 Chiang had explained that the militarization of society was one of the three basic elements in Fascism (the other two were a sense of national superiority and faith in the leader).[56] Five months later the New Life Movement was launched. Chiang now declared that the militarization of society was the chief goal of the movement. He claimed,

> In Fascism, the organization, the spirit, and the activities must all be militarized ... In the home, the factory, and the government office, regardless of place, time, or situation, everyone's activities must be the same as in the army ... In other words, there must be obedience, sacrifice, strictness, cleanliness, accuracy, speed, diligence, secrecy ... and everyone together must firmly and bravely sacrifice everything for the group and for the nation.[57]

This vision of the whole of Chinese society performing with the discipline, obedience and efficiency of a military camp was essential to the New Life Movement. Chiang stated,

> What is the New Life Movement that I now propose? Stated simply, it is to thoroughly militarize the lives of the citizens of the entire nation so that they can cultivate courage and swiftness, the endurance of suffering and a tolerance of hard work, and especially the habit and ability of unified action, so that they will at any time sacrifice themselves for the nation.[58]

He pointed out that the best examples were Germany, Italy and Japan. Chiang's paramount aim was clear – the creation of a strong national state.

The goal of the Fascist militarization of the nation was to turn men into fighters. 'Train strong bodies for the nation' went the well-aired slogan. Strong bodies were not only the source of high morale but also the source of national salvation. Health, strength and nationhood were indivisible.

> In order to become a healthy modern citizen, it is necessary first to have a strong and robust body; having a strong body, one then has a strong spirit; having a strong spirit, one can then acquire all the

abilities required to strengthen the nation, one can naturally defend the state and glorify the nation, help our state and country to forever accord with the world and never again suffer from the aggression and oppression of foreign countries or receive disdain and insults.[59]

The source of a healthy body, predictably and logically, was exercise. As Chen Lifu, the leader of the Nationalist Party, wrote in *Qinfen tiyu yuebao* (Qinfen Sports Monthly) in October 1934: 'Physical education is the only way to strengthen the body. With a healthy body one can achieve the intellectual and moral fulfilment.'[60] Simultaneously, Zhou Fuhai, the Director of Jiangsu Provincial Educational Council, wrote an article to explain the triangular relationship between exercise, the body and the New Life Movement: exercise was part of education. It promoted a healthy body as well as a healthy spirit. Both would lead to the fulfilment of the mission of the New Life Movement.[61]

On 2 March 1935 Chiang Kai-shek wrote an open letter to the nation entitled 'Promotion of Sport and Exercise' demanding the implementation of physical activity programmes:

> We must have a mass physical exercise campaign. From now on all the students and teachers of primary and middle schools, all staff of Party offices, social services and the army must participate in physical activity. They must choose one event as their regular exercise and without exception have their daily exercise time fixed between five and six o'clock every day. They are to be encouraged to do outdoor activities but they can do indoor exercise if the weather is not good. Physical exercise must be constant. The principals of schools, the heads of government offices and army officers must supervise and discipline their pupils and staff and report to their superior.[62]

On 19 April 1935 Chiang wrote a further letter to the public along the same lines to ensure the implementation of his demands.[63]

Chiang, head of state, made inspirational demands. Cheng Dengke, a professor at Nanjing University who studied physical education in Germany between 1929 to 1933,[64] made practical suggestions. He published an article in February 1935 in *Tiyu jikan* (Sports Quarterly) entitled 'Physical Education in Germany' advocating German militarized physical education.[65] In May, in 'On Militarized Sport and Exercise' published in *Qinfen tiyu yuebao*, he explained the difference between competitive sport and militarized physical exercise. He stated that competitive sport which came from the United States was not suitable for China. It advocated individualism and élitism. Militarized exercise was the best way to get the people to exercise their bodies *and* cultivated their patriotic spirit. It would teach them military discipline and Fascist obedience. It would produce fighters. What China needed was soldiers not players. Militarized physical education should be the backbone of Chinese physical training. He pointed out that the secret of success of Germany, Italy and Japan was military programmes and training systems.[66] Others had already taken up the same refrain. Dong Shaoyi, an influential physical educationalist and the Chinese IOC representative, had argued in an article in 1934, 'The Power of Promoting Sport', that 'Strong bodies were the foundation of reconstruction of our nation.' He continued, 'Look at Germany, since Hitler became the head of the government, nationalism is stimulated. Military training has become compulsory in schools. Germany, therefore, has become a strong nation.'[67] Cheng Dunzhen, another noted physical educationalist, claimed in his article 'On the Restoration of the Pride of the Nation', also published in 1934, that China should follow Germany's footsteps and train its people to be strong soldiers to defend the country so that the nation would restore its pride,[68] while in 1934, Zhejiang Province held a Pupils' Sports Essay Contest. Seven middle schools and 12 primary schools took part in the contest. The topic for the middle school was 'what kind of sport can save our country?' and the topic for the primary school was 'the relationship between sport and the restoration of the nation'. Most of the student essays argued that only militarized physical training could save China and restore the nation.[69] Cheng Dengke, mentioned above, the admirer of German militarized physical education, went further in the article 'How to use police and armed forces to promote sports among masses' published in April 1935. He set out a programme for militarizing people using the army and the police as instructors and monitors.[70] Shao Rugan, a physical educationalist and sports journalist, sang the same tune. In *Qinfen tiyu yuebao* in May 1935, in 'How to Promote a Mass Physical Exercise Campaign', he advocated the opening up of school playgrounds to ordinary people, the training of more physical educationalists and general participation in exercise, if necessary, enforced by police supervision![71] Military training was not a new phenomenon in modern China. At the beginning of the twentieth century it had dominated the physical education field. However, it was challenged in the May Fourth period when liberalism and individualism became favoured ideals and practices in the China of the 1920s. Military drill was attacked and eventually banned from the curriculum.[72] Games and modern sports were taught instead. During the 1930s, as stated above, when the country was in deep crisis, the ideal of the militarization of the national again was reborn. Chiang's call for a mass exercise campaign and others advocacy of militarized physical training were the products of the time.

In November 1935 the Nationalists held their Fifth National Congress; its manifesto announced: 'Mass training should be promoted. An emphasis should be laid on military training in order to cultivate the habits of the collective life, provide educational programmes for social organizations and enhance the potential for national independence and freedom.'[73] Following the call of the party, the state machinery moved enthusiastically. The

Nationalist Party established a Physical Education Department to promote military training among the masses. The Education Ministry gave orders to every provincial educational council to set up a Sports Council to promote the mass exercise campaign. By the end of July, 19 provinces and large cities had sports councils. A Physical Education and Sports Department was founded within the New Life Promotion Committee in 1935. The National Military Training Commission invited Cheng Dengke to be its head. In order to set up a network and make the state machine operate more effectively, in 1935, Chiang sent a telegram to the whole country suggesting the creation of a co-operation committee among the party, government, army and schools to promote military education and physical exercise at every level.[74]

A military education for the young was a crucial step in spreading Fascism. The Hitler Youth was a model for the Chinese. The Tongzijun became a popular youth organization in China. Originally the Tongzijun was an imitation of the British Boy Scouts. It was founded by educationalists in 1911 in Wuchang. It began as a small educational organization. Over the years it grew steadily in some cities and provinces. With a momentum imparted by enthusiastic Blue Shirts, the Tongzijun expanded dramatically during the 1930s. It appeared in almost every province and city. On 1 November 1934 Tongzijun's headquarters, the National Committee of Tongzijun, was established. Chiang was the Chairman. The committee set up a board, with the Minister of the Education as its head, in charge of all affairs of the Tongzijun in China. The Education Ministry issued a decree on the same day when the committee was established. It required all pupils of junior middle school to join the Tongzijun. It also stated that military training was compulsory for them. Pupils who joined the Tongzijun would vow to obey Chairman Chiang and the rules. Chiang himself approved the vow and the rules.[75] The responsibility of the Tongzijun was to educate boys to be patriots and to turn them into future soldiers through physical exercise and military training. In 1935 the publisher, Qinfen Books, published 151 books for the Tongzijun. Two thirds were on physical exercise and training.[76] The influential educationalist Liu Xuesong wrote an article in 1935 stressing the importance of moral and physical training for the young through the Tongzijun.[77] Now almost everywhere one looked, there were symptoms and symbols of a country in militarized transition. Boys wore uniforms, practised military drill and paraded through streets. Disciplined squads of these uniformed boys became icons of the new order. An American missionary in Huining recalled, 'At certain hours of the day – early in the morning, noon, and late afternoon – the streets were filled with lads in uniform . . . elementary school children . . . constructing tanks and warplanes and other war paraphernalia . . .'[78] A journalist reported in May 1934 that 'Mass meetings are frequently being held in public parks of Wuchang and Hanko. School children of all ages parade through the streets and are taught to march in very orderly fashion. Sometimes a lantern parade is organized.'[79] The government also held mass meeting to examine the results of the militarization of the young. When Zhejiang provincial government inspected the Tongzijun in April 1934, 1,000 boys took part the parade and 10,000 people watched.[80] A General Review of the Tongzijun took place in 1936 in Nanjing, the capital city, Chiang inspected 10,000 school children.[81] Photographs published in *Liangyou* (Good Friend) *Pictorial* in 1939 show that children between the ages of eight and twelve in Eastern Zhejiang were being organized and trained for the army. The magazine commented that their spirit, discipline and military skill could compete with the youth in Hitler's Germany and Mussolini's Italy.[82] John Israel in his book, *Student Nationalism in China, 1927–1937*, stated: 'The zeal of the Boy's Army in the urban middle schools of the lower Yangtze proved that military regimentation had considerable appeal for Chinese adolescents. Given time, Chiang might have developed a sizeable following of middle school youth.'[83]

At the same time the National Military Training Commission and the Ministry of Education in May 1934 issued the Regulation of Military Training in All Schools. Military training became compulsory. Students in universities and senior middle schools were to have two years' military training.[84] The following year, in teachers training colleges, six hours per week were added for military training.[85] Special summer training camps were also established in major cities where students received an additional three weeks to a month of military training.[86] It was reported that 'A new military spirit was abroad in the country: during the summer of 1934 college students were required to take military training for the first time in history; indeed this "militarization of the mind of China" might well prove to be the decade's most significant development.'[87] In Shanghai, military display competitions among schools took place between 1934 and 1936. The best display received an award.[88] In Zhejiang province in 1935 and 1936 middle school students took part in military training during their summer holiday.[89] A Jiangsu party newspaper proclaimed the importance of summer training and declared the young should receive both military and political training. After their training, it argued, they should be sent to convert peasants, workers, merchants, women and primary school pupils to the Nationalist Party's cause.[90] Chiang Kai-shek also urged students to use their summer vacations for social service under the leadership of the New Life Movement headquarters. The National Military Training Commission recommended that college and middle school students indoctrinate the citizenry in obedience to the party leadership, and promote the New Life Movement.[91] The teachers had their military training too. The slogan was 'to be a teacher, first be a student'. An advanced military training of all middle school teachers in Hubei province took place during the summer vocation in 1936.[92] Furthermore, when the Olympic Games took place in Berlin in 1936 China sent not only athletes but also a delegation of 34 influential physical educationalists to observe and learn from the physical education and training programme and system in Germany and other European countries.[93]

To cultivate the young was not enough. The New Life movement committee and the National Military Training Commission aimed to militarize the Chinese population with the ancillary goal of creating a people's militia of 12 million men.[94] The Headquarters of the New Life Movement in 1934 issued a militarization scheme 'with Fascist ideals as the foundation'.[95] It stated that ordinary citizens between the ages of 14 and 60 should show respect for the party and its laws and attend simple military training, air-raid and first-aid training. Teachers and students, for their part, should be obedient, wear uniforms, receive military training and reject smoking, drinking and dancing. Civil servants for their part should respect the national and the Nationalist Party's flags, show obedience towards superiors and wear uniforms.[96]

Members of the Blue Shirts played a key role in the militarization of the nation. Six of the 13 executive directors of the New Life Movement Commission were Blue Shirts members and majority of the middle and lower-ranking cadre in the commission were members of the Blue Shirts.[97] They created training programmes and opened training centres for military instructors. George Shepherd, a Protestant missionary, who in 1935 became one of the 'directors' of the New Life Movement, complained in 1936 that military officers dominated the Movement.[98] Some secretaries of the YMCA were concerned that the movement was 'really a blue-shirt movement, looking forward to the regimentation of the country under a sort of Fascist regime'.[99] *China Weekly Review* commented in May 1934 that the New Life Movement was the masterpiece of the Blue Shirts.[100]

The New Life Movement went out of fashion in 1937. There were several reasons: first, an anti-military atmosphere was growing. Some radical students began to view military education as a farce. Those who had vehemently demanded training found that instead of the instruction in military science and the use of weapons they had expected, they drilled, saluted, and wasted time in seemingly useless martial ritual. Many students were in open revolt against military training and considered their drillmasters power-hungry, though somewhat inept, conspirators.[101] Second, the Blue Shirts' control of the movement was never complete and the YMCA and Christian churches became increasingly involved in the movement and changed its direction.[102] Third, the Japanese army's invasion of China in 1937 resulted in open war between China and Japan. This forced the whole of the nation to unite and the Nationalists and Communists soon established the United Front. To fight against the Japanese and win the war became the priority of the nation. The New Life Movement and associated Fascist ideals, ideas and actions gradually lost their importance in the face of this national emergency.[103]

The war also sounded the death knell of the Blue Shirts. The Organization and the Movement were disbanded in the spring of 1938. There were several reasons: first, for the sake of the United Front the Nationalist Party and

Chiang himself had to stop anti-Communist and anti-liberalist action and ban the terror organization – the Blue Shirts. Second, power struggles within the Nationalist Party weakened the strength of the Blue Shirts.[104] The Blue Shirts gradually fell out of favour with Chiang Kai-shek when the political situation changed and when he wanted to demonstrate to the West, especially his American friends, that he was a sound democrat and a true Christian. Third, the Blue Shirts were an élitist organization, which lacked the support of the public. It required the support of a strong political leader. Otherwise, it had no future. However, the spirit of the Blue Shirts was carried on by the new Nationalist youth organization, the Three People's Principles Youth League, founded in May 1938. Five founders of the Blue Shirts were in its executive committee.

In summary, the Nationalists in China in the 1930s embraced the international Fascist movement with enthusiasm. The Blue shirts and the New Life Movement were Fascist creations. They, like the Fascist movement in Italy and Germany, established a revolutionary new social and ethical order on the basis of indoctrinated youth and mass mobilization. They used mechanisms of intensive social engineering and repression to maintain a one-party rule. They stressed militarism as a bastion of Chinese security, pride and independence. However, they were not simple copies of the Fascist movement in Italy and Germany. On the contrary, they were a Fascist movement with Chinese elements and characters drawn from a Confucian past to create a Fascist future. This fact demonstrates the multifarious forms that Fascism assumed in different national settings. As James S. Barnes stated:

> Fascists in each country must make Fascism their own national movement, which conforms to the traditions, psychology and tastes of their own land. Do not seize on the accidentals of the movement or you will be in danger, of missing the essentials. Remember that, though truth is universal, its acceptance need never make the world the same colour, for in its application to the individual case is born variety . . . One God in three persons.[105]

Nevertheless, in common with so many Fascist organizations across the world, the Blue Shirts considered male bodies as the property of the state, to be strengthened, disciplined and trained for martial expendability for the good of the state, with the result that sport of all kinds was assimilated into, and subordinated to, a militaristic cult in the interest of creating 'supermen' to bring about once again China's greatness.

Notes

I wish to thank my parents for providing me with the information about the Blue Shirts. I am grateful for my Chinese colleagues, Professor Fan Wei and Professor Yan Shaolu, for providing some source material, and Yan Xuening for providing an invaluable photograph for this essay.

1. Chiang Kai-shek, 'The New Life', in T'ang Leang-li (ed.), *Reconstruction in China* (Shanghai, 1935), p.33.
2. R. Griffin (ed.), *Fascism* (Oxford, 1995), p.15.
3. S. Turner and D. Lasler (eds.), *Sociology Responds to Fascism* (London, 1992), pp.11–2.
4. Z. Sternhell, 'Fascism', in D. Miller (ed.), *The Blackwell Encyclopedia of Political Thought* (Blackwell, 1987), p.148.
5. L.E. Eastman, *The Abortive Revolution: China under Nationalist Rule, 1927–37* (Cambridge, MA, 1974), p.xiii and ch.1.
6. Ludwig Rajehman's report is in League of Nations Archives, 5 February 1930, Eastman, *The Abortive Revolution*, p.2.
7. M.J.T. Shieh (ed.), *The Kuomintang: Selected Historical Documents, 1894–1969* (Michigan, 1970), p.152.
8. Quoted in Yang Kongta, 'Faxisiti zi mi' (The Fascist riddle), in *Shidai gonglun*, 16 (1932), Eastman, *The Abortive Revolution*, p.1.
9. 'Ranisha no soshiki to hanman konichi katsudo no jitsurei' (The organization of the Blue Shirts and examples of anti-Manchukuo, anti-Japanese activities) (hereafter RNS), in Ranisha ni kansuru shiryo (Materials on the Blue Shirts) (a specially bound volume of materials in the Toyo Bunko), p.11, Iwai Eiichi, 'Ranisha ni kansuru chosa' (An investigation of the Blue Shirts) issued by the Research Division of the Foreign Ministry, p.6, Eastman, *The Abortive Revolution*, p.40.
10. H.E. Salisbury, *The Long March: The Untold Story* (London, 1985), p.16.
11. Jerry Bernard Seps, 'German Military Advisers and Chiang Kai-shek, 1927–38' (Ph.D. thesis, University of California, Berkeley, 1972), pp.10, 35, 82 and *passism*, Eastman, *The Abortive Revolution*, p.39.
12. A.L. Strong, *China's Millions: The Revolutionary Struggle from 1927 to 1935* (London, 1936), p.403, A. Smedley, *China's Red Army Marches* (London, 1936), p.xvii, Salisbury, *Long March* p.16.
13. Seps, p.10, 35, 83 and *passim*.
14. Jin Feng, *Juntong sijutou* (Biography of the Four Heads of the Chinese Special Service) (Beijing, 1995), pp.64–5 (hereafter *Juntong sijutou*), Liu, Huijun, *Chiang Kai-shek and Dai Li* (Nanjing, 1995), p.22 (hereafter *Chiang Kai-shek*).
15. There is debate and confusion about the name of the organization. Some have argued that there was a proposal but no such organization existed. See Liu, *Chiang Kai-shek*, pp.22–3. I found that the Blue Shirts as a terror Fascist organization existed during 1930s. The name might be different from one place to the other, for example, Lanyishe, Fuxingshe, Lixingshe, but they belonged to the same organization and had the same leaders: Chiang and Dai Li. My parents were radical students in 1930s and they remembered that Blue Shirts were a major Fascist organization. Members of the Blue Shirts were terrorists and counter-revolutionaries. After 1949 when the Communists took over China, one of the targets, according to some official documents, was to eliminate counter-revolutionaries, and members of the Blue Shirts were included. See also Li, Jixin, *Zhongguo tewu* (Chinese SS) (Nanzhou, 1996), pp.101–4, Gan, Guoxun, 'Si "Lanyishe" binhui Liu Jianqiong' (Explanation of the Blue Shirts and recollections of Liu Jianqiong), *Zhuji wenxue*, 21 (1972), 11–6, Jin Feng, *Juntong sijutou*, p.64.

16 Eastman, *The Abortive Revolution*, pp.55–6.
17 Dai Li was the Head of the Second Section of the Military Affairs Commission's Bureau of Investigation and Statistics. He directed one of China's largest special service network. Zhen Jiemin was his assistant. Dai died in 1946 and Zhen became one of his successors. See Jin Feng, *Juntong sijutou, passim*.
18 Eastman, pp.34–44, Jin Feng, *Juntong sijutou*, pp.66–7.
19 'Guomindang yu faxishiti yundong' (The Nationalist Party and the Fascist movement), *shehui xinwen* (The Society Mercury), 4 (1933), 274.
20 Iwai Eiichi, 'Ranisha ni kansuru chosa', pp.38–9, Eastman, pp.43–4.
21 Editorial article, *Shehui xinwen*, 3 (1933), 147, Eastman, p.43.
22 Iwai, 'Ranisha ni kansuru chosa', p.188, Eastman, *The Abortive Revolution*, p.42.
23 Liu Chenchun, 'Yinho yiwang' (Memories at Yinho), *Chuanchi wenxue zoukan*, 6 (1966), 235.
24 'RNS', p.5, Eastman, *The Abortive Revolution*, p.45.
25 Editorial article, 'Minquan yu zuyi' (People's sovereignty and freedom), *Shehui xinwen*, 3 (1933), 147, Chen Qiuyun, 'Faxisiti zhuyi yu Zhongguo' (Fascism and China), *Qiantu* (Future), 2 (1934), 3, Eastman, pp.42–3.
26 Lu Kejen, 'Shehui minzhu zhuyi shifou keyi jiu Zhongguo?' (Can social-democracy save China?), *Shehui xinwen*, 3 (1933), 435.
27 'RNS', p.5, Eastman, p.46.
28 Editorial article, 'women xuyao zenyang de wenhua?' (What kind of culture do we need?), Shehui xinwen, 3 (1933), 354.
29 'RNS', p.25, Eastman, p.47.
30 S.C. Chu, 'The New Life Movement 1934–1937', in J.E. Lane, *Research in the Social Sciences on China* (New York, 1957), p.4.
31 Iwai, pp.22, Eastman, p.67.
32 Chu, 'The New Life Movement 1934–1937', p.3.
33 Minguo ershisannian xinshenghuo yundong zongbaogao (Complete Report of the New Life Movement of 1934) (Nanchang, 1935), p.66.
34 W.H. Chen, 'The New Life Movement', *Information Bulletin*, 2 (1936), 189.
35 M.C. Wright, *The Last Stand of Chinese Conservatism* (Stanford, 1957), pp.300–12.
36 Chu, 'The New Life Movement 1934–1937', p.4.
37 See *Xinshenghuo yundong shouce* (New Life Movement Handbook) (Nanchang, 1935).
38 See Chiang's speech 'The New Life Movement', p.34.
39 Chiang's speeches were included in the Completed Report of the New Life Movement of 1934, op. cit., see also Chu, p.3 and Chen, pp.190–1.
40 Chiang Kai-shek, 'The New Life Movement', p.41 and Chu, pp.3–4.
41 Chen, pp.197–200 and Chu, pp.4–5.
42 *New York Times*, 22 May, 1934.
43 T.S. Young, 'The Chinese have found their Leader', *China Weekly Review*, 78 (1936), 452.
44 Chiang Kai-shek, 'The New Life Movement', pp. 33–5.
45 Lin Yutang, *My Country and My People* (London, 1936), p.89.
46 J. Israel, *Student Nationalism in China 1927–1937* (Stanford, 1966), p.89.
47 See Helen F. Snow, *Is Youth Crushed again in China?* (Peiping, 1935), Israel, p.98.
48 Helen F. Snow (under pseud. Nym Wales), *Notes on the Chinese Student Movement, 1935–1936* (Madison, CT, 1959), pp.9, 24.
49 Helen F. Snow, *Is Youth Crushed again in China?*, p.99, Israel, p.99.
50 G.W. Shepherd, 'The Chinese Communists', in *China Christian Year Book, 1934–1935* (Shanghai, 1935), p.96.

51 Yu Wenwei, 'Zhonghua minzu xianzai xuyao hezong jiaoyu?' (What kind of education does the nation need?), *Qian tu*, 1 (1933), 3–5, Qiu Chun, 'Jiaoyu yu Zhonghua minzu xing zi gai-cao' (Education and the rebuilding of China's national character), *Qiantu*, 1 (1933), 10, Eastman, p.49.
52 Lin Shicun, 'Guojia zongdongyuan' (On the mobilization of the whole nation), *Qiantu*, 2 (1934), 4, Eastman, p.49.
52 Yu Wenwei, pp.3–6, Eastman, p.50.
54 Qiu Chun, p.10, Yu Wenwei, pp.3–6, Eastman, p.49.
55 Ai Jen, 'Zhongguo geming jinchenzhong zi jiaoyu wenti' (Education issues in the Chinese revolution), *Qiantu*, 2 (1934), 3–7, Qiu Chun, pp.11–12, Yu Wenwei, pp.3–6, Eastman, pp.49–50.
56 Iwai, pp.36–9, Eastman, p.68.
57 Iwai, pp.37–8, Eastman, p.68.
58 Chiang Kai-shek, 'Xinshenghuo yundong zi yaoyi', in Pei Qinghua (ed.), *Xinshenghuo luncong* (Selected works on the New Life Movement) (hereafter Selected works) (Shanghai, 1936), p.8.
59 Chiang Kai-shek, 'Lun xinshenghuo' (On the New Life Movement), in Pei Qinghua, *Selected works*, p.18.
60 In *Qin Fen tiyu yuebao* (Qin Fen Sports Monthly) (hereafter *Qin Fen*), 1 (1934), 10.
61 Zhou Fuhai, 'Zhongguo tiyu zi zhuixin shimin' (The New mission of Chinese physical education), *Qin Fen*, 1 (1934), 12.
62 Chiang, Kai-shek, 'Tichang tiyu tongdian' (On the promotion of physical exercise and sport), *Qin Fen*, 7 (1934), 1–2.
63 See the report in *Tiyu zhoubao* (Sports Weekly), 25 (1933), 51.
64 See Cheng Denke and Chen Weilin, 'Che Denke huiyi lu' (Cheng Denke's Biography), *Tiyu shiliao*, 14 (1989), 55–68.
65 Chinese Society for History of Physical Education and Sport (hereafter CSHPES) (ed.), *Zhongguo tiyu jindaishi* (Modern Chinese History of Physical Education and Sport) (Beijing, 1989), p.320.
66 Cheng Dengke, 'Du Fang Wanbang wen' (My view on Fang Wanbang's article), *Tiyu jikan* (Sports Quarterly), 3 (1935), 353–361.
67 Dong Shouyi, 'Tichang tiyu de yuandongli' (The original motivation of physical exercise), *Qin Fen*, 1 (1934), 26–7.
68 Cheng Dengzhen, 'Fuxin minzhu yu tichang guoshu zi yiyi' (On the restoration of the nation and the promotion of physical exercise), *Guosu zhoukan* (National Sports Weekly), 127 (1934).
69 Zhao Lin, 'Zhejiang jindai tiyu xiaoshiliao' (Modern exercise in Zhejiang), in *Zhejiang tiyu shiliao* (Archives of Zhejiang Physical Activities), 5 (1984) 32.
70 Cheng Dengke, 'Zheyang liyong junjin quanli fuzu minzong tiyu shi quanmin tiyuhua' (How to use police and armed forces to promote sports among masses), *Tiyu jikan*, 2 (1935), 179–187.
71 Shao Rugan, 'Ruhe tichang quanmin tiyu' (How to promote a mass physical exercise campaign), *Qin Fen*, 8 (1935), 53.
72 CSHPES, pp.104–5.
73 Shieh, p.160.
74 CSHPES, p.306.
75 Education Ministry, Taiwan, *Zhonghua minguo jiaoyu nianjian* (Educational Yearbook of the Republic of China), 5th edition (Taibei, 1984), pp.1785, 1790, 1791, 1908.
76 See *Qin Fen* 6 (1935).
77 Liu Xuesong, 'Kefou jiang tiyu Tongjun guosu dachen yipian' (Can we combine

sport, Boy's Army and the Chinese Wusu together?), *Tiyu jikan* (Sport Quarterly), 1 (1935), 7–10.
78 Dwight W. Edwards, '1934–35 Annual Report' (Peiping, 1935), in Historical Library of the Young Men's Christian Association, New York, N.Y.; Israel, p.99.
79 Unsigned, 'Chiang Kai-shek developing a Fascism à la Chine', *China Weekly Review*, 68 (1934), 387.
80 Seem *Zhejiang tiyu wenshi* (Archives of Zhejiang Sports History), 4 (1984), 34.
81 See *Liangyou* (Good Friend Pictorial), 121 (1936).
82 See *Liangyou*, 139 (1939).
83 Israel, p. 191.
84 Chengdu Research Institute of Sports History (hereafter CRISH) (ed.), *Zhongguo jindai tiyusi ziliao* (Historical Material of Sports History in Modern China) (Chengdu, 1988), pp.190–1.
85 See *Qin Fen*, 1 (1935), 93.
86 'Chiang Kaishek developing a Fascism à la Chine', p.387.
87 Quoted in James C. Thomson, *While China Faced West* (Cambridge, MA, 1969), p.168.
88 See *Lianyou*, 90 (1934).
89 See *Zhejiang tiyu wenshi* (Archives of Zhejiang Sports History), 4 (1984), 34.
90 See *Zhongyang ribao* (National News), 12 June 1934.
91 *Shishi xinbao* (China Times), 2 June 1936, *Zhongyang dangwu yuekan* (Central Party Affairs Monthly), 95 (1936), 558–9.
92 See Liangyou, 120 (1936).
93 'Jiaobu juiding fude kaoca tuanyuan' (The Education Ministry decided the members of the Delegation for the Research of German Physical Education), *Qin Fen*, 9 (1936), 864.
94 Iwai, p.156, Eastman, p.65.
95 'Chiang Kai-shek developing a Fascism à la Chine', p.387.
96 Chu, p.8.
97 Iwai, p.157–8, Eastman, pp.68–9.
98 Thomson, p.177.
99 Ibid., p.183.
100 'Chiang Kai-shek developing a Fascism à la Chine', p.387.
101 *Da gong bao*, 4, 6, 11 December 1934.
102 See Thomson, ch. 7 and 8.
103 Chu, pp.1–3, Arif Dirlik, 'The Ideological Foundations of the New Life Movement: A Study in Counter-revolution', *Journal of Asian Studies*, XXXIV (1975), 945–8.
104 Jin Feng, *passim*, Eastman, pp. 77–9.
105 James S. Barnes, *The Universal Aspects of Fascism* (London, 1928), p.241.

72

JAPANESE FASCISM AND THE TENNŌ IMPERIAL STATE

Tetsunari Matsuzawa

Source: *Papers of the Japanese Studies Centre* 10 (1984): 1–15. Translated into English by Valerie McGown.

Introduction

From ancient times to the present, ever since a class state was set up in Japan with the emperor as its crown, discrimination and oppression, anti-foreignism and overseas aggression and economic exploitation have existed. Moreover, it was the more or less intimate relationship between overseas aggression and domestic oppression which played an important role in the formation of the emperor system and the class state. In some cases, economic exploitation was also involved.

From the beginning of the modern period, the interrelationship between these three factors (that is, discrimination, oppression and exploitation) became even closer and more mutually reinforcing. First of all, political groups which have thus far won the struggle for leadership fix the boundaries of the State and the race quite strictly and thus clearly distinguish those on the inside as 'citizens' and those on the outside as others or 'outsiders'. At the same time, they consolidate their power by making the nation into a centralized system of government and by locking opposition forces and the interests of the people into a single network of parliament, political parties and elections. This is what 'modern' social science calls nationalism or the formation of a nation state.

Secondly, over quite a long period, which bridges this period of the establishment of the framework of the state, the relationship between capital and wage labour (exploitation) is shaped. A pool of free, property-less labour is forced off the land through discrimination and oppression or aggression and conquest, and as a result of the wheeling and dealing which occurs during this process, there is an amassing of wealth (which is frequently also accompanied by aggression and conquest, discrimination and oppression). Then, the two — capital and labour — are brought together and, quite rapidly, a mode of production arising from the relationship between capital and labour takes a dominant position within the national boundaries. The capitalists attain a position of power over the wage labourers.

From the very earliest stage, these two forms of power — political and social — join together and help each other both publicly and privately. Together they form the ruling class and come to govern over the ruled.

All these characteristics can clearly be seen in the formation of the Japanese 'nation state' since the period of the end of the Bakufu and the Meiji Restoration.

The 'anti-outsider' principle in the early modern state

In 1869, the Meiji oligarchy fought and won the *Boshin* (civil) War. The first thing they did was to qualitatively strengthen the colonial type of rule which, since the previous period, had been exercised over the Ainu people[1] (who were a different race), and over Ainu land. In the same year, they divided the whole of the Ainu lands into administrative regions and put pro-*Bakufu daimyō* in charge. The Commissioner of the Colonization Office of Hokkaidō who was appointed at the same time was given all inclusive powers by the central government, took leadership of the local *daimyō* and extended his control over all of the Ainu people and their territory throughout Hokkaidō. Thereafter, by means of the banning of the Ainu language and the enforcement of Japanese, the forceful imposition of a pattern of settled agriculture, discrimination, trickery and maltreatment, and physical destruction through alcoholism and veneral disease, they devised the extermination or total assimilation of the Ainu race. The land, in both name and reality, was taken as Japanese.

Then the clan bureaucrats turned their attention southward. At that time, in the Ryūkyūs, there was a strong sense of pride in that country as an independent monarchy. In response, first of all, in 1872, the Ryūkyū *han* was established, and in an unparalleled move, the king was appointed to the position of *king* of the *han*. Since this first step towards annexation met with fierce opposition, having created a diversion and sounded out the situation by despatching troops to Taiwan in 1874 (supposedly for the protection of the Ryūkyū people), the Meiji government finally made the Ryūkyūs part of Japan in 1879 under the threat of mobilization of armed force. At first, some of the people of the Ryūkyū group vigorously refused to become part of the modern Japanese state, but they were subjected to extreme discrimination and finally forced into its lowest strata.

Even with only this brief glimpse, one can see how conspicuous discrimination based on the anti-other or anti-foreign principle was in modern Japan. That is, what was more striking than anything else was the relationship by which intense discrimination and oppression, hostility and aggression towards 'outsiders' guaranteed a powerful cohesion and close integration within the 'in-group'. Firstly, this sort of relationship played a very important role in giving rise to a highly efficient form of exploitation. That is, naturally amongst those who held power, but also amongst the ruled, discrimination and oppressive attitudes were most marked towards not only the Ainu and the people of the Ryūkyūs but later also towards Koreans and outcaste *burakumin* people as well as the non-propertied class (especially the poverty-stricken) and women workers. Naturally, the compensation for the labour of the victims of such discrimination was extremely low. Conversely, because of this very discrimination and oppression, those who committed the discrimination and oppression came to evaluate themselves more highly and strengthened their mutual solidarity. But, there is also little doubt that, in this process, they lost any critical perspective towards the ruling powers and became increasingly obedient to the system. For example, most of the workers at factories such as the Yawata Steel, which, in the early period, had the very latest machinery, were caught in this trap. Seen from the capitalists' side, nothing could have been more convenient.

On the one hand, they could give the odd jobs and the worst jobs to those who were discriminated against at extremely low wages while on the other hand, they could, without worrying about the discriminatory, submissive and conservative workers such as those who worked in the highly modern factories, pursue higher productivity and raise larger profits. Without doubt, it could be said that integration based on the anti-other or anti-foreign principle was absolutely essential to industrial capitalism in 'modern' Japan. It is hardly necessary to point out that the existence of 'others' who are ruined is a precondition for the primitive accumulation of capital in the course of establishing a new state and system.

Secondly, integration based on the 'anti-outsider' principle was also used by the socially and politically powerful as the basis on which they governed the people.

In modern Japan, the activists who tried to oppose the government and the system were completely suppressed. Labelled as 'ideologues (*shugisha*), 'reds' and 'traitors', they were largely ostracized from civil life. In other words, the ruling powers drove a wedge of discrimination and division between the members of civil society and those outside it, stirred up anti-foreignism and thus achieved cohesion among the people in general. Moreover, this same device was incorporated into the very means of suppression itself. By skilfully differentiating the use of direct suppression such as imprisonment and torture, from conciliation and buying-off, the authorities divided the suppressed into the non-converted and the converted, caused discrimination and struggle between them and tried, by these means, to induce the converted to join forces with each other. Basically the same methods were used in the case of the Ainu, the people of the Ryūkyūs living in Japan, and later the Koreans, the outcaste *burakumin* and also the property-less, especially the poverty-sticken, and women workers. The very fact of being Ainu was enough to earn one contempt. People from the very fact of being Ainu was enough to earn one contempt. People from the Ryūkyūs and the Koreans were discriminated against as 'new citizens'; for example, in the words of landlords who rented rooms, 'No Ryūkyūans or Koreans need apply'. And the property-less class, the poverty-stricken and women were treated with contempt. Thus, by treating 'outsiders' in this way, the civilian population tightened their community-type (*kyōdōtai-teki*) bonds. It goes without saying that the ruling powers reproduced, promoted, encouraged and strengthened these relationships both directly and indirectly.

A constitution and a system of party politics based on it were introduced into the civilian society from which the Koreans resident in Japan, the property-less class and those who paid less than a certain level of tax were excluded. Although this system claimed to represent, indirectly, the opposition forces and the interests of the people, it was in reality a device intended to appease and induce acceptance. The ideology of this system was disseminated very early — already by the 1880's; and, between 1889–1890 and the Hara 'People's' cabinet of 1918 and the first general election of 1928, it gradually became established. It must be admitted that, within certain limits, a level of effective government was realized. The mode of existence of modern Japan was an oppressive system of control which discriminated subtly in the use of direct suppression and of conciliation and inducement. Integration based on the 'anti-outsider' principle was systematized and institutionalized.

Anti-foreignism, integration and the Emperor system

Naturally, when opposition to and disputes with other countries and peoples extended into fighting and war, anti-foreignism was greatly strengthened and integration was most tightly achieved. Accordingly, under modern Japanese industrial capitalism and its system of oppression and control, external aggression and war were welcomed, and frequently events were so arranged that they spontaneously occurred. Conversely, through the prosecution of external aggression and war, capitalism flourished and the system of oppression and control was further strengthened. However, in 'modern Japan', the most intense form of integration by anti-foreignism — external aggression and war — naturally was not the day to day means or policy for controlling the people. Only after having selected the most favourable time and calculating when the risk or danger was at its lowest would the ruling powers employ such extraordinary measures.

So, who or what was the actor responsible for making such judgements and calculations and serving the interests of capital? Who actually operated the system of oppression and control? The answer is none other than the political parties and the Meiji clan bureaucrats. But how could they possess the single, sufficiently united purpose needed to run such a large nation-state? As a matter of fact, no such unity was assumed in the imperial constitution and, indeed, it was frequently impossible to achieve a consensus of opinion among the leadership. As such times, it was the emperor who exercised his authority in unique ways. Itö Hirobumi, Inoue Kaoru and others who drafted the constitution, designed it in such a way.

There is a theory that the emperor was little more than a robot controlled by various political groups and restricted by the constitution, but such a theory is simply not tenable. This is because the state responsibilities of the emperor were specifically set out in the very constitution on the existence of which this theory rests. The emperor held sovereignty as head of state and also held ultimate responsibility for the army and navy. But most important of all is the fact that the emperor reserved the final right of approval or refusal. In other words, the political structure was such that all those who actually exercised authority were ultimately required to report to the emperor and submit to his sanction. Moreover, this was set down in the constitution. In the case of the third emperor of modern Japan, Hirohito, this ultimate right was exercised at least three times prior to the end of the Second World War. The first case was in 1928 when Hirohito used his power of refusal to dismiss the Prime Minister, Tanaka Giichi, on the occasion of the bomb incident in which Chang Tso-lin died. Tanaka was driven to an early death as a result. The next case was in 1936 at the time of the rather paradoxical uprising by the Young Officers (the as-yet immature supporters of fascist revolutionary theory in Japan) who mobilized troops in what they saw as an expression of their devotion to the emperor. The emperor berated the senior officers for their vacilation and ordered that they take command of the troops and suppress the rebellion or else, if they didn't take immediate action, he would take command in person. The third is the very belated decision to end the war in 1945 — though rather than a decision it was simply a matter of the emperor saying to Anami, the Minister of War who had advocated a policy of fighting to the last man on behalf of the emperor, 'It is enough'.

Along with possession of the power of this final sanction, came the function of coordinating the political groups within the ruling circles which had become divided and politicized and even fought among themselves, and of bringing together their mutually antagonistic views. It was not that he actively took this role upon himself but rather that the function of regulation and integration operated through those close to the throne, including the Keeper of the Privy Seal, the Lord Chamberlain, the Minister of the Imperial Household — the so-called imperial court group, and because other political forces sounded out the views 'from above' (that is, the emperor). Because they knew that the emperor held the power of final sanction, all those in power made up or changed their minds and also decided on the method and timing of announcements in accordance with his views. There were also some cases, however few, where the emperor's intentions were deliberately misrepresented and then communicated to others.

Last but not least, we come to the question of the symbolic role of the emperor. It is this which is the most important aspect. For all those who were involved in the system, the emperor was the embodiment of family affection. This was sometimes even raised to the religious level of representing him as the embodiment of compassion. But, in direct contrast, for those who were rejected by the system, or mercilessly slaughtered, from whom intolerable sacrifices were exacted, he was what the Chinese called '*tung-yang kuei*' or 'demon of the East' and the major target of revenge. This was apparent also in the individual acts of terrorism committed time and again by anarchists like Kanno Suga, communists such as Namba Daisuke and members of the movement for Korean independence, such as I-Bon Chan. In other words, Mutsuhito (the Meiji emperor), Yoshihito (the Taishō emperor) and also the present emperor Hirohito had two faces — on the surface, one of affection and compassion, but underneath, one of the demon. The emperor was, in short, the personification (assuming that the emperor was a kind of person) of integration through the 'anti-outsider' or anti-foreignism principle. This is obviously an antinomy, but such a paradox was virtually implicit in 'modern Japan', or possibly any 'modern' state. The paradox is to synthesize and regulate 'anti-foreignism' and 'integration', and furthermore to embody those functions in one figure. It is only possible to truly resolve this paradox by eliminating and overthrowing the state itself and its symbol.

For this modern Japanese state system with its peculiar characteristics, I will use '*Tennō* imperial state' as the most appropriate term. Since its creation, through its destruction and reconstruction, the state has combined external aggression/war, a capitalist economy and a system of oppression and control by means of the single thread of integration through anti-foreignism, and thus achieved the 'great prosperity' of today.

The nature of Japanese fascism

Certainly there are many similarities between the *Tennō* imperial state and Japanese fascism (both the movement and the system), in the methods of government. On the other hand, however, it is clear that major differences can also be seen. Under the *Tennō* imperial state, the anti-outsider or anti-foreign principle was one of the main factors in the integration of the state. However, under the Japanese fascist movement and, after 1937, government, anti-foreignism and aggression were the predominant fundamental principles.

In the case of the *Tennō* imperial state, it is clear that integration through anti-foreignism was based on discrimination and division. That is, the cohesion of the 'inside' was strengthened by forcing certain parts onto the 'outside'. Furthermore, this system took a number of different forms of expression — (industrial) capitalism, a constitutional monarchy-type party political system, and a system of oppression and control (largely bureaucratic in character) combined with intermittent overseas aggression or war.

These different forms of expression were closely intertwined to form the modern Japanese state. Normally, change or reformation of this system or state could come about through either

(i) the fixed course of constitution, parliament and elections, or
(ii) through compromise and dealings or collaboration between the disparate forces within the ruling circles — which could be broadly divided into two, i.e. the Meiji clan bureaucrats and the political parties, or
(iii) through the opportunistic and arbitrary judgement and decisions of the emperor and those close to the throne.

In the case of (ii), the political parties tried to use mass movements to apply pressure on the Meiji bureaucrats, as in the case of the People's Rights movement of the 1880s, the Hibiya Fire Incident of 1905, the Rice Riots of 1918 and the Defence of Constitutionalism Movement in 1912 and 1922. In these cases, the 'activity' of the party lobbyists and newspapers sympathetic to particular political parties was evident, but their autonomy and independence as popular movements was frequently lacking. Therefore, they did little more than provide the power or pressure which the political parties could use as basis in negotiating or dealing with other political forces. However, after about the middle of the 1920s, such a 'necessity' disappeared and the popular will turned to a completely different form of expression. Furthermore, the rebellion by the troops of the Chōshū *han* in 1869–70 and the samurai uprisings of 1874–77 were attempts at reformation using the armed forces (i.e. the military) and were important, but thereafter they completely disappeared from history and must be regarded as a sidetrack. After the First World War, there were many workers' and peasants' movements but opinions are divided on the question. For the purpose of this paper, I simply wish to point out that they usually took a representative form of organization like unions. I wish to make clear that even the very militant factory council system and factory representative system and even strikers' committees were a type of representative organization and not direct democratic movements.

Thus, the *Tennō* imperial state took a fixed form of expression and certain fixed procedures were required in order to change or reform the system. In addition, in the case of popular movements or armed rebellions, there was always a boss-type leader who expressed the interests of the participants on their behalf and represented them indirectly. Even in the case of the union movement, negotiation between groups by small numbers of representatives was the usual method.

Japanese fascism was decisively different. Like German and Italian fascism, it adopted anti-foreignism and aggression as its guiding principle. That is, in the first place, the vast majority of the people participate directly and fully in politics, and, of their own volition they engage in a passionate search for a political ideal completely different from any previously known. The persons who join such a movement are 'true believers'. They ignore the present system, structures and procedures, push aside the existing representatives and spokesmen, judge matters directly themselves and try to realize their idealism. Because they believe in their own subjective goals so strongly and deeply, they are unable to accept the existence of anyone who does not share their views. They feel that non-conformity itself must not be allowed to exist. They harbour a deep and abiding anger towards any non-conformist, attack and try to, or even actually do, obliterate such people as revolutionaries or, in the case of war, as foreigners.

The two main factions of Japanese fascism

Historically speaking, the Japanese fascist movement was born in the face of the threat of the dissolution of the *Tennō* imperial state which, at the end of the 1920s, was rocked by a period of panic and fear of the loss of its special interests in Manchuria and Mongolia. The Japanese fascist movement first appeared as a faction advocating 'return to the origins' which held up the close-knit community usually in a rural setting as an ideal.

Against an historical background which saw the intensification of class opposition and of internal divisions and conflict with the ruling class, Tachibana Kōzaburō, Gondō Seikyō and others proposed an end to all opposition and struggle, and because they thought that the panic [of the depression] was an indication of the fundamental destruction of the capitalist economy and the cities, they stood for anti-urbanism and anti-capitalism, for the elevation of farming, the villages and the peasants. In one word, through Tachibana's proposal of the 'ideal village' (*risō buraku*), and Gondo's 'self-governing community' (*shashoku jichi*) these two, who had been born out of the imminent collapse of the old system, ironically played a major role in accelerating its disintegration. It was an ideology which unmistakably proclaimed the disintegration of the *Tennō* imperial state.[2]

However, what was lacking was conscious systematic attention to the questions of what lay at the end of all their struggle, and of how to realize anti-urbanism and anti-capitalism — the elevation of 'farming' and the close-knit community.

They repeatedly failed even at the preliminary stage, i.e., they failed to fully appreciate the gulf between reality and ideals or aims. This failure was one reason why the various popular movements in which this faction became involved were soon stifled. Firstly, between 1920 and 1931, Tachibana and others set up the *aikyō kai* (love village society) with branches in local areas and the *aikyō juku* to train leaders. The *aikyō kai* was a type of cooperative association for which the 'self-governing communities' (*sha-shoku jichi*) had been the forerunner. Also, in 1932 the Gondō group (joined by some of the Tachibana group and also Wagō Tsuneo and Nagano Rō) organized mass action against the Diet, in the form of petition demanding the cancellation of rural debt. However, about the middle of this period, behind the scenes, between February and May 1932 Tachibana and Gondō joined up with the group of Inoue Nisshō and moved rapidly towards terrorism, in the blood brotherhood (*ketsumeidan*) incident and the May 15th incident. In any case, the lack of methodology, and the recognition of the tension in the situation and of the deadlock facing mass action, drew Tachibana and Gondō towards Inoue. With respect to Inoue, it was anti-urbanism, anti-capitalism and the desire to promote the value of 'farming', his theory of phenomenological monism based on the feeling of the unity of all creation and the attempt to realize this in the blood brotherhood-type groups, that drove him to join with Tachibana and Gondō. Although the phenomenological monism of Inoue with it philosophical and religious overtones lacked the historical approach of Tachibana and Gondō, the content is very similar to that of the close-knit community thesis of the latter two.[3] One could even say that the dissolution of all internal struggle through terrorism, the creation of internally close-knit communities such as the ideal village, the self-governing community or the blood brotherhood (*ketsumeidan*), was virtually the inevitable conclusion of the logic of the 'return of the origins' faction. Thus, this superficially peaceful and, at a glance even idyllic, theory of the 'return to the origins' faction of Japanese fascism, in fact, unmistakably harboured within it a vicious anti-foreignism and aggressiveness.

On the other hand, the 'controlled development' faction of Japanese fascism emerged after the historical and theoretical dissolution of the state had been publicly proclaimed and promoted by the 'return to the origins' faction. The institutionalization and integration of the *new* state and system was the historical mission of this faction and was indeed the objective task which confronted it.

The main theme of this group was the idea of a moral state and people. The state of being tightly organized and very closely and firmly integrated was itself highly valued. It was postulated that the new state and people which were to be created would constitute the realization of superior values because of

1 the dialectical *aufheben* (sublation) of opposites, e.g. Takabatake Motoyuki or
2 the realization of comprehensive order, e.g. Kanokogi Kazunobu or
3 of sharing the mission of saving mankind, e.g. Amano Tatsuo.

To put it another way, it was regarded as an expression of justice and morality. Two policy implications tended to follow from such a thesis. First was the establishment of a strong body politic supported by the spontaneous approval of the general populace. Specifically, having rejected the party political system and proposed a type of direct imperial rule, their basic idea was to replace those close to the throne and eliminate intermediate political forces. Secondly, economic regulation for the welfare of the general public was to be the goal. An economic system combining private ownership and a market economy with a planned economy was conceived. In this way, once a theoretically correct line was achieved, it was natural and inevitable that it would be forcefully disseminated. The practical and central leaders of the 'controlled development' faction of Japanese fascism called for its dissemination to Asia and the whole world. Ōkawa Shūmei issued a manifesto linking 'revolution in Europe' and 'the revival of Asia', which saw the destiny of the new Japan as to give birth to the 'dawn of a new world' joining East and West. Kita Ikki appealed for the revolutionary transformation of China and Japan and the waging of a war to smash inequality on an international scale by means of war to establish justice for all mankind.[4] Ishihara Kanji called for the building of a peaceful world from which war had finally disappeared, but this would result after the East Asian League, yellow eastern culture centred on Japan, had waged total war against white culture, the Western block centred on America.

In the case of these two factions of Japanese fascism, dedication or spiritual surrender to the emperor was more or less inevitable. The achievement of a close knit community which inevitably brought with it the obliteration of those different from oneself, or, to put it another way, the complete regimentation of the society, was a logical contradiction. This is also true of the high value placed on integration which did not permit the existence of non-conformists. As long as a certain part was discriminated against and forced to the 'outside', this could not be called *total* regimentation; nor is it possible for such a community to be truly close-knit. Similarly, attacking and destroying, eliminating outsiders and heresy could certainly not be called moral. If one follows the reasoning of the Japanese fascists, one inevitably runs into a wall midway. Inescapably, logical and rational thought is abandoned or despaired of and one has to seek a supra-metaphysical existence to which to dedicate and surrender oneself. Thus, the fascists were inevitably attracted to the emperor, who was the symbol and personification of the basic contradiction in the *Tennō* imperial state, because of the similarity of their own logical contradictions and because he was a familiar supra-metaphysical existence. And so they themselves came to believe and to be completely absorbed in him. The importing of the 'emperor' into their illogical reasoning almost inevitably constituted a milestone on the way towards total affirmation of the reality of the Tennō imperial state. The tendency, consciously or unconsciously, to ignore the gap between reality and ideal or goal was one axis of Japanese fascist 'thought'.

The active phase of the Japanese fascist movement following the Manchurian incident

With the Manchurian incident on 18 September 1931, Japanese fascism entered for the first time upon successful political action. In other words, the invasion of North-east China, by the Kwantung Army under Ishihara Kanji as officer-in-charge of the operation, was to be 'the final solution' to the Manchurian-Mongolian problem — that is, the problem stemming from fear of the loss of special rights and interests in the region. This military operation provoked a domestic incident — an attempted *coup d'état* which followed in October 1931. The October incident was the result of a brief and 'unholy' alliance between the two factions previously mentioned which quickly ended in failure. Nevertheless, as mentioned previously, between February and May, 1932, the terrorism in which Fujii Hitoshi and other young naval officers were also involved, spelt the death of party politics as well as bringing about 'conversion' of the *zaibalsu* and financial capital. This, together with the Manchurian incident, was a major step in moving the domestic system towards fascism. The active phase of the Japanese fascist movement began in the period from the Manchurian incident to the October incident, with the terrorism against individuals during February to May, 1932, the establishment of the puppet regime in Manchukuo in March, and then, in May, the assassination of Prime Minister Inukai who had only taken office in the previous December (in the May 15th incident). This was the beginning of the process by which the Japanese fascists caused the existing *Tennō* imperial state frequent severe shocks as they seized one concession (or rather fascist reform) after another.

What sort of a person was Ishihara Kanji — the elite military man who had given initial impetus to the beginning of the active phase of the Japanese fascist movement, or, to put it another way, the beginning of the process to accomplish the Japanese fascist reformation? How were his character and thinking formed? What was the structure and the religious and military-scientific background of his unique conception of 'Final World War'?[5]

Needless to say, because there were, both inside and outside Japan, people in important posts who supported or at least sympathized with this man and his thinking, it was possible for Ishihara and the Kwantung Army to act arbitrarily and take matters into their own hands. It is a fact that Ishihara himself, through the presentation of his theories and the utilization of his position, made a positive effort to create as many sympathizers as he could around him. This included the Staff Officers of the Kwantung Army under its Chief of Staff, Itagaki Seishirō, the Head of the Special Service Agency at Mukden, Doihara Kenji, and Hanaya Shō of the same Agency, the Commander of the 10th Infantry Regiment, Tōmiya Tetsuo, China Research Officer, attached to the General Staff and stationed at Mukden, Imada Shintarō, Squad Leader of the Mukden Military Police, Mitani Kiyoshi, the

Chief of Staff of the 16th Army Division, Okada Kikusaburō (who was in Mukden at the time), and Staff Officer of the Korean Army, Kanda Masatane. In addition, Amakasu Masahiko, who was notorious for the massacre of Ōsugi Sakae and others and who was a central fiure in the latter period of the *kyōwa kai*, and Nakano Kōitsu who was a powerful member of the right-wing civilian group, *daiyūhō kai*, were also closely involved. Ishihara tried to create an even wider organization or network of support around those who, in a narrow sense, had been the instigators of the Manchurian incident. His approaches to and discussions with members of the South Manchurian Railway Company's research section (Sada Kōjirō, Head) and other sections, and with another civilian right-wing group, the Manchurian Youth League, were for the same purpose. In part, these efforts met with success and, immediately after the 'outbreak' of the incident, the cooperation of many Japanese people (both those resident in Manchuria and others), and organizations especially among the employees of the South Manchurian Railway, the Youth League and the *yūhō kai*, was gained with relative ease. As long as the establishment of a puppet regime deviated slightly from the official policy of the Japanese state, that is, as long as it was a policy of the Japanese fascist revolution, the spontaneity and cooperation of sympathizers were necessary in order to establish a nation-state — at least until 1932. In this situation the conception or ideology of 'Utopia' *(ōdō rakudo)* which has as its banner 'interracial harmony' played an absolutely crucial role as a rallying call.[6]

So, historically, how was this ideology formulated within the society of Japanese residents in Manchuria? I wish to trace the process from its beginnings in the anti-party system movement of the mid-1920's and its subsequent divergence from that movement. Then finally I wish to look at the formation and function of the 'Inter-Racial Harmony' *(minzoku kyōwa)* movement against the background of the development and spread of Chinese nationalism, the inappropriate diplomatic response by the Japanese political parties, and the effect of the world depression. In a word, while this movement provided a basis of mass support for Ishihara Kanji's theories, it also later became an important link in his thinking.

Next, how did the contemporary society of north-east China react to this attempt by Japanese fascism to form a puppet state? In the first place, there was a section within the Korean and Chinese communities resident in Manchuria which supported this state and system.[7] Secondly, the vast majority of Korean and Chinese masses showed a fierce opposition to this 'state'. It was mainly an early anti-Japanese association of ruined peasants and former soldiers and some groups of Korean communists who constituted the anti-imperialist, anti-Japanese movement in the early stages. Later, the communists led by the Chinese who had abandoned the policy of soviets and turned to a united front, became the mainstream of the movement. However, they were all finally defeated by the Japanese fascist army. Japanese fascism expelled, separated or isolated, by armed force or by ideological or political means, everyone who opposed 'the state of Manchukuo'. It thus claimed to have created a utopian society. In other words, 'Manchukuo' was the embodiment of discrimination and anti-foreignism and the realization of these principles as a social system. It is precisely for this reason the Manchukuo is called the first practical test of Japanese fascism.

In Japan itself, there were various expressions of support for and opposition to the situation in Manchuria. Firstly, most of the young officers and the nucleus of the War Ministry and the General Staff Office publicly supported the actions of Ishihara and the Kwantung Army. In particular, the *isseki kai* largely agreed with their ideological position and also gave their actual cooperation. The groups within the Army called the *isseki kai* and the *sakura kai* were formed around the end of the 1920s. These groups tried to achieve some sort of reform by seeking to destroy the Chōshū faction's power, especially its monopoly on appointments, as well as the improvement and modernization of military equipment. They tried to use the 'Manchurian-Mongolian Problem' to make the breakthrough. At the very least, it is true that Ishihara was a registered member of *isseki kai* and that other members expected Ishihara to find a solution to the problem. Furthermore, in 1930, Lieutenant Colonel Hashimoto Kingorō formed the *sakura kai* which was the first fascist group within the army to take a grand stand on the slogan of 'Reconstruction of the State' (*kokka kaizō*). This was one of the groups which took a leading role in the October incident mentioned above. As well, within the bureaucracy or the political parties of the ruling group and also in the property-less class, there appeared people who, in a general or broad sense saw themselves as or were branded 'right-wing reformists' and who jumped on the band-wagon and gave a degree of support to the course of events from the Manchurian incident to the creation of the state of Manchukuo. Thereafter, the 'lessons of Manchukuo' had a not insignificant effect on the shift in direction of the *Tennō* imperial state towards Japanese fascism.

The rise of the control (*tōsei*) faction: Japanese fascism in power

The Manchurian experience was inherited mainly by those of the control (*tōsei*) faction which was formed around 1934. Earlier, around the end of 1931 and the beginning of 1932, young officers such as the Kita-Nishida group, the Ogishi group and others joined with a section of the senior army staff including Araki Sadao and Masaki Jinzaburō and formed the imperial way (*kōdō*) faction to plan the 'restoration' of the armed forces. Those who opposed these moves — Nagata Tetsuzan and others in the mainstream of the *isseki kai* and the study group of staff officers below the rank of major belonging to the War Ministry and the General Staff Office (including

Katakura Chū, Sanada Jōichirō, Sakama Junichi, Nakayama Genpu, Nagai Yatsuji, Katō Michio, Hattori Tokushirō, Nishiura Susumu, Wakamatsu Shichirō, Horiba Kazuo, Arao Kōkō, Tsuji Masanobu, Kumon Arifumi and Shimamura Nori) made plans for a counter *coup d'état*. The 'reformist bureaucrats' who belonged to the *kokui kai* or the Cabinet Research Bureau aligned and merged with the above groups to form the control faction. These events took place in the second phase — the phase of actual implementation of Japanese fascism as a political system. The imperial way (*kōdō*) faction, which was strongly influenced by the controlled development faction and which had placed stress on domestic reform, later developed into a movement for the 'clarification of the national polity' and then into a movement in support of Lieutenant Colonel Aizawa Saburō when Aizawa was on trial by Court-Martial for having cut down by sword and murdered Nagata Tetsuzan, central figure in the control faction, in August 1935. Finally, in 1936, with the February 26 incident, they made moves to implement their theory of a kind of direct imperial rule which was to be achieved largely by completely replacing the advisors to the throne. But even though they were able to mobilize a section of the regular troops to mount an attack and briefly to occupy the central parts of the capital, the attempt ultimately failed.[8]

In contrast, the plan for a counter-*coup d'état* was put into action and this saw the beginning of the period of the control faction's ascendancy. Japanese fascism was soon to reach its zenith. It was Ishihara Kanji, Miyazaki Masayoshi, Katakura Tadashi and others of the so-called Manchurian clique who again seized the spotlight as its first practitioners. They opposed the policies of the Hirota Cabinet, prevented the formation of a cabinet by Hayashi Senjūrō. Thus they created a pattern of integration based on threats. They silenced any who opposed them and eliminated all types of struggle by threatening, both publicly and privately, to use some form of armed force — techniques which had been tested and proved during their 'Manchurian experience'. The same can be said of their concept of a planned economy which was based on the thesis of the expansion of productive capacity. On the basis of his experience since the 1930s and with the help of the so-called 'Miyazaki Agency', Ishihara devised the conception of a 'National Defence State' (*kokubō-kokka*) which had its origins in the theory of 'Final World War'. Then, from the latter half of 1936, he made a determined effort to raise these ideas to the level of national policy and to implement them.

With respect to both the 'outside' (that is, Manchuria) and also the restoration of the 'inside' (that is, Japan itself), on the one hand, it could be said that Ishihara Kanji's schemes were half realized, but on the other, they were also half frustrated. A typical example is the plans for the development of the northern border areas at the end of the 1930s — plans which were controlled and promoted by a colonial bureaucracy which, contrary to his expectations, had grown enormously. The conversion of Manchuria into a huge anti-Soviet military base, which was the core of these plans, was precisely the pivotal point of Ishihara's long-cherished theory.

Ishihara Kanji's group which was known for the logical contradictions of its peculiar theories, in which military science and religious beliefs were mingled, and the peaceful unification of all mankind was to be achieved through a total war of carnage, dissipated its strength as the sequence of the war from the Chinese mainland in 1937 to South-East Asia and the Pacific region developed into a quagmire. The drive towards war against foreign countries greatly strengthened the oppression and control of the domestic system, and brought about the further development of the controlled or planned economy and the final extinction of all opposition struggle. And so a single, powerful but internally vacuous organization, the Imperial Rule Assistance Association *(taisei yokusan kai)*, which embraced the wishes and interests of all the people was created. Now the prosecution of a massive-scale war into which the military dragged the general populace took centre stage. The vast majority of the general public participated directly and completely in this war. With a subjective certainty in the propriety and morality of their actions, they sought with an intense fervour to achieve, *together* with the enemy, a state of happiness. To do this meant to commit murder and other extreme acts of anti-foreign aggression. In a word, this movement, this expression of the extraordinary, was institutionalized: the extraordinary became the ordinary, the normal. Now all that was necessary was to keep the system in constant motion. Thus, even at the zenith of Japanese fascism, there were nonetheless those who quite rightly pointed to the inadequate mobilization of the organization and the internal weakness of the system.

The movement by Ishihara (who had, by 1939, retired from the military) and others for an East Asian League must be considered against such a background. In order to overcome its internal weakness and to activate the domestic system and also to incorporate into the system the peripheral parts of an Empire which expanded endlessly — or, to put it more concretely, as one means by which the administration of the occupied territories could cope with the Chinese United Anti-Japanese Front — something like Ishihara's East Asian League movement or Nakano Seigō's *tōhō kai* was absolutely indispensible. The Tōjō regime which had its foundations in the *tonari gumi* (neighbourhood associations) and the Imperial Rule Assistance Association and which held absolute power, tried to suppress even the very limited power of Ishihara and Nakano as a critical force. However, as far as their actual function is concerned, ironically, it was with the assistance of Ishihara, Nakano and others, that the regime extended its advance step-by-step from East to South-East Asia. There must be no better proof of this than the fact that the theory of the 'Greater East Asia Coprosperity Sphere', which was the central ideology of this aggression, was actually a distorted version which had appropriated the essentials of Ishihara's theory of the 'Final World War'.

Notes

1. Ainu: the aboriginal inhabitants of Japan, whose numbers are concentrated in the northermost Japanese island of Hokkaidō.
2. For details on Tachibana, see my *Tachibana Kōzaburō: Nihon fashizumu genshi kaiki ronha* (Tachibana Kōzaburō: The 'Return to the Origins' Faction in Japanese Fascism), Tokyo, San-ichi shobō, 1972.
3. Concerning Inoue and the Blood Brotherhood League see my *Ajiashugi to fashizumu* (Asianism and Fascism), Tokyo, Renga shobō shinsha, 1979, esp. pp. 120–150.
4. On Kita Ikki, see ibid., pp. 179–235.
5. This essay was written as introduction to a larger work in Japanese. For a full discussion of the questions raised in this paragraph, see my *Nihon faschizumu no taigai shinryaku: Ishihara Kanji to 'minzoku kyōwa' undō* (Japanese Fascism's External Aggression: Ishihara Kanji and the 'Inter-racial Harmony' movement), Tokyo, San-ichi shobō, 1983.
6. On the ideology of 'utopianism in Manchuria', see the work cited in note 2 above, at especially pp. 151–178.
7. The circumstances which led Koreans or Chinese to support the new state are examined in detail in my latest book, cited in note 4 above.
8. See Suzuki Masasetsu and Matsuzawa Tetsunari, *Ni ni roku jiken to seinen shōkō* (The February 26th Incident and the Young Officers Movement), Tokyo, San-ichi shobō, 1974.

73

FASCISM FROM BELOW?

A comparative perspective on the Japanese right, 1931–1936

Gregory J. Kasza

Source: *Journal of Contemporary History* 19(3) (1984) 607–29.

Following Maruyama Masao, many scholars of Japanese politics identify the period from the Manchurian Incident in 1931 to the rebellion of junior officers in 1936 as that of 'fascism from below', i.e., the time when direct action by 'fascist' groups standing outside élite circles was a dominant factor in the political system.[1] By means of propaganda, intimidation, assassinations, and the plotting of several abortive coups, rightist groups contributed significantly to the breakdown of party government, to the pervasive sense of political crisis, and to the delegitimation of democracy, freedom, individualism, and internationalism in public discourse. Yet, while the historical importance of these groups is undeniable, there is little agreement on the proper comparative framework for their analysis. The term 'fascism' has frequently been applied, but its opponents have justifiably criticized its ambiguity in much of the scholarship on Japan. While some have retreated to a middle ground of referring simply to Japan 'in the era of fascism',[2] others have abandoned the concept altogether,[3] though without as yet arriving at an alternative comparative framework.[4] Unfortunately, most critics of the fascist concept have been as guilty of conceptual slackness as its proponents, since they censure the sloppy use of the term by others without offering any rigorous definition of their own. The debate has been further complicated by ideological tendencies, the critics often attributing currency of the term to Marxist influence (Japan's leftist intellectuals have always been divided on the relevance of the fascist concept), while some advocates of the fascist interpretation brand their opponents as apologists for imperialism (very rarely the case).[5]

If this debate highlights the need to employ a strict empirical definition of fascism, the conviction evident on both sides also tends to conceal our ignorance of most rightist groups active in interwar Japan. The debate over fascism has largely focused on the issue of whether the ruling Japanese regime could at some point be characterized as fascist — if a fascist regime would be one controlled by a fascist movement, one must agree with those who contend that no such regime was ever formed.[6] However, as was true of the right in most countries of interwar Europe, Japan's rightist groups were an important historical phenomenon in and of themselves, their failure to seize power notwithstanding. Though a few of the more prominent rightist elements have been carefully studied,[7] there were literally hundreds of active right-wing organizations, and as yet we have no real overview of their character or activities.

This article reanalyses the utility of the fascist concept as a comparative framework for the Japanese right in the early 1930s with the hope of filling some of the gaps in previous treatments of this question. A tight empirical definition of fascism has been drawn from the best of recent scholarship on inter-war Europe. The focus is not on the ruling regime but on rightist groups operating for the most part outside state élite circles. A broad overview of the right will be offered rather than a focus on one or two specific groups. Finally, analysis of the relevance of the fascist concept is complemented by an effort to suggest other lines of comparison where the facist framework does not appear applicable.

Identifying a fascist movement

The best empirical description of a fascist movement for comparative purposes is that offered by Stanley Payne.[8] His effort does not prejudge the issues of why fascist movements arose or what accounted for their success or failure in various countries. It does enable us to identify the type and to avoid confusing it with other movements that shared some but not all of its essential characteristics. Payne has organised the features of a typical fascist movement under three headings: the fascist negations, ideology and goals, and style and organisation. Though the reader should refer to Payne's own work for a full account, a brief review of these is offered for reference here.

The fascist negations are three: (a) antiliberalism, (b) anticommunism, and (c) anticonservatism. The first two involve what Juan Linz has called the 'rejection of the institutionalization of conflict and cleavages in modern societies'.[9] Fascism is politically antiliberal in its opposition to parliamentary government, which institutionalizes party conflict, and economically antiliberal in its opposition to an unfettered capitalist economy, which institutionalizes business competition through the market. Likewise, the fascist rejects communism for its doctrine of conflict between classes. The anticonservatism of fascism is best understood with reference to the second heading of ideology and goals.

Four traits are listed under ideology and goals:

(a) creation of a new nationalist authoritarian state based not merely on traditional principles or models;
(b) organization of some new kind of regulated, multi-class, integrated national economic structure, whether called national corporatist, national socialist, or national syndicalist;
(c) the goal of empire or a radical change in the nation's relationship with other powers;
(d) specific esposual of an idealist, voluntarist creed, normally involving the attempt to realize a new form of modern, self-determined, secular culture.

Fascist ideology is thus anticonservative in its opposition to the political and economic status quo, in its pursuit of markedly statist politico-economic models which do not constitute a return to the past (e.g., to nineteenth-century bourgeois constitutional monarchy), and in its espousal of non-traditional, secular principles of legitimacy for its programme.

Payne enumerates six elements of style and organization:

(a) emphasis on aesthetic structure of meetings, symbols, and political choreography, stressing romantic and mystical aspects;
(b) attempted mass mobilization with militarization of political relationships and style and with the goal of a mass party militia;
(c) positive evaluation and use of, or willingness to use, violence;
(d) extreme stress on the masculine principle and male dominance, while espousing the organic view of society;
(e) exaltation of youth above other phases of life, emphasizing the conflict of generations, at least in effecting the initial political transformation;
(f) specific tendency toward an authoritarian, charistmatic, personal style of command, whether or not the command is to some degree initially elective.

Most noteworthy for present purposes are the effort to organize a mass following and a party army (though most European movements failed to achieve these), openness to violent struggle, and the military style (uniforms, flags, salutes, marching in formation), which identified fascism as a distinctively radical and modern form of political movement.

Payne's typology also distinguishes two other species of rightist movement prevalent in the inter-war period: the conservative authoritarian right, and the radical right. This is a great advantage, since one reason the fascist concept has been overused is that scholars have had no conceptual tools to deal with other manifestations of the authoritarian right. Like fascism, the conservative authoritarian right and radical right were nationalistic, opposed to parliamentary government, and strongly anticommunist — elements of either might strike up ephemeral alliances with fascist movements. However, each diverged from fascism in fundamental ways. The conservative authoritarian right differed as follows: (a) it legitimized its programme with traditional religious or monarchical formulae; (b) it preferred to effect change without violent disruptions, minimizing legal discontinuity; (c) its organization of paramilitary units stopped short of challenging the supremacy of the armed forces, which were often viewed as potential allies; (d) it was much slower to seek a mass political organization, usually operating more through established élite groups than from the streets; (e) through anticonservative in its rejection of parliamentarism, it did not advocate a new and radical form of dictatorship — many proponents sought primarily to restore the influence they had lost with the development of parliamentary democracy and could therefore be considered reactionary; (f) its economic programme was largely designed to reinforce a traditional social hierarchy in danger of disintegration and was thus less extreme than that of fascism. The radical right differed from fascism in some of the same ways as the conservative authoritarian right, but it too was distinctive: (a) it usually used traditional principles to legitimize its platform; (b) it sought to eradicate existing liberal institutions and could be just as violent as fascism, but its preferred political alternative was partly reactionary, often some form of neo-monarchism; (c) even when terrorist tactics were embraced, it did not develop a party militia that might threaten the military — to the contrary, it often actively campaigned for military support and called for military government under certain conditions; (d) it was the least effective at organizing a mass base, and even more dependent upon élite manipulation than the conservative authoritarian right; (e) its economic programme paralleled that of the conservatives in seeking to replace class conflict with a more regulated structure, but one that would entail only modest transformation of the social hierarchy. In short, the radical right could approach fascism in its advocacy of extra-legal change and violence, but was closer to the conservative right in its more moderate positive programme, its more traditional basis of ideological legitimacy, and its neglect of mass politics in favour of élite manipulation.

To illustrate this conceptual triad, in Germany Payne sees the nazis as representing fascism, Hindenburg and Bruning as conservative authoritarian rightists, and von Papen and the Stahlhelm as the radical right. In Spain, the Falange is described as fascist, the CEDA as the conservative authoritarian right, and the Carlists as part of the radical right. We will now evaluate the utility of this conceptual framework for describing Japan's rightist groups in the 1931–1936 period.

Most new information presented below on the Japanese right was drawn from the records of the publications police, a division of the Home Ministry. In the early 1930s, the state enforced a system of post-publication censorship.

All publishers had to register with the police. Inspection copies of newspapers and current events magazines had to be submitted to officials simultaneously with publication, copies of books and other magazines three days in advance. The police examined all submissions and were empowered to inflict administrative sanctions or initiate prosecution for any contents threatening public order or undermining public morals. The police published monthly reports on censorship throughout the period under study, as well as six annual reports over 1930–1935.[10] Because rightist publications became a major source of violations during this period, they were segregated for special analysis in many of the reports. The authors of these documents, then, read more rightist literature than anyone else at the time or since. The reports were classified in the pre-war era and constitute a remarkably candid record. Though they do not go into great detail on individual movements, they contain a broad overview of all those rightist elements engaged in propaganda efforts. The materials must be supplemented with reference to other sources, both because some important rightist elements published very little (especially among the radical young officers' associations), and to guard against any systematic biases that may characterize official sources. On the whole, however, the materials are wide-ranging in their treatment of many rightist groups, and the police seem to have had little reason to lie to themselves regarding the purely descriptive traits of the rights publishers they portray. Their commentary does not touch upon every variable in Professor Payne's definition of fascism, but it does address a sufficient number to enable us to draw some significant, if tentative, conclusions.

The political and economic programmes

European fascist movements advocated the creation of a new powerful centralized authoritarian regime and a radical overhaul of the economic structure in the mould of state corporatist, socialist, or syndicalist ideas (thus Szalasi's 'Hungarian National Socialism', Codreanu's Romanian 'National Christian Socialism', Ledesma Ramos' Spanish 'National Syndicalism', etc.). Although a number of Japanese intellectuals and strategically-placed bureaucrats adopted similar ideas in the late 1930s, the data gathered by the publications police indicate that very few Japanese rightist groups espoused such radical positions earlier in the decade.

Over 1932–1935, the police divided the right into two main categories: pure Japanism and national socialism. Both were critical of party politics and capitalism, but the national socialist journals were singled out for the extremism of their positive programme. Influenced by the thought of Takabatake Motoyuki, Japan's leading national socialist intellectual and one-time translator of Marx's *Capital*, they proposed to eradicate capitalism and replace it with a planned state socialist economy; they were highly critical of private property, and they advocated nationalization of the means of production. Like the early northern wing of the Nazi Party under Gregor and Otto Strasser, Japan's national socialists took their socialism very seriously, and the groups harboured a number of ex-leftists. Their opposition to parliamentarism was uncompromising.[11]

Though some national socialist ideas found their way into the Japanist camp, as a rule the Japanists embraced more moderate positions. Most rejected party politics but not the Diet (only the Diet was inscribed in the constitution); they were in favour of keeping the good points of capitalism while compensating for its deficiencies, most supported only a 'lukewarm controlled economy', and many favoured the decentralization of authority.[12] Their theories were generally less systematic than those of the national socialists and often focused on vague prescriptions for spiritual renovation. Officials did not one or two exceptions to this general portrait among the Japanist groups. Most significant was the journal *Kaizo Sensen*, published by the Great Japan Production Party. It called for the complete eradication of capitalism and establishment of a new state-controlled economic system.[13] The police were careful to point out that the party's formal programme was more moderate and that *Kaizo Sensen* was apparently under the control of a faction strongly influenced by Marxism. It is significant that this journal was singled out as an exception, since certain elements within the Great Japan Production Party were involved in the only plot for armed civilian insurrection in the 1930s, the Shinpeitai Incident of July 1933. Most Japanist groups, in other words, did not share such revolutionary aims. The party split following the arrest of those members implicated in the incident. As the figures in Table 1 indicate, the pure Japanist groups far outweighed the national socialists in terms of publishing activity.

The agriculturist journals noted for 1934 and 1935 were largely offshoots of the rural depression, especially cruel in Japan's northeastern prefectures. Theirs was clearly not a fascist programme. They were opposed to western capitalism, materialism, urban culture, and the notion of a powerful central state, appealing instead for greater self-government in the farm villages.[14]

In 1934–1935, the publications police noted a split within the Japanist camp. One group was very conservative, reactionary, and 'idealistic' (*kannenteki*), the other more 'progressive' (*shinpoteki*) and outspoken on concrete political and economic questions — the progressive wing was becoming the dominant force.[15] This observation later developed into the distinction between the idealist right and the renovationist right, the two principal labels for rightist groups employed in the late 1930s. However, although the progressive right was said to borrow more from national socialism than the idealist right, this does not imply that most progressives were leaning toward a fascist programme — in fact, rightist publications on the whole 'markedly softened' their platforms over 1934–1935 in comparison to earlier years.[16] In 1935, the number of rightist periodicals, books, and propaganda sheets banned from circulation decreased for the first time in the decade, from 492 in

Table 1 **The Number of Active Rightist Periodicals by Political/Thought Tendency: 1932–1935**

			Political/Thought Tendency		
Year	Type of Journal	Total Active Journals	Pure Japanist[a]	National Socialist	Other
1932	Newspapers	27	11	2	14
	Magazines	32	11	5	16
	Total	59	22	7	30
1933	Newspapers	31	9	4	18
	Magazines	42	16	4	22
	Total	73	25	8	40
					Agriculturist[b]
1934	Newspapers	35	30	3	2
	Magazines	59	52	5	2
	Total	94	82	8	4
1935	Newspapers	43	37	3	3
	Magazines	47	42	2	3
	Total	90	79	5	6

Sources: Naimusho Keihokyoku, *Shuppan Keisatsu Gaikan*, 1932–1935.
[a] This category is usually rendered as 'pure Japanist' (*junsui Nihonshugi*), occasionally as 'Japanist', and once in the magazine classification of 1932 as 'pure Japanist/ultra-nationalist' (the latter term — *kokusuishugi*).
[b] This category is rendered as 'agriculturist' (*nohonshugi*) or 'agriculture self-governmentist' (*nohon jijishugi*).

1934 to 282.[17] We have an unusually detailed account of the reasons rightist publications were banned in 1935 — see Table 2. The paucity of sanctions for rejecting or slandering private property, the law and state authority, the courts, and the parliamentary system would indicate that few rightist groups endorsed a politico-economic programme as extreme as that Payne found to be characteristic of European fascist movements. Ben-Ami Shillony's study of the young officers' movement only confirms this conclusion. Though a few of the officers expressed approval for socialist ideas, for most the Showa Restoration they sought 'had no blueprint at all.'[18] As one of them put it, 'By the term resoration we meant an absolute monarch with an egalitarian people'.[19] No European fascist leader could have made such a statement. The publications police records and Shillony's research both second Maruyama's judgment that the radical and concrete positive programme put forth by Kita Ikki was 'an exception in right-wing thought'.[20]

The position on violence

The records indicate that the instigation of violence and sympathy for violent acts were fairly widespread in the Japanese right during 1932 and 1933. In 1932, for example, support for political violence accounted for 51 of the 64

Table 2 **Domestic Rightist Periodical Editions and Books Banned for Violating Regular Public Order Censorship Standards in 1935**

Standards	Newspaper Law		Publications Law		Total	% of Column Total
	Newspapers	Magazines	Magazines	Books		
Advocating:						
Illegal change	12	2	1	3	18	10.9
Direct action	29	7	0	3	39	23.6
Mass violence	1	0	0	1	2	1.2
Violent acts	3	0	0	0	3	1.8
Illegal movements	1	1	0	0	2	1.2
Crime	1	1	0	0	2	1.2
Criminals	5	0	0	0	5	3.0
Social unrest	3	1	0	0	4	2.4
War	1	1	0	0	2	1.2
Rejecting/slandering:						
Imperial family	16	7	0	2	25	15.1
Private property	1	0	0	0	1	.6
Law/state authority	2	1	0	0	3	1.8
Courts	0	1	0	0	1	.6
Parliamentary system	2	0	0	0	2	1.2
Military/war	2	0	0	0	2	1.2
Foreign policy	0	1	1	0	2	1.2
Disturbing/hindering:						
Constitution	5	2	0	2	9	5.4
Foundation of military	3	0	0	0	3	1.8
Military discipline	12	13	1	6	32	19.4
Foreign affairs	2	0	0	0	2	1.2
Business world	1	0	0	0	1	.6
Other	3	1	0	1	5	3.0
Total	105	39	3	18	165	99.6
% of row total	63.6	23.6	1.8	10.9	99.9	

Source: Naimusho Keihokyoku, *Shuppan Keisatsu Gaikan*, 1935.

rightist newspaper editions banned from circulation.[21] Some specifically applauded Prime Minister Inukai's assassination and the Blood Brotherhood (*Ketsumeidan*) murders of industrialist Dan Takuma and ex-Finance Minister Inoue Junnosuke. All but four of the 51 sanctions were levied against Japanist rather than national socialist journals. For example, all thirteen editions of the Great Japan Production Party's *Kaizo Sensen* were banned for supporting violence in 1932, as were seven editions of the bimonthly *Gekkan Nihon*, founded by Dr. Okawa Shumei, for the same reason.[22] This pattern continued in 1933.

The data in Table 2 indicate that support for violence was still the main reason for sanctions against the rightist press in 1935. However, officials noted a new moderation in the rightist position on violence in both 1934 and 1935:

> Seeing that even in the atmosphere of popular excitement after the Manchurian Incident the national reconstruction movement based upon direct action by *a few extremists* in the 5/15 Incident, Shinpeitai Incident, etc., ended in failure, it is evident throughout various articles that the rightist camp is aware it is now forced to make a great shift (*tenko*) in the movement's direction . . . (emphasis added).[23]

This shift was a turn by some of the more extreme groups to strictly legal methods (parliamentary action, circulating petitions) in an effort to overcome a general decline in right-wing activity and effectiveness.[24]

The data warrant only tentative conclusions regarding the prevalence of support for violent tactics. The use of official records on this point may be especially precarious, since it is well-known that some officials were sympathetic to rightist violence. It is difficult to judge the veracity of police records that speak of severe enforcement against rightist journals even indirectly encouraging violence in 1935,[25] though the mass arrest of rightist thugs in Tokyo in May of that year would tend to bolster the official claim. If one chooses to trust the records, then approval for violence was rare indeed — adding together sanctions for supporting illegal change, direct action, mass violence, violent acts, and crime, one comes to a total of only 57 infractions (for individual editions) by 90 rightist newspapers and magazines publishing in 1935 (see Table 2).

Another difficulty in using the figures for comparative purposes is that the records do not distinguish clearly between mere expressions of sympathy for the violent actions of others, and actual espousal of terrorism as one's own tactic for acquiring power (as found in European fascist movements). Many praising various acts of terrorism were undoubtedly individuals who would never have imagined committing such acts themselves. Note that if the police accounts are correct on the slackening of support for violence over 1934–1935, the usual historical periodization for the right may be in error. The February 1936 rebellion is most often cited as a turning-point for the right as a whole, denoting the end of violent challenges to state authority, but the censorship records suggest that most rightist journals had confined their appeals to legal means for some time; they lead one to conclude that the 1936 mutiny, plotted by 21 junior officers and a few privy civilians, was not representative of the right wing generally and may be much less of an historical crossroads than is usually thought.[26]

It is often remarked that the unique trait of some fascist movements was not the use of violence per se but the belief in its spiritually ennobling qualities.[27] There is no question that the Japanese rightists most directly engaged in violence — the young officers' groups — glorified terrorism and potential martyrdom as purifying acts of sacrifice for the nation. As one of the 1936 mutineers wrote to his mother just before his execution:

> In order for the empire to continue its advance in the way of the gods, and so that people, parents and children and brothers and sisters in harmony, may enjoy their work, rejoice in the flowers, amuse themselves with sake, and offer congratulations of 'Long Life!' to the imperial reign, a small number of people chosen by heaven must taste agony, suffer grief, abandon their lives, and break their bones. I, who hope for the honour of those loyal to that fate, think there is nothing I could be more thankful for than to have been born in Japan and to be able to die for the Emperor. The history of Japan is a trail of the lifeblood shed by our ancestors to protect and foster the national polity. Now our lifeblood will become the eternal prosperity of the imperial throne.[28]

(A rightist journal publishing this letter was prosecuted in court.) However, rather than place the young officers in the fascist category, this finding may call for revision of the hypothesis that the fascist exaltation of violence was unique.

Mass mobilization or elite manipulation?

A tactical focus on élite manipulation has been convincingly documented in many prominent rightist elements in the 1931–1936 period.[29] Some conservative rightist groups, like Baron Hiranuma Kiichiro's National Foundation Society, drew their membership primarily from élite circles. Even the more radical young officers and the civilians on their fringes, however, made no effort to organize a mass party or a militia to rival the security forces of the state. As much by choice as by necessity, they were typically small conspiratorial societies with no pretensions of promoting a social movement. Even with downtown Tokyo under their control, the rebels of February 1936 did not attempt to seize the national radio station or to distribute printed materials directly among the public.[30] Whereas fascists sought a mass movement to seize power for themselves, the young officers' project was more akin to the terrorism seen in western Europe today, designed for self-gratification and sensational publicity to influence the thinking and actions of others. When these groups spelled out a concrete goal at all, it was usually to provoke change at the top in the form of a military government to be led by senior officers, who definitely did not belong to fascist movements.

The data in Table 2 would seem to extend this portrait to the right wing generally. In 1935, there were almost no violations for promoting illegal movements or mass violence, whereas rightist infractions for disturbing military discipline were 19.4 per cent of the total. Articles in this category usually called for one or another military faction to take direct political action, thus representing a strategy of élite manipulation. However, police found that the general disillusionment with violent tactics among civil rightist groups in 1935 was associated with a growing interest in developing a mass base.[31] The failure of direct action to accomplish much in 1932 and 1933 led many to consider instead a legal path to influence based upon a wide popular appeal. The fact that such an appeal was then lacking came to be perceived as a pressing problem calling for a unified effort by the rightist camp, which was sorely divided at the time (and was to remain so).[32] One gets the impression that most groups perceived violent acts of rebellion and a mass movement as mutually exclusive strategies; those pursuing violent tactics like the young officers and their civilian collaborators shunned a mass base, while those beginning to contemplate a mass movement did so out of disenchantment with terrorism. There is lacking the fascist amalgam of a mass movement engaging simultaneously in legal and illegal methods to win power, the relative novelty of which caught so many of Europe's established political élites by surprise.

The early faith in the potential of small terrorist groups to effect change was partly due to Japanese historical traditions of revolt.[33] For other reasons as well, the strategy was bound to appear more realistic in Japan than it would have in most of inter-war Europe. In Europe, mass politics was generally more highly developed and established parties had mobilized most of the electorate; to challenge seriously for power required making room for oneself in a highly organized party system at the mass level. In Japan, party mobilization of sectors such as the working class and rural tenant farmers had just got underway in the 1920s, and after 1932 governments were formed entirely on the basis of closed élite interaction rather than popular approval — the notion that a few demonstrative acts might produce change by swaying those at the top was thus more feasible. A final reason for the perception of incompatibility between violent tactics and a mass movement was that public opinion was strongly unfavourable to terrorism. As Table 3 illustrates, the circulation of rightist publications plummeted in the wake of the 2/26 Incident. To organize a mass movement around violent opposition could not have appeared a very viable alternative at the time. It is perhaps no accident that the rightist movement which later came closest to winning mass support, the *Tohokai*, did not embrace violent tactics.

More research is needed to explore the possibility of fascist exceptions to the general pattern over 1931–1936. Logical places to begin looking would be among the national socialist groups and a few of the most radical Japanist organizations such as the Great Japan Production Party (the Shinpeitai plot envisioned the mobilization of 3,600 armed men). The data summarized above, however, do indicate that whatever rightist ambitions for a mass movement existed in the early 1930s, they were exceptions to the rule and, by all accounts, ended in failure. The results of general elections held in 1936

Table 3 **The Circulation of 'Thought' Newspapers Kept under Surveillance by the Tokyo Metropolitan Police: February–July 1936**

Month	Rightist Journals	Rightist Circulation	Leftist Journals	Leftist Circulation
February	51	892,340	34	165,700
March	50	439,315	34	207,700
April	49	324,090	33	221,700
May	47	309,260	33	232,300
June	45	267,420	32	245,600
July[a]	43	378,652	32	251,100

Source: Naimusho Keihokyoku, *Shuppan Keisatsu Ho*, no. 96, pp. 100–101.
Note: The one active anarchist newspaper was included in the leftist category in the table, though classified separately in the original document.
[a] Interest in rightist journals rose in July due to the executions of the ringleaders of the 2/26 rebellion and the assassin of General Nagata. No data are available for later months.

and 1937 make it clear that if the mainstream parties lost much of their political power in this period, it was not for having lost their electoral constituencies to the right. Nakano Seigo's *Tohokai* (Eastern Way Society) was the only incontrovertibly rightist group to break the so-called 'two per cent barrier' in national elections with but 2.17 per cent of the vote in 1937 and 3 per cent in 1942.

The formula for legitimacy

No fascist movement justified its programme with primary reference to traditional religious or monarchical principles. While religious elements might be present (Romania's Legionaries may represent the extreme of this tendency), and fascism was not incompatible with religious faith (Léon Degrelle and José Antonio Primo de Rivera, among others, were practising Catholics), fascism was never built upon a religious institutional foundation, and the attitude towards monarchism is one of the clearest dividing lines between fascist and non-fascist movements. Fascism was not simply a projection of traditional values into a modern political context. As Payne writes, 'Fascist philosophical ideas are often said to stem from opposition to the Enlightenment or the "Ideas of 1789", when as a matter of fact they are a direct byproduct of aspects of the Enlightenment and were derived specifically from the modern, secular, Promethean concepts of the eighteenth century.'[34] This was not the case with most right-wing ideas in inter-war Japan.

The publications police emphasized again and again that if there was one feature common to all rightist groups of the early 1930s — whether Japanist, national socialist, or agrarianist — it was the centrality of the Emperor in their ideological doctrines. In 1932, for example, officials summed up the guiding spirit upheld by all rightist newspapers as follows:

> Based upon the Japanese spirit, and recognizing the absolute sovereignty of the Emperor rooted in our national polity (*kokutai*), we look forward to the establishment of a political organization centred on the Emperor and the imperial family and to the realization of a social organization of co-prosperity and unity between the Emperor and his subjects; by these means we shall exalt imperial authority more and more, and we hope for the worldwide advance of the Japanese race.[35]

The young officers' groups too were fanatical Emperor worshippers.[36] One should note that as a transcendent and impersonal symbol, the throne was a rather malleable object of loyalty that could be invoked to many different purposes. There was nothing inconsistent between rightist reverence for the throne and rightist publications being banned for impiety when they called for elimination of the evil advisors allegedly blinding his majesty to the true state of the nation (see Table 2). One must also distinguish those rightist intellectuals who gave the throne a *relatively* less conspicuous place in their theories and drew most heavily from modern, secular doctrines such as social Darwinism and/or Marxism, e.g. Kita Ikki and some of the renovationist bureaucrats such as Okumura Kiwao.[37] However, imperial legitimacy was not invoked hypocritically as a mere expedient to achieve short-term goals. This is revealed by the immense impact of the Emperor's role upon the practical programmes of most rightist groups. The fact that the Meiji Emperor had proclaimed and thus sanctified the constitution was a major impediment to a complete renunciation of parliamentarism and to any proposal for a radically new political regime. For example, the idea of a single party movement to take over the state was rejected by many rightists for creating an impure filter between the Emperor and his subjects (a new shogunate) — this theme can be traced in the thought of the young officers, the agrarianists, and most importantly in the 'idealist' right-wing camp which later strongly opposed efforts to form a single party regime in 1940. The Emperor's status made it more difficult to borrow fascist ideas from Europe by the simple fact that they excluded monarchical rule. The *modus vivendi* Mussolini was compelled to accept with the Italian King was apparently not even a topic of discussion within the Japanese right — the notion of striking a bargain with the Emperor would undoubtedly have been perceived as sacrilegious.

Thus the formula for imperial legitimacy not only distinguishes the Japanese right from European fascism in and of itself, but also helps to account for other salient points of departure by most groups from the fascist pattern.

The sparse emulation of European models

The chronological development of the rightist press provides strong evidence that few groups were consciously imitating European fascism. Mussolini's takeover in Italy in 1922 did not have much impact in Japan,[38] and rightist publications were not a major factor in law enforcement or public discussion until the 1930s. In January 1930, officials counted only 27 right-wing newspapers and magazines, 21 of them published but once a month. Rightist groups had received a boost from the mass arrests of leftists in the mid- to late 1920s, but the police judged their influence to be 'feeble'.[39] State documents consistently cite the Manchurian Incident of September 1931 as the critical turning-point in rightist activity — this came sixteen months before Hitler's rise to power.[40] The data in Table 1 support this observation; rightist periodicals more than doubled between 1930 and 1932, and of the 22 leading right-wing journals identified in mid-1932, ten had started since the Manchurian Incident.[41] The end of party government in May 1932 was another important stimulus for the right, since it opened up new possibilities in domestic politics, but imperialism was the primary cause of expansion. It not only stirred nationalistic groups to greater efforts, but also created the readership for new journals appealing to the aroused patriotism of the average subject. Imperialistic issues favoured the right until mid-1933, especially the clash between Japanese and Chinese troops in Shanghai in early 1932, the founding of Manchukuo in July 1932, and withdrawal from the League of Nations in March 1933. There were no comparable international stimuli in 1934, and consequently there was no increase in rightist periodicals between 1934 and 1935. Contrary to the thesis of Barrington Moore, then, the publications police saw rightist growth as much more a function of foreign crises than of the domestic rural depression and corresponding strains in the land tenure system.

What of developments after the appearance of Hitler as a world leader? National socialist groups, never a dominant force on the Japanese right, faded even further into the background. There was no increase in the number of national socialist periodicals between 1933 and 1935, and the actual amount of their publishing activity decreased.[42] Of course, one need not advertise oneself as a facist or national socialist to imitate fascism — even the Nazi Party never called itself 'fascist'.[43] What, then, was the overall assessment of European fascism in Japan's rightist publications? In the early 1930s, police used the term 'fascism' rather loosely, applying it to the general rise of the right wing, to national socialist periodicals, and even to Baron Hiranuma's National Foundation Society.[44] But by 1935, official censors were using 'fascism' to refer to the politics of Hitler and Mussolini. Of 712 rightist books published in Japan in 1935, only eleven were devoted to 'research on fascism', compared to 217 on doctrinal matters, 89 on the Emperor-as-organ theory, 70 historical biographies, 67 on Far Eastern thought, 47 on politics, 40 on economic controls, and 30 on Japanese classics.[45] Officials noted not only the paucity of works on fascism, but also their critical approach to the subject matter — most opposed indiscriminate borrowing from foreign models in the name of Japan's unique spirit and Shinto traditions, reflecting a tendency toward anti-foreign attitudes.[46] Thus the development of rightist activism in Japan neither coincided with fascist fortunes in Europe nor was there much conscious emulation of fascist models in this period.

The data presented above do not speak to every variable in Payne's typology of the inter-war right, but the findings do suggest certain tentative lines of comparison. Candidates for the fascist category appear to constitute a small minority of Japan's rightist groups in the 1931–1936 period. Those approaching the fascist model were the relatively few national socialist elements that flourished mainly between 1932 and 1934, and a few exceptional Japanist groups, such as the extremist wing of the Great Japan Production Party involved in the Shinpeitai plot. Only these organizations may have met the fascist criteria of violent tactics, the goal of mass mobilization, and a radical positive politico-economic programme. Even in these cases, however, the reliance upon a traditional legitimacy formula would be at least one prominent point of divergence from fascism — further research might well reveal others.

The right radicals were also a minority in the rightist camp. The young officers' groups and the civilians associated with them (e.g., Okawa Shumei, Nishida Zei) fit Payne's description of this type rather well. The key traits of violent tactics, élite manipulation, traditional legitimacy, and the lack of an extreme positive programme were all present. Though few in number, the radical rightists made a strong political impact by means of terrorism and the sympathy they elicited from others.

Payne's new conservative authoritarian right describes the dominant rightist trend in Japan. Almost all the Japanist groups appear to conform to the general model; they embraced a more moderate politico-economic reform programme than fascism, a strategy of élite manipulation rather than mass action, and traditional monarchical principles of legitimacy. Despite signs of sympathy with the terror of the radical right in 1932 and 1933, the great majority did not adopt terrorist tactics as their own, and at least by 1935 most had clearly come to espouse non-violent means to influence. The dominance of this category was such that to locate the Japanese right around fascism at the centre would be something akin to locating the position of an elephant with reference to a fly perched on its back. In this period, neither the most numerous nor the most influential elements in the Japanese right were fascist.[47] The most fruitful comparisons with other countries, given relative levels of mass politics, might then be with some of the Eastern European states where fascism was similarly a minority wing of the inter-war right.

Having applied to Japan a typology derived primarily from European history, it may be useful now to turn the tables and ask whether the Japanese data do not perhaps suggest some refinements in the typology itself. Comparative frameworks are not designed to incorporate all the nuances of any one country's historical experience, but their value is certainly enhanced the closer they fit the historical particulars of the various cases under study. The greatest limitation of Payne's typology as applied to Japan is that it overlooks important distinctions within the new conservative authoritarian right. The typology compels us to place virtually all non-violent rightist groups in this one category, yet the political battles of the 1930s in Japan were largely fought *between* rightist forces that did not advocate violent political change. A common description of these forces divides them into 'idealist' and 'renovationist' camps, as noted above. Most groups in both camps used peaceful methods and all invoked imperial legitimacy, thus the conservative authoritarian right category, but their plans for the country were very different. Whereas the idealist called for a revival of traditional moral values largely within the existing structure of institutions, renovationist plans might extend even to a modified national socialism for Japan.[48] While the former understood their task largely as the restoration of something lost in the past, the latter saw their country as entering a new stage of history. To lose sight of the distinction between them would render the political history of late imperial Japan incomprehensible. It would seem that similarly important variations are overlooked in the conservative authoritarian right category as Payne has applied it to Europe. For example, Hindenburg, a true conservative, shares this label with the early Belgian Rex of the mid-1930s, which was a thoroughly fascist group but for its rejection of violence. This parallels the confusion of placing a conservative rightist like Hiranuma Kiichiro in the same conceptual compartment with a renovationist such as Nakano Seigo.

In conclusion, the Japanese experience seems to call for a four-part typology of the inter-war right. Violent rightist groups would be treated under the two headings of fascism and the radical right, as described by Payne. The non-violent right, however, would comprise both the conservative authoritarian right (as in Payne's account, the likes of Hindenburg and Hiranuma), and a renovationist authoritarian right. The term 'renovation' would be understood as falling between a *reform* programme intended to conserve a traditional social order strained by the development of parliamentary democracy, and a sweeping socio-political *revolution* of the sort demanded by fascism. It would encompass groups such as Nakano Seigo's Eastern Way Society and the early Christus Rex, which do not comfortably fit the other three categories, and for which the label 'conservative' can be fundamentally misleading. The addition of a 'renovationist authoritarian right' category might also be an invaluable tool for the comparative study of regimes in the inter-war period, since this political tendency was dominant in mobilizational military-bureaucratic regimes to appear in Romania, Poland,

Hungary, Portugal, and Japan. In these countries it resulted in new policy programmes and bureaucratic mass organizations designed partly to preempt a full-blown revolution, but also constituting significant and in some areas radical innovations in and of themselves, thus breaking from the mould of conservative reform.

Notes

Japanese names are rendered in the customary style, with family names given first.

1 Maruyama Masao, *Thought and Behavior in Modern Japanese Politics*, expanded edn, ed. Ivan Morris (London 1969), 26–33, 65–66.
2 E.g., Ishida Takeshi, 'Elements of Tradition and "Renovation" in Japan during the "Era of Fascism" ', *Annals of the Institute of Social Science* (University of Tokyo), 17, 1976. The eight-volume series on inter-war politics published by the University of Tokyo's Social Science Research Institute is titled *Fashizumu-ki no Kokka to Shakai* (The State and Society in the Era of Fascism).
3 E.g., Ito Takashi, *Nihon no Rekishi*, vol. 30, *Jugo-nen Senso* (Tokyo 1976), 19. Most American historians now working on inter-war Japan do not use the fascist concept as a principal theme in their work, e.g., Gordon Berger, James Crowley, Richard Mitchell.
4 Historian Ito Takashi has developed an alternative conceptual scheme around two pairs of variables: renovation versus status quo, and progressive versus reactionary. See his 'Showa Seiji Shi Kenkyu e no Hito Shikaku', *Shiso* 624 (June 1976). Ito's framework is extremely useful as an account of intellectual history, but his concepts are historically specific to Japan. As American critics of the fascist concept in Japan have pointed out, if fascism is judged inadequate, the need is to replace it with another conceptual framework of similar *comparative* range. E.g., see George Macklin Wilson, 'A New Look at the Problem of "Japanese Fascism"', *Comparative Studies in Society and History*, 10, 4 (July 1968); Peter Duus and Daniel I. Okimoto, 'Fascism and the History of Prewar Japan: The Failure of a Concept', *Journal of Asian Studies* 39 (November 1979).
5 For a description and defence of the Marxist approaches, see Abe Hirozumi, 'Nihon Fashizumu no Kenkyu Shikaku', Mibu Shiro, 'Nihon Fashizumu Kenkyu ni Yosete — Benmei Shikan Hihan', and Yoshimi Yoshiaki, 'Senzen ni Okeru "Nihon Fashizumu" Kan no Hensen — 1931-nen kara 1937-nen made', all in *Rekishigaku Kenkyu* 451 (December 1977).
6 This is not to ignore the interesting issue of functional equivalencies between the Japanese regime in the late 1930s and nazi Germany and fascist Italy. The Japanese were avid students of German public policy in particular and borrowed a great deal. However, as Juan Linz has noted:

> Even assuming that all anti-democratic movements and regimes aiming at the suppression of socialist and communist labour movements perform the same function, and that therefore the movements we have narrowly defined as fascist are only variants of the same genus, that is, functional alternatives in pursuit of the same policies, the question would still remain why there are alternative roads to the same goal. Why turn to fascism to defeat labour rather than to military-bureacratic dictatorship?

Linz, 'Political Space and Fascism as a Late-Comer', in Stein U. Larsen, Bernt Hagtvet, and Jan P. Myklbust (eds.), *Who were the Fascists?* (Bergen, Norway 1980), 170.

7 In particular, attention has been lavished on rightist cabals in the lower ranks of the military — see Hata Ikuhiko, *Gun Fashizumu Undo Shi* (Tokyo 1962), and in English, Ben-Ami Shillony, *Revolt in Japan: The Young Officers and the February 26, 1936 Incident* (Princeton 1973).

8 Payne, *Fascism: Comparison and Definition* (Madison 1980), 3–21. Payne himself has attempted to apply his typology of rightist groups to Japan, but without — I believe — much accuracy due to the paucity of reliable materials in English on the Japanese case. That was one inspiration for the present effort.

9 Linz, 'Some Notes Toward a Comparative Study of Fascism in Sociological Historical Perspective', in Walter Laqueur (ed.), *Fascism: A Reader's Guide* (Berkeley 1976), 13.

10 Both were prepared by the Home Ministry's Criminal Affairs Bureau (*Keihokyoku*). The monthly reports were titled *Shuppan Keisatsu Ho*, the yearly summaries *Shuppan Keisatsu Gaikan*, hereafter cited as *Ho* and *Gaikan*, respectively.

11 *Gaikan*, 1932, 260.

12 Ibid., 259–61; *Gaikan*, 1933, 244; *Gaikan*, 1934, 154, this last for the quotation on lukewarm support for a controlled economy.

13 *Gaikan*, 1932, 209; see also Maruyama, 30–31, and for the party mainstream's more moderate programme, 44.

14 *Gaikan*, 1934, 160–61.

15 Ibid., 218.

16 *Gaikan*, 1935, 43, 103.

17 *Gaikan*, vols. for 1934 and 1935.

18 Shillony, 76.

19 Quoted in ibid., 66.

20 Maruyama, 42.

21 *Gaikan*, 1932, 206, 213–16, 261–62.

22 *Gaikan*, 1933, 192–93, 196.

23 *Gaikan*, 1935, 109.

24 Ibid., 110.

25 Ibid., 221.

26 Earlier rightist violence was also the work of very few groups, and one should remember that rightist intimidation did not cease to be a force in Japanese politics after 1936; witness the takeover of party headquarters during Diet discussion of the State Total Mobilization Law in early 1938, and the threats against Konoe from radical elements in the 'idealist' right during formation of the Imperial Rule Assistance in late 1940.

27 Payne, 12; Eugen Weber, *Varieties of Fascism* (Princeton 1964), 34.

28 *Ho*, no. 95, 202.

29 Hata, 15; Maruyama, 52–57; George M. Wilson, *Radical Nationalist in Japan: Kita Ikki 1883–1937* (Cambridge, Mass. 1969), 49, 68.

30 Shiliony, 159–61, 183.

31 *Gaikan*, 1935, 43.

32 *Gaikan*, 1935, 109–10.

33 Shillony, 58–59.

34 Payne, 10.

35 *Gaikan*, 1932, 203, and see also 206; compare *Ho*, no. 17, 21 (printed in 1930), and *Gaikan*, 1933, 242.

36 Shillony, chap. 3; Wilson, *Kita Ikki*, 116–17.

37 See Wilson, *Kita Ikki*, 27–30; Okumura Kiwao, *Nihon Seiji no Kakushin* (Tokyo 1938), 3–46, 127–54.
38 Note that the earliest intellectual forerunner of Japan's new authoritarian right, Kita Ikki, penned his famous *Plan for the Reorganization of Japan* in the summer of 1919, before Mussolini's fascist movement had had any significant success or could have influenced its writing.
39 *Ho*, no. 17, 21–23.
40 *Gaikan*, 1932, 152–53.
41 Latter figures from *Ho*, no. 47, 127–36. Even in the book market, which is slower to react to current events, the Manchurian Incident made itself felt before the end of 1931. Nationalist and anti-Marxist books were 12 of the annual total of 614 books related to social thought in 1930, but rose to 69 of 686 in 1931 due to a boom after September. See *Gaikan*, 1930, 88, and *Gaikan*, 1931, 69–70.
42 E.g., see *Gaikan*, 1934, 225.
43 Stanislav Andreski, 'Fascists as Moderates', in Larsen, Hagtvet, and Myklbust (eds.), 53.
44 *Gaikan*, 1932, 258–64.
45 *Gaikan*, 1935, 46–47.
46 By contrast, the debate over fascism in leftist circles was lively, focusing on the issue of whether there was such a thing as fascism in Japan. Those who took the negative view argued that fascism was supposed to signify the rule of finance capital (the Comintern's view), not rule by a 'feudalistic' military-bureaucratic caste. The other interpretation was that although the bourgeoisie did not control the state, fascism, due to the peculiarities of Japanese capitalism, had presented itself within the power structure (rather than outside of it as in Europe) in the form of military-bureaucratic élites, for whom finance capital was a faithful servant. This was a state summary of arguments in leftist periodicals — ibid., 58–59.
47 Indeed, the more conscious emulation of fascism by groups such as the *Tohokai* and *Dai Nihon Seinen To*, which begins in 1936, may signify greater fascist influence at the grass roots level in the late 1930s than in those earlier years of so-called 'fascism from below'.
48 It is worth recalling that national socialism as a political programme pre-dated the appearance of fascist movements in Europe and was never their exclusive property — Eugen Weber and Professor Payne have both made this point. A number of Japanese also embraced revolutionary statist programmes for change without joining or advocating fascist movements.

74

Extracts from
THE COMING AMERICAN FASCISM

Lawrence Dennis

Source: Lawrence Dennis, *The Coming American Fascism*, New York Harper & Brothers, 1936, pp. vii–xiii 245–57.

Introduction

This book is addressed to the thoughtful who are not frightened by new and unpopular terms and concepts. If liberal capitalism is doomed, a fight for a lost cause will impose on mankind the most futile sort of suffering. The British Mercantilist System of the 18th Century and the Southern Planter-Slavery System of the pre-industrial-revolution period each fought on American soil an utterly futile and foolish war to save what was doomed by the inevitable and irresistible trend of social changes. If the present system, or more particularly, those features of it which are challenged by current trends be doomed, the longer and harder the fight waged to preserve it, the greater will be the suffering and losses of the people. Assuming that the old system is doomed, the basic premise of this book and an assumption which current events surely render probable enough to be entertained as an hypothesis in exploratory thinking about the near future, What are the possible alternatives to ultimate social disintegration and chaos? Most intelligent observers of the changing scene, whatever their personal preferences and prejudices, are agreed that, in the event the present system is not soon made to work better, the alternatives fall into the broad classifications of fascism or communism.

Precise definition of these two terms, now on every one's lips, should give us little concern. Officially, communism is whatever the latest encyclical from Moscow says it is, while the fascism of every fascist country is whatever its authorized fascist exponents proclaim it to be. Actually, of course, terms like communism and fascism, just as terms like Christianity, Americanism, or due process of law, must mean many different and often mutually exclusive things to different people. It is always possible to sustain two or more sides to an argument about the precise meaning of terms which, in the nature of things, cannot have a fixed definition like that of an English yard or a French metre. Still, if we are to have intellectual discourse, we must use terms like Christianity, fascism, socialism and so forth, in the expectation that other parties to the discussion will accept such terms in the sense in which they have come to be currently used and in the broad and almost undefinable sense in which we accordingly use them. Naturally, if a party to the discussion refuses to accept a term in a sense acceptable to the other parties, discussion must end.

In the case of the term fascism as applied to a social scheme yet to be developed in this country or as a term applied to the mere advocacy of such a scheme, it should be clear that no argument about the correct use of the term fascism can now be settled by an appeal to authority. Certainly Signor Mussolini, Herr Hitler or an American college professor who has written a book against fascism cannot be appealed to as an authority to define what fascism for America would be like. Obviously the official definition given the coming American fascism will be that of its authorized party exponents. This definition is not likely to call the American fascism by that name. It is much more likely to include an emphatic denial that the new American fascism is fascism. And it is fairly certain, if it follows the precedents of other important party platforms and propaganda, to say that the official American fascism, probably called by another name, is a great many things which it clearly is not.

This book is essentially one man's definition of what a desirable fascism, in his way of thinking, would be like. For obvious reasons, it cannot be a definition of the future American fascism, called by that or any other name. In discussing future social developments we can talk to some point about desirable and undesirable possibilities and probabilities. As these are largely matters of speculation and deduction from the limited field of the known to the unlimited field of the unknown and future unknowable, such discussions cannot deal in certainties nor can they to any good purpose give much time to questions of pure terminology respecting what admittedly lies still in the womb of time.

In this book, the system advanced is the thing, not the validity of the term used to describe or identify it. The reader is asked to remember that Italian fascism and German Nazism are not primarily the subjects of discussion. Correctly or incorrectly, the term fascism has come to identify in most people's minds many things and the general synthesis of ideas here advanced, all with exclusive reference to this country. The term, fascism, is therefore used chiefly as matter of intellectual integrity. I am fully aware and am incessantly being reminded that the term fascism is most unpopular at this time in the United States. I am also told that the thing itself is unthinkable in this country, an opinion which I find naïve. Nothing could be more logical or in the best political tradition than for a type of fascism to be ushered into this country by leaders who are now vigorously denouncing fascism and repudiating all that it is understood to stand for. Dr. Arthur Rosenberg, a communist sympathizer if no longer a member of the Party, points out in his admirable *History of Bolshevism* (Page 98) that the motto of the Bolshevist Revolution was not "The Dictatorship of the Proletariat. Down with Democracy!" but its exact contrary: "Long Live Democracy and Down with Dictatorship." The ideal fascism would be one which was honestly and truthfully presented to the people during its struggle for power. The fascism most to be feared is the fascism sailing under false colors. Such a type of fascism will be the worse for the duplicity of its leaders, and much of the blame will attach to those soft-thinking liberal leaders who have sought to make of fascism a synonym for all that is socially iniquitous instead of a descriptive for a rational and workable social scheme to which they happen to be opposed.

Both fascism and communism should be thought of as formulas of revolutionary social action for those of the under-privileged, dissatisfied and frustrated who have a will to power and a will, through the seizure and use of power, to change a situation they find intolerable, and, of course, to conserve a situation they find more satisfactory. Both fascism and communism are crisis formulas, that is to say, unlike formulas of liberal reform, neither has significance except in so far as it may have a chance of full realization as a new totalitarian or all-embracing social scheme. And, unlike liberal reform, neither has such a chance except in measure as the crisis of the existing system makes an entirely different system the alternative to chaos.

While fascism is to be thought of essentially as a formula for the frustrated in an extreme social crisis, it also has a strong appeal to many whose personal fortunes may still be far from desperate in such a crisis, as well as to national governments which may be interested more in conservation than further acquisition. Such persons, while moved by no feeling of frustration, still do not feel a zest for, or confidence in the outcome of, any fight to the finish under present world conditions between those in the house of want and those in the house of have. Interestingly enough, large numbers of extreme conservatives seem to share the understandable eagerness of the extreme communists for such a fray. The communists are entirely logical and loyal to self-interest in desiring and promoting wherever and whenever possible an intensification of class warfare. From it they have nothing to lose and, as a result of it, a chance to come to full power. The back-to-Hoover Republicans or back-to-Jefferson Democrats who would liquidate the New Deal or the back-to-liberalism British leaders who would liquidate fascism in international war stand only to lose by fighting those in the house of want, be they underprivileged nations seeking a place in the sun or the frustrated élite in liberal countries seeking an escape from the consequences of indefinitely prolonged depression. It is little short of astounding to see how the liberals of Downing Street, Wall Street and the Quai d'Orsay have been welcoming the comradeship in sanctions and arms of communist Russia against fascist Italy. (The fountain head of liberalism in America is really Wall Street or the eastern plutocracy, with its endowed and kept agencies of liberal indoctrination, the leading colleges and metropolitan newspapers.) These moneyed liberals who are seeking to use communist Russia in a war against fascism are singularly blind to their own interests, since they can never be comrades of communists. The liquidation of fascism where it is in power could only mean the succession of communism, and that could only mean the liquidation before a firing squad of property owners. And it is not to be supposed by the liberals of England, France, or even the United States, that they would long be safe in a world half-communist. The fact, of course, is that the liberals and conservatives, really two terms for the same people nowadays, as a whole, are still not sufficiently worried over the implications of present trends or over the ability of the system to stage a come-back. To those still in the house of have who are worried and humanely disposed at the same time, fascism makes an appeal which communism cannot make. Fascism does not expropriate all property rights or effect a wholesale liquidation of the owning and managing classes of the present order. And fascism does not mean a dictatorship by the leaders of the Marxist parties, falsely called by the communists a dictatorship of the proletariat.

Fascism is being widely denounced by liberals in the house of have and by their paid propagandists in the United States as being irrational as well as wholly evil. This book is an undertaking to rationalize fascism before it becomes an accomplished fact in the United States. The point of view from which the subject is discussed is that wherever fascism has happened, there has been reason for its occurrence and that wherever it survives, there must be reason in its use of power. Whether one wishes to go with and try to guide an important social trend, the ruling motivation in the writing of this book, or whether one wishes to oppose the trend, one can only profit from an attempt to understand it as a rational pattern of human behavior. It can serve no useful purpose, either of guidance or opposition, to pronounce fascism madness and fascists madmen.

As for the attempt to make fascism out to be a manifestation of mob madness or social irrationality, let it be borne in mind that fascism and communism, respectively, present a new social order, each with its own synthesis of values or ends and each with a highly rational scheme of social means to these ends. Each system of operating fascism and the Russian system of communism will be found to contain much that will be rejected by most Americans and much that would be inappropriate or down-right impracticable in this country. But it has to be recognized by any intelligent person that, so far as ends are concerned, the fascists know what they want, something which cannot be said of many liberal statesmen and something which is not rationally to be called a sign of insanity or irrationality. And, as for means to these ends, it can hardly be denied that fascism has had considerable success in fitting means to ends or in getting things done the way the leaders of action have willed. As much cannot be said of many liberal statesmen and as much cannot rationally be said of any one who is correctly defined as a lunatic or a moron.

Indeed, as to rationality, or fitness of means to ends, it has to be recognized that both fascism and communism are gigantic undertakings or adventures in what might be called sociological rationalization, corresponding to the sort of thing that has been carried so far in the advanced industrial nations in the fields of technology, having been given in Europe the name of industrial rationalization. Whether one starts out from the premise that the liberal ends, such as a chicken in every pot, equal justice under law, personal freedom, etc., etc., are well enough but that the social means to these ends are proving hopelessly ineffectual, or whether, like the communists, one starts out from the postulate that the ends of liberal capitalism are all wrong, the formula resulting from any thinking through of current problems of social ends and means is certain to be revolutionary. And in this fact resides the truth of the thesis of John Chamberlain's brilliant and inevitable "Farewell to Reform."

It seems likely that it will be as a radical program of sociological rationalization to bring our social machinery up to date or to make social and institutional means fit ends, that fascism will exercise a strong appeal in the United States. After many of our discontented and frustrated have experienced a few more disappointments with monetary schemes, economic specifics, and largesses of the public treasury to minority group interests, it is likely that they will see the logic of fascism as the only rationalized scheme of social means and ends, other than communism, which promises success. There can be but one refutation of the charge that the present system won't work and that is to make it work. Those who have been driven by the experiences of economic defeat and frustration to challenge the present system and seek a substitute cannot rationally be expected to respond to appeals to help make the system they are attacking work better. In other words, any rational discussion or analysis of fascism has to be conducted primarily from the point of view of the frustrated with a will to power and of those who feel neither able nor disposed to fight them and who also question the ability of the social order to buy them off indefinitely with government gifts financed by borrowing. Discussing fascism in other terms or from other points of view may faithfully and gratifyingly express one's own feeling about the matter but, so to relieve one's feelings about fascism will not throw much light on the logic of the situation as it must appear to those who will make an American fascism a reality, if it becomes a reality. And it is as a possible reality in the United States that fascism is most worth while discussing.

[...]

The élite assume responsibility

In the fascist view of the crisis of capitalism, the great initial problem of insuring order and welfare is that of getting the right élite in power under a right discipline and plan of national interest. Liberal theory, it will be remembered, considers the problem of order and welfare as largely one of getting the right set of rules and institutions and then letting the majority work out the good life through this system. The definition of the rules is supposed to be made by the courts, and the operation of the system is supposed just to happen as a result of the fortuitous concurrence of three separate branches of government and all the personal and impersonal factors of the national community, the whole acting autonomously and subject only to the rule of law which is, by definition, wholly impersonal. Consequently, liberalism is the most perfect social system ever conceived for allowing great power to be exercised by individuals and groups, chiefly through property rights legally enforced, with maximum irresponsibility of persons or groups for the social consequences of their acts.

The fundamental objectives of order and welfare are common to liberalism and communism as well as fascism. Fascism is distinctive from both, however, in that it recognizes and makes a cardinal point of the functions and responsibilities of the élite. The issues or choices are as to different sets of the élite who may rule, and of different systems of making their rule effective and responsible. There is no choice as to whether or not some group of the élite shall rule. The fallacy of the communist ideal of a classless society inheres in the fact that there must always be a ruling or managing class.

It is always, of course, the out-élite who put over a social revolution, whether they do so in the name of one group or another or of one set of principles or another. It is the contention of this book that fascism makes a stronger appeal than communism to the out-élite in America, though it is fully recognized that communism can have an appeal to certain members of the out-élite, as occurred in Russia. Fascism, or the out-élite making up fascist leadership, must make out a case for the rule of the fascist élite, not because the rule of the élite is a peculiarity of fascism, but simply because fascism—unlike liberalism and communism—frankly acknowledges, or rather boasts, that its élite rule.

It is one of the merits of fascism, and a part of its appeal, that its leaders do not dissimulate their rôle or try to place responsibility for their rule on a phantom of definition and assumption—such as, the majority or the proletariat. They do not stress a class war, though they naturally fight for their objectives as nearly every one else does. They do not stress a class war, because the formula of solidarity is a national union which includes all citizens. They do not demand a class monopoly of power, except in so far as the ends of order and administration require that the class of the most competent be entrusted with power necessary for efficient management.

The appeal of fascism to the out-élite is too obvious to need much persuasive statement. They have roughly the choices of fascism, communism, or slow degradation, as a necessary accompaniment to the present and unchecked decline of free capitalism. They must turn fascist in large numbers for reasons which make up the subject matter of most of this book. It is the appeal of fascism to the in-élite and the masses which calls for most explanation. One might as well recognize the divergence of interests at any given moment, as between the in-élite, the out-élite, and the masses who are not factually classifiable as being exceptionally influential or powerful as separate individuals or collectively as members of any group. The appeal of fascism to the masses has already been indicated somewhat briefly in the discussion of the question, "Why fascism instead of communism?"

The fundamental case is that the masses need the élite, and that that social system promises most in the way of welfare for the masses which best uses and disciplines the élite. So far as the welfare of the masses is concerned, the problem might with good reason be called largely one of getting the best out of the élite. From the point of view of mass welfare, the best that can be said for liberal capitalism in the days of its success is that it was singularly effective in getting the best out of the élite. The worst that can be said against capitalism today is that it is not getting the best out of the in-élite, and that it is getting nothing constructive out of the out-élite, so many of whom are jobless and functionless. If communism can get more out of the élite as a whole than fascism or liberalism, then communism should be the choice of the masses. As we already have remarked in comparing communism and fascism, it is difficult to see how communism can be expected to get the best out of the élite when it involves the liquidation of so many of them.

The moving spirits of an emerging fascism are, obviously, the quintessence of the élite of influence and power, as we are using these terms. If they were not, there would be no emergence of fascism. They are also likely to be mainly recruited from the over-numerous ranks of the out-élite, except for such members of the in-élite as are wise enough to join them. Their bid for the support of the masses consists chiefly in a sincere and soundly-motivated undertaking to run things better or, expressed in economic terms, to increase the material output by more efficient management.

Fascism lays emphasis on the gains to be realized by more honest and efficient management, which would come largely from better coördination of authority and integration of control. Fascism does not stress the benefits for the underprivileged to be derived from simple transfer of wealth from the rich to the poor. The people are made to see that wealth is income or production, and that an equalization of ownership followed by a heavy drop in production would leave the masses poorer than before.

In other words, labor is better off with seventy per cent of an output of one hundred than with one hundred per cent of an output of sixty. It is not to be supposed, however, that considerable redistribution of ownership and percentage shares of the total income is not effected by fascism. But fascism proposes to raise the living standards of the masses chiefly by making a more efficient use of the available factors of production, such a formula alone being considered by the fascists as capable of securing the fullest or the essential measure of coöperation by the élite.

In this connection, it is pertinent to refer to the frequently exploited device of comparing economic statistics of the fascist countries with similar statistics of the more prosperous nonfascist countries, and drawing from such comparisons conclusions invidious to fascism. No attempt is made in this book to go into comparative economic statistics. There would be no space for doing so. If fair and adequate comparisons were to be attempted, the results would be unreadably technical, and the conclusions too doubtful, to justify the average reader's outlay of effort.

The tricks that can be played with statistics are amazingly deceptive. A few general explanations about statistical comparisons invidious to the fascist countries will be briefly offered. The first and most important set of facts to bear in mind about the economic sequels of fascism are that fascism, thus far, has always taken over control in a moment of extreme crisis. It has had to carry on with whatever resources it has found and against whatever obstacles it has encountered; and most definitely it has not inaugurated its régime under the auspices of a smiling fortune such as beamed on liberal capitalism in its infancy.

Fascism, everywhere, has been born of harsh necessity and not the lucky strikes of explorers and freebooters seeking new trade routes and lands for conquest. For instance, before the War, Italy received a yearly gift of over a hundred million dollars of unearned money from remittances by Italian immigrants to the near relatives and dependents in the mother country. Since the War, the virtual stoppage of Italian immigration by American law has necessarily resulted in a slow drying up of this stream of income. Rising tariffs everywhere have also operated since the War to the extreme economic disadvantage of Germany and Italy, which used to depend on the profits of foreign trade to help defray the costs of supplying many deficiencies in raw materials.

Fascism did not produce these external economic pressures, which have been developing for a long time and which have grown acute since the War. Fascism is the answer to these external pressures. If one says that one prefers in place of fascism the lush days of 19th century liberal capitalist infancy, with all its faults, one has said absolutely nothing logically relevant by way of a criticism of post-War fascism. Nations have to choose what is attainable. Wishes for the unattainable are not arguments against fascism or in favor of liberalism.

Another consideration of which the comparers of fascist and liberal economic statistics fail to take account is that countries like the United States, Great Britain, and France have much larger accumulations of surplus than the fascist countries, with which to carry the economic crisis for a time in good style. The privileged liberal nations are likely to go completely fascist when and as this surplus runs low. Germany lost its surplus through the War, had it replaced partially for a brief spell by foreign loans, and when they stopped the country soon went fascist. Italy never had much of a surplus, and after the War it faced a harder world market in which to compete.

America, England and France have a chance in 1935 to initiate the social plan of fascism under vastly more promising auspices than marked its inauguration in the fascist countries. The whole point as to living standards is that whatever fascism provides ultimately in welfare for the masses must be determined as much by the resources of the moment, and the exigencies of the situation, as by the mechanics of fascism or the wishes of fascists in power. The defense of fascism in Italy is not to say that it has given the Italian worker a higher standard of living than British workers, including those on the dole, have enjoyed during the same period. For it has not done so. The defense of Italian fascism is that it has done a better job of social management than the preceding régime was doing, or would have done, in the situation fascism has had to face.

Comparisons of living standards and real wages are further complicated or invalidated by the unpleasant facts that, while the three leading liberal countries, the United States, Great Britain and France, did most of their land-grabbing before 1914 and are now anxious to have the present status quo respected, the fascist countries, having yet to achieve their necessary territorial expansion, hold different views about the inviolability of existing territorial arrangements. The military burdens imposed by the obvious necessity of expansion for the successful maintenance of nationhood must inevitably limit in the fascist countries the living standard which any social management by the élite can afford the masses. The costs of military preparations for expansion naturally levy a heavier percentage of income per capita in the under-privileged than in the privileged nations.

The prevailing opinion of the liberal countries, of course, is that the fascist countries do not have to expand. This opinion can be rebutted by arguments too lengthy to develop here. But why waste time arguing that the present fascist countries need to expand when every one knows that they will try to expand or perish in the attempt? And if they perish as nations in the attempt, there is not likely to be much left of western civilization in the now liberal countries after the attempt. Propositions for which nations fight rather than argue cannot be met with argument but must be met with concession and compromise, or else war. There is, therefore, no sense to any liberal argument intended merely to talk the underprivileged nations out of a will to expand. Further discussion of the international aspects of this question is left for the chapter on the international implications of fascism.

Here it need only be said in résumé that the demands of an expansionist policy on an underprivileged nation must render pointless all comparison of its living standards with those of privileged nations on the defensive. And it must be repeated that fascism has not invented national expansion. The liberal countries founded their prosperity on expansion, and cannot now make a desire by the fascist countries for expansion the subject of a reproach. The underprivileged fascist countries will have to pay more dearly in individual sacrifices for their bid for expansion than the now liberal nations had to pay for grabbing South Africa from the Boers, or Texas and California from Mexico, just as the American settlers in the middle of the 17th century paid more dearly for the rocky shores of New England snatched from the Indians than the American expansionists of 1848 had to pay for the fertile lands of Texas and California taken from Mexico in a war which was little more than a summer picnic. What the people have to pay in living standards for national existence and expansion is not determined mainly by the scheme of social organization but by the limits of their resources and the nature of the obstacles to their expansion.

Perhaps the strongest point in the fascist appeal to the masses, so far as the rule of the élite is concerned, is one seldom considered by critics of fascism and not always fully appreciated by the rank and file of fascists. It is the consideration that the élite are more dangerous to mass welfare when rendered desperate than when well treated and well disciplined. Fascism believes in providing ample and satsifactory functions or careers and rewards for the élite. Communism disclaims any such belief but practices it with great thoroughness. Liberalism disdains haughtily, though insincerely, any solicitude for the élite, and affects an attitude of neutrality and laissez faire so far as the personal struggle for existence is concerned. Liberalism assumes that the élite will make jobs or careers for themselves, unaided by the State, a sufficiently good assumption until the élite start making careers for themselves in social revolution or banditry or international war.

The association of the élite with banditry may seem incongruous to many modern minds, which are accustomed to think of the élite as bespectacled intellectuals or bejewelled merchant princes. It should be sufficient to bring such minds to a sense of reality by pointing out to them that practically all the proudest noble houses of Europe, or those whose patents of nobility were won by gallant exploits and not bought with money since the French Revolution, were knightly bandits and warriors, who derived much of their income from periodically shaking down the money lenders and the common people. The masses are vastly better off under a nationally disciplined élite than by being at the mercy of an élite engaged in private, gentlemanly warfare and knightly banditry.

From the point of view of mass welfare, if one's perspective takes in the history of several centuries instead of merely several decades of capitalism in its youthful upsurge, and if one's perspective includes the trends of the hour, it should be fairly clear that the best protection for the masses is to have the élite provided for with useful functions, and driven neither to orderly international warfare nor the still more inhumane conditions of private warfare. Any accurate sense of the laws of life, of the struggle for existence, of the survival of the fittest to survive, must tell one that if the élite do not find useful functions provided for them by a booming capitalism in expansion, or by a benevolent, paternal State with unlimited powers, the élite will ultimately find functions for themselves, as did their ancestors, the robber barons of medieval Europe, the piratical buccaneers of Queen Bess, or, still farther back, the strongest savages.

It is a curious insensitiveness to the logic of history and the struggle for existence which allows many muddle-headed sympathizers with communism or radical socialism to deride or denounce fascism for taking care of the élite. The safety and welfare of the masses depend on nothing so much as taking proper care of the élite in exchange for their social contributions and disciplined service of public order. If the élite return to the ways of their ancestors of only a few brief centuries ago it will be bad for a large number of them, but it will be still worse for those who are not of the élite or whose fangs are not so long and whose cunning is not so great. Any notion that the élite of the genus homo will ever exterminate each other and leave the weak of the same species to inherit the earth contradicts any expectancy based on natural history.

The great contribution of fascism to mass welfare is that of providing a formula of national solidarity within the spiritual bonds and iron discipline of which the élite and the masses of any given nation, every one in the measure of his capacity, can coöperate for the common good. The achievement of conceiving and realizing such a formula is the alternative to a return to the types of the struggle for existence which prevailed up to the rise of modern capitalism.

If the so-called friends of peace, or the liberal leaders of the Allied powers at Versailles, in 1919, and their several followings, had had any sense of the realities of the struggle for existence and had possessed a genuine passion for peace, they would have given more thought to political and economic formulas to provide places for the élite of the defeated enemy nations and the underprivileged Allied nations. They would have reasoned that, as wars are desired, planned and provoked by the frustrated élite who see in war opportunities they do not perceive in peace, the chief problem in ensuring European peace was that of fitting as many as possible of these potential war-makers into a peaceful scheme of things. This would have made it apparent that the survival of liberal republican government in Germany depended on nothing so much as on tolerable solutions for the élite. Questions of territorial rearrangements, war indemnities, and colonies, would have been discussed with consideration for this major imperative of preserving the peace in Europe.

But, as I have had occasion to learn from scores of conversation with some of the most eminent and influential of the liberal preachers of peace, the liberal ideology makes it impossible for them to see any connection between realities like the frustration of the élite and international war. Liberal ideology forces them to see peace, like every other desirable social result, as being principally a matter of legal enactment, contract, and judicial procedure. Hence the silly mania for the League of Nations and the World Court as means of preventing war, while half the graduates of German universities each year found no jobs. A mind properly formed in liberal ideology finds the greatest difficulty in grasping the idea that normal or average men would rather fight, whatever the prospects, and even would rather go into a fight with the certainty of death (which no one has in going into a war), than face the certainty of life-long frustration, defeat, and humiliation, with a strong probability of slow death by malnutrition or some one of the concomitants of prolonged poverty and frustration.

From the point of view of the masses, there is to be considered the question of controlling the élite, as well as getting the best out of them and keeping them from plunging the world into war or the cruder forms of the struggle for existence. In the matter of controlling or disciplining the élite in power, fascist technique or theory marks a great advance over liberalism.

Fascism uses the science of propaganda, indoctrination, education, group conditioning, and a rational scheme of personal motivations, to make the élite behave according to a desired pattern. Liberalism, on the other hand, relies chiefly on law courts and policemen to make the élite behave, quite forgetting that the élite must make, interpret, and manipulate any law-enforcement machinery. If an ideal pattern of behavior by the élite is left to law enforcement, and if law enforcement is a game, the élite will play to beat the game. If an ideal pattern of behave as desired in much the same way soldiers or other trained men behave. The trouble with liberal training of the professional élite, of course, is that they are not trained to be good citizens, as West Pointers are trained to be good soldiers. They are trained to make money.

On the score of conditioning the élite for social control, it has to be recognized first and foremost that there is no sure system of negatively controlling the élite. Education, indoctrination, and habit formation are the only scientific methods, and their effectiveness depends largely on the efficiency of the training. Communism certainly offers little to the masses in the way of control for the in-élite, as Trotzky and his fellow exiles, or millions of the slain by the Red forces, might testify. Fascism, as we have just observed, offers as its most promising instrument of control for the in-élite the motivations of self-interest and the logic of a scientific pragmatism. Fascism indulges in no such naïveté as attaching importance to constitutional or legal inhibitions on the élite, who, as long as they are powerful enough to be abusive, will be powerful enough to interpret or amend any constitution or law to suit their ends.

Under capitalism, as might be expected, the worst abuses of power are committed with the aid of the courts and law enforcement. Fascism attaches importance only to the guarantee afforded by a spirit of discipline by a consciousness of national solidarity, by a certain sense of noblesse oblige, and by the logic of self-interest under a given set-up for those who have power. These spiritual forces and fundamental motivations are the only measures of control for the élite, or the only effective safeguards against their neglect of duty or commission of errors and downright abuses.

Fascism, in other words, so far as the control of the élite in the national interest or the protection of the people is concerned, pins its faith on character, rather than on codes or on the training and spirit it gives the élite, rather than on the policeman it might put over them. Broadly speaking, the in-élite, as a whole, can be controlled or disciplined only by forces within themselves. External or institutional controls, like laws, courts, and police, are largely worthless for the in-élite, as a whole, for the simple reason that the in-élite themselves will operate such institutional controls. This is true equally under liberalism, fascism or communism.

While we are still on the subject of the fascist appeal to the masses, we should also stress the point that the élite, under fascism, are not an aristocracy of heredity except in so far as the qualities of the élite prove hereditary. Under fascism, every private carries a field marshal's baton in his knapsack. Fascism, to be true to its pragmatic principles and inner logic, must take care of the élite, and that means, of course, giving the élite, wherever found, the function and rewards appropriate to their possibilities of usefulness. The system is so organized that those in control have an interest in obtaining the best contribution of everyone, and consequently there is every incentive freely to admit to the functions of the élite all who are capable of exercising them. Fascism needs and uses all the élite it can command. Hence a fascist régime is likely to provide for the freest circulation of the classes or furnish the best facilities for persons of exceptional qualities to find their proper place in the scheme of things.

We have stated some of the more important elements of the fascist appeal to the masses. The welfare of the masses depends on the contributions of the élite, and on the élite being well enough cared for and disciplined under peace not to turn to war or the more primitive forms of the struggle for existence. It remains only to state a few important considerations which should make fascism appeal to the more intelligent of the élite who are still among the ins. At the outset, those whose one idea in the present crisis is to hold the fort until relief comes from another capitalistic revival, should be reminded that they are staking a great deal on an extremely uncertain event. About all that can be reasonably said for the happening of this happy event is that it has always happened before.

Then these stand-patters among the in-élite should be told that fascism is in no sense a fatal thing for them or their interests. We can well understand that they prefer liberal laissez faire to fascist discipline. But, after all, they should remember that fascist discipline may be self-administered, and that there will be no wholesale liquidation of the in-élite. It is also to be borne in mind that the sternest social or group discipline can be rendered agreeable to personal taste by the processes of scientific conditioning of the human personality. A scientist or a professional soldier who for years has been disciplined to certain habits will be made miserable, if not ill, by a life of complete idleness which so many persons crave. Disciplined service to the State or under State supervision, given the necessary conditioning, can afford to the élite the same degree of personal satisfaction found by so many of them at present in making money. The rewards of honor and power are equally gratifying and abundant under fascism or under liberalism.

And, most important of all, perhaps, are the considerations that, while revolutionary change is slow in getting started, it is extremely swift, once under way; that if the in-élite oppose fascism or fascist principles as long as possible, it may not be possible for them to jump on the band wagon of a swiftly emerging fascism at the last minute; and that, in the most happy circumstances of fascist success, the longer the in-élite stay out of the movement or oppose its principles, the less they will have to say about the formation of the new American fascism.

In 1935, a substantial number of the in-élite, adopting a clear-cut fascist ideology, could easily unite under a common political banner enough of the out-élite and the masses in a movement along orderly and non-violent lines of procedure to effect the most desirable sort of fascist revolution conceivable. The worse conditions become before fascism definitely emerges, the less the chances that its leadership, program, or methods will be agreeable to the in-élite.

Mr. Roosevelt, or the candidate of the Republican Party, or both, conceivably, could, by the middle of 1936, be offering to the American electorate what might be fascism in everything but name. It is not entirely improbable that Mr. Roosevelt may be pushed far in such a direction by the middle of 1936, especially under the pressure of world events. It is more improbable that a Republican candidate could be run in 1936 on anything but a platform of muddled liberalism. If capitalism cannot stage a full recovery, the in-élite will be far better off in the long run to join the ranks of a vigorous fascism at the start than to remain with a moribund liberalism until the ship sinks.

Whether the Democratic Party or the Republican Party, or both, turn towards fascism, and how far they move in that direction, will depend almost entirely on the in-élite, the consensus of whose opinions largely determines the platforms of both major parties. At present, the in-élite are combating fascism by name, and its ideology in all its phases, hardly less violently than they are attacking communism. Yet how infinitely better for the in-élite of the moment to have fascism come through one of the major parties of the moment than to have it fight its way to power as the program of the most embittered leaders of the out-élite. The old régime in France, at any time up to a few months before the outbreak of the French Revolution, could have averted that misfortune for themselves and their nation by merely initiating a régime comparable to that which eventually emerged.

From the point of view of the broadest consideration of all interests, and of the most humane interest, it seems clear that, if we are to have a social revolution, it is desirable to have its leadership representative of as many group interests as possible. By opposing fascism, the logical orientation for the out-élite, and communism, the program of peculiar though deceptive appeal to the masses, the in-élite are really condemning us to a dog-fight between the fascism of the out-élite and communism. What we need, of course, is a fascism of the nation, or a fascism which will embrace the largest possible number of the élite, which will have fewest enemies to liquidate, and which will attain most good will of the masses. Whether we get such a fascism or not at present depends mainly on the attitude of the in-élite.